The Making of Ireland

'Mr Lydon has written a comprehensive history of Ireland from ancient times to the present . . . a joy to read'.

Gordon Beadle, *State University of New York, Cortland*

'The author has produced a first rate general survey of Irish history which should take its place amongst the best of its kind. Lydon offers us a new standard for a single volume history of Ireland in a book which is graceful, suggestive and distinctive.

Sean Farrell Moran, *Oakland University*

The Making of Ireland provides an accessible history of Ireland from the earliest times. James Lydon recounts, in colourful detail, the waves of settlers, missionaries and invaders who have come to Ireland since pre-history and offers a long perspective on Irish history right up to the present.

This full survey includes discussion of the arrival of St Patrick in the fifth century and Henry II in the twelfth, as well as that of numerous soldiers, traders and craftsmen through the ages. The author explores how these settlers have shaped the political and cultural climate of Ireland today and charts the changing racial mix which fashioned the Irish nation. Lydon also follows Ireland's long and grievous entanglement with England from its beginning through to the present troubles.

The Making of Ireland offers a complete history in one volume. The nuanced narrative provides a coherent and readable introduction to this vital complex history.

James Lydon, formerly Lecky Professor of Modern History, Trinity College Dublin, and Fellow Emeritus, Trinity College Dublin.

The Making of Ireland

From ancient times to the present

James Lydon

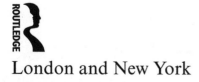

London and New York

First published 1998
by Routledge
11 New Fetter Lane, London EC4P 4EE

Simultaneously published in the USA and Canada
by Routledge
29 West 35th Street, New York, NY 10001

Typeset in Times by
M Rules
Printed and bound in Great Britain by
TJ International Ltd, Padstow, Cornwall

British Library Cataloguing in Publication Data
A catalogue record for this book is available from the British Library

Library of Congress Cataloguing in Publication Data

Lydon, James F.
  The making of Ireland: a history / James Lydon.
    p. cm.
  Includes bibliographical references and index.
  1. Ireland–History. I. Title
  DA910.L87   1998
  941.5–dc21   98–13707

ISBN 0–415–01347–x (hbk)
ISBN 0–415–01348–8 (pbk)

For Brendan Kennelly, my friend

Contents

Preface

This book has been a long time in the making. I am a medievalist by training and inclination. It was for that reason that I was originally asked to write a replacement for *A History of Ireland* by Edmund Curtis, the great historian of medieval Ireland. It was a long, hard task, making me fully aware of what the Bible (Ecclesiastes, 12.12.) meant by: 'One last thing, my son, be warned that writing books involves endless hard work, and that much study wearies the body'. My ignorance of most of the history of modern Ireland meant that I had to read what I could of the mass of literature which historians have produced in recent years in what can truly be called an historiographical revolution. I have been unable to resolve many of the problems encountered and can only hope that my interpretations will not cause too much offence. I am especially conscious that I have concentrated on political narrative, to the near exclusion of social and economic matters, except where they had an important impact on political developments. This was deliberate, otherwise the story would have been so long as to be unmanageable. Whether or not one agrees with Patrick Kavanagh that 'all history is legend . . . the only value of history is to stir the imagination' (*Kavanagh's Weekly*, 24 June 1952, p.2), there is no doubt that a journey through the history of Ireland will leave a deep imprint on the mind of the traveller. I hope that this account of my journey will convey something of the impression it made on me. Each person, in each generation, must discover the past.

October 1997
Trinity College, Dublin

1 Saints and scholars
Early Christian Ireland

The story of the Irish people begins about ten thousand years ago when the first men arrived from Europe to what was then probably already an island. These wanderers from middle Europe were nomadic hunters, using flint for their arrows and knives. In their search for food they gradually spread to different parts of the island, living from hand to mouth along the coast, by rivers and lakes, competing with animals for the food needed to sustain life. These hunters have left little trace other than the primitive flint instruments they used. Slowly they formed settled communities, living in circular huts made of saplings. During the millennia that followed, other men came to Ireland, who knew how to domesticate the animals needed for food and, more importantly, how to grow crops to add to their diet. New settled communities appeared, more permanent houses, burial places and religious sites. In many parts of Ireland megalithic tombs built of stone still survive, representing at once the graveyards of these distant stone-age people and their places of worship. In the Boyne valley the largest of them, elaborate in scale and plan, show evidence of a considerable technology, a delicate sense of design in the decoration widely employed and a sophisticated knowledge of measurement, all of which argues for an advanced civilization. The very size of some of them suggests a density of population and a developed social system capable of building such monuments.

By the time the great monument at Newgrange came to be constructed, in around 2500 BC, the people were growing wheat, as pollen analysis of turves on the mound has shown. But the Newgrange monument also shows that these people possessed an astonishing skill in engineering, sophisticated enough to manipulate huge masses of stone and to align the tomb so that the first rays of the sun on the morning of the winter solstice will shine through a special slit in the roof, along a passage for more than 60 feet, to focus on the most sacred spot at the heart of the mound, where no one would ever see it once the entrance was sealed and concealed. At the very depth of winter, when the dark was at its strongest, they captured and celebrated light. And where they thought no human eye would ever penetrate, they decorated the great stones of the tomb with abstract designs which can still set the imagination alight. While we may wonder at the religious impulse which drove the people to construct such massive monuments as Newgrange, they demonstrate the existence of large, settled communities with the necessary resources and leadership to provide and organize the considerable labour forces required for the construction over long periods of time and for the carriage of huge stones, often from long distances away. Wherever we find such clusters of different kinds of tombs, in many parts of Ireland, we have evidence of settlement, civilization and prosperity.

The tribes which settled down necessarily developed appropriate religious and secular institutions to govern their lives. But of these we know little, except what can be gleaned from much later, and suspect, literary sources. They practised agriculture and they developed technical skills of a high order which enabled them to work in gold, silver, bronze, and eventually iron. They perfected the art of pottery and became adept at the difficult medium of ceramics. They clearly had a keen sense of beauty which impelled them to produce artefacts which were purely ornamental in purpose. and possessed a sure sense of design. All of this argues for a high level of civilization, so that it is remarkable that they did not develop an alphabet for writing (apart from the crude ogham alphabet which was used for inscriptions on stone and possibly wood). It must be presumed that this was deliberate. The succeeding invasions and settlements of Celtic tribes continued to bring new skills and knowledge, but never the art of writing. The last to come, the Goidels, who imposed their own Gaelic culture over the island, produced a rich oral literature which, to judge from its later written forms, was derived from the common stock of heroic and mythical traditions which was shared by the Indo-European world. They also developed a complex and sophisticated legal system, preserved in a body of laws which was passed on orally through generations of the legal caste which was its custodian. Inaugural rites for the sacral kings, the privileges and obligations of the warrior aristocracy, the historical lore of sacred places, and the genealogies of kings were never committed to writing, but were handed on orally. While the rest of the civilized world was committing history, laws and literature to writing, Ireland was left without letters.

This suggests isolation from the world which Rome had conquered. But there is plenty of evidence to show that this was not the case. Trading links had long been established. Men from Ireland served with Roman legions. Others had gone raiding deep into Roman Britain and some were even to found colonies there. It was not isolation which made Ireland go her own way, but conservatism. By the time of the Christian era Gaelic Ireland had fossilized. What caused this situation to change radically was the arrival of Christianity, sufficiently strong in the island by 431 for the pope of the day to take notice and send a bishop. Christianity was not only to challenge the priestly caste with their mysteries, it offered new ideas which were to bring Europe into Ireland and eventually revolutionize existing institutions. This was a long process over many generations, sometimes requiring renewal from Europe in the future. But from the fifth century, when that process began, a new Ireland emerged.

We will never know when exactly the first Christians came to Ireland. The message of Christ may have been carried by traders, it may even have been brought by unremembered missionaries or brought home by Irishmen who had been converted in Europe. What is certain is that by the first quarter of the fifth century a flourishing Christian community was established in one part of the island. Prosper of Aquitaine, who wrote a chronicle in Rome in which he recounted events to which he was a witness, recorded that in 431 Pope Celestine sent Palladius as 'the first bishop to the Irish believing in Christ'. Not only is this the first authentic date in Irish history, it is a genuine record of the first Irish bishop. What became of Palladius is not known. It was not he who was subsequently remembered in Irish tradition as the first bishop but Patrick, regarded as the Apostle of Ireland and now the national saint. Traditionally said to have arrived in 432 and single-handedly to have converted the Irish before his death in 461, this Patrick and his mission may well be an amalgam of different evangelizers. But there is no doubting the authenticity of Patrick the Briton who worked in Ireland, probably in the mid-fifth century, and founded a church from which all modern Irish Christians claim descent. He left us a very precious record in his own words, now known as his *Confession*, with a letter which he wrote to a British chieftain named Coroticus, and possibly even some sayings which were carefully cherished and later written down in the great manuscript which we now know as the *Book of Armagh*, believed for centuries to be in the saint's own hand and therefore a very precious relic carefully preserved. From these, and from a cautious use of later literary sources, it is possible to reconstruct an outline of his achievement in Ireland and the legacy which he left after his death.

He was born, he tells us, in the west of Romanized Britain. His father, who was a deacon, had a small estate from which Patrick was captured by Irish raiders when he was 16. Taken as a slave to Ireland he spent six years there as a herd. During that time in captivity he rediscovered the lost faith of his childhood, when, as he says, God came 'and the Spirit was fervent in me'. One night in a dream a voice, which was to come to him again in later life and bring him back to Ireland, told him that a ship was ready to carry him to freedom. Patrick left his master, travelled 200 miles through unknown country, managed to get on board a ship, sailed for three days and, after landing, wandered with the pagan crew for another 28 days through a deserted country. During all that time God protected him and the pagans, once again confirming the trust of Patrick.

Eventually he made his way home to Britain and rejoined his family. But one night he had a dream in which he received a letter from a messenger from Ireland and on opening the letter he found that it was addressed to him by 'The Voice of the Irish'. As he read he imagined that he heard the voice of those who lived beside 'the forest of Foclut which is near the western sea', crying out to him, as though with one voice: 'We beg you, holy boy, to come and walk among us again'. The dreams continued, giving him no peace until he decided to return to Ireland.

Patrick insisted that he was a rustic, uneducated man, only fitted to be a bishop among the Irish because he was called there by God. This lack of learning, which may mean that contrary to later tradition he never studied in Gaul, was the cause of opposition to his mission in Britain, together with some unknown sin of his youth which seems to have indicated that he was unfit to be a bishop. It was in reply to such criticism that he finally wrote his *Confession* and justified his work as bishop on the ground that he was made one by God and that he was blessed with success. He wrote that he had preached the gospel 'to the point beyond which there is no-one' and described how he 'baptised so many thousands' and ordained clergy everywhere 'to serve a people just now coming to the faith'. He asked his critics to explain how it was that in Ireland 'those who never had any knowledge of God but up till now always worshipped idols and abominations' are now called by all 'the people of the lord and the sons of God'; furthermore, why was it that so many sons and daughters of Irish kings 'are seen to be monks and virgins of Christ?'. Clearly this must be the work of God.

But it was not achieved without great hardship and dangers. Like St Paul before him, Patrick was often persecuted and then saved by God. Yet undaunted by the many dangers which beset him he travelled to the most remote districts 'where no-one had ever penetrated to baptise or ordain clergy or confirm the people', for the salvation of the Irish. Through it he suffered acute loneliness, longing to see his homeland and his family, living 'among barbarous peoples, a stranger and an exile for the love of God'. If Patrick here emphasizes the loneliness of the exile, and thus gives first utterance to a cry which was constantly to be repeated in the future in the literature of Irish exile, and in particular missionary exile, he also admitted in a phrase in his letter to Coroticus that he now regarded Ireland as another homeland. 'We are Irish', he wrote.

None of this tells us much about the actual achievement of Patrick in Ireland. Both the *Confession* and the letter provide a rare insight into the mind and heart of a great European of the fifth century. We can reach back through the generations to the man. But apart from this, we learn little about the details of his life in Ireland or the character of the Christian church there. The obscurities and difficulties have given rise to what has been one of the most controversial problems in Irish historiography. But there is now general agreement that Patrick's mission was largely confined to the northern half of the island. Other missionaries, including perhaps Palladius, had been busy in the south. Leinster and Munster preserve some traditions of pre-Patrician saints. This rough division of Ireland into two separate areas of missionary activity not only mirrored the old division of Ireland into two halves, *Leth Chuinn* ('Conn's half') and *Leth Mugha* ('Mug's half'), north and south, but was also to be reflected in later ecclesiastical controversy between Armagh and Kildare.

Despite his claim to have baptized thousands and to have spread Christianity widely, Patrick does admit that he also met with stern resistance.

He seems to have been forced to conform to the social habits of the island, moving constantly from place to place with an entourage of young aristocrats and distributing gifts like any high-born nobleman. It was inevitable that in a society which lacked towns and the kind of centralized institutions on which Christian ecclesiastical organization was based, Patrick should find it nearly impossible to give his church an orthodox structure. He had to try, since it was the only structure he knew, and it made the process of conversion difficult and slow. The idea that the whole, or even the greater part of Ireland was converted by the time Patrick died is an invention of later hagiography designed to give Patrick heroic as well as saintly status. The group of late sixth century canons, ecclesiastical legislation later attributed to Patrick, Auxilius and Iserninus, show clearly that Ireland was still largely pagan. They also reveal a church organized as was the church elsewhere in Europe, ruled by bishops, each of whom was the authority in his own *paruchia* or diocese. Monasticism, with abbots, had its place in this organization, but it was still a subsidiary one.

This kind of church fitted uneasily into the Irish society of the fifth century. That society has been described, in a phrase which has become classical, as 'tribal, rural, hierarchical and familiar'. The whole of Ireland was divided into a large number of autonomous *tuatha* (literally 'peoples'), small communities with a *rí* ('king'). The king was elected from the royal lineage, chosen on the basis of his fitness to rule. He must be without serious physical blemish, a warrior capable of leading his people into battle, and pleasing enough to the local deity so that the land would be fruitful during his reign. The sacral nature of his kingship was symbolized at his inauguration by his solemn marriage to the goddess of his land, a custom which was so important that it survived the influence of Christianity until much later in the middle ages. For the new religion to gain even a foothold it would first of all have to overcome this pagan prop of kingship and gain the king himself.

The king was severely restricted by all sorts of taboos. For the most part he could not interfere with the affairs of a neighbouring *tuath*, even where he was able to exercise some kind of personal lordship over its king. This meant that Christianity had to expand from *tuath* to *tuath*. There could be no sudden, miraculous conversion of the island by the winning over of a great king. The church was based on the *tuatha*, so that the dioceses of the first bishops had to be coterminous with those basic political units. Because there was no urban or even nucleated centre of population within each *tuath*, since the people lived in scattered farmsteads represented today by thousands of surviving earthworks or *raths*, there was no Roman-style centre where the bishop could establish his cathedral and develop the rudiments of a sedentary administration. The bishop, therefore, was an awkward intrusion into the kind of social set-up which was typical of Ireland.

There was another feature which made it difficult for Christianity in its Roman form to be assimilated. Family and kin (*fine*) were all-important as the property owning unit and the guardian of the legal rights of members.

Land could not normally be alienated outside the *fine*, so that it was impossible to establish and endow a bishopric except within the kin, which was contrary to orthodox Latin practice. The many bishops, therefore, confined within their *tuath*, must have found it impossible to establish a satisfactory, independent, landed base for their authority, even after they had been given a status at law equal to that of a king. The sixth century canons already referred to indicate something of this. The bishop certainly had authority over all the priests and churches in his diocese and could legislate against outsiders coming in. But the whole tone of the legislation is defensive, betraying a lack of real confidence in the comprehensive authority of the bishop. And while monks were forbidden to baptize or receive alms, the monasteries were already endowed with property through the *fine*. Bishops could and did acquire property, but only on a restricted basis and with all the limitations imposed by the *fine*. It was much easier for the *fine* to endow a monastery and retain rights in the property thereafter. In the course of the sixth century, as the new religion began to spread, wealthy families began to endow monasteries. The Irish church slowly began to assume the strongly monastic character which was to remain its most notable characteristic until the great reforms of the twelfth century.

But in the fifth and sixth centuries there were still forces which were hostile to the reception of Christianity. Ireland had long possessed a learned class which, supported by the old religion, preserved in oral form the traditional and necessary lore handed down through the generations. Their prestige largely depended on this and the druids, poets and lawyers were naturally hostile to the new religion which threatened the very foundations of their place in society. The challenge was later represented in hagiography in such well known pieces as the confrontation of Patrick and the druids on the hill of Tara before the king. But it finds a truer echo in an anonymous poem written in the seventh century, satirizing a priest saying mass. The speaker is supposedly a druid who opposed Patrick:

> Across the sea will come Adze-Head,
> crazed in the head,
> his cloak with hole for the head,
> his stick bent in the head.

> He will chant impiety
> from a table in front of his house;
> all his people will answer:
> 'Be it thus, Be it thus'.

In time the new religion adapted itself to the peculiarities of Irish society and became popular. The learned classes too, at least outwardly, embraced Christianity. Hostility may have continued, but it was largely hidden. The conversion of the men of learning resulted in a marvellous fusion of Gaelic and Latin cultures which was to make the Irish church unique. There was no rigid separation of the sacred and profane in Ireland as happened elsewhere. It was the monks who wrote down and preserved for posterity the literature of the pagan past, the myths and the heroic tales. It was a great saint, Colum Cille, who was reputed to have defended and saved the *filí* ('poets', 'seers') of Ireland at the convention of Druim Ceata in the sixth century. In law the monk scholar was given a high status, equivalent to that held by the *file* who professed secular learning. The integration of Christianity with society, delayed because of the orthodox structure which the first generation of bishops imposed on the church, eventually produced a real enrichment of the native culture and tradition.

That culture exercised a profound influence on the church in Ireland, not least in making monasticism predominant. Abbots gradually replaced bishops in the hierarchy of authority and monastic filiations (*paruchiae*) were absorbing the older bishoprics. When and why this should have occurred is a complex matter. But there is no doubt that in the second half of the sixth century, or roughly a century after the traditional date of the Patrician mission, a number of great monasteries were founded which were to establish federations of houses under them. These, unlike the bishoprics, were not confined to one *tuath* or even one area. The greatest, the *paruchia* of Colum Cille, based on Iona, straddled Scotland, England and Ireland. Others had houses even further away on the mainland of Europe. The monastic *paruchia* had powers of expansion which no bishop could possibly possess. It was natural, in time, for the bishop to take second place to the abbot in most of the *paruchiae* of Ireland. The Irish church had thus become monastic in its structure and abbatial in authority.

The origins of Irish monasticism are lost in diverse traditions. Some have seen a strong eastern Mediterranean influence, echoing the asceticism of the desert fathers and preserving features which are more reminiscent of the Coptic than of the Latin church of the west. Others have argued for Gaulish origins, pointing to the probable sojourn of Patrick as a student there and the later cult of St Martin of Tours in Ireland. But there can be no doubt that in Irish tradition it was Britain which provided the model and probably the rule for the early Irish monastic founders. Most of them were subsequently associated with the church of Candida Casa ('the white house') at Whithorn in Galloway, as if somehow it was important to show that the saint had connections with a community which had a special place in Irish hagiography, which could refer to it simply as 'the great monastery'. Tradition also made much of the connection with Wales and with some of her great saints. But none of this is reliable and only Samson can be seen as a probable Welsh influence.

Within Ireland itself it seems as if some early monasteries began in much the same way as they did in the eastern church. *Fuga mundi* ('flight from the world') was an impulse which drove men to seek God and their own salvation in lonely places as hermits. The fact that *dísert* ('desert') is among the commonest ecclesiastical element in placenames indicates how widespread the flight to the desert was. Extreme asceticism, long to remain one of the chief characteristics of Irish monasticism, was adopted by many as a form of martyrdom, impelling them to leave the safety and security of *fine* and *tuath* and go into exile in another part of Ireland. They sought austere seclusion in the forest, in mountain valleys, on small islands off the coast. But not all were successful in escaping. Their fame as holy men attracted followers and, as the numbers grew, food, shelter and discipline had to be organized and a rule had to be provided. This is what happened to Coemgen (Kevin) who had a small hermitage at Hollywood in Wicklow. When his solitude was invaded by disciples, he fled across the nearby mountains into Glendalough. But soon more followed and the reluctant saint had to organize them into a monastic community, with himself as abbot. Even the hermitage on the forbidding rock known as Skellig Michael, rising sheer for nearly 800 feet from the sea about eight miles off the Kerry coast, grew into a monastic community.

Many of these monasteries, however, preserved some trace of their origins by retaining an eremetic as well as a coenobitic character. Right down to the end of the purely Irish monastic system, hermits existed within the community and individual cells remained the norm. This was also true of those monasteries which were founded in a more formal way by the great monastic founders of the sixth century. Enda was probably the first with his monastery situated on the barren ground of the largest of the Aran islands. Among his disciples were supposedly some of the greatest founding saints of all: Colum Cille, Brendan of Clonfert subject of the most famous of all Irish voyage stories, the *Navigatio sancti Brendani* ('Voyage of St Brendan'), Ciaran of Clonmacnois, and Finnian of Clonard. This last, however, far outstripped Enda as a teacher of Irish saints. Finnian's Clonard was the model for many other Irish monasteries and he himself was affectionately known as 'foster-father of the saints of Ireland in his day'. He combined the asceticism of Enda with an emphasis on the intellectual life, thus fashioning another characteristic feature of Irish monasticism.

During the sixth century, then, many of the great Irish monasteries were founded. Clonard, probably before 515, Clonmacnois (the largest of all), *c.* 555, and Clonfert *c.* 560 are only three of the multitude which eventually covered the entire island. They provided an outlet for the thousands who desired to find salvation through prayer, mortification and a strict rule governing their lives.

For some, however, this was not enough. The ideal of self-imposed exile by becoming a wanderer for Christ, was a powerful impulse to leave Ireland altogether. It was the greatest sacrifice a man could make. This was the *peregrinatio* ('pilgrimage'), a wandering at the will of God, seeking solitude across the ocean. It may have been partly inspired by, as it inspired in turn, a class of story which had already existed in pagan times, the *imram* ('voyage'). Such pagan voyagers pursued another world, often an island in the western ocean, with many adventures on the way. The entertainment value was high and Christian hagiography was not slow to adapt the form to saints and pilgrimage, of which the Brendan voyage is the most famous example. But the real-life pilgrims rarely enjoyed such adventures. As Bede said of Fursa, who first came to England and later moved to north-eastern Gaul, he went on his voyage because he 'desired the wandering life for the love of the Lord'. In fact he became a famous evangelizer, establishing the basis of a notable *paruchia* which eventually spread throughout the territories he had covered.

Fursa is typical of the way in which the Irish pilgrim became a missionary, bringing to Scotland, England, Gaul, parts of western and central Europe and Italy an Irish style of Christianity. Two names stand out: Colum Cille and Columbanus. The former belonged to the Uí Néill, the lineage of one of the most famous of early Irish kings, Niall of the Nine Hostages. He had other aristocratic connections, notably with the ruling family of Dal Riata in Scotland, among whom he was eventually to settle. He seems to have received some training as a poet and when he died in 597 one of the leading poets of Ireland, Dallán Forgaill, composed an elegy in his honour, *Amra Choluim Cille* ('The song of Colum Cille'), which is possibly the oldest piece of vernacular poetry in western Europe. Many poems subsequently attributed to the saint are spurious (though one long one, in Latin, which was an innovation in European literature, seems to have been written by him); but they show the early and persistent tradition that he was a poet. They are important, too, in conveying the loneliness which the pilgrims felt on leaving Ireland and they show an early sense of what, to some at least, it meant to be an Irishman.

Colum Cille certainly received a more orthodox training as a monk and a scholar. By 546, when he founded his monastery at Derry, he was already emulating others who are supposed to have been his companions under Finnian at Clonard. When, about 10 years later, he founded another monastery at Durrow, he seemed to be typical of the great monastic founders of sixth century Ireland. Yet shortly afterwards, in 561, he left Ireland and sailed for Scotland with a handful (the traditional 12) of followers. One later explanation of this abandonment of the path he had chosen to follow in Ireland is that it was a penance imposed on the saint for having caused the battle of Cúl Dreimne, fought by his lineage on his behalf. According to the story, Colum Cille copied a psalter of St Finnian's and refused to hand it over when he was discovered. Eventually the secular brehons gave a famous judgement, often quoted as the first case of copyright, that the copy belonged to the owner of the original, just as the calf belongs to the cow. When Finnian tried to execute the judgement, Colum Cille's family moved to protect him and his book. The result was the battle of Cúl Dreimne and the deaths of many. The penitent saint was later told by his *anam chara* ('soul friend', the typical confessor of the Irish church) that he must go into exile as a penance.

There seems no truth to this popular story about Colum Cille's motives in abandoning Ireland. His great biographer Adamnán, abbot of Iona, is categorical in stating that at the age of 42 the saint sailed to Britain 'wishing to be a pilgrim for Christ'. So he was going on a *peregrinatio*, seeking his desert across the ocean. Yet Adamnán twice dates this to the second year after the battle of Cúl Dreimne and in another context seems aware that the battle was somehow part of the circumstances in which the saint, now getting old by the standards of the sixth century, suddenly decided to become a pilgrim. Most likely, too, his departure was in some measure a response to a need felt in Dál Riata. Bede later wrote that he came as an evangelizer, to preach to the Picts. In Scottish tradition he has much the same place as St Patrick in Ireland, assuming the role of national apostle. All of this shows that the ideal of the *peregrinatio* was rarely achieved in practice. The pilgrim became the evangelizer, the desert all too often became the world of politics and intrigue.

Colum Cille established an important monastery on the island of Iona and from there he and his followers subsequently created a great *paruchia* which eventually spread from Kells and Durrow in the Irish midlands, through Scotland and down into northern England, helping to produce that cultural mix which was to result in the magnificent Hiberno-Saxon civilization of Northumbria. It has been estimated that altogether there were more than 90 places in Ireland and Scotland which were part of this Columban *paruchia*. Such a huge federation made Colum Cille, and his successors on Iona, important political as well as ecclesiastical figures. Colum Cille himself not only consecrated Aedán as King of Dál Riata by anointing him (the first recorded instance in Britain or Ireland), he also acted as envoy on missions to the Picts and to Ireland. When he spoke on behalf of the poets of Ireland at the convention of Druim Cett in 575, he was there mainly to negotiate on behalf of King Aedán of Dál Riata. Here, then, is no simple pilgrim, seeking his desert, but an aristocratic and learned head of a great *paruchia*, moving easily in the highest political circles.

At the same time Colum Cille emerges from Adamnán's *Life*, which is founded on an uninterrupted Iona oral tradition, as an austere but concerned father, who could be saddened because his monks in Durrow were being overworked in cold weather and whose humanity shines from almost every page. He is given no epic stature in the conventional way, but shown to have a concern for even the simplest creatures. He is a good representative of the paradox that baffles inquirers into early Irish Christianity, where the world seems to be able to intrude into the very heart of the monastery without destroying the desert which the monks found there.

Even more of a paradox is Columbanus, a Pauline character who still survives in his sermons, letters, rule and poems. They reveal a man with all the self-confidence of the early Irish church, a theologian who blundered into some of the great questions of his day, unorthodox in his views (as on the Easter question), outspoken and dogmatic, even when addressing the pope himself. He was aristocratic by birth, exceptionally well educated, especially in the Latin authors for which the Irish had a passion, but by inclination an ascetic and contemplative. He, too, decided to leave the bright prospects which Ireland offered and sail away 'for the love of God', as his biographer

Jonas tells us. Columbanus always stressed that while the pilgrim must pursue his own road to heaven, he must also help others on their journey. If the monk must first of all glorify God in contemplation, he must also, 'aflame with divine fire', become an apostle to others. So, in his view, the concept of the *peregrinatio* easily merged into that of mission. Yet he seems to have been less than enthusiastic as a missionary, to judge by his statement in a letter that he 'wanted to visit the brethren in order to preach the gospel to them, but Fidolius' telling me about their lukewarmness almost drove the thought from my mind'. Nevertheless, enjoying royal support in a number of kingdoms, he and his followers established a string of monasteries stretching from Annegray, Luxeil and Fontaines, to St Gall and as far as Bobbio in Italy. The names of some 63 immediate followers of the saint are known to history, who spread his influence from Gaul and the Rhineland, through northern Belgium, Germany, Switzerland and Italy. It has been estimated that after his death more than 50 communities followed his harsh rule before finally yielding to the less demanding, and more orthodox, rule of St Benedict.

Through the sprawling *paruchia* of Columbanus, Irish penetentials, auricular confession, private penance, and other important innovations in religious practice spread throughout the Latin church. In scholarship, book production and art the Irish monks left their mark on Europe. Many Columban foundations, such as Bobbio, became famous centres of learning, reflecting the saint's own inclination towards scholarship. He had been master of the school at Bangor and in his own rule he emphasized the importance of study. Jonas tells us that when the saint knew that he would die before long, he became more assiduous than ever in copying in the *scriptorium*. The organization of a *scriptorium* in the Irish fashion was often a primary task in a new foundation and the institution of a library a close second. The Irish missionaries soon became teachers as well, and not just of scripture and the Latin fathers, but of grammar and some earlier pagan writers, notably Virgil.

Colum Cille and Columbanus are only two of a flood of Irish monks who helped to evangelize, reform and educate large parts of Britain and the continent in the seventh and eighth centuries. Their foundations, widely scattered throughout Europe, and their cults which survive to this day in many places, are a testimony to their abiding influence in shaping the church as it developed in western and parts of central Europe. But their foundations performed another function, providing a refuge for pilgrims who continued to stream from Ireland. Such a man was Cummian who died at Bobbio sometime in the first half of the eighth century. A bishop in Ireland, he went on a *peregrinatio* at the advanced age of 78. He found his desert at Bobbio and lived there for another 17 years before he died. Cummian may not be typical, but many more like him kept open the contacts between Ireland and Europe. This allowed books and new ideas eventually to find their way back to Ireland, improving the quality and breadth of the learning already available there.

One of the most outstanding characteristics of the early Irish church was the importance given to study. In the Irish monasteries learning was almost venerated. Their schools became famous, not just in Ireland but abroad as well. Bede, the great Anglo-Saxon historian, tells us that in 664, when the great plague ravaged Ireland, many English scholars there fell victim. In a celebrated passage he describes how 'many English nobles and lesser folk' had gone to Ireland to study or to find a stricter way of life. Some stayed in one monastery, 'while others preferred to travel, studying under various teachers in turn. The Irish welcomed them all kindly and, without asking for any payment, provided them with books and instructors'. They continued to come to the end of the seventh century, because of the quality of learning available there. Pride of place was naturally given to the study of scripture and because the Irish scholar had access to a wide range of sources, especially in commentaries on the old and new testaments, he was able to produce a rich corpus of work devoted to biblical exegesis. Much of this was in the allegorical tradition which was the norm elsewhere, seeing scenes or incidents in the Bible as allegories for Christ, or the church and so on. But uniquely in the western church the Irish exegetes employed a more scientific method, that which was the norm in the eastern 'historical' schools, without resorting to allegorical interpretation. Thus one, anonymous, Irish commentator, writing *c*. 630, said that it was his purpose 'to explain the reason and order of actual events, excluding at this stage figurative interpretation'. This suggests a possible Greek influence and a knowledge of Greek. But it is not known if such knowledge went very deep. In Latin, however, the Irish were masters. They delighted in Virgil in particular and saw nothing wrong in combining a study of profane and pagan writers with the more appropriate sacred books. Their interests were also shaped by contact with Britain and Gaul, but especially by Spain. The writings of Isidore of Seville were quickly in circulation in Ireland and exercised a profound influence, not always for the better. The Irish were not content to accept what they received uncritically, but preserved a critical and independent spirit, even when dealing with established masters such as Priscian in grammar. If they were not always original, it is a mistake to think, as is commonly the case, that they were generally incapable of 'abstract thought' and so unable to make any notable contribution to philosophy, theology or jurisprudence. Early Irish law accepted the concept of 'natural law' and jurists developed legal concepts based on this, with the later Christian addition of the concept of a divine order underlying all.

If the Irish monk-scholars were excited by the mythology derived from the Graeco-Roman tradition, they were equally interested in their own vernacular oral tradition with its rich store of myth and pagan saga. This they exploited for the purpose of creating an intelligible history of Ireland which could be meshed with the more orthodox Christian view of world history. Here their achievement was immense. Not only had they to adapt the Roman alphabet to be able to write down the vernacular tradition, they had then to sort out the available material to provide a coherent story. Most important of all they had to fit this into a chronology based on the established order which was generally accepted by the Christian church. They thus established the basis for a chronicle of Ireland which in turn provided the framework for the more extended regional annals which are still a primary source for the early history of Ireland.

This interest in the vernacular, unique in the west, enabled the monks to preserve a great corpus of ancient literature which continues to delight readers. But they went further and created a vernacular literature of their own. Lives of saints, voyages, visions, new versions of pagan mythology, were all composed in Irish. Perhaps most important of all, in the eighth century they created a new Irish literary form, the lyric, in which they expressed their love of God in a new way by singing of nature in all its manifestations, simple as well as grand. Nowhere else at the time did poets celebrate nature in this way and it is a tribute to the originality and independence of the Irish monastic schools that they did so there.

At the same time the monasteries were centres of other arts. Illumination benefited from foreign contacts and Irish monks produced masterpieces of which the *Book of Durrow* is one of the earliest, reaching a peak in the incomparable *Book of Kells*. Metalwork, too, displayed the rich genius of the craftsmen, and great stone crosses, skilfully decorated and with splendid panels in relief, still reveal the skills of great schools of sculptors. The output of the *scriptoria* and workshops of the monasteries was of prodigious richness and indicates not only a high level of artistic achievement, but the wealth of many of the monasteries as well. The great federations were thus being seduced by worldly standards which inevitably led to a deterioration in the spiritual values which had been their justification. A competitive spirit developed which reflected the contemporary aggrandizement of not only secular but of ecclesiastical power as well.

There seems to be no doubt that with an episcopal–diocesan structure of the kind which the early missionaries had imposed on the young Irish church there came the concept of an organization based on a hierarchy of bishops, under metropolitans or archbishops. This notion of authority naturally gave rise to the idea of primacy: that one church, for historical reasons, was first among equals and that certain rights flowed from this. By the middle of the seventh century, or roughly two centuries after the Palladian–Patrician missions, two great churches were engaged in a propaganda war for the primacy. In the north, Armagh, and in the south, Kildare, were by then pre-eminent among the *paruchiae* of Ireland. The one claimed a special association with Patrick, Apostle of Ireland; the other with Brigit, whose cult was even more widespread. It was difficult for Armagh to claim, as it were, exclusive ownership of Patrick, since he was buried at Downpatrick and there was little historical justification for accepting Armagh as his principal church. In Brigit, Kildare had a much more convincing patron. A pagan cult had long since spread her name over many places, even in the northern half of Ireland. It was easy for the propagandists to claim these places for the *paruchia* of the Christian saint. Armagh had to create evidence for a similar widespread cult of St Patrick so as to justify the intrusion of its *paruchia* into remote places.

That they succeeded can be largely attributed to the work of two scholars, Tirechán and Muirchú, who between them laid the foundations of the legend of St Patrick, Apostle of Ireland. Even so, it is doubtful if 'history' alone would have given Armagh the edge in this struggle for primacy. Kildare was more orthodox by Roman standards, in the controversial matter of the dating of Easter for example. But Armagh had one great advantage in that she was adopted by the powerful Uí Néill dynasty whose political star was now in the ascendant. Kildare, in contrast, was connected with the Uí Dúnlainge, who were unable to establish a permanent claim to the provincial kingship of Leinster. Faced with successful Armagh expansion, even as uncomfortably close as Old Kilcullen only a few miles away, Kildare abandoned her extravagant claims in return for recognition of her own extensive *paruchia* within Leinster. Armagh was thus left in the second half of the eighth century to establish her primacy unopposed. The agreement between the two was symbolized in a famous passage added to the *Book of Armagh*, where Patrick and Brigit are called 'the pillars of the Irish' with 'such friendship of charity that they had one heart and one mind. Christ performed many miracles through them both. The holy man therefore said to the Christian virgin: O my Brigit, your *paruchia* in your province will be reckoned unto you for your monarchy; but in the eastern and western part it will be my domination'.

In seventh- and eighth-century Ireland, then, ecclesiastical aggrandizement in the last analysis depended on secular support. The political ambition of great dynasties determined the future structure of authority within the Irish church. This is hardly surprising, given the close link between the church and the ruling families. The emergence of some lineages into prominence naturally promoted the status of the attached churches, just as the existence of the more powerful *paruchiae* were a help in fostering the political ambitions of the local dynasts. But when the first missionaries came in the fifth-century Ireland was politically extremely fragmented. These missionaries encountered a society which looked back nostalgically to an heroic past, kept alive in the epic literature which was handed on orally from one generation to the next. This preserved the memory of great kingdoms and a warrior aristocracy fighting great battles. Even the Christian hagiographers of a later age could present the same unreal picture of a powerful King of Ireland presiding over a magnificent court at Tara, surrounded by warriors, druids and poets. Thus Muirchú, in creating a heroic St Patrick, presented Lóegaire as an emperor ruling from Tara 'the capital of the Irish'. As late as the twelfth century a scribe represented pictorially the seating list, in order of rank, in the banqueting hall at Tara during the reign of another legendary ruler of Ireland, Cormac mac Airt.

But the reality was very different. The hundred and more *tuatha*, or petty kingdoms, which covered Ireland were small, poor, and underpopulated. By the fifth century some larger groupings had emerged and these were recognized in laws which designated different grades of kingship to match the larger political units. The King of the small *tuath*, the *rí*, might accept the overlordship of a more highly ranked king, the *ruire*; and he, in turn, might acknowledge as lord a still higher king, the *rí ruirech*. Thus the laws recognized a hierarchy of political units from the province (the *cóiced*) to the over-kingdom of several *tuatha*, down to the simple *tuath*. The province might also demonstrate its existence by celebrating a great *óenach* (tribal assembly), such as the Oenach Carman of the Lagin held every three years. This was a mixture of fair, games, competitions and tribal parley, formally presided over by the King of Leinster and with the lesser kings of the province taking their places in a strict order of historical precedence. It tried to preserve the memory of a more heroic age and a ritual derived from a pagan past. It gave some kind of reality to the province of Leinster and to the dynasty which claimed to be its king.

In the centuries before the Vikings came to Ireland some strong lineages attempted to gain permanent control over the shadowy rights of provincial rulers. The most prominent of these dynasties in the south were the Eóganacht in Munster, based in Cashel from which they expanded through different segments to become the dominant lineage occupying the best land in the province. To the north the Uí Néill emerged from historical obscurity in the west to expand across the Shannon to Meath, forming the southern branch of a sprawling lineage; the northern Uí Néill expanded to dominate the area west of the Bann in Ulster. The kingship of Tara was the title aspired to by the Uí Néill and even though Tara was reputedly abandoned by the kings after being cursed by St Rúadán of Lorrha, the prestige of its name, because of its association with the heroic age, made it a title to be preserved. The Lagin, too, had laid claim to this title and it was largely at their expense that the Uí Néill expanded, forcing them to yield in a long series of battles. No one lineage was able to dominate the Lagin internally. The northern segments were claimants to the kingship of Leinster until the eleventh century, when the Uí Chennselaig of the southern Lagin were to predominate. West of the Shannon the Connachta over-kingship was to alternate between the Uí Briúin and the two branches of the Uí Fiachrach, with the former tending to become predominant. From them were to come the Uí Conchobair kings who were ultimately to seize permanently the provincial kingship and gain an overlordship over the other provinces as well.

There were dozens of lesser lineages, each trying to secure advantage at the expense of neighbours. Segments within the great lineages were seldom willing to accept the permanent ascendancy of one segment, the result was often chaos. There was no tidy or uniform growth of overlordship leading to permanent over-kingdoms or provincial kingdoms, much less a kingdom of Ireland with what later tradition called a 'high king'. One reason for this was the island's topography which made communication difficult and left many *tuatha* virtually isolated. Dense forests, vast stretches of peat bogs, mountains and drumlins made much of the country impassable at certain times of the year. They also provided a refuge in time of war. More than half the island was uninhabited, even if parts could provide rough grazing. The remainder of the island contained as much bad as good land. Even with a small population, then, the average *tuath* could provide little more than a bare subsistence for the inhabitants. In the circumstances many a *rí* was glad to enter into a subordinate relationship with the nearest wealthy neighbour. Such a relationship was personal and gave the over-king no authority over the *tuath* of the subordinate king. It was thus difficult for effective over-kingdoms to emerge, especially since the traditional laws made the *tuath* of each man the area to which his rights were confined. It was only when later kings were bold enough to defy tradition, broke with customary law and began to expel lesser kings and occupy lands that real over-kingdoms could emerge.

Within the *tuath* society was intensely status conscious. Each grade (king, nobility, commoners, unfree) was subdivided by status, which for most people was fixed by the value of property owned, mainly land and cattle, and for a member of the nobility by the number of *céli* (clients) he possessed. Skill in an art, craft, or learning could also determine status and one of the most interesting features of early Irish society was the existence of a special class, the *áes dána* (men of art), a learned class (including the clergy) which was given a high status. It was status which fixed honour and accorded it a value, usually defined in numbers of cattle. Thus a simple *rí* of a *tuath* had an honour-price of fifty or so cows. The importance of honour-price was that it limited a man's value at law, as a witness, a surety, an oath-taker. It also fixed compensation, and naturally had political implications, limiting the role a king could play in external relations.

The king was limited in other ways. He had no standing army, nothing like a police force, no civil service. He was neither a judge nor a law-giver, empowered only to issue temporary ordinances in an emergency. As the office was elective, the would-be king had to buy support and thus made himself dependent to a degree on his supporters. The royal *fine* (kin – the extended family which was the land owning group) could split into factions and challenge for the office. Succession disputes were a source of weakness internally and in a later age could be exploited by neighbours powerful enough, if they had the necessary resources, to intervene and exert subordination as the price of support.

So long, then, as the traditional laws were respected, the *rí* was severely restricted in political action. Once the laws were written down in classical law tracts, by about the middle of the eighth century, they were given immutable status and were expounded by conservative legal scholars. While society changed, the laws remained sacred and unchangeable. They thus ceased to reflect contemporary society from the late eighth century onwards and it is clear that strong rulers were then ignoring customary limitations and relying on force to achieve their political ambitions. The Irish annals began to reflect the change. New titles were devised to indicate that a *rí* of a *tuath* had been forced to accept the overlordship of a more powerful neighbour: he might be called in Latin a *dux* or in Irish a *tigerna* or *tuísech* (lord). The higher title of *rí* came to be reserved for the most powerful dynasts who were to establish genuine and permanent overlordships covering a wide area.

In ecclesiastical circles, too, something of the same break with traditional values can be seen. The creation of an extensive *paruchia* almost inevitably involved the filiation in some kind of power struggle with others, as we saw in the case of Armagh and Kildare. But it went on at a lower level as well. Monasteries seeking prestige had to compete with others for property, privilege and rights. This was partly the reason why lives of saints were written in the idiom of the old heroic tales, for it was necessary to show the saint as superhuman, a great miracle worker and a great intercessor before the throne of God. His monastery would benefit accordingly, attracting pilgrims seeking the help of the saint. His relics would be more valuable, in demand not only for purely ecclesiastical purposes but for healing, to add weight to an oath, even to lend assistance in battle. With the help of historians the saint's name might even be attached to a *lex* or *cáin* (law) which could be proclaimed in his name and provide his monastery with an income. The most famous of all, the *Cáin Phatraic*, was promulgated by Armagh over much of Ireland. There were many lesser ones, more limited in the area they covered. Initially these *cána* were designed to promote peace, a kind of truce of God, so as to ameliorate the effects of war. But in time they came to be regarded as a tribute which the monastery had the right to levy and the word *cáin* itself came to have this meaning. It is clear, too, that the *cáin* could only be promulgated with the connivance of the secular authorities, who would hope to benefit. Indeed since many of the monasteries were already being absorbed into the greater lineages, the promulgation of *cána* was increasingly done to foster purely secular interests.

The pursuit of material gain was not the only way in which the church manifested increasing secularization. By the eighth century many of the monasteries were being run almost as family estates. It had been common for abbots to be chosen from the same lineage as the founder. On Iona all the abbots, with only two exceptions out of twelve, down to 724 were from the same kin as Colum Cille. They were celibate and in orders. But increasingly abbots married, did not take major orders, and passed office to sons. Hereditary succession became common and, as in the secular world, this often led to quarrels involving different segments of a lineage and could end in bloodshed. In 783 what the annals call a *bellum* (war) took place at Ferns between the abbot and another faction. Worst of all, monasteries went to war with each other. In 764 when Clonmacnois and Durrow fought each other it was reported that 200 of the *familia* of the latter perished.

Increasing secularization did not necessarily mean that all spiritual values were abandoned or that ascetic standards fell everywhere. Even the most secularized of the monasteries supported anchorites. But there does seem to have been an increasing awareness among some monks that there was a decline in standards and a need for a return to earlier practices. In the second half of the eighth century a remarkable ascetic reform began which lasted for nearly a century. The reformers borrowed a secular term to designate themselves as *céli dé* (clients of God), implying that they had entered into a special contract of service with God, analogous to that of *célsine* (clientship) between a *flaith* (lord) and his *céle* (client) in the secular world. It lacked the organization of a cohesive movement and it ultimately wasted away as a consequence. But before then the reformers had fired the imagination of many and led a return to earlier asceticism and the anchorite life. Máel-ruain founded a monastery at Tallaght and made it a centre of reform. His disciple Duiblitir founded another at Finglas. These monasteries became known as the 'two eyes of Ireland'. From them reform was carried as far away as Terryglass, on Lough Derg on the Shannon, and Loch Cré, near Roscrea. The reformers looked on the body as a possible occasion of sin and therefore prescribed austere penances to keep it under subjection. Cross vigils, flagellation and other extreme forms of asceticism were practised. Women were to be shunned and Sunday, as the Lord's Day, must be strictly kept, almost as a Jewish sabbath.

But we must not overstress the asceticism of the reformers. They were much concerned with liturgical practices and above all with prayer, which should be at the centre of every monk's life. They were not true puritans. One of the records of their teaching, the 'Rule of the Céli Dé', said that 'the kingdom of heaven is granted to him who directs studies, and to him who studies, and to him who supports the pupil who is studying'. This ready acceptance of study as a part of God's work is very typically Irish and shows that the reformers wanted no radical departure from the Irish tradition. The communities which accepted all or some of the teaching of the *céli dé* continued to maintain a scriptorium, collect literature, and put it into great books. They made room for the anchorites, maintained them and admired them. There was no forced uniformity and no attempt at centralization; each reformed house went its own way. This is reflected in the poetry which depicted the anchorite and his relations with God. He might be noble born, with a diet of salmon, honey and strawberries; or of a more lowly origin, living on watercress and what he can find in the surrounding forest. The one might drink beer, the other confine himself to pure water. But both desire solitude, 'a secret hut in the wilderness' or a 'hut in the wood, none knows it but my lord'; there they feel close to God and can pray undisturbed. For both prayer is the heart of the matter.

One of the most famous of the *céli dé* was Oengus, who wrote a calendar of saints (*Félire Oengusso*) in the late eighth or early ninth century. In the prologue he included a poem which celebrated the passing of the old pagan centres with their kings and the triumph of the new Christian monasteries with their saints. King Ailill and his fort at Croghan have vanished; it is to Clonmacnois that kings now come. Navan fort has been destroyed, with ruins everywhere; but Glendalough remains, so big that half the world seems to be there. But that world of saints and scholars was already under attack from the ambition and greed of powerful lineages and secularized churchmen. Ireland's 'golden age' was being tarnished. Soon it was to be shattered by a new scourge which was to lash the Irish church, the pagan Vikings who descended in hordes to loot the exposed and unprotected monasteries wherever they were accessible.

2   The Viking impact

The sudden appearance of Viking raiders in the Irish Sea was the start of a new phase in the development of Ireland. For many generations the island had been spared the barbarian invasions and settlements which had shattered local communities all over Europe and helped to shape the new kingdoms which were to emerge from the ruins of the Roman empire. Ireland had gone her own way unimpeded. But the raid on Lambey Island in Dublin Bay in 795 was the beginning of a process which was to change all that. The raiders were Scandinavian, possibly the same group which had sacked Lindisfarne on the other side of England in 793. These were the Vikings who were to leave such a profound impression on the Irish consciousness that they came to represent the very essence of evil and bloodthirsty vandalism, not to be equalled until Cromwell came more than 800 years later. When an Irish king in the early fourteenth century wished to impress upon a contemporary the iniquity of the English in Ireland he wrote that they were 'more wicked than the inhuman Danes themselves', reflecting the folk memory of the Viking terror.

Those who first invaded Ireland were in fact Norse, not Danish. They also plundered the remote monasteries on the Atlantic islands of Inismurray and Inisboffin in 795 and from then on Viking raiders were to sack monastic communities all around the Irish coast. These raids were part of a wider series which devastated people and property in England and along the Frankish coast. Small bands, often in only one ship, snatched booty from unprotected monasteries and carried it home. When they could find no precious metals or valuable jewellery they took food and slaves, sometimes held people and valuable objects such as relics to ransom. Often they destroyed wantonly, especially books upon which they placed no value; always they seemed bloodthirsty and savagely destructive, killing, burning and levelling.

No place near the coast was safe, especially monasteries on isolated islands which were most at risk. Iona was raided in 795, in 802, and again in 806 when nearly 70 members of the community were killed. So great was the danger that precious Colum Cille relics were removed for safety to a new church far inland at Kells in Ireland. Bangor, with its school, was attacked two years running: in 823, when scholars were killed and the precious shrine of Comgall was destroyed, and in 824. Even the small community of hermits perched high on Skellig rock off the Kerry coast did not escape and suffered in 824. Viking ships, with their ferocious animal heads for bowsprits, appeared out of nowhere and left smoking ruins behind them. Only a stormy sea, when the ships could not travel, meant safety and a quiet night for the monks. Deep in Europe an anonymous Irish monk remembered the terror and recalled the feeling which the sound of a howling wind brought:

> There's a wicked wind tonight,
> Wild upheaval in the sea;
> No fear now that the Viking hordes
> Will terrify me.

During the first phase of the Viking onslaught, which penetrated only short distances inland, it was impossible to provide any kind of warning which would cover the whole coastline. With their great mobility and superior weapons the Vikings seemed to be irresistible. Even when they moved inland, little protection could be offered against them by local rulers. Armagh was raided three times in one month in 823. Occasionally a small raiding party was trapped inland and destroyed – for example, one in Ulster in 811 and others in Connacht and Kerry in 812. But with the Scandinavian settlement of the northern islands and the Hebrides providing bases closer to Ireland, larger forces began to appear and a more terrible period of Viking raids began. In 827 the Irish annals reported a fleet of 60 ships on the Boyne and another fleet on the Liffey. Even larger fleets began to appear – one of 120 in 849. The Vikings now began to use the rivers, especially the Shannon, to plunder sites far inland. They made the rivers their highways, where necessary using porterage to get the ships through waters which were not navigable. In 863, using the Boyne, they plundered the ancient sites of Newgrange, Knowth and Dowth. They also began to place fleets on the larger inland lakes – one on Lough Neagh in 839, for example. The following year that fleet wintered on the lake, which changed the character of Viking raids. From now on the raiders wintered in Ireland and quickly established permanent settlements. The earliest of these *longphorts* (defended places where their ships would be safe) were situated along the east coast, Dublin being the most famous. Later some of them were to grow into Ireland's first real towns but in the mid-ninth century their character was entirely military and from them the Norse were able to mount sustained and more destructive attacks. At this time it seemed as if they might easily conquer and colonize large parts of Ireland, particularly in the northern half which bore the brunt of the attack. This is how it seemed to observers abroad. A Frankish chronicle reported in 847 that 'the Irish, who had been attacked by the Northmen for a number of years, were made into regular tribute-payers'.

That was an exaggeration which hid an important development, when some Irish allied with the Vikings and at the same time continued their own internal struggles. Intermarriage took place, resulting in a mixed Hiberno-Norse race which was bilingual, even if a commentator scornfully described their Irish as *gioc-goc* (pidgin Irish). There may even have been closer ties, resulting from fosterage which in Ireland could be more binding than blood-relationship: in some annals the Hiberno-Norse are referred to as 'foster-sons of the Norse'. Some, too, must have been converted to Christianity, which may have helped them to be assimilated. The annals had consistently called the Vikings *geinte* (gentiles, that is pagans), but later dropped the term in favour of the more popular *gaill* (foreigners), suggesting that they had at least lost paganism as their most distinguishing characteristic.

But most Scandinavian settlers kept to themselves. The ninth-century cemetery which was excavated at Islandbridge near Dublin showed that the settlers there brought Scandinavian women with them when they decided to remain permanently in Ireland. It also revealed in the profusion of swords and other weapons that the settlement was primarily a military one, for all that there was evidence of other crafts as well. In the mid-ninth century the Vikings were still foreign, pagan and military intruders, bent on loot and destruction. In this they were eminently successful, despite the occasional defeat which some of them suffered. In 845 the Uí Néill over-king Máel Sechnaill captured and put to death by drowning a Viking leader named Turgéis by the Irish. In a later propaganda history, *Cogadh Gaedhel re Gallaibh* (The war of the Irish with the Foreigners), written in support of the Munster O Briens, Turgéis was depicted as a superhero, a sort of Viking high king who almost conquered the whole island. But the real man was of much less stature. His death made little difference to the other Vikings who continued with their onslaughts.

One result of the destruction of the monasteries was a new exodus of Irish monks to Europe. Some scholars fled the terror, bringing to safety precious books and the learning they contained and they found a ready welcome in the schools of the west. But they also continued the older tradition of pilgrimage, though its character had changed. The tombs of earlier Irish saints were now attracting pilgrims, such as that of Fursa, who died in 650, at Peronne. It became such a noted Irish centre that it had a cult of St Patrick and was popularly known as *Peronna Scottorum* (Peronne of the Irish), until it was destroyed by the Vikings in 880. There were many other places ruled by Irishmen who tried to preserve the kind of abbatial authority familiar to them at home. Ultimately, however, they had to yield to the more orthodox system of episcopal authority, particularly in Germanic lands which came under the influence of English missionaries. Virgil of Salzburg had ruled his diocese as abbot from the monastery of St Peter's, with another Irishman, Dubdagrecus (Dub-dá-chrich), as bishop to perform necessary episcopal functions. Not for many years did he yield to pressure from Boniface, the primate. This was typical. But before the end of the eighth century Irish missionaries in Europe had conformed to the idea of episcopal authority, just as their monasteries were adopting the Benedictine rule which was now the norm.

Virgil of Salzburg first achieved notoriety at the court of Pipin. He was a learned scholar, with a particular interest in cosmography, and author of an influential work supposedly edited by St Jerome from a pagan original. As a scholar he also typified the change which was taking place in the character of Irish missionary activity in Europe. Irish monks were now coming as teachers. There were Irish scholars at the court of Charlemagne and some were to play an important part in the revival of learning associated with that emperor and his successors. When Charlemagne looked for someone to take charge of his palace school he chose the Englishman Alcuin. But Alcuin was the product of an Irish education, he brought an Irishman, Joseph, to help him, and his successor as head of the school was another Irishman. The script invented in Ireland was brought to Europe by Irish scribes and can still be seen in surviving manuscripts in the great libraries of Europe. Even though it was overtaken by the Carolingian minuscule, it left a permanent mark on European scripts, in particular its system of abbreviation which was universally adopted. In manuscript decoration, too, Irish influence can be seen and the insular tradition brought by Irish master painters had a lasting effect. Even music was influenced by Irish teachers, one of whom was the author of the earliest treatise on polyphony, which was brought from Ireland.

Some Irish scholars flocked to the new centres of scholarship, hoping to benefit from the new learning available there. This might suggest that at home learning had gone into decline as a result of the Viking raids, a view expressed in ninth century Europe by a writer who poured scorn on Irish scholars, 'workers without skill and teachers without learning. . . . To go to the end of the world and visit Ireland is a great toil without profit'. Yet learning of a high standard was still available in ninth-century Ireland, despite the impact of the Vikings, capable of producing scholars and poets who greatly impressed their peers in France. Men like Clemens, the head of the palace school, or Dungal, who wrote a treatise on the eclipse of the sun at the request of the emperor in 810, or Dicuil, who wrote the best geographical treatise to survive from the early middle ages, were scholars of wide learning which they brought from Ireland. Many of them were accomplished poets. One, Donatus (probably the same Irishman who was Bishop of Fiesole from 826 to 877), wrote a life of Brigit in Latin verses which displays the ease and fluency of a master. The most outstanding of these poets was Sedulius, called Scottus (Irishman), one of an Irish colony at Liege under the patronage of Bishop Hartgar. Sedulius wore his learning lightly, writing wittily to his patron of the burden of work placed on his shoulders and ending: 'Muse, tell my lord bishop and father his servant is dry'. He was a unique voice in his time, anticipating the later goliardic poetry. But he was much more than the greatest poet of his generation. A master of Greek as well as Latin, a biblical scholar of note, a commentator on Virgil, Ovid, and especially Horace (to some extent his model), he was the author of *On Christian Rulers*, one of the first 'mirrors of princes'. Sedulius combined his great learning with a deep spirituality which was very Irish, aware of his own sinful nature and his need of God:

I read or write, I teach or wonder what is truth,
I call upon my God by night and day.
I eat and freely drink, I make my rhymes,
And snoring sleep, or vigil keep and pray.
And very ware of all my shames I am;
O Mary, Christ, have mercy on your man.

Towering over all his contemporaries was the mighty figure of John Scottus (who called himself *Eriugena* or scion of Ireland). He was the leading figure of another circle of Irish scholars at Laon, where the palace school was situated and of which he was the most famous teacher. In a long scholarly career as philosopher and theologian he left an abiding mark on the intellectual history of Europe. Like Sedulius he was a poet, if not a great one, and was unique in his ability to compose verses in Greek. His deep knowledge of that language enabled him to make available for the first time in translation works which were to have a profound influence, most notably the work attributed to Dionysius the Araeopagite, the disciple of St Paul, which was subsequently to be so important in shaping medieval thought. But it was his own original works which marked his genius, like his commentaries on the gospel of St John or the theology of Boethius. He also engaged in polemic against the greatest heretic of the day, which helped to shape his own theology. Out of this he provided the first great synthesis of theology, unequalled until that of Aquinas in the thirteenth century. This was his most important work, *De Divisione Naturae* (On the division of nature), which went far beyond the comprehension of contemporaries in its daring speculation and erudition, so that it quickly came to be regarded as unorthodox. Even as late as 1225 it was condemned by Pope Honorius and remained banned for centuries.

John himself would have protested his orthodoxy, just as he proclaimed his Irishness. He was a product of conservative monasticism, and when in the prologue of his great work he wrote 'I offer this work first of all to God' (though dedicating it to Wulfad 'my beloved brother in Christ and fellow-searcher for truth') he was echoing the age-old monastic identification of work with prayer. Like all the Irish monks who went to Europe as teachers and scholars John retained a commitment to his spiritual calling. He does not seem in any sense a refugee. Neither does Sedulius, although he was Irish enough to celebrate in a poem a defeat of the Vikings at home, with the victors 'quaffing the blood of a savage oppressor' and 'three times ten thousand' lying bloody 'on that dread field'. Sedulius in fact may first have come to Europe as part of an embassy from Ireland to the court of Charles the Bold in 848. According to French annals which recorded the event, the Irish came to announce a victory over the Norse and requested free passage for their king to make a pilgrimage to Rome.

But in Ireland in that year the Norse had suffered not one but four important defeats. Two of these were gained by the Uí Néill under Máel Sechnaill in Meath and by the Eóganacht near Cashel. So the tide began to turn against the Vikings in Ireland. Irish kings were adapting to the situation, exploiting it to their own advantage in the struggle for overlordship. Viking settlements were shown to be vulnerable and they were also weakened by dissension amongst themselves. In 851 the first Danish fleet arrived in Irish waters and violently attacked the Norse of Dublin. Other Norse retaliated and soon there was bloody war between the two groups, distinguished by the Irish as *Dub-Gaill* (Black Foreigners) and *Finn-Gaill* (Blonde Foreigners), no doubt because of predominant hair-colouring. The Irish took full advantage of this dissension, even helping one side against the other. By 866 the Uí Néill king Aed Findliath cleared the Vikings out of their northern settlements, raids noticeably slackened and the number of attacks on monasteries began to decline. Increasingly, too, the Norse were diverted to involvement in local politics. In 860, for example, the Dublin Norse allied with Aed Findliath in his attempt to wrest Uí Néill overlordship from Máel Sechnaill and during the second half of the ninth century they were frequently involved in Irish dynastic struggles. Nevertheless, it is hardly a coincidence that the decline in Viking raids on Irish churches was contemporary with increased activity in Europe, where richer churches were just as vulnerable. It is likely that many of the Vikings of Ireland were attracted away by the wealth so easily procured elsewhere.

In the popular mind the Vikings of the ninth century were savage heathens who seemed to have a special hatred for Christianity. *A furore Normannorum libera nos Domine* (From the fury of the Northmen deliver us O Lord) was the pious ejaculation which represented the fears of many in Ireland. At the same time another prayer for deliverance 'from a flood of foreigners and pagans and tribulations, from plagues of fire and famine and disorders' hints that not all of the disasters of that terrible time were to be attributed to the Vikings. Irish kings, as we have seen, were complacent about using the foreigners as allies in their power struggles and such men certainly played their part in causing havoc and ruin in many parts of Ireland. A bizarre example is Fedelemid mac Crimthainn, the Eóganacht King of Cashel from 820 to 847. In his obituary in the annals of Ulster he is called *optimus Scottorum, scriba et ancorita* (the best of the Irish, scribe and anchorite) and elsewhere he is referred to as a bishop, which is doubtful. But as king he was especially violent, responsible for the destruction of more churches than any Viking. In 823 he burned Gallen 'with its entire habitation and its oratory', the same year in which in conjunction with the abbot of Armagh he promulgated the *Cáin Phatraic* (Law of Patrick) in Munster. Fore was burned in 830, Clonmacnois in 832 and again in 833, when many of the community were killed. Durrow suffered similarly in the same year. In 836 he sacked Kildare and captured the abbot of Armagh, seized the abbacy of Cork and took the abbot away to Cashel where the annals record that he 'died without communion'. Two years later he usurped the abbacy of Clonfert. He was clearly not worried about possible repercussions, disregarding the vengeance of the great saints whose churches he sacked. But according to reports in the annals his violent sacrileges were finally revenged in 844, after he had sacked Clonmacnois yet again. He was pursued by an outraged St Ciaran, who wounded him with his crozier, a wound from which Fedelmid eventually died.

Fedelmid was, in fact, pursuing an aggressive policy of expansion, trying to establish Eóganacht overlordship beyond the traditional Munster boundaries. There was precedent for this. In 721 an earlier King of Cashel, Cathal mac Finguine, had challenged the Uí Néill in alliance with the King of Leinster and according to the southern annals of Inisfallen had procured the submission of the Uí Néill king. He invaded Meath again in 733. A century later Fedelmid was pursuing the same goal. In 830 the southern annals record the defeat of a combined Uí Néill and Connacht army. Then in 838 they record that there was 'a great assembly of the men of Ireland in Clonfert', where the King of Tara submitted to Fedelmid, 'so that he became full King of Ireland on that day'. If it is difficult to accept this literally, there can be no doubt that Fedelmid was a key figure not only in the history of the Eóganachta of Cashel, but also in the struggles of expanding dynasties which were eventually to lead to the attempt to create a kingship of Ireland. Not only did he not attack the Vikings; he did not scruple to use them if need be. He raided widely over the midlands and deep into Uí Néill territory and took hostages from the King of Connacht.

Another King of Cashel, Cormac mac Cuilennáin, also challenged the Uí Néill. He was certainly a bishop, a distinguished scholar who was reputedly the author of many works (notably *Cormac's Glossary*). But he was also an aggressive expansionist. In 907 he put a fleet on the Shannon and raided the midlands and Connacht, taking hostages and defeating the Uí Néill. The following year, 908, he was defeated and killed at Belach Mugna (in county Carlow) by the combined forces of the Uí Néill and the Laigin. This battle is significant for many reasons. It devastated the Eóganacht of Cashel and the next Munster King of prominence, Cellachán, came from a different segment. Although he too followed an aggressive line against the Uí Néill, using the Waterford Vikings, he was no match for the northerners. He was taken prisoner and held for a time in Meath. He found difficulty in retaining the over-kingship of Munster, being confronted by Cennétig, the King of Dál Cais. Even though Cennétig was defeated, his son Mathgamain seized the kingship of Cashel in 963, which shattered the power of the Eóganachta. It was with the Dál Cais that the future lay.

This development was indirectly the result of the battle of Belach Mugna. But that battle had another significance. It was fought as a result of the Eóganacht invasion of Leinster and it is likely that what was at stake was the overlordship of that province. Should it go to the Eóganacht king it would be an enormous boost to his aggrandizement at the expense of the Uí Néill. The defeat of Cormac mac Cuilennáin not only destroyed Eóganacht dreams of expansion into the northern half, it confirmed the supremacy of the Uí Néill King of Tara, Flann Sinna, who well knew the importance of Leinster. His Uí Néill predecessors had often tried to extend their lordship over Leinster and had even tried partition in 818. They had also gained prestige in containing the Vikings. Most importantly they had succeeded in gaining the submission of the King of Munster. This was achieved by one of their greatest kings, Máel Sechnaill, who had executed the Viking leader Turgéis. After taking hostages from Munster in 854 and 856, a large-scale invasion in 858 finally reduced the province to submission. The following year Munster ceded the kingdom of Osraige to Tara and for the first time Munster acknowledged an Uí Néill king as superior. When he died in 862 Máel Sechnaill was called King of Ireland in the annals. His successor, Aed Findliath, was unable to maintain this position, though he did succeed in consolidating his over-kingship in the northern half. He also had notable success against the Vikings and forced them to abandon their settlements in the area under his suzerainty. It was the next King of Tara, Flann Sinna, who was the victor of Belach Mugna in 908. Previous to that he had forced the King of Connacht to submit and in 902 the Norse were forced to abandon their most important settlement in Ireland, Dublin.

At the beginning of the tenth century, then, it seemed that the Uí Néill kings of Tara were well on the way to establishing an over-kingdom which would embrace much of Ireland and that they had neutralized the Norse threat. In the whole of Ireland, now, there were only about a dozen kingdoms which were politically important. In these the kings had been strengthened by the theory of kingship being enlarged, so that their rights and power were emphasized, and not just the more traditional duties. Royal authority was being defined in a series of texts which were drafted by ecclesiastics who were jurists. These churchmen acted as advisors to the greater kings and instructed them in kingship. The most important churches actively associated themselves with the powerful local dynasts and promoted their interests. Armagh identified with the Uí Néill and the abbot of Armagh was present at the assembly of 859 which ceded Osraige to the over-kingship of Máel Sechnaill.

It is important, too, that the concept of an Irish nation came to be defined. We can see it already in existence in an early seventh century text which talks about 'the nation without law'. The classical law tracts also show the same awareness when referring to the 'custom of Ireland' or ' the jurisprudence of the land of Ireland'. As we saw earlier Muirchú in the mid-seventh century, writing about St Patrick, could refer to Tara as 'the capital of the Irish'. In the poetry attributed to Colum Cille there is a keen awareness of Ireland and of being Irish. This recognition of the Irish as a race distinct from all others was a necessary part of the development of a history of Ireland which the monk-scholars elaborated to fit in with the Christian scheme of universal history. By the mid-seventh century an origin legend, of the kind which each dynasty was able to provide for itself, had been constructed for the people of Ireland. This provided an ancestor in Míl of Spain and through him it was possible to trace ancestry back to Noah. For centuries afterwards the legend was refined and elaborated until it was included into the twelfth century *Lebor Gábála*

Érenn (*Book of the Conquests of Ireland*), a synthetic history of the Irish people. By then the idea of a high King of all Ireland (árd rí Érenn) was being given reality by different dynasts and it was important to push the idea as far back in time as possible. But that was to falsify the past. The concept of an árd rí who ruled Ireland did not exist in the earlier period and the very title, although used of some Uí Néill over-kings, could also be given to minor kings and even to the Norse King of Dublin.

But in the early tenth century the future seemed to lie with the Uí Néill kings. In 916 Niall Glúndub (Black Knee) became over-king. Three years later he was dead, killed by the Norse leader Sitric at the battle of Islandbridge near Dublin. This was a dramatic reversal of Uí Néill fortunes and it marked a significant and dangerous renewal of Viking activity in Ireland. Left without land to colonize in the west, and with few easy targets providing rich booty, the Vikings returned in force to Ireland. In a graphic phrase the twelfth-century *Cogadh Gaedhel re Gallaibh* (The war of the Irish with the foreigners) described the sea vomiting them on the shores of Ireland, so numerous were they. In 914 large fleets began to land on Ireland, the first at Waterford. Munster suffered most at first, further weakening the Eóganachta. In 917 Niall Glúndub came to their assistance and even laid siege to Waterford. But by now there were too many new Norse settlers spreading out through Munster. Apart from small inland settlements, there were larger ones in Dublin, Wexford, Waterford, Cork and Limerick, which in time grew into wealthy towns and petty kingdoms. King Niall in 917 was depending on the help of the Lagin, but in a battle fought near St Mullins (County Carlow) the Norse totally defeated the King of Leinster with terrible slaughter. Ominously, the annals recorded the appearance of a comet, a bad omen, in that year. The Norse leader, Sitric, then pressed on and occupied Dublin where he rapidly established a powerful new kingdom. In 919 Niall Glúndub, with other northern kings, came south to face Sitric and suffered defeat and death at Islandbridge.

Under Sitric, Dublin was to go from strength to strength. Raiding parties penetrated far inland, sacking Armagh for example in 921, and there can be no doubt that had Sitric concentrated his energies on Ireland he would have been a formidable threat to the provincial kings in their ambitions. But he preferred to seek his fortune in York, where he ruled until 927. This Dublin–York connection was maintained, to the detriment of Dublin. Each Dublin king in turn tried to move on to York and finally, in 937, they suffered a disaster in the battle of Brunanburh at the hands of King Athelstan. If this battle was a crucial milestone in the emergence of England, it was hardly of less importance in the history of Dublin. In 938 the Uí Néill over-king Donnchad attacked Dublin and moved on to sack the land to the south. Still the Dublin kings continued to meddle with York and left themselves open to attack in Ireland. So Dublin gradually became less important in Irish politics, declined somewhat as a military power, and became more of a mercantile centre with trading links all over the Viking world.

Apart from that, Dublin had also dissipated its energies in trying to win some kind of hegemony over the other Viking colonies in Ireland. But they never met with permanent success and it merely contributed to the bitter quarrels which weakened Viking settlements with no love for one another. Although the Viking presence in Ireland was greatly augmented in the tenth century, the different groupings could not coalesce and in the end were to be dominated by the leading Irish kingdoms. They continued to be a menace however and Viking raids could still inflict suffering. In 950, for example, the Dublin Norse set fire to the round tower in Slane killing the people who had taken refuge there. Such round towers were themselves a symbol of continuing Viking aggression. They are assumed to be the *cloictech* (house of bells) often mentioned in the annals as attached to a monastery, but it is hard to believe that such massive, high stone towers were laboriously constructed simply to serve as belfries for the monks. It seems certain that they were primarily intended to provide refuge for people and valuables during attack. While their precise chronology is obscure, the first half of the tenth century was a period when many were built, coinciding with the renewed Viking terror and suggesting that they were intended as places of refuge.

The Viking impact was marked in other ways. Obviously many monasteries disappeared for ever. Nendrum, on an island in Strangford Lough, was attacked around 820, partly destroyed, and subsequently rebuilt. A stone wall was added for protection, as well as a tower. But in 874 it was sacked and burned, the abbot was killed, and the monastery was abandoned for good. This must have happened to many other communities, so that the number throughout Ireland was drastically reduced. The larger ones survived and became even more important as centres of learning and the arts, but the constant destructive attacks necessarily took their toll. Manuscript illumination sharply declined as the marauders took a particular delight in 'drowning' (as the annals put it) fine books. So did the art of metalwork, which provided valuable loot for the raiders. From the period after 800, comparatively few manuscripts survive today and while this is certainly the result, in part, of natural loss through the passage of time, it also reflects the results of Viking depredations. Work in stone, however, is not subject to the same danger and there was no decline in sculpture, which may even have secured greater patronage as a safer medium. The high crosses in particular show a continuity which was not interrupted by the raiders. They also preserve their native character and show little sign of Viking influence. It was not until the late tenth and eleventh centuries that a pronounced Scandinavian style appeared in Irish art.

This suggests that before that the Scandinavian settlers had, for the most part, held themselves aloof and that very little integration had taken place. Some certainly had; there had been some intermarriage. and a few had been converted to Christianity. Olaf Cuarán, King of Dublin, retired to die on the monastery of Iona. Traders, too, had clearly influenced commercial life. For the first time coins circulated in Ireland, first pennies of English manufacture and then, from the late tenth century, those produced by the Norse mint in Dublin. New words came into Irish from Norse which show the character of the influence: *pingin* (penny) and *margad* (market) are two. Others show a borrowing of terms relating to ships and shipping, such as *bád* (boat) and *ancaire* (anchor). There is no doubt that Irish kings also learned the true value of ships in warfare from the Vikings. On a more mundane level a scatter of Norse placenames, such as Leixlip, Howth, or Wicklow, give some evidence of Scandinavian penetration. More interestingly the names of three provinces, Ulster, Munster, Leinster, are a combination of Irish and Norse elements.

While all of this in sum may seem impressive evidence of Scandinavian integration, there is more which shows the opposite. Experts have estimated that altogether less than 50 borrowings from Norse came into the Irish language. Placenames, with few exceptions, remained staunchly Irish, even within the vicinity of Dublin itself, which was never given a Norse name. Not until the end of the millennium did the settlers forsake their pagan gods and adopt the Christian God of the Irish. Their culture remained essentially foreign until the eleventh century, even though there was some exchange of form and design among artists. Overall their impact on Ireland was largely destructive, even when allowance is made for the positive contribution they made to the island's economy. Because of them the character of warfare in Ireland became more savage, less discriminating in its victims, larger in scale and duration. The Irish, who even before the Vikings came to teach them were already abandoning traditional respect for holy places and people, soon began to match the foreigners in making war. As a result, the struggles of the great lineages for overlordship were given a new impetus and the suzerainties which they established were made more effective.

Nowhere can this be better seen than in the remarkable ascendancy of the Munster dynasty of Dál Cais. By the beginning of the eleventh century it had produced a king who had managed to make himself the greatest king in Ireland, Brian Borúma, who could confidently take the title of *Imperator Scottorum* (Emperor of the Irish). What is astonishing is that was not until 934 that his father Cennétig was able to become King of Dál Cais, the first of his segment to do so. His rise to power was meteoric, so that before he died in 951 he had become strong enough to challenge, albeit unsuccessfully, the Eóganacht of Cashel for supremacy in Munster. One explanation offered for this quick aggrandizement is that it was achieved with the help of the Uí Néill, who were anxious to distract the Eóganacht king from any further attempts at expansion into Meath. There may be some truth in this. But the very weakness of the Munster kings was enough to provide an opportunity to aspiring challengers. Cennétig of Dál Cais was simply in the best position to make the most of the opportunity. Other lineages had become so segmented that they were incapable of either blocking his way, or providing an alternative challenge to the weakened over-kings of Munster.

If Cennétig failed in his challenge, he had at least made an impression. The

Uí Néill King of Tara seems to have taken fright at the monster (as he saw it) he had helped to create, if the argument of earlier Uí Néill support for Dál Cais is true. At any rate, he invaded Thomond ('north Munster', the area then dominated by Dál Cais) in 950–51, killing two sons of Cennétig. That he did this at the very time when his own kingship was being challenged by a rival Uí Néill segment shows clearly his anxiety at Cennétig's rise to power. No wonder Cennétig on his death was called 'royal heir' of Munster by the annals of Inisfallen. By 963 his son Mathgamain, with the support of lesser kings, was able to seize the kingship of Cashel. As he grew stronger, he became more anxious to expand his power. Almost inevitably rivals appeared and, as so often happened, they sought Viking help. By the mid-tenth century the Viking settlement in Limerick, founded in 922, had grown in wealth and power, with its fleet dominating the lower Shannon. In alliance with Mathgamain's rivals, the Limerick Vikings met the Dál Cais in battle at Saloghead, in county Tipperary, in 967. Mathgamain showed his new strength in a famous victory, moving on to Limerick the following day. The city was taken, looted and burned. Later, Mathgamain expelled its king, after again defeating him, though he was unable to prevent him from returning in 969. Limerick was bitterly hostile to Dál Cais and always willing to join an alliance against Mathgamain, as it did in 974. But the Dál Cais king was now strong in east as well as west Munster. Not only was he able to procure help from the Déisi in the east, he made the Waterford Vikings his allies as well. He showed his authority in a more meaningful way in 973, when the abbot of Armagh came on a visitation to Munster. He clashed with the abbot of Emly and it was Mathgamain who arbitrated the dispute, finding in favour of Armagh. It was only through treachery that he was brought down in the end, when he was captured in 976 and handed over to his bitterest enemy who immediately killed him. Two years later the treachery was avenged in battle by Mathgamain's brother Brian, his successor in Dál Cais. As a result of that battle Brian became King of Munster and began straight away to consolidate his power in the southern province.

Brian Borúma was the most remarkable man in Irish politics of the tenth century. As with many great men of the past, reality has been so heavily encrusted with legend that it is now impossible to identify the real man. The later O Brien propaganda of the twelfth century tried to show Brian as an Irish Alfred the Great, fighting the Norse throughout his youth, even when he was left with only a tiny following of men, living in the impenetrable woods of Thomond to carry on the struggle against the hated foreigners. He was the champion who saved Ireland from the Vikings, finally defeating them in their last attempt to conquer the country, and at the same time preventing the triumph of the evil forces of paganism over the Christianity which had earned Ireland such fame abroad. Like Alfred, too, he was depicted as a great educator, bringing learning back to his people. He was a builder of churches, patron of the arts, in every way a great 'culture king' and not merely a great warrior. In all of this there is also a deliberate modelling of Brian on the great

Charlemagne, saviour of Europe. It is the image of Brian which has persevered to modern times and it is not easy to discredit it totally. Brian was a
great warrior, a shrewd politician, statesmanlike in his dealings with churchmen, kings and foreigners, able to achieve a degree of success in the attempt
to establish a kingdom of Ireland that was quite without precedent.

Even before his brother Mathgamain was killed, Brian had begun to show
signs of his ability and had won a place of prominence among the Dál Cais.
After he succeeded his brother, he killed the Norse King of Limerick and, in
a rapid series of battles, established himself firmly as King of Munster. By
983 he had obtained the submission of Leinster and taken hostages. Soon he
was following the traditional Munster path of expansion into the northern
half. This meant challenging Máel Sechnaill, the Uí Néill King of Tara. In
988 Brian raided Meath, working from a fleet which he had based on Lough
Ree. Máel Sechnaill retaliated by invading Munster in 989. For some years
the two greatest kings in Ireland engaged in hostilities, with Connacht and
Leinster suffering from the attacks and counter-attacks. All the time Brian's
power was growing, so that by 997 Máel Sechnaill was willing to face reality
and come to some kind of arrangement with the Munster king. A meeting
between the two took place near Clonfert and both agreed to acknowledge
the other's rightful sphere of influence: Máel Sechnaill was to be supreme in
the northern half of Ireland, Brian in the southern half. In recognition of this
arrangement, Brian received from Máel Sechnaill the hostages taken from the
Norse kingdom of Dublin and Leinster. The following year Brian, in turn,
gave Máel Sechnaill the hostages he had taken from Connacht.

This was an extraordinary achievement for Brian. In a comparatively short
time he had made himself over-king of the southern half and had forced the
over-king of the Uí Néill to recognize this as a reality. Máel Sechnaill was no
mean opponent. In 980 he had defeated the Dublin Norse, aided significantly
by Norse allies from the Hebrides, and in the following year he had captured
Dublin itself. He repeated this feat nine years later and imposed a famous tax
of one ounce of gold on every garth in the city. By then the Norse of Dublin
had established their own mint and were becoming wealthier by the year as
their trade grew. This wealth naturally attracted the attention of Irish kings
and in 995, Máel Sechnaill captured the city for the third time. On that occasion he brought away with him from the city two important trophies, the
ring of Thor and the sword of Carlus, twin symbols of Norse rule and religion. So that despite being weakened by opposition from other segments of
the Uí Néill, Máel Sechnaill was able to retain his position as King of Tara
and the most powerful king in Ireland, until he found himself confronted by
Brian Borúma.

The 997 arrangement could only be temporary at best. Both kings were
ambitious and strong, not likely to accept a permanent limit being set on their
kingship. So although they had honoured the agreement by handing over
hostages, and had even marched together against the Norse of Dublin, one or
the other would eventually feel strong enough to assert his superiority. The

chance first came to Brian. In 999 he had to face a Leinster revolt, backed by the Norse of Dublin, who chaffed under the dominance of the recently obscure Dál Cais. Brian reacted swiftly, marching to Leinster and crushing the rebels in a major confrontation at Glenn Máma, probably near Saggart in county Dublin. He marched into Dublin, where he remained for more than a month. Both Máel Morda of Leinster and Sitric of Dublin were forced to accept Brian as over-king and gave hostages in recognition of that fact. Now he felt strong enough to move on and challenge Máel Sechnaill for a greater prize. He called on Leinster and Dublin for support, summoned men from Munster, Osraige, and south Connacht and invaded Meath. But one part of his army was defeated in a skirmish and Brian, cautious as ever, withdrew. Two years later he was back, this time forcing his way via the Shannon through Athlone and compelling Máel Sechnaill to recognize him as over-king.

This great turning point in Brian's career is almost casually recorded in the annals, which simply tell how the Munster king took the hostages of Máel Sechnaill and of Connacht. But they conceal the dramatic turn-about in the fortunes of Máel Sechnaill who failed to procure the support of other Uí Néill segments and was left alone to face Brian and his superior forces. There was a later tradition that Brian magnanimously allowed Máel Sechnaill one month to gather support from the northern half, which he failed to do. The Uí Néill King of Ailech, Aed, is supposed to have replied to the request for help by saying that 'he would not risk his life in battle against the Dál Cais in defence of the sovereignty for any man'. In other words, he would help to protect the kingship of Tara when his dynasty was on the throne, but not when the southern Uí Néill occupied it. Whatever the truth of the story, it does reveal the fatal flaw in the position of the great over-kings, who were never able to establish any kind of real overlordship on a permanent basis, even within their own lineages. Ireland remained politically fragmented. Local particularism was still a prime fact of political life. Even when faced with life or death struggles against Viking invaders, small Irish kingdoms could still attack one another, heedless of the consequences provided that there was immediate gain. Rarely could they unite, never for very long.

Brian Borúma always had to contend with this fragmentation, even before he became over-king of southern Ireland. His power was limited, depending always on his personal intervention. It could never be delegated. Even the Viking settlements were beyond real control, except when he personally forced submission from them for limited periods. On occasion he might have to negotiate and accept compromise; sometimes he had to bargain. In 990, for example, Vikings captured a famous scholar at Roscarbury and demanded a ransom for his release, which Brian had to pay before the man was handed over on Scattery island on the Shannon. Whatever this may reveal about Brian's regard for scholarship, it does show that his kingship was limited in action.

After the capitulation of Máel Sechnaill in 1002, Brian pushed on into the north trying to make his over-kingship a reality. Even though he had men from Munster, Connacht, Leinster, Meath and Dublin, he was unable to exact hostages from all of the north. He tried again in 1004 and failed. The following year he switched tactics, going a different way and spending a week in Armagh, publicly recognizing its ecclesiastical primacy. Securing the support of Armagh was a shrewd move and his gift of 20 ounces of gold was a small price to pay. Visiting the library he was shown its most precious treasure, the *Book of Armagh*, believed to have been written by St Patrick himself. To commemorate the occasion his scribe, Máel Suthain, penned an entry in the book which referred to Brian as *Imperator Scottorum* (Emperor of the Irish), undoubtedly the king's own choice of title. What exactly it was meant to convey is obscure – perhaps 'king of the kings of Ireland', a title used by another Irish king 200 years later. But it was no more than a title. In this year, 1005, Brian gave it some substance by taking hostages from the greater kings in Ulster, with the exception of one dynasty, the Cenél Conaill, in the west. He came back again in 1006, taking more hostages but still failing to force the Cenél Conaill into submission. In 1007 he marched into Ulster yet again and received more hostages. But still Cenél Conaill held out, as they did in the face of yet another Dál Cais expedition in 1008.

So, in every year after the submission of Máel Sechnaill in 1002, Brian Borúma marched into the north to procure submissions. He displayed frantic energy in these royal circuits and showed fierce determination to succeed. But ultimate success eluded him, as the Cenél Conaill held out. In 1011 he made a supreme effort, this time combining an attack from the sea with the customary overland expedition. He not only managed to defeat the Cenél Conaill, taking enough booty to recompense the cost, but also succeeded in capturing the king and brought him back to Thomond where he forced submission from him as the price for his release. He had now managed to gain the submission of all the leading kings in Ireland, taking hostages as the symbol as well as the guarantee of his overlordship. In some areas, therefore, he had justified his title of *imperator* and was giving substance to the concept of a king (or high king, as he came to be called) of Ireland.

Yet in reality he had only the shadow of power. Not even he could bring true order into the maelstrom of Irish politics. There were no institutions of government which would enable him to rule from a distance or to delegate authority. Hostages were a poor substitute and were no guarantee of submissions wrung from unwilling kings only after the expensive use of force. Brian had to go to Ulster year after year, and still he could not be sure that the submissions so hard won would last for any length of time. Always there was the danger that one leading king or another would challenge his position, just as he had done with Máel Sechnaill. It came in 1012, when the northern Uí Néill king, Flaithbertach, tried to establish a new hegemony in the north with himself as leader. Máel Sechnaill resisted the new aggressor when he invaded Meath in 1013, but was unable to block the advance of Flaithbertach and had to retreat. In the same year the annals record that Brian built many fortresses in Thomond, almost as if he feared invasion from the north. But he also took the offensive, not in the north as one might expect, but in the east in Osraige and, through his son Murchad, in Leinster. Brian joined his son in September 1013 and together they laid siege to Dublin up to Christmas. Failing to take the city they lifted the siege and returned to Munster.

It is clear that Leinster, with the Norse of Dublin, had also repudiated the supremacy of Brian and that this was the reason for his invasion. They knew that he would be back the following spring when conditions would be better. So they looked for allies. The King of Dublin, Sitric, sailed to the Orkneys and made a bargain with Earl Sigurd to come to Dublin with his fleet on Palm Sunday 1014. He also negotiated an alliance with the Vikings of the Isle of Man. Máel Morda for his part tried to engage the support of south Leinster kings, but without success. Brian, too, began to prepare for battle. Now that his supremacy was under challenge his support fell away. No northern king would agree to help and only two of the lesser Connacht kings were willing to support him. Osraige held aloof and so Brian had to rely mostly on his own Munster forces. He did get help from Máel Sechnaill and Meath, but just before the battle was joined they left the field and returned home. What happened is not clear. It may be that Máel Sechnaill saw an opportunity for himself presented by the challenge to Brian and hoped that defeat might lead to a revival of his own fortunes, but we do not know.

On Good Friday, 23 April 1014, one of the most famous of all Irish battles was fought at Clontarf, north of Dublin. The numbers involved were large by contemporary standards, the contest lasted for an unprecedented day, the slaughter on both sides was terrible, and most of the leaders were killed. The Leinstermen and Norse were completely routed. But the victory was soured by the death of Brian Borúma, killed by one of the retreating Norse. His body was carried in solemn procession all the way to Armagh, almost as if he were too important to be buried at Clonmacnois or any other holy place in the south. This unprecedented act must have given the dead king, and the battle where he lost his life, a special significance in the eyes of contemporaries.

Before long the battle passed into legend and with each passing year it was invested with increasing import until it became 'the greatest battle in the western world'. It was not only in Irish tradition that Clontarf was given this legendary place. Scandinavian tradition, too, saw it as an epic encounter where great issues were decided. In both literatures, the battle is preceded by signs of doom: contestants are drenched with showers of blood, attacked by spears which leap from walls, ravens with iron beaks fly at them. The twelfth century *Book of Leinster* sees Brian as a sort of crusader, through whom 'the spells of heathendom were vanquished for ever by the superior powers of Christianity'. The Icelandic saga of *Burnt Njal*, which incorporates an earlier Brian saga, also depicts him as a great Christian king who 'died but saved his kingdom'. The same saga tells how Sitric of Dublin persuaded Sigurd of the Orkneys to come to Ireland by offering him 'the kingdom', as if the prize at stake at Clontarf were Ireland itself.

It is not easy to see how the importance of Clontarf was inflated so quickly in this way, if the battle simply resulted from Leinster's repudiation of the supremacy claimed by Brian Borúma. Nor is it clear why the Vikings of the Orkneys and the Isle of Man came to Clontarf. But it is surely significant that while the Irish annals make no mention of the foreigners between 1002 and 1012, they suddenly emerged again in 1013 when a great fleet invaded Munster and it looked as though the Viking terror was about to begin all over again. During those years England had been invaded and was conquered in 1013 by Svein Forkbeard, King of Denmark. He was succeeded as King of England by his son Canute. This may well have stirred ambitions in other Viking hearts and brought them to Ireland. In retrospect it was very likely seen as a renewal of Viking, pagan expansion which threatened Ireland, so that Brian at Clontarf was easily seen as a saviour. It was all grist to the mill of the propagandists, both Irish and Scandinavian, who were trying to use history to bolster their own particular causes.

In Ireland that cause was the ambition of twelfth-century kings who were trying to set themselves up as kings of Ireland and were looking for historical justification for their actions. But to credit Brian Borúma with the creation of a national monarchy is to distort his achievement. He had come a long way before he died and had shown what a strong, ambitious ruler could achieve. But that was far short of a kingship of all Ireland. By 1014 the island was still politically fragmented, for all that the great over-kings had managed to accomplish, and it was likely to remain so until institutions of government were developed through which a king could rule from a distance, gain control of land which was the basis of all wealth, become a lawmaker so that he might exploit as well as protect his people, and control the resources necessary to secure the substance of power for his family necessary to guarantee that it would inherit his kingship. Much of this was already happening. But it was in the years after Clontarf that a kingdom of Ireland, with a hierarchical national church to match, began to be transmitted into fact.

3 Church reform and political change

After Clontarf the hegemony created by Brian Borúma fell apart. His son Donnchad succeeded him as King of Dál Cais, but he had to fight off a challenge by his half-brother Tadg. The fatal tendency for segments of lineages to fight among themselves was once more in evidence. Máel Sechnaill of Meath, who had evaded Clontarf, reaped his reward by meeting no strong opposition to his rule, and until he died in 1022, he remained Ireland's most powerful king. But even he was in no position to take up where Brian Borúma had left off and it was a long time before another Irish king was successful in laying effective claim to the kingship of Ireland. This was a period of rapid political change in the provinces.

Brian's own line in Dál Cais suffered many vicissitudes, It was not until 1025 that Donnchad had Tadg killed and was able to assume the undisputed kingship of Munster. He then began to expand, taking hostages from Connacht and Leinster and even from Meath. But he was unable to maintain this momentum, or to overcome challenges from Osraige and a revived Eóganacht of Cashel. Other provincial kings began to interfere in Munster, first Leinster and then Connacht. Still Donnchad persevered, calling himself 'king of Ireland' in the shrine he provided for the celebrated Stowe missal. But it was an empty boast. Even in Munster his lordship was shaky. Eventually his nephew Turlough, son of the murdered Tadg, rose to confront him. By 1059 Donnchad's position was so weak that he was forced to submit to the King of Connacht. Four years later, in 1063, he handed over the kingship of Munster to his nephew Turlough and a new round of dynastic struggles began.

In Leinster, meanwhile, the first of the Uí Chennselaig dynasty became king in 1042. This was Diarmait and for the next 30 years he was to manipulate the internal rivalries of other lineages, especially in Munster, to his own advantage. He asserted his authority over the Norse cities of Waterford, Wexford and especially Dublin. Their existence was now turned to advantage, economic as well as military. Diarmait even made himself King of Dublin for a time and inserted his son there as his regent. He attacked Meath, a sure sign of his ambitions to expand beyond the limits of his provincial kingship. He allied with Connacht and, more importantly, with Turlough O Brien in his

struggles for the kingship of Munster. As a result he became the most powerful king in the southern half of Ireland. It was time to strike for a bigger
prize. In 1067, when Connacht (already weakened as a result of invasion by
the northern Uí Néill) was torn by internal struggles, Diarmait and his allies
crossed into the province in a bid for power. But the intrusion was a failure
and Dermot had to withdraw. Five years later he was killed in battle near
Navan, while attempting a new expansion northwards, an event noted far
away in Mainz by the scribe of the Irish *inclusus* (enclosed hermit) Marianus
in the margin of his chronicle: 'the year of the killing of Diarmait King of
Leinster'. His death was also recorded in the Book of Leinster, where he was
awarded a significant new title: *Rí hÉrend co Fressabra* (king of Ireland with
opposition).

That was no empty boast by a later Leinster propagandist. During his
reign Diarmait had made himself the strongest king in the south and had
shown a willingness and capacity to extend the limits of his kingship northwards. If it was an exaggeration to invest his rule with a greater territorial
extension than in fact it possessed, at least the tag 'with opposition' clearly
indicated that there was no willing acceptance by other dynasts in Ireland. In
fact Turlough O Brien seems to have consistently accepted a subordinate
position as King of Munster, and regularly allied himself with Diarmait
whenever the Leinster king decided to assert a lordship over a wider area of
Ireland. Diarmait, while not able to repeat the achievement of Brian Borúma,
had pointed the way to others and the new generation of provincial kings was
not slow to follow his example.

Chief among those was Turlough O Brien. After the death of Diarmait in
1072 he felt free to assert himself and immediately invaded Leinster, taking
hostages and exacting submission. Dublin, too, capitulated and in 1073
Meath fell. Before the end of the same year he had marched into Connacht
and established his authority there. At last a true heir to Brian Borúma had
appeared in the person of his grandson. He showed his power by promoting
a new division of Leinster and installed his own son Muirchertach as King of
Dublin in 1074. He invaded Connacht again in 1076, exacting submission. In
1079 he even expelled the King of Connacht. His authority, if shaky at times,
was ruthlessly imposed. Only in the north did he fail, though northern kings
attempting to gain support in local struggles did come south to him in
Munster and made submission. When Turlough died in the summer of 1086
he was called *rí Érenn* (king of Ireland) in the annals of Ulster, a clear indication that even the north accepted him, in some sense, as an over-king. No
less significantly he was called 'magnificent king and noble King of Ireland'
by the great Pope Gregory VII.

Turlough's career shows the possibilities and limitations facing an Irish
provincial king in the late eleventh century. He had to be prepared to impose
his lordship in a never-ending series of invasions of subordinate kingdoms
and could never hope to achieve any kind of permanent ascendancy. But he
could go close enough, if he had the necessary energy and resources. What he

could not do was to ensure that his heir would inherit his status and be able
to carry on where he left off. On Turlough's death not even the kingship of
Munster passed intact to his heir. It was divided between three sons, one of
whom, Muirchertach, had to struggle hard before he was finally able to
assume unchallenged the kingship of Munster in 1093. The disorders in the
southern province naturally presented others with an opportunity to free
themselves from O Brien overlordship. Both Leinster and Connacht challenged Muirchertach, who also had to face a new threat when Munster was
invaded by the northern Uí Néill king, Domnall Mac Lochlainn, to whom he
submitted in 1090. Despite this setback, Muirchertach showed that he was a
worthy successor to his father. Taking advantage of an internal struggle for
power in Connacht in 1092, he invaded the province in force and exacted submission. In 1093 he returned to crush a revolt and installed a new subordinate
king. The following year he showed his new strength by expelling the Norse
King of Dublin, killing the King of Meath, and partitioning that kingdom
between two new dynasts subordinate to himself. He campaigned in
Connacht again in 1095 and set up a new king. He had already made Leinster
subject to his overlordship and was now ready to face the northern kings,
especially Domnall Mac Lochlainn, the dominant ruler in the northern half.
A series of invasions, by sea as well as by land, proved fruitless. Not even military forces from Dublin, Leinster, Meath and Connacht, as well as his own
Munster, could enable Muirchertach to force Mac Lochlainn into submission.

This obsession with the north, the incessant expeditions with their high
cost and severe loss of life, may have sapped the energy of O Brien and
diminished his resources. He also had to face the effects of bad weather,
severe enough to cause death throughout Ireland according to the annals,
famine, and a great plague which lasted for two years, 1095–96. His prolonged absences from Munster also made it increasingly difficult for him to
fend off potential rivals, in particular the brother who had first challenged
him after the death of his father, Turlough. Finally, in 1114, severe illness
weakened him further and he was deposed by his brother Diarmait. Even
though he was restored the following year, he was expelled again in 1116. He
entered the monastery of Lismore, presumably to end his days making his
peace with God. He did not die there, however, but at Killaloe, witnessing the
ignominy of a Connacht invasion of Munster, the destruction of the ancient
O Brien capital at Kincora, and the occupation of Killaloe itself by the King
of Connacht.

With Muirchertach O Brien the great days of Munster as a prime force in
Irish politics came to an end. A new star had appeared in the west and the
future lay with him. But it was the O Brien kings who had shown how much
was possible. They had become kings of Ireland, even if 'with opposition',
and it was only a matter of time before someone would make a kingdom of
Ireland a reality. For this new institutions were essential. They were already
developing. The O Brien kings deployed huge forces, by Irish standards, in

many of their campaigns and this could only have been achieved through intermediaries working under their control. That presupposes some machinery through which control could be exercised. So, too, did the partitioning of kingdoms, the creation of puppet kingships, not to mention the constant negotiations which had to be maintained. They corresponded with the Archbishop of Canterbury, probably with the pope, and with other important people in England. In 1088 Muirchertach supplied William Rufus in England with timber to roof Westminster Hall. In 1102 he arranged the marriage of his daughter to Arnulf of Montgomery, probably as part of an alliance in support of the rebellion of Arnulf's brother, the Earl of Shrewsbury, against Henry I of England. The subsequent embargo imposed by King Henry on trade with Ireland suggests as much. Interestingly, too, the man employed by Arnulf to negotiate the marriage with Muirchertach was Gerald of Windsor, the steward of his castle of Pembroke, and ancestor of the Geraldines who were to dominate the English invasion and much of the subsequent history of medieval Ireland. Muirchertach also married another daughter to the son of the Norse King Magnus Barelegs and thereby seems to have gained an important ally in his struggle for dominion over the north of Ireland. He made Limerick something like his capital, breaking with the tradition of his ancestors who clung to the unsuitable Kincora. He also exploited the resources of other Hiberno-Norse cities, especially Waterford and Dublin. Indeed the latter almost seems to have begun to assume the status of a national capital which had to be controlled by any king with ambitions to be King of Ireland. More than anyone it was the O Briens who gave Dublin this new status. Muirchertach twice took over its kingship, exploited its resources, patronized its church, and visited and stayed there often. In 1111 he stayed there for three months up to Christmas Day.

The O Briens also used the church to their own political advantage. Accepting the primacy of Armagh and guaranteeing its rights in the areas under their control was one way of promoting the idea of a kingship of all Ireland. The revolutionary programme which in the twelfth century was to establish a new national hierarchical structure in the Irish church, reflecting the strongest political overlordships in the new metropolitan sees, all under the new primatial authority of Armagh, inevitably was a powerful stimulus to political unity as well. But before that, churchmen had looked to secular lords to carry through reforms and in turn offered the assistance of their own powerful influence. In 1050 the O Brien King of Munster presided over an assembly of clergy and laymen at Killaloe, which 'enacted a law and a restraint upon every injustice' in an attempt to quell civil disturbance. When Muirchertach O Brien made peace with his brother Diarmait in 1093, it was achieved with the help of the church and was guaranteed by 'the relics of Ireland, including the Staff of Jesus, as pledges'. This great Armagh relic, reputedly the staff given to St Patrick by an angel, was in constant demand as a pledge in secular agreements. It was also a symbol of Armagh's authority in Ireland. When Turlough O Brien received the submission of Máel Sechnaill of Meath in 1079, it was in the presence of the abbot of Armagh and guaranteed by the same Staff of Jesus.

This church support was an essential ingredient of post-Clontarf political development. Conversely secular backing was necessary for the transformation of the Irish church, which was a reflection of the changes which were taking place in Europe. A reforming papacy, through a new administration, was reaching out to the furthest parts of Europe, and Ireland, once described by Pope Honorius I in the seventh century as 'isolated at the uttermost ends of the earth', was not too remote to be involved. Monasticism, too, was reformed and the arrival of the first Benedictines, followed by Augustinian canons regular and Cistercians, was to have a profound effect on the future Irish church. For change to happen there had to be a need expressed in Ireland, churchmen willing to receive new ideas and ecclesiastical structures from abroad, and channels of communication through which they could be transmitted. It is an extraordinary fact that despite the increased secularization of the Irish church in the centuries before Clontarf, and the enormous damage inflicted by Viking war bands and native marauders, there was still a deep level of spirituality to be found and a devotion to the old 'desert' ideal. The Irish life of Colum Cille shows clearly how vital religion still was in the tenth century Irish church, with its strong emphasis on pilgrimage and the older forms of piety. Even when secularization engulfed the monasteries and saints' lives were written for material gain, the spirituality was not altogether muffled. The late ninth-century 'Tripartite Life of Patrick' was written to buttress Armagh's claims to jurisdiction and property, so much so that churches were carefully listed and located, sometimes even with precise measurements. Yet that same life contains the famous 'Breastplate of St Patrick', a prayer of intense spirituality which is still popular with devout Christians. Another writer expressed the ideal life of contemplation proper to a monk: 'to be sitting awhile, praying to God'.

The continuing vitality of Irish scholarship is also well attested. Irish scholars were in touch with the court of Athelstan in England and with the continent. The monastic schools could still attract scholars from abroad, such as the Welshman Sulien, Bishop of St David's. His son later wrote that 'moved by the example of his fathers, eager for learning, he went to the Irish, renowned for their marvellous wisdom'. He studied in Ireland for 10 years before returning home to pass on the knowledge he had acquired. Irish scholars went abroad and brought back the new learning. Glendalough, in 1106, was using textbooks currently in fashion in Europe. Armagh in 1138 had available notes taken at a lecture given by Peter Lombard in Paris in the same year. Another Irish monk in the early twelfth century transcribed the most famous work of theology ever produced by an Irishman, John the Scot's *De divisione naturae*, and there is other evidence of Irish interest in current theological problems.

Despite the ravages of the Vikings, then, from the tenth to the twelfth centuries Irish scholarship continued to flourish. True, the number of schools declined as a result of the raids, and only the larger monasteries (Armagh, Lismore, Clonmacnois, Clonard, Kildare and Glendalough being the most famous) continued to have important schools. There was even an attempt to raise Armagh to a privileged position in 1162 when the synod of Clane decreed that only graduates of that school might be masters in Irish monasteries. Armagh, to judge by an entry in the annals, had its special student quarter, one third of which was reserved for students from England.

There are many signs that post-Clontarf Ireland was responding to the new ideas which were transforming Europe. Irish pilgrims were amazed at the new buildings which they saw on the road to Rome or Compostela. St Malachy visited Clairvaux while it was being rebuilt and elsewhere saw churches in the new style being erected. St Bernard tells us that when he returned to Ireland 'it seemed good to Malachy that a stone oratory should be erected at Bangor like those which he had seen constructed in other regions'. He was opposed by the conservative locals, one of whom asked him why he 'thought good to introduce this novelty into our region? We are Scots, not Gauls. What is this frivolity?'. But other 'frivolities' were also introduced from abroad which led to a whole new style (Hiberno-Romanesque) of design and decoration in ecclesiastical buildings. Kings vied with each other as patrons, seeking masterpieces which would reflect their status and enhance their prestige. They also encouraged lay craftsmen, so that monasteries in the future no longer had a monopoly. Lay scribes, too, were patronized and families of scribes were to dominate letters in the future. But in eleventh- and twelfth-century Ireland it was still the monastic scribes who were dominant. They spared no effort in labouring in the scriptorium and they were conscious that their work was for the enrichment of others. One wrote: 'I send my little dripping pen unceasingly over an assemblage of books of great beauty, to enrich the possessions of the men of art – whence my hand is weary with writing'.

It is clear, then, that Ireland shared in that twelfth century renaissance which was transforming so many aspects of European life. But the Irish were not content to be mere recipients of new fashions from England or the continent. They adapted them to fit in with their own rich inheritance. At the same time they discovered their own past and vigorously set about preserving the written tradition (*senchas*) for the future. So that at the time when great classical stories such as the siege of Troy or the wandering of Aeneas were introduced into Irish, scribes were compiling massive collections of traditional lore, while others were composing what became the great Fenian cycle of poetry. An abbot of Terryglass, Aed mac Crimthainn, compiled one of the greatest of these collections, now known as the *Book of Leinster*. It included the most famous tale of the Ulster cycle, the *Táin Bó Cualnge* (the cattle raid of Cooley), which depicts a purely pagan Ireland from the heroic past. At the end the scribe added: 'But I, who have written this history, or rather fable, give no belief to the various incidents related in it. For some things in it are the deception of demons, others poetic inventions; some are probable, others improbable; while still others are included for the delight of fools'. Abbot Aed respected tradition, even where it offended his Christian sensibilities or his educated sense of what was reasonable. Another scribe defended the traditional arts of *eólas* (learning) and *filidecht* (poetry), which preserved so much of the pagan ethos of Ireland, and wrote that 'though the faith came, these arts were not put away, for they are good'. The interests of such scholars was truly Catholic and they were not afraid to combine the search for truth in sacred literature with the most lively interest in the profane. The same Abbot Aed of Terryglass received a letter from Bishop Find of Kildare, to whom he had lent his still uncompleted *Book of Leinster*, asking for the conclusion of a 'little story' in the unfinished book and requesting that 'the poem book of Mac Lonáin' might be sent to him 'so that we may study the meaning of the poems that are in it'. And one of the great reforming bishops of Munster, in the course of a letter to Archbishop Lanfranc of Canterbury seeking clarification of some thorny theological and liturgical problems, also asked about certain 'questions of secular letters' (as Lanfranc put it in his reply, when prudishly refusing to deal with such matters).

This independent spirit, typical of the spirit of the older Irish monastic scholars, was matched by a self-confidence which bordered on the arrogant. The ability to make fun of themselves is a measure of the confidence of the scholar monks. Much of the scholastic tradition was parodied in the anonymous *Vision of Mac Conglinne*, an irreverent and at times blasphemous satire of the twelfth century. Everything is fair game for the author – the forms and motifs of literature, the schools, the genealogies, the monks, and especially the hermits and ascetics. Voyage and vision literature is marvellously lampooned, with Mac Conglinne being guided by a phantom called 'Dirty-belch, son of Fluxy', instead of the conventional angel. He voyaged in a boat made of beef and other meats, through a sea of milk, landing on an island made of food and inhabited by a hermit. The ascetic lived close to a church entirely constructed of rich foods, wore lumps of butter on his head and bunches of leeks, and blessed the voyager with the invocation: 'Be thou under the safeguard of good food'. When he sent him on his voyage the hermit again blessed him: 'Be thou under the protection of smooth juicy bacon. Be thou under the protection of hard, yellow-backed cream', as he put a gospel book made of bacon and sausage around his neck.

When the hermit first appeared he had stuffed into his boots the reading which he enjoyed in his hermitage, the *Táin* and three others of the greatest stories from the heroic age of pagan Ireland. No scripture, hagiography or other literature suitable for a holy man there. It seemed that the Irish church had lapsed into a self-indulgence far removed from the asceticism of the great days of monasticism. The contrast was sharply pointed out by a monk critic:

Those venerable who did God's will
At time's onset,
Needy, naked, sore and filthy,
Not fat of belly they.

He wrote on the 'venerable' of his own day, 'with silk, sarsamat, satin', sitting on soft couches after drinking, 'held fast by the devil'. The writer was expressing what many of a puritanical outlook felt when they looked at the state of the church and religion in eleventh-century Ireland. When pilgrims began to travel abroad again, and when Irish monks came into contact with reformed monasticism abroad, they became critical of what was the norm at home. These contacts with Europe were to generate a great movement for reform which was to have a revolutionary effect on the Irish church.

The new upsurge of Irish pilgrims was mainly the result of guarantees of safe passage procured from the emperor Conrad in 1027. Before that, pilgrims often faced death, like one Colman who was murdered in Austria in 1012 while on his way to the Holy Land. Subsequently miracles were attributed to him. The emperor, Henry II, had his body brought to Metz and the Irishman, as Kilimann, became one of the patron saints of Austria. But after 1027 pilgrimage was safer and many more left Ireland. Some were royal pilgrims, such as Sitric, King of Dublin, who, accompanied by the King of Brega, visited Rome in 1028. On his return he gave a site for the new church of Holy Trinity in Dublin, which became the cathedral church of the new diocese of Dublin. Some royal pilgrims never returned to Ireland. After he was deposed in 1064, Donchad O Brien of Munster went to Rome and died there. But most of them, like Sitric, came back and brought with them new attitudes towards many traditional values. It is reasonable to suppose, too, that through these pilgrimages the papacy established contacts with Irish rulers who might be useful instruments in helping to reform the Irish church.

But long before this Irish monks had been to Rome, some dying there like the abbots of Bangor and Terrglass in 929. In the next century there was even a community of Irish monks in their own house in Rome. Known as 'Sancta Trinitas Scottorum' (Holy Trinity of the Irish), this Irish monastery was an important channel of communication with Ireland. So, too, were the other Irish houses which were founded further north in Europe, many by pilgrims on their way to Rome. Such a pilgrim was the monk Muiredach (*Marianus*) who with his companions settled near Ratisbon. From this first house other Schottenkloester (Irish monasteries) were established at Wurzburg, Vienna, Nuremburg, Erfurt, and even as far east as Kiev in Russia. These communities retained an Irish character and remained in touch with Ireland. One of the most famous of these monks was another Marianus (Máel-Brigte), an *inclusus*, or hermit, walled off from the rest of the community at Fulda, and compiler of a well-known chronicle which included the record of important events in far-off Ireland. His scribe made a significant entry on the margin of a page, recording the date, the death of the King of Leinster, and adding that 'this is the first year I came from Scotland [Ireland] in my pilgrimage. And I have written this book for love of you [Marianus] and of all the Scots, that is the Irish, because I myself am an Irishman'. These Irish monks in the heart of Europe not only kept in touch with home, they could sometimes influence developments there. The famous Cormac's chapel on the Rock of Cashel certainly shows the influence of German romanesque and there can be no doubt that reforming ideas were also passed along this route to Ireland, where they helped to invigorate that revolution which was to transform the Irish church.

The most important single influence, however, came from a source much closer to Ireland. The Norman conquest of England brought to Canterbury as archbishop Lanfranc, a canon lawyer and convinced reformer, a man determined to uphold the primacy of his see against the protests of York. This led him, in 1072, to claim authority over Ireland as well. It is doubtful if this bogus historical claim was ever intended to be exercised in practice, but it did give Lanfranc an interest in the state of the Irish church. His predecessors seem to have actively involved themselves in the new Dublin diocese, established after Sitric's pilgrimage to Rome in 1028. When the people of Dublin presented Patrick for consecration in 1074, they told Lanfranc that 'we have always submitted to the government of your predecessors from whom we remember that we received ecclesiastical dignity'. Lanfranc in reply said that he had consecrated Patrick 'according to the custom of our ancestors'. And the new Bishop of Dublin took an oath of obedience to Canterbury ('I promise that I shall obey you and your successors in all things which pertain to the Christian religion') as did the four bishops who succeeded him, until Dublin was raised to the status of an archbishopric in 1152. Occasionally other Hiberno-Norse sees similarly professed obedience: Malchus, first Bishop of Waterford in 1097, and Patrick of Limerick in 1148. But, in general, the Dublin bishops were the only ones regularly to swear obedience, and they did so willingly: 'We have always been willing subjects to your predecessors', the clergy and the burgesses (as they called themselves) of the city wrote in a letter to Canterbury in 1121.

When Bishop Patrick returned to Dublin after his consecration in 1074, he brought with him two letters from Lanfranc. One was addressed to Godfraid, King of Dublin, called 'glorious King of Ireland' by the archbishop in diplomatic flattery. The second letter was much more important. This one was to Turlough O Brien, similarly addressed as 'magnificent King of Ireland' and clearly seen by Lanfranc as the most powerful secular support for reform in the Irish church. It drew attention to abuses ('some things have been reported to us that displease us'), particularly the way the law of marriage was being applied, so that it was 'rather a law of fornication'. The king was requested to summon an assembly of bishops and senior clergy, to preside over it himself with his nobility, and to 'strive to banish from your kingdom these evil customs and all others which are forbidden by the laws of the church'.

This was momentous advice and might immediately have provided Ireland with the normal European institution through which reform could be initiated. It was all the more important for it was followed soon after by a letter from the greatest reforming pope, Gregory VII, which among other matters reminded the king, and the bishops and abbots of Ireland, that their obedience was due to the successor of St Peter in Rome. But nothing happened, whether because Turlough lacked the heart for reform, or more likely because he saw little gain for himself from such an effort in his struggle for political ascendancy. It was his son Muirchertach O Brien who was eventually to summon the kind of assembly which Lanfranc had urged. This was 27 years later, in 1101, at Cashel, after further prompting by the saintly Anselm, Lanfranc's successor at Canterbury.

Shortly after his consecration in 1093, Anselm wrote a letter to the bishops of Ireland asking for their prayers and urging them to turn to him if they needed advice in difficulties. By now there was certainly a bond between Canterbury and the Irish church which went beyond the traditional link with Dublin. When Malchus was presented as Bishop-elect of Waterford, the signatories to the letter to Canterbury included the Munster bishop Domnall Ua hÉnna (who had earlier corresponded with Lanfranc on some liturgical and canonical matters), Máel Muire Ua Dúnán, Bishop of Meath, and Muiredach O Brien. The last two were to play leading roles in the revolution in the Irish church. Ua Dúnán seems to have been transferred to Munster after the death of Bishop Domnall and to have presided, with Muiredach, over the council of Cashel in 1101. In one source he is described as 'chief legate, chief bishop and chief senior of Ireland, with authority from the pope himself'. He was the first papal legate in Ireland, which would make the council of Cashel all the more important. Muiredach O Brien, too, was seen by Canterbury as a key figure. He had received letters from Anselm urging him to correct abuses within the church, especially those relating to the laws of marriage and the position of bishops.

The decrees of the council of Cashel show that the reformers were mainly concerned with the same sort of problems which preoccupied the church elsewhere – simony, the freedom of the church from secular taxation and the civil courts, the right of sanctuary, the celibacy of the clergy. But the terminology employed showed the peculiar character of the Irish church, with authority still vested in abbots (often laymen and usually married) and no territorial dioceses. Nor did the council make any real attempt to reform the marriage law in any meaningful way. While promulgating the forbidden degrees of kinship within which marriage could not be contracted, the council still allowed for easy divorce, retained some traces of polygamy, and left the Irish marriage laws gravely in conflict with the orthodox Christian ethic. Secular rulers, however, refused to be confined to strict monogamy and indissoluble marriage and no reformer was ever able to implement fully the canon law in this respect.

For all its shortcomings, the council of Cashel was an important event. It demonstrated the will to reform, brought influential churchmen into the movement, and showed Muiredach O Brien with the capacity to provide the necessary secular leadership. Perhaps most important of all, it showed in the presence of a papal legate that reform was now an organized, purposeful movement in the European tradition. Máel Muire Ua Dúnáin, the legate, must be seen as exemplifying a new breed of bishops who were now to drag the Irish church into the twelfth century, under the auspices of Rome and, more immediately, Canterbury, and with the support of O Brien and lesser rulers in the south.

The most interesting group were the bishops of the Hiberno-Norse sees, most of whom were Irish Benedictine monks from English reformed monasteries. Bishop Patrick of Dublin was a monk of Worcester, his successor Donngus was one of Lanfranc's monks at Canterbury, and his successor Samuel was a monk of St Alban's. The first Bishop of Waterford, Malchus, was a monk at Winchester. The most remarkable was Gilbert, Bishop of Limerick, who became a friend of Anselm's following their meeting at Rouen in Normandy, probably in 1087. This friendship was probably responsible for Gilbert's nomination as papal legate in succession to Ua Dúnáin, and it was he who thus presided over the revolutionary synod of Rath Breasail in 1111, which gave a wholly new structure to the Irish church. Probably by way of preparation for that momentous event, Bishop Gilbert composed an extraordinary tract, *De statu ecclesiae* (On the state of the church), which fitted the new canon law into the traditional structure which divided society into those who pray, those who fight and those who work. Not until the advent of Aquinas in the next century was this piece of ecclesiology to be surpassed. In twelfth century Ireland its impact was shattering. He wrote it at the request of many of the clergy, with all the authority of a legate, and addressed it 'to the bishops and presbyters of the whole of Ireland'. Behind the complexities of the argument of the text lay a simple message: the church is to be ruled by bishops, and the number of bishoprics must be limited, of fixed territorial limits, and organized into metropolitan provinces under a primate of all Ireland.

The assembly which met at Rath Breasail in 1111 under the legate Gilbert and Muirchertach O Brien, divided the Irish church into two provinces, following the traditional secular division into northern and southern halves, with Armagh as the metropolitan see in one and Cashel in the other. Then each province was further divided into twelve dioceses, which in turn were allocated to the different provincial kingdoms. Each diocese was given carefully defined boundaries. The surprising thing is that so much of this was successful. No less than 17 of the dioceses established at Rath Breasail were to preserve their identity throughout the centuries. The modifications which were subsequently made to the Rath Breasail structure were largely the result of political pressure and were, for the most part, stabilized at the later synod of Kells-Mellifont.

One reason for this success was that the reform movement was no longer an exclusively southern phenomenon, though it was still dominated by Munster personalities. Among the 50 bishops present at Rath Breasail was Cellach of Armagh, a member of the Uí Sinaich family which had controlled the abbacy of Armagh for over 100 years. The abbots had all been laymen and it was Cellach who broke with tradition by taking holy orders when he inherited the office in 1105. The following year he went further by accepting consecration as a bishop. Significantly, this happened when he was in Munster, the home of reform. His unification of the abbacy and bishopric made possible the creation of a new diocese at Armagh. But, more than this, his presence at Rath Breasail brought Armagh, with its unique position in the Irish church, into the reform movement. Without Armagh that movement could never have hoped to make any real progress in Ireland as a whole. Now with Cellach the movement took on a new dimension. From Armagh, too, came the greatest of all reformers, Malachy, who was a student there when Rath Breasail was convened. His father was the *fer léginn* (the head teacher) at the Armagh school. Later in life Malachy met and was befriended by St Bernard, probably the most famous man of his generation. After his death St Bernard wrote the life of his friend. From it we learn that Malachy, while still a young man, attached himself to 'a holy man, most austere in life, a pitiless castigator of his body'. This was the hermit Imar, who lived a life of austerity in the Irish desert tradition. Malachy, then, inherited that strange combination of worldly scholarship and asceticism which marked the greatest Irish saints. He attracted the attention of Cellach, was ordained *c*. 1119, and at the age of 26 was put in charge of the new diocese when Cellach went as metropolitan to Dublin in 1121.

According to St Bernard he now instituted a whole series of reforms in the archdiocese, in liturgy, the administration of the sacraments, and the regulation of abuses. When Cellach returned, Malachy went south to the monastery of Lismore, to study there with Malchus, who had made the monastery a centre of reform ideology. By 1124 he was Bishop of the new diocese of Conor and abbot there of the ancient monastery of Bangor. Now he was faced for the first time with the kind of fierce opposition reformers were encountering from entrenched conservatives protecting local vested interests. St Bernard did not mince his words in describing how, when Malachy began his work, he 'understood that he had not been sent to men, but beasts. . . . They were Christian in name, but in fact they were pagans'. Political upheaval also made life difficult. Bangor was destroyed and Malachy fled south to Lismore. Here he gave full rein to his ascetic inclination, gathered some followers, and founded a new monastery at an unknown location, possibly close to Cashel. He had abandoned the work of reform.

But he was not allowed to remain in seclusion for long. Before he died in 1129 Bishop Cellach had designated Malachy as his successor in Armagh. Malachy resisted, not least because the Uí Sinaich had immediately installed their own successor to Cellach in the Armagh abbacy. Eventually, in 1132, at the urging of Gilbert of Limerick, still the papal legate, Malachy reluctantly accepted consecration as Archbishop of Armagh and in 1134 was installed there, despite the opposition of the local ruler. But he never managed to win acceptance and, in 1136, he was ousted by the abbot, Niall, resigned his archbishopric in favour of Gelasius, abbot of Derry, and retired to Bangor once more, which he made into the centre of the bishopric of Down. Before long he was on the move again, walking to Rome to procure from the pope two *pallia* (palls) for the metropolitans of Armagh and Cashel, the symbols of their special authority sanctioned by the papacy. Apart from his meeting with the pope, the journey was memorable for Malachy because of his visit to the Cistercian abbey of Clairvaux and encounter with St Bernard, and another visit to the Augustinian abbey at Arrouaise. As a result, the first Irish Cistercian house was founded at Mellifont, from which the Cistercian rule was quickly spread throughout the Irish church. No less significant was the introduction of the canons regular of St Augustine and the rule of Arrouaise, which was to provide some of the new cathedrals, such as Holy Trinity in Dublin, with regular chapters. These new religious orders, with the Benedictines who had arrived earlier in 1127 when a Savigniac house was founded in Down from Furness, were to transform Irish monasticism and be instruments of reform.

Malachy's encounter with the Cistercians had also reawakened his inclination towards the strictest monastic life. But Pope Innocent II refused to free Malachy from his holy office, appointed him papal legate, and sent him home to Ireland with instructions to convene a synod which would make a formal request for palls and for papal confirmation of the new ecclesiastical structure in Ireland. It is not clear why the pope refused to ratify the Rath Breasail decrees, and it is strange that it was not until 1148 that the new papal legate summoned the necessary synod. Even stranger, it met at the most unlikely place, Inis Patraic (St Patrick's isle, off the coast of Dublin), was much smaller than earlier assemblies, and did not have a secular ruler participating. Nevertheless it made a formal request for the palls and delegated Malachy to go to Rome. But he died on the way at Clairvaux, in the arms of St Bernard, on the night of 1 November 1148. He was buried before the high altar in the abbey church, an indication of the love of Bernard and the community for this man from the remotest part of Europe. When St Bernard died, five years later, he was buried beside his friend. Malachy continued to be honoured by the Cistercians, who spread his cult and were responsible for his canonization in 1190. He is still an honoured saint in the Cistercian calendar.

St Malachy represents all that was best in this reform movement and displays its essential Irish character. But he also demonstrates the importance of the European connection and the continuing interest of the papacy. Soon after his death the rulers and clergy of Ireland, probably in some unrecorded assembly, formally requested the pope to send them a legate. He came in 1151, Cardinal John Paparo, and in 1152 he summoned the last of the great reforming synods. This met at Kells and later sessions were held at Mellifont. It passed decrees against simony, usury and sexual immorality, and instituted a system of tithes. This latter was important for it suggests that the reformers were aware of the need to establish a proper parochial system for the cure of souls. Equally important, the synod dealt with the vexed question of the marriage law, though the precise formulation is not known. Most important of all, the legate revealed that he had brought, not two palls as requested, but four. In addition to Armagh, confirmed as the primatial see, and Cashel, there were to be two metropolitans, at Tuam in Connacht and, more surprisingly, at Dublin in Leinster. Tuam was chosen because of its connection with Turlough O Connor, now high king with opposition. The choice of Dublin is a clear indication of its importance as a metropolis in Irish politics and was probably the price that had to be paid for weaning it from ecclesiastical dependence on Canterbury. The creation of two additional ecclesiastical provinces necessarily meant altering the diocesan structure established at Rath Breasail. Eleven suffragan sees were now allocated to Armagh, five to Dublin, 12 to Cashel, and six to Tuam. With some minor changes, this arrangement was to remain unchanged during the middle ages, which in itself is a good indication of the success of the reformers. Despite local vested interests, and the opposition of some of the old monastic foundations, the new diocesan structure was pushed through with remarkable speed. Some of the high crosses of this period vividly represent the triumph of the new hierarchical structure by highlighting the figure of a bishop with a new-style crozier, emphasizing his authority in the new scheme of things. The satirist who composed *The vision of Mac Conglinne* thought it worthwhile making fun of the new system of tithes, as if the very success of the reform at that level demanded ridicule. All the outward signs were of success. New reformed monasteries were founded, new churches in the continental fashion were built. Abuses had been tackled, canon law procedures imposed, all with the backing of important secular rulers.

Yet there were signs that at a deeper level the reformers had failed to change fundamentally the character of Irish Christianity. Popular lives of saints, written at the height of the reform movement, reflect traditional material values and customary attitudes which seem unaffected by the reforms. Financial rights are set out, as are secular claims, in the traditional manner. Erenaghs continued to administer monasteries as married men and monastic office remained hereditary in many places. In Killaloe, long after the reform, the same families continued to retain many of the same offices in hereditary succession. The new monasticism, especially the Cistercian, failed to conform absolutely to the European norm and soon traditional features of Irish monasticism appeared which were to debase, in foreign eyes, the ideal which all were supposed to embrace. The Irish monks refused to conform and clung stubbornly to their own ways – often living in separate cells (and not dormitories as the rule prescribed), embellishing their churches with forbidden decoration, maintaining a lifestyle that was often at variance with the rule.

Even at diocesan level, where reform was most successful, reorganization was painfully slow. In almost all cases, cathedral chapters were not established until after the English invasion, which meant that bishops lacked the normal corporation to assist in administering the diocese and in performing the liturgy adequately in their cathedrals. Much more seriously, however, there is no evidence that any real parochial organization was established in most parts of Ireland before the English created parishes as part of the new manorial structure in the fees which were the normal pattern of settlement. This can only mean that, in many places the cure of souls was neglected, the old ways maintained, and the kind of abuses condemned by Lanfranc and Anselm remained. This was certainly the view taken by outsiders, not least by the papacy, and it was to lead to a proposal in 1156 that Henry II of England should invade Ireland 'to enlarge the boundaries of the church, to restrain the downward course of vice, to correct evil habits and introduce virtue and to increase the Christian religion'. That was how the famous privilege *Laudabiliter*, issued by Pope Adrian IV, expressed it when licensing an invasion of Ireland. In papal eyes, the reform had signally failed and the implication is that this was because, ultimately, secular authority in Ireland was either too weak, or too reluctant, to help to implement the reform in the areas under their control.

Yet we have already seen that, in the early days of reform at least, this was not true. The O Briens were willing partners in the work of reform and may even have seen the reformers, with their foreign education and advanced ideas, as useful allies. The hierarchy of authority advocated by Gilbert in his *De statu ecclesiae*, where the primate is made to correspond to the king, and to whom is reserved the special privilege of ordaining and crowning the king, may well have seemed appropriate to rulers who were trying to extend their authority in an orderly fashion to embrace the whole of Ireland. An established primacy in the ecclesiastical order would facilitate the creation of a primacy in the secular world, even if it were to be one 'with opposition'.

Muirchertach O Brien certainly seems to have gained from his support of the reformers. When he died in 1119 all the annals, even the northern ones, styled him 'King of Ireland', a striking testimony to the universality of his rule. But he had already seen a rival dynasty appear in the west and, in the person of Turlough O Connor, this family was to go even further in the political process leading slowly to a kingdom of Ireland. When a fragment of what was supposed to be the 'true cross' reached Ireland and O Connor had it enshrined in the beautiful cross of Cong, he added an inscription asking for a prayer for himself as 'king of Ireland'. In the year after Muirchertach O Brien's death in 1120, O Connor celebrated the *Óenach Tailten* (Fair of Tailte) in the belief that by convening this assembly of all Ireland he was exercising an ancient prerogative which belonged to the King of Ireland alone. Later, in 1168, his son Rory also convened it and used it to summon a royal council to meet at Athlone to levy a tax on the whole of Ireland, again demonstrating his prerogative as King of Ireland. Both were accepting the view of twelfth-century historians that a high kingship of Ireland had existed from the distant past, with national institutions such as the *Óenach Tailten* which gave it public expression. When Gilbert of Limerick gave to the primate of all Ireland the sole responsibility for crowning the king he was lending support to this view of Irish history and to current political theory.

Turlough O Connor represents how radically the kings of twelfth-century Ireland were departing from the restricted kingship of an earlier time. They gave laws, imposed taxes, granted conquered land, frequently by means of elaborate charters issued by their writing office, divided kingdoms, deposed kings and installed puppet kings, developed new governmental offices which allowed them to rule through intermediaries (especially the *airrí*, or royal governor, and the *rectaire*, a lesser official who was prominent in the king's home kingdom). With greater resources they made war on a more extended scale, maintaining a standing army, garrisoning fortified places, hiring mercenaries, buying military allies, and even using naval forces on an unprecedented scale. Expensive cavalry was now used, so much so that a new royal official, 'commander of cavalry', made his appearance. Some built castles, expanded navies and deployed them in inland waters and Turlough O Connor, if we are to believe the annals, even went so far as to divert the river Suck for military purposes. Perhaps more than anyone he went closest to making the high kingship a reality, firmly based on his own unassailable control of Connacht. He tried to protect himself behind a ring of fortresses (some of which are called castles in the annals, suggesting that they were built of stone, unlike the normal earthworks), using the Shannon as a natural boundary. He was an outstanding soldier, especially notable for his exploitation of naval forces.

Early in his career he partitioned Munster, so as to weaken the O Briens. He restored the Eóganacht of Cashel as rivals in the south, or Desmond, setting up the Mac Carthys as kings there and leaving the O Briens as kings of north Munster, or Thomond. He had already tried this policy of partition in Meath in 1115. In 1125 he repeated it in a spectacular fashion, expelling the king and dividing the kingdom into four parts, three of which he gave to lesser kings of the same lineage and the fourth to his ally Tiernan O Rourke of Breffny. A year later he installed a son as King of Leinster and Dublin. But he was expelled within a few years and O Connor was forced on the offensive again. He was never, in fact, able to relax, secure in the knowledge that he had achieved any sort of permanent ascendancy in the other provinces. Again and again he led expeditions into Munster, trying to keep it partitioned and thus weakened, so as to be able to devote himself to Leinster and the north. He succeeded up to a point, but in the end his settlements always broke down. In 1131 he was faced by a grand alliance, resulting in an invasion of Connacht from north and south simultaneously. O Connor recovered and, at the cost of endless negotiations and regular campaigns, he managed to assert his superiority. He relied heavily on allies, none of whom were ever constant. The most regular, Tiernan O Rourke of Breffny, was to prove himself false on a number of occasions and defected to the enemy when it was politic to do so. Even enemies did not remain constant. Dermot Mac Murrough, King of Leinster, had more reason than most to hate O Connor. When his brother Enna died in 1126 O Connor invaded Leinster and installed his son in place of the obvious Uí Chennselaig successor, Dermot. When the 'stranger in sovereignty' was deposed, O Connor again invaded the province in 1128 and wasted it from north to south. Despite this, and later incursions at the expense of the Uí Chennsalaig, Dermot Mac Murrough was not a regular opponent of

O Connor's rule. He sometimes even supported him and benefited accordingly. In 1144, for example, he shared in the division of Meath when O Connor gave him the kingship of half of the eastern portion. Like the other Irish over-kings, Mac Murrough was an opportunist, willing to attach himself to the dynast best able to promote his interests. If that were the current high king, well and good; if not, then Mac Murrough did not hesitate to join the opposition.

There is no real pattern either in the rather confused politics of the period. Turlough O Connor was consistent throughout in his struggles to maintain his high kingship, whatever the opposition. He had his ups and downs, in no regular sequence, as he tried to keep Munster neutralized through regular partition, make Leinster dependent, destroy Meath by division, and leave himself free to concentrate his attention on asserting lordship over the north and thus validate his high kingship fully. He was never able to do this, through a long reign which began in 1106, when he became King of Connacht, to 1156 when he died while planning yet another all-out assault on the north. During those 50 years he faced different alliances of enemies, with ever-changing combinations of forces. He brought the kingdom of Ireland one step nearer to reality and left to his son Rory a firm base on which to build when his turn came.

From that perspective one can discern some purpose in the complex manoeuvring of Irish dynasts throughout the period. Mastery within one's own province, often within one's own lineage, was the first priority, and then an advance to the high kingship. Generally it was the O Connors of Connacht, Mac Lochlainns of the north, Mac Murrough of Leinster, and the O Briens and Mac Carthys of Munster who were the primary characters in the drama. The sudden expansion of Breffny also made Tiernan O Rourke a central figure in many of the great events of the age. Some curious patterns can also be discerned. Whenever an over-king gained any kind of ascendancy, he made it his business to weaken potentially dangerous kingdoms by deposing the ruler and resorting to partition. Munster was divided by O Connor in 1118, and again in 1121, 1151, 1153. Leinster was divided in 1127. The rich kingdom of Meath, containing some of the best land in Ireland, occupying a position of great strategic importance between north and south, and home of the ancient royal site of Tara, was frequently partitioned: by O Connor in 1125 and 1144; by Mac Loughlainn in 1150; by both jointly in 1152; by Mac Loughlainn in 1157 and 1161. Greedy hands regularly tried to obtain possession of some part of those rich lands and use them to their own advantage. Sometimes, too, the new religious foundations benefited. Tiernan O Rourke granted lands along the Boyne, between Navan and Dowdstown, to the Augustinian canons of Navan. It is noticeable, too, how often Dublin was involved in the ambitions of the candidates for the high kingship, because of her great wealth and military (especially naval) resources. In 1154 Mac Lochlainn gave the enormous *tuarustul* (a retainer paid to a subordinate) of 1,500 cows to Dublin. But even that huge amount was exceeded by Rory O Connor in 1166 when he gave 4,000 cows. To put these figures into a meaningful perspective, the *tuarustul* given by O Connor to O Carroll in that same year was 240 cows. When the men of Meath had to pay a large compensation to O Connor for the murder of his son, they gave him 400 cows.

After the death of Turlough O Connor in 1156 a more definite pattern appeared in Irish politics. Although his son Rory became King of Connacht, the initiative now lay with the most powerful king in Ireland, Muirchertach Mac Lochlainn of Tír Eógain. When the Cistercian abbey of Mellifont was consecrated in 1157, Mac Lochlainn was there as high king, foremost among all the notables who attended. He subsequently defeated O Connor, procured submission and hostages from him and from all the important kings in Ireland, and thus asserted his high kingship. Realizing where the future lay, Dermot Mac Murrough became his ally and remained constant until both fell together in 1166. O Connor remained the chief challenger and he, too, now had a firm ally in Tiernan O Rourke. At the highest level, Irish politics had resolved itself into a clear struggle between two major groupings, with the high kingship as the prize for the chief protagonists and a share of the spoils for their principal supporters.

Mac Lochlainn had no doubts about his supremacy. In a charter conveying land to the Cistercian abbey of Newry, which he founded, he styled himself *rex totius Hibernie* (king of all Ireland) and addressed himself to all his 'Irish magnates, sub-kings, princes, dukes, clerks and laymen, present and future'. The land in question was not in Mac Lochlainn's own kingdom, but in the territory of a dependent king, and the grant was made 'by the unanimous will and consent' of that king and the other 'kings and magnates' dependent on Mac Lochlainn. This suggests that not only did the high king grant lands held by his sub-king, but that he had an institution by which consent could be obtained. In fact there is other evidence which shows even greater control over dependent kings, of a kind which could only have resulted from cen-tralized systems of government supporting the provincial kings. When Dermot Mac Murrough confirmed a grant of 14 townlands made by the dependant O Ryan lord of Idrone, he called himself *rex Lagenensium* (king of the Leinstermen) and addressed all his 'kings, dukes and earls'. He confirmed that the original grant had been made 'by our leave' and he authenticated the charter by his personal seal. The use of a seal is another indication that new instruments of government were being forged in Ireland, possibly under the influence of foreign religious orders which were being established in many parts of the island. In another Mac Murrough charter, to his new foundation for the Augustinian canons regular at Ferns, one of the witnesses was Florence 'chancellor of the king'. This grant, too, was made 'by the counsel and assent of my princes and nobles' at Ferns, clearly implying some kind of consenting council. Most important of all, the charter provided for the free election of the abbot by the religious, but added that after the election, and before the consecration by the bishop, 'he shall be presented to me or my heirs or their seneschals in recognition of our lordship so that with our permission the bishop may ordain him'. Irish kings, like their European counterparts, were establishing lordship over land, insisting on their rights over holders of major benefices, firmly controlling dependent kings and lords while providing some mechanism for procuring counsel and consent, and developing institutions of government necessary to maintain their rule.

In other respects Irish kingship was still conservative and traditional modes were respected, even if only to procure added strength from historic precedents. The continuing use of essentially pagan inauguration rites, involving ceremonial marriage to the goddess of the land, is evidence of that. Not all the old taboos had been swept away by the radicals of the twelfth century. Certain conventions were still binding. In 1165 Muirchertach Mac Lochlainn faced revolt by some of his sub-kings, as a result of which one king, Eochaid of the Ulaid (roughly that part of Ulster east of the Bann), was taken prisoner by O Carroll of Uriel. Elaborate arrangements were then made for the release of Eochaid and the final agreement was solemnly guaranteed by a number of notables, including the Archbishop of Armagh. But the following year Mac Lochlainn outraged public opinion by breaking the guaranteed agreement, taking Eochaid prisoner and blinding him. Mac Lochlainn was abandoned on all sides, faced widespread revolt, and was killed in battle by one of the guarantors, O Carroll, joined by Tiernan O Rourke.

Rory O Connor, supported by O Rourke, had already been sniping at Mac Lochlainn, even though they had been defeated by him in 1159. They now moved rapidly, invading Meath and moving on to Dublin, which now received that great *tuarastal* of 4,000 cows. Joined by Dublin forces, the army moved into Uriel where O Carroll submitted and handed over hostages. Leinster was then invaded and more submissions procured. Ossory was next and then O Connor swept in a great arc home to Connacht, before leading an invasion against the Cenél Conaill in west Ulster, who submitted and gave hostages. O Carroll meanwhile had marched against Mac Lochlainn and killed him. O Connor was now supreme, acknowledged as high king. His ascendancy also meant the triumph of O Rourke, just as the fall of Mac Lochlainn inevitably meant trouble for Mac Murrough. He now faced a revolt by the old enemies of his lineage in north Leinster. Dublin, now bound to O Connor, also turned on him. Tiernan O Rourke, joined by Meath, marched against him. The enmity between these two had been made more bitter by a famous incident which occurred in 1152, when the Leinster king abducted Dervorgilla, wife of O Rourke, and carried her off to Ferns. Even though she was restored the following year, the insult to O Rourke's pride and dignity was unforgivable. Now that he had his chance he prepared to take full revenge. He destroyed the fortress at Ferns and acting as agent for the high king banished Mac Murrough from Ireland. The invader then partitioned that part of Leinster traditionally held by the Uí Chennselaig, giving one part to a brother of Mac Murrough and the other to the King of Ossory. Deserted on all sides, with no hope of getting help now that the supremacy of O Connor was widely recognized, Dermot Mac Murrough took the momentous decision to seek help abroad and, early in August 1166, he sailed to Bristol. Some in Ireland lamented his departure. In a comment on his banishment the scribe of the *Book of Leinster* ends: 'Alas! O lord, what shall I do?'

Rory O Connor was now undisputed ruler of Ireland. He made a triumphant circuit of the island and in a great assembly at Athlone, which recognized him as high king, he levied a tax on the 'men of Ireland'. In 1167 he presided over another assembly, this time of important clergy and secular lords of *Leth Cuinn* (the northern half), at Athboy in county Meath. He then proceeded at the head of an army, which included contingents from every important kingdom in Ireland, against Niall Mac Lochlainn who had challenged his supremacy. Mac Lochlainn was now King of Cenél Conaill as well as the Cenél nEógain, but he was forced to submit to O Connor. Once more, the traditional policy of partition was employed. Rory left half of his kingdom to Niall, but gave the other half to Mac Lochlainn's arch enemy in the north, Aed O Neill. There was no real opposition left and Rory O Connor was at last the high King of Ireland 'without opposition'. In 1168, to signify this, he celebrated the *Óenech Tailten*. He became patron of the school of Armagh and, in 1169, made available an annual grant for the teaching of students from Scotland as well as Ireland. He supported the building of the new Romanesque cathedral in Tuam, his capital, and it was during his reign that the great doorway of Clonfert cathedral was carved.

The success of O Connor seemed to bring to an end the great dynastic wars of the twelfth century and the struggle for the high kingship. But soon a new element was added which not only renewed the struggle, but was to transform the political future of Ireland. In August 1167, Dermot Mac Murrough returned from his exile and began the process of recovering his kingdom in south Leinster. Rory O Connor was once again faced with an enemy. The difference this time was that Mac Murrough was no longer relying solely on his own people in Uí Chennselaig. He had brought with him a small force of Flemings from south Wales. More importantly, he had a firm promise of armed support from a number of magnates of Norman stock, of whom Richard fitz Gilbert, Earl of Pembroke, was the greatest. Known in Irish history as Strongbow, Richard was to help secure the recovery of Leinster and Dublin by Mac Murrough, encourage his expansionist policies, marry his daughter Aoife, succeed him in Leinster, and as his heir was to press on with the traditional Leinster aspiration to a higher kingship. His very success brought Henry II to Ireland to establish his rightful lordship there. In this way Ireland became attached to the English crown and her future history became inextricably bound up with that of England.

When Dermot Mac Murrough went to Bristol in 1166 he was going to a city with which he had many connections, not least because of Dublin. He stayed with his friend Robert fitz Harding, reeve of Bristol, a wealthy merchant to whom Henry II was much indebted. It was certainly he who advised the Irishman to go to the king and seek help, though it is also possible that knowledge of the papal privilege *Laudabiliter* and the earlier plan for an invasion of Ireland by Henry may have influenced Mac Murrough. At any rate, when he finally caught up with the king in Aquitaine, Mac Murrough became his 'vassal and liegeman', was rewarded with royal gifts and, most important of all, was given a letter under the great seal which authorized any subject to help Mac Murrough in the recovery of his kingdom. With this licence and promises of land in Ireland, Dermot was able to recruit help in Wales, most importantly Strongbow. But more significant for the future were the Geraldines who were to found some of the most important lineages in medieval Ireland. The first to be recruited, with a promise of Wexford and the two cantreds adjoining the town, were Robert fitz Stephen and his half-brother, Maurice fitz Gerald. Another, Raymond fitz Gerald (usually called le Gros), was a nephew of Maurice. He married Basilia, sister of Strongbow, and formed one important link between the Geraldines and the future lord of Leinster. Hervey de Montmorency, an uncle of Strongbow, married Nesta the daughter of Maurice fitz Gerald, further strengthening the link. Another nephew of Maurice was Robert de Barry, whose brother Gerald, better known as Cambrensis, was the author of *Expugnatio Hibernica* (The conquest of Ireland), the most important primary source for the early history of the English in Ireland. Another leader was Meiler fitz Henry, a son of a half-brother of Robert fitz Stephen, himself a bastard son of Henry I. So the men who led retinues to Ireland in the first series of landings were all related.

When the news of Dermot's return was broadcast, O Connor and O Rourke moved to confront him in Leinster, forcing him to submit, to give hostages to O Connor, and to compensate O Rourke for the abdication of Dervorgilla years before. He was now reduced to the status of a petty King of Uí Chennsalaig and O Connor moved to deal with Munster in 1168. It was divided yet again, half to the sons of Cormac Mac Carthy, and the rest to Donal O Brien, called 'the great', a king who was to play a prominent part in southern politics from now on. The following year, O Connor was involved with Meath, where the king had been killed. This time, when he partitioned Meath, he retained the western half for himself and gave the other half to his ally O Rourke. O Connor was now at the height of his power and his high kingship had been secured on a seemingly permanent basis.

But in May 1169 another force of English mercenaries landed at Bannow bay in county Wexford, led by Robert fitz Stephen and Maurice Prendergast, with Hervey de Montmorency representing the interests of his nephew Strongbow. With their help, Mac Murrough captured Wexford, gave it to fitz Stephen, granted the cantreds between it and Waterford to Hervey, and then invaded Ossory and even beyond it into the modern county Kildare. The English had rapidly shown their military superiority and Mac Murrough was quick to capitalize. He was generous with his rewards, leaving no doubt of his rights of lordship over conquered lands. Even so, he was not able to retain the services of all who had come to Ireland to help him. In the course of the

Ossory campaign, Prendergast and his men deserted him and defected to the Ossory side. Already the English, like their Viking predecessors, were becoming enmeshed in local politics and making their services available to the highest bidder. But this did not halt Mac Murough. He seemed to be irresistible in Leinster, so once again O Connor and O Rourke, joined by the forces of Meath and Dublin, combined to check him. Mac Murrough submitted once more, gave his son and heir, Conor, as hostage, and formally agreed that no more foreigners would be introduced. The whole arrangement reflected O Connor's self-confidence. He clearly saw no real threat to his high kingship from Mac Murrough and his English. The following year he was in Munster, campaigning against O Brien, who seemed to him far more dangerous. He may have been aware that O Brien now had English support from a contingent led by fitz Stephen. But this does not seem to have worried O Connor or to have been deemed worthy of comment by the Irish annals. On the broad stage of Irish politics the English presence was of little account.

But the summer of 1170 changed that. First Raymond le Gros and his men landed in Wexford, and then, in late August, Strongbow arrived with his army. So far, the contingents arriving had been modest enough: three shiploads with fitz Stephen, two with Prendergast, another two with Maurice fitz Gerald, and two more with Raymond le Gros. Some knights, some mounted archers, and a larger number of foot archers, armed with the formidable longbow, probably amounted to no more than a few hundred in all. But if few in number, they proved devastatingly effective in Irish warfare. The knights in particular, fully armoured on huge horses, demolished local opposition where conditions were favourable to a controlled charge. Elsewhere, the archers were able to destroy an enemy without coming to close quarters. With larger numbers it should have been obvious that the English would prove formidable. Strongbow brought over 1,000 men, including 200 knights. This was no mere band of mercenaries, but an invading army. The cost was high, with Jewish money-lenders providing Strongbow with the necessary capital. He was staking all on success in Ireland. He came as an ally of Mac Murrough, lured in part by marriage to that king's daughter and the promise of succession in Leinster. Under him, all the earlier contingents of English united to augment his army and turn it into a force which could not be ignored. He even brought the defector Prendergast and his soldiers back to Ireland. It is doubtful if any Irish king, even O Connor, could have defeated this army in open battle. Knights and archers in combination made up the most formidable fighting machine in western Europe.

They quickly showed their power in Ireland. The second Scandinavian city, Waterford, was taken. There Strongbow married Aoife, the daughter of Mac Murrough, and became heir to Leinster. But Mac Murrough's ambition, and now doubtless Strongow's, went beyond Leinster. This powerful English army, allied to his own of Leinster, could bring the high kingship itself into his hands. First Dublin would have to be taken, as had been the case with so many challenges in the past. So the combined forces, Irish and English, marched on the chief city of Ireland. O Connor appreciated what was afoot and determined to prevent them from approaching Dublin. He collected the largest possible army and deployed it south of the city to cut off all approaches. But Mac Murrough found a route through the Wicklow and Dublin mountains and before O Connor knew it the enemy was before the walls of Dublin. The city was taken on 21 September 1170 and was never again, until 1922, to be free of English control. Mac Murrough and Strongbow now had the three chief cities of Ireland firmly in their grasp and controlled the country in between. Now was the time to expand, with O Connor and his army discomfited. Ossory, Meath and Breffny were invaded in turn and submissions procured in the traditional Irish fashion. O Connor retaliated by executing his Leinster hostage, Mac Murrough's son. But there was no stopping the challenge that way. Only the onset of winter prevented further expansion by Mac Murrough and his army now retired to the safety of Leinster.

By now Henry II had become alarmed at what was happening in Ireland. Helping Mac Murrough was one thing; conquering land, capturing cities, possibly establishing an independent English kingdom was quite another. He had no reason to trust Strongbow, long since out of favour since his attachment to King Stephen in the civil war. It was time for the king to establish his authority over his subjects in Ireland, including Mac Murrough who had become his vassal in France. As a first step, Henry placed an embargo on all shipping to Ireland. That this was defied only increased his alarm. He then ordered all his subjects to return from Ireland under threat of forfeiture. Strongbow sent messengers saying that he would put at Henry's disposal all that he now possessed in Ireland. But neither he nor the others obeyed the summons by Henry. The murder of Thomas à Becket at Canterbury on 25 December 1170 probably forced a decision from the king. Going to Ireland would put him, temporarily at least, out of reach of the immediate consequences of that crime. At the same time he could deal with Strongbow and the others.

The extent of Henry's alarm, and his determination to be master, are demonstrated by the thoroughness of his preparations for an expedition to Ireland. Stores and equipment on a massive scale were collected from many parts of England, including siege-towers which could also be used for building operations, and a huge fleet of 400 ships was assembled. This took many weeks and demanded the attention of many royal officials, especially in the shires. Henry's expedition was not the result of a sudden decision, hastily prepared and inadequately fitted out. On the contrary, it was well planned and superbly organized. It may be that the death of Mac Murrough in May 1171, and the succession of Strongbow in Leinster, was what made Henry finally fix on a date.

During the summer, events moved rapidly in Ireland. There was a revolt against Strongbow in Leinster. More seriously, O Connor marched on Dublin with a host of allies and placed the city under siege with Strongbow inside.

For two months the Irish were content to wait and starve the besieged into surrender. In desperation Strongbow even offered to accept O Connor as his lord, provided he could retain Leinster. This was not just a repudiation of Henry II, but a startling recognition of the high kingship of O Connor and the superiority of the forces under his control at that time. But O Connor rejected that radical proposal and instead offered Strongbow Dublin, Waterford and Wexford, which had always been in foreign hands. Not satisfied with this, Strongbow decided to risk all on a sudden attack. Late in the evening, when it was least expected, the English rushed out of the city. They caught many of the Irish, including O Connor, bathing in the Liffey, killed many of them and got back safely into the city with an enormous booty, sufficient to help them withstand a siege for many more weeks.

Strongbow had won a victory of great psychological value and a dejected O Connor abandoned the siege. The English were now confirmed in possession of Dublin and were able to regain control of Leinster. This success enabled Strongbow to detach O Brien from O Connor, though the fact that the men were married to sisters also probably helped. O Brien then forced the King of Ossory to come to terms with Strongbow. This was important, since it gave Strongbow some of the security he needed if he had to leave Ireland to make his peace with Henry II. He had proved himself to be master of Leinster, had shown his ability to hold Dublin, Waterford and Wexford, and had demonstrated his capacity to expand, in the tradition of his Leinster predecessors, along the road that would lead to a higher prize.

But however successful Strongbow may have been in Ireland, he could not treat Henry II, now preparing his massive expedition, as if he were another O Connor. He had already offered all that he had won in Ireland to the king. Now he travelled to meet him and submit in person. When he encountered Henry, probably near Gloucester where the army was mustering for Ireland, he was well received. The king accepted his oath of fealty and granted him Leinster as a fief, retaining the Hiberno-Norse towns and their extensive lands as a royal demesne in Ireland. So Strongbow's new fief was immediately reduced. But he was well satisfied with what he retained. By any standards Leinster was large and wealthy, with some of the best land in Ireland, crossed by navigable waterways and serviced by the three most advanced ports in Ireland. The potential was obvious and both Strongbow and his successor William Marshal were quick to build on that.

King Henry, meanwhile, had received messengers from the Ostmen (as the Norse were now called in Ireland) of Wexford, asking him to intervene and telling him that they were holding fitz Stephen as a prisoner for him. He also seems to have received an embassy from Irish kings, begging his protection against the English. And in the background, despite the difficulties caused by the murder of Becket, there was the papal licence to invade Ireland in *Laudabiliter* and the promise of a welcome from at least some of the more radical reformers among senior churchmen. He was not, then, simply coming to Ireland as a foreign aggressor, intent on conquest and dominion. His motives were mixed and it is likely that he begrudged the time, energy and resources that he would have to waste.

He landed near Waterford on 17 October 1171. His army was huge – contemporaries put the numbers at 4,000, including 500 knights, which may seem exaggerated. But the scutage levied in England indicates that many tenants-in-chief served in person and the extent of the preparations, not least the large fleet assembled for transportation, confirm that the forces engaged were formidable. This, then, was a large-scale invasion of Ireland. It established Henry as effective feudal lord of Ireland and opened a whole new era in Irish history.

4   The feudal lordship

King Henry's immediate problem on landing in Ireland was to secure a firm base for himself. The two Hiberno-Norse towns of Waterford and Wexford provided this and he also retained extensive lands in between. This was later augmented by Dublin and the old Ostman kingdom, which included much of the modern county together with Wicklow east of the mountains as far south as Arklow. All of these lands in the east and south-east became extensive royal demesne. In addition, the king retained exclusive rights over the forest, which also provided a useful source of patronage for the future. He confirmed Strongbow in possession of the rest of Leinster, for the service of 100 knights. He also received the submission of Donal Mac Carthy, King of Desmond, who swore fealty, promised a yearly tribute and gave hostages. Other Irish kings quickly followed suit. Donal O Brien, King of Thomond, and lesser nobility submitted while King Henry was on his way to Cashel. Later, while he was journeying to Dublin, all the important Leinster nobility similarly submitted. So did O Rourke of Breffny, O Carroll of Uriel, and finally, if we are to believe Gerald of Wales, O Connor himself submitted to representatives of the king at a special ceremony on the banks of the Shannon. All of the Irish nobility, with the exception of the two great northern lineages of Cenél nEógan and Cenél Conail, freely submitted, accepted Henry as their lord, swore fealty, promised tribute, and gave up hostages. In this way, and because the Ostmen of the towns and the recently arrived English also submitted to him, Henry became effectively *dominus Hibernie* (lord of Ireland). Thus was Ireland 'conquered'. It remained to be colonized by new settlers over the next few generations.

Henry's purpose in going to Cashel via Lismore was to arrange a church synod, after discussion with the Bishop of Lismore, who was the papal legate, and the Archbishop of Cashel, where the synod was to be held. It was summoned on 6 November and was in session later that winter. Only the Archbishop of Armagh was an absentee, because of his great age, and he later consented to all that was done at Cashel. The king was represented by the abbot of Buildwas, an English Cistercian abbey with important Irish connections, and the archdeacon of Llandaff. The synod passed decrees covering a number of matters which had been the concern of the earlier generation of reformers: abuses of the marriage law; administration of the sacraments and the conduct of the liturgy; freedom of the church and clerical privileges; the payment of tithes. But the most important thing to happen at Cashel was that the Irish bishops accepted Henry as lord and drew up a report for the pope on the state of the Irish church. This was quickly carried to Rome by the archdeacon of Llandaff, who personally enlarged on the abuses and gave the pope a horrifying picture of conditions in the Irish church. King Henry now emerged as something of a crusader, rescuing the church and ending abuses, enthusiastically supported by the Irish clergy. There can be no doubt that this was why he made the summoning of a synod one of his first priorities in Ireland and that its success helped to secure for him papal absolution for the murder of Becket in May 1172. In September the pope congratulated him because he had 'magnificently triumphed over the disordered and undisciplined Irish' and had subjected 'this people to your lordship' in order to eradicate vice. Other letters to the clergy and separately to the 'noblemen, kings and princes of Ireland' gave papal approval for the new lordship established in Ireland and the fealty sworn to the king, and warned the laity 'to preserve unwavering and inviolate the fealty which you have sworn on the gospel to so great a king, with appropriate submission'.

This was a triumph for Henry and it clearly stated papal approval, based on the supposed rights of the pope over all islands in the world, for the new lordship of Ireland. There were consequences for the church, as well as the laity, in this. The logic of the position taken by the Irish bishops implied that English practice would henceforth be followed in the Irish church. This was explicitly stated by Gerald of Wales in his account of the synod of Cashel, when he commented that 'all divine services are to be carried out in all parts of the church in Ireland . . . according to what the English church observed. For it is right and just that, as by divine providence Ireland received her lord and king from England, she should also submit to a reformation from the same source'. Inevitably, then, the Irish church was to be anglicized, as well as feudalized, and this was to be an important element in the social as well as the political revolution which was to transform Ireland.

Meanwhile, King Henry had been busy in other ways. He celebrated Christmas in Dublin, holding court in a pavilion specially built in the Irish fashion and set up outside the city walls. He entertained his new Irish subjects in particular during the traditional public ceremonies associated with the feast. In a quieter way he consolidated his authority. A charter gave to Dublin the liberties of Bristol and set the bounds within which the municipality was to function as a royal borough in the future. This was the first such royal charter ever sealed in Ireland and it was the precedent which led to the creation of other new boroughs as the land was settled by feudatories, as well as the raising of existing Ostman towns to borough status. Henry was no revolutionary, anxious to wipe out existing institutions. Rather he confirmed them, subject to his own authority. Religious corporations like Holy Trinity (Christ Church), St Mary's abbey, or All Hallows in Dublin were confirmed in their landed possessions. The indigenous inhabitants of Dublin, the Ostmen, were not dispossessed and existing burgage plots were respected. But the city was now part of the royal demesne and whatever rights it was to possess would be held at farm, at an annual rent, from the king. Henry put a constable, Hugh de Lacy, in charge of the city in his name. He also gave Wexford and Waterford into the charge of members of his household, important officials who would make sure that in these two ports the king would retain an entry into Ireland if ever he were faced with revolt.

The need to consolidate his new lordship by some sort of military occupation was Henry's prime concern after he had received the submissions of the leading men, both English and Irish. That was why he had brought such a large army to Ireland, with the equipment necessary for building castles (probably of the simple earthwork or motte and bailey type), as well as laying siege to castles which refused to surrender. Gerald of Wales relates that it was his intention during the summer of 1172 'to fortify with castles, settle in peace and stability, and altogether to mould to his own design . . . his Irish dominion'. But he was given no time. Papal legates were demanding his presence in Normandy. Worse was the news of the rebellion being stirred up by his sons. Ireland would have to wait.

Before he left, however, he granted the whole of Meath, as it existed before the partition of 1169, to Hugh de Lacy for the service of 50 knights. Hugh belonged to one of the great families of England and had accompanied the king to Ireland as intimate and a member of the royal household. He was a man to be trusted. The grant of the enormous fief of Meath, stretching from the Shannon across Ireland to the mouth of the Boyne, was not just a reward for loyal service. It was also designed to block Strongbow from expansion in the traditional Leinster way, facing him with an English lord just as powerful as he and loyal to the king. Henry further made de Lacy his Chief Governor (later called the Justiciar) in Ireland, as well as constable of Dublin.

When Henry II sailed from Waterford on 17 April 1172 he probably knew that he was leaving an untidy situation behind him in Ireland and there is some indication that he planned to return. There was by this stage a strong English presence in Ireland, dominated by Strongbow, the Geraldines, and de Lacy. Henceforth the island would be divided between them and the Irish nobility, most of whom had already submitted to the foreign king. The nature of that submission has been disputed. Henry's language, like that of most of his followers, was French. The language in which he kept a record of his transactions was Latin, written by his clerks, while that of the local nobility was, of course, Irish. Professional interpreters, called latimers, were employed and they saw to it that diplomatic niceties and political exchanges could be understood by both sides. Such latimers had served the king well in his dealings with Welsh princes in the past, while they had also been employed by Mac Murrough and Strongbow to good effect long before the king came to Ireland. So there should have been little, if any, confusion in the exchanges between Henry II and the Irish. In describing the submission of Dermot

Mac Carthy, Gerald of Wales writes that he was bound by an oath of fealty and 'the bond of subjection', as well as hostages and an annual tribute. The same term, 'bond of subjection', is also used of Donal O Brien's submission, as well as of Rory O Connor's. Simple fealty, rather than the more formal homage, was the norm. But the Irish kings henceforth held their kingdoms under Henry at an annual rent.

In the case of O Connor, Gerald is more specific: he 'became dependant for the tenure of his kingdom on the king as overlord'. In the future, when the evidence is fuller, the Irish kings were sometimes treated as vassals of the crown, owing military service and liable to taxation like other tenants in chief. They also enjoyed the full benefits of English law like other subjects of the king. They, for their part, were anxious to possess charters confirming them in possession of their lands as hereditable fees.

After Henry left Ireland, Strongbow, de Lacy and the other English leaders got on with the business of securing possession of their fiefs and settling them in the English fashion. In Leinster there was little resistance from the resident Irish, who were easily accommodated within the new system. They were addressed in charters equally with English, Welsh, and Flemings, and there is no evidence of the kind of racial tension which was to poison relations in the future. Strongbow had married an Irish woman, Aoife, who became the countess Eva, and many lesser men followed his example. The result was a second generation of English settlers in Ireland who were half Irish, spoke Irish often as their first language, and inevitably identified with Ireland and Irish ways in a manner impossible for their fathers. In Meath, Hugh de Lacy also married an Irish woman in 1180, the daughter of the high king Rory O Connor. This, coupled with the vigour and success with which he pursued his right to the ancient, undivided kingdom of Meath, and the fact that he achieved a high status among at least some of the Irish (the annals actually referred to him as 'king of Erin'), gave rise to gossip so that, as Gerald of Wales tells us, 'he was strongly suspected of wanting to throw off his allegiance and usurp the government of the kingdom, and with it crown and sceptre'.

Such gossip was malicious, but it illustrates the misunderstanding that was to bedevil Anglo-Irish relations in the future. Distance, slow communications, and eventually sharp cultural differences were to make for an uneasy relationship. When the settlers, despite links with England through family, land and loyalty to the crown, became increasingly Irish in their ways, they rapidly assumed an identity of their own which made them a distinct group. As a 'middle nation', a term they applied to themselves, neither wholly English nor Irish, but what we would call Anglo-Irish, they were to shape their own political future, accepting the lordship of the king but insisting on Ireland's own ways.

All of this was in the future. But its genesis is to be found in the early years of the conquest, when the settlers were forced to adopt some Irish ways, not least in warfare and relationships with others. From the beginning they had to be partly assimilated into the culture of the Irish so that, from the perspective of England, they began to appear ever more distant and degenerate. The essence of the change was expressed by Gerald of Wales in a famous speech which he gave to Maurice fitz Gerald during the siege of Dublin by Rory O'Connor: '. . . just as we are English so far as the Irish are concerned, likewise to the English we are Irish, and the inhabitants of this island and the other assail us with an equal degree of hatred'.

In another speech, Gerald reports fitz Stephen as saying that by their helping Mac Murrough, Ireland might be united 'and sovereignty over the whole kingdom will devolve upon our race for the future . . . if by our present assault the kingdom of Ireland is forever preserved for us and our descendants, then what renown we shall win'. Such words were read in England, where they caused some anxiety. But if such high ambitions were far from the reality of the situation confronting the English in Ireland, they do illustrate the energy, purpose and lust for land which drove them on. They could not be kept within the bounds established by Henry II in 1172. They were drawn into the volatile politics of Ireland and exploited that situation to their own advantage. After he murdered Tiernan O Rourke during a meeting in 1172, whether by accident or design is immaterial here, Hugh de Lacy pressed on to the Shannon. Not even a long absence in Normandy, when he and Strongbow brought an army from Ireland to support Henry II, could halt the momentum of conquest in Ireland. Raids in the Irish fashion produced booty, especially cattle, and led to the incastellation of lands designed to hold them as fiefs for the settlers. Raymond le Gros raided into Decies in Munster, plundered the ancient monastery of Lismore, and brought a huge prey of cattle to Waterford. The Irish reacted. Early in 1174 Donal O Brien inflicted a heavy defeat on a mixed English and Dublin Ostman army camped at Thurles. Rory O Connor took advantage of the absence of Hugh de Lacy to invade Meath and destroyed his chief castle at Trim. The following year the English restored their lordship in Meath, hanging the O Melaghlin king at Trim. In October le Gros marched against O Brien, took Limerick and garrisoned it. He was provided with guides by the King of Ossory and, more importantly, was joined by Rory O Connor who, according to the annals, had actually initiated this move against O Brien. From the Irish perspective, the English presence was merely an added element in the age-old dynastic warfare which had characterized the struggle for the high kingship.

Meanwhile a new agreement, preserved in a charter issued under the great seal of England, was reached between O Connor and King Henry on 6 October 1175. In this, the so-called 'treaty of Windsor', Henry recognized that O Connor, his 'liege King of Connacht', should be king under him and hold his kingdom 'well and in peace, even as he held it before the king entered Ireland, but paying tribute for it'. This tribute, one hide from every 10 beasts slain, was also to be paid by the other Irish kings through O Connor, who was recognized as some sort of mesne lord between them and Henry. Meath, Leinster, and that part of Munster which lay between Waterford and Dungarvan, were to be immediately under Henry. This was an explicit recognition that Ireland was now divided, the Irish part under O Connor and the English part outside his immediate suzereignty, and both parts under the lordship of the King of England. Finally, the high king was to make sure that those Irish who had fled before English advances should return to 'the lands of the King of England's barons'. The invasion may have caused a refugee problem, but there was no intention of clearing out the Irish population from conquered land. Rather it was intended that there would be a strong indigenous element, and with it a pronounced Irish culture, in any feudal settlement.

Rory O Connor had the Archbishop of Tuam, the abbot of Clonfert, and his own chancellor, master Laurence, as his representatives negotiating this new arrangement in England. Among the witnesses to the charter was Laurence O Toole, the Archbishop of Dublin. This is a possible indication that Irish ecclesiastics had been involved in promoting this rapprochement between Henry and Rory, probably in the interests of peace in Ireland. If so, their attempt failed, largely because those in Ireland refused to make it work. The death of Strongbow in April 1176, leaving a minor as his heir, created a vacuum and removed a restraining influence. The Mac Lochlainn King of Cenél nEógan invaded Meath and caused settlements to be abandoned. Early in 1177 John de Courcy led a raid on the north, captured Downpatrick, and soon was busy establishing for himself what amounted to a principality in the area east of Lough Neagh and the Bann. Individual enterprise was once more asserting itself in Ireland, threatening the stability of the lordship. As before, the king intervened to regulate the lordship in his own fashion. At a council in Oxford in May 1177 he divided Munster in two: Desmond was granted to Robert fitz Stephen and Milo de Cogan, Thomond ultimately to Philip de Briouze. He gave 'custody' of Waterford to Robert le Poer and confirmed the earlier grant of Meath to Hugh de Lacy. Most important of all, he granted the lordship of Ireland to his nine-year-old son John. His intention was that John should become King of Ireland and all the grantees were made to do homage to him, as well as to Henry, for their Irish lands. This creation of an appanage was part of a wider plan to hold together the vast territories, often called the Angevin empire, under Henry's lordship, by entrusting them to the government of different sons.

It was not until 1185 that John came to take possession of his new lordship. He was as well prepared as was possible at that time. The new Archbishop of Dublin, John Comyn, the first English cleric to hold office, was sent ahead in 1184 to prepare the way. Messengers were dispatched to Rome seeking a crown from the pope and recognition of John's kingship of Ireland. Experienced members of the royal household were assigned to accompany the new lord to Ireland, some of whom, like Gilbert Pipard or Bertram de Verdon, were to found important lineages in Ireland. Ralph Glanville, the king's justiciar in England, in whose household the young John had been partly educated, travelled as far as Milford Haven with the expedition. All of this was to help create a centralized administration in Ireland. Also with

John were some close companions, most notably Theobald Walter, who established the Butler family in Ireland, and William de Burgh, founder of another great family in the lordship. Not least importantly, John was also given a large army, the equal of that which came with his father in 1171.

John spent eight months in Ireland. None of the Irish lieges came and submitted, possibly because he alienated some of them by his boorish behaviour shortly after arriving, but more likely because they were reluctant to accept his lordship. Hugh de Lacy had by then established a position of pre-eminence in Anglo-Ireland, both because of his own extensive lordship in Meath and because of the patronage he had exercised as chief governor on behalf of the king. He had also won some respect from some Irish. Gerald of Wales wrote that he gained the support of Irish lords 'by generous treatment and flattering them with his friendship', and that he had the most important of them as his allies. John later complained that it was de Lacy who prevented him from assuming his rightful role as lord of Ireland, which may be true. John certainly concentrated his attention on the south, away from de Lacy's immediate sphere of influence, building castles at Tibberaghny, Ardfinan and Lismore, where they at once provided a shield for his own Waterford demesne and springboards for further expansion. He also made extensive grants in the modern counties of Clare, Limerick, Tipperary and Offaly to Theobald Walter. Other grants were also made to William de Burgh and Philip de Worcester. Further north, Bertram de Verdun, John's marshal, and Gilbert Pipard were given lands which were later augmented in Louth, Monaghan and Armagh.

By the time he left Ireland on 17 September, John had greatly extended the feudal area through his many speculative grants, that is grants of land which subsequently had to be conquered and occupied by the grantee. While in Dublin he had also issued charters confirming earlier grants by his father, established an administration to look after his rights, particularly financial, as lord, and made a critical intervention in ecclesiastical affairs by issuing a charter uniting the see of Glendalough with Dublin. His departure from Ireland was sudden and he made little use of the resources provided by his father. But for all that, his expedition was not a complete failure and left a permanent mark on the developing feudal lordship.

After 1185 the initiative lay with the feudatories in Ireland. Hugh de Lacy was murdered in 1186 by an Irishman, supposedly in reparation to St Colum Cille for the desecration of his church at Durrow, where de Lacy was building a castle. It was the new men who from now on were to push ahead with military occupation. Many of these had landed interests elsewhere, but increasingly they concentrated their energies on Ireland. They exploited every advantage, not least the traditional antagonisms among the leading Irish families. Thus William de Burgh married a daughter of Donal O Brien and, with his consent, was able to build a castle on the Shannon estuary. O Brien hoped that this would provide a protection for him against his traditional enemy, Mac Carthy. Internal dynastic quarrels, in particular succession disputes among different segments of royal lineages, were also adroitly used by the English. Connacht provides the classic example. Early in the 1190s William de Burgh procured a charter granting him Connacht. In 1200 he led an army into the province, with strong support from his O Brien inlaws, in aid of Cathal O Connor, who accompanied him. De Burgh deposed the reigning O Connor king and installed Cathal in his place. The following year, while de Burgh was campaigning in west Cork with O Brien again in support, the deposed O Connor, Crobderg (red hand), returned to claim Connacht, this time with the help of John de Courcy and Hugh de Lacy II. Then, in 1202, de Burgh invaded Connacht again, on this occasion in support of Crobderg against his former protégé and installed him as king. Until he died in 1223 Cathal Crobderg retained the kingship of Connacht, managed to get a charter from King John in 1205, was granted Connacht in fee in 1215, and successfully passed on his kingship to his son Aed. But there were recurring disputes in Connacht, with the de Burghs regularly playing the part of kingmakers and their enemies among the colonial nobility backing O Connor challengers.

As always, the Irish split along traditional patterns and regularly combined with English forces. There was never clear division along racial lines. Political expediency, territorial gain, military supremacy – these were the determining factors. Nor was there any unity among the English, who frequently took opposing sides with Irish allies in the effort to win and hold land and influence. By the time John became King of England in 1199, marches (frontier lands which were being contested) had appeared in many parts of Ireland, providing occasion for war, treachery and death. There were, of course, large areas which were being successfully colonized and socially transformed and already they were known in official terminology as *terra pacis* (land of peace), in contrast to the *terra guerre* (land of war) which was still under the control of the Irish. But ambitious men like Theobald Walter, William de Burgh, John de Courcy and Hugh de Lacy the younger, were energetically pushing forward the frontiers of the so-called land of peace and in the process were creating a situation which made it increasingly difficult for the king to exercise efficient lordship.

King John made it his business to remedy the situation. In 1204 he ordered the construction of a large castle in Dublin, ostensibly to provide a safe place for his treasure, but eventually to become the centre, as well as the symbol, of English government in Ireland. He pushed ahead the development of a royal exchequer, with a staff and system of records capable of exploiting his financial rights in a lordship which was growing in prosperity with each year that passed. He continued to develop the system of local government, where necessary making the great feudatories in their fiefs his instruments. The law of England was made the law of Ireland and was enforced through a system of courts and justices who looked to the king himself as the supreme arbiter. A justiciar presided over all, even the lordship's army, in the name of the king. The process of infeudation meant that all land in Ireland was held of the king in return for specific services, mainly military, giving him the right to look for financial subsidies and to demand counsel whenever it was needed. This latter provided the justiciar with the means of consulting with the greater tenants in a council which was to evolve into parliament. The justiciar also presided over a smaller, secret (privy) council which met regularly and provided day-to-day advice. Even before he became king, John had mints at Dublin, Limerick and Waterford, of which only the first continued to issue coins into the early thirteenth century.

Perhaps most importantly of all, the king appointed as justiciar men who were loyal and devoted servants, the two most prominent of whom (John de Gray and Henry de Londres) were careerists looking for high office in the church as well as the state. Through them he began to control the great feudatories of Ireland, some of whom had displayed an independence which was intolerable. In Ulster, John de Courcy had minted his own coins, at Downpatrick and Carrickfergus, with his own name on some, and even seems to have adopted the name *princeps Ulidiae* (Prince of Ulster), if we are to trust Jocelin of Furness, who dedicated his 'Life of St Patrick' to him under that title. The king used the ambitious Hugh de Lacy to get rid of him, rewarding his service with the earldom of Ulster in 1205.

The most powerful noble in England, William Marshal, had married Isabella de Clare, the heiress of Strongbow, and through her had acquired vast estates in John's dominions, not least in Ireland where she had inherited Leinster. Marshal fell into disfavour with the king and came to Ireland in 1206, where he spent much of his time until 1212. While devoting himself to the economic exploitation of his lands, creating boroughs and new manors, he was harried by King John's justiciar. In 1208 he and Walter de Lacy were forced to accept new charters which curtailed their franchises. Resentment was now reaching boiling point among the Irish magnates, incensed at the activities of the justiciar. There seems to have been a plot, involving a de Lacy, to organize a rebellion which would have the support of John's greatest enemy, King Philip of France. Later in the same year, William de Briouze, formerly a favourite of King John's but now being sought to answer for maligning the king, fled to Ireland. He was given asylum by William Marshal, who held some land of him, then went to his son-in-law Walter de Lacy in Meath, and was finally promised every help by Hugh de Lacy in Ulster. The king took fright at these rebellious developments in Ireland. He decided to come in person to deal with the problem, an indication of how seriously he viewed the situation. On 20 June 1210 he landed near Waterford with a large army (including siege specialists) and all the stores and equipment he would need for a long campaign.

John spent just nine weeks in Ireland. He enjoyed a huge military success, taking Meath and Ulster into his hands, forcing de Briouze, Walter and Hugh de Lacy to flee for their lives from Ireland. William Marshal had been reconciled with the king and accompanied him on the campaign. The more important Irish kings submitted and O Connor, with others, joined the royal army on the march to Carrickfergus castle in Ulster. The whole campaign had been a diplomatic as well as a military triumph for King John; by the time he returned to England, the whole of Anglo-Ireland was firmly under royal control. The great lordships of Limerick, Meath and Ulster had been forfeited or were in royal custody, and of the great fiefs only Leinster remained under the immediate authority of its lord. But the king had done more than just suppress rebels or potential rebels. He had brought legal experts with him to Ireland and while in Dublin he issued a charter, which the leading magnates swore to observe, stipulating that the common law of England would be observed in Ireland and outlining the main rules of that law as it was to be applied in the lordship. This precursor, at least in part, of the more famous *Magna Carta* (Great Charter) issued in England in 1215, greatly strengthened the authority of the king's government in Ireland while limiting the seigniorial jurisdiction exercised by the magnates on their manors.

From then on the magnates gave no cause for alarm. They supported the king in England with a strong military backing when there was imminent danger of a French invasion in 1213; they protested vigorously in the same year when the pope proposed to free all John's subjects from their allegiance; and when England was plunged into civil war and partly occupied by the French at the end of the reign, none of them availed of the opportunity to rebel in Ireland. So confident was John of his success in Ireland that he began to restore lands to many tenants in Meath and Ulster who had been dispossessed because of their involvement with the de Lacy rebellion. Even Walter de Lacy was restored in Meath. Only Hugh de Lacy was left in exile. Prisoners were released and hostages restored. When King John died England was in turmoil, but Ireland was quiet. The Anglo-Irish nobility from now on concentrated their energies on consolidating their hold on the lands they occupied, gaining new lands, and turning all to profit. It was to be a long time before an English king faced the kind of crisis in Ireland which King John had successfully overcome.

In part, this was because the English government was careful to mollify potential resentments. *Magna Carta*, with all that that implied, was rapidly extended to Ireland and new charters were issued, furthering the ambitions of settlers to gain more land, or introducing new blood where there was no competition for land. During the minority of Henry III, when William Marshal was regent of England, the latter used his powers to his own benefit and that of his friends in Ireland. After his death, when Hubert de Burgh headed the government in England, the de Burgh interest in Ireland was promoted. Their attempt to expand into Connacht at the expense of the O Connors met with Anglo-Irish opposition, led by Richard Marshal when he came to Ireland. But he was treacherously killed during a meeting on the Curragh on 1 April 1235, some said with the connivance of the young King Henry, and stability was restored. The new king pressed ahead with reforms of the Irish administration, creating a chancery with its own great seal,

expanding the Dublin exchequer, and developing the courts which administered the common law. He ordered the building of a great hall in Dublin
castle, which was intended to provide a suitable setting for his court when he
came on his proposed visit to Ireland. That visit never took place. Instead,
in 1254 he gave most of the land of Ireland, together with lands in Wales,
Scotland, the Channel Islands and Gascony, to his heir Edward. Lordship of
Ireland was still reserved to the king, unlike in 1177 when it was vested in
John. Indeed the 1254 charter was unambiguous in stating that the land of
Ireland should never be separated from the crown of England, an important
statement of the inalienability of crown lands. It was a milestone in the his-
tory of the constitutional links binding Ireland and England.

Despite the legal position, in practice the young Edward very soon began
to act as if he were in fact lord of Ireland. Something of a condominium
resulted and divided responsibility meant that the quality of Irish
government deteriorated. It was not until after he became king in 1272, and
thus the legitimate lord of Ireland, that Edward began to reform the state of
Ireland. A succession of strong chief governors, beginning with his friend and
fellow crusader Geoffrey de Geneville (who became lord of Trim when he
married one of the de Lacy co-heiresses) and ending with John Wogan, succeeded in restoring good government, increasing revenues substantially
(always a good yardstick with which to measure government efficiency), and
providing the king with much surplus revenue. The lordship made an important contribution to England's war effort, especially during the last decade of
Edward's reign. Anglo-Irish served in Wales and Flanders; military supplies
and enormous quantities of grain, beef and other foodstuffs were shipped at
the expense of the Dublin exchequer to English armies in the field as far away
as Gascony. Major expeditionary forces served in Scotland in 1296, 1301, and
1303. Nothing better illustrates the success of the colonization of Ireland. It
was the result of the steady expansion of the manors of the settled areas
which had gone on continuously for much of the thirteenth century.

This was the result, in part, of the consolidation of older grants and, in
part, the taking up of new grants of land. The most spectacular was the
grant of Connacht to Richard de Burgh in 1227, though even as late as 1276
the whole of Thomond was granted to Thomas de Clare, a younger brother
of the Earl of Gloucester and a friend of the king. By then much of the good
land was occupied by the settlers and only part of the north, west and south-
west was still dominated by the old Irish lineages. There were, of course,
areas within feudal Ireland which were still in Irish hands, such as the highlands of east Leinster which came uncomfortably close to Dublin, or the
poorer lands to the west of the province which contained some of the largest
stretches of bog on the island. These Irish enclaves were to pose problems of
defence and peace-keeping in the future. But for much of the thirteenth century they made little impact on the lands of the settlers who were
transforming much of the landscape of Ireland.

Land without men to work it was useless and, right from the beginning, efforts were made to keep the indigenous population, as far as possible, on the land. Some of these became free tenants, most were reduced to serf status, unfree, as betaghs (*betagii*). In practice this meant little difference to their way of life and many of them were better off than the poor English cotters who provided the bulk of the labour force to work the lord's land. The greatest disability which the Irish had to endure was to be left outside the common law. At first the Irish, like the Ostmen, had enjoyed the benefits of English law, but from the mid-thirteenth century onwards the Irish as a race, with few exceptions, were allowed no recourse to the law of Ireland or the king's courts. At best this was an inconvenience, at worst it could lead to injustice. One could buy a charter of denizenship, but as this was an expensive business it was only for the few. This led to many in the settled areas taking English names and passing themselves off as Englishmen, necessarily with the connivance of their neighbours on the manor. Behind many an English name on lists of tenants lurked an Irishman and most manors would have had a substantial Irish element in their populations.

Nevertheless there is evidence of a considerable migration of English peasants into Ireland. They had to be offered powerful inducements to come to such a strange and often hostile land. When Buildwas abbey in the 1170s was offered a large endowment of land in Wexford for a new Cistercian foundation, the abbot sensibly sent a monk to survey the place. His report painted a grim picture which was enough to dissuade the abbot from all thoughts of accepting the gift. It spoke of 'the waste of the place, the sterility of the lands, and the ferocity and wildness of the local inhabitants'. This was typical of the way Ireland was commonly perceived in twelfth-century England, a backward place inhabited by wild Irish. Despite this, land-hungry peasants were persuaded to immigrate by the offer of light labour services, compared with the more heavy ones demanded in England, and more especially by the offer of burgage tenure, a privilege which gave them many desirable liberties not normally available to them in rural England. So they came in numbers, settling most heavily on the better lands in Leinster, Meath and Munster, though penetrating as far west as Erris in Mayo and Dingle in Kerry.

They brought with them the kind of agricultural expertise required to make their new lands profitable. Land was cleared, drained, ploughed and sown, enough grain was produced to make a large surplus available for market and more cattle were reared than ever before, mainly because the settlers were able to feed them through the winter by using hay. There was a spectacular increase in the number of sheep, kept mainly for wool which was now in demand by the cloth manufacturers of Europe. Before the end of the thirteenth century great numbers of fleeces were being exported, mainly by Italian merchant companies attracted by the growing Irish economy. Italian bankers, too, of firms in Lucca and Florence, were much in evidence, supplying the capital necessary to promote this agricultural revolution.

The new lordships, organized into manors on the English model, provided the kind of infrastructure which made possible the economic boom. Rivers were made more navigable, new roads were cleared and bridges built, markets and fairs were created in a network which covered the colony, boroughs were encouraged by enterprising lords. Many of these boroughs were established merely to attract settlers and never developed into true towns. But at points most favourable for trade new towns were established in large numbers. The king developed his own towns (Dublin, Wexford, Waterford, Cork and Limerick) by giving them charters of liberties to encourage economic growth. Lords like Marshal (New Ross, Kilkenny), de Lacy (Drogheda), de Burgh (Galway) or Bermingham (Athenry) were quick to follow and soon the colony was dotted with market towns. Into them poured the produce of neighbouring manors and luxury goods imported from overseas. Some basic commodities like salt, wine and iron were also imported, often in return for Irish grain, wool or hides.

The resulting prosperity was reflected in the new stone buildings which went up in the thirteenth century. While most lords of manor were content with modest stone houses, the more important built castles in the latest fashion; Trim castle is imposing even in a ruined state today and many lesser ones appeared on the landscape of Ireland. Later in the century, Richard de Burgh brought over the man who had designed the great Welsh castles for Edward I and employed him in designing new fortresses in Connacht. The new wealth enabled lords to endow new religious foundations, not just by the well established Cistercians or the Augustinian canons, but by Hospitallers, Templars and other exotic importations. During the thirteenth century the new orders of friars arrived and the Franciscans and Dominicans in particular set up friaries in many of the new towns. The church itself, heavily endowed with land even before the English came, became increasingly wealthy and could afford to follow the European trend in building. Dublin got not one but two new cathedrals (Holy Trinity and St Patrick's) and Kilkenny under Marshal boasted one of the most beautiful of all. These were smaller in scale than their English or French counterparts, but they faithfully reproduced the latest fashion in ecclesiastical architecture, even importing stone from England (Holy Trinity) and skilled masons to work it so as not to appear too provincial to the casual glance. The more humble parish church was also up to date, most of them being newly built to serve the parishes which were created as an integral part of the new secular manors.

Wherever the colonists settled, therefore, they transformed the local secular and ecclesiastical scene. The prosperity which they generated was not only to make the local lords more wealthy, it also provided taxable wealth which the absent lord of Ireland was able to enjoy. King John drew substantial revenues from Ireland and his successors, Henry III and Edward I, followed suit, so that Ireland became a useful source of revenue to financially hard-pressed governments in England. In the early fourteenth century, radical reformers known as the Ordainers in England complained that a 'wrong use' had been made of Irish revenues, resulting in 'default of money' in Ireland, so that good government had become difficult there and 'the residue of money of the issues of Ireland had so far not sufficed for keeping the peace there'. Nevertheless, the exploitation of Irish revenues by the king continued, though before long the economic depression of the fourteenth century and increasing civil disorders produced a dramatic decline in Irish revenues and left the Dublin government dependent on the English taxpayer.

But throughout the thirteenth century the Irish lordship had prospered. There was a forward movement of colonization, directed by some great personalities at the head of important lineages. Hugh de Lacy was restored to his earldom of Ulster and before he died in 1242 he had pushed its borders westwards. He left no heir and it was the de Burghs, first Walter and then Richard (known as the 'Red Earl') who brought the earldom of Ulster to its greatest power. All the leading Irish nobility of Ulster owed these earls military service, and the greatest of them all, O Neill, even acknowledged that he held his kingship from de Burgh. In 1268 in a formal charter he agreed that if he defaulted in his obligations the earl 'shall be free to throw me out of the kingship . . . and to give it to whomsoever it shall please him'.

But the de Burghs were also lords of Connacht, with the exception of an area bordering the Shannon known as 'the king's cantreds', portion of which continued to be held by the O Connors. In Connacht, too, the de Burghs managed to dominate the Irish for the most part, exploiting lineage factions, making kings and deposing others. An early fourteenth-century Irish tract from Galway spoke approvingly of 'our own foreigners' and praised them for having learnt the ways of the Irish. As in Ulster, the Irish owed some sort of military service to the lord. In 1310 the annals record that there was not one of the O Connor townlands 'without its permanent quartering, nor a *tuath* free from exaction, nor a prince free from oppression, so long as William Burke was in control of them'. This was William de Burgh, first cousin of Earl Richard, called *liath* (grey) by the Irish. Married to Finula O Brien, he is a good example of the settler who was half-Irish, easily adopting Irish ways when it suited, but still English (or *gaill*, foreign), identifying with Dublin – he acted as deputy to the justiciar in 1308–9 – and beyond that with the king in England. He was the ancestor of the Burkes (the Mac Williams upper and lower) who were to dominate Connacht politics to the end of the middle ages.

The other important settler family in Connacht were the Berminghams of Athenry. The more important segment of that family was based in Tethmoy, on the border of Meath and Kildare, where they became closely associated with John fitz Thomas, who became first Earl of Kildare in 1316. The Geraldines had participated in the conquest of Connacht, with the huge manor of Sligo as their major holding. The ambitions of John fitz Thomas led him into a conflict with the de Burghs and in the settlement which ended the quarrel in 1298 he withdrew from Connacht, leaving it henceforth to be dominated by the de Burghs. He built up a power base in the midlands, centred on Kildare, from which succeeding earls were to play a major role in the history of Ireland.

To the south, other Geraldines were important in the expansion of the colony into south west Munster. One segment acquired a collection of estates in Limerick, Kerry and Cork, and even to the east in Waterford, which were gradually welded together to form the lordship subsequently held by the earls of Desmond. Others acquired lands in north Kerry and Limerick which provided lordships in the future for the knights of Glin and the lords of Kerry. Thus, the Geraldines of the first invasion had established themselves in different segments throughout the midlands and in Munster. In the Earls of Kildare and Desmond they provided leading figures in the politics of Anglo-Ireland in the later middle ages. The other family which was equally prominent in politics was that of Butler, founded by Theobald Walter who came to Ireland with the Lord John in 1185. He had been granted the eastern part of the old kingdom of Limerick, which never was realized. It was in Tipperary that the Butlers became dominant. In 1328 James Butler was created first Earl of Ormond and the earldom eventually expanded eastwards to include the valuable lordship of Kilkenny, which became their capital, with many other scattered lands as well.

These great families, with their many segments, were predominant in the colonizing of Ireland and they gained most in the parcelling out of lands by successive kings. But there were many lesser lineages, each dominant in its own locality, who were a necessary part of the expansion of the lordship. The le Poers (Powers) were important in the south, with the Barrys, Roches, Cogans, Cantetons (Candons) and Purcells. Others of prominence were the Harolds, Archbolds, Lawlesses and Rochforts in Leinster; the Mandevilles, Logans and Savages in Ulster; Tuyts, Flemings, Petits in Meath; Exeters and Barrets in Connacht. But even these are only a few of the complex networks of interrelated families who held much of the land and therefore the wealth of Ireland. They sometimes broke into factions, dabbling in the politics of the Irish lordships and occasionally drawing swords against each other.

In the thirteenth century, for example, the de Burghs and Geraldines engaged in what almost amounted to a civil war. In December 1264, Maurice fitz Maurice took prisoner the justiciar, Richard de la Rochelle, along with some of the leading magnates and confined them in his castle at Lea. Immediately there was reprisal when the Geraldine manors in Connacht were attacked by the de Burghs and before long much of Ireland was plunged into civil war. It was with difficulty that the magnates were persuaded to accept an uneasy truce in a parliament summoned the following year, which revealed an alarming number of tenants dispossessed of their lands during the disturbances caused by the war. The quarrel was renewed later when John fitz Thomas seized the Earl of Ulster and held him prisoner for months, again in Lea castle. During that time, according to the Irish annals, 'all Erin was thrown into a state of disturbance'. Official records support this. Taxes could not be collected, the exchequer recorded, 'on account of the war and the capture of the Earl of Ulster'. Special payments had to be made to members of the council for leading armed men to 'various parts of

Ireland . . . to establish the king's peace which had been disturbed by the taking of the Earl of Ulster'. A graphic phrase in the official record of the eyre of Kildare sums it up. Referring to the period after de Burgh's capture, it calls it simply 'the time of the disturbance'.

The same record shows another side of the quarrel, with fitz Thomas on the rampage with the O Connors in Kildare, killing, looting, and burning. Other English and Irish joined in the disturbances and they spread to other parts. This encouraged the O Byrnes, O Tooles and Mac Murroughs of the mountains, who had been at peace since 1283, to attack the rich English settlements within striking distance. In Connacht the quarrel involved the O Connors. Later in Thomond the Geraldines supported one O Brien segment against another which had the backing of de Burgh. In this way magnates exploited Irish dynastic succession disputes to their own end, often prolonging them needlessly.

Nor did the magnates hesitate to use the local Irish lords to score off Anglo-Irish adversaries, even where this meant damage and even destruction of feudal settlements. In 1273 the mayor of Carrickfergus accused the Mandevilles and other Ulster magnates of procuring O Neill and other Irish to invade 'the king's land', so that they 'brought into it homicide, burning and robbery', all because the earl's seneschal had tried to levy debts which the magnates owed the king. The seneschal was William fitz Warrin, with whom the Mandevilles had a bitter and prolonged quarrel.

The Irish, for their part, were quick to take advantage of such quarrels. In the second half of the thirteenth century lost ground was gradually recovered by some of them, settlements were looted, pitched battles were fought and won, and old institutions were revived in places. In the middle of the century a new generation of Irish leaders began to appear, frustrated by the failure of their fathers' attempts to gain permanent possession of their lands within the English system. Some of them, in the words of a poet, made the sword their charter. In Connacht, Aed O Connor, even before he became king in 1265, led a military revival which was to be climaxed by the destruction of a de Burgh army at the battle of Ath in Cip, near Carrick-on-Shannon, in 1270. He married a daughter of Mac Sorley of the western isles of Scotland in 1259 and with her received a dowry of 160 galloglas soldiers. These were the first of the fearsome Scottish mercenaries who were later to pour into Ireland, providing Irish chieftains (and later Anglo-Irish as well) with full-time professional soldiers.

In 1258, together with the son of the O Brien King of Thomond, Aed met with Brian O Neill, King of Tyrone, at an important conference at Caeluisce, near Belleek. The high kingship was revived and in an unprecedented gesture the two leading dynasties of Connacht and Munster accepted Brian as high king. Henry III confirmed the existence of this new status when he subsequently complained that O Neill had 'presumptuously styled himself King of the kings of Ireland'. O Neill had already been attacking settlements in the north; now, fortified by his new status, he went on the rampage. But in 1260 he was defeated and killed at the battle of Downpatrick. Many of the Connacht Irish nobility, who had been led to the battle by O Connor, also fell. O Neill's head was subsequently taken to Dublin and then sent to the king in England, suggesting that the government had got a fright.

Two years later the high kingship was offered to King Haakon of Norway, who seems to have been willing to revive old Norse ambitions in Ireland, in return for expelling the English. Nothing came of this and it was not until the early fourteenth century that a similar offer was made to the King of Scotland, the great Robert Bruce. He liked to pose as a man who would deliver the Irish from their bondage, writing to them as their kinsman, claiming that he and they were all of the one nation, bound together by a common culture and common ancestry. He sent his brother Edward with an army to invade Ireland in 1315 and it was he who was solemnly inaugurated as the last high King of Ireland in the spring of 1316. That winter, King Robert himself arrived with reinforcements and the two brothers began a royal circuit designed to win support in the old way from the Irish chieftains. Instead they found the Irish divided, some making use of the disturbed conditions to score off the Anglo-Irish, others fighting among themselves, and some (like the dominant segment among the O Briens) positively hostile. There was no real support for the Scots, whose invasion coincided with the worst famine to hit Europe in the middle ages, and the grand enterprise ended in dismal failure at the battle of Faughart in October 1318. Edward Bruce was killed, his army destroyed, and the greatest single threat ever presented to the English lordship in medieval Ireland was at an end.

There was to be no united Irish effort against the English. That there was a national consciousness fostered by the men of letters, is undoubted. However much the Anglo-Irish may have adopted Irish ways, they were still *gaill*, foreigners, different to those whose ancestry reached far back into the Irish past. When Pope John XXIII issued a general condemnation of all supporters of Bruce, the Irish king Donal O Neill replied in a famous 'remonstrance', defending his right to cede his kingship of Ireland to Bruce and condemning the English for their failure to deal justly with the Irish. There is no doubting the sense of nationality and pride in the Irish past which runs through the document, and the venom towards the Anglo-Irish is quite explicit. They have, it was claimed, 'eagerly lusted for our land' and there 'is no hope whatever of our having peace with them . . . for we have a natural hostility towards each other arising from the mutual, malignant and incessant slaying of fathers, brothers, nephews and other near relatives and friends'.

But such attitudes rarely generated political action. The Irish, and indeed the Anglo-Irish, followed the course most convenient to them in the localities, each man trying to gain advancement sometimes by cooperation, sometimes by violence, often by treachery and bad faith. The gruesome murder of the O Connors by Peter Bermingham while entertaining them in his castle at Carbury in 1308, when thirty in all were killed, was a notorious example of how a marcher lord could best deal with his local enemies. That the Irish council approved is certain and they subsequently rewarded Bermingham with the usual 'head money' (*capitagium*) paid as a bounty to those producing the heads of notorious Irish felons. Popular approval for the murder was demonstrated in an elegy written when Bermingham died, which praised him for hunting the Irish 'as hunter does the hare' and especially for his massacre at Carbury.

Treachery was not all on one side however, and the violence which resulted was not easily contained. It contributed to the growth of crime in the late thirteenth century which swept Ireland, in common with England and much of western Europe, and for which governments had no answer. In Ireland the criminal was often indistinguishable from the local mandarin and his retinue. Whole families were brought to court on criminal charges and early four-teenth century parliaments had to adopt the radical solution of making what were called 'chieftains of great lineages' responsible for errant members of the family. The problem was aggravated by the proliferation of what were called 'idlemen', junior members of families, landless and without prospects. Many joined the retinues of local lords who were forwarding their ambitions, or protecting their interests, through the use of armed retainers. Most of these were Irish 'kernes' and they were often supported by billeting on a helpless population, the taking of illegal prises, and the issuing of what were in effect licences to commit crime through a system of avowery, by which the lord promised to protect them and compensate their victims if the law was able to take its course. Whole communities could be terrified, unable to retaliate.

But occasionally there was a spirited reaction, a famous example occurring in 1329 at the Earl of Louth's manor of Braganstown. The murder of a man of Ardee by some of the earl's kernes had resulted in the townsmen finally taking the law into their own hands. They killed as many of the hated retain-ers as they could lay hands on, including some who had sought sanctuary, in a state of terror, in the local Carmelite church. With others from county Louth they pursued the remainder of the kernes to Braganstown and when the earl contemptuously refused to hand over the kernes the enraged mob murdered him, his brother, eight others of his name, Talbot of Malahide and 12 other gentry who were staying at the castle, as well as more than 150 others whose names are not known, including a famous Irish harper with 20 of his pupils.

Retinues of armed men, of mixed race, the raw material of what historians have called 'bastard feudalism', remained a permanent feature of medieval Irish society. They provided a ready instrument for making war, which became endemic in the lordship. Long before the end of the thirteenth cen-tury the terms *terra pacis* (land of peace) and *terra guerre* (land of war) became part of the official terminology normally employed by the government. While they optimistically identified the former with the English and the latter with the Irish, the terms do display a consciousness that war in some form was a normal part of Irish life. In the famous 1297 parliament, when representatives of the shires were present as well as the magnates, the problem was highlighted. Much of the burden of defence and peace-keeping was thrown on the local communities, with the government retaining a supervisory role and confining itself to large-scale expeditions against more important Irish enemies. By then, too, the term *inimicus* (enemy) was being increasingly applied to Irish felons or rebels so that, before long, the two terms, Irish and enemy, became almost interchangeable. While the horrific concept of the Irishman as a 'natural enemy' was slow to grow, it did emerge in the late middle ages. It developed out of the increasing violence which prevailed in the marchlands of late thirteenth-century Ireland.

The same parliament of 1297 highlighted another feature of contemporary Ireland. In a celebrated statute it condemned as 'degenerate' those settlers who had taken to Irish fashion in dress, hairstyle and mode of riding. Because they were easily mistaken for Irishmen, they were sometimes killed on the spot and this could give rise to blood-feuds between families. The nervous, almost siege-like, mentality revealed in this legislation is an interesting commentary on the dangers of life on many manors where stray Irishmen might be killed on sight. Even within easy reach of Dublin, places like Saggart were regularly raided by hungry Irish from the mountains. In the early 1280s the tenants complained to the king and asked for succour. They had been burned out of their homes, they said, 'with many of our fathers, brothers and relatives killed', and for the past seven years had to take refuge where they could, so that their land lay waste and uncultivated. They listed some of their losses – 3,000 sheep, 200 cattle, 200 pigs, 100 horses, as well as corn burnt or carried away and other goods stolen. About 10 years previous to this a royal official referred to Saggart as 'near to the land of war', and that within 10 miles of Dublin.

But even more revealing is the term 'degenerate' employed by the parliament, meaning that by adopting Irish fashion the people concerned had lost their very identity as Englishmen. Almost from the very beginning of colonization there was some degree of assimilation to the Irish way of life. Intermarriage, the racial mix on many manors, even the simple need to communicate, made many settlers bilingual. Not much literature in English has come down to us from medieval Ireland, but the chance survival of a late thirteenth or early fourteenth collection, urban in origin, demonstrates the use of words in English which are direct borrowings from Irish. A satire on the people of Kildare, for example, uses the word *corrin* for a small cup, which is a straight borrowing from the Irish diminutive *cuirín*. The most famous of all poems included in this collection, *The land of Cokayne*, shows in both form and content that the author was familiar with the Irish tradition of satire and was influenced by it even when composing in English in an international genre. Nicknames used by the settlers betray a familiarity with the Irish language, like William Slab of the manor of Ballymore Eustace; and there are many like John Bán, William Beg and Henry Óg who combined English and Irish forms of their names.

What was most worrying to the government was the more insidious effect, as seen from Dublin, of Irish law on the common law introduced from England, which could be altered to suit the circumstances of the colonists in Ireland. For example, in order to prevent estates going to heiresses and being partitioned, the law of primogeniture might be put aside. Crime was frequently punished by fine, even in the royal courts, in place of the death penalty demanded by the common law. Worst of all was the growth of march law, a hybrid derived from the needs of the frontier conditions prevailing in many parts of Ireland. It was this law which tolerated the actions of marcher lords and their retinues of idlemen and kernes which the common law would have outlawed. It allowed for the kind of relationship with Irish enemies, 'in the manner of the marches' as one official record phrased it, which the Dublin government found difficult to stomach. In distant Westminster, where it was impossible to imagine the stress of life in the Irish marches, march law (like Irish law, which Edward I had once described as 'detestable to God and contrary to all laws') was outrightly condemned.

Cultural assimilation, even if only to a limited degree, and the growth of march law could often mean more harmonious relations with the Irish. But, long before the end of the thirteenth century, there was much evidence of racial tension in Ireland, based on antagonisms bred in wars, raids, murder and theft. Its extent should not be exaggerated, for many Irish and Anglo-Irish were able to live in peace with each other. But many others, for one reason or another, found co-existence impossible. This can be clearly seen even among the religious orders. The Cistercians had split along racial or cultural lines early in the century. Even before the English arrived tensions between the French and Irish monks had developed during the building of Mellifont. It was natural for the Irish to resist the importation of foreign styles, well illustrated by St Bernard in his 'Life of St Malachy', where he described the reaction to the new style of stone church which Malachy wanted to build in his diocese of Connor. The locals would have no new fashion imposed on them by the saint and one of them told him tartly: 'We are Irish, not French'. Such conservatism remained a source of tension when the Irish monks refused to conform to the Cistercian norm in every detail.

It burst into violence during the so-called Mellifont conspiracy in the early thirteenth century, when houses of the Mellifont affiliation rebelled against a succession of visitors sent by the general chapter from Citeaux, even resorting to violence to prevent entry into the monastery. The general chapter, as it told the pope, was careful to select visitors of different nationalities – 'Irish, Welsh, English, Flemish, French, Lombard and many from Clairvaux itself' – in case the Irish might believe that national bias was influencing any action taken. But to no avail. Many houses refused to accept English monks. Even as late as 1321, despite all the efforts of visitors from the mother house, racial bias was still being applied. Edward II complained to the general chapter in that year that in many houses in Ireland 'it has become the practice that no one is admitted to the religious habit unless an oath is taken, or it be known on evidence or common knowledge, that he is not of the English nation or related to the English'. Among the Franciscans, too, national divisions appeared, exploding violently in 1291 when the provincial chapter met in Cork. Irish and Anglo-Irish friars fought, some were killed, and peace was restored only when the secular arm intervened. During the Bruce invasion many actively supported the Scots and were condemned by the pope. In 1324 the provincial chapter, meeting in Dublin, tried to intrude Anglo-Irish friars into a number of 'pure Irish' friaries, mainly in the west, but division along racial lines persisted.

The Anglo-Irish, for their part, often reflected the same racial bias. It was expressed in its most exaggerated form in the Kilkenny parliament of 1310 which enacted a statute forbidding 'all the religious who dwell in a territory at peace or in the English land, to receive into their order or into their profession any save those who are of the English nation'. Five bishops were present at that parliament, including the Archbishop of Cashel, who was Irish, and assented to the statute. The legislation was quickly revoked, but it reveals the extent to which the nations had been polarized within the church. In the fourteenth century it became common to speak of the *ecclesia inter anglicos* (church among the English) in distinction to the *ecclesia inter hibernicos* (church among the Irish), almost as if they were two distinct churches indeed.

There were compensations. Cultural differences could enrich as well as divide. Not all religious men took too seriously the dangers of acquiring Irish ways. The unknown friar who wrote *The land of Cokayne*, a late thirteenth- or early fourteenth-century satire, could make fun of the traditional mores of Irish Cistercians, mocking their strict asceticism and chaste lives. The walls of the abbey are constructed of pasties, fish and rich meat, the shingles of cakes. Wine flows endlessly, precious stones are everywhere and even the trees are made of ginger. The miraculous ability to levitate, so beloved of pious hagiographers, is mercilessly lampooned, with the young monks flying out to play every day, faster than any hawk. In their play they join with the young nuns from a nearby nunnery as they timidly swim in the local river. Each of the monks takes a nun back to the monastery and there teaches her 'an orison' which makes a mockery of the vow of celibacy.

But behind the banter in the poem a strong anti-Irish, as well as anti-Cistercian note can be detected. However much the process of assimilation nibbled away at the colony, many of the Anglo-Irish remained strongly antagonistic towards all things Irish. More and more the Irish as a race came to be seen as natural enemies; they were also seen as unreasonable. A statute of the 1297 parliament speaks of them 'rushing instantly to war' because they were *leves* (not capable of controlling themselves as reasonable beings, excitable, capricious, fickle). This was no new attitude. It is found in the writings of Gerald of Wales who said that the Irish were 'a race consistent only in their fickleness', 'unreliable', 'of unstable temperament', as well as being 'wild' and 'barbarous'. One of the Cistercian visitors during the

Mellifont conspiracy wrote that the Irish were a 'bestial people' (*gentes bestiales*), meaning that emotion rather than reason governed them. The same term 'bestial' was used by Edward II in a letter to Pope John XXII. In the later middle ages the same attitude was expressed by the English term *wylde* (wild), or sometimes the French *sauvage* (savage). In official eyes this meant that the Irish could not be trusted, that agreements with them would not last unless they could be enforced. If relations with the Irish were not carefully controlled by the Dublin government, instability would prevail. Hence the insistence by successive governments that there must be no parleying with the Irish except under licence. Until such time as they were taught what later generations called 'civility' they were not fit to be trusted.

The Irish, for their part, took a no less jaundiced view of the Anglo-Irish. The author of the 1317 remonstrance wrote of their treachery and lack of good faith. He even went so far as to say, doubtless with his tongue in his cheek, that 'the holy and dove-like simplicity' of the Irish people had been 'altered into a serpentine craftiness through daily life with them and through their bad example'. In general the Irish men of letters felt so confident of their superiority that it was not until the seventeenth century that they thought it necessary to defend such a self-evident fact. Like the Anglo-Irish they believed that they had a monopoly on integrity, reason and civilized manners.

In day-to-day life, of course, both nations (to use a term that they would have used of themselves) were able to exist, if not in harmony at least in understanding. But the attitudes reflected by notions of superiority were nevertheless important and were often invoked at the highest level to justify policy or political expediency.

5 The two nations

Ireland's relationship to the English crown was clear and unambiguous in theory. The King of England was lord of Ireland and he had a duty to protect his subjects there. When Edward II sent the statute of Winchester to Ireland in 1308 to help in maintaining the peace there, he said that he was all the more anxious about it 'because we are hereto bound by the bond of an oath'. This reference to his recent coronation oath, which made him the protector of the realm, showed an awareness that Ireland was now inseparable from the English crown, a fact which had been spelt out in the 1254 charter in which Henry III granted the land of Ireland to his son Edward. It was to the crown, then, that the liege people of Ireland looked. The king was the ultimate source of justice, patronage, reward, protection and, where appropriate, retribution. It was to him, and only to him, that homage was due. If his subjects in Ireland had a responsibility to help him to protect his lands, defeat his enemies, and generally to support him in his 'time of necessity' (the legal formula used at the time), then he in turn was bound to guard their rights and above all protect them in their property. Edward III admitted as much in 1357, explaining why he did not 'provide defences and other remedies, as behoves us' for his people of Ireland. Three years later a message from an Irish great council sought 'succour and remedy' to be provided 'as a noble and gracious prince is bound to do for his subjects'. More than a century later an Irish parliament, in another message to the king, argued that he was 'bound to the defence of the land of Ireland by reason that it is one of the members of his most noble crown and eldest member thereof'.

But there was another reason why the King of England should have some regard for the protection of his lordship of Ireland. In the later middle ages, with the growth in national consciousness and increasing concern for security, Ireland assumed a new role. The anonymous author of the early fifteenth century *Libelle of Englyshe Polycye* wrote that 'Ireland is a buttress and a post under England' and warned the English council to look to its defence, lest it fall into the hands of England's enemies. Long before that, however, the Scots had exposed the same danger, when Robert Bruce had tried to involve Irish and Welsh citizens in a common attack on the English. The invasion of Ireland in 1315 was an indicator of how serious the threat was, even if the crisis which followed was ultimately contained. Some Anglo-Irish supported the Scots, others adopted an ambiguous position, and the leaders of the great lineages were forced to swear a special oath of fealty to Edward II and to hand over hostages as a guarantee of loyalty. When King Robert of Scotland suddenly appeared in Ulster again in 1327 the two governments in London and Dublin were thrown into something of a panic. Robert Outlaw, the Irish chancellor, was sent to the north for discussions with the men of Ulster, whose loyalty was suspect. Outlaw was ordered that he was to 'look into their hearts' and determine their intentions about resisting the Scots. There was a rumour in circulation that Bruce intended invading England via Ireland, linking with the Welsh on the way, and this was taken so seriously that the government began to defend the outskirts of Dublin against his advance. The potential of Ireland as a backdoor to England was already a fact of Anglo-Irish relations. In the event the threat was neutralized and the crisis passed.

But Scotland continued to exercise an influence in the north of Ireland. A common language and a rich literature inherited from the past, incorporating a common history, with a professional caste preserving and enlarging it in common, linked the two Gaelic communities of Ireland and Scotland together. The presence of large numbers of Scottish mercenaries, the famous galloglas, in the households of most heads of important northern lineages strengthened the link. The west of Scotland and the Gaelic north of Ireland formed a distinct cultural region and for centuries traffic across the narrow sea bound them together.

There was another community in Ulster, however, part of the de Burgh earldom, whose links were with England, via Dublin and the rest of Anglo-Ireland. However qualified the loyalty of its magnates, by tradition and culture it formed part of the wider world which embraced the dominion of the King of England. It was no more remote from Dublin than other Anglo-Irish communities in the west and south. Like them it was subject, however fitfully, to a royal administration which worked through institutions imported from England and which embraced all the king's subjects. Certain forms were observed governing inheritance, taxation, the making of war and the preservation of the king's peace. To that extent there was uniformity, just as there was among the Irish communities. Indeed those communities were also in theory part of the king's lordship and their lords, too, had been the king's lieges from the beginning of the conquest.

But there was one fatal flaw in the relationship between the crown and the Irish. The king's law, the common law of England, was never fully extended to them as it had been to all his other subjects, including the Ostmen of pre-conquest Ireland. Up to about the middle of the thirteenth century the Irish seem to have enjoyed the benefits of English law, but thereafter, for the rest of the middle ages, they were left outside the law. Except in some individual cases, where charters of denizenship had been purchased, the Irish were treated as aliens and were left outside the law, under their own brehon law.

After the failure of an attempt in the 1270s to purchase the benefits of the common law for all free Irishmen, two systems of law (as well as the banned, unofficial system of march law) continued to exist side-by-side in the lordship.

Two jurisdictions naturally created impossible problems for governments, not least because criminals could too easily escape from the common law area into areas where that law did not reach. In the wider context of Anglo-Irish relations, however, the results were even worse since the king could never deal with the Irish solely within the feudal framework as defined by the law of England. One can see something of the problem in the gradual emergence of the concept of the Irish as 'enemies', while the term 'rebel', which in the thirteenth century had been more frequently applied to disturbers of the peace without racial distinction, came to be confined to those who were English by blood. In the fourteenth century, the regular distinction between 'Irish enemies' and 'English rebels' neatly made the point: the former were regarded as aliens, outside the law, while the latter were denizens, governed by the same law which bound the king's subjects everywhere.

The absurdity of the division of Ireland into two jurisdictions was emphasized by John Darcy in 1328 when he was being reappointed to the office of chief governor. He made it a condition of his appointment that all Irishmen should be given the same status at law as Englishmen. Three years later, in 1331, a famous ordinance proclaimed that there should be *una et eadem lex* (one and the same law) for all, so that henceforth all free Irishmen should have English law; but it was too late. The Irish lordships continued to function under brehon law and even in Anglo-Irish communities where there was a substantial Irish population, brehons were retained to administer their own law. The situation was made even more complicated by the growth of march law in many areas where heads of lineages imposed arbitrary burdens on the people, such as the system of coign and livery which enabled them to maintain their armed retinues. Richard fitz Ralph, the great Archbishop of Armagh, denounced it as the law of the devil, but to no avail. It continued to spread, even in areas close to Dublin itself. In the middle of the fourteenth century, the cities of Ireland sent a petition to Edward III complaining bitterly of the erosion of English law and of the existence of 'diversity of law' (they listed common law, Irish law, march law) which made good government impossible. Justices, even when they bothered to visit the shires to administer justice, no longer exacted the penalties demanded by the common law for misdemeanours. The petitioners looked back nostalgically to happier days when, they thought, the common law of Ireland was enforced throughout the lordship.

But the fact was that, by the early fourteenth century, Ireland was no longer amenable to the same kind of uniformity which had seemed possible in the earlier stages of colonization. The island had never been wholly conquered and gradually the areas under English dominion had been reduced. Outside the ports and a few other towns, the island was now dominated by the great lineages, Irish and Anglo-Irish, and it was with their heads ('chieftains' or 'captains') that the real substance of power lay. As early as 1278 an Irish parliament invoked the brehon law principle of kin responsibility and made the heads of Irish lineages who were in the king's peace responsible for criminals within their lordship. But within a few years heads of Anglo-Irish families were also authorized to bring their criminals to justice. In 1310 and again in 1324 parliament made the Anglo-Irish 'chieftains of great lineage' responsible for the misdemeanours of members of their clans. This was explicit recognition of the importance of those lineages in the structure of society and of the government's dependence on them. Increasingly they were empowered to arbitrate local problems, parley with local enemies, benefit from local taxation, and generally to govern their own areas, provided that they accepted the overriding authority of the Dublin government and, behind that, the supreme authority of the king as their lord.

Ireland, then, was a land of regions, dominated by lineages who controlled the real sources of power – land and armed retainers. Each region had its own dynamics, largely determined by the struggles for dominance among the most important families. The creation of new earldoms in the wake of the Bruce invasion of 1315 and as part of an attempt to stabilize unruly Ireland gave an added importance to some of the Anglo-Irish magnates. John fitz Thomas was belted Earl of Kildare in 1316; John de Bermingham Earl of Louth in 1319; James Butler Earl of Ormond in 1328; and Maurice fitz Thomas Earl of Desmond in 1329. But these were, to some extent, counterbalanced by the decline in the vast earldom of Ulster and lordship of Connacht after the Scottish invasion, not helped by the near senility of the 'red' earl and the youthful inexperience of his heir of sixteen who was murdered in 1333. The earldom passed by marriage to Lionel, son of Edward III, and remained in absentee hands to the end of the middle ages. It never recovered. Elsewhere, partitions gravely weakened some of the older lordships, so that Wexford, Kilkenny, Carlow, Meath and the more recently created de Clare lordship west of the Shannon were all to show evidence of neglect and decline as the fourteenth century wore on.

One result of all this was that there was a scramble for power and security among the Anglo-Irish magnates. The fact that the English government of Edward III was reluctant to confirm their new status and to tolerate the consolidation of their authority locally, made them nervous and aggressive in their pursuit of security. This was a violent age, made worse by dissensions between the great families. Sometimes their faction fights amounted to civil war. In 1327, the Kilkenny chronicler, John Clyn, reported that 'the most savage war began between the Geraldines, Berminghams and their followers on one side against the Powers and those of de Burgh on the other'. Lesser lineages joined in, like the Walls, St Aubyns, Keatings, and soon the whole of south Leinster was ablaze. The first Earl of Desmond engaged in open war against the king's government in Ireland, terrorized communities all over the south, and even, it was alleged, plotted to make himself King of Ireland, with provincial kingships going to allies as a reward for support. There were frequent disturbances as factions grouped around one family or another, sometimes reflecting political quarrels which had flared up in England. All the time within their own lordships, where they often enjoyed palatine authority, the great lords were stabilizing their power.

At the same time, the Irish lords were taking advantage of weaknesses in marginal land and new march areas. They, too, were creating new hegemonies which in some respects were a throwback to the dynastic struggles of the twelfth century. The Anglo-Irish presence added a new dimension, however, and the growing involvement of some settlers in the politics of Gaelic Ireland made the situation more complex. The appearance of 'English rebels', hardly to be distinguished except in name from 'Irish enemies', reflects not only the continuing gaelicization of the settlers (the 'degenerates' of parliamentary terminology) but also the interlocking ambitions of many families in the struggles for power. Professional poets composed suitable verses to mark important events in the careers of their patrons or to encourage support by using models from Ireland's heroic past, or resurrecting, even fabricating, historic claims to grandiose titles, of which the supreme one was the kingship of Tara. If an Anglo-Irish patron paid the appropriate fee, he too could be the beneficiary of such a piece of propaganda. One cynical versifier even reminded an Anglo-Irish patron not to be too worried if in another poem he promised that the Gael would banish the gaill from Ireland: 'it is our fashion' he disarmingly said, and people got what they paid for.

Some of the more important Irish lords used prophecy and legend in much the same way as Arthurian lore or legends about Charlemagne were used elsewhere. In 1387, O Neill posed as a new Cú Chulainn and, in a specially-built house at the site of Emhain Macha (the prehistoric Navan Fort near Armagh which had particular associations with the heroic kings of the past), celebrated the great deeds of the Red Branch 'knights', who had supposedly once guarded the north from all danger. We might almost see something of the same tradition of propaganda in the evidence of the Limerick jury that the rebellious first Earl of Desmond had wished in 1327 to restore the ancient provincial kingdoms of pre-Norman times as part of a new kingdom of Ireland with himself as high king. Preposterous the suggestion may have been in the real world of 1332, when the jury presented its evidence, but it is a good indication of the climate of political opinion amongst a community fairly remote from Dublin.

But there was more to it than appears on the surface. In 1330 Edward III had assumed personal control in England, arrested and then executed Roger Mortimer, who had been exercising royal patronage in Ireland in order to win support there. The new king naturally wished to undo what Mortimer had achieved by dispensing favours and in 1331 sent a new justiciar, Anthony Lucy, to restore royal authority in Ireland. The attack on Desmond was part of that process. So was the arrest of lesser magnates like Henry de Mandeville, Walter de Burgh, and Walter and William de Bermingham. The latter was executed in July 1332, an event which shocked Anglo-Ireland. But it showed clearly that the new king and his new Dublin Government were not going to tolerate what we might call casual treason in Ireland. Edward even planned a royal expedition to his lordship, reminiscent of King John's decisive intervention in 1210. In the event he did not have to come. He went to Scotland instead and so secure was his new influence with the leading Anglo-Irish that in 1335 they joined him on campaign there.

Yet those same magnates were already assuming a position which made them resentful of undue interference from England in their affairs. Ham-fisted attempts at reform by officials from England seemed to threaten local interests. The arrival of 200 Welsh archers with a new justiciar in 1337 was sufficiently novel to be commented on by the Kilkenny chronicler Clyn and signified a new show of force by the king. More sinister was the insistence that only English-born officials should be justices in Ireland, which showed mistrust of Irish-born ministers of the crown. Worst of all was what hap-pened after Edward III purged his administration in England in 1340–1. A similar purge was extended to Ireland and a series of drastic measures threat-ening the foundations of many a noble family reached a dramatic climax with the resumption by the king in July 1341 of all grants of lands and liber-ties in Ireland made since the accession of Edward II on 8 July 1307. This horrific act threatened nearly everyone who mattered in Ireland. There was an immediate explosion in the Dublin parliament in October. When it moved to Kilkenny the king's ministers were too frightened to attend and the Anglo-Irish who were present resolved to send messengers to the king seeking redress. They pointed out to him that:

'whereas divers people of your allegiance, as of Scotland, Gascony and Wales, often in times past have levied war against their liege lord, all the time, sire, your English liege people of Ireland have conducted them-selves well and loyally towards their liege lord, and always will do so, if God please'.

They also attacked the incompetence of his ministers in Dublin, denouncing them to the king.

In the process of debate which produced this Anglo-Irish reaction they found a new political voice. The Dublin chronicler recorded 'notable and manifest division between the English of England and the English of the land of Ireland' because of the crisis. But he reflected a much more serious devel-opment in the Anglo-Irish position when he added that 'a great dispute arose in the land and the land of Ireland was on the point of separation from the hands of the King of England'. This called in question the constitutional link which bound the lordship to the English crown. It can hardly represent the considered view of the Anglo-Irish, but it certainly indicates that some at least were frustrated enough to adopt so radical a stance.

What it really represents, however, is an outraged reaction to the policy of revoking old grants. It also manifests an Anglo-Irish hostility towards interference by English-born officials who were held responsible for policies which threatened local interests. The crisis brought into the open anti-English feelings which had been dormant for years. The Anglo-Irish had long since identified with Ireland as their *patria* (homeland). On a celebrated occasion in the Dublin parliament of 1324 the seneschal of Kilkenny, Arnold Power, tried to rouse anti-English feelings against the English Bishop of Ossory, whom he called 'some tramp from England'. He reminded those present that Ireland 'has always been called the 'Island of the Saints'. Now this foreigner comes from England and says we're all heretics and excommunicates . . . Defamation of this country affects every one of us, so we must all unite against this man'.

Such feelings were to be generated again whenever local resentment at rule by Englishmen was aroused. In 1364 the king referred to 'divers dissensions and debates between the English born in England and the English born in Ireland' which in the past had caused 'hurt and peril' in Ireland. He feared that this animosity would do even more damage unless a speedy remedy was found. Two years later the famous statutes of Kilkenny showed that the problem was far from solved. Parliament enacted that in future there was to be no distinction between the English born in Ireland and English born in England, that the former were not to be called 'Irish dog' or the latter 'English clown', but that all were to be known by the same name, 'the English lieges of our lord the king'. Feelings were running high when 'English' and 'Irish' were used as terms of abuse.

Nor were such feelings easily assuaged. Later in the fourteenth century when another English chief governor, William of Windsor, was openly confronted by Anglo-Irish opposition which came to centre on their refusal to agree to new taxes, the king made what was an unprecedented demand. On 6 October 1375, at a parliament in Kilkenny which again refused to grant a subsidy, the king's special ambassador, Nicholas Dagworth, announced that clergy and commons would now have to elect representatives to attend a special assembly in England where the king would preside in person. This caused a sensation and when elections were subsequently held, opposition was rampant. The magnates and commons of Louth, for example, declared *una voce* (with one voice) that 'according to the rights, privileges, liberties, laws and customs of the land of Ireland, from the time of the conquest and before' they were not bound to attend parliaments in England. They would do so only 'out of respect for the king', though they refused to give their elected representatives power to agree to taxation.

The Anglo-Irish were giving voice to their distinctness, as other colonial communities were to do in the future. Their emphasis on the liberties, laws and customs of Ireland emphasized their constitutional position. In 1381 the Irish prelates and clergy went even further when they protested to the king that they should not be bound by any statute of an English parliament in which they were not represented. Finally, in 1460, this constitutional position was given its extreme expression when an Irish parliament declared Ireland to be 'corporate of itself' and bound only by the legislation of its own parliament.

But if the Anglo-Irish protested their independence of an English parliament, they still respected their relationship with their lord the king. Even in 1376, while saving their 'privileges and liberties', they said that out of respect for the king they would comply with his request. Earlier in 1341 when complaining bitterly to Edward III against 'those who are sent out of England to govern them, who have little knowledge of your said land of Ireland', they boasted of their constant loyalty to the king. They saw no contradiction between maintaining their own identity as a separate community, even to the extent of insisting upon being bound solely by their own parliament, and at the same time affirming their allegiance to the crown. It was, of course, very much in their own interest to do so. In 1360 a great council at Kilkenny elected the chancellor and three others to inform the king of the perils facing the land of Ireland and his lieges there 'who are on the point of being lost' unless he provide 'succour and remedy'. The message ended with a plea for help to be provided 'as a noble and gracious lord is bound to do for his subjects'. This was a cry which was to be repeated by the Anglo-Irish in years to come.

They had reason to worry in 1360. Their message to the king presented a sorry picture of the state of Ireland, oppressed by the burden of defence against the Irish at war who were threatening, the king was told, to conquer the land. They complained in particular of depopulated lands and for this they blamed most of all the pestilence which 'was so great and so hideous among the English lieges and not among the Irish'. This was the Black Death, the great plague which swept across Europe with terrifying effects before it reached Ireland in the summer of 1348. It spread rapidly from the ports on the east coast and devastated the English settlements. People believed that no one could survive. In Kilkenny, Friar Clyn reported the terror and the very high mortality. Before he succumbed himself, he wrote that he was leaving some parchment so that his work of recording might be continued 'if perchance any of the race of Adam may be able to escape this pestilence'.

But the Black Death was only one manifestation of a plague that was pandemic, striking with devastating effect every few years. In 1361 as many as 20 per cent of the population were struck down. In the hundred years between 1349 and 1450 it has been estimated that the population of Europe fell between 60 per cent and 75 per cent and most of this in rural areas. The effects of recurring plague were cumulative. But it was all the worse since the pandemic followed a series of disastrous famines, including the worst one of all in 1315–17, which in Ireland coincided with the horrors of the Bruce invasion. In Dublin, in the late thirteenth century, it was reported that starving people cannibalized the bodies of criminals hanging from gibbets. The price of basic foods rocketed in the first half of the fourteenth century and bad weather and poor harvests led to famine and death in a seemingly inevitable cycle. By the time the Black Death struck Ireland in the mid-fourteenth century Irish society was in a state of shock.

One effect was the production of deserted villages and depopulated lands. Starvation led many to abandon the countryside and seek help in the towns. High wages made labour more mobile and already devastated lands were further weakened by labour moving to better conditions. Many began to leave Ireland and the emerging cloth industries of England attracted immigrants. A pattern of migrant labour that was to be a feature of later centuries was firmly established in the fourteenth century. But perhaps most of all it was the endemic war and associated crime which dislocated population. Refugees fled from the land of war to the land of peace and no amount of parliamentary legislation could force them back. Gaps appeared in the *frontura* (frontier) between colonized lands and those beyond. To contemporaries it appeared that such undefended gaps left the way open to Irish enemies, who were quick to take advantage. Whenever an Irish parliament catalogued the woes of Ireland and the straitened circumstances of the land of peace, the absence of tenants in areas which had once been part of the settlement and the presence of undefended lands came high on the list of complaints, especially lands in the hands of absentees. So it was in 1360. The remedy sought was for the king to send 'a good and sufficient chieftain', well supplied with fighting men and treasure.

The king's response to this request for help was spectacular and marked a decisive shift in Anglo-Irish relations. In 1361 he sent his second son Lionel, Earl of Ulster and later Duke of Clarence, with some 200 men at arms (or heavy cavalry) and 700 mounted archers. Small as this force may seem in comparison with the English armies which fought in France, it was unprecedented in Anglo-Irish relations since 1210 and was to place a heavy burden on English taxpayers, of which they soon complained in parliament. It marked the beginning of a period of heavy subsidization of Ireland and an all-out attempt to push back the frontiers of the land of war and expand the land of peace through the recovery of territories lost to the Irish.

Lionel was not only commander-in-chief of the expeditionary force, but also lieutenant of the king with wide powers as befitted a royal head of Government. As chief governor he tried to reform the Irish administration as well as conquer land with his English soldiers. In both he had some modest success. He captured Mac Murrough of Leinster, for example, recovered land in Munster and expanded the area in which revenue could be collected by the exchequer. Administrative reform, despite tension between Anglo-Irish and English officials, improved the state of Irish finances, though anything gained was swiftly swallowed up by the demands of the army. There can be no doubt, however, that Lionel's most lasting achievement was the body of legislation produced by the parliament which he summoned to Kilkenny in 1366. These statutes of Kilkenny were confirmed in future parliaments and came to have a status in Ireland not far short of *Magna Carta* itself. They were not innovatory, being largely a codification of existing legislation dealing with problems of long standing in the lordship: 'the good government of the land and the quiet of the people' was how the preamble expressed their purpose. In particular they focused on what had been called degeneracy by an earlier generation and established rules to preserve the English culture of the colony in language, dress, custom and anything else which might be regarded as distinct from Irish. They were at once an admission that the Gaelicization of the settlers had reached crisis proportions in the eyes of officialdom and a confident assertion of the essential English and therefore superior character of the colony in Ireland. They should be seen, therefore, not as an attempt to cut losses and preserve a small part of the island for English culture, but as a triumphant assertion of English ascendancy based on the success of unprecedented military intervention. There was to be no pulling back and the new policy of military intervention, paid for by England, was to be maintained.

Edward III was later to say that his hope was that Ireland might become profitable to the crown, as it had been in the past. This was his justification to the English parliament for spending such large sums of money on the pacification of the lordship. Stability would increase revenues and produce a surplus which would be available when war with France inevitably broke out again. Budgets prepared in England to plan expenditure show how high a priority was temporarily being given to 'the war in Ireland'. When Lionel was recalled from Ireland in 1366, because the king wished him to marry the wealthy niece of the Visconti ruler of Milan, there was an interval before another military chief governor contracted to serve in Ireland. During that interval, with the English army withdrawn, there was a sharp deterioration in the condition of the colony. Nevertheless, when William of Windsor was appointed chief governor and military commander in March 1369 he was again supplied with a substantial, if reduced, army at a cost of £20,000 before the end of June. If his subsequent attempts to raise supplementary revenues in Ireland by means of parliamentary subsidies made him run foul of the colonists, so that he was withdrawn in 1372, he was reappointed in 1373. Once more he was given substantial forces and was heavily subsidized.

In a short period, 1361–76, over £91,000 was spent on wages alone for the armies sent from England to Ireland and more than £71,000 of this came from the already over-burdened taxpayers of England; no wonder the commons protested in the Westminster parliament. To get these figures into perspective, we should remember that the recorded receipts at the Dublin exchequer averaged £2,000 per annum. So that by Irish standards this expenditure by England was of massive proportions. The surprising thing is that, despite the strain imposed on English resources by the long war with France and Scotland, the subsidy was sustained for so long. Successive English governments lived in hope that the heavy expenditure would be justified in the end by large profits coming out of Ireland. So, when Richard II's favourite, Robert de Vere, was made marquis of Dublin in 1385, granted Ireland for life, and given lavish grants to maintain a huge force of 500 men at arms and 1,000 archers for two years, he was expected to conquer Ireland and provide the king with 5,000 marks a year out of his conquests.

But the reality was very different. The massive military interventions failed in their main purpose of achieving stability. If anything, the state of the colony deteriorated further. Irish needs simply swallowed money and there was never enough. Money began to run out and soldiers deserted for want of pay. When Mortimer was appointed chief governor in 1379 his contract awarded him a stipend of 20,000 marks. But when he suddenly died in 1381, his pay was already 10,000 marks in arrears. He even had to lend the king £1,000 to help pay the cost of his own expedition. Significantly, after his sudden death, both Desmond and Ormond flatly refused to head a new government, however temporarily, because of the grave personal financial risks involved. Still the English Government optimistically continued its policy of heavy subsidies. In 1392 Gloucester was granted 34,000 marks and as late as 1398 Surrey contracted for 11,500 marks a year.

The second half of the fourteenth century, then, had seen a dramatic turnabout in Anglo-Irish relations. As lord of Ireland the King of England was manifestly accepting his obligations to protect his lieges there against the enemies who threatened their lives and properties. Yet for all the money which had been poured into Ireland the condition of the colony continued to deteriorate. Such was the pressure from Gaelic Ireland that only by paying the equivalent of 'protection money' could many communities survive. Castledermot, for example, had to pay 84 marks to Mac Murrough in 1392 and while the townsmen desperately sought to raise the money they suffered the added indignity of having to hand over one of themselves as surety for payment. In 1385 the Irish parliament sent an urgent message to Richard II begging him to come 'in his own person to survey and visit his said seignory' and to save it from the threat of conquest which was believed to be imminent. Failing that, he was to send 'the greatest and most trustworthy lord of England'. But it was not until 1394, when peace with France provided the opportunity, that the king decided to come to Ireland.

Richard II's expedition must be seen as the climax to the policy of military intervention practised since 1361. But it was much more, for the king was determined to re-establish by force his lordship over the whole of Ireland and to restore a unity which all the inhabitants, Irish as well as Anglo-Irish, would share as the king's liege subjects. The fact that he came himself, the first king to do so since John in 1210, is an indication of how determined he was. So, too, were the preparations for his expedition and the enormous amount of money spent on wages, equipment, transportation and food for what was to be the largest army ever to come to Ireland in the middle ages. It numbered more than 5,000 troops, led by the most important magnates of England and backed by the full resources of the royal administration.

In Leinster Richard soon showed his military strength and skill in crushing Mac Murrough and the leading chieftains and forcing them into submission. Harassing raids, in which villages were burned, cattle preyed and people killed, were so effective that it took only 10 days to achieve complete victory. In January and February 1395 Mac Murrough, O Byrne,

O More, O Toole, O Nolan and leading Leinster Irish formally swore oaths of liege homage, recorded for posterity by a notary and, in addition, promised to hand back to the king all land usurped by them in Leinster. They were to accept the king's wages, help to conquer other lands held by rebels, and were given the option of holding such lands as tenants-in-chief of the king. Mac Murough was confirmed in his possession, through his Anglo-Irish wife, of the important manor of Norragh, O Byrne of lands near Wicklow, and O Toole was licensed to carry on a lucrative trade with the important Anglo-Irish towns of Leinster.

There was action in Munster as well, where some of the Mac Carthy lineage and others were forced to surrender. But on the whole the spectacular success in Leinster was sufficient to demonstrate the power of the king and his determination to reimpose his lordship. As a result, Gaelic Ireland, through the heads of the leading lineages, submitted to Richard in a long series of negotiations, followed by formal ceremonies in which oaths of liege homage were sworn, all formally recorded for posterity by a notary. Some of the more important, such as O Neill, O Brien and O Connor, were knighted by the king and ceremonial robes were distributed to signify the new and intimate relationship which had been established. Many of them admitted past rebellion, excusing themselves because of wrongs suffered at the hands of Anglo-Irish lords. Niall Mór O Neill wrote to Richard begging him to act as 'shield and helmet of justice between my lord the Earl of Ulster and me'; O Connor Faly wrote that if he had offended in the past it was because 'I found none to do justice between the English and me'. All were willing to accept a new relationship with the King of England, legally defined and based on oaths of homage, which would re-establish the sovereignty of the king as lord of Ireland, embracing Irish and Anglo-Irish alike as liege subjects of the crown; for this the king would do justice to all. He wrote to the English council on 1 February 1395 and said that 'these Irish rebels are rebels only because of grievances and wrongs done to them on one side and lack of remedy on the other'. Such an admission was unprecedented and shows Richard's totally new and radical approach to the problem of Ireland. He had already, in the same letter, distinguished between three classes of people in Ireland: 'wild Irish our enemies, Irish rebels, and obedient English'. This separated out the 'wild Irish' like O Donnell, who had not submitted, from the great majority of the Irish who were 'rebels' and thus within the law.

When Richard sailed home to England, an Irish annalist recorded that he went 'with power and honour from all Irishmen, as he deserved', unstinting praise from the voice of Gaelic Ireland. Six months later, in November 1395, the king wrote to O Neill urging him to visit Westminster as soon as possible and thanking him for remaining loyal. Richard's personal intervention had been spectacularly successful. Despite the problems which beset him in England, he maintained his interest in Ireland, which was given a priority unprecedented in Anglo-Irish relations. Fees were paid for a time to some leading Irish captains. Donough O Brien visited England in February 1396 and was granted 80 marks per annum. He returned there in August, this time with Thomas Kavanagh representing Mac Murrough and 10 others who represented lesser lineages. The Leinster settlement seemed to be holding well. So, too, were other new relationships which had been established with Irish lords. O Carroll of Ely, for example, also visited England, was warmly received by the king and accompanied him to Calais in December 1396.

But appearances were deceptive. A crucial element in the new royal settlement was the Anglo-Irish nobility and, to a lesser extent, those absentee lords who had been persuaded by King Richard to give personal attention to their Irish estates. Men like Desmond and Ormond were essential to the new arrangements and they naturally took the opportunity to bolster their own position, if necessary at the expense of the Irish chieftains who had submitted to the king. In Ulster Mortimer lost patience with the slow and delicate methods of royal diplomacy which tried to secure the handing over of supposedly usurped lands. He raided into Longford and Cavan, defeating the O Farrells and O Reillys. He made an unprovoked attack on O Neill, accompanied by Ormond, Kildare and other Anglo-Irish.

Slowly, then, Gaelic Ireland reverted to a state of rebellion and Richard's grand design began to founder on Anglo-Irish ambitions and opportunism. Even administrative reforms, which the king had initiated as part of his new policy for Ireland, failed to be realized in the face of entrenched Anglo-Irish opposition. As the king's domestic problems worsened, he was unable to find time or resources to face up to the growing problem of Ireland. A projected expedition late in 1397 had to be cancelled. Leinster in particular was in a state of war and, when Mortimer was killed in a skirmish near Callan in July 1398, it marked the end of Richard's settlement. Rebellion spread as antagonisms involved more people on both sides. But not until the death of John of Gaunt in 1399 did the king feel reasonably safe in leaving England. He landed at Waterford for the second time on 1 June.

Again he brought a large army and was well equipped, even shipping canons and gunpowder to Ireland. But, in contrast to the first expedition, this time his army met with disaster in Leinster. It was harried all the way to Dublin, starved for lack of adequate supplies, and utterly failed to force the Leinster Irish into meaningful negotiations. Meanwhile, England was invaded by the future Henry IV and Richard hurriedly had to abandon Ireland to its own devices, while he sought to protect his crown in England. His failure and death finally smashed all hope of a continuation of his radical policy for Ireland. There the Anglo-Irish and Irish lords were left to look after their own interests, with the government concentrating on the limited objective of supervising the needs of the communities near to Dublin and maintaining some semblance of royal authority in the lordship beyond.

The new Lancastrian dynasty which seized the English crown was both chronically short of funds and fearful of enemies who threatened the security of the realm and the shaky hold of the new ruler on the throne. Because of the latter fear, Henry IV could not afford to take any chances with Ireland. He sent his 13-year-old son, Thomas, to govern the lordship, placate Anglo-Irish opinion, and ensure that no threat would come to England from that side of the Irish sea. But shortage of money meant that inadequate funding was provided to maintain the new government in Dublin. Thomas was left so short of cash, despite the large sums promised in his contract, that he had to pawn his jewels and plate to raise the money. By 1407 his arrears had climbed to over £20,000 and years later he was still trying to procure payment for these old debts. Other chief governors similarly suffered, the pauper Lancastrian government could no longer afford to allocate to Ireland anything like the subsidies invested by both Edward III and Richard II and the radical departure of 1361 had to be reversed.

In Ireland, therefore, the Dublin government had to trim its sails. An abnormally low income, rarely much above £1,000 per annum, meant that military operations had to be confined in the main to defence, with occasional forays into Irish territories not too far away. What were known as the 'four loyal shires' of Dublin, Meath, Louth and Kildare became the focus of attention. Yet even this area became too large for the limited resources of the government and by the middle of the fifteenth century a much smaller district, known as the Pale (probably in imitation of the better known Pale of Calais) emerged as the part of Ireland which was the most immediate concern of the Dublin government. A new, fortified frontier was created, running from Dundalk inland to Kells via Ardee, then south to Naas and Ballymore Eustace before turning east to the sea at Dalkey, skirting the Dublin and Wicklow mountains on the way. Castles and fortalices were constructed along the frontier, some other parts were entrenched, important bridges were guarded, and watchmen were paid to light warning beacons in case of attack. While the main concern of the inhabitants seems to have been to prevent raiders from driving cattle out of this area, which was the purpose of the trenches they dug in places, there was also the need to offer some protection against raiders who spilt blood. The chief governors in particular were faced with this responsibility. Success or failure in office might be measured by the extent to which they managed to protect the Pale and safeguard the inhabitants within.

Beyond the Pale, Ireland was, for the most part, left to the lineages which controlled the regions, provided that the nominal authority of the king's government was respected. But increasingly in the fifteenth century both the English and the Irish governments displayed an anxiety to prevent the Englishness of the lordship from being diluted. Repeated attempts were made to force emigrants to England back to Ireland, especially artisans and skilled labourers. At the same time, Irish legislation was trying to prevent the exodus from Ireland, even to the extent of the government appointing officials to inspect ships and confiscate those discovered to be carrying unlicensed emigrants. But the attraction of good jobs and wages in England proved to be irresistible and no government was ever able to prevent this movement of labour. One result was a scarcity of skilled labour in parts of Ireland, which hit nascent industrial growth.

More serious was the scarcity of tenants, a phenomenon which had become apparent as long ago as the early fourteenth century. But with a population decimated by plague, famine and the misfortunes of war, further decreased by refugees from the land of war and migration to the comparative security and fortune to be had in England, more land fell vacant. In the area which became the Pale it soon became obvious that the only source of tenants for many gentry was what a statute of 1476 called 'divers persons of the Irish nation' who came to 'occupy the land as husbandmen'. An earlier statute had complained of 'a great multitude of Irish people, mostly strong young men and women' who were brought into 'English country', so that the country was 'overwhelmed with them'. Because they brought threshed corn in the autumn to Irish enemies, thus strengthening them, parliament feared what it called 'a covert conquest'.

This was an exaggeration, as were the many reports of the growing number of Irish 'spies' now residing among the loyal English. But parliamentary legislation continued to reflect such fears and to demonstrate an obsession with the preservation of all forms of English identity, even in the most artificial way. Native Irishmen living among the Anglo-Irish were compelled to adopt as surnames the name of an English town or trade and thus disguised would somehow become 'English' and thus 'loyal', instead of an 'enemy', and acceptable. Generations earlier, many Irish living on manors had hidden their identity under false English names so as to enjoy the benefits of the common law, which was restricted to 'English by blood'. But their descendants in fifteenth-century Ireland had nothing to lose, since they had access to that law and the king's courts and were no longer subject to the same kind of discrimination.

Fear of 'Irish enemies' was rampant in official circles and manifested itself in England even at popular level. It was a time when contempt for foreigners was rife in England and resentment at Irishmen taking well-paid jobs, securing public office (Bristol for a time had an Irish mayor), or occupying places at the universities or inns of court in London, was to be expected. Speaking an outlandish language (Irish or an archaic English dialect which seemed little different to many ears), wearing a strange fashion in clothes, different even in hairstyle, Irish visitors – Gaelic or Anglo-Irish – all seemed foreign and therefore vaguely threatening.

Even as far back as the thirteenth century, strong anti-Irish feelings had manifested themselves at Oxford, resulting in riots, mayhem and even death. Classed as *Hibernienses* (Irishmen), the university authorities drew no distinction between Gaelic and Anglo-Irish students. In a world where Latin was the formal medium of communication and where the feast of the national apostle, St Patrick, was wildly celebrated by both 'nations', such a blurring of distinction was understandable. By the fifteenth century, with the growth of national xenophobia in England, it was natural for the English to manifest strong anti-Irish feelings. The accusation of being a 'wild Irishman' was enough to land the person so charged in prison. Irish or Anglo-Irish (it made no difference) were banned from the universities and, what was more serious, from the inns of court which provided the only professional training in law.

In 1440 a new low was reached when the Anglo-Irish were formally classified as aliens, which brought forth a bitter protest from the Irish council in 1441 that Englishmen born in Ireland should have the same rights in England as Englishmen born in England. The Anglo-Irish naturally resented being classed as foreigners and it was one of the factors which helped to stiffen their own sense of Irish identity, which for long had been growing in the frontier conditions which prevailed in Ireland. It was soon to find expression in an extreme form with the radical declaration of corporate identity in the parliament of 1460.

At the top level, the Anglo-Irish magnates formed a ruling caste which was careful to emphasize allegiance to the crown on the one hand and a formal antipathy towards Gaelic Ireland on the other. From 1297 onwards, parliamentary statutes had outlawed Gaelic customs, dress, language, and much else among the Anglo-Irish. The official view was that the Irish were in the strictest sense uncivilized, wild or savage, even bestial (meaning that emotion rather than reason governed their actions). Above all they were enemies, indeed 'our natural enemies', as they were called in an official record of 1537. Therefore they must be extirpated, hunted 'as the hunter doth the hare', according to a poem eulogizing Peter de Bermingham after his death in the early fourteenth century. He received high praise as such a hunter, most notably for his murder of 30 leading members of the O Connor lineage while they were his guests at a Trinity Sunday feast in his castle of Carbury in 1305. More than a century later the greatest Anglo-Irishman of his day, the fourth (or 'White') Earl of Ormond, was urged to treat Irish enemies in much the same way when they fell into his hands: 'Erase them all out of the root, as the gardener does the nettle'. The advice came from a Dublin notary, James Yonge, in *The governance of princes* which he wrote for the earl in 1420. In it he also reminded his patron 'that a prince should not trust to his enemy' and that the only time that Irish enemies were 'true to you or your father' was when 'you were stronger than they'.

Such a philosophy was intended to guide a great nobleman like Ormond in shaping his attitude towards the Irish. Yet in his own great Butler lordship a strange mixture of English and Irish customs, reflecting a tenantry of different ethnic origins, helped him to rule. A series of ordinances enacted by assemblies representing communities in Kilkenny and Tipperary reveal a society in which Irish no less than Anglo-Irish elements are prominent. In particular the system based on coign and livery, the amalgam of customs by means of which troops were maintained for the defence of the lordship, was highlighted. As in other parts of Ireland, the Butler lordship survived because Irish custom was exploited to augment the lord's traditional feudal, or English, rights. The communities, through representatives, gave their consent to the imposition of coign – that was the parliamentary, or English tradition; but what they agreed to was Irish. The Butler lordship perfectly illustrates this fusion of two traditions which all over Anglo-Ireland was enabling lordships to enjoy a new stability, and thus prosperity, in the fifteenth century. Ormond even retained his own brehons to administer Irish law to those of his Irish tenants who used it.

It is clear, too, that some degree of cultural assimilation had already taken place, the result of intermarriage as much as anything else. Even before the fourth earl's death in 1452, the head of the Polestown Butlers, Edmund mac Richard Butler, often served as his deputy in Ormond during the earl's frequent absences in England. Edmund perfectly illustrates the process of acculturation which for long had been prominent in even the greatest of lineages. He had been fostered (an Irish practice which had been specifically outlawed by parliament from 1366 onward) by a famous Archbishop of Cashel, Richard O Hedigan, who reared him as if in an Irish household. He spoke Irish, loved the literature and history of Ireland's past, and commissioned the writing of a famous compilation of Irish literary and historical matter, driving on the scribes in his anxiety to have the finished work. When he was held prisoner by the Earl of Desmond, after the battle of Pilltown in 1462, this same treasure was demanded by the earl as part of his ransom to secure release. Desmond in turn placed a very high value on this book and had some passages which had faded through use lovingly restored. When Desmond himself died in 1468 he was praised by an Irish man of letters, almost as if he were an Irish lord: 'bountiful in bestowing good gifts on both laity and clergy, and on all the learned, both antiquaries, poets, and aesdanas ('men of art', the learned men) of all Ireland'.

Yet people like Butler or Desmond never sought to lose their Englishness or to deny their true allegiance to the crown. Butler fought the battle of Pilltown in support of his Lancastrian king, Henry VI, against the Yorkists of Ireland who had helped to put Edward IV on the throne. In the terminology employed by Irish writers they were always *gaill* (the traditional word for foreigner) and only on very rare occasions were they referred to as *errenaig* (Irishmen). At the same time they were not seen as English, for whom the word *Saxin* (Saxon) was reserved. Indeed from the perspective of Gaelic Ireland they truly appear as a 'middle nation', a term which the Irish remonstrance of 1317 says they coined for themselves: they were distinct from both the Gaels of Ireland and the Saxons of England.

The Anglo-Irish perspective was no different. Stressing their Englishness – a William Power of the leading Waterford lineage was sent to gaol in 1371 because he could not speak English and was only released when he found pledges that he would apply himself diligently to learning the language – they still identified themselves with Ireland as their *patria* (homeland). They were proud of their own history in Ireland, since they came as conquerors in the twelfth century. When James Yonge was writing his book for the Earl of Ormond, he was constantly reminding him of Irish history and showed a pride in his nation which was typical of educated men of his class. He also castigated what he called 'divers English captains' for their failure to punish Irish enemies and resented their ineptitude, which was clearly the result of their ignorance of Ireland. Such resentment of hamfisted English officials was bound to have political, if not constitutional, implications and was part of the long tradition of self-sufficiency which made the leaders of the Anglo-Irish community anxious to be masters of their own fate – albeit constantly reminding the King of his obligation as their lord to succour and protect them.

It was also a manifestation of their will to power, to control the Dublin government as a source of power, for material profit and gain. The prevalence of faction in fifteenth-century Ireland also contributed, since English officials almost inevitably became enmeshed. When James Yonge vented his spleen against English officials, he certainly had in mind the Talbots and their supporters who had challenged the supremacy of his patron the Earl of Ormond. He even went so far as to write that he was unwilling to say any more about their incompetence – it was 'perilous to rehearse', he wrote, as if he feared for his own life. While his fear is exaggerated, it does represent the intensity of the attacks which the factions engaged in the struggle launched on each other.

Sir John Talbot came to Ireland as chief governor in 1414. A famous soldier, his main task was to force the Irish, especially those on the borders of the later Pale, into submission. There had been some previous success. In the winter of 1401, O Connor of Offaly, O Byrne of Wicklow, and Mac Mahon of Uriel (who was given the barony of Farney in Monaghan in a bizarre attempt to settle, as the government thought, friendly Irish to guard the land of peace) were forced to seal treaties, as was O Reilly of Breffny the following spring. But Talbot went much further. Not only did he force Mac Mahon, O Byrne and O Reilly to submit again, he did so with the help of O More of Leix, who was obliged as part of the terms of his submission to supply two 'battles' (450 men) of horse and foot to join the chief governor on campaign. Further north, O Hanlon on the Ulster border had his land devastated and had to sue for peace. Then the great Ulster lords – O Neill, O Neill Boy, McGuinness, O Donnell and Maguire – took fright and made their peace. By 1419 Talbot had captured the ruling Mac Murrough, fortified the crucial bridge at Athy, and seemed well on the way to securing peace for all the borderlands which had been disturbed for so long. He had successfully fulfilled the first duty of a chief governor, to secure peace, and was therefore praised and supported by many of the residents of the land of peace.

But already he had encountered the outright opposition of Ormond and a fierce struggle for control of the Irish Government ensued. There was certainly a bitter personal animosity between Talbot and Ormond, exacerbated when the earl's lands were taken into the king's hands by the lieutenant. Talbot had also inherited lands in Ireland and was in one guise a returned absentee. He also wasted no time in using his office to further his own and his family's interests in Ireland, exploiting patronage (such as the awarding of lucrative marriages or wardships) to build up support. It was this which made enemies of the Butlers. They, too, had enemies who were quick to take advantage of their discomfiture. Ireland, like England, was faction ridden at the time, when lineages in mafia fashion extended family control over whole territories. They burdened communities with their armed retinues of kern and galloglas, exploited coign and livery and other customary (if still illegal) exactions as a form of taxation, extracting protection money from those who could afford to pay. Control of office was a vital element in the process of exploitation. With the greatest of the lineages, such as the Butlers, control of central governmental office became crucial. Talbot's exploitation of office was naturally, therefore, bitterly resented.

The quarrel dragged on for years, with accusation and counter-accusation of oppression and misgovernment flying across the Irish sea. Treason was alleged, not to mention peculation and abuse of power. Even when the two principals, Talbot and Ormond, came to an agreement in 1444 with the marriage of the lieutenant's son to the earl's daughter, the two factions continued to struggle. Because it involved so many, and important, persons, contemporaries blamed it for many of the ills which beset the lordship. Archbishop Swayne of Armagh complained bitterly in 1427 that 'this debate betwyx these two lords is cause of the great harm that be done in this country', so that 'the English ground that is obeying to the king's law in this land, as I suppose, is not so much of quantity as is one shire in England'.

Behind this power struggle, one can also detect something that went beyond the merely personal. Supporters of Ormond argued that chief governors should be left in office for longer periods. Frequent change was a cause of weakness. This proposition was attacked by their opponents as nothing less than an attempt to restrict the authority of the king in Ireland. In 1429, the Butler faction demanded that in future the king should not receive any charges or accusations against a chief governor, until these had first been examined and upheld by an Irish parliament. Their opponents counter-argued that in this way the truth would never be known, since Ormond packed parliament and thus made it an instrument of his will.

Both sides stressed the importance of direct access to the king, acknowledging his supreme authority as lord of Ireland. But at the same time they seem tacitly to have accepted the authority of the Irish parliament, now claiming a monopoly over taxation and a legislative independence which had roots deep in the past. One of the more significant incidents occurred in 1418 when Talbot's deputy uncovered what he claimed was a conspiracy and arrested the Earl of Kildare (father-in-law of Ormond) and Sir Christopher Preston. It had been reported that they intended to seize the deputy, kill his retinue and then nominate a chief governor of their own. When he was arrested, Preston was found to be carrying documents which were considered to be incriminating and they were exemplified to be produced in evidence at his trial for treason – a copy of the English coronation oath and a tract known as *Modus tenendi parliamentum* (How parliament should be held). The latter is a highly controversial document, both as to origin, date, and relevance to fifteenth-century parliaments, Preston's was an Irish version and was clearly regarded as subversive. Shortly before this, in December 1417, a great council meeting at Naas had proclaimed the superiority of parliament. Before too long an Irish parliament was to declare that Ireland could only be bound by statutes enacted by the lords and commons of Ireland.

The man who was responsible for creating the circumstances which allowed such a radical declaration to be made was Richard, Duke of York, who came to Ireland in 1449 as lieutenant. In part this was a manoeuvre by the Lancastrian government in England to get him out of the way and perhaps, with luck, even embarrass him politically by failure to cope with the problems of Irish security. York had been vociferous in the opposition to the failings of the current administration in England and was to become the leader of the faction which would lead England into the civil war known as the 'War of the Roses'. In 1447, when he was appointed lieutenant, he was also next in line to the throne. As grandson of Roger Mortimer he had also inherited the vast Mortimer estates in Ireland, which included the earldom of Ulster and the lordships of Connacht and Trim. He made an immediate impact. A successful campaign in Ulster gained the submission of all the leading Ulster chieftains, including O Neill. The great Leinster chieftains followed, led by Mac Murrough. The Yorkists were ecstatic and published the great news in a series of propaganda releases, designed to magnify York's success, and proclaiming in 1449 that 'with the might of Jesus ere twelve months come to an end the wildest Irishman in Ireland shall be sworn English'.

But this sense of achievement was misplaced. Not for the first, or the last, time were English officials deceived by appearances in Ireland. The Yorkists proudly listed the chieftains who presented the duke with 3,626 cattle. But most of these came from rivals to the current chieftains (or 'captains of nations') – such as Fergal O Reilly (the unsuccessful rival of Aedh Ruadh Mac Mahon of Monahan). They were bribes intended to involve the chief governor, who happened also to be Earl of Ulster and Lord of Trim, in factional politics. But York was no de Burgh, anxious to pose as effective ruler of Ulster and to enjoy the traditional rights of earl there. Instead he allowed O Neill in practice to rule the earldom in his name.

What York did gain was a promise from O Neill of all the ancient military services due to the earl, which in 1449 were specified as 500 cavalry and 500 foot, armed with lances, axes and bows, to serve in Ulster without wages and at the duke's wages outside; this was more to York's purpose. While in Ireland he was intent on building up support among the nobility and gentry, which would provide him with protection and a power base in the future should the need ever arise. He was well aware of his precarious position in Ireland, where lack of money was causing problems. Even his own lands in Meath were attacked and York complained of the king's failure to pay him money owed. He knew that failure in Ireland would gravely compromise his reputation in England. In one letter he wrote that 'it shall never be chronicled nor remain in scripture, by the grace of God, that Ireland was lost through my negligence'. He would go back to England to protect himself, where the rebellion of Jack Cade, claiming to be an Irish Mortimer and related to York, further complicated matters. Before he left, the Earl of Ormond, certainly the most powerful of the Anglo-Irish nobility, sealed an indenture with the duke, binding him for life 'to do him service as well in war as in peace, as well in England when he shall happen to be there as in Ireland'. It was Ormond, too, who was left behind by York as his deputy.

But within two years Ormond was dead and his successor as earl was his son, James Butler, recently belted Earl of Wiltshire in England, where he had emerged as a leading opponent of York. The Irish Butlers followed his lead and became supporters of the Lancastrians. Traditional rivalry, allied to the successful diplomacy of York in gaining widespread personal allegiance while in Ireland, meant that most other important lineages, led by the Geraldines of Kildare and Desmond, became Yorkist. Thus the growing split between Lancaster and York in England was reflected in Ireland, where it coalesced with older traditional groupings. By the time events in England had forced York to flee for his life in 1459, his supporters in Ireland were in firm control of the government there.

Attainted by the Coventry parliament, York chose to take his chance in Ireland, and not in Calais which supported him. He sent his son and the Earl of Warwick there, while he came to Ireland seeking a safe refuge. He made the right choice. Early in 1460 an Irish parliament not only confirmed him in office as lieutenant (thus defying the king and parliament in England and ignoring his attainder), but it also protected his person by declaring treasonable any action against him. When an unfortunate messenger arrived from England with orders for the duke's arrest, he was summarily executed for treason.

In order to legitimize such a refusal to be bound by a statute enacted by an English parliament or to carry out an order issued under the great seal of England, the Irish parliament had to proclaim formally that Ireland was bound by Irish legislation only and that its seal had primacy over others. This it proceeded to do in the very first session, with the famous statute which declared:

> 'That whereas the land of Ireland is, and at all times has been, corporate of itself by the ancient laws and customs used in the same, freed of the burden of any special law of the realm of England save only such laws as by the lords spiritual and temporal and commons of the said land had been in council or parliament there held, admitted, accepted, affirmed and proclaimed, according to sundry ancient statutes thereof made'.

The king's seal of Ireland was the one 'to which all the said subjects ought to do lawful obedience'. Another statute seemed to challenge directly the king's authority by establishing an Irish mint to produce a new coinage for the lordship, which was intended to bolster the Irish economy by making the export of bullion less attractive than formerly. There were technical reasons for this but, in addition, a new Irish coinage, with its own distinctive design and Irish names like 'Patrick' would symbolize the new order initiated with the arrival of York and represent the independence of the land of Ireland from the land of England.

Designed to protect York, the 1460 statutes nevertheless proclaimed the independence of the Irish parliament. Anglo-Ireland had long since used parliament to voice political grievances and ambitions. Even in the early fourteenth century the 'custom of Ireland' had been proclaimed as the touchstone for testing the validity of specific English statutes in Ireland. When shire communities refused to answer royal summonses to send representatives to England in 1375, it was because of the 'liberties, privileges, rights, laws and customs of the land of Ireland'. The 1460 statute similarly emphasized the 'ancient laws and customs' which made Ireland corporate of itself. It is clear that such a theory of the constitutional relationship of Ireland to England was academically respectable, even if repugnant to royal judges sitting in royal courts in England. The greatest expert had unambiguously accepted the separation of the land of Ireland from the kingdom of England. Sir John Fortescue gave it as his considered opinion that:

'the territory of Ireland is separate from the kingdom of England, for if a tenth or fifteenth be granted here, it shall not bind the people of Ireland, and if a statute be made here, it shall not bind those in Ireland, unless they approve it in their own parliament, even if the king under his great seal shall send the same statute to Ireland'.

Such high doctrine may have been far from the minds of those who attended the 1460 parliament. York certainly had other things on his mind, plotting an invasion of England with Warwick, organising military support from his Anglo-Irish sympathizers, making provision for his future. He was naturally anxious to call on those who had sealed military indentures with him now that the testing time had come. Parliament willingly assented to legislation giving leave of absence to all who wished to sail with him to England. In the event no help was required. Warwick defeated the royal army at Northampton on 10 July and by October the king agreed that York and his heirs would succeed to the throne of England. This settlement quickly broke down, hostilities were renewed and in December York was killed in battle at Wakefield. But in March 1461 the Yorkists won a decisive victory at Towton and York's son became Edward IV of England.

Ireland had played a significant role in the events leading to this Yorkist ascendancy. York himself had exploited his advantage there, even to the extent of seriously compromising the authority of the king in the legislation of the 1460 parliament. His enemies were no better. It was reported in England that Henry VI had written to his Irish enemies, 'which never King of England did heretofore', urging them 'to enter into the conquest of the said land'. Queen Margaret also tried to stir up rebellion in the lordship. The age-old conflict between Butler and Geraldine lineages was given new meaning by the Lancastrian–Yorkist power struggle. Apart from a brief alliance to counter the threat of the Talbot faction, the Butlers and their supporters were consistently hostile to the Geraldines and loyal to the house of Lancaster.

Now they were to lead an invasion from England and generate a wide-spread rebellion in Ireland. In 1462 Sir John Butler, heir to the executed fifth earl and claiming to be the sixth earl, invaded the south with what the record calls 'a great multitude of Englishmen'. Waterford and New Ross were taken. There was rebellion in the Butler lands in Kilkenny and Tipperary and further north where, it was later reported to Edward IV, 'the commons of the county of Meath to the number of 5,000 made insurrection and rising'. The situation was extremely dangerous and it was the decisive defeat of the rebels by the Earl of Desmond at the battle of Pilltown (near Carrick-on-Suir) which averted the crisis. According to a message from the Irish parliament in 1463, this dangerous insurrection was put down only 'because of the continual war had all the last summer by the said deputy (Desmond)' and because Desmond remained in the field as long as was necessary 'at his own proper cost with his men to the number of 20,000'. The Irish Butlers were now attainted with their cousins in England, their lands confiscated and their traditional enemies rewarded for their support of the new Yorkist dynasty. A Geraldine ascendancy was now inaugurated which was to dominate the politics of Anglo-Ireland for many years to come.

6   The Geraldine supremacy

The seventh Earl of Desmond, Thomas fitz James fitz Gerald, was, on the face of it, an odd choice to head the Irish Government. His family, unlike the Kildare branch of the Geraldines, had never been involved in government, except for the second earl who had briefly acted as justiciar in 1367–9. Though the earl was head of one of the great Anglo-Irish lineages, ruling a lordship which extended from Kerry and Limerick through Cork as far as west Waterford, the family had long concentrated its energies on the south-east, well away from the centre of English government based in Dublin. It was also the most Gaelicized of the great Anglo-Irish lineages. The third earl, Gerald fitz Maurice, was eulogized by an Irish writer as 'a witty and inge-nious composer of Irish poetry', for which he earned a reputation which, as Gearóid Íarla, has lasted to the present day. He was, an Irish annalist recorded, 'one of the English nobility that had Irish learning and professors thereof in greatest reverence of all the English of Ireland'. In December 1388, despite all legislation forbidding fosterage, he procured a licence per-mitting him to send his son to O Brien of Thomond 'to be brought up and educated and there to remain as long as he should think fit'. The impact of such a fosterage was to last for life. In Irish society foster-brothers were if any-thing closer than blood-brothers. For someone like Desmond this could cause acute problems in the future, when a choice might have to be made between two allegiances, the Irish and the English. In one of his own compositions, addressed to his foster-brother Mac Carthy, he exposed this dilemma: '. . . because I feared the anger of the Saxon king, I preferred to go against my brothers [the Mac Carthies], no matter what they thought of me, than to be held under duress by the Saxon king in London'. His descendant, the seventh earl, had no such fear. He had earned the gratitude of Edward IV, as the par-liament of 1463 pointed out in a message to the king, having restored the land to 'reasonable peace and tranquillity', and it behoved the king 'to have him in tenderness and special favour and him thereupon heartily thank and reward after his most wisdom and bounty'.

But though the king showered gifts on him, he was not fully convinced that Desmond was the right man to be deputy. He warned the earl that he must not depart from the English mode in governing Ireland and specifically demanded that he end the burden of coign and livery. The implication was that the earl might seek to introduce outlandish and illegal exactions such as were traditional in his own Gaelicized earldom. The king's fears were only too well founded. Desmond not only failed to remove illegal exactions, he extended them into the Pale and thus alienated the gentry of the area. In the summer of 1463 a Drogheda merchant, James Dokeray, went to England to complain of coign and livery imposed by the deputy on the king's subjects in Meath. Since King Edward was lord of Trim, there was a particular interest in this complaint. Other charges were made against Desmond, serious enough for parliament, which he controlled, to ask the king to pay no attention. The English-born Bishop of Meath, William Sherwood, who had been close to the king's father, now emerged as leader of the opposition and went to England to lay charges against the deputy. But Desmond managed to clear his name and was retained in office. The king had been made aware of his deficiencies and had been led to believe that there was a considerable opposition to the deputy within the Pale.

Yet there was much to be said for Desmond's government. He helped to bring outlying regions closer to Dublin for a time, more elected representatives turned up to his parliaments and legislation became more comprehensive, embracing more of Ireland than usual. He was certainly not overtly displaying any tendency to use his office in the interest of family or friends. Nor could he be accused of being in any sense pro-Irish. Quite the opposite, for his legislation was more rigorous than was customary in trying to impose English norms and practices on the Anglo-Irish and to outlaw Irish customs. He even demanded that outlying communities should cease to pay black rents (protection money paid to local Irish lords) and instead pay equivalent sums into the exchequer. As earl, he was praised among the Irish for his generosity to poets and for his learning in Irish, English and Latin; but as deputy there is no evidence that he ever gave vent to this interest by dangerously giving encouragement to Irish culture. When he promoted a scheme to found a university, it was Drogheda which he chose diplomatically as the site for the new foundation. Had he enjoyed continued military success and kept at bay the Irish neighbouring the Pale, it is unlikely that his government would ever have been successfully challenged. But failure in 1466, culminating in his ignominious capture by the O Connors of Offaly, made the king listen to the opposition and determine to replace him.

The man chosen was Sir John Tiptoft, Earl of Worcester, notorious in England as 'butcher' because of the number of Lancastrians he brought to the scaffold. But he was also a humanist who had studied in Italy for two years and had a high reputation as a Latin scholar. A bibliophile who amassed a great collection of books, some specially commissioned and skilfully decorated, Tiptoft was no mere soldier sent to ride roughshod over Desmond and the Anglo-Irish nobility. Indeed, not long after he arrived in late September 1467, the new deputy cooperated with others, including the Earl of Kildare, in founding a fashionable chantry in Dunshaughlin. He held a parliament at Dublin in December and during the first session no provocative legislation was introduced. No sign of any animosity between Desmond and the Geraldines was evident. His administrative experience in England, where he had served the king as treasurer, among other offices, was utilized in Dublin to reform the administration and create a new efficiency, but not in such a way as to drive local office-holders into opposition. When parliament went into recess for Christmas all seemed well.

The next session was switched to Drogheda, which had been at the centre of opposition to Desmond. On the first day, 4 February 1468, a bill was rushed through attainting the earls of Desmond and Kildare, together with Edmund Plunkett, the seneschal of Meath, of 'horrible treasons and felonies contrived and done by them, as well in alliance, fosterage and alterage with the Irish enemies of the king, as in giving them horses and harness and arms, and supporting them against the king's faithful subjects'. That Desmond had maintained close relations with some Irish was undeniable. In 1463 Dokeray had accused him of being 'councilled, ruled and governed by the king's great traitors and rebels' and it can hardly have improved his image when O Donnell and other Irish enemies, as well as English rebels, came to Dublin in that summer and there, in the words of an annalist, 'adhered to him'. But this was no justification for a charge of treason five years later. More serious was an accusation, made apparently about this time, that Roland fitz Eustace, a former deputy and current treasurer, had urged Desmond to make himself King of Ireland. The charge was preposterous, but it suggests a well-coordinated conspiracy against Desmond which may have included Tiptoft. Another tradition implicated Queen Elizabeth who was said to have been slighted by Desmond and was using Tiptoft to exact revenge, though there is no real evidence to sustain this. Whatever the reason for the attack on Desmond, and it may simply be that the king had decided to be rid of him and dealt with him in much the same way as many a nobleman had been dealt with in England by Tiptoft, Desmond was taken from his confinement in the Dominican friary in Drogheda on 15 February and immediately executed.

It shocked the whole of Ireland, Gaelic as well as Anglo-Irish. An annalist wrote that not only Ireland itself, but the whole of Europe as far as Rome 'was filled with sorrow and affliction'. An Anglo-Irishman wrote that he was 'made a martyr of Christ'. Years later, Richard III wrote that he had been 'extorciously slain and murdered by colour of the law . . . against all manhood, reason and good conscience'. There was a violent reaction to the execution. Desmond's brother, Garret, came as far north as Meath 'burning, wasting and destroying'. Parliament reported to the king that he brought with him from Munster 20,000 galloglas and 2,000 horsemen. The treasurer, fitz Eustace, freed Kildare from prison in Dublin and together they came 'with such fellowship as they could make' to help Garret. He was also joined by O Connor Faley and Kavanagh, presenting a formidable challenge to the government. Tiptoft had brought 500 archers with him from England and they now proved their worth. He succeeded in defeating Garret, but disturbances spread to other parts. O Reilly raided into Louth, Garret raided Tipperary, O Neill killed the seneschal of Ulster and reportedly massacred 500 men, and the Leinster Irish went into revolt. In this dangerous situation, with trouble escalating everywhere, Tiptoft accepted Kildare back into the king's peace (he was later formally pardoned by Edward IV), on condition that he would use his influence with both Irish enemies and English rebels who were 'bounden in affinity to him', in order to procure 'tranquillity and peace for the king's subjects'. Later, when parliament reversed his attainder, Kildare had to promise 'to make the Irishmen of Leinster to be at peace according to his power'.

Here was an explicit recognition of the beneficial widespread influence of the Geraldines. Through their connections, it was believed, peace could be maintained at no cost to the king. It brought Kildare to the forefront of Irish politics. Garret was kept busy in Desmond where he had to face problems of his own until his nephew James, son of the murdered earl, finally succeeded to the earldom. The government recognized James as eighth Earl of Desmond and even sent ambassadors to negotiate with him, but it was to no avail. Desmond now turned his back on Dublin, later refused to be reconciled despite Richard III's attempts to woo him, and for all practical purposes abandoned his allegiance. So Kildare was left to assume political leadership when the time was right.

Tiptoft was still in favour. There was no criticism from Edward of his summary execution of Desmond, nor was criticism to be expected. When Tiptoft had returned to England from Italy and was appointed treasurer and constable in February 1462, he was commissioned to try all cases of treason without a jury, 'summarily and plainly without noise and show of judgement'. His execution of Desmond was done in that spirit and the king continued to trust him. When Tiptoft's first son was born in Dublin, Edward sent the father a great cup as a special present for the baptism. He remained as head of the Irish government until 1470, when he returned to England of his own volition and then became a victim of the violence which marked the triumphant Lancastrian celebration of the readeption of Henry VI in October. To the delight of the London mob, Tiptoft was publicly executed on the fourteenth of that month. By then Kildare was in control of Ireland and the long ascendancy of his family had begun.

Tiptoft had left a deputy, Sir Edward Dudley, behind him in Ireland. But sometime in the late summer, and certainly before 13 October 1470, the council in Dublin elected Kildare as justiciar. The timing was significant. On 2 October Edward IV abandoned England; four days later Warwick entered London, took Henry VI from the Tower and the readeption commenced. It was not until 26 November, when parliament was finally able to assemble, that Henry was formally declared to be king. Obviously Kildare and the Irish council kept themselves informed of what was going on in England. When the earl held a parliament in November, at a time when he must have known that Henry VI was back in power, the formal record of its proceedings stated unambiguously that it was held 'in the tenth year of the reign of King Edward IV, before Thomas fitz Maurice, Earl of Kildare, justiciar of the said lord king in his land of Ireland'. On 26 November, ironically the same day as parliament in England declared Henry VI to be king, Kildare's parliament ordered a new coinage to be struck for Ireland, bearing the legend 'Edward by the grace of God King of England and lord of Ireland'. So that on the face of it, the presumption must be that Kildare was still recognizing Edward IV as king, despite events in England. However, that parliament which authorized the new coinage bearing the name of Edward added 'or the name of any other king for the time being'. Kildare was nothing if not cautious, waiting to see which way the game would go in England.

Meanwhile, he used parliament to annul all laws enacted under Tiptoft which were derogatory to himself and his family, to procure all Tiptoft's Irish property, and to secure for his heir, in the event of his death, immediate livery of all his inheritance. The new Lancastrian government confirmed him in office as deputy, at some date before February 1471, so that there was no suspicion of him as a dangerous and confirmed supporter of the house of York. The rapid change in political fortune in England, which finally saw the restoration of Edward IV and the decisive defeat of the Lancastrians in April 1471, seems to have caused no ripple in Ireland.

There Kildare was kept busy trying to cope with widespread disorder. Among other measures, he persuaded parliament to provide him with a permanent retinue of 80 archers for the protection of Dublin, Meath, Louth and Kildare, an important development in the creation of a standing army which would be as much an instrument of Geraldine policy as a protection for the hard-pressed inhabitants of the Pale. At the Dublin parliament of 1474 a new military order was created. Known as the Fraternity (or Guild) of St George, it was to consist of 12 of the most important men of the Pale, with Kildare as master, and a permanent force of 40 cavalry, 40 'pages' and 120 archers, to be supported from the receipts of a new poundage levied on imports and exports. Parliament even proposed to the king that a conquest of Ireland was possible, if he provided sufficient means, pointing out that the 'first conquest thereof was obtained with a small number of English men at which time all the land was under Irish obeissance'. Good government thereafter would produce an annual income of 100,000 marks. But, typically, the same message containing this euphoric speculation complained of the 'piteous decay' of the land and his subjects there and warned that without relief 'they may no longer endure under his obeissance or ligeance, or by distress to depart out of the land'. Such a threat, however improbable, that they might be forced to transfer their allegiance – they do not even hint at to whom – is consistent with the ambiguous stance so often adopted by the 'loyal' Anglo-Irish. The message ended by reminding the king that 'of every right the realm of England is bound to the defence of his land of Ireland by reason that it is one of the members of his most noble crown and oldest member thereof'.

The king made a positive response. Sir Gilbert Dagenham, who carried the message from Dublin, returned in the autumn of 1474 with 400 English archers (parliament had asked for 1,000). He was also appointed chancellor, an indication that the king was not entirely happy with Kildare in charge in Ireland. Before he sent a further force of 220 archers in April 1475, the king replaced Kildare as deputy by Desmond's old enemy, Bishop Sherwood of Meath. But Kildare could not be kept out of office for long. Sherwood was deputy to the nominal lieutenant of Ireland, the Duke of Clarence, who was executed for treason in February 1478. Sherwood's patent of appointment naturally lapsed and the Irish council immediately seized the opportunity of the vacancy to elect a new chief governor and chose Kildare as Justiciar. But almost immediately the earl died (on 25 March) and at once the council elected his son Gerald to take his place in office. This was the eighth earl, famous in tradition subsequently as 'the great earl', who was to govern Ireland under four kings – Edward IV, Richard III, Henry VII, and Henry VIII. The actions of the council in these successive elections show the influence of the Geraldines and their dominance over Irish politics. It was confirmed in the most dramatic fashion shortly afterwards. On 6 July Lord Grey was appointed deputy by the king, thus replacing the justiciar Kildare. With a new force of 300 archers (a measure of the reliance the king placed on him) he arrived in Dublin in late August. Grey was met with outright resistance by Kildare's supporters. The constable of Dublin castle, seat of government and official residence of the deputy, demolished the drawbridge and refused access to the new deputy. The chancellor, Roland fitz Eustace, the father-in-law of Kildare, withheld the great seal from Grey, thus making government virtually impossible until a new great seal could be provided. The treasurer quickly assigned all revenues, so that nothing was left for the deputy.

The technical excuse for all of this was that Grey's appointment was conveyed under the privy seal, and not the great seal of England, which was not acceptable to the Irish council. To make matters worse, Kildare had summoned a parliament which met at Naas in late May, adjourned to Dublin in July and to Connell in September. Grey then summoned a parliament to Trim in November, which in turn was adjourned to Drogheda and finally to Dublin. Grey called Kildare's assembly a 'pretended parliament' and proceeded to annul all its legislation. The king was thus faced with an unprecedented situation, with two parliaments claiming validity for two sets of statutes which were contradictory. Early in 1479 Kildare went to England, was interviewed by the king, made such an impression that he won Edward's support, and was appointed deputy in place of Grey. It was an extraordinary *volte face* by the king.

Edward decided that both sets of statutes should be annulled and gave Kildare a set of 'directions' resolving the confusion which had arisen. These contained specific instructions for statutes to replace some of the more important acts in dispute. This anticipation of what was to be established as normal procedure by the famous Poynings' law at the end of the next century, whereby all bills introduced in the Irish parliament had first to obtain the assent of the king, is a good indication that Edward IV was determined to assert his ultimate authority as king. When Kildare subsequently summoned a parliament, a number of bills were presented by the commons which were based on the king's instructions. But Kildare ignored some of the more contentious instructions which would have resulted in legislation intended to limit his authority in Ireland. He thus showed that whatever the king might decide in England, the initiative in Ireland still lay with him.

Kildare had succeeded not only in regaining office and thus vindicating the actions of his supporters, not far short of treason, he had also defied the king's wishes with impunity. Though the king had appointed Sherwood as chancellor, fitz Eustace was retained as treasurer and, after Sherwood's death in 1482, Kildare was once again able to dominate the council without opposition. The king wanted a strong authority in Ireland and this, it was now abundantly clear, could best be provided by Kildare. He was part of the system of captaincies and lineages by which Ireland, Anglo-Irish as well as Gaelic, was effectively governed. A central authority in Dublin was far removed from most of the local centres of power and only a man who was himself intimately involved with the leading nobility could hope to exercise any real authority, however fleeting, on behalf of the king and the organs of central government. The alternative was massive military intervention from England, which Edward IV could not afford, and without wholesale institutional and legal changes even such an intervention would not have succeeded.

But King Edward had always shown some awareness of his special position in Ireland as Earl of March and Ulster. In 1463 he sent what the annals call 'the donative' to Henry O Neill of Ulster, namely 'eight and forty yards of scarlet and a collar of gold'. The king was tacitly accepting the reality of the situation in most of Ulster, where O Neill's supremacy was a fact of political life, in the hope of preserving some shadow of his own special position there. At the same time he was anxious to preserve the remnants of the Anglo-Irish community there and protect the marches of Louth and Meath from harrowing attack, though O Neill gained considerable reward in the form of black rents from the communities protected. In 1474 he was officially styled 'the king's friend', an unprecedented title for an Irish lord. Even more extraordinary, in 1480 he was formally thanked by the Dublin parliament for 'the faithful service' done to the king and his liege people.

It is important to realize that in Ulster, where most of the earldom was now firmly under the dominion of the revived O Neill hegemony, part of the modern county Down remained Anglo-Irish and retained a strong English character to the end of the middle ages. Communities there needed to be protected, just as much as did those closer to Dublin. The great Irish recovery, which in the fourteenth century had led to the re-occupation of lands in many parts of the island, had been most successful in those areas which had been comparatively thinly settled during the period of English expansion in Ireland. But where the original settlement had been deep and thorough, where new fortified towns and strong castles appeared, Irish chieftains failed to penetrate permanently. Throughout the lordship, often far away from Dublin, there were pockets of colonists surviving like small islands in an Irish sea. There were larger communities, too, self-sufficient and managing to co-exist with Irish lordships, usually with a mixed population and a hybrid culture. The Butler lordship was a good example. North Tipperary was lost in the fourteenth century, but elsewhere in south Tipperary and Kilkenny the settlement survived. The Irish population was integrated into a feudalized society, providing tenants and artisans for many of the manors in the lordship, while retaining their own language and distinctive culture. Here and elsewhere there was a stable population on the land, century after century, which, in the long term, was to help to protect the community during times of great social upheaval in Ireland.

Such lordships were ruled almost like petty states and were an essential element in preserving some form of stability in the dangerous world of the fifteenth century. From the middle of that century there has survived the set of ordinances which the Earl of Ormond had promoted so as to help in preserving peace within the lordship and defending it against enemies from outside. One ordinance stipulated that the earl should hold an assembly every year, to which he would summon representatives, 'both spiritual and temporal', just as the king did in his parliament. Here laws would be promulgated and taxes granted, a clear indication of the autonomy of the earl within his own lordship. It was people like Ormond who maintained some kind of order and stability within Ireland, however weak the king's government in Dublin might be.

One sign of the new stability was the economic recovery of the fifteenth century, manifested not only in the new enclosure of land for tillage and a growth in commercial activity, but physically demonstrated in the rash of new and restored buildings which appeared all over the island. Elaborate new friaries, new parish churches, massive restoration projects in older religious houses, a multitude of new stone tower houses – all point to the ready availability of the necessary resources in money, materials and labour. The patronage which generated this building boom was itself a sign of new optimism, demonstrated in the founding of chantries, the commissioning of literary works, and the compilation of new libraries of books for the future.

Even lower down the social scale the wills of Dubliners show unmistakably all the signs of a wealthy bourgeoisie anxious to secure future happiness through the lavish endowment of religious enterprises before they died. Nothing better illustrates the self-confidence and civic pride of late medieval Dublin than the elaborate regulations by the municipality for the annual Corpus Christi procession, involving a multitude of guilds, each with its own contribution to make to the spectacle and drama of the day. The glovers were to provide Adam and Eve 'with an angel following bearing a sword'; the weavers, Abraham and Isaac 'with their altar and a lamb and their offering'; skinners, house-carpenters, tanners and embroiderers, 'the body of the camel and Our Lady and child well apparelled, with St Joseph to lead the camel, and Moses with the children of Israel, and porters to bear the camel'. Other towns, such as Kilkenny, had their own spectacles. Most show the same signs of prosperity and optimism, despite the apparent anarchy which abounds in the annals of the time. If, like Waterford and Cork, they occasionally complained of isolation and dangers, begging remission of debts to the Irish exchequer, it was often a case of 'putting on the poor mouth'. Like other communities in Ireland, they were adept at protesting their hardiness in resisting the tide of rebellion which they said threatened to engulf them and at the same time looking for help and reward.

But there was a price to be paid for the stability provided by the great lords and communities would often bitterly complain about the cost. The frequent condemnations of coign and livery, the system which allowed the billeting of soldiers and horses on the people, as well as taking the food necessary to sustain them (to take 'man meat and horse meat' as a fifteenth-century bishop put it) was to no avail against the practices which lords exercised in their own domains. These had become customary long before the end of the fifteenth century, part of an elaborate series of 'exactions' which the nobility, Anglo-Irish as well as Gaelic, imposed to support their retinues of armed men, in addition to enabling them to enjoy a standard of living proper to men of their rank. These lords, in the network of lordships which covered the island, were the props of peace.

They could also be agents of disturbance. Quarrels were frequent, if usually confined regionally. This was only to be expected in an age where crime was rampant, so that all men went armed, and injury done by one man to another could quickly involve the lineages of both, making the subsequent fighting difficult to contain. The greater the protagonists, the greater the disturbance. Untold damage was done by feuds among the Anglo-Irish lineages, of which that between the Butlers and the Geraldines (especially the Desmond branch) was the worst. It lasted for generations. A demented Bishop of Cloyne was driven, in 1380, to insert a passionate outcry in the liturgy, when celebrating mass in Dublin castle: 'O eternal God, there are two in Munster who destroy us and our goods, namely the Earl of Ormond and the Earl of Desmond with their followers, whom in the end the Lord will destroy, through Jesus Christ our Lord, Amen'. Despite repeating his prayer on successive days, the bishop's hope was not realized. Fighting broke out at intervals and resulted in widespread destruction. In 1447 Desmond, accompanied by some important Irish chieftains, such as O More of Leix and Mac Gillapatrick of Ossory, invaded Kilkenny and Tipperary. It was reported to the king that in Kilkenny alone 76 towns and 16 churches were destroyed, many were killed and others taken prisoner, cattle and goods were carried away, and that the liege people were now nearly destroyed.

Alliances were made and unmade with bewildering frequency. There seems to have been little coherence in the ever-changing pattern of groupings. If, among the Anglo-Irish, affiliations could often rest on one lord's ambition to achieve office or secure control of patronage, among the Irish, too, alliances could often reflect memories of past glories, however distant to the realities of fifteenth century Ireland. When Turloch O Brien became a vassal of Henry O Neill in 1463, in the traditional way by accepting *tuarastal* (ceremonial wages), he was hoping for help against common enemies in the O Donnells and the Burkes of Mayo. But he was also, by this symbolic act, consciously renouncing ancestral claims to the kingship of Ireland. When, in 1466, he formed an imposing alliance of the Irish chieftains of Leinster and Munster which devastated large areas, so that he gained control of Limerick and south Tipperary, with the city of Limerick forced to promise a black rent of 60 marks a year, there was talk of bringing him to Tara and making him king. But he had already acknowledged the superior claims of O Neill, a fact emphasized in a ceremonial ode which urged O Neill to become the husband of Banba, or King of Ireland.

Henry O Neill, however, was a realist, content to exercise control in Ulster. However much the poets and antiquarians may have fantasized about reviving the kingship of Tara, none of the provincial dynasties ever took seriously the aspirations towards national unity which such fantasies expressed. They knew that the balance of power in Ireland would not permit such a development. Not only were the most powerful Irish lineages (O Neill, O Donnell, O Connor, O Brien, Mac Carthy, Mac Murrough Kavanagh) held together in a delicate, if changeable, system of dependency, the Anglo-Irish (Kildare, Desmond, Butler, Burke) were also locked into the same system. The great lordships, the myriad of lesser 'countries' (as they were called in the 1515 report on the state of Ireland) with their 'captains' or chieftains, were governed according to notions of authority which were alien to the common law tradition of England. Centralized government, based in Dublin, could have little direct impact on these regions, except through the occasional use of force. It was this which made the Earl of Kildare, himself a part of the system, an obvious choice to represent royal authority in Ireland. Even within England itself, outlying districts or marches were increasingly left to be controlled, in the king's name, by the powerful local magnates. To that extent, reliance on Kildare was not totally at variance with notions of government in late fifteenth-century England.

The vast landed wealth possessed by the earls of Kildare, strategically concentrated on the marches south of the Pale and dominating Butler lands as well as those of Irish lords, provided the basis of power. Control of government was used to augment the Kildare lands and the exploitation of patronage was fully used to win support and alliance. Such control was exercised through the council, which was dominated by Kildare supporters. Despite royal intervention, the earl generally managed to maintain his nominees in office and through them made the council, and even parliament of which it was still the core, an instrument of his power. It might be argued that this was essential to the implementation of the king's authority, through the deputy, in the regions. But it could also be used to preserve the continuation of Kildare rule, through the rise and fall of governments in England. The mythical 'Statute of Henry fitz Empress', under which the Irish council was empowered to elect someone as Justiciar to 'keep' or 'guard' the lordship during a sudden vacancy in the deputyship, was adroitly exploited in favour of the Kildares. In 1485, the critical year of the Tudor accession in England, Kildare put through the Irish parliament an act which confirmed this 'statute', and which also listed the members of the council who *ex officio* were to form the college of electors. Having named the individuals, stipulating that they were to retain their offices for life, it enacted that in the event of any of them vacating office, replacement was to be in the gift of Kildare.

Through his own family, Kildare also established a relationship with many of the leading Irish and Anglo-Irish families of Ireland. He himself was married to Alice fitz Eustace; his sister Eleanor to Conn O Neill, whose son (later the first Earl of Tyrone) married his first cousin, the earl's daughter Eleanor; and other sons and daughters were married into the families of O Donnell, Mac Carthy, O Carroll, O Connor of Offaly, O Kelly, Piers Butler (subsequently Earl of Ormond), Fleming, Burke, Darcy and Plunket. In 1499 he fostered his son with O Donnell. This network of family connections made it easier for Kildare to promote the king's peace and, if occasion demanded, to augment the forces at his disposal. The battle of Knockdoe in 1505 is a striking example of his capacity in raising a mixed army of Irish and Anglo-Irish allies.

Others were bound to the earl in a more dependant relationship, well illustrated in the Kildare rental of 1518. In a section entitled 'Duties upon Irishmen' are listed all the Irish lordships paying protection money to the earl, including all the important ones bordering the Pale. Prominent among the names are Mac Murrough, O Toole, O Byrne, O More, O Connor, O Farrell, O Reilly, Mac Mahon, all promising money or some tribute in kind to the earl each year. Even as far away as Leitrim Mac Rannall promised yearly 'a shilling for every quarter of land which belongs to O Ruark or Magrdhnaill . . . in consideration of the earl's defending and assisting them against all men subject to his authority'. In some cases, too, payment was conditional on the earl holding office as deputy, the amount to be reduced by half if he ceases to head the government. Nothing better illustrates the importance to the Earl of the chief governorship of Ireland. It is notable, too, that Anglo-Irish were willing to pay for protection, even a Bishop of Waterford and the prior of the Augustinian priory at Duleek in Meath.

But if the eighth Earl of Kildare thus occupied a position which made him supreme among the nobility of Ireland, so that he was the only one ever to be called Mór (great) by the annalists, and if from time to time he caused anxiety in England, he was never the 'all-but-king' of later tradition. After the death of his first wife he married the king's ward, Elizabeth St John. His son and heir Gerald was left to be brought up at court in England, playing a leading part in the ceremonies at the funeral of the king's eldest son Arthur in Worcester cathedral in 1502. In the following year, at the age of 16, he married another ward of Henry VII, Elizabeth Zouche. The English connection was valuable to Kildare. At no time did he seek to renounce it. If he seemed, at times, to defy the king's wishes and to be pursuing an independent policy of his own, it was no more than might be expected of a powerful and ambitious subject, not easily amenable to the control of a distant king. He never defaulted in his allegiance to the crown. Attempts by Edward IV, Richard III and Henry VII to cut him down to size were never wholly effective and he was always restored with his powers little impaired.

The accession of Richard III immediately presented Kildare with a challenge to his authority in Ireland. The new king was anxious to regain the initiative in his lordship and had appointed a new chancellor. But Kildare, who had earlier appointed his brother to the same office, refused to admit the king's nominee, claiming the right to do so under the terms of the statute fitz Empress. This direct challenge to the royal authority could not go unanswered and Richard quickly established through the courts the royal prerogative in this matter. He retained Kildare in office, accepted his choice of chancellor, and made a bargain when Kildare visited England in 1484. But the king was biding his time. He had already sent one embassy to Ireland on a preliminary inquiry into government there. Now he sent the Bishop of Annaghdown on a mission to contact English rebels and dissidents such as the Earl of Desmond, as well as leading Irish enemies such as O Neill in Ulster, in a massive attempt to bring as many as possible back into the king's allegiance. This was a return to the radical policy of Richard II and, if successful, would not only have re-established royal authority over much of Ireland, but in the process would have made Kildare, and indeed his like, superfluous to the king's needs in Ireland. Fortunately for Kildare, the arrival of Henry Tudor in England and the subsequent dethronement and death of Richard, restored the status quo.

The greatest crisis in his relations with the crown arose from his involvement in two Yorkist plots to topple the first Tudor monarch. The Battle of Bosworth in August 1485 brought Henry Tudor to the throne, Kildare had known what was in the wind. On 6 June, in anticipation of a possible change of dynasty in England, he had taken the precaution of getting parliament to have 'confirmed, ratified and made good and effectual in law' the statute of Henry fitz Empress, thus securing his own continuity in office in Ireland, whatever the outcome in England. In March 1486, the new king confirmed him as deputy. Whatever deposit of sympathy for the house of York remained in Ireland was slow to manifest itself. Everyone, Kildare included, seemed to accept the new dynasty without question. Then, early in 1487, an Oxford priest arrived in Dublin with a 10-year-old boy who claimed to be Edward, Earl of Warwick and true heir to the throne. This pretender, now known to be Lambert Simnel, was immediately given protection by Kildare's brother the chancellor, and it was he who summoned support. Kildare was cautious at first, not wishing to be involved without some positive insurance of effective support for the pretender. Margaret, Duchess of Burgundy, sister of the late Edward IV, and other Yorkist sympathizers soon provided what was needed and on 5 May 1487 Martin Schwarz and 2,000 mercenaries landed in Dublin.

The waverers were now convinced. The boy was solemnly crowned as Edward VI in Christ Church on 24 May, in the presence of Kildare and many other notables, ecclesiastical as well as lay. There could be no going back now. An army was assembled, including Anglo-Irish as well as Irish troops in addition to the German mercenaries, and on 4 June it invaded England. Among the leaders was Kildare's brother, the former chancellor, who was killed along with many more from Ireland when the Yorkist force was finally beaten at the crucial battle of Stoke. In Ireland, Kildare summoned a great council in the name of Edward VI, issuing letters in his name under a new great seal which carried an effigy of the boy king. Most interestingly, the royal style used called Edward 'by the grace of God King of England, France and Ireland' (not the traditional 'lord of Ireland') and Kildare was styled 'lieutenant of our kingdom of Ireland'. The Dublin mint issued a new coinage in Edward's name and, more astonishingly, so did the Waterford mint, suggesting a Geraldine attachment before the city (the *urbs intacta* of Tudor propaganda) threw in its lot with Henry VII. The implication that Edward VI had been crowned King of Ireland, as well as the fact that Kildare now enjoyed the higher office of lieutenant, suggests that there may have been hard bargaining before the pretender was crowned. But there is too little evidence to draw any conclusions about the nature of any radical change which may have taken place in the constitutional relationship between England and Ireland.

What is clear is that Kildare, as always, exploited the situation in his own interest and that his support of the Yorkist plot was not just out of a sentimental regard for that house, still less a conviction of the legitimacy of the Simnel claim, but a calculated gamble. It did not come off. Yet he was still holding his position even four months after the battle of Stoke. A letter from Henry VII to the mayor of Waterford tells how Kildare and other traitors had planned 'the destruction of our person and the utter subversion of our realm' and 'unto this day uphold and maintain the same'.

Sometime after that the earl began negotiations with the king, received letters of pardon on 25 May 1488, and settled back into office. There is no indication that the king had replaced him during the long interval. He sent a special envoy, Sir Richard Edgecombe, on a mission to Ireland to negotiate more exact terms of submission with the rebels. But when Edgecombe reached Dublin in July he was treated with contempt by Kildare, who refused to accept the conditions demanded by the king. According to Edgecombe, he and the other leaders said that rather than accept, 'they would become Irish every of them'. This again was typical of the Anglo-Irish, always ready to threaten withdrawal of allegiance if their position was threatened. Eventually they took an oath of allegiance, promising not to support rebels in the future, and with this the envoy had to be content. Kildare was retained in office, despite the protests of the citizens of Waterford, who feared retaliation for their loyalty to the king, and the outright warning of Archbishop Octavian of

Armagh that if the earl should 'obtain the governorship of Ireland by royal authority and appoints the chancellor of Ireland at his own pleasure, I have no hope of peace in Ireland'. Kildare visited the king early in 1489 and was lavishly entertained at Greenwich, when (so the story goes) the pretender was brought from prison to wait on him at table. He regained the confidence of the king and was soon back in Ireland, involved once more in the complex politics of the lordship.

In July 1490 Henry summoned Kildare to England, suggesting that he come within 10 months. There was no sense of urgency here, no hint that the king was worried about his Irish deputy, but Kildare was loath to go, and for good reasons. In June 1491 the Dublin parliament sent a message to the king, asking him to excuse the deputy, saying that the danger to the Pale was too great. Kildare also wrote, adding that he had to intervene in Munster and Connacht, and he was supported in this by letters from Desmond, Roche, Coursey and Sir Piers Butler. There was no reply from Henry, still seemingly complacent about Ireland. Then, in November, Perkin Warbeck, who claimed to be Richard Duke of York and was yet another pretender to the English crown, escaped from the Tower of London. He arrived in Cork, was enthusiastically received and soon had the active support of the Earl of Desmond. Warbeck later claimed that Kildare had also helped him, a fact strenuously denied by the deputy: 'I never lay with him, nor aided, comforted, nor supported him with goods nor in no other manner wise'. But at the very least his role was ambiguous.

The king acted decisively. In December 1491 he sent James Ormond (a bastard son of the sixth earl) and Thomas Garth to Ireland, with a retinue of 200 and orders to defend Tipperary and Kilkenny. This was Butler territory and clearly the king was ensuring that in the event of a Geraldine rebellion, this part of the lordship would be held for the crown. Waterford, too, would be protected. Not until June 1492 did Henry dismiss Kildare from office, by which time Warbeck had left Ireland and the main danger seemed to be over. Authority was now divided between the Archbishop of Dublin, Walter fitz Simons, who replaced Kildare as deputy, and James Ormond who took the odd title of 'governor and treasurer' (*gubernator et thesaurarius*). Other new appointments removed Geraldine supporters, thus ending the earl's vital control over the Irish council.

A near civil war ensued between the old Butler and Geraldine factions and their supporters. Even on the streets of Dublin rival gangs came to blows. O Brien supported the Butlers, O Connor of Offaly the Geraldines. When Garth invaded Offaly, Kildare took him prisoner and hanged his son. Between March and June 1493 an alarmed King Henry sent three retinues, 400 in all, with cannon, guns and wagon loads of ammunition. Still the fighting went on. In June another fracas on Oxmantown Green in Dublin resulted in the deaths of a former mayor and other citizens.

The failure of fitz Simons and James Ormond to exercise any real control had become blatantly obvious. During the summer of 1493 they were replaced by Gormanston and the main irritant to Kildare was removed. He had long since been pardoned by the king, who seems to have accepted his assurances that he had never been involved with Warbeck. In the autumn of 1493, together with Gormanston, Garth and others, he went to England to confer with the king. Ormond and fitz Simons had crossed earlier. The king was now deeply concerned about Ireland. He had spent about £4,000 on armed intervention and while this had blunted rebellion, it had failed to curb the widespread disorder in Ireland. Besides, Warbeck was still at large, gathering support, a threat so long as he was free. Ireland might again become a backdoor to England, so Henry adopted a radical change in policy. As he wrote to the King of France on 10 August, he intended to pacify Ireland, especially that part inhabited by 'Irish savages', and send 'a good and sufficient army accompanied by good and great persons as well for war as for justice'. It was a return to the old policy of direct military intervention, coupled with a thorough reform of the administration.

There can be no doubt that in adopting this course King Henry was following the advice of the large Anglo-Irish deputation which had gone to confer with him in 1493. Kildare would play a key part, using his influence not only with Desmond, but with the other Anglo-Irish and Irish lords with whom he had relations. He would also participate in the military operations which the new policy might demand. But he would act under a new deputy, Sir Edward Poynings, who had been appointed on 12 September 1494. With about 400 men, Poynings landed at Howth in October. In November he moved against Ulster, accompanied by Kildare and James Ormond. But while the lands of O Hanlon in Armagh were being ravaged, a quarrel between the deputy and the earl brought the campaign to an abrupt end. Kildare was later arrested, attainted of treason by the Irish parliament, and sent as a prisoner to England in March 1485. But within a few months an English parliament abrogated his attainder and by August 1496 he was on his way back to Ireland as deputy.

Earlier in Ireland his arrest had led to a Geraldine rebellion, which kept Poynings busy. In July 1495 Warbeck invaded the south-east and Poynings had to move south to lift the siege of Waterford, which was successfully accomplished. Warbeck made his way through Ireland to Scotland but, after his failure in Munster, he no longer presented a real threat to Henry. To that extent, at least, the Poynings expedition to Ireland had been a success. But the cost had been way beyond anything the English government had invested in Ireland since the fourteenth century. About £23,000 had been spent by the hard-pressed Henry, almost up to the level of Edward III's expenditure on the Clarence expedition in the 1360s. Such expenditure could not be sustained.

The king had anticipated this and Poynings had been accompanied by a number of experienced English administrators to initiate long-needed reform in Ireland. Already the 1493 parliament had begun the process with an act of resumption which had massive implications. Not since 1341 had the like been tried. The main thrust of the reform programme, however, was financial, designed to make Ireland pay her own way. There was spectacular, if temporary, success. Exchequer revenues were pushed as high as £3,055 in one year, well over double normal receipts. At the same time, careful housekeeping reduced expenditure. But still the cost of maintaining even a small English army in Ireland was well beyond the resources of the Dublin exchequer. In February 1496 Henry had to send £2,500 and in May a further £3,000. It was time to return to the old policy of reliance on a local magnate, able to keep order without the help of large financial subventions from England. Only Kildare could fill that role. He was given the king's cousin in marriage, left his eldest son with the king, and on 5 August 1496 was reappointed deputy. Far from reducing his powers, the king in fact extended them in the new patent. Kildare was granted the office for an unprecedented 10 years, allowed to appoint to all ministries with the sole exception of the chancery, and given a grant of all lands which he might secure from the enemies and rebels of the king. It was a restoration which left Kildare in control of the council as before and thus able to ensure the continuity of his government. He was also granted all Irish revenues without being accountable, which removed yet another check on his independence.

Henry VII's experiment in old-fashioned direct rule had come to an end, but it left an important legacy. While in Ireland, Poynings summoned a parliament which met in Drogheda in December 1494 and this assembly passed the act which ever since has been known as Poynings' law. Probably the most famous single act in Irish parliamentary history, it declared that henceforth no parliament could be summoned except by the king's prior consent, and that no bill could be introduced except for those already approved by the king and his council in England. The reason for this is obvious. Never again would an Irish parliament be used to give legitimate authority to a pretender. But the effect, in the long term, went far beyond the simple purpose for which the act was designed and was to have repercussions in Irish parliamentary history down to the eighteenth century. The actual wording of the act was very cumbersome, indicating that its framers were not at all sure of the procedure to be followed in actually administering the new law in the future. Time revealed that it was virtually impossible to proceed, as had been customary for some time, by bill arising out of private petition, even for the greatest in the land. In practice, bills tended to be initiated by the king, so that parliament became much more than formerly an instrument of the royal will. It virtually ceased to operate as a court and its long-established judicial function had to be taken over by chancery in particular. The number of parliaments fell dramatically. Before 1494, except for a couple of years, parliament met annually. After 1495, during the 41 years prior to the reformation parliament of 1536, only eight were summoned. And after the great burst of activity during the period 1541–3, only four parliaments met during the 70 years before 1613.

The other piece of legislation of Poynings' parliament which had important consequences for Anglo-Irish relations was the statute which annulled the 'pretensed prescription' of York's 1460 parliament, which had made it high treason to attack any person under the English great seal. The same statute also enacted that the great seal of England, the privy seal and signet were to be obeyed in Ireland. Finally, it decreed that 'all statutes late made' in England were 'from henceforth to be good and effectual in law, and over that be accepted, used and executed within this land'. This seems to apply only to recent English legislation, and not to be concerned with the more important general point raised by the 1460 declaration. The doubt remained, so that the question of the application of English statutes in Ireland became more than a matter of antiquarian interest at a later stage of Irish history.

The great bulk of the legislation of Poynings' parliament was designed to preserve law and order and to re-establish the authority of the king. With Kildare back in the saddle, if anything strengthened by the traumas of recent years, the traditional system of government was resumed. While Dublin was still the capital, it no longer was the centre it had once been. When the Earl of Surrey came to Ireland in 1520, he found Dublin castle so ruinous that he had to begin a programme of reconstruction. The records, too, were in a shambles. Kildare was constantly on the move, sometimes engaged in campaigns all over the lordship, sometimes marching with great splendour in what resembled royal progresses through the countryside. He enjoyed great success, extending the scope of royal (and his own) authority well beyond the limits of the Pale.

But there were never-ending problems, defying the kind of temporary military intervention which had long been the custom with chief governors. Submissions were equally temporary, no lasting peace could be secured in any region and O Brien in particular posed real difficulties. In 1506 he built a new bridge across the Shannon, bypassing Limerick and giving himself a new access to the midlands and to Munster. Such was the threat posed by this to the peace that it even alarmed the English council. At a meeting on 3 December 1506 it decided on a plan for Ireland and informed the king accordingly. The king had gained 'little advantage or profit' from the armies which had been sent 'divers times into the land of Ireland for the reduction of the same'. He must 'make a voyage personal in his most noble person for the repress of the wild Irish and redress and sure reduction of all the said land'. He would need 6,000 'well chosen men and no less' for his army, apart from others engaged in transporting men and supplies. He was also told that three 'great guns', as well as no fewer than 900 other guns, would be needed. But subsequently financial arguments prevailed and the plan was dropped.

It was in 1510 that O Brien showed his power, using his new bridge to strike. Kildare was able to call on O Donnell and Desmond and so was able to lead a formidable army against him. But the force was ambushed by O Brien, who inflicted severe losses. It was an ominous sign that not even Kildare, with all the resources he could call on, was able to extend royal authority too far beyond the Pale and its marches. Any success was temporary, but he was constantly trying. In 1511, while on yet another campaign, he was shot by O More of Leix. The wound seriously hampered him until it finally caused his death on 3 September 1513.

He had enjoyed a remarkable career, spanning 35 years, during which he showed consummate political skill. He knew how far he could go in his dealings with the king, always relying on his belief that in the end he would be indispensable. Years later, in 1534, one of Cromwell's spies reported that the ninth Earl of Kildare had been encouraged into rebellion by being told that:

> 'you shall be more esteemed in Ireland to take part against the king. For what would you have been if your father had not done so? What was he set by until he crowned a king there, took Garth, the king's captain, prisoner, hanged his son, resisted Poynings and all his deputies, killed them of Dublin upon Oxmantown Green, would suffer no man to rule here for the king, but himself? Then the king regarded him, made him deputy and married your mother to him'.

This may be a distortion, but it contains more than a grain of truth. In many ways Kildare was conventional in the manner of his age. He planned a fashionable collegiate church for his principal seat at Maynooth, endowed a new chapel at Christ Church, left the usual gifts to the cathedral in his will, took a fierce pride in his family (he wrote to his supposed relations, the Gherardini of Florence, in 1507, boasting of his house and ancestry), and in Maynooth he built up a fine library of books in Latin, French, English and Irish, including Virgil, Juvenal and *Cuncullyn's Actes*. But in politics he was an opportunist, daring rebellion when he felt the gain to be worth the risk. He left this casual attitude towards rebellion to his son the ninth earl, and he in turn was to encourage his son Thomas to follow the same path. But by 1534 the Geraldines were dealing with Henry VIII, Cromwell, and a new order in England which, for one reason or another, could not tolerate the traditional attitude towards royal authority in Ireland. In the end it meant disaster for the house of Kildare and indeed for the old policy which for so long had preserved a balance of power in the lordship.

The ninth earl, also Gerald, succeeded his father as deputy in 1513 and Kildare rule continued without a break. A product of England, where he had spent his formative years at court, married to a royal ward and acquainted with many of the people who now mattered (including the new king, Henry VIII), Kildare was still a true Geraldine in outlook. He, too, had a hot-and-cold relationship with the king, being pushed aside whenever the English government was pressed by circumstances to interfere in Ireland. But Henry VIII had no wish to be drawn into a consideration of the lordship's problems, despite the flood of complaints, plans of reform, or programmes for the redress of Ireland which flowed across the Irish sea. There were occasional flurries of interest, which led to statements of policy and direct intervention, but the cost was always prohibitive and financial considerations always dictated the restoration of Kildare.

In 1519, after a volume of complaints against the earl, he was summoned to England and the council there discussed 'how Ireland may be reduced and restored to good order and obedience'. The result was a decision to send a lieutenant, with a substantial retinue and the new artillery which had revolutionized siege warfare. The choice fell on the Earl of Surrey, a soldier of experience and high reputation, who was given the impossible task of restoring the king's authority throughout the lordship. When he landed on 23 May 1520 he had 700 troops, including 400 of the royal guard for whom special uniforms had been provided. He quickly moved out of Dublin, first northwards, receiving the submissions of both O Neill and O Donnell. He raided Leix, moved into south Leinster and Munster, making contact with the Butlers, Desmond and the Mac Carthies. Despite appearances, however, he was not enjoying much success and was certainly not improving on Kildare.

In the autumn of 1520 he received a famous message from the king, outlining a policy for Ireland. Henry emphasized that in contacting the Irish captains to bring them 'to further obedience' and 'the observance of our laws', Surrey must proceed rather 'by sober ways, amiable persuasions, founded in law and reason, than by rigorous dealing . . . or by strength or violence'. After a remarkable passage extolling the 'rules of law', without which the weak suffer and no man is safe ('realms without justice be but tyrannies and robberies'), the king went so far as to suggest that 'if their [the Irish] laws be good and reasonable, they may be approved'. The was a far cry from Edward I's condemnation of Irish law as detestable to God, and even went well beyond what Richard II was prepared to concede, when he promised justice to aggrieved Irish chieftains.

There was a sting in Henry's message, however, which gave a hint of the more authoritative attitude of the future. Surrey was to tell the Irish that 'we, being their supreme lord and prince, though of our absolute power we be above the laws', will not deprive them of what is rightfully theirs. This claim to absolute power was a new fact in Anglo-Irish relations. The king's absolutism placed him above the law and so he could dispossess the Irish no matter what legal title they possessed. Henry also spelt out clearly to Surrey that he would not tolerate 'an appearance only of obeisance', without obeying the law, accepting the justice of the king's courts and restoring 'such dominions as they unlawfully detain from us'. To 'spend so much money for the reduction of that land' for false submissions 'were a thing of little policy, less advantage, and least effect'.

Surrey quickly discovered that Henry was unwilling to provide the kind of financial backing his policy required. In June 1521 he informed the king of the alternatives. A rapid conquest of Ireland would require at least 6,000 men; a slower, piecemeal one would take 2,500 men over many years. Vigorous incastellation and a programme of building new towns, with colonization by new English settlers, would also be essential. All of this would be prohibitively expensive, difficult to carry out, and would take a minimum of 10 years. Surrey knew well what the royal response would be. Henry withdrew from his ambitious new policy, returned to the tradition of Anglo-Irish government, and appointed first Piers Butler and then, when this was a clear failure, Kildare as deputy. But the earl had to accept Butler as treasurer and the situation quickly became impossible, given the violence and animosity between the two.

Henry VIII was now determined to make his mark in Europe, and was also occupied with the Scots. He had little time, and fewer resources, to spare for Ireland. When the Butler–Geraldine faction fighting reached its peak, the king summoned the two chief protagonists, Kildare and Ossory (Sir Piers Butler) to England. Various measures were then tried in Ireland, including the reappointment of Ossory, again a failure, and the odd experiment of government by a 'secret council' of ministers. When this failed, it was decided to send Sir William Skeffington as deputy, and with him Kildare, who promised that he would employ himself 'for the annoyance of the king's said rebellious subjects of the wild Irishry'. He seemed to be indispensable to the security of the Pale. He was certainly incapable of sharing power with anyone. Despite complaint, he was again appointed deputy in July 1532 and was back in Dublin in August, once more in sole control. All that the frequent change of government had achieved was a weakening of the royal authority in Ireland. Despite the many plans, programmes and instructions, there was no consistent policy for the lordship, except to fall back on Kildare.

But the advent to power of Thomas Cromwell in England, who from this point was given charge of Ireland in the English council, led to closer control of Kildare's actions and more supervision through royal agents reporting directly to Cromwell. There were more complaints about the deputy's failings, and especially about the feud with Butler. Steps were taken to appoint ministers more directly under Westminister's control, thus loosening Kildare's grip on the Irish council.

In 1533 the king married Anne Boleyn and a breach with Rome, as well as with Queen Catherine's nephew, the Emperor Charles V, was inevitable. The implications for England's security were considerable and it was important that Ireland should not provide a possible location for international plots against the king. Desmond had long since entered into treasonable negotiations with the King of France and then, more to the point, with Charles V of Spain, who sent an envoy to Ireland to reconnoitre. Reports from Ireland that Kildare was plotting treason and had removed the king's guns from Dublin castle to his own castle at Maynooth, convinced Cromwell that he must be replaced. Kildare's reluctance to answer a summons to England added to the conviction. But Kildare was still supremely confident and given the power to appoint his own deputy in Ireland during his absence, he chose his inexperienced son Thomas, Lord Offaly ('Silken Thomas'), and in February 1534 he arrived in London.

It was a mistake, his 'manyfold enormities' were now proved against him and he was forbidden to return to Ireland. Still free in London, he had no difficulty in communicating with his son in Ireland and later evidence argued that Kildare had urged Thomas into rebellion. Thomas feared for his father's safety, particularly after he learnt that Skeffington was to be appointed deputy. He also had information, indiscreetly committed to writing by Skeffington's secretary, that he and his five uncles and others of his family were, if possible, to be arrested, brought to England, and there executed. The council which his father had left behind to guide him advised rebellion. So on 11 June, in a dramatic gesture before the Irish council, Thomas resigned the sword of state and publicly defied the king. He also issued a proclamation that all Englishmen should leave the lordship at once, on pain of death, this led directly to the capture of Archbishop Alen of Dublin, who was then murdered. Thomas also denounced Henry as a heretic, demanding oaths of allegiance to pope and emperor, as well as to himself. In the hope of getting help from abroad, he was trying to associate the rebellion with Henry's enemies and giving it the appearance of a religious crusade.

It was only when news of all this reached England that Henry arrested Kildare on 29 June and confined him in the Tower. He was already a sick man, the result of a wound received long before and he died on 30 September. By then the rebellion was widespread in Ireland, Thomas had large forces at his disposal and the English government was astonishingly slow to react. The rebels were in control of the Pale, though they failed to take Dublin castle, and they dominated much of Leinster as well. They were supported by the most important Irish chieftains and only in the Butler territories was there any real resistance. The king's authority was on the point of collapse. An independent Ireland, possibly under the pope or the emperor, seemed not impossible. But it is most likely that until news of Kildare's death was received, his restoration to power was what was really hoped for.

The arrival of Skeffington in October, however, changed everything. He brought a large army of 2,300, indicating the king's determination not to yield to Thomas, no matter what the cost. Thomas now realized that he was fighting for his life. With all the leading Irish, except O Donnell, supporting him, the rebellion had taken on something of the character of a war of independence. But, in one way or another, during the winter of 1534–5, most of Thomas' allies deserted him. Skeffington, known as the 'gunner' in Ireland because of his expertize with artillery, had brought the very latest weaponry to Ireland. When the ground was suitable in spring, he advanced on Maynooth and in March the hitherto impregnable fortress fell. The rebellion collapsed and in August Thomas surrendered.

The Kildare rebellion marks a turning point in Anglo-Irish relations. For one thing it committed the king to a new and radical policy for the lordship – the creation of a refurbished English administration in Dublin, backed by the presence of an effective standing army, heavily subsidized by the English tax-payer, and all under the direct control of the English government. But it meant, too, a break with the past in another way. The full rigour of the law was employed against those who rebelled. Imprisonment, attainder, execution and confiscation of lands were the order of the day. The use of force and the manipulation of the law to gain political ends were given a new meaning by the ministers of the crown in Ireland. When Thomas surrendered on 24 August 1535, he embarrassed the government because of the conditions attached, namely the promise of life and limb. The king was strongly advised from Ireland that if ever 'the said traitor do repair hereunto any more, the king's grace hath wasted all this labour and cost'. The old pattern of pardon and restoration simply could not be repeated. Norfolk, who as Earl of Surrey had been the king's deputy in Ireland, wrote urgently outlining three possible options to the king: an immediate execution, which would surely cause widespread war in Ireland; a pardon, which would be 'the worst example that ever was, and especially for that ungracious people of Ireland'; and imprisonment for a time, until Ireland got quieter and then execution, when there was nothing further to be gained by sparing Thomas any longer. This was the course followed.

After imprisonment for 16 months Thomas, now tenth Earl of Kildare, and his five uncles were executed on 3 February 1537. A contemporary account tells how they were 'drawn from the Tower unto Tyburn and there all hanged and headed and quartered, save the Lord Thomas, for he was but hanged and headed'. In Ireland, between 75 and 100 others were also executed, a small amount, it has been argued, when the numbers who rebelled are taken into consideration, perhaps as many as 5,000 in all. The king's revenge was modest by his own standards. But this was Ireland, not England, where for many generations rebellion and rebels, even when attainted of treason, had been pardoned and often restored to office. In 1534 Henry VIII was advised that:

'to this time, where many men have been taken and part of them indicted of felonies and treason, if they be poor wretches not having lands nor goods nor friends, then shall they have the extremities of justice; but if he be a great man having land or goods whereby your deputy may be pleased, then shall this malefactor have pardon'.

The execution of Desmond in 1468 was still remembered and Anglo-Irish history recorded the shock which greeted the execution of William Bermingham, an ally of the first Earl of Desmond in rebellion, in 1332. But in the new Ireland, executions were to become commonplace, as the king's justice reached further into the lordship and the full rigour of the law was employed in dealing with subversives, religious as well as political, Irish as well as Anglo-Irish. A new concept of nationality was to be forged.

7   The end of the old order

In June 1535 a commission was issued for the suppression of the convent of Augustinian nuns at Grane in county Kildare. There had been proposals earlier for dealing with the problem of religious houses situated on the border of Irish 'countries', which might be a danger to the Pale by offering support to Irish enemies. In 1534 Sir Patrick Finglas raised an alarm about 'divers abbeys adjoining the Irishmen' which 'give more aid and supportation to those Irishmen than to the king's subjects'. The flight of tenants into the comparative security of the Pale, and even across the Irish sea, had long since caused something of a demographic crisis among the Anglo-Irish. In 1528 a Welsh official wrote of a colony of 20,000 Irish 'rascals' in Pembrokeshire alone, no doubt a great exaggeration. But it illustrates how serious the problem appeared to contemporaries. Even as far back as 1297 the Irish parliament had complained of the effects of this kind of dilution of a population supposed to preserve English culture in an alien Gaelic environment. Two and a half centuries later the situation had worsened. Now the Irish were encroaching everywhere and tiny communities in comparatively well-to-do religious houses could do nothing to resist the tide. Better to suppress them and grant their properties to men who would protect the land and attract new English tenants.

This was the thinking behind the suppression of Grane in 1535. It was granted to Lord Leonard Grey, the new marshal of the army sent to combat the Geraldine forces in Ireland. But the commission also saw Henry VIII exercising the powers which the act of supremacy (enacted the previous November in England) had conferred upon him as head of the church. Yet it was not until May 1536 that an Irish parliament enacted that Henry was also 'supreme head in earth of the whole Church of Ireland'. This supremacy act and other legislation necessary to give it effect was put through parliament with speed, and almost no opposition, during the first session. Only some of the proctors of the lower clergy protested, but they hardly mattered. A peculiar Irish survival of medieval parliamentary representation, they were shortly afterwards eliminated from parliament altogether. From now on the king was head of the Irish church, which was under his sole jurisdiction. The Church of Ireland, in its new form, was legally established almost unopposed.

It was in the second session of the reformation parliament that opposition to ecclesiastical legislation really emerged. It came when a bill 'for the suppression of certain monasteries' was challenged. It was not the suppression itself which was resented, but rather its economic consequences for those with a vested interest. Bills relating to taxation and customs duties were similarly opposed. What the opposition feared was the loss of valuable monastic leases and the acquisition of properties by new English officials now in control in Dublin. Resentment of English-born intruders was already strong. Somewhat later, in 1545, Archbishop Browne wrote to the king: 'To be plain with your majesty I think that they [the Anglo-Irish] be weary of us all that be English men here'. But economic gain was an even sharper motive. Once the fears of possible loss were assuaged, the Anglo-Irish quickly agreed to the suppression in a later session. The emergence of an opposition in parliament was an indication of Anglo-Irish resolve: where their interests were concerned, they were not going to be forced against their will. There was also opposition to secular legislation in this reformation parliament of 1536–7, and the king was forced to pay heed to it.

But so far as ecclesiastical or reformation legislation was concerned, it seemed to be of little concern to them. The only real opposition came from the lower clergy, and they paid the price. The commons and the upper house, including the higher clergy, acquiesced. To accept the royal supremacy seemed academic to them, a definition of the rights of the lord of Ireland who was their protector as well as their source of patronage. It might even be said that the members of parliament saw this as yet another dispute with the papacy about jurisdiction, part of a controversy which went back into the dim reaches of the past. There was no Pilgrimage of Grace in Ireland. Even though the Kildare rebellion was given a religious gloss, it was less from conviction than to win support from lower clergy at home and papal forces abroad. But when Archbishop Browne and others later began to give practical effect to reformation legislation in a heavy-handed way, they met with stern resistance from conservative Anglo-Irish. Religion and politics became enmeshed, as they had been in the Kildare rebellion (when many supporters, and especially from the lower clergy, joined because they genuinely believed that Henry was a heretic and had forfeited the lordship of Ireland which they believed he held of the pope) and its sequel the Geraldine league. There could be no going back. Henceforth Irish politics was given a religious dimension which was often a decisive element in the future.

If self-interest and political motives were reasons for religious change, there were other reasons why the Protestant reformation had no easy passage in Ireland. There was no real tradition of religious dissent, much less heresy, anti-papalism or even strong anti-clericalism at popular or even academic level. Nor does there seem to have been any importation of the new Lutheranism by means of European contacts, in the way in which Christianity itself had first found its way to Ireland in the distant past. Popular religion was focused on the parish and its church, where in many areas the Observantine friars were in control and a high level of spirituality was maintained. Apart from some exceptions, like the shrine of Our Lady at Trim and the popular Staff of Jesus in Holy Trinity, Dublin, there were no great centres of pilgrimage and there does not seem to have been a particularly strong attachment to local cults. When the reformers later moved to destroy images of saints and other expressions of former cults, there was little or no popular reaction.

In Gaelic Ireland in particular, and that meant the greater part of the lordship by the time of the reformation, clergy and community were closely knit. Among the higher clergy, hereditary succession to office was commonplace, with married clergy often members of the dominant local lineages. Clerical celibacy existed, but more as an ideal than a norm. Married clergy were so common that names like *Mac an Easpaig* (son of the bishop), *Mac an tSagairt* (son of the priest) or *Mac an Phríóir* (son of the prior) became established forms. Celibacy and chastity were by no means identical. In one of the annals a clerk with 12 children was praised as 'a gem of purity and a turtle-dove of chastity'.

Outsiders, of course, were appalled by such deviations from the strict tenets of the canon law of the church. As had happened in the twelfth century, and regularly in the centuries which followed, orthodox administrators formulating ordinances in provincial or diocesan synods frequently condemned 'abuses' which contravened what elsewhere were ecclesiastical norms. The impression was easily created that the Irish church was in a chronic state of decay and needed reform. Even the very fabric of many ecclesiastical buildings, decayed and in need of repair, seemed to suggest the same need of renewal and renovation in the church. But where the evidence allows us to peep, we can see that the state of the Irish church was no worse than elsewhere, and in many respects much better. The spectacular success of the Observantine friars, somewhat like the Céli Dé of an earlier age, shows vigour and vitality at the popular level unmatched elsewhere. The way in which religious poetry used commonplace social customs in a normal literary context (the death of Jesus on the cross was likened to the payment of legal compensation for wrong done) shows how alive religious feeling was. Far from being totally depressed, the church in late medieval Ireland manifested many signs of vigour.

In Anglo-Ireland, too, there were signs that not all was stagnation. The decline of religious houses, where communities fell away to tiny numbers in the demographic crisis of the later middle ages, when vocation to the regular life went out of fashion, should not be taken as evidence of religious decline generally. The new parish churches, distinctive in style and decoration, the refurbishment of some religious houses, the endowment of chantries and colleges, the growth of cults of new saints, the spread of religious guilds – these are signs of vitality. The Earl of Kildare's library provides evidence that religious polemic was imported, with books like *The declaration of the gospels*, *The King of England his answer to Luther* and *Sir Thomas More his book against the new opinions that hold against pilgrimages*. Many monasteries, too, had extensive libraries of books, which unfortunately were lost when the houses were suppressed or demolished during the reformation. The libraries contained a treasure of religious works for those who cared to read them.

It is wrong, therefore, to exaggerate the decline of the church in late medieval Ireland and to assume that a reformation was much in need and would find a ready audience. To accept Henry VIII as head of the church meant little to most people, especially among the Anglo-Irish. For long they had been pressing for a positive political initiative which would 'civilize' Gaelic Ireland, by force if necessary. To that extent the king's new ecclesiastical role could be seen as part of the process of change which had to be implemented in the wake of the Kildare rebellion. Apart from the dissolution of religious houses, which came slowly and caused little popular opposition, there was no obvious break with the past. Religious practices remained the same as always. Initially, therefore, many conformed and accepted, if they were ever really aware of it, the break with the pope. Doctrinally, under Henry VIII, the Irish church still remained close to Rome. And for those clergy who refused to conform, punishment was mild. There were no martyrs as yet.

But there were signs of some unease. Archbishop Browne's implementation of the reform programme was based on authority and royal sovereignty. Ireland must be made to conform to English practice. In 1533 an English parliament had defined the 'realm of England' as 'an empire governed by one supreme head and king unto whom a body politic be bounden and ought to bear, next to God, a natural and humble obedience'. The lordship of Ireland was part of that body politic. What has been called the concept of unitary sovereignty, or the unitary state, whereby the king was to be master in the one state under his dominion, meant that royal supremacy in the church must be extended in a meaningful way throughout Ireland. So Archbishop Browne of Dublin, who led the campaign of reform in 1538, invoked penal laws and the secular arm to enforce the reformation programme. This now included liturgical reform, devotional changes, the circulation of English prayers, the condemnation of images, some aspects of confession, and the much-abused practice of indulgences. Fear, not reason, was to be the instrument used. In effect, too, this authoritarian approach was one of anglicization, with the Irish church made to conform to the Church of England. At one stage Cromwell, the mind behind this programme, intended to extend the jurisdiction of Canterbury to Ireland, a gambit which not even the most fanatical of the twelfth century reformers had ever dared to make. But Bishop Staples of Meath, in the summer of 1538, was critical of this approach. He wrote that it was commonly said that 'the supremacy is maintained by power and not by reason and learning'; that the new programme was giving scandal; and that what should be diligently sought was acceptance of the royal supremacy of the church.

It must be said, too, that this reformation programme was confined to the area where effectively the king's writ ran. Such opposition as it encountered there came for the most part from the lower clergy. The friars in particular preached against the new order, even within the Pale. Outside, they were active in encouraging rebellion. One report from O Donnell's country claimed that the lower clergy everywhere 'preach daily that every man ought, for the salvation of his soul, fight and make war' against the king and that all who died in the attempt would go straight to heaven. But such attempts to introduce the counter-reformation into Ireland had small success while Henry VIII was alive. It was later, when fundamental doctrinal and liturgical changes were imposed, with Puritan elements to the fore, that resistance became widespread and led to a return to the former recognition of papal, as against royal, supremacy in the church.

This had obvious implications for Anglo-Irish loyalty and posed a dilemma of fundamental importance: how to square loyalty to the pope in the spiritual sphere with loyalty to the crown in the secular. Religion became a basic ingredient in the already complex mix of Anglo-Irish politics. When news of the death of Edward VI reached Kilkenny in July 1553, Bishop Bale found his priests celebrating the event, many in the taverns of the town, hoping 'to have their masses again'. It was even rumoured that Ireland was to have her own king. English garrisons were attacked and soldiers killed.

In Gaelic Ireland there was another pattern, the dissolution of religious houses, for example, took a different course. More than half of the monasteries, and over one third of the friaries, had been suppressed by the time Henry VIII died. But most of these were in the Pale and the English districts outside. Beyond, the process of suppression was much slower and depended on the success achieved in extending the authority of the king's government in Ireland. Some religious houses survived into the seventeenth century. Most were dissolved as the process of anglicization was pushed through the Irish and degenerate English countries. Inevitably, the suppression and the wider religious change of which it became a part, were identified with the political change threatening the independence of the nobility.

For there was another 'reformation' which in the reign of Henry VIII was not so much concerned with the church and her institutions, as with the 'wild Irish' and those whom Bishop Bale termed the 'tame Irish' – those Anglo-Irish who were degenerate and particularly resentful of the new English being settled in Ireland. The reform of Ireland was above all to teach the Irish civility and reason. It was the opposite of 'conquest'. William Thomas, writing of Henry VIII shortly after his death, told how he had

> 'brought that nation, from rude, beastly, ignorant, cruel and unruly infidels, to the state of civil, reasonable, patient, humble and well governed Christians, not for the desire of dominion, or for the increase of revenue, but for God's honour and for Christian peace'.

Ignoring the sanctimonious tone, and the deliberate portrayal of the Irish as pagans, we can see what reformation meant to those who preached it.

But there was another and harsher way to bring Ireland, and especially the Gaelic part, within the body politic which acknowledged the supremacy of the king in all matters. It can be seen in the aftermath of the Kildare rebellion, in the manner in which the new deputy Lord Grey conducted his administration. He was extraordinarily active in his military operations during the years 1538–40, pushing across the Shannon as far west as the city of Galway, through Munster, north as far as Armagh, and even (in 1540) deep into O Neill's territory when he drove as far as Dungannon. His energy recalled the great days of Kildare's perambulations through the lordship, so that a Butler could say of him that 'my lord deputy is the Earl of Kildare newly born again'. Irish lords who had been forced into accepting harsh terms of submission, or threatened with Grey's strong-arm methods, reacted through what is known as the Geraldine league.

Its instigator was Manus O Donnell, lord of Donegal, who married Eleanor Fitzgerald, widow of MacCarthy and aunt of the Kildare heir, Gerald. Through this marriage, Manus became the protector of Gerald, gave him asylum and eventually procured his safe passage to France in 1540. A formidable alliance of Irish chieftains was formed to protect the Geraldine heir, sought everywhere by government agents, and to resist the assertion of ecclesiastical supremacy by Henry VIII. An alliance which brought together the most important lords, some of them bitter rivals for generations past – O Neill, O Donnell, O Connor of Sligo, O Connor of Offaly, O Brien of Thomond – together with many lords of lesser rank, like O Rourke, Maguire and McDermott was, for the government, an alarming development in Irish political life. An invasion of the Pale in August 1539, when a large prey of cattle was taken, indicated the scale of the danger. Hampered by the huge booty, the Irish were surprised by Grey at Bellahoe on their way home and routed. But the alliance was not to collapse, in 1540, with the Geraldine withdrawal, the league became a purely Gaelic movement of independence. There was even a revival of a proposal to make O Neill high king at Tara, with a restored Earl of Kildare as a vassal lord. But this unprecedented alliance was not tolerant of such traditional fantasizing and gave expression to a political programme of a more realistic kind. This included a plan, disturbing to the government, to offer the Irish crown and formally transfer allegiance to the King of Scotland. The ghost of Bruce was abroad again.

In a letter to King Henry in July 1540, O Neill condemned Grey's aggressive policy and suggested that only through a more conciliatory approach could peace be restored. There seems little doubt that it was fear of the implications of what Grey was doing, threatening the security of the lords in their own countries, and in the longer term perhaps even the legality of the tenure of their lands, that really prompted the formation of the Geraldine league. Its success posed a greater threat to the English lordship than had the Kildare rebellion of a few years before. There was a real fear abroad, especially within the Pale, that this unusual alliance might succeed in its challenge to the crown. More realistically, it was appreciated that Grey's hard line would drive the Gaelic world into further resistance and would achieve nothing at great cost. A letter to Henry in December 1539 put it neatly: 'Without a general reformation the king's majesty shall vainly consume his treasure in this land'. Grey was withdrawn, to be subsequently charged with treason and executed in June 1541. The appointment of Sir Anthony St Leger as his successor marked a decisive shift in policy whereby Gaelic Ireland would be brought, through the consent of the chieftains, into a new and more intimate relationship with the king.

To that extent the Geraldine league had a dramatic success. It had manifested a new Irish sense of nationality which had expressed itself in political as well as military terms. For the first time there was a widespread and cohesive alliance against the crown, with old rivalries and bitter enmities buried, even if only for a time. The instinct of self-preservation was stronger than pride or jealousy. This new political awareness was also prepared to exploit deep-seated religious fears, by denouncing the king as a heretic. A captured messenger from O Neill to the O Tooles in April 1539 confessed that the leaders of the league 'call all Englishmen heretics' and accounted the king 'the most heretic and worst man in the world'. If the leaders were cynical in making use of the strong attachment to Rome among the local clergy, and presumably their flocks, throughout the Gaelic world, they were giving substance to an attitude which saw the king and the whole English nation as a new kind of enemy.

The only way to establish the royal supremacy was to disabuse the Irish leaders of this notion. Force alone would not do it, even at impossible cost. It was stated in 1541 that:

> 'Irishmen will never be conquered by religious war. They must be instructed that the king intendeth not to exile, banish or destroy them, but would be content that every of them should enjoy his possessions, taking the same from the king . . . and become his true subjects, obedient to his laws, forsaking their Irish laws, habits and customs, setting their children to learn English'.

So, they must be wooed. The key principle was tenurial, giving the lords of countries a legal status as tenants-in-chief of their territories under the crown. Known as 'surrender and regrant', the new policy would have the lord surrender all rights in his land, so that he might have letters patent granting him legal title to the land, holding it in perpetuity directly from the king. The English norm of primogeniture would be established, in place of the Irish practice of election, and a new stability would be created. In addition, the lord would adopt a new English title, appropriate to his status, which would bind him to the king. There were other conditions attached. In 1541, for example, Manus O Donnell also agreed to 'recognise and accept the king as his liege lord and king'; not to ally with but to fight rebels; to renounce the 'usurped primacy and authority of the Roman pontiff'; to attend, when summoned, hostings in person, with 70 cavalry, 120 kern and as many galloglas, for one month at his own expense; to attend parliament; to send one son to England, there to be 'reared and educated according to English manner'. Con O Neill also promised to encourage tillage and build houses for his tenants, and to obey the king's laws, answer his writs and attend his courts in Dublin and elsewhere. Usually the military service attached to the tenure was substantial, acknowledging the traditional services which the Irish lord had customarily demanded within his lordship. But to compensate for this, rents were light because of the absence of a cash economy in many places.

This policy was not of the king's choosing. Instead he was reluctant to accept it and was cynical in his approach. He insisted that if conquest ever became a feasibility, the new grants should not rule out the expropriation of the tenants. The real architects of this radical programme were the deputy St Leger and especially the Anglo-Irish Sir Thomas Cusack, later chancellor. Despite the opposition of hardliners in the Dublin administration, they finally persuaded the king to follow this road of conciliation. In its early stages it met with great success. As with Richard II long before, St Leger began with a sharp campaign in Leinster in the autumn of 1540 and brought Mac Murrough, O Connor and O More to submission. The first 'renounced the name of Mac Murrough', promised to hold his lands by knight service, to obey the king's laws and to 'prosecute all others of their nation that should disobey the same'. Lesser lords also came in. Turloch O Toole promised submission in similar terms in November and was sent to England to be received by the king, who approved the terms in January 1541. The O Byrnes quickly followed. The year 1541 began with a spectacular success, when the Earl of Desmond was reconciled after his family had been estranged for generations. His example helped to persuade Mac William Burke and, a year later, Murrough O Brien, to negotiate terms. Lesser men continued to seek terms. MacGillapatrick, having agreed by indenture to renounce his Irish title, use 'English habits and manners', introduce English agriculture and style of houses, use the king's laws and courts, obey his writs, and hold his land by knight service, was ennobled as Baron of Upper Ossory and subsequently sat in the upper house of the Dublin parliament. In August 1541 Manus O Donnell submitted and finally, after an unprecedented winter campaign, Conn O Neill came in on 28 December.

The way was now clear for fully implementing the surrender and regrant policy, with the great lords presenting themselves to do homage to the king in England. Desmond went first, followed by O Neill. This was sensational, as the French ambassador in London reported to his king. St Leger boasted that 'it cannot be known that ever any O Neill repaired in person before this to England'. O Neill had asked for the title of Earl of Ulster, but this the king refused. He said that it was 'one of the great earldoms of christendom and our proper inheritance'. Instead he was belted Earl of Tyrone. Later O Brien was made Earl of Thomond and MacWilliam Earl of Clanrickard. Three Magennises had been knighted with O Neill and others, like Macnamara, with O Brien. Small wonder that it was now claimed in England that there never had been 'so great a conquest of Ireland'.

It remained to complete the programme in Ireland itself. Each lordship had to be dealt with separately, with complex internal problems to be sorted out. A good sign of progress was the attendance of the new nobility at Dublin. Both O Neill and O Brien were made members of the Irish council. In July 1543, O Neill and O Donnell submitted differences between them to the council for arbitration, attended in person and there concluded a formal settlement.

Meanwhile there was another part of the programme which had to be implemented. Three months after St Leger arrived in Ireland the Irish council proposed that Henry's style should change from 'lord of Ireland' to 'King of Ireland'. Echoing a suggestion made by Bishop Staples in 1538 to change the title so that the Irish might have 'a great motive to bring them to obedience' (and incidentally disabuse them of the notion that Ireland was held as a lordship from the pope), the council argued that 'they that be of the Irishry would more gladder obey your highness by name of King of this your land, than by name of lord thereof'. It was the logical conclusion to the surrender and regrant programme and was in no way a device initiated by the king as a way of supplanting papal overlordship, though it was a bonus that it had that effect. Indeed Henry VIII pretended to be furious when informed of the proposal and wrote to the Irish council, rebuking them for having 'devised by an act, to invest in us the name and title of King of Ireland' and complaining that Irish revenues were not 'sufficient to maintain the state of the same'. But in reality he had made sure when the heads of bills for parliament had been presented to the English council that the bill proposing to make him King of Ireland was given primacy.

On 18 June 1541, after an address by the speaker, Sir Thomas Cusack, a bill was presented in the Dublin parliament that Henry and his heirs 'should from thenceforth be named and called king' of the realm of Ireland. Describing the great occasion in a letter, St Leger told how the bill was first presented in the house of lords,

'which once being read and declared to them in Irish, all the whole house most willingly and joyously agreed to the same. And being three times read, and with one voice agreed, we sent the same to the lower house, wherein likewise it passed, with no less joy and willing consent'.

Not the slightest opposition manifested itself to this momentous change. On the Sunday, 'all the lords and gentlemen rode in procession to St Patrick's to hear a solemn mass sung by the Archbishop; and after the mass, the said act proclaimed there in presence of 2,000 persons and Te Deum sung, with great joy and gladness to all men'.

One radical result of this act and of the surrender and regrant programme was to give a new legal status to the Irish population. Cusack argued before the English council that 'where before they were taken as Irish enemies', they were now 'accepted as subjects' and that this was the best way 'by good wisdom, to continue them in peace and obedience'. According to St Leger, there was a substantial Irish presence in the 1541 parliament, which is presumably one reason why the Earl of Ormond translated the speaker's address and the chancellor's reply into Irish, and why the bill was read in the upper house in Irish only. So that others could attend parliament, St Leger held sessions at Limerick, where the O Briens and Macwilliam Burkes attended, and at Trim, where most of the Irish lords of Leinster, as well as O Neill and O Donnell, were present. So, for the first time in the long history of the Irish parliament, Irish lords in numbers joined their Anglo-Irish peers in the upper house. It was a momentous development and it made the 1541 parliament one of the most remarkable ever summoned in Ireland. It signified the success of the surrender and regrant policy, with the astonishing spectacle of former rebels – O Neill, O Donnell, O Brien, Desmond and Burke – now willing to travel to Dublin and other centres at the government's wish. The Irish council even proposed that each of the important Irish lords be provided with property in or near Dublin, so as to facilitate attendance at meetings of the council 'for affairs of the realm'. When St Leger was called to England in the spring of 1546, he summoned a council to Dublin. Among those who attended were O Neill, O Brien, Desmond and the leading Leinster captains. Cusack was able to assert the triumphant success of the conciliation policy by declaring that 'those which could not be brought under subjection with 10,000 men, came to Dublin with a letter, which is no small comfort to every faithful heart to see'. He wrote that at the council meeting he 'could perceive none of better conformity than those Irish lords, promising to help to see the country defended, as need shall require from time to time, to the uttermost of their powers, till the return of my lord deputy'.

Yet within a few short years it had all turned sour. While St Leger was in England the conservative hardliners, led by Sir William Brabazon, the vice-treasurer, controlled the administration. Whether through bungling or, as has been argued, through deliberate provocation, O Connor and O More were driven into rebellion and St Leger returned to find them in open war. It may be, too, that the reduction of the English garrison in Ireland to 500 men had something to do with it, and the withdrawal of other troops to serve in France and Scotland exacerbated the situation. Whatever the reason for the outburst of violence, St Leger was given little time to repair the damage. Within six weeks of his return to Ireland, Henry VIII was dead.

Somerset became protector in England and under him there was a return to the policy of coercion in Ireland, backed by strong (and costly) military intervention from England. Even though retained in office as deputy, St Leger was gradually superseded in practice. The appointment of Edmund Bellingham as deputy in April 1548 signalled the radical change. A soldier, Bellingham was a throwback to an earlier style of deputy. He had already been sent to Ireland as Captain-General, with troops, supplies, and money and his mission was to restore peace by force. During the summer of 1548 he fought through Kildare, Leix and Offaly as far as the Shannon, suppressing the rebellion. Both O More and O Connor were forced to surrender, sent to England, and there held prisoner. Cahir O Connor suffered a worse fate, which showed the new rigour being applied. After being made to do public penance in Dublin, he was executed.

Bellingham also began a new policy of military occupation, building new forts in Leix and Offaly, followed by the introduction of new settlers into the lands of rebels in Offaly and west of the Barrow. When St Leger was reappointed deputy, he was instructed to confiscate the whole of the countries of O Connor and O More and to allocate them to new tenants. This was the complete abnegation of surrender and regrant and its replacement by plantation. Conquest, garrisoning and plantation were to become the key elements in the new policy for Ireland. The Irish were once again forced to think in terms of fighting for survival, if possible with foreign help. The English ambassador in Paris reported from the French court in June 1550, that an Irish agent was saying

'that the whole nobility of Ireland, from highest to the lowest, had conspired to rid themselves from the yoke of England; and that it was time for them to do so, for otherwise, little by little, they looked for none other but to be driven out of their ancient possessions, one after the other, in such sort as had lately been served to O'More and O'Connor.'

In April 1551 he reported that Cormac O Connor was then in France seeking help. This return to foreign intrigue was an inevitable consequence of the new policy of repression being pursued in Ireland.

There was also a huge financial cost, which the limited military success could hardly justify. From 1547 until the death of Edward VI in July 1553, nearly £250,000 was spent on Ireland, most of it on the army; of this, some £150,000 had to come from England. A debased coinage and inflation exaggerated the figures; but the escalation of military expenditure year-by-year was very real and the size of the standing army exemplifies this. In 1534 there was an army of 500 men in Ireland; by 1547 it was 800; by 1551 it had climbed above 2,600; and by the early 1580s it had reached 6,000 – not including the families, camp followers and servants accompanying the troops. Ireland was once more a burden on the English taxpayer, just as she had been in that other classic period of direct military intervention in the fourteenth century, and there was to be no real let up. Between 1555 and 1565 the cost of the army in Ireland came to an average of £24,326 annually, of which nearly £21,000 had to come from England. By the end of the century, the government of Queen Elizabeth was spending massive sums on the war in

Ireland – £200,000 in 1600–01, and about £1 million in all in the war with Hugh O Neill.

Bellingham was also responsible for a radical change in promoting the reformation in Ireland. He used the royal prerogative to secure reforms which showed the influence of continental Protestantism, thus alienating large sections of the population. The new *Book of Common Prayer* was introduced and orders were issued for the abolition of 'idolatry, papacy and the like'. A side effect was the creation of the first printing press in Ireland in 1551 to make copies available. But these, of course, were useless to the Irish-speaking population and their circulation only helped to make the process of religious alienation more pronounced. The introduction of the *Second Book of Common Prayer* in 1552, which substantially changed the liturgy and its rites, caused more trouble, not least among a conservative clergy. Before the Marian restoration of Catholicism in 1553, with the queen's instruction that henceforth religious practice would be that 'of old time used', the damage had been done. Rightly or wrongly, liturgical change, introduced with repressive measures, came to be associated with a colonialism which threatened not only the lands and titles of many in Gaelic Ireland, but lives as well.

The Anglo-Irish, too, were resentful of change. In Primate Dowdall of Armagh they found an uncompromising defender of the conservative liturgy. His cousin was that same Sir Thomas Cusack who had been the chief architect of the moderate surrender and regrant policy. It was to him that Dowdall wrote, after an acrimonious confrontation with Archbishop Browne and other reformers, in the presence of the deputy in St Mary's Abbey in Dublin, that he 'would never be bishop where the holy mass was abolished'. Rather than conform, he went into exile in Europe.

He was reinstated when Queen Mary, still the supreme head of the church in Ireland, exercised her powers to restore Catholicism. Unlike in England, the Marian restoration produced no martyr in Ireland, a sure sign of how little progress had been made in converting the population, clerical as well as lay, to the new Protestant ways. But within six years Queen Elizabeth was on the throne, the act of supremacy (which imposed an oath on all ecclesiastics, office holders, those suing for livery of lands, and those taking university degrees) was forced through the Dublin parliament. An act of uniformity restored the English prayer book and made attendance at the new liturgy each Sunday compulsory for all, under pain of a fine of one shilling.

But to enforce the Elizabethan settlement it was necessary to mount a programme of persuasion and coercion far beyond the resources available, either in men of the right calibre or suitable ecclesiastical structures. A catechism in Irish (which has the distinction of being the first book printed in Irish) did not appear until 1571 and it was not until 1603 that a *New Testament* in Irish was printed. Although new parochial schools began in the 1570s, it was not until 1592, with the foundation of Trinity College, that provision was made for Protestant education at university level. There was little evidence, too, that prescribed penalties were imposed on those who failed to observe the law in religious matters. Too many of the people who mattered, even within the Pale, were recusants. In 1580 a Protestant fanatic, Barnaby Rich, could report that the whole country

> 'does swarm with Jesuits, seminaries, and massing priests, yea, the friars and these do keep such continual and daily buzzing in the poor people's ears that they are not only led from all duty and obedience of their prince, but also drawn from God by superstitious idolatry and so brought headlong by heaps into hell.'

From the beginning of the reformation great stress had been laid on the importance of education in the process of change. An act of 1538 proposed the setting up of schools in every parish to promote the English language and through it religious change. But it was mainly Catholic teachers who established schools, like that which Peter White opened in Kilkenny in 1565. One of his best known pupils was Richard Stanyhurst; others were some of the leading Catholic missionaries who came back to Ireland later – Archer, Comerford, Lombard, Strong and Walsh. There were very few Protestant schools which could successfully compete with the Catholic ones, and because Dublin University was not founded until 1592, there was a continuous flow along traditional routes to pursue a higher education in Catholic Europe. Some, too, entered the new Jesuit colleges and the secular English college at Douai. Late in the century new Irish colleges were founded, both to meet the needs of the Irish mission and to educate the sons of Irish gentlemen: Salamanca in 1592, Douai (where the teaching of Irish to English-speaking students was part of the curriculum) in 1594; and a host of others, as many as 20, during the following century.

These colleges provided priests educated in the new Tridentine discipline and orthodoxy for the Irish mission. Led by the Jesuits, the counter-reformation began to make inroads in Ireland. During the reign of Elizabeth, however, the number of priests returning was small and if some of them played a conspicuous part in politics in the name of religion, most were concerned with checking the spread of heresy and looking after the spiritual wellbeing of the people. Neither they, nor the Catholic laymen who were educated abroad, identified with the militant tendencies of leaders who were using religion as an excuse for rebellion. But imbued with the spirit of the counter-reformation, fully adhering to the concept of freedom of conscience, and adopting the Bellarmine principle of dual loyalty, they were able to initiate a debate among the Anglo-Irish for religious toleration to be coupled with loyalty to the crown.

The position of the Anglo-Irish community – the 'middle nation' of an earlier period – had become increasingly difficult by the middle of the sixteenth century. Their identification with Ireland did not change. It was still their *patria* (homeland), in the words of one of them their 'native country' for which they had a 'natural affection'. As early as 1533 the Anglo-Irish author of a treatise presented to Cromwell wrote that he desired nothing more than 'the weal of my native country . . . as I was born there', a sentiment later echoed by Primate Dowdall when he was wrestling with his conscience. They still held aloof from the 'wild' Irish and considered the decay of 'the English tongue, the English rule, the English habit' as a primary cause of the decline of the medieval colony. So Dowdall argued in 1558, when he expounded to the queen's council his ideas as to how Ireland and the Irish might be 'reformed'.

Significantly, in discussing the Irish of Ulster, he indicated a shift in attitude towards the Irish in general by adding 'whom you call the wild Irish'. These were distinguished from the rest of the 'mere Irish', who were now in theory as secure under the law as were the Anglo-Irish and were therefore reformable. This was a logical development of the ideology underlining the surrender and regrant policy. Indeed another Anglo-Irish writer of the mid-sixteenth century, in addressing Irish lords called them his 'dear countrymen', who owed loyalty to their 'own mother Ireland'. Later in the century, Richard Stanyhurst showed that his attitude did not mean cultural assimilation in any marked degree. He could take pride in the glories of the Gaelic past, defend the 'ruder part' of the people of Ireland against the snide remarks of outsiders and argue that if the right guidance was made available to the Irish, then within two or three generations Ireland would 'be reckoned civil as the best part of Germany'. He wrote of 'the love I bear my native land', castigating those whom he called 'Ireland men . . . in no wise Irishmen'.

But he deplored the spread of the Irish tongue like a cancer within the Pale, and he called on all Anglo-Irishmen to shun it if they wished their *respublica* to survive. Even after he had gone into exile as a Catholic, he failed to identify with those Irish who were seeking in the name of religion to break with England. He was at the court of Philip II of Spain when an embassy from Gaelic Ireland arrived, offering him the kingdom of Ireland, and Stanyhurst immediately felt impelled to warn the king 'of the fickleness and weakness of those people'. It was only towards the end, when Hugh O Neill was seemingly invincible and the full weight of the counter-reformation was thrown behind the rebellion in Ireland, that he felt that he could wholeheartedly identify with the Irish attempt to break the connection with the English crown.

Stanyhurst represents the dilemma of the Anglo-Irish community, especially within the Pale. Catholic by conviction, identifying with the kingdom of Ireland, resentful of too much interference from England and particularly of the 'new' English officials and others who were settling in Ireland, they were still proud of their Englishness and anxious to retain their loyalty to the crown. This placed them apart – 'Anglo-Hiberni' according to Stanyhurst, though 'Newer Irish' according to his later critic Philip O Sullivan Beare, and 'Old English' (or more accurately Old *Gaill*) according to Geoffrey Keating. Even those who, like the third Earl of Desmond in the fourteenth century, had been sufficiently assimilated to compose poetry in Irish, could still display a sense of otherness. Christopher Nugent, a member of one of the most important Pale families, writing his Irish poems in exile around 1570, referred to Ireland as 'the land of *Gaill* and *Gael*', preserving the cultural distinction which for centuries had separated the two nations of Ireland.

Faced, then, with the problem of 'nationality with loyalty' (the famous phrase used by the great Irish historian Lecky of the Protestant patriots of the eighteenth century), the Anglo-Irish community, particularly of the Pale, were increasingly alienated by the new policy which favoured colonization of the lands bordering the Pale, from which they were largely excluded, and by the consequences of the change in policy towards the 'mere' Irish from conciliation to conquest and plantation. To implement this harsher policy, it was necessary for the new English officials to try to avoid the horrendous cost falling solely, or even mainly, on England. As the English garrison grew in numbers, the local community had to help to maintain it by what was called 'cess'. This was the medieval royal prerogative of purveyance, coupled with the obligation to military service which lay on every liege subject; it was particularly harsh in the Pale, where the burden largely fell. It has been estimated that in 1561 it cost about £20,000, which even in an affluent society would have been an intolerable imposition.

While the Anglo-Irish community had its well-to-do section, particularly among the merchants of the towns, it certainly did not have the wealth to sustain such a high level of what, in effect, was general taxation. Small wonder that the volume of complaints grew increasingly shrill. In 1576 a joint petition of 'the inhabitants of the English Pale' to the deputy Sydney and the council complained that 'for some years past we have been oppressed with cesses and exactions . . . whereby we are reduced to great decay and poverty'. Exaggerated it may have been, but it represents the anger and disillusionment of the men of the Pale with the Government. To them it must have seemed as if the worst excesses of coign and livery were being revived, like some dreaded ghost from the past, and, just as their ancestors had laid that ghost to rest, they too initiated a campaign which used parliament to fight their cause.

Constitutional resistance, based on their rights as subjects of the crown in a kingdom independent of England, fed by precedents provided by lawyers trained in the best traditions of the English inns of court, and fired by the history of their own community in Ireland from the time of Henry II – this was the road which the moderate party chose to follow. In Perrot's parliament of 1585–6 the speaker Walsh, himself a nominee of the Government, delivered a long address setting out the constitutional position. No Government could be autocratic, using power in an arbitrary fashion, king, lords and commons legislated together in parliament. The subject was protected by his status under the crown and there could, therefore, be no discrimination against one in favour of another. He even quoted an ancient sage: 'Better to save one citizen than to overthrow a thousand enemies'. The implications for relations with Gaelic Ireland were clear, since the Irish, too, were now 'citizens' of the state – 'this body politic', as he called it. All members of the body politic must be accepted by the Dublin government 'without any differences or distinctions of persons'. The queen was 'head of this body politic'. This echo of the 1460 declaration (Ireland was 'corporate of itself') was drawing on a long tradition of political autonomy, expressed through an independent parliament, and laid the constitutional basis of opposition to unacceptable programmes of reform for the future.

But such opposition needed parliament as a medium and there were few parliaments summoned in Ireland, and those were still controlled by the operation of Poynings' law. One alternative was to revert to an earlier practice of direct petition to the crown, using family ties or personal connections at court, or even the more formal channels of legal process, to subvert pro-grammes initiated by chief governors in Ireland. At this the Anglo-Irish became adept, drawing on experience gained by lawyers in the London inns of court. It was, however, an expensive tactic, slow and time-consuming, sub-ject to the whims of political change which might have nothing to do with what was happening in Ireland. There was another way, again an inheritance from the past, and that was open defiance and, if need be, rebellion. To the men of the Pale such a course was unthinkable, since loyalty to the monarch was the bedrock on which their constitutional position was founded. But the growing influence of counter-reformation ideas, brought back to Ireland by young students educated abroad, encouraged some to regard rebellion as a legitimate means of dissent.

During the first phase of the counter-reformation in Ireland the pope's envoys would not countenance rebellion against legitimately constituted authority, even if heretical. Archbishop Creagh of Armagh excommunicated Shane O Neill for this very reason and said that he hoped that his successor in Ulster would be 'true to his natural queen and crown of England, whom the lord God maintain now and forever'. That was in 1566, but the position changed, especially after Elizabeth was excommunicated in 1570. Now called 'the pretended queen' by the pope, her Catholic subjects were thus released from their allegiance.

In the summer of 1580 two of the leading Pale families were involved in rebellion. James Eustace, Viscount Baltinglass, and William Nugent, a brother of the Baron of Delvin, led an insurrection which was quickly put down. Baltinglass marched under a papal banner, announcing that no woman 'uncapax of all holy order' could ever be head of the church in Ireland. Worse, he proceeded to ally himself with the O Byrnes, traditional enemies of the Pale and in particular of his own family, who had suffered much from their raids in the past. In one memorable engagement, reminiscent of what happened centuries before, Fiach MacHugh O Byrne inflicted an ignomin-ious defeat on the army sent against him in his fastness of Glenmalure in the Wicklow mountains. His name passed into folklore and the victory of Glenmalure was used to inspire generations of rebels in the future. No wonder the deputy who had suffered the disgrace reacted furiously against those who had precipitated the crisis in the Pale. Baltinglass escaped to the continent, but Lord Grey instigated a reign of terror to root out the other subversives. The Earls of Kildare and Delvin were both arrested for treason; other Nugents were executed; members of suspect families, especially lawyers, were rounded up, charged, imprisoned, and in some cases put to death. Lands were confiscated and then distributed by the deputy to the army. Altogether 20 members of leading families were executed before Grey's fury could be checked. The Pale was deeply shocked.

It was against this background that a new deputy, Sir John Perrot, held the parliament of 1585–6, in which the men of the Pale mounted a constitutional opposition. Perrot had intended to enforce the oath of supremacy throughout Ireland and now this opposition in parliament became closely identified with recusancy. Their defence of Catholicism became inextricably intertwined with their political stance. That much, at least, had been achieved by Baltinglass. From now on the Anglo-Irish recusants were vehement in their adherence to the old religion, coupled with a defence of their concept of the body politic, resentful of ill-conceived interference by new English elements in Ireland. They were still, for the most part, opposed to any involvement with Gaelic Ireland in opposition to the crown, resentful of being identified simply as 'Irish' by ignorant commentators in England, and insisted (as a 1598 'discourse' put it) that they were 'the extract of the English nation' in Ireland. Significantly, the same author used, possibly for the first time, the label by which they came to be identified in the following century: 'Old English'.

Gaelic Ireland, of course, had no such inhibitions about armed resistance. By the time of the Baltinglass revolt, war had become almost endemic. Lord Grey's secretary was the famous poet Edmund Spenser and in his *A view of the present state of Ireland* (1596) he wrote of what he called 'the contagion' of rebellion from which 'there was no part free . . . but all conspired in one to cast off their subjection to the crown of England'. There was no coherent movement of independence, as Spenser suggested, except that defence of the old religion did provide a common purpose. But for years there had been widespread resistance to the threat posed to Irish chieftains by the forceful extension of English law and custom. Bellingham's intervention in Leix and Offaly, the dispossession of the O Mores and O Connors and their eventual resettlement 'beyond the bog', the planting of a colony which would protect the frontiers of the Pale, and the introduction of an English garrison to hold down the country, based on new fortresses, frightened Irish lords elsewhere.

By the time Elizabeth succeeded Mary as queen in November 1558, England was committed to a policy of repression and Ireland had become the 'problem' that was to bedevil Anglo-Irish relations for centuries to come. England could neither pull out and let Ireland go her own way – such an abrogation of responsibility was inconceivable, even if it was also politic with foreign enemies waiting to use her as a backdoor – nor extend royal authority throughout Ireland, except at a cost that was almost equally inconceivable. The Earl of Sussex, who was deputy in 1560, expressed a sentiment which was to be repeated many times in the future, when he wrote of Ireland 'which I have often wished to be sunk in the sea'. Frustration was to be the lot of many a chief governor.

When Sussex wrote this he had been deputy for four years and had vigorously campaigned throughout that time – twice against the Scots in Ulster, against O Connors in Offaly, O Neill in Tyrone, O Mores in Leix, and in Thomond in support of the new, loyal, O Brien earl. But it was Shane O Neill, son of the first Earl of Tyrone, who was the greatest problem. The death of Conn O Neill in 1559 left a vacancy, since his heir designate Matthew had died in the previous year. Who should succeed? Shane was the obvious candidate, not least because he was legitimate. But he had already made it clear that he wanted no part of the kind of tenurial relationship which had existed between his father and the crown. Rather he hankered to be an old-style chieftain, 'captain of his nation' in the Irish fashion, heir to the kingdom of Ulster with all the traditional rights and services due. When the English government insisted on the full application of principles derived from feudal law, which contravened Irish customary rights, a clash was inevitable. An instruction of May 1560 recognized Shane's nephew, now Baron of Dungannon (the title held by the heir designate to the earldom of Tyrone) as the person 'to whom by law and the grant of Henry VIII the earldom of Tyrone belongs' and by August the queen ordered his institution 'being the heir by right'. But Shane was all the time protesting his rights. There was a long exchange of letters between him and the queen and her advisors, with O Neill displaying an adroitness at diplomacy that must have astonished his adversaries. He expressed a desire to visit England, asked for money, even for an English wife; he began to impress the queen.

Meanwhile Sussex was trying to isolate him in Ireland, using O Donnell, the Scots and lesser chieftains against him. Ulster was invaded, Armagh garrisoned, and O Neill's army defeated. Sussex was able to boast that 'never before durst Scot or Irishman look an Englishman in the face in plain or wood since I was here'. But it was a delusion, Shane O Neill came back against the military odds, so that the deputy had to write bitterly that 'the fame of the English army – so hardly gotten – is now vanished, and I wrecked and dishonoured by other men's deeds'. Attempts to solve the problem by assassinating O Neill failed, a peace was concluded and finally O Neill appeared, under a guarantee of safe return to Ulster, at Elizabeth's court. There he made his case (he had been elected captain by his people), outwitted treacherous attempts to keep him in London, had his authority vaguely recognized, though he was refused the earldom, and even had his expenses paid. He claimed to rule as his dynasty had ruled for generations over the whole of Ulster and all its chieftains, except for O Donnell's country and part of Antrim.

When he returned to Ireland, Shane began to put his claims into practice. He also revived old animosities towards the O Donnells and attacked the Scots in Antrim. On 25 April 1566 he wrote to Charles IX of France, asking him for 5–6,000 well-armed troops to help in expelling the English and offered to become a subject of the king. By now Sussex had been succeeded in office by his brother-in-law, Sir Henry Sidney, a former vice-treasurer and a man with a considerable experience of Ireland.

Sidney believed that he had the answer to the problem of Ireland, which was in part based on a radical proposal first put forward by Sussex in 1562, and which would ultimately lead to the conquest of the island, begun as far back as the twelfth century but never brought to completion. In Ulster it would mean the removal of O Neill and the introduction of new English colonists. The new deputy therefore demanded a larger army, a regular supply of money and the full support of the English council. His intervention in Ulster would be decisive. He marched through O Neill's country and was spectacularly successful. But it was not he who finally brought down Shane O Neill. During an invasion of Tirconnell, O Neill was surprised by O Donnell near Letterkenny and his army was cut to pieces. Advised to seek help from the Antrim Scots, he used Sorley Beg MacDonnell, his prisoner since 1565, as a bargain to secure a force of galloglas. Instead he was treacherously cut down while being entertained at a banquet and his head was sent to Dublin, where it was triumphantly displayed on the castle wall. Four years later it was still there, according to Campion who claimed to have seen it, a mute testimony to the folly of resisting the military might of England.

Yet Shane's death settled nothing in England. A posthumous act of attainder in the Dublin parliament of 1569 proclaimed that:

> 'the name of O Neill, with the manner and ceremonies of his creation, and all the superiorities, titles, dignities, preeminences, jurisdictions, authorities, rules, tributes and expenses, used, claimed, usurped, or taken by any O Neill, as in right of that name . . . of any of the lords, captains, or people of Ulster, and all manner of offices given by the said O Neill, shall from henceforth cease, end, determine, and be utterly abolished and extinct for ever'.

Nothing could be more final. Sidney addressed the parliament, making it clear that he had only begun the conquest of Ireland and warning his Anglo-Irish listeners that the Irish were the common enemy, 'a sort of barbarous people, odious to God and man, that lap your blood as greedily as ours'. Yet Shane's successor, Turloch Luineach, had already been elected and inaugurated O Neill in Ulster, and although he made his peace with the queen in June 1572, he remained a captain in the Irish fashion. In 1569 he married Agnes Campbell, the widow of James MacDonnell and sister of the Earl of Argyl, who brought him a formidable force of 1,200 galloglas, which he augmented through the recruitment of other mercenaries to 3,000 and more. With this army he was impossible to crush and Ulster was left to go her own way, for the time being at least.

Sidney had other problems to deal with by then. His proposed conquest of Ireland, the creation of new presidency councils to govern Munster and

Connacht, and the radical scheme for colonization based on private enterprise, had all produced a violent reaction in Anglo- as well as Gaelic Ireland. His determination to break the power of the magnates (the traditional captains of nations as well as the newer nobility) was essential to his concept of civility which he felt bound to extend throughout Ireland. The common law was to be enforced, wherever possible, so that the Irish would be kept 'in dutiful obedience and civil quiet without permitting any more their brehon law to be used amongst them'. Society would be transformed on the English model. This would be done in Munster and Connacht through the aegis of provincial presidents and councils. These would, first of all, achieve military dominance and then undermine the power of the magnates, not least by reducing their rights of jurisdiction in old franchises – 'their pretended palatine liberties'.

In Connacht the presidency was established in December 1569 and was first limited to the earldoms of Clanrickard and Thomond. Under Sir Francis Fitton the province was shired, Irish laws and customs were prohibited and the chief landholders were made to give recognizances for good behaviour, all with the support of Clanrickard. Coign and livery were to cease, leading to a general disarmament. There was acrimony over the appointment of sheriffs. But it was Fitton's insensitive attempt to impose religious change which caused trouble. He went on circuit through Connacht, visiting 'sundry and many of the idols and images in their churches and committed them to the fire, and expelled and discharged sundry of the friars of Athenry and Kilconnell'. Attempts to impose a land tax based on ploughlands led to outright hostility, before he went back to England in 1574.

It was Sidney himself who continued the work, placing Thomond under the Munster presidency, establishing the county boundaries of Galway, Mayo, Roscommon and Sligo, introducing the common law, securing the submissions of chieftains in the north as well as the south of the province, and all the time curbing the power of the great lords. Under the new president, Sir Nicholas Malby, who was given 300 troops, resistance was crushed. It was he who first came to an arrangement with the landholders in 1577 that all the traditional exactions of the lords, especially coign and livery and including the controversial cess imposed to support the English garrison, would be commuted into an annual rent. In return, the presidency would see to defence in place of the lords who had traditionally done so.

This 'composition' was, in the first instance, designed to weaken the power of the same lords by striking at the traditional support of their armed retainers. By 1585 a new and more moderate composition of Connacht was introduced. This retained the rent of the 1577 composition, 10 shillings per quarter of land, which went to the government. But in addition, a new, second rent was now added which was paid to the lords as compensation for the traditional rights which they had lost. It undermined the Sidney policy of weakening the lords, who were to regain their dominant position through the wealth generated by the new rents. No wonder that an English critic of the composition wrote that it had raised the great lords 'higher than ever they were in riches, authority and number of followers'. It left the Anglo-Irish and not the new English dominant in Connacht. Not until the next century did they feel that their titles to their land were threatened.

It was otherwise in Munster, where the new presidency went disastrously wrong. The first president in 1566 was Sir Warham St Leger, son of the former deputy and architect of the moderate surrender and regrant policy. But persistent Desmond-Ormond disputes wrecked his chances of success and the presidency foundered. The activities of English adventurers in colonizing projects were now causing some alarm among the Anglo-Irish. When Sir Peter Carew came to Ireland in 1568 with claims to land in Munster and Leinster, held by his ancestors in the distant past, alarm grew. He successfully defended a claim to the manor of Maston in county Meath, held by the important Pale family of Cheevers. This caused a panic and when Carew went on to press his claims to the barony of Idrone, in county Carlow, the Butler overlords were outraged. Carew moved into Idrone and then laid claims against Sir Edmund Butler, brother of the Earl of Ormond, for adjoining land. Fearing that he would receive no justice in the royal courts, Butler took up arms. The absence of the earl, who might have restrained him, did not really matter. Given the long tradition of open warfare in which the Butlers had participated for generations, in particular against their Geraldine enemies, and which no government had ever been able to stamp out completely, Sir Edmund was not departing radically from family habit. His war, he said disingenuously, was not against the queen, but against Carew and those who threatened Ireland 'and mean conquest'.

There was another revolt in Munster, led by James Fitzmaurice Fitzgerald, cousin of the Earl of Desmond. The earl was now a prisoner in London and in his absence James was elected captain of the Geraldines. By 1569 he was openly defying Sidney and the Dublin government. He seems to have been in earnest when he raised his rebellion to the level of a religious crusade, condemning the queen as a heretic who was trying to force the Irish 'to forsake the Catholic faith by God unto his church given'. A meeting of rebel leaders decided to seek Spanish help and offer the Irish crown to Philip II. Maurice Mac Gibbon, the Catholic Archbishop of Cashel, led a delegation to Spain, where they were received by the king. They presented a memorial on behalf of 'the nobles and people' of Ireland, asserting their will 'to remain firm, constant and unshakeable to the faith and unity of the Catholic church, as also to persevere even to their last breath in their immemorial obedience and attachment to the Roman pontiffs and the apostolic see'. They condemned the schismatics Henry VIII, Edward VI and Elizabeth, and offered the crown to 'any Catholic and valiant prince' nominated by Philip. This remarkable renunciation of the queen's authority, supposedly signed by four Archbishops, eight bishops, and 13 'nobles', is a milestone in the history of the counter-reformation in Ireland and it gave the rebellion the character of a religious war supported by the church.

But in Munster itself the immediate cause of the war was the aggressive policy of Sidney, which seemed to threaten legal titles and the very basis of magnate power. Certainly the government's response showed that there was no room for diplomatic niceties or moderation. When Humphrey Gilbert was appointed as colonel of the province, with a brief to suppress the rebellion by force, he was given extraordinary powers by Sidney in September 1569. Martial law was introduced. Gilbert was authorized to proclaim as outlaw or rebel anyone 'that is a notorious offender or malefactor or shall wilfully refuse to come to answer the law'; to knock down the castle of any 'rebel or suspect person'; and to 'annoy in every way any such malefactor by fire and sword according to the quality of the offence and to use any kind of punishment upon the suspected person'. Gilbert made full use of his powers and war became total, so that non-combatants suffered equally with those who fought. Sidney reported that force was used against 'man, woman and child', so that 'the name of English man was made terrible to them'. One of Gilbert's lieutenants justified the slaughter of non-combatants, 'so that the killing of them by the sword was the way to kill the men of war by famine'. The same writer gave a horrific description of how each day Gilbert decapitated those who had been killed and had the heads laid out on each side of the approach to his own tent, so that any who wished to visit him had to 'pass through a lane of heads'. This brought 'great terror to the people when they saw the heads of their dead fathers, brothers, children, kinfolk and friends lie on the ground before their faces, as they came to speak with the said colonel'.

If it is hard now to understand the attitude which could commend such brutality, it is important to remember that to Sidney, Gilbert, Carew and others who came from Protestant England the Irish were never to be regarded as Christians. Their outlandish practices had long since condemned the Irish Catholics in the eyes of orthodox Catholicism. To extreme Protestants they were pagan, so that Sidney could readily compare Shane O Neill with the Huns and Turks. He also called him 'that cannibal', a term signifying the ultimate barbarism. If the Irish, then, were pagan and barbarous, there was no way they could be brought to civility except by the sword. Only then could they be converted to Christianity. So the normal moral law, which restrained indiscriminate killing, did not apply. When Barnaby Rich heard it argued that the English were 'too severe' in Ireland, he replied that the Irish were not to be treated like human beings. They 'live like beasts, void of law and good order . . . more uncivil, more uncleanly, more barbarous and more brutish in their customs and demeanours, than in any other part of the world that is known'.

Such an attitude was convenient, of course, to men who wished to expropriate landholders. When Carew wrote that one of his purposes in Ireland was 'the suppressing and reforming of the loose, barbarous and most wicked life of that savage nation', he was not only stressing the English mission of 'reform' or 'bringing civility', but was also emphasizing that it came after 'suppressing'. The whole structure of Gaelic or Gaelicized Ireland would have to be changed, English laws introduced, and then civility taught. In Munster it was not until a new president was appointed in 1576 that the policy of undermining the social structure of the province, and especially that based on brehon law, was taken in hand. But even then the chosen method was brute force rather than what Henry VIII had termed 'amiable persuasion'. Sir William Drury, the new president, not only indicted the Earl of Desmond and other lords for imposing coign and livery, he boasted that in less than two years he had executed 400 'masterless men'. His ruthless imposition of rents on the chief men of the province, the demolition of their castles, and the disbanding of their private armies naturally alienated many of them.

When James Fitzmaurice Fitzgerald invaded Munster in July 1579, having spent two years in Spain unsuccessfully trying to organize an expedition to Ireland, he was joined in rebellion by some of the disaffected, most notably Desmond. The invading force was pathetic: one ship and three fishing vessels with a total of 70 men, including the Bishop of Killala and a Spanish friar. Despite an elaborate proclamation calling on all Irishmen to forget their quarrels and take up arms, under the papal standard, to fight a just war against Elizabeth, few heeded the call. When Fitzmaurice was killed in a skirmish with some of the Burkes in August, Desmond was forced to assume the leadership of the rebels. Proclaimed an outlaw, he appealed for allies 'to join the defence of our Catholic faith against Englishmen who have overrun our country'. In Leinster, Viscount Baltinglass answered the call and joined forces with O Byrne.

In September 1580, a small papal force of 600 Spaniards and Italians landed at Smerwick harbour and occupied the old fort known as Dunanoir (the golden fort). There they were trapped, cut off by sea by English ships and facing the new deputy, Lord Grey, with his guns and an army of over 6,000 men. Their position was hopeless and they surrendered unconditionally, Grey immediately sent enough men into the fort to execute the disarmed garrison. In one of the most infamous massacres in Irish history 500 were slaughtered. What the poet Spenser, who was present with Grey at the time, called 'that sharp execution of the Spaniards at the fort of Smerwick' has ever since stained the reputation of the English commander. But he had promised no quarter, had procured from the foreigners an admission that they were 'not any lawful enemies' but 'adventurers', and they were therefore not entitled, he claimed, to 'either custom of war or law of nations'. Given the situation in Munster, where Desmond and his allies still posed a threat, Grey felt that there was only one course to take. In the words of Spenser, 'there was no other way but to make that short end of them which was made'.

Nothing illustrates more clearly the cold ruthlessness of Grey. No rebel, Irish or Anglo-Irish, and no foreign ally, could expect mercy. James, the younger brother of Desmond, was hanged and quartered in Cork. Others submitted, leaving Desmond to be hunted as a fugitive through the wilderness until he was finally assassinated, stripped of all his noble trappings, in the winter of 1583. By then Munster had been devastated by a war of extermination, made worse by the terrible famine which gripped the land. The population was reduced to the most miserable condition, recounted by Spenser in the most famous and most emotional passage in his *View*. Describing Munster as 'a most rich and plentiful country, full of corn and cattle', he told how a year and a half of war had brought the inhabitants

> 'to such wretchedness, as any stony heart would have rued the same. Out of every corner of the woods and glens they came creeping forth upon their hands, for their legs could not bear them. They looked anatomies of death, they spoke like ghosts crying out of their graves, they did eat of the dead carrions, happy where they could find them, yea and one another soon after in so much that as the very carcasses they spared not to scrape out of their graves, and if they found a plot of water cress or shamrocks, there they flocked as to a feast for the time, yet not able long to continue therewith, that in short space there were none almost left and a most populous and plentiful country suddenly left void of man or beast. Yet sure in all that war there perished not many by the sword, but all by the extremity of famine, which they themselves had wrought'.

Desmond's death in 1583 was followed by his attainder in the 1586 session of Perrot's parliament. With him were attainted a total of 139 rebels, as well as others unknown. All forfeited their 'honours, castles, manors, messuages, lands, tenements, rents, reversions, remainders, possessions, rights, conditions, interests, offices, fees, annuities, and all other their hereditaments, goods, chattels, debts and other things . . . which they . . . had to their uses'. As a result nearly 600,000 acres of land escheated to the crown.

But already a scheme of plantation had been worked out in London. The land was divided into 'seigniories' of 12,000, 8,000, 6,000 and 4,000 acres each, with appropriate rents for the different divisions. The 'undertakers', all English, had to guarantee that no land would be leased to native Irish. The number of families required to settle the land was worked out, the cost of moving them to Ireland, and what each family would need in the way of provisions to enable them to survive. In the spring of 1584 the work of surveying and fixing boundaries was begun, though it was not until 1586 that four surveyors arrived in Munster to commence work on the ground. But when only 60,000 acres had been dealt with the survey was abandoned and the undertakers were left to agree on divisions among themselves.

That was a recipe for trouble and it led to conflict, litigation, and an inability to occupy much land. The inadequacies of the scheme were exposed. Social engineering on the ambitious scale envisaged by the original plantation plans was quite beyond the capacity of the governments in London and Dublin. To confuse matters further, many of the dispossessed petitioned against undertaker claims and a surprising number subsequently had their petitions upheld. Some undertakers lost badly as a result. For example, in 1591 the privy council upheld a petition against Henry Cuffe, who had been granted 12,000 acres in Cork, so that he lost all but 1,953 of those acres.

There was no wholesale expropriation of the existing Irish tenants, many of whom remained in occupation, often paying rents to undertakers who tried to make the best of a bad job. So there was little real plantation of English tenants. Those who did settle in Munster were surrounded by Irish and when rebellion returned to the province once more in 1598, they were too few to be able to defend themselves and their new settlements. The main purpose of the plantation scheme, anglicization, was thoroughly defeated.

By the time of the Munster plantation, an Elizabethan conquest of Ireland seemed not far from completion. Despite the strong Anglo-Irish reaction to the new oppressive policies of the government, resulting in five distinct Anglo-Irish rebellions between 1568 and 1574, the three provinces of Leinster, Munster and Connacht had been largely reduced to obedience. When the remnants of the great Spanish armada of 1588 were shipwrecked off the coast of Ireland, with the loss of about 25 ships, the survivors got short shrift everywhere except in north Connacht and Munster. The strong arm of the president, Sir Richard Bingham, kept Connacht quiet. He dealt ruthlessly with dangerous foes. On 22 September 1586, for example, he put to the sword 2,000 Scots, including women and children accompanying the galloglas, when they arrived in Mayo to take service with the Burkes. For this – 'the only piece of service, next to Smerwick, that has been done in this land in many years', according to a contemporary – Bingham was reprimanded by the government. But he continued to have his way, applying martial law and cutting legal corners, so that even north Connacht was finally brought under control.

Only in Ulster did the old Gaelic system substantially survive intact. A proposed presidency council had come to nothing. But there had been some experiments with colonization. First, in 1571, Sir Thomas Smith, one of England's leading intellectuals, undertook to colonize a large area based on the Ards peninsula in county Down. In a novel experiment, which would later be copied for other projects in the New World, he issued broadsheets in a propaganda campaign designed to persuade merchants to invest money and gentry to lead tenants as colonists. Nearly 800 men eventually assembled at Liverpool early in 1572 to go to Ireland and a great deal of money was contributed by investors in joint-stock to finance the enterprise, with Smith himself heading the list with £450. But a long delay, and the appointment of Smith as ambassador to France, led to many defections and eventually only 100 men landed in Ulster in August 1572. In the end the whole enterprise fizzled out.

A more extensive effort at colonization was led by Walter Devereux, Earl of Essex, who attempted to occupy Clandeboy in August 1573. The rights of the local Irish, in particular Sir Brian O Neill, were put on one side. But the whole enterprise was a disaster, costing the queen £21,250 and the total cost to all concerned was well in excess of £100,000. It also left in Ulster a legacy of hatred, after senseless acts of treachery which achieved nothing. The seizure of Sir Brian O Neill (who was later sent to Dublin for execution) and his wife, and the slaughter of 200 of his followers, at a parley in the winter of 1574, was only exceeded by the massacre of the population of Rathlin Island, including women and children, about 600 in all, in July 1575. This was in direct contradiction to the bland assurances Essex had given the queen, when he was proposing colonization, that he would not redden his hands with more blood 'than the necessity of the cause requires'. His death in September 1576 was a relief to all.

But the damage had been done. An Irish annalist described the execution of O Neill as 'a sufficient cause of hatred and disgust (of the English) to the Irish'. Such hatred was growing, generated by the harsh policies pursued by the English in Ireland. It was a fact accepted by the New English themselves. In 1572 the deputy, Sir William Fitzwilliam, wrote that the names of 'England and English were waxing generally and in toto apparently hateful' to the Irish. The first man to exploit this hatred and turn it to profit was Hugh O Neill.

Hugh was the grandson of the first Earl of Tyrone and a son of the first Baron of Dungannon. His father had been killed by Shane O Neill in 1558 and his brother, the second Baron of Dungannon, by Turloch O Neill, so there was no love lost between these two. Hugh was educated in England, acquired English ways, and after he returned to Ireland served the queen in Munster. He cooperated with Essex in his colonization project and took his place in parliament in 1585. His usefulness to the Government was apparent. Seemingly English in sympathy, antagonistic towards Turloch O Neill, a model of civility in a hostile and barbarous land, he could clearly be trusted to promote the queen's peace in Ulster. In 1587 he was made Earl of Tyrone, with the reservation that his authority should be confined to the earldom, whose boundaries were to be clearly defined, and not extend to any of the traditional vassal chieftains of the O Neill.

But the earl had already been made tanist, or successor, of Turloch O Neill in 1584 and would therefore be inaugurated O Neill, with all that implied, at some date in the future. His ambitions were centred on Gaelic Ulster, and not on a diminished, anglicized earldom. The Englishness was a veneer. Yet he was patient, calming the queen with assertions of loyalty, complaining of the lack of civility among his people, offering in 1590 to 'renounce the name and title of O Neill', to 'have his country made shire ground', and to accept for himself and his tenants the same principle of composition as had been imposed in Munster and Connacht. In 1561 he had married Mabel Bagenal, sister of Sir Henry Bagenal, marshal of the army, and in 1593 he assisted Bagenal in his attack on Fermanagh. On 13 August 1594 he unexpectedly appeared at a council meeting in Dublin, explaining the reasons for his absence hitherto, protesting that 'her majesty's displeasure has been my greatest grief' and offering his services in war. Yet the following June he attacked and defeated Bagenal's army at Clontibret in county Monaghan and within days was publicly proclaimed a traitor. Almost on cue, Turloch O Neill died in September and Tyrone immediately succeeded him as O Neill.

Tyrone had acquired in England a military expertise which he put to good use in Ireland. He showed his abilities in Munster while fighting for the queen. In Ulster he painstakingly built up an army of his own on English lines, importing modern arms and ammunition from Scotland, and augmenting the traditional force of galloglas from the western highlands. His victory at Clontibret in 1595 showed how strong he was. A contemporary report warned that his rebellion would cost the queen more than any previous war, for

> 'educated, more disciplined, and naturally valiant, he is worthily reputed the best man of war of his nation. Most of his followers are well-trained soldiers, using our weapons; and he is the greatest man of territory and revenue within that kingdom, and is absolute commander of the north of Ireland'.

By then the earl was leading a confederacy of Ulster chieftains in rebellion, defending the province from anglicization, in correspondence with Philip II of Spain on behalf of 'the whole Irish nobility', offering him the kingdom of Ireland, and posing as the defender of the old religion. The rebellion was to spread, involving more and more of Ireland, and Hugh O Neill was to come closer than anyone before to the ideal of a national leader against English oppression.

At first his concentration was on Ulster. There he was followed by the leading Irish chieftains, most notably his two sons-in-law, Hugh Roe O Donnell of Tirconnell, who had been succoured by Tyrone after his spectacular escape from Dublin castle in the winter of 1591, and Hugh Maguire of Fermanagh. These had buried traditional rivalries and made common cause against English attempts to insert garrisons and subvert Gaelic institutions in their countries. Others like O Rourke and MacMahon, had joined them, so that by the time O Neill openly rebelled in 1595 the whole of Gaelic Ulster was prepared for war. To make sure that he had time to gather as much support as possible, O Neill entered into protracted negotiations with the government. He insisted that he was representing all the chieftains in rebellion and at a later stage in the negotiations he and O Donnell demanded that the Leinster rebels, including Fiach Mac Hugh O Byrne, should be covered by whatever treaty resulted. It is significant, too, that the two main demands of the rebels were that 'no garrison, sheriff or other officer' should remain in their countries, and that 'all persons may have liberty of conscience'.

This latter demand would seem to indicate that the rebels' claim to be defending Catholicism was no mere ploy to engage foreign help for a religious cause. An appeal by O Neill and his confederates to 'the gentlemen of Munster' on 6 July 1596 called on them to join in making war on the English in defence of 'Christ's Catholic religion'. This appeal did not go unheeded and attacks on English settlements in Munster began. In Leinster O Byrne rose again.

But there was no Anglo-Irish response. They were convinced that O Neill was insincere in his Catholic protest and there was no papal support such as might convince them that the rebels were fighting in a just cause. Indeed it was not until Peter Lombard of the University of Louvain became O Neill's personal representative in Rome late in 1599 that the pope began to listen to appeals from Ireland. Lombard worked assiduously, briefing the pope and anyone likely to influence him on what was happening in Ireland. He even wrote an account of Ireland's history and geography that was designed to show that O Neill and his allies were fighting for 'the vindication of the Catholic religion, the glory of God, the liberty of their country and their own security'. This association of the Catholic faith with liberty was the main purpose of Lombard's propaganda. Pope Clement VIII was at last convinced and in April 1600 issued an address to the Irish people which proclaimed the war against Elizabeth to be on the same level as the war against the Turks and granted a plenary indulgence to anyone who helped O Neill.

But nothing would persuade him to excommunicate those who were helping the queen in Ireland, especially those Catholic Anglo-Irish who were supporting the English forces. Even the nomination of a papal nuncio, which would enhance the prestige of the rebellion, was delayed and the man finally chosen, the Italian Jesuit Mansoni, was unsuitable and unwanted in Ireland. Before the nuncio left Spain, news of the disaster at Kinsale reached the pope in Rome. Clement expressed his grief, but did nothing. Finally, when James VI of Scotland succeeded Elizabeth a few days after her death in 1603, Clement voiced his 'inexpressible joy', convinced that by the providence of God, James had 'now become the most powerful King of the three kingdoms of England, Scotland and Ireland' who would deal favourably with his Catholic subjects. But King James I of England did the opposite, outlawing Catholic priests, fining anyone who succoured them, rewarding informers, Clement's hopes were shattered. The lack of a more positive papal response to the rebellion in Ireland had finally produced the inevitable result.

There is some evidence that O Neill was ambitious to win more than Ulster for himself and freedom of religion for all Catholic subjects. In 1595, after openly identifying with the northern rebellion, he appointed the Bishop of Killaloe to argue his case for help with the pope. In his letter the bishop first asked the pope to annul 'the bull of Adrian IV granting dominion over Ireland to Henry II', free Ireland from English jurisdiction, excommunicate all supporting the English and grant indulgence to 'those who join O Neill and his army against the English'. If he did so, 'all Ireland from the youngest to the oldest will in a short time take up arms against the English and with the help of God will shake off their yoke and drive them from Ireland'. He also presented a petition from the 'bishops and princes of Ireland . . . to appoint the Earl of Tyrone King of Ireland'. All were willing to obey him as 'the one to whom the kingship of Ireland belongs by right of descent'. The bishop can hardly have been reviving O Neill claims to the old high kingship of Ireland without the knowledge and consent of Tyrone. But it may have been nothing more than a device to claim some kind of legitimacy for the rebellion. It is unique to this occasion and in the diplomatic correspondence with the papacy and the Spanish court there is no mention of it. But it does give some credence to Anglo-Irish fears.

Meanwhile, O Neill had made good use of the time won by the continuation of the truce. On 14 August 1598, together with O Donnell and Maguire he destroyed an army of 4,000 commanded by Bagenal at the battle of the Yellow Ford in county Armagh. More than half the force was lost. Bagenal himself was killed and most of the equipment fell into Irish hands. It was a famous victory and the results were immediately apparent. Connacht now fell under the control of O Donnell; O More attacked the Leix-Offaly settlers; Munster was invaded by a northern army and the settlers there either murdered or forced to flee for their lives. Far from completing the conquest of Ireland, as had seemed so imminent a short time before, Elizabeth now found herself facing the prospect of a collapse of her authority throughout the island. It was no time for parsimony and, after sending reinforcements in the winter of 1598–9, nearly 10,000 men in all, she appointed a new chief governor in March 1599. This was Robert Devereux, the second Earl of Essex, her great favourite. With him came a massive force of nearly 17,000 men, by far the largest army sent to Ireland by England. His mission was immediately to face O Neill, crush him and force him into submission.

But Essex proved to be no military tactician. Instead of going north, he divided his army, placing some in garrisons and leading the remainder on what amounted to spectacular and costly, but useless, progresses through Leinster and Munster. Worse, other armies suffered defeats which London regarded as shameful in Wicklow, Louth, Kildare and most spectacular of all in Roscommon, where O Donnell destroyed Clifford in the Curlew mountains. Clifford was killed with nearly a third of his men. The queen was furious and ordered Essex to move into Ulster. O Neill met him at Carrickmacross in county Monaghan, held a parley, and then astonishingly persuaded Essex to agree to a truce. Later in London, when Essex was accused of treason, it was stated that O Neill had promised the earl that if he would 'stand for himself' the Irishman 'would join with him'. Philip II's agent in Ireland also reported that 'O Neill had almost prevailed upon the Earl of Essex to desert the queen's cause and join that of your majesty and surrender all the realm to you'. Whatever the truth, there is no doubt that Essex made a fool of himself in Ireland. Worse, he had deserted his Irish post despite the queen's specific instructions not to do so. Not for the first, or the last, time was an English reputation ruined in Ireland.

With the departure of Essex, the ascendancy of O Neill was confirmed. In the winter of 1599–1600 he made what amounted to a triumphal progress south into Leinster and Munster as far as Kinsale; at the same time negotiations with Spain were stepped up. In the hope of persuading the Spanish king to send an army to Ireland, there was sustained diplomatic activity. In September 1596 ships with arms and ammunition had arrived in Donegal, in

October a fleet had been assembled and sailed for Ireland; but fierce storms forced the ships back and the mission had to be abandoned. When Philip II died in 1598 it seemed that a Spanish army would never land in Ireland. More arms and ammunition were sent in 1599 and again in 1600; but no army. On 24 April 1600 Matthew de Oviedo, sent to Ireland by Philip III, reported to the king: 'As the oft-promised aid from Spain was hourly expected, when we arrived with empty hands, only again to repeat the old promises, they were overcome with sorrow and dismay'. He emphasized that while 'O Neill has overrun all Munster' and 'O Donnell has subjected Connacht', and both 'are full of courage, they cannot prevail over the other chiefs and their followers, who fear the long delay in the arrival of succour and suspect that they are being played with'. Reinforcements were an urgent necessity and Oviedo asked for 6,000 men. He told the king that with them he 'may carry through an enterprise which will bridle English insolence in Flanders and secure Spain and the Indies from molestation'.

The force of the last argument carried weight. In January 1601 the treaty of Lyons between France and Savoy suddenly freed Spain from an obligation to send troops to Archduke Albert and the decision was taken to send 6,000 men to Ireland. By August, 43 companies, numbering 4,432 men in all, were assembled at Lisbon and sailed to Ireland under the command of Don Juan del Aquila. A storm detached four ships, with 674 men as well as vital supplies, so eventually a depleted force landed at Kinsale on 21 September. By October, disease and mishap had taken their toll, so that only about 2,500 men were fit for battle. These were poorly equipped and as each day passed the number was further reduced. Frantic messages to Spain went unanswered. It was not until December that six ships, with about 600 men and badly needed supplies and arms, managed to reach west Cork, miles away from Kinsale. Their arrival did lead to a west Munster rising in support of O Neill and gave hope of an ultimate Irish victory. But by then Aquila and the Spaniards were trapped under siege in Kinsale.

The arrival of Aquila at the other end of Ireland was a blow to the rebels in Ulster. But when he submitted to siege there was consternation. O Neill and his allies knew well that whatever success they had enjoyed in the past would be swept away unless they gained a decisive victory over the English. The only hope of that lay in a joint operation with the Spaniards, for by 1601 the situation in Ireland had changed dramatically. The appointment of Lord Mountjoy, a soldier as well as administrator, as deputy in January 1600, with the subsequent appointment of Sir George Carew as president of Munster, had given the English forces badly needed leadership. A naval expedition in May was successful in landing a large force of 4,000 men and in establishing a base near Derry, while another army under Mountjoy pushed northwards by land. He failed to penetrate O Neill's territory, but pursued a scorched earth policy designed to starve the population into surrender. Ruthlessly maintaining the pressure, burning houses, cutting harvests and driving off stock, Mountjoy raided through Leinster as well as into the north. Already the policy was working. Sir Arthur O Neill, the son of Turloch, and Niall Garbh O Donnell, cousin of Hugh, submitted and were soon followed by others. By October Mountjoy had succeeded in penetrating beyond Newry and had demolished O Neill's defences on the Moiry pass.

Meanwhile Carew had destroyed the alliance in Munster. Both O Neill and O Donnell failed to stiffen resistance by raids into the south. By the time the Spaniards arrived in September 1601, Munster was lost to the rebellion. Widespread support in Munster had been the basis of the decision, supported by O Neill and O Donnell, to land there. When the northern leaders finally realized that support in Munster had collapsed, it was too late to divert the Spaniards to land further north. Mountjoy, too, had anticipated a Munster landing and refused to be diverted to Ulster. He even took men from the northern forts, risking all on facing a Spanish invasion in the south. The risk was well justified when he was able to pin Aquila in Kinsale, placing an embargo by sea so that ships could not sail into the port. There was nothing the northern leaders could do but try to make contact with the Spaniards. Even before the siege of Kinsale began on 26 October, O Donnell had set out with his troops on the 23rd. A week later O Neill and his army followed.

It was the greatest march in Irish history to that date and it meant leaving their bases in Ulster open to attack in the event of failure. But a victory over Mountjoy would certainly have turned the war in their favour and would have freed the Spaniards to fight with them throughout Ireland. Further Spanish help would then seem certain, to carry the war into England itself, and the independent Catholic Ireland O Neill had fought for would be a reality. But a series of mistakes, and not least a fatal tactical blunder by O Neill himself, gave the victory to Mountjoy and virtually ended the greatest rebellion the English had ever faced in Ireland. Aquila made honourable terms, sailed home with his forces virtually intact, and was not only cleared of any suspicion of misconduct, but was praised by a subsequent royal inquiry in Spain. The expedition to Ireland may not have achieved a victory in the field, but it certainly benefited Philip III in his dealings with England.

For O Neill, however, Kinsale was the ultimate disaster, O Donnell left immediately for Spain, where he died the following year, vainly seeking further help. Mountjoy took precautions against a future invasion, building a string of forts, before turning his attention to Ulster. O Neill was forced to abandon Dungannon and took refuge in the woods to the north. Once again the English wasted the countryside, starving the people to shut off support for the rebels. In a symbolic gesture, Mountjoy demolished 'the chair wherein the O Neills were wont to be created' at the age-old inauguration site at Tullahogue. It marked the end not only of the hegemony which O Neill had created, but centuries of Gaelic tradition. Ulster was now to be anglicized with a vengeance, once O Neill's resistance was overcome.

O Neill had no option but to negotiate terms of submission. In England Elizabeth was dying, unknown to the chief protagonists in the war in Ireland. Befuddled with age, she finally instructed Mountjoy to offer a pardon to

O Neill. By the time he formally submitted at Mellifont in October 1603, the queen was dead. Considering all that had happened, O Neill was leniently treated, even if personally humiliated, Mountjoy's secretary described how he was made to kneel for an hour 'making his penitent submission to her majesty'. He had to give up his Gaelic title, and with it his ancestral rights, allow sheriffs and garrisons into his territories, and renounce the King of Spain. Later O Neill travelled to England with Mountjoy and was graciously received by James I. He had preserved his earldom intact and, at the expense of abandoning Gaelic institutions, was made the sole owner of his lands and guaranteed in his authority locally. The same generous terms were extended to Rory O Donnell, brother of the late Hugh, who was elevated to the earldom of Tyrconnell in 1603. There was no attempt to organize Ulster into a presidency on the model of Munster or Connacht.

Yet Irish lordships had been wiped out everywhere and land was mostly held according to English law. This land was now garrisoned to an extent unimaginable even a generation earlier. To that extent Elizabeth, at enormous cost in money, and an even greater cost in Irish lives lost through the wars and resultant famines, had conquered Ireland. The old division which had lasted for centuries between Gaelic and feudal Ireland was now all but obliterated. In Ulster the great chieftains had become peers of the realm. The province was shired into nine counties, with sheriffs and the whole apparatus of English local government. For a time O Neill managed to preserve his status in the new circumstances, effectively ruling over three counties. But the pressure of the forces of anglicization was inexorable, establishing the rights of freeholders to the lands they occupied, irrespective of the proprietary rights enjoyed by their lords under Irish custom. A proclamation of 11 March 1604 declared that all persons in the realm were the 'free, natural and immediate' subjects of the king, and not the subjects of any lord or chief. The common law of England was imposed, insisting that land descend through a system of primogeniture. The main protagonist was the gifted Sir John Davies, solicitor general, who was determined, as he said himself, to make the Irish 'become English'. The shadow of Carew and claims to land which might be upheld in English courts loomed again.

O Neill became involved in a dispute with his son-in-law O Cahan over land confirmed to the earl by the treaty of Mellifont. In July 1607 he was summoned to London with O Cahan to have the dispute resolved. The possibility of the decision going against him was enough to worry the earl. But a more serious possibility, given what had happened to others throughout the sixteenth century, was that he might be detained in London and prevented from returning to Ireland. As far back as December 1605 his son Henry had become the colonel of an Irish regiment serving with the Spaniards in the Netherlands. This had compromised O Neill and raised the suspicion that he was once again seeking Spanish help in a new rebellion. The award of an annual pension of 4,000 ducats by the Spanish Government did nothing to allay such fears.

When Maguire went to Europe in 1607 alarm grew. It was known, too, that O Donnell was planning to go abroad and the English government grew increasingly suspicious. The sudden return of Maguire in August, with transport for O Donnell to Europe, created a problem for O Neill. If he remained in Ulster, with the others plotting in Europe, there was no way that he could dispel the suspicion that he was involved in a Spanish plot. He suddenly decided to join O Donnell, Maguire and other chieftains and abandon Ulster. On 4 September 1607 they sailed from Lough Swilly and left Ireland forever.

This 'flight of the earls' marked the end of an era. One of those on board was Tadhg Ó Cianáin, a professional historian employed by Maguire. He compiled a diary of the journey into exile as far as Rome and provided a glimpse of the trials, as well as the minor triumphs, of the exiles. The pain of separation was especially cruel. He had left his own wife behind and there is no evidence that he ever saw her again. The earls had their immediate families with them and were received with honour in Rome. But they died in exile there, O Donnell a few months after they arrived and O Neill in 1616.

Their tragedy was personal. But Gaelic Ulster, abandoned by most of the traditional leaders, suffered more. The annals of the Four Masters recorded the events which led to the flight in sober terms, but they could not forbear from a great wail of sorrow at the implications of the event: 'Woe to the heart that meditated, woe to the mind that conceived, woe to the council that decided on, the project of their setting out on this voyage'. A poet cried: 'Tonight Ireland is desolate . . . no reciting of poems of praise, no relating of stories at sleeping time, no interest in consulting books, no harkening to genealogies'. It was a cultural disaster and the beginning of a process which was to drive the Gaelic tradition from its traditional, aristocratic fastness to a more popular level and end the endowments which had kept it alive from time immemorial.

Sir John Davies put another gloss on the flight in his official report to England. Everyone in Ireland, he wrote, was glad to see Tyrone banished, 'which the best army in Europe and the expense of two million of sterling pounds did not bring to pass'. O Neill had found that 'the law of England, and the ministers thereof, were shackles and handlocks unto him, and the garrisons planted in his country were pricks in his side'. Now it was hoped that the government

'will work a greater miracle in this kingdom than ever St Patrick did, for St Patrick only banished the poisonous worms, but suffered the men full of poison to inhabit the land still; but his majesty's blessed genius will banish all those generations of vipers out of it, and make it, ere long, a right fortunate island'.

In abandoning Ireland, O Neill and the others had provided the long-sought opportunity for wholesale colonization and anglicization in depth of their lands. No wonder an Irish poet composed what was a national lament, *Mo thruaigh mar táid Gaoidhil* (Pitiful are the Gaeil), bewailing the disappearance of honoured customs and habits, the land conquered and no relief in sight: 'If providence has ordained that Ireland – a new England in all but name – should be in the hands of enemies in their time it is fitting to bid farewell to the isle'.

8　A new Ireland

On 17 September 1607, less than a fortnight after the flight of the earls, Sir Arthur Chichester (who had been appointed lord deputy in 1605) submitted proposals to the privy council in England for the disposal of the lands of those who had fled. In December the fugitives were indicted for treason, their lands declared forfeit, and plans were rapidly put in hand for colonization. When Sir Cahir O'Doherty, lord of Inishowen, alarmed at the prospect rose in rebellion, the government's resolve to plant was strengthened. By September 1608 a preliminary survey of six Ulster counties – Armagh, Cavan, Coleraine, Donegal, Fermanagh and Tyrone – declared most of the land escheated to the crown. Within a few months detailed plans for planting the escheated lands were published, a new survey was undertaken, the area was mapped and divided, and by 1610 lands were being assigned. The plantation of Ulster was now underway, an undertaking which was to change the face of northern Ireland and with effects which have lasted down to the present time.

Despite the reservations of Chichester, it was the method of wholesale expropriation of the Irish, forcefully advocated by Sir John Davies, which prevailed. Ulster was to be anglicized, not by 'civilizing' the Irish, but by saturating the province with colonists who would introduce settlers from England and Scotland. Social engineering on this scale demanded the most careful planning. Three commissions of 1608, 1609 and 1610 did the fieldwork and provided the planners with the information needed if the kind of mistakes made in the earlier Munster plantation were to be avoided. Above all, exact cartographical information was required. Between August 1609, when the commissioners under Chichester and Davies reached Armagh, and 29 September, when the work was completed in Cavan, a survey of the land to be planted was reduced to maps. By March 1610 these maps, with accompanying inquisitions, were safely in London. No wonder Davies was well satisfied with his work. In a letter to England he wrote that he wished 'that his majesty, with one of his far-seeing glasses, could see his commissioners and other his ministers here in Ulster, everyone performing his several duty'. As a result, he wrote, 'the plantation itself will succeed and be fully accomplished'. Later he boasted of the success of the inquisitions which provided the crown with legal title and took pride in the cartographic survey which had been so 'exactly and particularly done' that 'the most obscure and unknown part of the king's dominions is now as well known and particularly described as any part of England'.

His optimism was misplaced. Persistent rumours that Tyrone was going to invade Ulster was only one fact which led to 'no small discouragement of the plantation'. A more important weakness were the surveys which, because of their inaccuracy, resulted in most grantees receiving more land than the acreage stipulated on paper. One result of this was that native tenants remained on many lands. So the original plan for the removal of the natives (with the exception of a small number of 'deserving Irish', who were to be given lands elsewhere) and their complete segregation from the new Protestant (and therefore by definition 'loyal') settlers from England and Scotland, was never realized. It also proved economically more attractive to retain native tenants, even despite fines and government pressure. So, instead of the neat scheme of plantation envisaged by the planners, with undertakers holding blocks of land farmed by imported tenants in the English fashion, there was a mixture of the old and the new throughout most of the confiscated area.

Nevertheless new towns and villages were built to plan, lands were enclosed and tillage became more widespread, markets and fairs proliferated, and the province was given a new basis for the kind of economic development which was to provide a rich return for those who had invested their money in plantation. The incorporation of towns – Dungannon in 1612, Coleraine, Londonderry and Belfast in 1613 – was one measure of progress. Altogether 16 of the proposed 25 new boroughs were incorporated and each was built according to a uniform plan. Some were substantial. By 1616 Derry had 215 new stone houses inside the walls. This had risen to 265 12 years later and the rapid expansion of suburbs indicated pressure on space within the walls. In most of the new towns, however, the number of houses was less than 40 and in some cases was less than the planned 20. Population varied from one place to the next. In 1630, for example, Enniskillen had only 60 adult males and that was fairly typical. But Virginia in the same year had only 19. It is clear that the optimistic plans for a controlled migration had come unstuck.

Despite this, there was a very large influx of new people into Ulster, much of it into areas outside the six counties comprising the area it was originally proposed to plant. Thousands of Scots, for example, poured into Down and Antrim, reinforcing the already significant Scottish element in the populations. Strongly Protestant in character, they were to introduce a radical element into the area which helped to make the north-east prosperous as well as ethnically different. The Scots also came in substantial numbers as tenants on the new estates in the planted area. Such was the level of emigration that in 1636 a proclamation banned any Scot from coming to Ireland without licence. But they continued to come throughout the century and the Scottish colony grew to be almost a little Scotland beyond the sea. The

'Scottish nation in the north of Ireland', as it called itself, formed a powerful political as well as religious presence in Ulster. By the 1640s, Presbyterians had become dominant among the Scots and henceforth Presbyterian Ulster was to provide a powerful religious, political, radical and even military voice in Ireland. A social revolution of immense significance for the future of the province, and indeed of the island at large, had taken place.

Other parts of Ireland were also planted. Crown title to lands was established and then parts of Wexford, Longford, Leitrim, Ely O'Carroll, King's County, Queen's County and Westmeath were granted to undertakers. Many of the native Irish were expropriated and thus a reservoir of resentment created which was later to supply a source of disaffection. Plans to settle Connacht failed, but in Munster the interrupted plantation of the previous century was renewed. By the 1630s the evidence suggests that as many as 20,000 settlers there enjoyed a level of prosperity which made it the most affluent of all English overseas settlements. As happened in Ulster, the newcomers did not confine themselves to the lands officially designated for plantation, but settled throughout the province wherever conditions suited. And, just as Ulster was to become almost an extension of Scotland, Munster moved ever more closely into contact with the south of England.

It seems clear, then, that quite apart from the planned migration which resulted from the plantations in Ulster, Munster and other localities, there was an extensive movement of British tenants and artisans to other estates in Ireland. With a small population, perhaps as low as 750,000 in 1600, and a density of only about 20 per square mile in rural areas, landowners were naturally anxious to encourage settlers who would help to make their lands profitable. An Earl of Thomond imported Dutch settlers and there were other occasional exotic importations. But the vast majority were Scots and English. An estimate of the total number of such immigrants before 1641 is as high as 100,000.

Such a large number was bound to dilute the native population in some parts of Ireland and to buttress the Protestant faith. In addition, emigration from Ireland helped that process. By about 1630 the flow of emigrants to America and the West Indies, mainly Catholic, though with some Presbyterians, and largely of indentured servants, was well established. Later, particularly in the 1650s, others were forced by government decree to migrate to Barbados, mainly priests, friars and schoolteachers. Both Sweden and Denmark, too, were able to recruit successfully in Ireland. Chichester claimed that, during his 11 years in office in Ireland (1605–16), he helped to recruit no fewer than 6,000 for Sweden. One large contingent of 1,600 was led by an O'Hanlon nephew of the Earl of Tyrone. There was, too, a continuing Catholic exodus to Spain, the Lowlands, France and Rome. Clerics and scholars, all Catholics, went in droves. Because those who entered military service rarely returned to Ireland, official policy encouraged them to go.

The influx of new settlers into Ireland, coupled with the emigration of many Irish Catholics, diluted the Catholic population. But despite this, Ireland still remained largely papist and many of the Protestants who came in were dissenters. Where the real revolution was accomplished in the century after Kinsale was in the ownership of land, on a scale unique in Europe. In 1610 about 2,000 Catholic gentry owned most of the land; by 1641 they still held 59 per cent; in 1660 only 22 per cent; and by 1703 as little as 14 per cent. Such a transformation was catastrophic and provided the basis for an anglican ascendancy which was to dominate Ireland in the next century. Yet it was by no means inevitable that a change in ownership on such a scale would happen and Catholic Ireland had gone to extreme lengths in order to keep possession.

These Catholics were, of course, mostly of the old stock, Irish or Anglo-Irish, settled in Ireland for many generations. Despite sharing a common religion, however, the Anglo-Irish still clung to those notions of superiority which marked them off from the Gaelic Irish. They began to call themselves 'Old English', not only to distinguish themselves from the New English, and generally Protestant, arrivals, but also from their Irish co-religionists. For centuries the Irish had been labelled as 'enemies', the very epitome of disloyalty. Now that their Catholic faith had caused their own loyalty to be questioned in England – no government could forget that a pope had excommunicated Queen Elizabeth and that Catholics in Europe were constantly intriguing to subvert the legitimate ruler of England – the Anglo-Irish had somehow to square loyalty to the pope with loyalty to the crown. Bellarmine's principle of 'dual loyalty', based on freedom of conscience, may have provided a comfortable theological basis for steering a middle course, but was hardly likely to ease official doubts.

So they stressed their Englishry as an antidote to their Catholicism. 'England is our mother', cried Patrick Darcy in the Irish parliament. They referred to 'the famous people of England from whose loins we are descended'. When a Protestant royal official wished to insult them deeply in the 1641 parliament, he could think of no better way than to label them 'Teigs' (a pejorative term used for the Irish). The Old English members whom he thus described were outraged. Their loyalty was in no way endangered by their Catholicism and should never be questioned. Even at the end of the seventeenth century, after suffering the trauma of dispossession and legal discrimination, the Old English author of the Jacobite tract *A light to the blind* (probably Nicholas Plunkett, a descendant of one of the great old families of the Pale) could write of the 'true conquerors' of Ireland in the twelfth century who were Catholics and

'annexed the Irish crown to the English diadem ... Their posterity have continued in sole gallantry and loyalty even to this day, propping the true kings of England at the hazard of their lives and fortunes, while the upstart Protestants have of late years endeavoured to cast down those crowned heads, and actually prevailed'.

Yet there were others, mostly those who went to Europe and were influenced by the counter-reformation, who experienced something of a crisis of identity. Geoffrey Keating, a scion of an Old English family, was strongly influenced by the new history then in fashion in Europe, where the *patria* (or fatherland) was regarded as the proper subject of the historian's craft. National histories were being widely produced. Keating set out to write a history of his native Ireland, adopting the new standards, distinguishing between primary and secondary sources, emphasizing the importance of a correct chronology, and constructing a coherent narrative. As was the fashion, he wrote in a high style, but in Irish rather than Latin, and his work has remained a classic in that language.

Exploiting the twelfth-century *Lebor Gabála* (Book of invasions), which tried to provide a suitable place in the history of the Irish nation for the Goedelic invaders of Ireland, by inventing a history which would enable them to take their place among the non-Gaelic indigenous inhabitants, Keating was able to fit his own remote ancestors, the English invaders of the twelfth century, into the diversity which made up the people of Ireland. This emphasis on a series of invasions of Ireland by different people, was nothing new in the Anglo-Irish tradition. In earlier times Anglo-Irish patrons had paid for praise-poems which similarly emphasized Ireland's population developing from successive invasions, including that of the English. Thus Old English exclusiveness could be maintained, while at the same time their identification with the historic Catholic Ireland would be unquestioned. For these Old English, Ireland was their *patria*. Keating went to the trouble to write its history because, he tells us, 'I deemed it was not fitting that a country so honourable as Ireland, and races so noble as those who have inhabited it, should go into oblivion without mention or narration being left to them'. He deliberately set out to defend Ireland against those who had calumniated her, from Cambrensis to Camden and others.

Keating, like William Nugent before him, and another famous Old English exile Pádraigín Haicéid (Hakett), also composed poetry in Irish according to the strict forms of the rules of the conventional bardic schools, implying that he had received part of his early education in one such school. In particular, those three were responsible for the revival of exile poetry of a kind which had not been composed for many years. All three, despite being from long-established Old English families, were well trained in the most conservative branch of the Gaelic educational system. They were by no means unique, as the poetry of the Kerry Old English Piers Ferriter reminds us.

Long before this the 'middle nation' of medieval Anglo-Ireland had assimilated much of the Gaelic culture and the Irish language was used by many almost as a mother tongue. About 1564 Christopher Nugent, the future Baron Delvin and thus one of the most important men in the Pale, provided for Queen Elizabeth a primer of the Irish language so that she could speak a few appropriate words to distinguished Irish visitors. Suitable phrases were chosen and arranged in three columns headed *Iryshe, Latten, English* – for example 'Cones ta tu: Quomodo habes: How doe you'. Nugent tells us in a preface that this was the method employed to teach his great-grandmother Irish and she was the royal ward Elizabeth Zouche, who was given in marriage to the Earl of Kildare by the king. In this way, he says, she learnt 'to read, write and perfectly speak the tongue' – proof, if ever needed, that a good knowledge of Irish was required to live at the highest social level in early sixteenth-century Ireland. Another great-grandson of the same Elizabeth Zouche, the Jesuit William Bathe, used the same family method in 1611 when he wrote *Ianua Linguarum* to help students of the Irish college of St Patrick at Salamanca acquire a knowledge of Latin or a second language. His book went through no fewer than 30 editions before the end of the century and was widely used for many years in Europe as the standard method for teaching a foreign language.

From the Irish perspective, too, the Old English as Catholics, and in sharp contrast to the new Protestant foreigners who had crowded into Ireland, were now more clearly seen as 'of Ireland' and therefore 'Irish'. Poets who in the past had consistently referred to them as *gaill* (foreigners), no matter how much acculturation may have Gaelicized them, now began to reserve the term *gaill* for the New English in Ireland. In contrast the term *Éireannaigh* (Irish, of Ireland) was applied in common to Irish and Old English alike. And even more strikingly the poets, when appealing for unity among *Éireannaigh* against the New English, now included the Old English, descendants of the first English settlers, among the Irish who must be united.

Literary convention, then, mirrored a radical change in attitude which was slowly taking place in Gaelic Ireland. But it took a long time and the traditional mistrust which had for so long been the hallmark of Irish perception of the Anglo-Irish could not be completely eradicated. Even when the traumatic impact in Ireland of the puritan revolution in England forced all Catholics to unite in a common cause, there was still a deposit of distrust which could frustrate leaders of rebellion. Behind the unifying force of religion there was often the reality of ethnic differences, sharpened by worry over material loss or gain, which revived age-old feelings of distrust and even hatred. It was not until they were socially depressed after the catastrophes of the seventeenth and eighteenth centuries that the Old English gradually became indistinguishable from the Irish. Before then many still retained the stereotypical view of the Irish as essentially disloyal.

If the Old English emphasized the disloyalty of the Irish as a group, it was because it was in their own interest to do so. They had been considerable gainers in every move to expropriate native landowners. No Irishman of Gaelic origin, no matter what his status, was in theory free of the taint of disloyalty. An O'Brien Earl of Inchiquin, a Protestant, had to face the charge of being Irish and therefore partially disloyal. He replied that it was 'not his fault but his misfortune'.

In fact, however, many Irish families were just as determined to prove loyalty to the crown. The surrender and regrant policy applied in the sixteenth century had proved so successful that in the early seventeenth century an

O'Brien Earl of Thomond and a Burke Earl of Clanricard were sufficiently trustworthy to be appointed respectively as governors of Munster and Connacht. Further down the social scale an O'Hara of Sligo could serve as an MP for the county in the parliament of 1613–16. The accession of James I to the English throne was an occasion for poetic offerings from Gaelic Ireland which depicted him as the rightful spouse of Ireland and gave him a suitable genealogy tracing his line back through the Gaelic rulers of the past to their great ancestor Míl of Spain. To him, then, obedience was due and, indeed, to his successor Charles I. Even in 1641 the rebels claimed not to be against the king but rather his evil advisors and later the Irish were to declare publicly their loyalty to the crown. The motto of the Catholic confederation of Kilkenny, which included Irish as well as Old English Catholics, was *Pro Deo, pro rege, pro patria Hibernia unanimis* (United for God, for king, for the fatherland Ireland).

Often, too, the distinction between Irish and English was blurred. All of the Irish leaders of the 1641 rebellion belonged to and were accepted by the propertied class. By education and upbringing they could hardly be distinguished from their Old English peers. Some of them, notably Sir Phelim O'Neill, Rory Maguire and Philip O'Reilly were members of the Irish parliament. When the time came the Old English members of parliament could not be prevailed on to condemn them as rebels. Instead they referred to them as 'discontented gentlemen'. Intermarriage, too, made for a racial mix. If Ulick Burke was Earl of Clanricard, he had three English grandparents and he himself was married to the daughter of an English earl.

The New English, too, quickly identified with Ireland. Even Sir John Davies, the chief architect of the Ulster plantation, showed some sense of identification when he protested in the English House of Commons against some legislation affecting Ireland and defended the independence of the Irish parliament. This phenomenon of English newcomers identifying with their adopted land and defending its distinction continued. A good example is Aubrey Mervyn, a native of Hampshire and English born and bred. In the Irish parliament of 1641 he not only defended the distinct law and constitution of Ireland, but did so in a manner which had a long tradition behind it, calling Ireland his mother:

'This kingdom, personated in the sable habit as a widow, with the dishevelled hairs, seems to petition your lordships, that since she is a mother to most of us, yet certainly a nurse unto us all, you would make some order for redress of her tyrannical oppression'.

Later, in 1660, he was also an active participant in the Protestant convention in Dublin, mainly New English in composition, which claimed that under 'the laws and laudable custom and constitution of this nation' Ireland was governed by the legislation of its own parliament. This remarkable echo of the constitutional sentiments of the 'middle nation' of late medieval Ireland went down well in that later assembly and Mervyn was consequently elected Speaker of the House of Commons.

The use of labels such as 'Old English' or 'New English' blurs a distinction which in the long term was to be even more important. What marked off most native Catholic Irishmen, of whatever race, from immigrants and others who were Protestant, was religion. The provost of the new Trinity College in Dublin, William Temple, explained this fact of life to English critics in 1620. His college could not attract large numbers of students because the Catholic education system funnelled students to Catholic colleges in Europe, while the official system, which was Protestant, mainly catered for immigrants. When the Cromwellians later officially classed the grandchildren of Edmund Spenser as 'Irish papists', they were emphasizing that it was this religious distinction that mattered, rather than that between different ethnic groups in Ireland.

The difference was sharpened by polemic. In Trinity College there was a 'Chair of theological controversies', the holders of which entered into debate with Catholics, in print as well as from the pulpit. Such debates gave the Church of Ireland a keen awareness of its distinction and helped to widen the religious difference between Catholic and Protestant. The one was accepted in much of Ireland, the other was not. In 1634 the Protestant Bishop of Kilmore, William Bedell, wrote that the 'popish clergy' had the 'love of the people', not least because of 'our extortions upon them' and because of 'the very inborn hatred of subdued people to their conquerors'. The Church of Ireland, therefore, naturally became orientated towards England and English settlers, divorced from the majority of the native population. A theological justification for Protestant ascendancy identified popish idolatry and superstition with the work of the Antichrist. Those who looked to Rome were so corrupt that they could not be saved. They were predestined for damnation, never should they be tolerated. The Bishop of Derry in the early seventeenth century expressed this view succinctly: 'If the pope be Antichrist, then those that be found to be resolute Antichristians, that is the recusant priests, ought not to be favoured or spared in a Christian Commonwealth . . . For what fellowship can there be between light and darkness?'. This was an attitude which seemed to be confirmed by the events of 1641, when the Irish Catholics rebelled and in so doing demonstrated that any tolerance extended to them cost the people of God dearly.

Such an attitude helps to explain why the Church of Ireland pressurized the Dublin administration to impose legal penalties on those 'addicted to popery'. In July 1605 the Government banished Catholic priests and ordered attendance at Protestant church services under pain of a fine of 12d. For a time this was rigorously enforced and churches in Dublin were full. The discovery of the 'gunpowder plot' at Westminster in November 1605 supported those who wished to extend no tolerance to Catholics. But once the outcry in England died down, James I, who wished to be moderate and believed in persuasion, ordered Dublin to pursue a less rigorous policy.

In any event, in the localities the Catholics had continued to practice their religion publicly. Masses were widely said in private houses, though increasingly in 'chapels' (to distinguish them from the 'churches' which were now in Protestant hands) built as places of Catholic worship. Before long a parish system was restored. From 1618 onwards a resident Catholic episcopate was reestablished. By 1637 there were 42 parish priests in the diocese of Elphin, for example, and in 1639 the Bishop of Waterford reported that he had 45 parishes staffed by 59 priests, in addition to about 40 religious. About the same time there were 56 priests in Tuam, 52 in Ardfert, and 47 in Killaloe. Even in Dublin itself Catholics greatly outnumbered Protestants, save in a few city parishes clustered around the castle. A majority of the 24 city aldermen were Catholic and still controlled the wealthy religious guild of St Anne in St Audoen's parish. The income from the property of the guild continued, as in the past, to support six priests to sing mass for deceased members and not until the lord deputy intervened in the 1630s did the priests (tactfully referred to as 'singing men') cease to perform this function.

And yet, there were laws against recusancy which could always threaten the individual Catholics who refused to conform. In Dublin the Castle Chamber court, which was not bound by normal common law procedures, was used to inflict crippling fines and often imprisonment as well. One famous victim was Francis Taylor, a Dublin Catholic alderman who spent seven years in prison before dying there in 1621. His death for his faith was widely reported, not only in Ireland but throughout Catholic Europe as well. An even more famous martyr was the aged Franciscan Bishop of Down and Connor, Conor O'Devany, who was hanged in 1612 for treason. A popular cult of the martyred bishop spread widely, not least among the Old English, and stiffened resistance to attempts to enforce the recusancy laws.

It is understandable, then, that religion and politics quickly became meshed in Ireland. The Old English had to use their still very considerable wealth and standing in the community to ensure that the practice of their religion was not an occasion for prosecution. In doing this they did not move any closer politically to the Irish. Sharing a common religion was not enough in itself to bring them together and even in religious matters there could be sharp divisions. The Old English were firm supporters of the counter-reformation and the new Tridentine discipline made more rapid progress among them than in areas still controlled by the Irish clergy. The deep-rooted division which had existed for centuries could not be permanently bridged and the bitter differences which were exposed after the rebellion of 1641 showed how far apart the two communities were.

Long before that, however, the Old English had tried to secure religious toleration by constitutional and legal means. Sir Patrick Barnewall, of the old Pale family, began the process in 1606 by arguing that the council had acted unlawfully in fining and imprisoning recusants. But it was the summoning of a parliament in 1613 which provided a notable opportunity for the Old English to mount opposition to the imposition of stricter religious conformity. The presumption was that there would be a Catholic majority, but the creation of about 40 new parliamentary boroughs changed that. These were 'rotten boroughs', designed to provide secure seats for reliable Protestants, especially members of the Dublin administration. There would be an assured Protestant majority in the new parliament. Of the 232 members returned, 132 were Protestant. More significantly: of those 63 came from Ulster, where only one Catholic was returned. When parliament met to elect a speaker, the Old English protested. They then proposed Sir John Everard, a former justice of the king's bench who had resigned because he refused to take the oath of supremacy as demanded by law. The government proposed Sir John Davies. While those in favour of Davies were signifying their vote by leaving the chamber, the Catholics seized the advantage and forcibly thrust Everard into the speaker's chair. The Protestant majority, returning to the chamber, took Davies, who was no lightweight, and dumped him in Everard's lap. Thus was the solemn business of parliament begun. A scuffle followed, Everard was thrown out and the Catholics withdrew. They refused to return and thus made the parliament ineffective. A bitter battle was then fought over the new boroughs and what the Catholics claimed were electoral irregularities, as a result of which the Protestant majority was reduced to six. More important, King James saw to it that proposed anti-catholic legislation was withdrawn. The king pronounced that it was not his intention to 'extort any man's conscience'. On the face of it, the Catholic parliamentarians had won an outstanding victory and had shown how constitutional opposition, even if accompanied by unseemly bickering, could get results.

But the king, in fact, had no intention of extending toleration to those holding public office. All must take the oath of supremacy. In 1614 in a public address to a deputation from the Old English members of parliament, he accused them of being 'only half-subjects of mine' and said that they had given their souls to the pope. In practice, however, he had to take a more tolerant view. He needed to procure parliamentary consent to a subsidy and this necessitated some compromise on religion if the consent of the Catholic members was to be gained. There was no extension of the penal laws, but neither was there any amelioration of existing laws. And with the subsidy voted, there was no longer any need of parliament, which had lasted for only 11 weeks in three sessions in 1613–15. Some other way would have to be found if the Old English were to continue using constitutional means to procure reform of the laws against them.

England's foreign policy provided some hope of leniency in administering the laws against recusancy. The attempt to procure a Spanish marriage for the heir to the throne in the early 1620s made it politic to exercise greater toleration in Ireland. When the Spanish match failed, so that the humiliated Charles called for war, an attempt was made to arrange a marriage with the sister of the King of France. Charles I succeeded his father in March 1625, married Henrietta Maria in May, and by September was at war with Spain.

Since Catholic Ireland, and especially the Irish part, had strong links with Spain, it was recognized that it might well be a source of danger in the war. It was said that if Ireland were invaded, the enemy 'by that means [would] have the backdoor of Ireland kept open as a bridle upon England'. There was every reason, therefore, to avoid measures which would arouse Catholic opposition. When, despite the marriage to Henrietta Maria, England went to war against France early in 1627, there was even some need for a cooperative Ireland.

As always, England's difficulties were Ireland's opportunity. Already in the autumn of 1625 a prominent Old English landholder, Sir John Bath, made it plain to a member of the English government that a policy of discrimination had bred mistrust among the Old English and that institutions like the new court of wards were seen by them as a threat to the property they held. 'By this means', he said, 'many mens' lands are taken out of their hands . . . it is commonly spoken that any man exposed thereunto will be by likelihood driven to forego his land in a short time'. The English government was convinced and the council decided that 'the Irish of the English race' should in future be treated favourably. For a time the government even agreed to use 'trained bands' of soldiers for the defence of Ireland, paid for and led by the Old English. But in the end this was too much for the Protestants to stomach, 'for thereby we would have put arms into their hands of whose hearts we rest not much assured'.

To defend Ireland, Charles decided to augment the standing army to 5,000 foot and 500 cavalry. This had to be paid for and the king listed 'matters of grace and bounty' which he was prepared to grant in return for a suitable financial subsidy towards the cost of defence. There were some radical concessions to Catholics, such as the abolition of religious tests for all practising law, appointments to office, and, most important, for all inheritance. The recusancy fines were to be suspended. Now, after making his offer, all the king could do was to sit and wait. As he expressed it in a letter to Buckingham, in terms which reveal something of his true attitude to the Old English, '. . . Ireland being the only egg we have sitten upon, and having a thick shell we have not yet hatched it'. But the Old English were not satisfied. The government had refused to trust Catholics in defending Ireland and they now demanded that the king should openly recognize the loyalty of the Old English by reviving the 'trained bands'. To complicate matters further. The Church of Ireland denounced the proposed suspension of recusancy fines as a grievous sin. The primate, Ussher, preached a sermon on the subject, rebuking those 'who from worldly ends like Judas, sell Christ for thirty pieces of silver'.

By the time Charles agreed to receive an Irish delegation in June 1627, an English failure to succour the Huguenots of La Rochelle had exposed Ireland to the threat of invasion yet again. When the delegates appeared in England in January 1628, eight were Old English Catholics and three were Protestants. The negotiations ended with the delegates agreeing to an annual subsidy of

£40,000 for three years in return for concessions. These were contained in 'His majesty's instructions and graces' which were despatched to the Irish government on 24 May. There were 51 'graces' in all, some of which redressed selected Catholic grievances. An oath of allegiance replaced the oath of supremacy for inheritance and admission to legal practice; trust in Catholic loyalty was implied in the agreement to appoint some Old English commanders of army companies; security of land title was guaranteed to all landholders of more than 60 years standing. But recusancy fines were not suspended and public office was still withheld from Catholics. Many of the 'graces' dealt with quite trivial matters and while Catholics did secure some major concessions, the dominant Protestant position was maintained in Ireland.

The 'graces' were to be confirmed in the next Irish parliament. Meanwhile the first £40,000 subsidy was to be collected and parliament was summoned by the lord deputy, Falkland. Writs for elections were issued in the summer of 1628. But this contravened the procedure which Poynings' law of 1494 had made mandatory – before a parliament could be summoned in Ireland all bills initiating legislation had first to be transmitted to England for approval by the privy council. Falkland, in his ignorance, had forgotten that this statute was still in force and so, on 20 October 1628, the parliament was indefinitely postponed by proclamation issued in Ireland. By then some representatives had already been elected and, naturally, the king's sincerity was questioned.

Despite their reluctance to do so, the Old English were of necessity contributing to the support of the army. Partly this was the result of being more or less held to ransom by soldiers who were difficult to control; but mainly it was because they did not wish to jeopardize those 'graces' which, however imperfectly, were extended to them in practice. When in April 1629 the treaty of Susa ended the war with France and the treaty of Madrid the war with Spain in the following year, there was even less reason to summon a parliament to give statutory force to the 'graces'. By mid-1630 the Irish government was openly proclaiming that there was no need to summon another parliament until financial considerations made it necessary. By then it was clear to the Old English that the most important of the concessions won from the king, confirmation of titles to land, was not going to be extended to them. There would be no statute of limitations. Worse, in June 1631, Sir Charles Coote, vice-president of Connacht, presented a scheme for plantation. Though his actual proposals were not acceptable to the English government, the planting of selected parts of Connacht did become official policy. The following year it was decided to reimpose recusancy fines with rigour. Already well known houses of religious orders were closed and by February 1631 the government was satisfied that all 'mass houses' had been shut.

This renewal of anti-Catholic activity, coupled with the indefinite postponement of parliament, not only demonstrated the incapacity of the Old

English to win concessions by constitutional means or to have their loyalty and therefore reliability officially recognized, it also confirmed the Protestant character of the new Ireland. Coincidentally the king announced the appointment of a new lord deputy in January 1632. This was Thomas, Viscount Wentworth, who was committed to support Charles I in ruling without parliaments. Interest of the crown was to be paramount and Ireland would be used, in Wentworth's own words, 'to supply the king's wants'. As a member of the Irish committee of the English privy council he already had a considerable knowledge of Ireland and was determined to force both communities, Catholic and Protestant, to accept government wishes to make Ireland a source of revenue to the crown, which would help the king to dispense with parliament and the subsidies it provided in England. A new policy, characterized as 'thorough' by commentators, would make the whole of Ireland, Irish, Old English, New English, subservient to the crown. In this he may not have been wholly novel, since his predecessors had initiated schemes of plantation and economic policies which anticipated what Wentworth would try in his attempt to exploit Ireland fully in the interests of the king. But he did realize that if the great potential power of the crown in Ireland could be fully utilized, then it would be possible to test experimentally there solutions to problems which could then be applied successfully in England. That was novel and indeed was to be used again by Henry Cromwell and later still when Charles II and James II both tested in Ireland a policy of 'catholicizing' before attempting it in England.

What Wentworth attempted to do in Ireland, then, became an issue in England. His determination to secure the rights of the crown, and indeed of the church, meant, as he told Archbishop Laud, using 'a little violence and extraordinary means' and this also against the New English settlers in Ireland. If, by securing royal interests, he made a profit for himself, so much the better. When his machinations procured the dispossession of the O'Byrnes in Wicklow and £2,000 a year in rents for the king, his reward was £1,000 a year for himself and two manors in that county. It supports the view of one contemporary that Wentworth was 'a servant violently zealous in his master's ends and not negligent in his own'.

In fact, he made a fortune from his office in Ireland, including an income of £13,000 a year from various sources. He resisted interference, not just because it might hinder good government, but because it prevented him from exploiting patronage for his own profit. He became one of the richest men in England, with an annual income of £19,000 a year. No wonder he had a high estimation of the office of lord deputy, well demonstrated when he set about building an official residence. This was the vast house – more properly a palace – which he planned to construct at Jigginstown in county Kildare. Its enormous proportions, 390 feet by 120 feet, make it the largest residence ever built in Ireland and one of the first to employ brick in its construction. It perfectly represents not only Wentworth's good taste, but his grandiose ideas as well.

At first Wentworth enjoyed the goodwill of the Catholics who hoped that the more important 'graces', such as inheritance without religious tests, confirmation of land titles, and the freedom for Catholics to practice law, would be given statutory force by parliament. Wentworth, for his part, soon realized that only through parliamentary subsidies would he be given the financial freedom he needed to pursue his policy of 'thorough'. The summoning of a parliament, then, was agreed to by him as a seeming concession to the Old English demand. It was summoned to meet on 14 July 1634. In the first session the Catholics were allowed to draw up a programme for converting the 'graces' into law. In return they consented to a request for six subsidies to be paid over four years. Worse, agreement was given to a bill which, unknown to them, was to be used by Wentworth to exploit defective land titles in the interest of the crown. By the time parliament was dissolved in April 1635, Wentworth had achieved the financial concessions which would in future make him independent of parliament, as well as the necessary legal authority to enable him to pursue a rigorous land policy.

Almost immediately he showed his hand. Inquisitions, conducted in his presence to intimidate juries, established royal title to lands in Mayo, Sligo and Roscommon. But in Galway the jurors refused to be intimidated, even when faced with imprisonment and the enormous fine of £4,000 each. Wentworth, enraged by the embarrassing delay, refused to back down. When the Galway landholders finally discovered that the king, to whom they sent a delegation to offer proof of their titles and trusting in royal honour, in fact backed his governor in Ireland, they had to give way. The jurors finally surrendered and in return for freedom and reduced fines found the king's title. They were even forced to acknowledge in the castle chamber court that their fines and imprisonment had been just. Wentworth's contempt for them could hardly have been more manifest. In a letter of October 1636 he called them 'a company of unconscionable and inconsiderable persons' and his total disregard for their rights and dignity was a warning to all of where resistance to him could lead.

Wentworth intended to use the new royal titles to proceed with a plantation of selected parts of Connacht. In this he showed a total disregard for the Old English who controlled large parts of the province and in particular the town and county of Galway. Thus he alienated them at the very time when they were already suffering from the effects of a series of harvest failures in 1629–33 and a serious economic crisis which hit landowners all over Ireland. The Old English now could be under no illusion about Wentworth's plans for Ireland. Nor could the New English settlers expect to benefit. It quickly became obvious that the confiscated lands would not go to them but rather to English courtiers who would be more amenable to the kind of Ireland the deputy had in mind. Worse, he soon showed that the New English too could lose lands. Clever manipulation of the law, the use of procedure outside the common law, even duplicity, beat New English landholders, like the powerful Earl of Cork, at their own game. This proved particularly successful in the recovery of much church property from great settlers like Cork, or lesser landowners like the one in Munster who wrote: 'We are like to suffer very much misery between the church and the subsidies. The one, I think, will take from us all our lands and the other all our monies'. No wonder such people grew to hate Wentworth. In England, too, there was alarm over the way the deputy seemed to be perverting the common law and the bishops' demands for restoration of lands and it was this which gave some basis of truth to the charge against Wentworth (then the Earl of Strafford) later at his trial that he had tried to subvert the law.

At the same time Wentworth was determined that the acts of uniformity and supremacy should be fully implemented. The Church of Ireland, too, must conform doctrinally to orthodox Anglicanism as laid down in 1604 for the Church of England. Calvinism was to be rooted out and the more Arminian orthodoxy which Archbishop Laud was promoting must be adopted. Many Protestants, and not least Ulster Presbyterians, felt threatened. Like the Catholics they no longer felt completely secure in their titles to land and in religious belief they were equally subject to pressure to conform. They were also dismayed to see, as they thought, that Wentworth apparently tolerated a leniency towards Catholics, as a result of which religious orders expanded rapidly. In 20 years the Franciscans increased from 200 odd to 1,000 and many friaries were reoccupied. But Wentworth never relented in his view that religious conformity was necessary and in his determination that as soon as circumstances allowed it, he would enforce it with all the rigour at his command. Neither did he remove any of the disabilities which threatened Catholics. Security of tenure was withheld, they were still excluded from public office and the perks that went with it, and were discriminated against in many other ways. So while Catholics may have been mostly free to practice their religion, they were still subject to religious discrimination and were increasingly conscious that their freedom would be threatened when Wentworth chose to impose uniformity.

In a few years, then, Wentworth had gone far towards achieving his primary objective in Ireland. He had built up an efficient administration, getting rid of the worst New English elements which had exploited office to their own ends and at the expense of good government. He had brought about a steady improvement in the Church of Ireland, not least by promoting a better ministry and making it financially independent – all this clearing the way for the imposition of religious conformity on all communities in Ireland. Land confiscations had provided the opportunity for importing more suitable tenants, and at the same time augmented royal revenues through increased rents. Financial self-sufficiency made him independent of parliament. By 1638, when he appointed John Ogilby master of revels – the first Dublin theatre had been opened in St Werburgh street the previous year – to entertain Dublin's high society, he seemed sufficiently confident of his political success to devote attention to lighter preoccupations.

But Wentworth also succeeded in doing the seemingly impossible. He galvanized the dissident elements on the island into joint opposition. Not only were Irish and Old English later to join forces for the first time, but Old English were to be joined by New English Protestants in what might be seen as an unnatural alliance. For Wentworth's steady progress of 'thorough' had alienated each group in turn, whether through religious persecution, a loss of land and other sources of profit, dismissal from office and destruction of vested interests. Across the Irish sea, too, events were rapidly leading to a confrontation between king and subjects which was to have a marked impact on Ireland. The attempt to force a Laudian brand of religion on all became a source of grievance to puritans. There was a riot in St Giles in Edinburgh in July 1637 when the new *Book of common prayer* was introduced. This new liturgy not only gave offence to Presbyterians, it convinced the Scots that they must unite in opposition to the growing authoritarian nature of royal rule from England. The result was the National Covenant of March 1638, designed to oppose the imposition of religious change on Scotland.

It was only to be expected that there would be repercussions in Ulster among the large Scottish and increasingly Presbyterian population. There was a report that some in the diocese of Raphoe were being wooed to join the covenant. While the Scots in arms were confronting the king, Wentworth in May 1639 began systematically to force all Scots over 16 years old in Ulster to take an oath of loyalty, the infamous 'Black Oath', and faced with the army most subscribed. By then the treaty of Berwick gave the king the time he needed to prepare to bring the Scots to heel. At last Wentworth was to be given the opportunity to show that the Ireland he had created would supply Charles I with material assistance, as he expressed it, 'to enforce those gain-sayers (the dissident Scots) to due obedience, and settle the public peace of all your kingdoms'.

Wentworth was now summoned to England to consult with the king, was created Earl of Strafford early in 1640 and raised to the higher dignity of lord lieutenant in Ireland. It was largely his influence which convinced the king that at all costs the full authority of the crown must be preserved. With the Scots still in arms, the only way this could be achieved was by force and for this money would be needed. There was no way out of summoning a parliament, in Ireland as well as in England, to provide the subsidies required. A large army of 9,000 was to be raised in Ireland, to be paid for by six subsidies spread over three years. Wentworth was confident that, as in 1634, he could manipulate parliament, opposing Catholic members to Protestant, and through the election of a sufficient number of governmental candidates securing a balance of power for himself. By the time he returned to Ireland on 18 March 1640 parliament had already assembled and the new lord lieutenant quickly succeeded in procuring a promise of four subsidies and began arrangements to raise the new army.

He left Ireland, for good, on 3 April, convinced that he could repeat in England the success he had enjoyed with the Irish parliament. But there he failed. Instead of being compliant, the English parliament turned on the king. The Commons not only refused assistance, but made it clear that Charles should compromise himself by offering terms to the Scots. On 5 May, barely three weeks after it had assembled, parliament was dissolved. But already some of its leaders were in communication with the Scots, who now began to see that they might enjoy some English parliamentary support in the solution of their quarrel with the king. On 20 August a Scottish army crossed the river Tweed and just a week later defeated the royal army near Newcastle-upon-Tyne. The king was left with no choice but to summon another parliament to seek help. When the Scots agreed terms for a truce on 21 October, Charles was obliged not only to leave them in occupation of part of the north of England, but also to pay them £850 each day. When parliament (the famous 'Long parliament') assembled on 3 November, the Commons were thus given some element of control over the king.

In Ireland, meanwhile, the army was mustered at Carrickfergus in July. Although too late to help the king against the Scots, their availability for use in future engagements forced the English parliament to devote some attention to Ireland. That the army was largely Catholic increased its potential danger to those opposed to the king. It was believed that this Irish army would be used in England. For this reason, if for no other, it was imperative to end Strafford's authority in Ireland and proceedings for his impeachment were instituted. Coincidentally the Irish parliament had prepared a remonstrance which was a fierce indictment of Strafford's earlier arbitrary government. Its substance was communicated to the English commons and when the third session of the Irish parliament began in January 1641, most of its energy was devoted to the preparation of evidence for use in the impeachment of Strafford in England. It did not matter that little of this evidence stood up in court when Strafford was brought to trial at Westminster on 22 March. The Commons passed a bill of attainder against him a month later and on 12 May he was executed on Tower Hill.

With Strafford out of the way, the catalyst which brought Catholic and Protestant opposition together in parliament was removed. The New English looked to the English parliamentary opposition as their hope for a restoration to power in Ireland and the preservation of the Protestant dominance there. Many New English had retained links with England and some had connections in the new House of Commons there. This New English interest can be represented in the person of Sir John Clotworthy. He had been a member for Antrim in the Irish parliament of 1634. A planter, with strong Presbyterian sympathies, he was returned to the English House of Commons, where he was the seconder of Pym's proposal that a special parliamentary committee should set up to deal with Irish affairs. In his address to the house he was strongly anti-Catholic.

Not surprisingly, the Old English took fright at this New English influence at Westminster and saw in the king, who now clearly needed Irish support, their best hope of survival. As well as lobbying him again to secure statutory recognition of the 'graces', they fell back once more on their old ploy of constitutional opposition. To offset any possible legislative interference by the dangerous English parliament, they produced a remarkable defence of the legislative independence of the Irish parliament. This was mainly the work of the Galway lawyer, Patrick Darcy, who was also a landholder anxious to protect Old English land titles in Connacht from the prerogative courts by subordinating them to the law and to parliament. The New English, hoping for an endorsement of their dominant position and of their plans for future profit at the expense of the Old English by English statutes, were naturally unwilling to give support to the Darcy position and temporized until parliament was adjourned on 7 August. By the time it reassembled again on 16 November, rebellion had broken out in Ulster and attacks on Protestants there revealed the deep religious gulf which existed between the different communities.

The origins of this rebellion are complex. A number of Irish Catholic gentry, mainly of Ulster, met on 5 October 1641 and plotted an armed rising to commence on 23 October. They would seize Dublin castle, as well as taking by force the most important fortified places in Ulster. A drunken Owen O'Connolly revealed the plan to take the castle, so that it and the capital were saved. But the rising began in Ulster as planned. The leaders of the rising never considered themselves to be rebels, insisting that, as Owen Roe O'Neill put it in 1643, '[we] do really fight for our prince, in defence of his crown and royal prerogatives, which we shall continue and die to the last man'. Sir Phelim O'Neill even claimed that Charles I himself had actually authorized them to fight the English in Ireland and produced the evidence. That this commission was fraudulent was beside the point. It was believed to be genuine in England, where it compromised the king until the day he lost his head. In Ireland it gave a spurious respectability to the insurgents, making it easier for conservative Catholics to join cause with them.

It is significant that the terms of the royal commission ordered the leaders not to 'meddle' with the Scots in Ireland. There is evidence which supports the genuine efforts of the leaders to protect the Scottish settlers in Ulster. In Cavan, for example, in December 1641, Philip O'Reilly warned his cousins 'not to meddle with any of the Scottish nation except they give cause'. A month earlier Turlough O'Neill had apologized for the death of some Scots, massacred after surrendering to his men, and he uttered the pious hope that 'both nations being formerly one should still so continue like brothers'. This startling echo of Robert Bruce's insistence in 1315 that Scots and Irish were one nation, conveniently overlooked the fundamental religious difference which now, apart from anything else, kept the two apart. In a reply he was told that such sentiments were 'resolutely scorned by the Scottish nation'. Whatever motives were publicly proclaimed for taking up arms, 'the liberty of our consciences' was always prominent. The Catholic clergy justified the rising because it was in defence of the Catholic faith, a view subsequently endorsed by the Kilkenny convention of Catholics late in 1642.

That same Kilkenny convention expressed the basic conservatism of the rising by publicly confirming ownership of land as it existed on 1 October 1641. All the leaders of the rising were propertied Irish, acceptable to Old English and government alike. They held extensive tracts of land, sat in parliament, married into the best Old English families, served as officers in the king's army, and generally belonged to a class which, though Irish in name, had long protested its loyalty and in that at least was not to be distinguished from fellow-Catholics among the Old English. They were gentry. They were not radicals, seeking to overthrow the Ulster plantation, from which indeed some of them had profited. That, at least, was the way the Old English of Leinster preferred to see things.

Yet it is difficult to believe that men like Sir Phelim O'Neill or Rory O'More did not have ambitions to recover lost ancestral lands. When O'More told Maguire that the 'smallness of my now estate' contrasted sharply with what his family had held in the past, he voiced a bitter grievance which lurked behind the loyalist facade of many a 'deserving Irishman', as they had condescendingly been termed by the architects of plantation. When Owen Roe O'Neill returned from Europe and became the natural leader of the dispossessed Irish, he can hardly have had any other objective in mind than the recovery of the position held before the flight of his uncle, the Earl of Tyrone, had prompted wholesale confiscation.

Lower down the social scale, the Irish suffered from the activities of ever more numerous settlers, pushing aside the restrictions of plantation policy and fully exploiting the favourable opportunities presented by conditions on the ground in an Ulster far removed from London. The resultant injustices rankled with the native population. They were left with the worst land. More was demanded from them for shorter leases. They were not only dispossessed, but exploited as well. Small wonder that they, too, like the gentry above them, were ambitious to recover lost lands.

It is an undoubted fact that the early days of the rising were marked by cruelties inflicted on Protestant settlers. The gross exaggerations subsequently publicized as anti-Irish propaganda should not blind us to the facts. There is plenty of evidence, for example, that many of the victims were stripped naked, as if to humiliate them publicly before they were punished by torture, or death, or in most cases expulsion from home and property. Many perished in the harsh winter conditions. But stripping was also a public demonstration that such Protestant settlers had come to Ireland with nothing and was a manifestation of the deep hatred felt for them by the dispossessed Irish. The population increase in Ulster, where the worst of the atrocities occurred, had grown by as much as 50 per cent and had led to a dramatic increase in the demand for food. Any harvest crisis was therefore bound to have widespread repercussions, as had happened in 1627 when there was a major failure. Such harvest failures bred violence locally, when there was a scramble for food and certainly generated increased hostility towards the newcomers in the areas affected. The north Antrim farmer who swore in a deposition that he rose in rebellion 'only after the husbandry failed' was reflecting what may well have been a widespread phenomenon.

If the leaders, then, were in no sense radical, the same cannot be said of the rank and file among the rebels. The conservatism of the leaders was proclaimed in their consistent loyalty to the crown and to their inherited religion. They had no wish to see the lot of the lower orders of society improved. The imposition of English common law and the banishment of the old Irish social order had already done enormous damage to the age-old privileges of the Irish gentry. They themselves belonged to the upper class and had no wish to further damage their inherited social privileges. But they were unable to control resentment from below, especially in the early days of the rebellion in Ulster. The country people also feared the puritans and stories from England led some to believe that all Catholics were to be massacred. They felt no loyalty to the English king, some believing that the King of Spain, or one of the 'old stock', even Sir Phelim O'Neill, should be offered the crown. All Scots and English settlers should be driven out, except for a few craftsmen who would be kept as slaves! It was a common enough belief that it was God's will to clear Ireland of heretics and that this justified indiscriminate attacks on all Protestants. So when Turlough O'Neill ordered that 'no Scotsman should be touched by any of the gentry', he realistically referred to 'what hurt others should do to them'. In another letter the writer apologized: 'We are sorry that some lewd people have spoilt without authority'. Clearly the 'gentry' and the 'common sort of people' were not of one mind as to how the Protestants should be treated and it proved impossible to prevent violence being widely inflicted on helpless settler families.

There is no way of knowing exactly how many Protestants lost their lives during the early days of the rebellion. Research has shown that in county Armagh the number of settlers murdered varied from 17 per cent to 43 per cent from area to area – horrific figures. It may have been that as many as 4,000 died at the hands of Catholic fanatics and that twice that number perished through exposure – it was an exceptionally hard winter – and lack of adequate sustenance. Refugees poured into Dublin and Drogheda, from where most of them made their way to England where stories of a massacre of Protestants in Ireland quickly spread. News of the atrocities first reached parliament on 1 November 1641 and no time was lost in spreading the stories, deliberately sensationalized to inflame public opinion against the Irish. Pamphlets poured from the presses recounting in lurid detail the barbarities reputedly perpetrated by the Catholics in Ireland. *Bloody news from Ireland, or the barbarous cruelties by the papists used in that kingdom*, published on 1 December, is a fairly typical title. Nothing was spared the reader, especially the supposed cruelties inflicted on women. Wives were raped before their hapless husbands, as were children before their parents. Babies were torn from their mothers' wombs. Horror was piled on horror. The presence of destitute refugees in many localities, each with a tale more lurid than the rest, added to the general impression of a massacre on a terrible scale. When

Alice Stonier returned with her five children to her native parish of Leek in Staffordshire, after spending eight years in Ireland, she was destitute and petitioned for relief. Her husband had been killed and she had been robbed of all she possessed and was driven from her home by 'the barbarous rebels', forced to fly to Dublin like 'many others', a city which was packed with refugees she said. From there she and the others had been sent to find succour in the counties of their birth.

The presence of so many refugees gave substance to the fear that England might be invaded and the Protestant population murdered as part of a great European Catholic conspiracy. Memories of the massacre of St Bartholomew, as well as the horrors of the Thirty Years' War, prepared public opinion for the worst. The citizens of London petitioned the House of Commons as early as 11 December 1641, crying that they did not know 'how soon they may feel the like cruelty and inhumanity from the papists, and their adherents, as those in Ireland have done'. It was even believed that the pope had proclaimed a holy war against all Protestants. But the real danger was seen to come from Ireland, as the nation was reminded on 14 November 1641: 'Ireland is not unfitly termed a back door into England; and of what dismal portendance it must needs be to you and your nation, to have the pope keeper of the keys of your back door, I shall not need to represent unto you'. So aid must be sent to the Protestants in Ireland to prevent the rebels there from making England 'the seat of war'.

This was a far cry from the complaisant attitude of the previous year when, on 17 April, in an address to the 'short parliament', the Speaker remarked that England 'had but two back doors. Ireland was one, and was civilized and from charge become an aid, Scotland was the other'. Now the Scots were friends and the Irish enemies. To whip up support against them pamphlets continued to pour from the presses and circulated widely, exaggerating wildly the number of Protestants massacred in Ireland. As the flood of pamphlets swelled the number of dead grew. In August 1642 the English parliament put it at 154,000. By 1647 *A prospect of bleeding Irish miseries* asserted that 'there hath been at least two hundred thousand Protestants slain and most inhumanely massacred by the barbarous and blood-thirsty Rebels', a figure which the poet Milton also accepted and propagated. It was to no avail that even in England the stories of atrocities were denied, as in a tract of January 1642, published in London, 'plainly demonstrating the falsehood' of the circulating pamphlets. Bishop Bedell's son-in-law, Clogy, who had been strongly anti-Catholic, later described how the bishop was allowed to shelter distressed Protestants for eight months in Cavan and how he and his family, with 1,200 others, were escorted to safety in Drogheda. They travelled for seven days, accompanied by 2,000 rebels who 'were very civil to us all the way, and many of them wept at our parting from them, that had lived so long and peaceably among them, as if all had been one people with them'.

But it was the image of massacre which remained. There had been strong anti-Irish feelings in England for many years into the past, dormant for long periods but always available to become virulent at the slightest provocation. No tale of Irish barbarism had been too outrageous to believe. When troops from Ireland were stationed in different localities, feelings ran high. In 1628, in the village of Witham in Essex, there was a riot on St Patrick's day. A letter described how the Irish soldiers billeted there celebrated the feast 'after their country manner wearing in their hats ribboned crosses'. A local boy mocked them by tying a similar red cross to a dog's tail, driving the frightened animal to run amok among the soldiers. 'Thereupon enraged, they fell violently among the inhabitants, whereby, it is said, there were on both sides between thirty and forty slain'. This was a gross exaggeration of what actually happened. But it illustrates how quickly an incident could be exploited against the Irish, and especially Catholics. In parliament the number supposedly slain was solemnly recorded and members gave voice to their fears.

The same sort of climate in 1641 was ready to entertain the worst possible reports from Ireland. When Sir John Temple in his definitive *The Irish rebellion*, published in 1646, put the number murdered during the first two months of the rebellion at 150,000, this became a fact which few denied, public opinion was inflamed and revenge was demanded. Temple himself recommended that when peace was restored 'there may be such a course taken, such provision made, and such a wall of separation set up betwixt the Irish and the British, as it shall not be in their power to rise up'. Anti-Irish feeling was rampant. In Britain, in retaliation for the supposed massacres, Irish were butchered and throughout the war which followed in Ireland horrific acts of barbarism were perpetrated, reminiscent of the worst days of the war in Munster in the previous century. Soldiers in Leinster, where few if any Protestants had earlier been massacred, were ordered to 'kill and destroy rebels and their adherents and relievers', to destroy 'all places of refuge' and also 'to kill and destroy all the men there inhabiting capable to bear arms'. For many years on 23 October (the day the massacre was supposed to have commenced and coincidentally the day on which a Catholic plot to take Dublin castle was prevented) an anniversary sermon was preached in each church in Ireland keeping alive the memory of 1641. In 1661 William Lighburn preached a sermon in Christ Church, telling the congregation to remember 1641 when 154,000 were massacred in Ulster, condemning Catholic beliefs which 'teach and warrant them to be perfidious, bloody and cruel to us' and warning his listeners that 'they cannot propagate their Catholic doctrine but by our destruction: if the Protestants stand, Rome must fall; but if Rome stand, Rome will be contriving our fall'. In 1746 the Catholic historian John Curry is said to have been moved to research the massacres after he heard a young woman exclaim, after emerging from hearing the annual 23 October sermon, 'Are there any of those bloody papists in Dublin?' Even as late as 1792, when Ireland was again filled with rumours of rebellion, Lord Westmoreland reported that 'you cannot have any idea of the alarm in every part of the country, men, women and children dream of 1641'. Stories of the brutalities of the 1641 massacres had become deeply embedded in popular Protestant memory and were always there to feed strong anti-Catholic feelings. They helped to justify the savagery of the Cromwellian campaign and the confiscations which followed.

The 1641 rebellion, then, only confirmed what many people in England had long feared. Irish papists were cruel, treacherous, and given half a chance would murder all Protestants even within England itself. In December 1641, therefore, parliament determined that henceforth popery would never be tolerated in Ireland. More serious, for the Old English in particular, was the passing into law of the act for adventurers in March 1642, under which two and a half million acres of Irish land, to be confiscated because of the rebellion, would be placed on the market for Protestant investors. The land was equally distributed in the four provinces and most of it at that time was in the hands of Catholic landholders who had so far held aloof from the rebels. Such a huge area of land would produce the money for the suppression of the rebellion in Ireland and thus for the extirpation of popery there. In the event, most of the money raised was diverted by the parliamentarians into their war against the king, though the 'adventurers' who had subscribed it retained their vested interest in Irish land and thus in the suppression of rebellion there.

The rebellion had also provided parliament with a convenient propaganda weapon against the king, who was compromised by the supposed commission under the great seal brandished by the leaders, as well as by their regular insistence that they were in arms defending the royal prerogative. In the heated political climate generated by the massacres, the matter of the extent to which the king could trusted became vital. Charles was accused of favouring, if not actively supporting, the rebels. He was thus a danger to the nation and to parliament its defender. Any army sent to Ireland must therefore be under the direct control of parliament. This blatant intrusion into the royal prerogative split parliament, so that a royalist party began to emerge there. Gradually the country moved towards civil war and in this the situation in Ireland had played a crucial role.

Meanwhile the rebellion there had spread rapidly. Having taken most of the forts of Ulster in a matter of days, the rebels spread southwards on 31 October, took Dundalk and then Ardee. By early November they were in control of Armagh, Monaghan, Cavan, Tyrone, Fermanagh, Donegal, Leitrim, Longford and even part of Down. Later in the month parts of Derry, Sligo and Roscommon had joined in. On 12 November part of Wicklow had risen and soon Louth was aflame. Next Carlow, Kilkenny and Wexford were in rebellion and then the countryside northwards almost to the walls of Dublin itself. The defeat at Julianstown of an army sent north to protect Drogheda not only provided the rebels with arms, ammunition and money, it humiliated the government and alienated potential support.

This was made worse by the excessive rigour of Sir Charles Coot who, late in November, led an army to relieve Wicklow castle. In Newcastle and Wicklow he hanged not only what he called suspected spies, but innocent men and women, leaving behind a reputation for cruelty which was still remembered at the end of the century. This fuelled Catholic fears of indiscriminate retaliation by the government and led some Old English in Louth and Meath, where Catholics still held over 80 per cent of the land, to join the rebellion, assured that defence of their religion and lands was consistent with defending the royal prerogatives. The oath of association which the rebel leaders made all followers swear included, after the defence of 'the public and free exercise of the true and Catholic Roman religion', a further promise to 'bear faith and allegiance to our sovereign lord King Charles, his heirs and successors' and defend them 'against all such as shall directly or indirectly endeavour to suppress their royal prerogatives'.

Soon most of the lords of the Pale, fearful of what the future held, joined the rebels. One message to Dublin claimed that they joined together to protect their very lives. In Westmeath and Kildare the Old English quickly joined. But all the time they tried to preserve their separate identity, so that they were reluctant to be wholly submerged in the rebel army (even if, significantly, it was now called the 'catholic army') which was led by Sir Phelim O'Neill and was largely Irish in composition. The Old English tried to retain their own command, as in Meath where Fingall and Gormanston were the generals in command, so as to preserve an identity separate from the Irish.

By December Sligo, Mayo and Roscommon were lost to the rebels. In the new year, 1642, parts of Galway were lost, as was Clare. Munster was slower to react, though the defection of Donough MacCarthy, Viscount Muskerry, at the end of February was decisive. Convinced that the cause of the rebellion was, as he said, 'the apparent ruin and destruction threatened to Catholic religion, king and country', he joined the rebels. By the middle of March nearly the whole province was lost.

With all these territorial gains, it was necessary to devise some sort of government to administer the area. In March 1642 it was, surprisingly, the Earl of Clonricarde who proposed a system of councils, arranged hierarchically from county to province to national level. An Armagh provincial council at Kells on 22 March, presided over by Archbishop O'Reilly, endorsed a proposal for a council of clergy and laity to govern the country. In May, a national clerical assembly, again under the presidency of O'Reilly, met at Kilkenny and as a result a meeting of the 'lords and gentry of the confederate Catholics' later assembled in the same city. Together they established a provisional government, with a supreme council and a quasi-parliamentary elected general assembly. Local government was to be provided by provincial and county councils.

The first assembly met on October 1642. By then the situation had changed. For one thing, civil war had broken out in England. King and parliament were now engaged in a war to the finish. Ireland, already a pawn in the political jostling which had preceded the war, now became more important than ever. The rebels in Ireland, both Irish and Old English, had consistently protested their loyalty to the crown and indeed their determination to guard the royal prerogatives from parliamentary attack. In that sense they were 'royalist' rather than 'parliamentarian'. But the king continued to retain his own government in Ireland, now headed by the Duke of Ormond, with its own army fighting the rebels. And there was gradually built up another army in Ireland, controlled by the English parliament, which was augmented by the army of the Scots, led by General Robert Munro, who landed at Carrrickfergus with 2,000 men in April 1642. Now the Kilkenny assembly decided to assume control of the rebel armies, which had already suffered serious setbacks.

The Ulster leaders had earlier taken the initiative by recruiting Owen Roe O'Neill, who returned from the Netherlands with some other junior officers who had served with him in the Spanish army there. A distinguished soldier, he had been in contact with Ulster since the previous year and when he landed in Donegal in July 1642 he brought a professional military expertise which had been lacking hitherto. Soon after, Col. Thomas Preston, another officer in the Spanish army, landed at Waterford. Both men represented the two traditions, Irish and Old English, which now were joined, however reluctantly, in rebellion. Owen Roe was a nephew of the Earl of Tyrone and thus was seen by the Irish as their destined leader in the war against England. Preston was a brother of Lord Gormanston and so was seen to represent the Old English community, in particular that of the former Pale. Both complemented each other. Preston, too, had brought the arms and artillery which O'Neill lacked. But age-old antagonisms die hard and the two former colonels, rivals since their days in the service of Spain, could not cooperate. Neither would serve under the other. Behind each lay centuries of enmity and not even the need to defend Catholicism could bring Irish and Old English together in real unity. The *unanimis* which the 'confederate Catholics' so confidently inscribed on the seal of their association proved to be a chimera.

There could be no army of resistance under a single command and centrally directed by a Catholic government united in purpose. O'Neill retained his own command in Ulster, Preston in Leinster, and just to complicate matters further Munster was under the command of Garret Barry. Despite the fact that all claimed to be fighting on behalf of the king, the royal army in Ireland under Ormond, who was appointed lieutenant-general, fought to contain them. He had organized the defence of Dublin against the rebels, relieved Drogheda in March 1642, and supplied garrisons in Kildare in April. Already Munro had recaptured Newry and other places in Ulster. But even this Protestant unity was to fall apart with the outbreak of civil war in England. It was inevitable that the king should try to exploit the royalist Protestant army in Ireland on his side and before long try to reach some sort of accommodation with the Catholic forces. When he failed to defeat the parliamentary army, his only hope seemed to lie in negotiations with the confederate Catholics, which might produce an army to fight for him in England. Such a plan, of course, confirmed all that the puritans had feared, but the king had little choice.

The confederates had always protested their loyalty to the crown. It was in the oath of association and it was in the first public declaration which justified the taking up of arms: 'we, the Roman Catholics of this kingdom of Ireland, have been continual, loving and faithful subjects to his sacred majesty'. And in the motto of the confederates 'for king' came only after 'for God' and before 'for the fatherland'. So there seemed every reason to expect that King Charles would find a receptive and loyal following when in January 1643 he instructed Ormond, Clanricard and five others to discuss their grievances with representatives of the Catholics. Then, in April 1643, he further commissioned Ormond to parley for a truce with the rebels. But protracted negotiations soon revealed that the confederate Catholics were determined to use the king's difficulties to secure major concessions, of a kind which Charles inevitably found excessive and impossible to concede.

The Old English dominated the Kilkenny assembly. With their long political experience and their knowledge of a constitutional process from which the Irish had for the most part been excluded, they had little difficulty in exercising control. This manifested itself in the Kilkenny protest against the 1642 adventurers' act, when it was argued that the English parliament could not legislate for Ireland. The confederates printed the argument produced by the Old English Catholic lawyer from Galway, Patrick Darcy, during the last session of the 1641 parliament, that only an Irish parliament could legislate for Ireland. In a remonstrance of 17 March 1643 they declared that

> 'this your majesty's kingdom of Ireland in all succession of ages since the reign of King Henry II . . . had parliaments of their own, composed of lords and commons, qualified with equal liberties, powers, privileges and immunities with the parliament of England, and only dependent of the crown of England and Ireland'.

And when, in 1649, the confederates eventually concluded a treaty with Ormond, it contained a specific provision that parliament might issue a declaration 'concerning the independency of the parliament of Ireland of the parliament of England'. This reiteration of the famous declaration of the 1460 Dublin parliament that Ireland was 'corporate of itself' and bound only by the legislation of its own parliament, is a testimony to the persistence of the tradition of independence among Old English parliamentarians. Loyalty to the crown, to which Ireland was annexed, did not mean being subject to an English parliament.

But in the political climate of the 1640s such notions were repugnant not only to the English parliamentarians, but to the king himself. He had notions of divine right which made it impossible for him to yield to such demands and thus, as he saw it, diminish his sovereignty. As in the past, in the matter of the infamous 'graces', he played for time and relied on promises. But the confederates refused to be taken in by promises and supposed good intentions. They demanded positive action. They wished to have an independent parliament which would safeguard their rights. Secure tenure of lands and protection against future reprisals were also required. But in addition, not only did they demand the abolition of penal laws and the admission of Catholics to state offices, they also sought the acceptance of Catholic clerical ownership of all lands and buildings repossessed by ecclesiastics since October 1641 – all of this to be enacted into law so that there would be no betrayal later.

These demands really reflected Old English interests. If they were resentful of upstarts from England who had usurped their hereditary position and threatened their lands – the remarks of one that 'the Earl of Cork reputed worth £20,000 a year in 1641, though not worth £100 when he went to Ireland' reflects their resentment – they had no desire to remove the injustices perpetrated against the Irish. There would be no going back to undo the massive land confiscations from which they themselves had profited. Neither, indeed, for all their loyalty to the old religion and their demands for repeal of penal legislation, did they wish to see the Catholic church restored fully to her old position. Many had acquired church lands in the not too distant past and had no wish to lose them. The Old English really sowed the seeds of their own destruction as an identifiable group with their selfish, conservative demands during the time when they controlled these negotiations with the king.

When delays and difficulties prevented the negotiations from being speedily concluded, Ormond was made the scapegoat. Certainly he allowed his genuine attachment to anglicanism and consequent distaste for Catholicism to inhibit his actions. But he was also compromised by the problem of communication. Within Ireland Dublin could reach Kilkenny in three days at most and sometimes, remarkably, in one day. But between Dublin and Oxford, where the king now had his headquarters, the problems of communication were legion, not least because of the dangers of parliamentary patrols on the mainland and their naval forces patrolling the Irish sea. Not only were long delays inevitable, many messages went astray or, worse, fell into enemy hands. Since Ormond would never act on his own initiative, this was disastrous. Because he saw Charles I as an absolute ruler, with divine right, he would never move without receiving royal instructions. On 2 November 1644 he wrote: 'And if his majesty will have me to change my course so here, as be most for his advantage in England, or least hurtful to him, it is of necessity that I receive clear instructions'. The fate of Strafford always provided a salutary warning.

A further complication was that the queen, Henrietta Maria, after she returned to France in the autumn of 1644, tried to influence both Ormond and the confederates, and indeed the papacy, in arranging a settlement. Both Pope Urban VIII and Pope Innocent X also intervened, as did the French and Spanish Governments. All of this made for unnecessary complications and made agreement more difficult. In Ireland there was an added problem when the papal envoys, first of all Scarampi and then the notorious Rinuccini, involved themselves in trying to shape the ultimate agreement. Both believed, rightly, that Charles could not be trusted, and that the Protestants (in Ireland as well as in England) would never allow him to honour his promises to Irish Catholics.

Rinuccini was of critical importance after he arrived in Ireland as papal nuncio on 12 November 1645. He gradually gained a dominant role in the affairs of the confederates, alienating the Old English who had been so prominent in the business of the supreme council and general assembly, using the weapon of excommunication ruthlessly to secure a harder line in dealings with the king, even imprisoning dissident council members who accepted the settlement of which he disapproved.

When Charles surrendered into the hands of the Scots and was eventually handed over to the parliamentarians in January 1647, the war was lost in England. But in Ireland the Catholics were still in control of much of the island. In June 1646 O'Neill had won a remarkable victory over the Scots at Benburb, near Armagh, and was then in a position to achieve a military ascendancy that would finish Munro in Ulster. Instead, he marched south to join Rinuccini and placed his army at the nuncio's disposal. The essential incompatibility of the Irish and Old English was out in the open. The general assembly in October 1642 had solemnly proclaimed that all distinctions were to disappear: 'And it is further ordered and established, that there shall be no distinction or comparison made betwixt Old Irish and Old and New English, or betwixt septs or families, or betwixt citizens and townsmen and country-men, joining in union . . .'. Such a vision of Catholic harmony was an illusion. The fundamental division among the confederates could not be per-manently bridged. When O'Neill marched south instead of following up the victory at Benburb in Ulster, he made it perfectly clear that, to the Irish, Rinuccini was the man who was in command. Much later, when Irish poets came to comment on the disaster which ultimately followed the defeat of the confederates, it was the failure of many Catholics to accept the direction of Rinuccini which was blamed. The terrible Cromwellian pogrom and confis-cation was seen as the vengeance of God. The sin of the few was responsible for the suffering of the many. A work published in Lisbon in 1645, written by an Irish Jesuit, and circulating in Ireland shortly afterwards, shows how irrec-oncilable the two Catholic factions really were. The author, Conor O'Mahony, not only denounced the Protestant New English, he attacked the Catholic Old English as well. He was so impressed by the independence of Portugal that he demanded that a native Irish king be elected in Ireland, Charles I overthrown, and a fully independent Ireland established.

A younger Owen Roe O'Neill in 1626 had drafted a plan for an invasion of Ireland which would have established a republic. By 1646 his views had tem-pered, but his religious beliefs were stronger than ever. Influenced in his early years by Irish Franciscans at Louvain and Brussels, who were strong advo-cates of counter-reformation in Ireland, to be achieved by any means, it was natural for him to break with the confederates when they betrayed this ideal by accepting less than adequate guarantees on religion from Charles I.

Backing Rinuccini, who was refusing to accept this inadequate settlement, seemed sensible. But it was militarily disastrous. A proposal to join with Preston in attacking Dublin foundered and when Ormond handed over Dublin to the parliamentary army in July 1647, it marked the beginning of the end.

Confederate negotiations with Henrietta Maria in France and the pope in Rome also betrayed anxiety and, yet again, conflict between Old English and Irish aspirations. Rinuccini caused further alienations by excommunicating all who assented to a truce which the confederates concluded with Inchiquin, who had just defected from the parliamentarians and joined the king, in May 1648. The nuncio denounced the Old English confederates – 'those people are Catholic only in name' – and then was forced to leave Kilkenny. When, at the very end of 1648, news arrived from London that the king was to be put on trial, it precipitated an agreement between Ormond and the confederates in Ireland. A treaty was signed in January 1649 and the government of the confederates was dissolved. The king was executed on 30 January, an event which the Ulster presbytery condemned in the strongest terms, accusing the parliamentarians that 'they seek not the vindication, but extirpation of laws, and liberties, as appears by their seizing upon the person of the king', and for which they in turn were denounced by Milton as 'these blockish presbyters of Clandeboy'.

Ormond attempted to gather all the royalist elements in Ireland together under his leadership. But Rinuccini left Ireland at the end of February, O'Neill refused to cooperate and the lord lieutenant had to make do with diminished armed forces. He still had a military superiority over the enemy outside Ulster and recaptured some lesser places, such as Drogheda and Dundalk. In July he advanced against Dublin, which he himself had handed over to the army of Jones barely two years previously. But on 2 August the royalist army was routed at the battle of Rathmines and a fortnight later a huge army of 12,000 men from England landed unopposed at Ringsend. It was led by Oliver Cromwell. Ireland was about to be conquered and retribution exacted for all the wrongs, real or imaginary, done to Protestants since 1641. Nemesis was at hand.

Cromwell to this day is a dominant figure in the popular mythology of Ireland. He left an imprint on the Irish imagination which has never been exorcized. 'Cromwell came over and like a lightning passed through the land', wrote Bishop French of Ferns in exile. With probably the finest body of professional soldiers in Europe, each man driven by a fanatical hatred of popery, and with his own proven military skills, there was no doubt that a speedy campaign of attrition was going to bring the rebels to heel. After landing Cromwell made a speech to the people of Dublin in which he announced his purpose as

'the great work against the barbarous and bloodthirsty Irish, and all their adherents and confederates, for the propagating of the gospel of

Christ, the establishing of truth and peace, and restoring that bleeding nation to its former happiness and tranquillity'.

Belief in providence was fundamental. God would always look after his own, which is why the army was distressed later when a plague which had hitherto been confined to the Irish struck them, thus removing 'that distinction and difference which formerly He . . . kept between us and the people of this nation'. Still, when they 'thought fit to take the field' it was 'to attempt such things as God by His providence should lead us to upon the enemy'. In coming to Ireland Cromwell followed providence. He wrote to a friend that 'truly our work is neither from our brains nor from our courage and strength, but we follow the Lord who goeth before, and gather what He scattereth, that so all may appear to be from Him'.

But the deliberate massacre of the Drogheda garrison in September, followed by the slaughter of many innocent civilians, quickly revealed the ruthless side of Cromwell. It was partly justified by him as a necessary demonstration of severity which would 'tend to prevent the effusion of blood for the future' – as dubious an excuse as the one made centuries later when the first atom bombs were dropped on more innocent civilians. Cromwell revealed a more likely motive for his action when he wrote that it was 'a righteous judgement of God upon these barbarous wretches, who have imbrued their hands in so much innocent blood'. Simple revenge was one motive and God was on his side. Recounting how in St Peter's church, where mass had been celebrated the previous Sunday, 'in this very place near 1,000 of them were put to the sword, fleeing thither for safety', he wrote that this 'great thing should be done, not by power or might, but by the Spirit of God' and 'therefore it is good that God alone should have all the glory'. That the people of Drogheda could not have been involved in the earlier massacre of Protestants was beside the point; all Catholics shared in the collective guilt and deserved punishment. Later, in October, his army ran amok in Wexford and as Cromwell wrote 'put all to the sword that came in their way . . . not many less than two thousand'. He informed parliament that he had hoped to take the town without ruining it

'hoping the town might be of more use to you and your army, yet God would not have it so, but, by an unexpected providence, in His righteous justice, brought a just judgement upon them, causing them to become a prey to the soldier, who in their piracies made a prey of so many families, and made with their bloods to answer the cruelties which they had exercised upon the lives of divers poor Protestants'.

There was little of the same indiscriminate killing subsequently, though no priest was safe. During the winter months a succession of towns surrendered to Cromwell's army – New Ross, Cork, Kinsale and Bandon. Then in March Kilkenny yielded and on 9 May Clonmel. When, after nine months in Ireland,

Cromwell sailed for England on 26 May 1650 he had broken the back of the rebellion and left it to Henry Ireton, his son-in-law, to complete the new conquest of Ireland. After that a more satisfactory revenge could be taken for 1641 with the extirpation of popery on the island. When on 16 August at Denfermline, in order to secure the support of the Scots, Charles II agreed to withdraw all the promises of his father to the Catholics of Ireland, there remained no hope of Catholic emancipation. The king lumped all together, Irish and Old English, as 'bloody Irish rebels, who treacherously shed the blood of so many [of his] faithful and loyal subjects'.

In January 1650, while at Youghal, Cromwell wrote that he came to Ireland 'by the assistance of God, to hold forth and maintain the lustre and glory of English liberty in a nation where we have an undoubted right to it' and made no secret of the fact that there would be massive confiscation 'by escheating the lands of those who had a hand in the rebellion'. But 'liberty' did not mean freedom to attend mass. When the New Ross garrison surrendered, they asked for liberty of conscience. To this Cromwell replied: 'I meddle not with any man's conscience. But if by liberty of conscience you mean liberty to attend mass, I judge it best to use plain dealing and to let you know, where the parliament of England have power, that will not be allowed of'. There would be no clergy left in the land to celebrate mass. Many had been killed or executed during the war and many more were later transported across the Atlantic to work on plantations. Still more, perhaps even as many as 1,000, were allowed to emigrate to Catholic Europe. Even though some clergy managed to survive all this their number was pitifully small and totally inadequate to serve the large Catholic population. They lived furtive lives, travelling by night under cover and mostly saying mass in lonely guarded places. It was natural in these circumstances that, with the virtual disappearance of the parochial system, all kinds of irregular practices should emerge and that Irish Catholicism should acquire the popular, at times almost superstitious character it retained for many years. But there was no real attempt to convert the masses to puritanism and before very long economic and entrepreneurial interests came to predominate in what has since become known as the Cromwellian settlement.

The war had devastating effects on the population. According to Sir William Petty, the famous cartographer who was responsible for the Down Survey, 616,000 had been lost out of a population of 1,466,000 and these for the most part were Irish Catholics. Of the 850,000 remaining in 1652, something like 160,000 were Protestant. The 1642 'adventurers' act' had already committed two and a half million acres of Irish land to those English Protestant adventurers who had subscribed money to put down the rebellion. But in addition there were many soldiers who had served in Ireland, between 33,000 and 35,000, who were to be paid in land, so as many acres again had to be found for them. Altogether nearly half of Ireland was confiscated by the English parliament and all of this was transferred from Catholic into Protestant ownership. Thus, at one swoop, Protestant control of most of the land of Ireland would be established. Moreover, the majority of the Catholic landowners, by being forced to vacate their estates and migrate across the Shannon into Clare and Connacht, would be isolated from political influence, leaving the best land in Ireland, for the most part, in the hands of reliable Protestants. So that while in 1641, at the outbreak of the rebellion, about 59 per cent of the land had been in Catholic hands, by the end of the interregnum in 1660 they held only 22 per cent. The collapse of their political power can be simply illustrated. In the 1634 parliament two-fifths of the commons were Catholic; in 1640 they had shrunk to one third; in 1661 only one Catholic was elected to parliament.

The plan of confiscation was basically very simple. About one hundred people were named (including Ormond, Clanricard, Inchiquin) who were refused pardon, were to be executed and have all their estates confiscated. Others who were active in the rebellion before 10 November 1642 (the day the first assembly of confederates met in Kilkenny) or who had even assisted the rebels, were to receive the same treatment. All other landowners who had fought, either as royalists or confederates, against the parliamentarians were to be pardoned, lose their lands, but be compensated with land in Connacht. Most iniquitous of all was the treatment of Catholics who had never fought against the parliamentarians, but who could have been shown not to have demonstrated 'constant good affection' towards parliament. They, too, were to lose their lands and be similarly compensated in Connacht. There would therefore be a wholesale transplantation of Catholic landowners to Connacht – hence the saying 'To hell or to Connacht' – and their places would be taken by loyal New English Protestants.

In the event it did not work out like that. It was 'old Protestants' or 'ancient Protestants', as they began to call themselves in the 1650s, that is Protestant settlers who had been in Ireland before the confiscations, who were the real gainers. Even as early as 1642 the Earl of Cork had seen in the rebellion what he called 'a fit opportunity . . . to root the popish party of natives out of the kingdom and plant it with English Protestants'. Men like him had long since become adept at exploiting land confiscations to their own advantage. They did so by getting close to power. In the early, radical phase of the new Cromwellian policy, such men were seen to be untrustworthy, largely because of their past royalist affiliations, and thus had to be excluded from power in the revolution that was shaping a new Ireland. Newcomers from England would replace them. A new Commonwealth was to be created in Ireland that would make sure that past mistakes, which had allowed the 1641 rebellion to take place, would never be repeated. Ireland would be united to England in a new way. Thirty elected representatives would attend a new parliament of 460 in England and in fact they took their seats in 1654, 1656, 1659.

There is evidence that Cromwellian policy in Ireland was at times so radical because social experiments were conducted in almost laboratory conditions. Here might be tested notions which, if successful, might later be introduced into England. If a perfect Commonwealth could be established in

Ireland, encompassing fundamental changes in religion, education, administration and the law, then the revolution in England could be strengthened by imposing what had already been proved successful in Ireland. Army radicals tried to push aside old Protestants to achieve the necessary changes and it was they who effectively ruled Ireland until about 1655. Religious differences hindered their cooperative efforts, however, and Henry Cromwell restored old Protestant, civilian influence. So the radicals were slowly replaced, partly because Cromwell himself (who was made lord protector in December 1653) was at heart a constitutionalist and not happy with what was in effect a military dictatorship. His son Henry became lord deputy of Ireland in 1657 and lieutenant the following year. He was sympathetic to and supportive of the old Protestants. He even had some sympathy for Catholics, which emerged in the autumn of 1657 when he expressed regret at the oath of abjuration which the 'act for convicting, discovering and repressing of popish recusants' required of Catholics. In one way or another many old Protestant estates were saved and in many cases the owners even managed to augment them in the market of Irish lands which quickly developed when 'adventurers' and soldiers looked for a quick sale of lands allocated to them. Prices plummeted as sellers tried to find buyers and this, of course, played into the hands of the old Protestants.

At the same time the 1652 'act of settlement', dispossessing Catholic landholders and resettling most of them across the Shannon, was implemented. A 1653 civil survey of 27 counties (excluding five western counties for which the 1636 Wentworth survey was already available) related in great detail for each parish in every barony the value of all the land and property held by each proprietor. This made available detailed information on how much Catholic land was available for confiscation. But it was the remarkable 'Down Survey' carried out by Petty, mapping 22 counties in detail, which provided the most accurate information. The original intention was to remove all Catholics to the west, where they would be confined while the rest of Ireland was occupied by Protestants. But while most of the landowners were removed, and indeed the wealthy Catholic townsmen as well, the new proprietors successfully petitioned that 'ploughmen, husbandmen, labourers and artificers' should be allowed to remain to make the land profitable. So an elite of about 3,000 Catholic landowners were shifted and a substantial Catholic population left behind to provide tenants and labourers for the Protestant estates. Indeed many of the soldiers who retained land married Catholics, despite stringent government efforts to prevent this, and many of their children in the next generation were papist.

During the interregnum of 1649–60, then, a revolution occurred as a result of which a new Ireland emerged. Protestants now occupied most of the land outside Connacht and controlled absolutely the politics of the island. They had gained a position of strength which was the foundation of that ascendancy which was to be the dominant feature of society in the future. Although they numbered less than one in five of the population, the

Protestants had succeeded in establishing a Protestant state. In the next century Jonathan Swift, with his usual acerbity, expressed pithily what the Protestants had gained:

> 'The Catholics of Ireland . . . lost their estates for fighting in defence of their king. Those who cut off the father's head, forced the son to flee for his life, and overturned the whole ancient frame of government . . . obtained grants of the very estates the Catholics lost in defence of the ancient constitution, and thus they gained by their rebellion what the Catholics lost by their loyalty'.

9   A Protestant kingdom, 1660–91

Charles II was proclaimed king in Dublin on 14 May 1660, only six days after his proclamation in London. This restoration of the monarchy, in which Ireland played a crucial role, was the result of a period of instability and political jostling which followed the death of Oliver Cromwell in September 1658. His son Richard succeeded him as protector in England and in Ireland another son, Henry, headed the government. But the leaders of the army and the less radical parliamentarians failed to agree and during the second half of 1659 rapid political change posed the threat of an army dictatorship in England.

In Ireland the 'ancient Protestants', already strengthened by the support of Henry Cromwell, became anxious about their future. When the army dissolved the rump parliament in England in October, anxiety gave way to fear of the possible consequences of the legal and constitutional uncertainty which now existed. Partly in response to General George Monck's declaration from Scotland in support of parliament and his specific appeal to the army officers in Ireland to join him, some officers decided to seize power. They were also frightened by the attempts of the republican Edmund Ludlow, who took command of the army in Ireland in 1659, to reform (as he saw it) the army by weeding out 200 officers who had been appointed by the moderate government of Henry Cromwell, replacing them with radicals who were convinced republicans and unlikely to accept a restored monarchy. This was the reason for the dramatic seizure of Dublin castle on 13 December by a group of officers fearful of their future and who then issued a proclamation that the castle was now held in the name of parliament. Very quickly most of the other garrisons on the island were seized by supporters of parliament. Having arrested those to whom the government had been committed, they proclaimed that the ruin of liberty, as well as religion, had thus been prevented by providence.

This success in Ireland caused General Monck to observe a day of thanksgiving in Scotland and greatly strengthened his resolve. Three men now exercised effective power in Ireland through control of army administration – Lord Broghill (a son of the Earl of Cork) in Munster, Sir Charles Coote in Connacht, and Colonel Cooper in Ulster. These men aimed to ensure that what had been achieved in Ireland during the protectorate of Oliver Cromwell would be safeguarded. In particular they were anxious to protect land acquisitions, as the instructions given to a special embassy to the council of state in London, late in 1659, made clear. One instruction specifically sought an act of parliament confirming all grants of land, as well as all leases, made since 19 April 1653. In a famous declaration published in February 1660, first Coote and 54 officers stationed in Dublin, and then Broghill and 45 officers in Munster referred to the calamities caused by the purging of parliament in 1648 and the consequent uncertainties under the law: 'Powers have made laws, and subsequent powers disowned and nulled what the preceding powers had acted; that now the questions are not so many, what is the meaning of the law as what is the law'. Not only had the law in many instances been put aside, so that their very liberty was threatened, they were particularly agitated because of new and excessive taxes imposed on Ireland by a Westminster parliament in which they were not even represented. The Dublin declaration in its prologue went so far as to refer to 'our now dying liberties and freedom' which had not yet been 'utterly razed and defaced' and therefore it was possible that 'by the wisdom of a full and free parliament they may be again renewed and firmly established'.

This radical hint that an independent Irish parliament might be restored was given greater force when, on 7 February 1660, a convention met in Dublin, with 137 members representing the old parliamentary constituencies. There was a violent reaction by the Commonwealth government in England. General Ludlow was sent back to Ireland, but he was barred from landing in Dublin and failed to make any impression on what was happening. Events in Ireland now seemed to be outside the control of the council of state in England.

The amount of time devoted to commercial matters and to taxation in the convention showed the extent of 'ancient' Protestant influence and their concern for their own material benefits. The Old English constitutional position was restored when the convention asserted that because Ireland was a sovereign state it had the power, as well as the right, to tax itself. In place of the taxes imposed by Westminster it then proceeded to institute a poll-tax, which was to the benefit of the landed gentry and wealthy merchants alike. Significantly, too, it restated the old arguments about the independence of the Irish parliament and, most memorably, the age-old protestation that Ireland was not bound by the acts of an English parliament.

It also favoured a restoration of the monarchy which would provide a stability based on law and thus protection of the vested interests of Protestant settlers, 'ancient' and Cromwellian alike. The restored monarchy, it was urged, would legitimize the *status quo* in Ireland, thus preserving both the land settlement and Protestantism. When the convention, on 14 May, proclaimed Charles II King of Ireland, it organized a huge procession through the city during which the proclamation was publicly declared at famous landmarks. A great celebration followed, with the ringing of bells, bonfires, fireworks, free wine in abundance, and a public entertainment through the streets in the style of the old miracle plays to act out the obsequies of the Commonwealth. A contemporary described 'the solemnization and funeral of a certain monster they called the Commonwealth, represented by an ugly misshapen body without an head, but with a huge insatiable belly and a prodigious rump'. In the end the monster was destroyed, torn to pieces by the mob and then publicly burned.

The programme of the convention, then, was nothing less than a general settlement in church as well as state, to restore some certainty where uncertainty had become the norm, to provide some sort of guarantee that would bring back and preserve religious orthodoxy of a more moderate Protestant character. With the Presbyterian element more dominant than the episcopalian it seemed plain enough what this meant. But in time what contemporaries began to call the 'prelatical' party came to dominate the convention, especially when the restoration of the monarchy seemed more assured. When Charles II was proclaimed king in Dublin on 14 May 1660, the convention arranged for a thanksgiving sermon to be preached in Christ Church cathedral by Henry Jones, described as 'bishop of Clogher'. Jones had indeed, when dean of Kilmore, succeeded to the bishopric of Clogher in pre-Cromwellian days. But he later changed sides, became scoutmaster-general to the Irish army under the Commonwealth, and was now (like so many of the 'ancient Protestants') backing the restoration of the old Protestant establishment. He later, in 1661, was consecrated Bishop of Meath. By 21 June when 'commissioners' appointed by the convention presented to the privy council in London a set of proposals, they included one requesting 'that the Church of Ireland be resettled in doctrine, discipline and worship, as it was in the time of your royal father of blessed memory'. Further, they asked that 'Godly, learned, orthodox and preaching ministers of the gospel be settled there as speedily as may be in a parochial way and supported by tithes, glebes and other legal maintenance'. Soon new clerical appointments to vacant bishoprics and deaneries followed and an episcopal Church of Ireland was re-established.

All of this reassured Protestants who were worried about their legal title to land, especially those 'ancient Protestants' who felt threatened by the radicalism of the 'new Protestants' or Commonwealth supporters who might destabilize society and thus upset the land settlement. No wonder that they rejoiced in the restoration of the episcopacy, celebrated in 1661 by the new dean of St Patrick's, William Fuller, in a new anthem:

Now that the lord the mitre has restored,
which with the crown lay in the dust abhorred.

More symbolic of the new ecclesiastical order was the ceremony in St Patrick's on 27 January 1661, when no less than two archbishops and 10 bishops were consecrated. With Dean Fuller all could celebrate when they sang:

Angels look down, rejoice to see
Like Heaven above, a hierarchy.

The restored episcopal hierarchy signified not just a restoration of the
Church of Ireland to its former status of ascendancy, but the restoration of
the 'ancient Protestants' to their position of dominance within the new state.
Whatever hopes the Presbyterians and other dissenters may have had from
the new monarchy were dashed. Shortly after the spectacular consecration
ceremony in St Patrick's, the issue of a proclamation against meetings of
'papists, presbyterians, independents, anabaptists, quakers and other fanatical persons' made it clear who was now in the ascendant, as did the legislation
of parliament in May 1661 ordering all to conform to the church as by law
established.

Long before this, in April 1660, the king had issued the famous declaration
of Breda, promising pardon to all who had opposed the Royalist cause. Later,
in August, an 'act of free and general pardon, indemnity and oblivion' was
published in England, but those who had joined in the rebellion in Ireland were
specifically excluded. Then, on 30 November, Charles made a declaration confirming adventurers and soldiers in the lands in their possession on 7 May
1659, though the lands of what were called 'innocent papists' were excepted.
This meant, in effect, that only a negligible acreage of land would be available
to provide for those Catholics who had supported the monarchy and who had
been promised restoration in that November declaration. For of the 33–35,000
Cromwellian soldiers who had been paid by grants of Irish land, about three-
quarters had sold their shares in the Irish land market, mainly to those who
now were determined to protect the settlement. Such men, 'ancient' Protestants
and Cromwellians alike, had most to lose if a royal declaration concerning
'innocent papists' was ever given full effect.

This helps to explain the fierce Protestant reaction in Ireland to the king's
feeble attempts to implement that section of his 1660 declaration. Catholics
had naturally taken an initiative in trying to persuade Charles and his council in England that religious toleration should now be extended to them and
that they should be restored to their confiscated lands. But they were inept in
their attempts at persuasion, emphasizing their rights and the king's duties
towards them, instead of laying the real stress on their continuous loyalty and
asking for grace. No wonder the royal patience wore thin. When it snapped,
Sir Nicholas Plunkett, of the old family of the Pale, was the luckless victim.
Appearing before the privy council, he was suddenly confronted with embarrassing evidence of past indiscretion, to say the least. A document under his
signature of 1647 was produced, offering Ireland to the pope, or if he refused
it then to any Catholic ruler in Europe who would protect it. That was the
end. He was banished from the court, Catholics were forbidden to petition
the council further, and the royal assent was given to the highly contentious
bill of settlement, sent over from Ireland in accordance with the provisions of
Poynings' law.

This act of settlement, published on 31 July 1662, was designed to give effect to the November 1660 declaration. It was followed by the opening of the first court of claims in September, to hear the evidence of those claiming to be 'innocents' and thus entitled under the act to restoration of their lands. A decree of innocence would entitle the claimant to immediate repossession of his lands, at the expense of the Cromwellian owner, of course, who would in turn be compensated (or 'reprised') elsewhere with land of equal value. But where to find suitable lands in compensation remained a problem. As Ormond observed cynically, 'there must be new discoveries made of a new Ireland, for this old will not serve to satisfy these engagements. It remains, then, to determine which party must suffer in the default of means to satisfy all'.

It is not surprising, then, that there was violent Protestant resistance to the court. Even while the court was sitting there were rumours of plots, confirmed in May when a plan to seize Dublin castle was uncovered. Led by Colonel Thomas Hood, in support of the claims of Cromwellian soldiers, there were eight members of parliament involved, three of whom were hanged in July. But it was believed that even more important people were implicated, such as Orrery (the former Lord Broghill). The king could no longer ignore the groundswell of Protestant opinion in Ireland. Parliament itself was now exclusively Protestant, since the one Catholic returned, Geoffrey Browne, never took his seat. On 21 August 1663 the court of claims was adjourned, a bare eight months since it first started hearing pleas. By then about 850,000 acres had been returned to Catholics. But no further claims were heard – Petty estimated that no less than 8,000 claims from Connacht alone remained unheard – and Protestant ascendancy over Irish land was confirmed. Where Catholics had held about 59 per cent of the profitable land in 1641, which had fallen to a mere 8 per cent by 1660, the bulk of it in Connacht, after 1663 they held about 20 per cent.

One result of this partial Catholic recovery of land was to accentuate the ancient division between Irish and Old English gentry. Among the 'innocents' restored by the court of claims were only two O'Neills, two McCarthies and two O'Briens (of whom one was a Protestant). In contrast there were large numbers of Old English: 15 Plunketts, 13 Nugents, 12 Roches, nine Dillons and many Fitzgeralds and Butlers. It was almost as if race was more important than religion in settling claims. But the effect was to reassert Anglo-Irish dominance and to confirm Irish suppression. One result was the appearance of 'tories', Irish brigands who moved outside the law and raided settlers occupying their former lands. Others managed to become tenants of the new owners and thus as tenant farmers secured possession of at least part of their lost estates. But Protestant ascendancy was confirmed. Not even the 1665 bill of explanation, which sought to force the Cromwellian settlers to surrender a third of their lands to provide for the restoration of 'innocents', succeeded in seriously altering the Cromwellian land settlement. As Petty remarked, it was a game which the English had won and they had 'a gamester's right at least to their estates'. Not all the 'gamesters' had gained. Bribery, family influence, and best of all a connection at court had helped some to gain most in what was more of a game of chance than a genuine land 'settlement'. Some years later the Earl of Essex was more realistic when he compared the tortuous process to 'flinging the reward upon the death of a deer among a pack of hounds, where every one pulls and tears what he can for himself'.

For one reason or another large numbers of Catholics remained on the land. Even in the towns, with the exception of Dublin, they continued to form the great majority of the population. The laws against recusancy were still on the books and the oath of supremacy was still demanded of all office holders. The king was disposed to be tolerant, however, and there was no sustained effort to make Catholics conform and, as the law demanded, attend Church of Ireland religious services. Besides, there was the added complication of what precisely was the strict legal position. If, as had been argued in the 1660 convention which led to the re-establishment of an independent Irish parliament, English statutes did not bind Ireland, then the penal laws of England could not be strictly enforced on the island.

Religious toleration became the norm. The old problem of loyalty remained, however: how to reconcile loyalty to the pope as head of the church with loyalty to the king as head of state? An assembly of Catholics in Dublin in 1666 accepted that in purely temporal matters the king exercised divine right and, more to the point, denied the power of deposition to the pope. But this did not go nearly far enough for the government and so Catholic loyalty remained a dubious commodity. A more radical proposal, composed by the Franciscan Peter Walsh in a 'loyal formulary or Irish remonstrance', and signed by some of the clergy as well as a number of laymen, not only denounced papal claims to the right to absolve Catholics from the king's authority, but proclaimed that all kings, no matter what their religion, were lieutenants of God here on earth. Walsh's remonstrance became a bitter bone of contention, denounced by Rome and the vast majority of the Catholic clergy of Ireland. Some, especially among the Franciscans, continued to support the radical position of the remonstrance, not least in Europe where polemic later raged. Even as late as 1680 when a 'poor, old and feeble Franciscan friar' appealed to Ormond for help, he wrote that 'I am and was of Peter Walsh's Remonstrance for which I suffered much to this day from the contrary sort'.

For most this was largely an academic question. Individual Catholics made their own way. For the old gentry who had come down in the world the loss of status was almost as hard to take as the loss of land. For many others, their status as tenant farmers provided them with a good life and, as always in a period of revolutionary change, there were some who exploited the situation to their own benefit. A vicious contemporary satire in Irish, *Pairlement Chloinne Tomáis*, attacked those farmers and artisans who, despite being Catholics, had prospered from the change. Not only had they turned their backs on their hereditary lords, they had proved themselves economically successful in competition with fallen gentry. They imitated the English and the satire lampoons them as peasants who were brutish and quarrelsome, dressing ridiculously in an attempt to be fashionable, totally lacking all refinement and manners. The composition clearly shows the kind of attitude which the Irish upper classes had towards the peasants.

It must be remembered that, in the Irish world before the extension of the common law of England, the nobility had virtually exercised the rights of tyrants. The peasants had few rights and owned little, so it was they, more than anyone, who benefited from the anglicization of large parts of Ireland which followed plantation. Under the new regime they were freed from the hereditary services which their lords had exacted and were free to profit from the demand for labour and even tenants which the new landlords represented. The change was momentous. A new class of Irish peasant emerged, greedy for land and willing to bow to every new regime in order to achieve their ambition. Only in religion, and possibly because there was never any great pressure on most of them to change, did they remain staunchly conservative. The English language, out of touch for most of them, became the badge of respectability and social conformity. Those who could speak it were a source of envy. In the *Pairlement Chloinne Tomáis* a travelling tobacco-seller in Munster is interrogated by the only peasant in the area who claims to know English. Tomás is the wonder of the neighbourhood. After returning the greeting of the pedlar in his finest English ('Pleshy for you, pleshy, goodman Robin'), Tomás is complimented in Irish by a neighbour: 'By my mother's soul you have swallowed the best of English'. Told to ask the price of the tobacco, he questions: 'What the bigg greate órdlach for the what so penny, for is the la yourself for me', which the pedlar rightly translates as asking 'how many inches is worth the penny'!

The ability to speak English was seen as a necessary qualification for entry into the new commercial world which was emerging in Ireland. For, despite all the death and destruction, the wars, famines and disease, the country recovered and developed. After the restoration the population was not far off two million. In 1672 Petty estimated that 150,000 immigrants had arrived in the previous 20 years. The furnaces of industry demanded charcoal and this led to the destruction of most woodlands. One result was that many wild animals disappeared and in 1710 what was reputed to be the last wolf in county Cork was killed. More importantly, forest clearance helped agriculture, so that grain export expanded dramatically, in addition to the traditional trade in wool, hides and skins. When English legislation prohibited the export of cattle and sheep to England, new markets for salted meats were found and a huge expansion in the dairy industry and the export of butter resulted. Irish agriculture was acquiring what became its characteristic stamp.

Nowhere is this growth more obvious than in the towns, which expanded greatly through economic development. Dublin was not only the largest city in Ireland, it became in size and importance second only to London. After 1660 the population, then about 17,000 trebled and perhaps even reached Petty's estimate of 60,000. One simple statistic illustrates this growth: before 1670 only one bridge spanned the Liffey, by 1685 five were necessary because of expansion. As the capital, Dublin was in a privileged position and the splendour of the viceregal court attracted the cultured as well as the wealthy. Dublin University was also expanding, with about 300 students and new buildings. The new Dublin Philosophical Society, founded by William Molyneux in 1685 in imitation of the Royal Society of London, and in close association with Trinity College, quickly provided a forum for academics and intellectuals. Late in the reign of Charles II the same Molyneux could boast about Dublin: 'We are come to fine things here in Dublin, and you will wonder how our city increases sensibly in fine buildings, fair trade, and splendour in all things – in furniture, coaches, civility, housekeeping'.

Such pride was justified. But the good life was enjoyed, at the upper level of society at least, by those who belonged to the established church. Regardless of the king's increasing interest in Catholicism, the realities of political life in Ireland made it difficult for him to extend any great favours to his Catholic subjects there. Toleration in religious practice was one thing: restoration of land and office was a different matter altogether. But then, in May 1670, King Charles signed a notorious secret treaty with Louis XIV in which he agreed not only to join the French in a war against the Dutch, but also to become a Catholic. This was followed in March 1672 with a 'declaration of indulgence' under which all penal laws affecting Catholics and dissenters were suspended. The effect in Ireland was immediate and a more liberal regime was instituted. But then the failure of his new foreign policy forced the king to give way to new anti-Catholic pressures in England. Despite the nominal extension of the new measures to Ireland (such as the order in late October that all upper clergy and regulars were to vacate the kingdom by the end of the year), in practice the old liberal attitude continued.

What really brought about a change in attitude was the plot, revealed in 1678 by Titus Oates, that the Catholics of England planned to murder the king. As always, events in England had an impact on Ireland. News of the 'popish plot' caused such fear that many Protestants fled from rural areas to the security of nearby towns. In Dublin a nightly guard of 500 men had to be provided, despite which terrified people made constant complaints to officials of priests illegally meeting and arms being stored by Catholics, none of which could be verified when search parties were sent out. An Irish scapegoat had to be found and the choice fell on Oliver Plunkett, the Catholic Archbishop of Armagh. He was arrested and accused of planning, with Jesuit help, a French invasion of Ireland and of organizing no less than 70,000 Catholics to rise in support. The only evidence produced was supplied by disaffected Irish Franciscans and others from Gaelic Ulster who had suffered from the reforming zeal of this descendant of one of the greatest families of the Pale. The charge was so ridiculous and the so-called evidence of the witnesses so obviously the result of personal hatreds – they were dismissed out of hand by

Ormond, the lord lieutenant, in a letter: 'They find it more honourable and safe to be the king's evidence than a cowstealer' – that the case against Plunkett was adjourned at Dundalk. But the archbishop was brought to London, indicted, convicted in June 1681 without any credible evidence against him, and then executed. Even on the scaffold the archbishop made a speech in which he affirmed that had he been tried in Ireland the charges against him would have been instantly dismissed by a Protestant jury. There is much truth in that. In Ireland, despite some increase in crime because of the prevailing conditions, there was a general respect for the law by governors and governed alike. If a chief governor admitted in 1674, with some exasperation, that 'the truth is, a little more severity must be used here than I conceive it requisite in England', the rule of law was in fact rigorously upheld and legal formalities observed. So it is most unlikely that a conviction of Plunkett would have been secured in Ireland. Even Charles II had no doubt of his innocence, but he did nothing to save him.

Back in Ireland there were further repercussions. Mass houses were ordered to close, bishops and regulars to go overseas, and weapons held by Catholics to be handed over. Some clergy were imprisoned and the Archbishop of Dublin, Peter Talbot, brother of the future Earl of Tyrconnell and formerly chaplain to the queen, was confined until he died. But generally there was no real enforcement of penal laws. The Archbishop of Cashel was able to write to the pope that the Irish government had not 'given credence to the calumnies' against Catholics and so 'has not oppressed us at all so much as in England'. Even the discovery of yet another 'plot' in the summer of 1683, the Rye House Plot, did not produce any strong anti-Catholic reaction in Ireland.

The more liberal treatment of Catholics in Ireland was not to the liking of many Protestants. While repeated reports of Catholic rebellions, plots and massacres of Protestants may seem so far-fetched as to be incredible, it must be remembered that memories of 1641 and all that happened afterwards were still vividly alive. Captain Thomas Walcott in 1672 gave voice to his constant anxiety:

'The cause of his fear and trouble [was] that remembering how the Irish papists had in 1641 murdered his father, and turned all his children a-begging, whereof he being one and a spectator, he believed their principle were the same now as then'.

Others gave voice to similar fears.

Yet the harsh realities of economic life made most Catholics secure. As the great majority of the population, the growing prosperity of the kingdom depended largely on them. Ormond, the lord lieutenant, did not mince words in condemning Protestant landowners who, he said, 'pretend that they cannot sleep for fear of having their throats cut by the Papists'. He pointed out that those same landlords 'are the men who brought them to inhabit their houses in towns and to plant and labour their lands'. So, while fear of Catholics was still prevalent, the Protestant community had little option but to accept them in their midst. As long as they were kept in their place and not given the means to threaten either the economic, political or military superiority of the Protestant elite, then they could be tolerated. Some Protestants went even further than mere tolerance. In November 1686 the provost of Trinity College, Robert Huntington, wrote in a letter, in the context of producing an Irish translation of the Bible: '. . . methinks the Nation should make their language triumphant also, and the rather, because their [sic] are Laws against it. For why should a free people retain any marks of Slavery'.

It was the growing influence of the king's brother, James Duke of York, an avowed Catholic, which threatened to upset the balance so successfully maintained in favour of the Protestants in Ireland. The attempt to enlarge the Catholic element in the army caused particular alarm. After the restoration of the monarchy the Irish Catholics who had served with the exiled Charles became a problem. Irish Catholic regiments and their officers were no longer considered safe, and certainly not for service in Ireland. They were banished to Tangiers in north Africa, where they remained until 1684, when the fortress was handed over to the Moors.

But with the advent of the Duke of York to a dominant influence over the king, a promotion of Catholics to prominence in the civil and military administration of Ireland was decided upon. Here the influence of Richard Talbot, a close friend of York's, was decisive. One ploy was to remove from the lord lieutenant in Ireland control over army commissions and place them in the king's hand, in effect under York's control and therefore mostly at the disposal of Talbot, who used them to good effect. After the accession of York as James II in 1685 Talbot was given control of the Irish army and in little more than a year he not only had promoted Catholics to make up more than half the total of officers, but nearly 70 per cent of the lower ranks were Catholic as well. No wonder that Protestant alarm escalated and that Catholic euphoria grew in the expectation that the recovery of lost lands would follow. In June 1686 the secretary of the lord lieutenant, the Earl of Clarendon, reported that 'the Irish talk of nothing now but of recovering their lands and bringing the English under their subjection, which they who have been the masters for above 400 years know not how well to bear'. Under a Catholic king, and with the help of Talbot, the Irish Catholics believed that the Protestant achievement of the seventeenth century could be overthrown and the rightful ascendancy of the Catholic majority on the island at last be established.

But for this to be achieved, it was not enough to promote Catholics in the army, in the judiciary, in local government and in all levels of the civil administration. All of this would count for little so long as Protestants held most of the land of Ireland. So, the lands and even the buildings held in such abundance by the clergy of the established Church of Ireland must be transferred into the hands of the Catholic clergy. More importantly, the land settlement must be reversed and wealth concentrated in Catholic hands. This was well appreciated. Late in 1686 the lawyer Richard Nagle told Tyrconnell that 'nothing can support the Catholic religion in that kingdom but to make the Catholics there considerable in their fortunes, as they are considerable in their number'. This alone would make a Protestant king in future 'allow them a toleration as to their religion'.

The policy of James II in England after his accession in 1685 greatly encouraged the Irish Catholics. He believed that his own conversion was God's way of easing the lot of Catholics in England. Once king, he vigorously pursued a policy of ending discrimination in law against Catholics and, because he needed support, against dissenters as well. In so doing he alienated his Tory support and gave credence to the Whig warning of what England could expect of a popish king. What was happening in Ireland seemed to confirm the worst fears. If Catholics were given a near monopoly of office there, would not the same thing eventually happen in England? When in September 1688 he ordered four regiments of Irish Catholics to be brought to England, he appeared to be preparing for a challenge to his programme as any Catholic autocrat in Europe might do.

But in fact King James had proceeded with some caution in Ireland. He sent the Earl of Clarendon, a staunch Anglican, as lord lieutenant and even though Tyrconnell in practice was able to proceed with his programme of promoting Catholics, the lord lieutenant was able to calm Protestant fears somewhat by passing on the royal assurance that 'whatever imaginary (for they can be called no other) apprehensions any man here may have had, his majesty hath no intention of altering the acts of settlement'. Land in Protestant hands was to be guaranteed. When in 1687 Tyrconnell was made chief governor, the first Catholic to hold that office since the reformation, he was given the lower status of lord deputy (instead of lord lieutenant), a token reassurance to Protestants.

But many saw his appointment as the triumph of Catholicism. The diarist John Evelyn recorded the appointment as 'to the evident ruin of the Protestants in that kingdom'. Some showed their fear by abandoning all they possessed and sought refuge in England, America or, more significantly, in Holland where they offered their services to William of Orange. The reconsecration for Catholic use of the chapels at Dublin castle and the royal hospital at Kilmainham symbolized the great change that they believed was taking place. New appointments of Catholics gave them control over local as well as the central administration in Dublin. This Catholic control of the localities was to manifest itself most blatantly when elections to parliament were held, securing an overwhelming Catholic majority.

The growing number of refugees from Ireland helped to sway public opinion in England against James and the spectre of a Catholic monarchy in the future. In June 1685 the queen, Mary of Modena, gave birth to a son and a Catholic successor to James was assured. The arrival of troops from Ireland in September only inflamed the situation, especially when some were involved in riots, such as happened when one of them attacked a Protestant church in

Portsmouth. The king's use of Irish Catholics alienated many in the English army so that when William of Orange landed in Devonshire in November 1688 he met with only token resistance. Most of the Irish troops subsequently got away from England, some to Ireland and more to France, with no real attempt to prevent them from leaving. There was little King James could do to halt the invaders and eventually, on Christmas Eve, he abandoned England altogether and sought refuge in France.

If England quickly united behind William of Orange and soon accepted him and his wife Mary, the Protestant daughter of James II, as king and queen, the same was not true of Protestant Ireland. It is a mistake to see the Protestants there as a coherent group, united in opposition to Catholics. A large migration of Scots into Ulster during the 1680s (and later during the 1690s) added a strong Presbyterian element. By 1689 there were 86 ministers serving their communities and by 1702 this had significantly increased to 130. To the anglicans, these dissenters were hardly any less of a threat than the Catholics. Even among the members of the established church there was no guarantee of a united opposition to James. Most of them continued to affirm their loyalty to the Stuart dynasty on the English throne. Even in Ulster there was no single, outright opposition. When Derry closed its gates against the Catholic Earl of Antrim on 17 December 1688, it was not because of any rooted opposition to James II, but rather because of a panic created by the revelation of a supposed plot to massacre Protestants. The citizens, in fact, behind the closed gates proclaimed their loyalty to King James and swore 'to persevere in our duty and loyalty to our sovereign lord the king'.

Even when in 1688 rumours circulated widely that a terrible massacre of Protestants was planned, repeating the horrors of 1641, there was no immediate panic. Only about five per cent of the Protestants fled to England, and most of them left because of the great increase in lawlessness and disorder which affected Catholics just as much. If anything, Protestants looked to their legitimate king, James II, to restore the rule of law in Ireland and many welcomed him for that reason when he arrived in Kinsale in March 1689. He was to be their protector. One Protestant agent reported that 'if anything doth better the Protestant condition it will be the king's being here', and that after he landed James was 'much troubled to hear that the English hath been ill dealt with and promiseth that he will take course to order things better than before'.

But the king failed to control the violence and this was certainly one reason why some of those Protestants who had supported him switched their allegiance to William. It was, as one of them put it, because 'we have no civil government among us'. If anything, the presence of so many hated French troops in the king's following increased the belief that further disorder, and not less, would result from his presence in Ireland.

More than anything else, however, a bill introduced in the Dublin parliament on 10 May 1689 alienated Protestants and drove them into opposition. This was designed to repeal the acts of settlement and explanation which formed the basis of the restoration land settlement. It thus threatened the very basis of Protestant power in Ireland and, in effect, faced them with a real Catholic ascendancy that would eventually wipe them out. This was demonstrated in no uncertain way in an act of attainder against more than 2,000 who were accused of adhering to William. Referring to the 'most horrid invasion of the king's unnatural enemy, the prince of Orange, assisted by many of his majesty's rebellious and traitorous subjects', the act was designed to proclaim those listed as traitors, subject to the death penalty and, perhaps more importantly, the confiscation of all they possessed. No wonder that William King, the dean of St Patrick's, said that it was an act unparalleled since ancient Rome, designed to accomplish the extirpation of all Protestants in Ireland. Later, the commons in the Williamite parliament of 1692 rejected a bill which provided for the common hangman to burn the records of the 1689 parliament because 'the house found it for their majesties' service and the honour of the Protestants of Ireland to preserve the records of the Irish barbarity'. So Ireland, like England, became polarized between Jacobites and Williamites.

This parliament of 1689, known as the 'patriot parliament' since it was so christened by Thomas Davis in the nineteenth century, is unique in many respects. It was the only one (apart from that summoned by Richard II when he was in Ireland in the late fourteenth century) which was opened by the king in person; and it was more representative of the whole of Ireland than any assembly before modern times. But it was anything but 'patriot', with the members pursuing selfish ends and wasting valuable time when the war required their energies elsewhere. As the Protestant Bishop of Meath exclaimed during yet another interminable debate on the land settlement in the House of Lords: 'Is it now time for men to seek vineyards and olive yards when a civil war is raging in the nation and we are under apprehension of invasion from abroad'? Of the 230 (from a full quota of 300) returned to the commons, all save six were Catholic. Of those about two-thirds were Old English, the remainder bearing old Irish names. Thirty-five sat in the upper house, with the Old English again predominant and only four Protestant secular peers in attendance. A remarkable feature, however, was the absence of the Catholic bishops, who had not been summoned, and the presence of the Protestant bishops of Meath, Cork, Ossory and Limerick. Three others, including the Archbishop of Armagh, were formally excused from attending because of sickness or age.

As was to be expected, the Catholics made the repeal of the restoration land settlement their first aim. While it is true that the Old English were quite genuine in their attachment to Catholicism, for many the recovery of their land was, if anything, more important. This had been the case even earlier in the century when the protection of their lands, rather than the defence of their religion, had turned them into rebels. When Robert Talbot said that 'he would not lose one acre for all the mitres in Ireland', he was expressing the views of many others. Perhaps not many would have joined him when he proclaimed that it was 'indifferent to him if mass was said in Christchurch or St Patrick's or his own bedside'. But 40 years later his successors were determined to use the advent of a Catholic king to recover the lands they had lost. How this was to be done led to interminable squabbles and delays while personal interests were advanced, before finally the Acts of Settlement and Explanation were repealed.

Before that, in order to clear the way, it was enacted that Ireland was not bound by English statutes. This declaratory act, a throwback to the famous legislation of 1460 and a prelude to much constitutional controversy in the future, was regarded by James II as prejudicial to the royal prerogative. He was reluctant in the extreme to give his assent, as indeed he was averse to the overthrowing of the land settlement. But in the circumstances he could not refuse. He subsequently showed his reluctance when he proved unwilling to establish a special court where those who had claims to land could have their title examined. Significantly, however, he did refuse to allow the repeal of Poynings' law, even though he was aware, as he said himself, that the Irish regarded it as 'the greatest sign and means of their subjection to England'. The fact was that he looked on Ireland as simply a base from which he could recover England and his Dublin parliament must not be allowed to do anything which might make that restoration more difficult to achieve. As the Comte d'Avaux, who had accompanied him to Ireland from France, reported to Paris,

'his heart is too English for him to agree to anything that could displease the English. He still counts on being reestablished soon in the kingdom of England and . . . will do nothing to remove Ireland from its dependence on the English'.

Contrary to expectations, the parliament did not replace a Protestant domination with a Catholic one. The fact that James summoned the Protestant bishops, but not the Catholic ones, was a clear indication that, while he might be anxious to ameliorate the lot of Catholics at law, he was not anxious to alienate his Protestant subjects by significantly diminishing their rights. His refusal to accept legislation that would favour French as against English economic interests, in relation to the export of wool for example, showed that he was determined to retain control of the Irish economy in English hands. When James opposed a bill barring the export of wool to England and favouring export to France, d'Avaux wrote that 'he has a heart too English to take any step that would vex the English, and that holds up the woollen business'. But the passing of the act of attainder destroyed whatever hopes he had of retaining Protestant support. His attitude during the sessions of parliament also helped to disillusion some of his Catholic supporters in Ireland.

Meanwhile a war had broken out in Ireland which was to make the legislation of the 1689 parliament ineffective. When James landed in Kinsale he brought with him French troops and supplies of war. This radically changed attitudes in England. Like it or not, William III and the English parliament now had no choice but to regard Ireland as a major player when war was declared against France in May. As one MP said: 'If Ireland should be lost, England will follow'. A measure of that worry is that parliament voted over £700,000 for the taking of Ireland. And when William later announced that he was going in person to Ireland, parliament voted the even larger sum of £1,200,000.

William had come to England in the first place because he believed that it was his mission to prevent the French under Louis XIV from dominating Europe and in particular the Dutch Republic. He saw himself as God's chosen instrument and believed that only he could humble the French king. He was part of the grand alliance which included the Holy Roman Emperor and the King of Spain, as well as the Protestant Dutch and English. With the French now involved in Ireland, which James II hoped would provide him with the resources with which to regain Scotland and then England, a military reduction of Ireland became vital for the Williamites – not just to end Jacobite ambitions, but also to bring to an end the territorial ambitions of the French.

'The war of the two kings', as it became known in Irish, was thus a major event in late seventeenth century European history. But its local dimension was also important, for it amounted in the end to a struggle between Catholics and Protestants for supremacy in the kingdom of Ireland. With French help the Jacobite army was reorganized at a level of 35,000 men and eight major convoys of ships brought all kinds of war supplies. In 1689, for example, the French landed 16,000 sabres, 3,000 swords, 5,000 muskets, 1,000 pairs of pistols, 500 carbines, 500 flintlocks and 100,000 rounds of ammunition. In 1690, in addition to arms and ammunition, ships brought tents, clothing, hospital supplies, carts, harness tools, flags and flour. Many French experts (generals, engineers, artillerymen and commissaries) as well as troops arrived, together with Irish, English and Scottish officers from abroad. The Jacobite army was a formidable force, more than adequate to take, hold and garrison the whole of Ireland for James II and that is what nearly happened. When they routed the Williamites at the 'break of Dromore' in March 1689, it was a preliminary to the regaining of authority over the whole of Ulster. But two famous events changed the course of history and helped to prevent James from holding Ireland. Both Derry and Enniskillen successfully resisted and defied all attempts to take them and later, in a major head to head confrontation at the river Boyne, King William defeated King James and caused him to abandon Ireland altogether.

The siege of Derry has passed into the folklore of Irish history. It was more incompetence and inexperience on the Jacobite side than anything else which prevented the city from being taken. There were 7,500 soldiers defending Derry, a city with strong walls and 20 guns to beat off attackers, so a direct attack was going to prove difficult. But with over 30 thousand refugees added to the inhabitants, shortage of food quickly became a problem. When a boom was constructed by French engineers across the Foyle, about two miles from the city, strong enough to prevent any relief arriving by boat, a blockade was bound to succeed in the end. Not only did food supplies disappear, with even rats, cats and dogs eventually scarce on the ground, but ammunition, too, began to run out. Fever and dysentery also took their toll. One of the governors, Reverend George Walker, published a famous price-list of dogs, cats, rats and mice – a quarter of a dog fattened by eating the bodies of slain Irish cost 5s.6d. – and immortalized a certain 'fat gentleman' who hid himself from his neighbours, already looking at him with what he said were greedy eyes. On 30 June, Conrad von Rosen, one of the Jacobite commanders, issued a desperate proclamation that if, by the following day, the city had not surrendered, then he would round up all the Protestants he could find and drive them into the walls. On 1 July he carried out his threat. Men, women and children in large numbers were forced under the walls in the hope that the garrison, in pity, would open the gates and allow them into the city. At the very least, this would worsen the shortage of food and thus hasten capitulation. But the reply of the garrison was simple. High up on the walls a gallows was erected and the threat to hang all prisoners within Derry was enough to force the besiegers to allow all the poor Protestants huddled beneath the walls to return to their homes.

The siege continued and thousands died of disease and starvation. The continuous bombardment created appalling conditions, destroying shelters and making it difficult to bury the dead. Then, on 28 July, in sheer desperation with a last attempt to save the city from being starved into surrender, three ships laden with provisions came up the Foyle and tried to break the boom. Even though the wind had dropped and Jacobites on both banks maintained a non-stop barrage with cannon and muskets (the captain of one ship was killed), two of the vessels finally got through. The *Mountjoy* (a significant name) from Derry and the *Phoenix* from Coleraine were carried on the incoming tide on a flat calm and reached the quay safely. Starving Derry was saved and on 31 July the Jacobites broke camp and set off for Lifford.

Meanwhile Enniskillen had become the centre of resistance by Protestants of south Ulster and north Connacht. Through control of Ballyshannon they had access to the sea and thus to supplies. While the siege of Derry progressed, all attempts to dislodge the Enniskillen-based Williamites failed. Eventually the king sent Viscount Mountcashel, Justin MacCarthy, at the head of a large force of 5,500 men to end the problem. But instead, on 31 July (the same day that the besieging army abandoned Derry), at Newtownbutler, the Jacobites were routed. MacCarthy, badly wounded after showing great bravery, was captured. Over 2,000 of his men were reported killed and 500 taken prisoner. All the cannon and the baggage train were seized. It was a disaster and so, three days after the relief of Derry another great Williamite victory helped to finish King James' hopes of recovering Ulster.

It was now that King William sent a formidable force to Ulster under the command of the veteran Duke of Schomberg, a Protestant refugee from the

French king's service after the revocation of the edict of Nantes. He marched towards Dublin, but was halted at Dundalk by an outbreak of dysentery or typhus. Whatever the disease, it destroyed thousands and left him perilously weak. By late September James himself led an army of 20,000 northwards from Dublin and faced Schomberg at Dundalk. But instead of attacking the Williamites, James did nothing for a fortnight. It was a disastrous military decision which allowed Schomberg to withdraw to the safety of Ulster, where eventually nearly half of his forces perished.

In England the House of Commons demanded an inquiry into the bad management of the army in Ireland and reluctantly William decided that the only answer was to take command himself although advisors were against this. Apart from the dangers from Jacobite activists in England and threatening squabbles between Whigs and Tories which demanded his attention, he would be unable to participate in the summer offensive against Louis XIV in 1690. This, he wrote to the elector of Bavaria, was 'a terrible mortification' to him, to be forced to go to Ireland where he would be 'as it were out of knowledge of the world', unable to help in the common cause against the French. But he had no choice. In another letter he wrote that the Irish expedition had been mishandled by Schomberg and that 'nothing worth while would be done' unless he went there himself. Nothing illustrates better than this how important affairs in Ireland had now become, not just in an English or Irish context, but to the very future of Europe as well.

Preparations for the expedition were on a massive scale. In addition to 6,000 English troops sent to swell the Williamite army in Ireland, another 7,000 were hired from Denmark, together with contingents from Switzerland, Germany, Scotland and, of course, Holland. In all about 37,000 were ready for his leadership when he landed in Ireland in June 1690. He also brought £200,000 in cash and vast quantities of arms and stores were shipped, as well as 500 wagons and 2,500 draught horses. A famous Dublin physician, Sir Patrick Dun, was put in charge of a special mobile field hospital to travel with the troops; and for the king's personal use, so that he might remain with his troops on the march, a special portable wooden house was designed by Sir Christopher Wren.

On the Jacobite side, too, troops were imported. In March 1690 in Cork a French fleet of over 6,000 landed, half of whom were Germans and Walloons. To the dismay of King James, most of those were Protestants. In exchange a total of 5,387 Irish troops were sent to France, so that the Jacobite army in Ireland was not really augmented by this import of troops.

On 16 June King James rode out from Dublin at the head of his army to meet William and block any advance from the north towards Dublin. With 25,000 men he pushed on past Dundalk to the Moiry Pass where a skirmish with some Williamites persuaded him that it was not a good point at which to meet the enemy. So he retreated back towards Dublin and then decided to make a stand on the southern bank of the Boyne, where he would enjoy a good strategic advantage. The Williamites came south and on 1 July 1690 the two armies met in the most famous battle in Irish history. James was defeated and fled to Dublin, then to the south where, on 4 July, he sailed with the French into exile. In Europe news of the victory was celebrated as an important success for the Grand Alliance by Catholics in Spain and Austria, where *Te Deums* were sung in thanksgiving in the cathedrals. The battle of the Boyne deserved the notoriety it received. Not only had two kings joined battle to see who would rule in England, but troops from many parts of Europe had fought in remote Ireland for a cause which would determine whether France would be dominant.

But the battle of the Boyne was less significant in the history of the struggle within Ireland itself. Despite the huge forces involved, only about 1,000 Jacobites and 500 Williamites were killed; most of the Jacobite army escaped to fight another day. William next failed to take Athlone in mid-July and then in August, thanks largely to the military skills of Patrick Sarsfield, Limerick held out against him. The Williamites lost 2,000 out of an army of 25,000. The line of the Shannon held and when William sailed to England on 5 September he left the Jacobites still in control of a large part of Ireland.

Despite the hardship of winter, the Jacobite army survived and continued the fight, greatly helped by bands of raparees, local guerrillas who lived in the Williamite area and did untold damage in raids and ambushes. In May 1691 a French general, the marquis de St Ruth, landed in Limerick and took command of the Jacobite army. On the other side the Dutch commander Ginkel, at the head of 20,000 men, began to move west to drive the Jacobites out. On 30 June, after a huge effort, he took Athlone and crossed the Shannon, St Ruth stood to meet him near Aughrim in county Galway and battle was joined on 12 July. The French general was killed and the battle was lost. Nearly 7,000 Irish died with him. On the Williamite side, by comparison, only about 700 were killed and 1,000 wounded. It was the worst disaster in Irish military history and made a Williamite victory in the Irish war inevitable. If the Boyne passed into Protestant folklore, then Aughrim became part of the Catholic Irish folk memory, kept alive by poets and story-tellers as 'Aughrim of the slaughter'.

With the army now shattered, there was no hope for the Jacobites and a week after Aughrim, Galway surrendered. A month later the siege of Limerick began, on 14 September Sligo surrendered and, finally, on 3 October 1691, the Treaty of Limerick was signed and the war was over. When on 22 December Sarsfield, followed by 12,000 Jacobite troops, sailed for France, the Williamites were left in complete control of Ireland. The Irish soldiers formed a distinct group in the French army and right up to the eighteenth century there was regular recruitment from Ireland. In Spain distinctive Irish regiments served until 1818 and elsewhere in Europe, especially in Catholic states, Irish troops served with distinction. These were the 'wild geese' who with other Irish emigrants were to make such a unique contribution to the development of Europe in the eighteenth century. It was one of the more significant results of the Williamite victory in Ireland.

If the war was over, the cost was high. In money it cost the government of William III more than six million pounds. Louis XIV, too, spent more than 890 thousand livres, which certainly came to more than one million pounds. As for James II, in Ireland he found that what an Irish Jacobite called 'the sinews of war', or ready cash, was in short supply. For various reasons little more than £450,000 hard cash seems to have been in circulation and much of this was unavailable to the king. In desperation he resorted to what we now know as 'gunmoney', though at the time it was usually termed 'copper' or more commonly 'brass' money. On 18 June 1689 a royal proclamation declared that 'we have ordered a certain quantity of copper and brass money to be coined to pass current . . . for remedy of the present scarcity of money'. Cannon were melted down, many specially imported from France for the purpose, as well as bells, ordnance and in particular any copper or brass objects that could be found, such as cooking vessels which were found in abundance. Exactly how many coins were minted is not known, but it is estimated that they had a total face value of about one and a half million pounds. For a time this 'false money' had a wide circulation at face value, but in the end, for various reasons (not least the fact that French troops were always paid in silver coins sent to Ireland by King Louis), there was a wild devaluation of the brass money. High inflation followed and a monetary disaster resulted.

In other ways, too, this war of the two kings was costly. Altogether about 25,000 soldiers were killed in battle. Many thousands more perished from disease. Countless civilians were killed, or died as a direct result of the war. The hearth tax returns show that between 1687 and 1694 the numbers of households able to pay fell by a third. Soldiers, like locusts, devoured what food they could find, leaving nothing for the people in the affected areas. A Williamite officer described the horror he witnessed:

'These wretches came flocking in great numbers about our camp devouring all the filth they could meet with. Our dead horses crawling with vermin, as the sun had parched them, were delicious food to them; while their infants sucked those carcasses with as much eagerness, as if they were at their mothers' breasts'.

As had happened before, the country and the people gradually recovered. But there was no general recovery for the Old English Catholic elite. The Old English author of 'A light to the blind', written soon after this, argued that 'the just interest of the crown of England is only preserved in Ireland by maintaining in a high state the true conquerors of that kingdom', the Old English, who were descended from those who 'by their blood annexed the Irish crown to the English diadem'. Describing those original conquerors as Catholics who had come to Ireland with Henry II, the author told how their descendants propped up the kings of England, losing life and possessions in the process, while the upstart Protestants who deposed kings actually profited from their treason. The outcome of the war, then, was a Protestant domination which might have been overturned had the Jacobites prevailed. Writing shortly after the event, William King had no doubt about its significance: either the Catholics or the Protestants 'must be undone', as he put it ('There was no medium but either we or they must be undone'). Both could not survive in post-Boyne Ireland.

If this Protestant supremacy was to be guaranteed, then their control over land would have to be maintained. Even before the war came to an end with the surrender of Limerick, Jacobite lands in areas under Williamite control were being seized by Protestants. In particular the lands of some leading Jacobite peers such as Tyrconnell, Gormanston, Clancarty and others who had been indicted for treason in England were taken into custody. Despite insistent demand, there was no general attainder act of the kind passed against Protestants in the Dublin parliament of 1689. Individual Jacobites were indicted in the areas under Williamite control, roughly twenty counties, and these numbered in excess of 2,000. Altogether, between those indicted in England and Ireland, including those who were outlawed for high treason abroad, about 4,000 were convicted. But many of those had no land, so that in the end about 1,700,000 statute acres were confiscated. Then in the Treaty of Limerick the Williamite commander, Ginkel, with the king's approval, offered generous terms to those surrendering. They were to be pardoned and, in return for a simple oath of allegiance, were to be guaranteed possession of their property as held in 1685. This, of course, applied only to those who did not accept the offer of free transportation to France. In addition to the individuals surrendering in Limerick, the treaty also guaranteed security in possession of their property to 'all such as are under their protection in these counties' (that is, Limerick, Galway, Mayo, Cork, Kerry and Clare), as well as the inhabitants of all places garrisoned by the Jacobites, like Limerick and Galway. This important qualifying clause was omitted when the text was sent to England for ratification by the king. But King William, to his honour, reinstated it before sealing the agreed terms. Unfortunately when the terms were finally given legal ratification by the Irish parliament in 1697, that same clause was once again deliberately omitted, thus depriving many Jacobites of its protection. This famous 'omitted clause' was subsequently used in Catholic propaganda and deservedly gained those responsible a dishonourable name in history. Years later at the battle of Fontenoy between the English and the French in 1745, the battle-cry of the Irish Brigade was: 'Remember Limerick and the treachery of the English'.

In fact, its omission did not result in a very large loss of lands to Catholics. As well as that, King William, through royal pardons, restored estates of about 142,560 statute acres to 24 individuals, such as Lord Bellew, Viscount Dillon, or Richard Talbot of Malahide. In the special court which heard claims arising out of the terms of the treaty, all but 16 of 1,283 claims heard were upheld, involving 848,500 acres. By far the greatest Catholic estate thus restored belonged to the third Earl of Antrim. There was also one Protestant, an MP in the Dublin parliament of 1689, who regained his land under the treaty. In the end, therefore, despite all the best efforts of Protestants in England, but especially in the Irish parliament, no more than 600,000 acres were actually confiscated. When sold, these brought in well over £700,000, far short of the huge sum eagerly anticipated to help pay the enormous cost of the war in Ireland.

In 1688 about 1,300 Catholics owned 22 per cent or nearly a quarter of the profitable land of Ireland, about 1,700,700 acres in all. By 1702, when William III died, that Catholic share had fallen to 14 per cent. But by the beginning of the last quarter of the eighteenth century, as a result of erosion under penal laws, the proportion had declined still further and only about 5 per cent of profitable land remained in Catholic hands, which was the English traveller Arthur Young's estimate when he visited Ireland in the 1770s (he later published an account of his visit, *A tour in Ireland*). This terrible decline was another result of failure to honour the terms of the treaty of Limerick. The second article had guaranteed that 'the Roman Catholics of this kingdom shall enjoy such privileges in the exercise of their religion, as are consistent with the laws of Ireland, or as they did enjoy in the reign of King Charles II'. This would have made them secure in their faith. The ninth article, too, was important for laying down that other than the oath of allegiance, no other oath would be required of Catholics.

Yet in the years after 1691, Catholics were discriminated against. In 1695, for example, parliament passed an act which disarmed Catholics and made it illegal for them to possess a horse worth more than £5; another act made it unlawful for them to send their children abroad for their education. In the same parliament the commons tried to introduce legislation ordering all members of religious orders to leave Ireland, but failed to get the consent of the English privy council. Two years later they succeeded and extended it to bishops and higher clergy generally; hundreds were expelled and many more left of their own accord. Only those few who were successful in finding safe hiding places survived. When finally, in the 1697 parliament, a bill was belatedly introduced to confirm the terms of the Treaty of Limerick both of these articles were omitted and the toleration promised to Catholics was withheld.

Thus the defeat of the Jacobites in the war of the two kings confirmed the dominant position of Protestants in the kingdom of Ireland. Control of most of the land was the single most important fact in creating their ascendancy. They had a monopoly of education, of office at central and local level, of the professions, and of the leading roles in domestic and international trade. Old English Catholics who refused to conform gradually lost status and became merged with the Irish population. By the time parliament assembled in Dublin in 1692 it had become a totally Protestant assembly. The kingdom of Ireland was truly, and seemingly eternally, a Protestant one.

10 Protestant nationalism and the Anglican ascendancy

On 23 October 1692, assembled in St Andrew's church in Dublin, the Irish House of Commons listened to a sermon preached by their chaplain, Dr Edward Walkington. He reminded his listeners that they had 'all the blessings of other governments, without any of their mischiefs'. In particular, he boasted of 'the authority of our representatives in parliament securing us from the encroachments of an arbitrary prerogative, which makes our laws, our liberties, our estates and our religion too, our own'. These, he said, were 'so fully our own, that they can't be touched, but pursuant to our laws to which we ourselves have given our consent'. This extraordinary echo of the earlier 'middle nation' of the medieval lordship protecting its ancient customs and liberties, which could only be changed by legislation of its own parliament, had no actual basis in the realities of political life in Ireland in 1692. It was giving voice to a kind of constitution to which the House of Commons may have aspired, but which was still restricted by the control exercised by the Dublin administration and ultimately by the government in England.

Yet during the course of that 1692 parliament the Commons had shown evidence of their desire to make their parliament once again an instrument of Government as it had been in the distant past. The lord lieutenant, Viscount Henry Sidney, in a letter to London wrote that they 'talk of freeing themselves from the yoke of England, of taking away Poynings' Law'. It was a fact that as long as this law was in operation, no Irish parliament could ever be fully independent. Writing to Swift in October 1711, Archbishop King informed him that the repeal of Poynings' law was

> 'a thing which is universally desired here, for on our side it would tend mightily to the liberty and flourishing estate of the country . . . My lord lieutenant looks on it as an attempt to become as much as possible independent of England and the commons say it's their birthright'.

But in 1692 there was no evidence that repeal of this basic law was seriously contemplated and Sidney's report was an exaggerated, even hysterical, view of what was going on in Dublin. Lawyers among the commons did encourage the view that they could and should initiate legislation, but only within the confines of Poynings' Law, by drafting 'heads of bills' (as had been done in the years after 1494) which could then be vetted by the privy council in London. The current financial crisis and the need to raise revenues in Ireland in the aftermath of a hugely costly war gave them their chance. They refused to accept two money bills introduced by the government, insisting that only they had the right to initiate legislation which gave rise to new taxes. In rejecting a bill to tax corn, the commons said that they did so 'because it had not its rise in this house'. This insistence on parliamentary control over taxation was fundamental. It guaranteed that parliament would have to be summoned in Ireland on a regular basis, which would inevitably give it a role in the future government of the kingdom.

This parliament was wholly Protestant. Ironically, in view of the debate about the efficacy of English legislation in Ireland, it was an English law of 1691 which made it impossible for Catholics to take their seats. No one could hold public office or become an MP who refused to take an oath against transubstantiation and against the power of the papacy. So the parliament of 1692 represented the Protestant nation. When a pamphlet (*Account of the Sessions*) was published, after parliament was suddenly prorogued by Sidney, the author referred to 'the misfortune of this nation', by which he meant the Protestant people of Ireland. Anti-Catholic feelings ran high among the members, reflecting the attitude of most Protestants on the island. Bishop Dopping of Meath had been suspended from the privy council after he preached a sermon in which, according to the lords justices, he uttered 'the most bitter invectives against the whole body of the Irish' and continued 'stirring up the people . . . to continue their animosities against them'.

It is easy to understand why anti-Catholicism should have been so pronounced. In the aftermath of the Jacobite war Protestant fears of a Catholic backlash were very real. The restoration of the exiled Stuarts, backed by Catholics in Europe, was a real danger. When war resumed in 1702, a climate of anxiety was created in Ireland. A minor French victory in 1704, wrote one correspondent, 'did much to exalt the papists in this kingdom, that they grew insolent'. When news reached Ireland of a French fleet sailing to Scotland, another correspondent wrote that the Catholics became 'insolent and foolish'. Even after a treaty between England and France in 1716 began two decades of peace, with the French ceasing all support for the Pretender, Irish Catholics continued to hope for an invasion. In 1721, for example, when Louis XV came of age as King of France, Archbishop King reported how it was expected that his coronation oath, in which he swore to extirpate heresy, would mean a renewal of support for the Stuarts. This was 'a notion got into Papists' heads', he wrote, and they 'depend on it as certain'.

The continuous recruitment of Catholics for service in France, as many as 20,000 according to some estimates, naturally caused great alarm, especially when it was believed that such volunteers were really intended for service in the Stuart cause. In the 1720s and 1730s it came to about 1,000 annually. If such soldiers were often recruited for service other than against England, there was a belief among Protestants that many young Irish Catholics were attracted by the possibility of fighting for the Stuarts at some time in the future. It was reported by an informer, Henry Murphy, in 1714 that men recruited in Wexford were told that 'they were to serve King James the Third and that they would not fight a battle till they had landed in England or Ireland'. In county Waterford in that same year a young man was told that he and others recruited 'should all return to Ireland again in less than a year's time, with an army to destroy and root out all the Protestants there'. There was certainly more than an echo of 1641 there. The cries in Irish of the Irish brigade at the battle of Fontenoy in 1745 – 'Remember Limerick and the treachery of the English' – show how strong anti-English feelings still were.

One simple illustration of the continuity of fears of a Jacobite restoration and consequent disaster for the Protestants of Ireland is the history of Sir John Temple's *The Irish rebellion*. First published in 1646, it was subsequently the origin of most of the stories of the torture and massacre of Protestants in 1641. Whenever a fear of a new threat to Protestants emerged, a new edition of Temple's book appeared. The Jacobite threats of 1713, 1714, 1724 and 1746 saw new editions, with a new subtitle added which made vividly clear the nature of the fear: *An history of the attempts of the Irish papists to extirpate the Protestants*. Hardly less important in keeping alive Protestant memories of Catholic attacks and a hatred of the Stuarts was William King's *The state of the Protestants of Ireland under the late King James's government*, which some publishers issued in a joint edition with Temple's book. Published in 1691, within a year four editions of King's work had appeared and there were 10 in all by 1768. Because King James had 'designed to destroy and utterly ruin' the Protestants, their religion, and their property, he had been rightly resisted. King argued that 'every Roman Catholic king, if he thoroughly understand his religion and do in earnest believe the principles of it, is obliged to be able to destroy his Protestant subjects' and after 1691 this is what a Jacobite threat represented to the Protestants of Ireland.

Outnumbering Protestants by three to one, Catholics seemingly posed a genuine threat and so had to be contained. Laws were devised to prevent them from ever again threatening an Anglican ascendancy by excluding them from all political power. This meant that they must be excluded not only from parliament, but from 1728 onwards they also lost the right to vote in parliamentary elections. This loss of franchise, while it did not affect very many because the number of Catholic freeholders had greatly declined by then, was pernicious in its effects. It deprived many Catholics of the opportunity to become tenants, since Protestant landlords tended to give leases to those whose vote they could control, that is to Protestants rather than disenfranchised Catholics. This was later condemned by Edmund Burke, who wrote that

'the taking away of a vote is the taking away the shield which the subject has, not only against the oppression of power, but that worst of all oppressions, the persecution of private society and private manners'.

Catholics were also excluded from all office, from the armed forces and from the legal profession where they might be able to exploit the law in their own interest. It was easy to do this by making mandatory an oath which no sincere Catholic could take, denying transubstantiation, accepting as not only superstitious but idolatrous the celebration of mass in the Roman rite, and denouncing the worship of the Virgin Mary or any other saint. The Catholic gentry, who were the traditional and natural leaders of their people, were attacked by measures which depressed them socially and economically. With the concentration of all office as well as military power in Protestant hands, Catholics were denied access to the means of exercising political power.

But the real basis of power was land. Most of the sitting members of the 1692 parliament were landlords as well as Protestants. They subscribed, even if unknowingly, to the argument of John Locke, the most influential philosopher of the time, that the end of government was protection of the rights and property of the governed. In Ireland this meant protection from Catholics. In 1715 Archbishop King was quite explicit: 'Not only our religion and liberty, but estates depend on the revolution'. Five years later he wrote that if others 'may make terms with the Pretender, or imagine that they may do so . . . no Protestant in Ireland can have any hope or view that way.' When, in a letter to Swift, he wrote that the ownership of land was what mattered in Ireland, he emphasized that these were estates

> 'which are all claimed by the forfeiters and nothing can restore them but the Pretender nor anything take them from us but bringing him in . . . Here is the true source of the zeal and violence of the Protestants of Ireland. Remove the fear of the Pretender and you may lead them like a dog on a string.'

Parliament enacted a series of laws in the years after 1691 which are usually referred to as 'penal laws', just as the period itself is referred to as a 'penal era'. But much of this legislation was haphazard, in no sense a code or systematic, enacted at different times in response to particular problems. Indeed contemporaries such as Archbishop King did not consider them to be even 'penal' and people of the time generally referred to them as 'popery laws'. Legislation of this kind was by no means unique to Ireland. In France the laws against Protestants were much more severe and were applied more stringently. In Spain, the Empire and elsewhere Catholics persecuted Protestants in the same way. But the difference in Ireland was that members of the established church were in a great minority.

Given the real fears that existed in 1692 and afterwards, the 1695 bill which forbade Catholics to keep weapons or a horse valued at more than £5 is understandable. The legislation was called *An act for the better securing the government by disarming papists* when it was first printed in Dublin. The purpose of another 'Act to restrain foreign education' was also security, to prevent contact with Catholics abroad, and especially in France. It was extended to include Catholics teaching in Ireland itself, though Catholic schools had in fact been illegal for generations past. This measure was not very effective; by 1731 an official 'Report on the state of popery' revealed the existence of 549 Catholic schools. As such places were illegal, the real number was probably much higher. Not only was religious instruction made available, some of these schools provided a surprisingly high standard of education. In 1731 the Protestant Bishop of Ossory reported that in a local Catholic school six out of the 30 pupils attending were taught Latin by the master. So, whatever the purpose of the 1695 legislation, it certainly failed to prevent young Catholic boys, even in poor rural areas, from being educated in their religion and providing the church with the intelligentsia needed.

The 'banishment act' of 1697, which banished bishops and regulars, was potentially disastrous for Catholics and was designed, with other penal laws, to create circumstances in which Irish Catholicism would wither away and the people be converted to the reformed religion. Locke, who exercised great influence on important members of the established church, such as Archbishop King of Dublin and Bishop Dopping of Meath, had reasoned that no one could be born a papist. So, if there were no Catholic clergy and if the people were surrounded by a totally Protestant environment, Ireland would inevitably become a Protestant kingdom in one, or at most two generations. That there was a desire to convert the people seems undoubted. Some Protestant churchmen believed that a mass conversion was not only desirable, but an obligation laid on them to bring the Irish to what Bishop Wetenhall of Cork, in his famous 1691 sermon commemorating 1641, called 'the truth and power of the reformed religion'.

In the event it was not possible to implement fully the relevant penal laws and although there was a genuine attempt to convert the Irish through a missionary effort, involving Irish speaking ministers and the publication of Irish translations of the Bible, the *Book of Common Prayer*, and the Protestant catechism, it never really got the whole-hearted support necessary and it died before the end of the first quarter of the eighteenth century. By 1727 Archbishop Synge of Tuam, one of the greatest advocates of a strong conversion policy, had to admit that all he could do for Catholics now 'to awaken you out of that religious lethargy in which the generality of you seem to me to be' was to offer prayers for their conversion.

The failure to enforce the strict letter of many of the 'popery laws' quickly became apparent. As early as 1704 all Catholic priests still in Ireland were ordered to register and provide security for their good behaviour. No less than 1,089 did so, among them three bishops and many regular clergy. Given that many regulars would have preferred to remain outside the law, rather than risk what revealing themselves for registration might entail, the number still in Ireland was probably very much higher. In 1731 another inquiry revealed 254 friars in addition to 1,445 secular clergy. As large parts of the country made no returns, the number was much higher. Certainly by 1750 there were about 800 regulars among the Catholic clergy of Ireland. This means, too, that the Catholics were well looked after. Given a Catholic population of about 1,750,000 in 1731, it means there was one priest for every 1,000 Catholics or so. No wonder that Archbishop King wrote despairingly to the Archbishop of Canterbury in 1719 of the terrible dilemma which faced the Protestants if they remained a minority, however powerful, within Ireland: 'How [will] the Protestants . . . secure themselves, or England secure Ireland when the commonalty are all papist?'

One answer was to make sure that the Protestant hold on most of the land of Ireland was not only maintained but increased. The 1697 parliament enacted that any Protestant marrying a Catholic woman was to be 'in law deemed and esteemed to all intents, constructions and purposes, to be a papist'; and if a Protestant heiress married a Catholic, then the estate must go to her nearest Protestant relative. More draconian was the law of 1703 that land held by a Catholic was to be equally divided among all his male heirs on his death, and prohibiting Catholics from inheriting land held by a Protestant, or from purchasing or even long-leasing land from anyone. The effect of this was terrible. In 1703 Catholics still held about 14 per cent of the land; by 1776 this had fallen to only 5 per cent. In 1791 the lord lieutenant put it bluntly when he said that in Ireland 'every man holds his estate and political consequence by dispossession of Catholics'. Anglican ascendancy rested on Catholic exclusion in law.

This legislation put terrible pressure on Catholic landholders to conform. As early as 1731 the 'convert rolls' list a total of 704, among them the leading gentry families of Blake, Browne, Burke, Butler, Dillon, French, Kirwan, Martin, Nugent, Taafe. Condemned by some of their contemporaries as hypocrites, for many it was the only way they could provide a secure future for their families. The Protestant poet Piaras Mac Gearailt (Piers Fitzgerald) conformed to save the remnants of the once extensive Fitzgerald estates in county Cork. For this he was attacked by Thomas Barry and in reply published an answer in Irish verse in which he wrote:

> Going over to Calvin
> Is my cross to carry
> Because my children's loss
> Of acres and herds
> Left my life a stormy
> Heartstream of tears.

He complained of the long years of persecution and told God that if He did not 'trample on these foreign boors' then all landowners would have to follow his 'sad move'. And throughout the poem the deep hurt, the sickness, and the fear of God come through strongly. The father of a more famous man, Richard Burke, had also conformed in order to be able to practise law.

For the most part those who conformed were not condemned by their Catholic contemporaries, who well understood the pressures they were under.

The subsequent careers of such families as the O'Haras of Sligo, Mathews of Tipperary, or Martins of Galway testify to this. They never lost the support of their Catholic tenants. On the Protestant side, such converts were usually well received. As one Protestant wrote in 1711, through conversion the children of the convert would get 'the advantage of an education in our church . . . and may prove to church and state'. Certainly the attractions were great and by the time the 'convert rolls' were completed a total of 5,870 were listed.

The overwhelming majority of Catholics, however, remained firm in their religion. Apart from a few zealous churchmen there was no widespread desire among the Protestant population at large to make a real effort at mass conversion. Indeed many of them would have seen this as a threat to their own position of privilege. Archbishop King was quite scathing when he condemned the justices of peace who 'make no other use of our popery acts but to oppress the poor people'. Far from wishing to convert Catholics and end popery, such people 'take care to cherish and support it, alleging that papists make the best tenants, as indeed they pay more rent and are greater slaves to their landlords than Protestants would ever be'.

Because those with an education were excluded in law from government, the army and the legal profession, many Catholics were forced to emigrate or to channel their energies and resources into commerce and industry. One significant fact which created a favourable economic climate was population growth. From about 1.7 million in 1672 it grew to 2.8 million before the end of the first quarter of the eighteenth century. This was a phenomenal development and it was partly responsible for the growth of towns, an expanding commercial industry and a general increase in prosperity. The export of wool, but especially butter and live cattle, was an area in which Catholics prospered. To such an extent were they successful that as early as 1718 Archbishop King could write that 'the papists have been made incapable to purchase lands, have turned themselves to trade, and already engrossed almost all the trade of the kingdom'.

While the bishop may have exaggerated, there is no doubt that outside Dublin, and Belfast of course, Catholics in other cities and towns did gain extensive trading interests. The great George Berkely, Bishop of Cloyne, in his *The Querist* published in 1750 asked if the ports of Galway, Limerick, Cork and Waterford were not the 'keys of the kingdom'? It was, he said, the merchants who 'are possessed of these keys; and who are the most numerous merchants in these towns?' In 1762 the corporation of Galway complained that only 350 out of 14,000 inhabitants were Protestants, so that Catholics not only controlled most of the town's wealth, but were thus able to exercise 'considerable influence and power over the indigent Protestant townsmen'. Even in Dublin, where Catholics were very much a minority, Edward Byrne of Mullinahack had become the wealthiest merchant in the city before the end of the century, reputedly worth well over £400,000 before he died. He was reputed to have been paying £80,000 and more per annum in duties to the

Irish exchequer. He was also chairman of the Catholic Committee in 1792, when it was accused of inciting disturbances in the country. But, significantly, the committee replied that they 'would suffer more by one week's disturbances than all members of the two houses of parliament'.

Despite the loss of land, many Catholic families retained a position of wealth and continued to dominate many localities by the end of the century. In different parts of Ireland they were bound together in marriage, trade, financial dealings, and often through eminent success abroad, especially in French commerce. In Nantes, for example, the richest port in early eighteenth century France, the Macnamaras controlled the richest firm. Others dominated the East India Company and many purchased lands on the continent and acquired rich plantations overseas.

Despite the continuous penal legislation, then, it is evident that many Catholics prospered and even acquired some degree of influence outside political circles. This is reflected in their ability to support, however modestly, the hierarchy of bishops and the large number of priests who provided pastoral care. Chapels and mass houses, however humble, were maintained. In Dublin, even quite early in the eighteenth century, the chapels were substantial buildings, well furnished and decorated, and maintained in a good state of repair. In poorer parts chapels were simpler, sometimes with mud walls and a thatched roof. Occasionally even such simple buildings could not be provided and mass was said in the open, upon 'mass rocks', the memory of which is still kept alive in folklore. But however humble, the fact is that places of worship were provided as was a clergy to serve the needs of the people.

For the most part, then, Catholics were allowed to practise their religion openly and even the laws against regular clergy were rarely invoked. Mendicants, such as the Dominicans, were able to work without risk, sometimes relying on the help of well disposed Protestants and, where necessary, bribing officials to turn a blind eye. When the Mayor of Galway reported that the sheriffs had searched what he called 'the reputed friary in Back Street', which was in fact an Augustinian house, he added that they 'could not find or discover any of the said friars'. But an entry for November 1731 in the Augustinian ledger tells us why: 'November 9th . . . a bottle of wine for ye sheriffs . . . 1s. 1d.' Another entry in the ledger of the Dominican friary in Galway records the expenditure of 2s. 2d. 'for claret to treat the sheriffs'. Orders like the Dominicans were able to hold provincial chapters regularly, communicate with Rome, and generally carry on almost as if the 'popery laws' were in abeyance. By the 1730s there were 182 members of the Irish province and no fewer than 35 friaries on the island.

It is not surprising, therefore, that in 1732 the vast number of households were still Catholic – 38 per cent in Ulster, 77 per cent in Leinster, 89 per cent in Munster and 91 per cent in Connacht. It is significant that however disadvantaged most of them were, they still managed to provide for their spiritual well-being and in so doing came close to their clergy in a unique manner which was to deepen the bond in the future. As a parish priest in the west of Ireland told a visitor in the late eighteenth century: 'the people give the fruit of their labours liberally to me and I give them my time, my care and my entire soul . . . Between us there is a ceaseless exchange of feelings of affection'. The majority of his parishioners were poor peasants, tilling the land for little more than a bare subsistence living. Most Catholics, even in the towns, were labourers. In Armagh, for example, just over 41 per cent of the 499 households were Catholic in 1770. The occupation of a third was described as 'labourers', compared with just over three per cent of Protestants. Given that legal sanctions, as well as established tradition, barred Catholics from the professions as well as government, it is not surprising that they were generally poor and the Protestants richer.

Having gained a pronounced ascendancy, it was easy for Protestants generally to be tolerant of Catholic neighbours and to allow them a degree of religious freedom in contradiction to the 'popery laws'. But from time to time, especially when the Jacobites seemed to threaten danger, there could be tensions which might explode into religious persecution. The case of Father Nicholas Sheehy in Clonmel showed how easy it was for Catholics to suffer when disturbance was interpreted as having a foreign origin. In the 1760s, county Tipperary was rent by agrarian troubles which were largely Catholic in origin. Even though they were a protest at upsetting changes in rural society, they were seen by many Protestants as being politically motivated and as representing a new visitation of the 1641 massacres. In Dublin the parliament characterized the disturbances as a 'popish insurrection'. Father Sheehy was identified as 'a very capital ringleader of those insurgents' and brought to trial in Dublin in 1776. When the main witness failed to appear the case was dismissed. But very quickly he was charged with the murder of this witness. During the trial evidence was presented that Sheehy attended a meeting at which those present swore that 'they would be faithful to the French king, conquer Ireland, and make it their own'. Father Sheehy was found guilty and was hanged, drawn and quartered in Clonmel. Even if there is evidence that he had been involved in resistance to the payment of tithes and so had acquired a notorious reputation – his own vicar-general refused to give evidence of his loyalty at the trial – there seems no doubt that the charge of murder was fabricated so as to get him out of the way.

An even more traumatic event occurred in 1720 when the Jacobite James Cotter was executed on the charge that he had raped his Quaker mistress. Leading Protestants from county Cork made every effort to see that the death penalty was not implemented. In arguing for a reprieve it was said that the judges had refused to show him 'that tenderness . . . on his trial as is usual in cases of life and death', such as would normally have been shown to someone of his social standing had he been a Protestant. But the lord lieutenant refused mercy, having been convinced by others that Cotter was politically dangerous and should be disposed of. The fact that the lord lieutenant was married to the grand-daughter of John Lisle, the notorious regicide who had been murdered by Cotter's father, Sir James, in Lausanne in 1664, hardly helped either. In Catholic circles it was certainly believed that he was executed because he represented one of the few surviving Catholic landowning families in county Cork, and one with strong Gaelic sympathies to boot. Up to 20 poems in Irish survive which convey the widespread dismay in Cork at his execution. In one, the poet Seán Clárach Mac Domhnaill gave voice to the common view that this was judicial murder and wrote: 'Sound sleep is far from the Irish when the jury of the Quakers is in supreme authority in Cork' and there were anti-Quaker riots even as far away as Dublin.

Cotter's execution caused some dismay even among the Protestant gentry of county Cork, the very people who had tried to save him from the gallows. At the upper levels of society religion was not normally the kind of barrier it was in law. In 1751, for example, Mrs Delany, wife of the Dean of Derry, entertained a Poor Clare nun to dinner, visited the convent, took tea with the nuns in their parlour, and even played the organ in the convent chapel. But at a time of political tension Protestant anxiety became a reality and Catholics might suffer.

Among the Protestants of Ireland there was by no means unanimity. Members of the established church were hardly less suspicious of Protestant dissenters, and especially Presbyterians, than of Catholics. In 1704 this was manifest in a damaging test act against dissenters which stipulated that only those who were prepared to take a sacramental test could be eligible to sit in parliament or a municipal corporation, hold political office, or be commissioned in the army. This act was not repealed until 1780, so it effectively excluded Protestant dissenters from public life.

It also encouraged many to emigrate, especially to America, where they could find the kind of toleration not to be had in Ireland. This emigration continued, almost unchecked, until the outbreak of the American revolution in 1775. Numbers grew until it was estimated in 1770 that about 12,000 were leaving Ulster every year. Many of these were pursuing jobs, especially the weavers who left in large numbers after the linen industry in Ireland ran into trouble. But many were also anxious to find the kind of rights in law which were denied to them at home. When a Presbyterian minister in 1720 led his congregation across the Atlantic, he proclaimed that they were departing so as 'to avoid oppression and cruel bondage, to shun persecution and designed ruin'.

Even if exaggerated, this shows that Presbyterians in early eighteenth century Ireland felt hardly any less disadvantaged than Catholics under penal laws. It encouraged a radical element to the extent that some were even willing to join with Catholics in the late eighteenth century in demanding political reform. It also helped to shape a strong sense of ethnic identity among Ulster Presbyterians. In Glasgow university in 1722, Presbyterian students from Ulster were enraged when two of them who appeared before the lord-advocate were officially designated 'Irishmen': they insisted that their Scottishness should be recognized, as was normally the case when each student was officially enrolled by the university as '*Scotus Hibernus*' (Scots-Irish).

As long as Protestant dissenters, as well as Catholics, were denied full civil rights, the members of the established church enjoyed a dominance in the political and social life of Ireland which was unprecedented. One sign of this was the obligation on all dissenters to pay tithes to the anglican clergy, which also made them subject to the ecclesiastical courts. An anglican ascendancy had been created in Ireland, partly by the operation of the penal laws and partly through a process, especially after the 'glorious revolution' of 1688 had been successfully defended in Ireland, by which control of most land had passed to the members of the established church before the end of the seventeenth century.

This position of ascendancy manifested itself in many ways, not least in the Irish parliament which became at once its greatest symbol and the most powerful means of maintaining it. When Anthony Dopping, Bishop of Meath, published *Rules and customs of the house gathered out of the journal books from the time of Edward the Sixth* in Dublin in 1692, he provided badly needed information on parliamentary procedure for the novices who sat in the Dublin parliament of that year. But more interesting is the fact that this procedural handbook was attached to an edition of a famous medieval tract on how parliament should be held. This was *Modus tenendi parliamentum*, a text which was regarded as so subversive in 1419 when it was found in the possession of Sir Christopher Preston that the government of the day had it exemplified to be brought in evidence against him at his trial for sedition. That this Irish version was published for the first time in 1692 is indicative of the new attitude of independence, even defiance, which manifested itself in parliament that year. It is a coincidence that the exiled James II, writing in that same year with the advantages of hindsight and his own experiences in Ireland, warned his son that when he regained his kingdom and sought to improve Ireland, he might support the Protestants there 'for the good of trade and the improvement of that kingdom'. But he added a warning that they were not really to be trusted because they were 'ill principled and republicans'.

However askew that judgement may be, it does reflect one reality of Irish Protestant ambition at the end of the seventeenth century. Preaching before the members of the House of Commons on 23 October, less than three weeks after parliament had opened and only 11 days before it was prorogued by the lord lieutenant, the chaplain, Edward Walkington, gave public voice to the core of that political ambition. The new constitution would protect the Protestants of Ireland, their liberties, their religion, their estates, their very lives, from all laws save only those to which they had given their consent.

To a very limited extent, Irish parliaments under William III did succeed in adhering to the principle of consent to legislation. Through a procedure by which the House of Commons drew up 'heads of bills' in which details of proposed legislation were presented in an orderly fashion before it was discussed by the council, they did participate in initiating legislation. So, even though most legislation continued to originate in council, a beginning had been made in making parliament the real source.

What brought matters to a head was the insistence of the English parliament on its right to legislate specifically for Ireland. In 1697, owing to the conviction in England that the Irish woollen industry threatened the English one, it was decided that it should be suppressed and Ireland would be compensated by encouraging the linen industry there. A bill was introduced in the English parliament which would prohibit the export of wool from Ireland. It failed, but it generated a dispute which led to a pamphlet war in which Irish writers defended the woollen industry as essential to the well-being of Ireland and English writers attacked the Irish parliament in particular. William Molyneux, who represented Dublin University in parliament, was quite scathing about the English view of the woollen trade, 'their darling mistress and they are jealous of any rival'. More importantly, he published his celebrated reply to England's claims to the right to legislate for Ireland, *The case of Ireland's being bound by acts of parliament in England, stated*, a great classic which is still consulted by scholars interested in the history of the medieval parliament. It was subsequently condemned by the English House of Commons as

'of dangerous consequence to the crown and people of England by denying the authority of the king and parliament of England to bind the kingdom and people of Ireland, and the subordination and dependence that Ireland hath and ought to have upon England as united and annexed to the imperial crown of the realm'.

Molyneux was a friend of John Locke, with whom he was in regular correspondence, and he made use of his *Two treatises of Government*, where the English thinker argued that because there was a contract between ruler and ruled, government could only be by the consent of those governed. Molyneux used this notion in *The case* and in so doing gave the first public estimation of the Englishman as a major political thinker by using his ideas of natural right claims in print for the first time in a significant context. He was also responsible for persuading the provost of Trinity College to put Locke's *Essay on human understanding* on the curriculum of the university. Molyneux argued that 'liberty seems the independent right of all mankind' and that it was 'against reason and the common rights of all mankind' to make English statutes binding on Ireland. Taxation without consent was unnatural, 'To tax me without my consent is little better, if at all, than downright robbing me'. Legislation without representation was not natural.

But the main thrust of his argument was historical, invoking precedents from the past to support the case against England's right to bind Ireland through parliamentary statutes. He was able to draw on the valuable work of his brother-in-law Anthony Dopping, who had produced his edition of the *Modus* in 1692, and of his father-in-law Sir William Domville, a former attorney general for Ireland, who knew the official records and had amassed a valuable collection of documents from them. Many of these supplied Molyneux with the material he needed from the middle ages to demonstrate that Ireland was not bound by any statute save those enacted in an Irish parliament.

In England, as might have been expected, there was an immediate reaction in a number of pamphlets denouncing and attempting to disprove the contention of Molyneux. With titles like *The history and reasons of the dependency of Ireland*, some authors also used evidence from medieval records to show that Ireland had always been bound by English statutes. In parliament, as we have seen, *The case* was denounced as dangerous, though for some reason the normal consequence of such a denunciation was not followed, so it was not burned by the common hangman. But more significantly, in an address to the king, the commons warned that Molyneux was not voicing a personal opinion but that his 'bold and pernicious assertions' were representative of the views of the Irish House of Commons. In the following year, 1699, the English parliament gave its real answer to the challenge when it legislated against the export of Irish woollens. By then Molyneux was dead, but his book lived on and had a profound influence not only in Ireland but in America where it has been seen as an important contribution to that 'government by consent' argument which led to the American revolution. In Ireland many editions were produced before the independence of the Irish parliament was finally conceded in 1782.

There were other strands in that development which also had their origins in the Irish Protestant determination to extend the parliamentary benefits of the 'glorious revolution' to Ireland. Because no Irish parliament had met between 1666 and 1688, there was no Irish House of Lords to act as a final court of appeal, so naturally such appeals had been referred to England. But a conflict between the Bishop of Derry and the Irish Society of London over land leases and fishing rights led to a confrontation between the two parliaments. The bishop was William King, the later Archbishop of Dublin, and he appealed the case to the Irish House of Lords, which decided in his favour. But in 1698, after the Society had lodged an appeal in the English House of Lords, that body decided that the Irish house had no right to hear an appeal. That started the dispute, which dragged on, through other cases, until the Irish House of Lords composed a 'representation' to George I in England, asserting their rights as the final court of appeal in Ireland. In the course of the argument they claimed (just as Molyneux had done in *The case*) that ever since the Irish princes had voluntarily submitted to Henry II in 1172 a contract existed under which

'the people of Ireland obtained the benefit of English laws, and many privileges, particularly that of having a distinct parliament, here as in England, and of having weighty and momentous matters relating to this kingdom treated of, discussed, and determined in the same'.

This insistence on Irish parliamentary independence, where matters should be 'determined', produced a reaction in England which led in 1720 to the passing of 'An act for the better securing the dependency of the Kingdom of Ireland upon the Crown of Great Britain'. This famous declaratory act, usually known as the 'Sixth of George I', ended the matter as far as the British government was concerned.

The reaction in Ireland was dismay. Robert Molesworth, who had sat in parliament with Molyneux and who had won an international reputation because he had been a leading figure in the attack on absolutism in Denmark, warned that if this led to direct taxation by the British parliament it 'would use us like those slaves which at present they declare us to be'. William King realized that there was indeed great danger to Ireland if they submitted to what he considered to be the illegal authority claimed by the British parliament. He regretted that age now prevented him from the kind of vigorous opposition which the legislation demanded and he wrote that 'no man ought to be silent when the liberty of our country and the being of our parliament is at stake'. How right he was the public outcry over the infamous 'Wood's halfpence' (1723–5) soon made plain. King was still strong enough to play a leading role in the opposition, which finally was successful. But an even more famous critic had emerged, his own Dean of St Patrick's, Jonathan Swift.

In 1722 the British government issued a patent for the minting of copper halfpence and farthings, which eventually ended in the possession of William Wood. There was a serious shortage of silver coins in circulation in Ireland and Wood's copper coins were supposed to provide a remedy. But, as Archbishop King said, 'we have more halfpence than we need already. It is true we want change, but it is sixpences, shillings, half-crowns and crowns'. For sound monetary reasons the measure was opposed by responsible officials in Dublin, which caused great concern in London. Officials there were especially angered when the Irish revenue commissioners actually questioned the right of the London treasury in the matter. Opposition by the Irish parliament was one thing; but a lack of support, and indeed even outright condemnation by government officials in Dublin was alarming. It caused the lord lieutenant to complain in 1723 that too many 'natives' were in important positions and this, he wrote, had produced 'very mischievous consequences to the British interest'. In 1723 the Irish parliament protested to the king, on a number of different grounds, about the circulation of Wood's coinage. But the British government refused to withdraw the patent, though the amount to be minted was reduced. This failed to pacify the Irish parliament and the publication of a series of pamphlets helped to inflame public opinion against the measure.

By far the most important of these pamphlets was a series of *Drapier's letters*, first published in the course of 1724. Though supposedly written by a Dublin tradesman, M.B. Drapier, it was well known that the author was Dean Swift and it was not the first time that Swift attacked England. When he published his *A proposal for the universal use of Irish manufactures* in 1720, in which he strongly defended the 'traffic of our wool with France', Swift argued that it 'has been our only support for several years, furnishing us with all the little money we have to pay our rents, and go to market'. Because English statutes tried to regulate Irish trade, Swift denounced this notion and was in effect replying to the declaratory act published the previous month. He urged the use by all of goods manufactured in Ireland, because he had seen the straits of the poor, especially the unemployed weavers living in the vicinity of St Patrick's.

Swift was always concerned for the poor. Whenever he could he walked instead of taking a coach and gave the money saved to some poor person. He only spent one third of his income on himself, giving another third to charities and saved the remaining third for a charitable foundation on his death, which provided the funds for St Patrick's hospital. In 1729, after a famine in which the poor starved, he published a satire which savagely attacked a society which could tolerate such suffering. Under the title *A modest proposal* he put forward a scheme to solve the problem by slaughtering one-year-old children and then using the flesh to make 'a most delicious, nourishing and wholesome food'.

But in 1720 he was more forthright. His tract contained a strong attack on England as the cause of the poverty and that was enough to have it condemned by the government. An attempt was made to prosecute the printer, Waters, for what was called a 'seditious, factious, and virulent pamphlet'. It is a measure of the strong anti-English feelings aroused by Swift that a grand jury could not be found willing to convict the printer. But a more serious argument used by Swift in asking 'whether a law to bind men without their own consent' can be binding in conscience raised the more fundamental issue of England's right to legislate for Ireland. Swift was using an economic problem for political propaganda and he even wrote a satirical poem, 'An excellent song on a seditious pamphlet', making political capital out of the attempted prosecution of the printer Waters, ending each stanza:

> We'll buy English silks for our wives and our daughters,
> In spite of his Deanship and journeyman Waters.

His skill as a versifier was often pressed into service to influence public opinion. But the letters he wrote as Drapier, the first of them entitled *A letter to the shopkeepers and common people of Ireland, concerning the brass half-pence coined by Mr Woods*, were much more overtly political and anti-English. The fourth letter, published in October 1724, was addressed 'to the whole people of Ireland', by which he meant, of course, the members of the established church, and argued strongly against the English claim that Ireland was a 'depending kingdom'. It was, he wrote, 'manifest by the laws of God, of nature, of nations, and of your own country, you are and ought to be as free a people as your brethren in England'. Once again the government tried to prosecute the printer, Harding, and two grand juries in succession refused to indict, so that he was discharged in the end. A Dublin ballad demonstrated Swift's popularity:

> Fair liberty was all his cry;
> For her he stood prepared to die,
> But not a traitor could be found
> To sell him for six hundred pounds.

His propaganda had won a huge public demand for the cancellation of the proposal to mint the copper coins and in the end the English government had to concede defeat, an enormous achievement for the Protestants of Ireland. The dean had proved to be what he himself wrote in his epitaph, a 'strenuous champion of liberty'.

Liberty did not yet mean, however, an independent Irish parliament. Ireland remained subject to the legislation of the British parliament in which the Protestant community was not represented. The logic of that position demanded consent to legislation through Irish representatives at Westminster and that implied union. There had been some tradition of proposals for such a union in the past, most notably from Sir William Petty in the late seventeenth century. He argued that not only would a union of the two kingdoms bring economic benefits – '[the] wealth of both peoples united will increase faster than of both distinct' – but the political gains, too, would be immense. Protestants would gain, Catholics would be politically weakened so that rebellion could be prevented, and a union 'of all his majesty's territories' would greatly strengthen England. The successful defeat of the Jacobites again fostered notions of union in the 1690s, even to the extent that in Lisburn one cleric gave a new name to Ireland, calling it 'Britland' in the parish register. Molyneux in *The case* argued that if Ireland were to be bound by English statutes, then the people of Ireland had the right to be represented in the English parliament. 'This, I believe, we should be willing enough to embrace, but this is an happiness we can hardly hope for'. He was expressing what was by then a widely held opinion. When the Irish House of Commons sent their congratulations to Queen Anne on the union with Scotland, they added a prayer that God 'might put it in your royal heart to add greater strength and lustre to your crown by yet more comprehensive union'. The House of Lords, too, expressed the same hope that the queen 'will perfect this great work by bringing her kingdom of Ireland also into the union'.

In his own inimitable fashion Swift expressed his feelings in an allegory which he called *The story of the injured lady, being a true picture of Scotch perfidy, Irish poverty and English partiality*, which contrasted the way Ireland and Scotland were treated. He depicted Scotland as an unattractive woman, 'with bad features and a worse complexion'; yet she was chosen by the gentleman (England), instead of the lady (Ireland) who was much superior not just in appearance, but fidelity as well. The lady was cast off and ruined.

But England was not interested in a united kingdom of Britain and Ireland. Not until the second half of the century did English politicians come to see political gain in such a union and by then opinion in Ireland was in favour of their own fully independent parliament. In a sense this had always been the real preference. In fighting legislative control from England the notion of natural right, liberty and consent, could sometimes best be argued through a demand for representation in England. This was the case with those who have been called 'commonwealthmen', arguing for constitutional as well as commercial equality with the English. As one correspondent put it in 1708, it was 'slavery to be governed by laws made without representation'. But for most of those concerned about politics this meant government by laws made in a representative Irish parliament. The stronger identity with Ireland became among Protestants, the greater the emphasis on this notion of parliamentary independence. When they came to see themselves as consti-tuting the Irish nation, it was natural for them to insist that this nation should be represented in its own parliament, as had always been the case since Henry II accepted the voluntary submission of the Irish princes in 1172 and in return conferred on them the benefits of English law and institutions includ-ing their own parliament. So the argument went; the last thing they were was a colony. When arguing in 1698 that Ireland was a separate kingdom and that the royal style included 'king of Ireland' Molyneux wrote:

> 'Is this agreeable to the nature of a colony? Do they use the title of kings of Virginia, New England or Maryland? . . . Have we not a parliament and courts of judicature? Do these things agree with a colony?'

When William King, the future Archbishop of Dublin, wrote in May 1698 that 'I would rather suffer anything than betray my country', he was voicing a sentiment of attachment to the *patria* which was increasingly common among the leaders of the established church. Robert Huntington, who became provost of Trinity College in 1683, wrote in a letter that 'the nation should make their language triumphant, and the rather because there are laws against it'. He was concerned with the Anglo-Irish, or English of Ireland, rather than the native Irish. William Molyneux always saw himself as an Englishman of Ireland, very different to the native Irish, and of course Catholic, population. Yet when he promoted the publication of Roderick O'Flaherty's *Ogygia, seu rerum Hibernicorum chronologia* in 1685, he wrote a letter to his brother praising the book and referred to 'the profound antiqui-ties of our country'. In the same year he called Dublin and Ireland 'our city and nation'. William Domville, who was a second-generation settler, when protesting Ireland's legislative independence of England, argued that the practice of 'our forefathers' was that they enacted the laws that bound them. And Swift, whose father had been born in England and who had himself spent much time there, in writing about the fifteenth century Anglo-Irish called them 'our ancestors'.

The Protestant nation thus identified with Ireland and, as was the case with their predecessors in the middle ages and the Old English of a later era, this meant taking a pride in Ireland's past history. One manifestation of this was the popularity of Keating's history and demands for a translation in the late seventeenth century. Another sign was the number of family histories produced. More unusually it sometimes led to an interest in and knowledge of the Irish language, or in the collection of old Irish manuscripts containing important historical texts. This could lead to an even closer identification with Ireland, when the newcomers might see themselves as the natural replacements of the old ousted heads of lineages. Arthur Brownlow, an Ulster settler, showed some awareness of this at the end of the seventeenth century when he translated an Irish poem he had found:

> And when she [Ireland] had thrust those natives from her arms
> She foreigners embraced with all her greatest charms,
> Cherished them most that did her greatest harms.

Brownlow had learnt Irish, collected manuscripts (including the famous Book of Armagh, which he rearranged into its correct form) and translated poetry, because he identified with Ireland and its history and became in some sense a 'foreigner embraced' by his adopted country.

From the perspective of England the ambiguity of the Protestant position and ambitions in Ireland were clear and obvious. In 1726 when Swift listed what he called 'Irish grievances', he gave primacy to the fact that in England 'all persons born in Ireland are called and treated as Irishmen, although their fathers and grandfathers were born in England'. Not only were they Irish, they were also seen as colonists, dependant on England and therefore subject in much the same way as a child to its parent. Like a child, the Irish Protestants also could be irresponsible and in need of correction. It was partly for this reason that so many Englishmen were appointed not only to the best posts in government and administration, but to so many of the high offices in the Church of Ireland as well. It was the persistence of this attitude which helped the Protestants of Ireland to develop a sense of being Irish, of being not only 'the whole people of Ireland' as Swift insisted, but the Irish nation itself.

Faced with this attitude, and with the Irish parliament gaining some degree of independence in money matters in particular, it became necessary for the English government to find some way of controlling or managing that parliament. This was done through what became known as 'the undertaker system', whereby carefully selected Irish politicians were promised a large share of official patronage and some say on policy in return for 'undertaking' to provide a majority in the Irish House of Commons. Since it was the commons who brought forward 'heads of bills' on which legislation was subsequently based, it was they rather than the House of Lords who had to be managed. Because the lord lieutenant was normally unfamiliar with Ireland, was in residence only when parliament was in session (that is for about eight months in two years) and could not attend parliament himself, it was necessary for him to employ managers of the commons. This was done almost from the time of the 1692 parliament.

By then something like a party system of Whigs and Tories was emerging which made management practical. But such party divisions were really ephemeral and most members of parliament were normally pursuing self-interested policies, looking for gain of one sort or another and were thus liable to be managed by those who controlled patronage. The lord lieutenant, usually a well-connected member of the English nobility, was a powerful figure. A member of the English cabinet, until the 1770s when he remained in Ireland, the lord lieutenant might regard the office as, in effect, a banishment from the political centre in England. But enjoying a huge salary (£20,000 in 1783), large financial allowances, and access to other sources of wealth which gave ample opportunity to help relatives, as well as oneself, the office was in fact a valuable one. With extensive powers, giving control over most offices, the lord lieutenant was in a position to exercise patronage in support of British interests in Ireland and, using the undertakers, secure a government majority in the Irish House of Commons. He could also exploit the useful connections of some individual members of parliament, in particular the powerful primate Archbishop of Armagh, always an Englishman chosen less for his ecclesiastical expertise than his political competence and, where possible, the powerful speaker of the House of Commons.

Such a person was William Connolly, speaker from 1715, as well as first commissioner of revenue. Connolly also held office as lord justice – one of the two lords justices who headed the Dublin government when the lord lieutenant was absent from Ireland. He was thus in a commanding position. A man of quite humble origins, he made a fortune by speculating in land and became the richest man in Ireland. In 1722 he commenced the building of Castletown, the first great Palladian house in Ireland. This great house was a fitting symbol of his leading position in Ireland and the dependence of the chief governor on his services. When he died in 1729 he was succeeded as speaker by Henry Boyle, who held the office for all of 23 years.

Boyle was at the centre of a major confrontation between the commons and the government, which centred on the money bill dispute of 1753. Two years previously, when a surplus in the treasury was available, a bill setting aside part of the money toward payment of the national debt was sent to England under the Poynings' law procedure. When it was returned by the British privy council a clause had been inserted giving the royal consent to the expenditure. In other words, where the commons claimed that the right of disposal did not lie solely with the crown, the privy council said that it did. At the time the commons accepted the revision and passed the bill into law. But in 1753, when a similar bill was returned from England with the royal consent clause inserted, the Irish House of Commons rejected the bill by 122 votes to 119. There were wild celebrations in the streets of Dublin, where the result was seen not just as a defeat for the government, but as a reassertion of the rights of the Irish parliament. A year later Lord Chesterfield in a letter to the Bishop of Waterford reflected on the outcome: 'The question is by no means how Ireland shall be governed but by whom'. It was regarded as a victory for what was known as the 'patriot' element in the parliament. 'Patriot' clubs were formed in many parts of Ireland and the Protestant nation identified with the victory. No wonder that the chief secretary, Lord Sackville, wrote in December that 'the cry throughout the country is "Ireland for ever" and sometimes with the addition of "down with the English"'.

This confrontation and the 'patriot' victory showed that the government was not always able to manage the parliament with the undertaker system and its control of patronage. It also showed that there was still a brand of Protestant nationalism which could find an outlet in parliament, where pro-Irish and anti-English sentiment could find a form of expression. To that extent at least parliament in eighteenth century Ireland could from time to time represent popular views. But parliament was in no real sense representative, except that whatever those elected decided was binding on the communities which elected them. The franchise was so restricted that only a small proportion of people actually had the vote. There was no secret ballot. For much of the century Catholics, and even Protestants married to Catholics, could not vote. Protestant dissenters were discriminated against through the operation of the 1704 sacramental test. Because the county elections were confined to the 40-shilling freeholders, most people, even members of the established church, were ruled out.

Apart from all that, elections in the 32 counties which returned two members each were largely controlled by landlords. This was even more so the case with the 117 boroughs returning two members each. Most of these so-called 'boroughs' were practically owned by members of the upper class. Altogether 300 were elected (including two from Trinity College) and the majority was firmly in the control of a small number of families. In 1736, when he was nearly 70, Swift wrote a vicious satire on parliament, which he called 'the legion club' (because it was inhabited by a legion of devils, like the possessed man in the gospel):

> As I stroll the city, oft I
> Spy a building large and lofty.
> Not a bow-shot from the College,
> Half the globe from sense and knowledge.
>
> Tell me what this pile contains?
> Many a head that holds no brains.

The members were a 'rout and a rabble', 'three hundred brutes' with nothing better to do than engage in 'wild disputes', roaring their lungs out about 'privilege of parliament'.

> Let them with their gosling quills
> Scribble senseless heads of bills.

Swift was especially vicious about individual members whom he named, unfit to be there, like 'Sir Tom, that rampant ass' (Sir Thomas

Prendergast), who was 'sprung from papists and a regicide'. Indeed some seats were virtually hereditary possessions. Small wonder that when the government in London was seriously considering implementing a union of the two kingdoms later in the century, it was reliably informed that the purchase of 20 individuals would secure the necessary support for a safe passage of a bill through the House of Commons.

There was one other feature of the Irish parliament which is important: from 1714 onwards each parliament sat throughout the whole reign of the current monarch. Thus when George I died in 1727 parliament was dissolved and then elections were held to form a new parliament which lasted until George II died in 1760. During the 33 years of that parliament no elections were held, even where members consistently failed to attend for years at a time. They remained members until they died and only then was a by-election held. So once the composition of a parliament became fixed, it was virtually impossible to change it. No matter how efficient the control exercised by the government through the undertaker system, parliament remained ultimately in the hands of the landlord class.

It also met regularly every two years, so that for the first time a permanent building had to be found to house it adequately. This was provided when the magnificent parliament building which still stands on College Green was constructed, with no money spared, from 1729. It also gave public expression to the fact that Ireland was no mere colony, but a kingdom with its own parliament which represented not just that anglican ascendancy which dominated the politics of eighteenth-century Ireland, but an even narrower landlord–gentry ascendancy. The magnificent houses and gardens which that class constructed throughout the island were a witness to that fact. When parliament in 1758 established 'the commissioners for making wide and convenient streets' in Dublin, it began the completion of a process which was to make Dublin one of the finest capitals in Europe, worthy of the Ireland of the eighteenth century. In 1806 a German stationed in Ireland for a time was sufficiently impressed to write that:

'Dublin is more beautiful than London. It has broader streets, taller and more uniform houses, and fine squares . . . Of very special note is the street in which the former parliament-house is situated; it displays a definite grandeur of the kind one fully expects in capital cities'.

11 The emergence of Catholic Ireland

In February 1768 the Dublin parliament enacted legislation which limited the lives of future parliaments to eight years. This Octennial Act had a profound effect, since frequent elections to parliament were bound to make aspiring MPs more conscious of public opinion and therefore, even if only to a very limited extent, make the House of Commons in its legislation more responsive to the articulated public aspirations of the people of Ireland. Potentially, then, it might augment the role of the 'patriots' who claimed to represent Irish aspirations to freedom from constitutional dependence on the British parliament. What is surprising is that this important piece of legislation was the achievement of the new lord lieutenant, Lord Townshend, the first of his kind to reside permanently in Dublin during his period in office.

Appointed in August 1767, it was Townshend who broke the back of the undertaker system in parliament and made Dublin castle an independent power broker in Irish politics. His immediate purpose in dealing with the Dublin parliament on his arrival in Ireland was to persuade it to agree to provide the money necessary to increase substantially the standing army. This would mean raising the military budget by as much as a third and to achieve this he was dependent on the successful management of the House of Commons by the undertakers. Townshend was also determined to weaken parliament's role in money matters by increasing the 'hereditary revenue' of the crown in Ireland and thus make the king less dependent on the commons for grants of money. But in November 1769, when the commons rejected a money bill, they gave as the reason the fact that the bill had not originated with them. This was a reassertion of Irish parliamentary control over finance and therefore another challenge to the executive in Dublin and ultimately to the British insistence on Ireland's colonial status. Townshend, who was determined to maintain that status, turned on his parliamentary managers, the undertakers, who had failed to procure him a majority in the commons for the bill. He prorogued parliament and in the interval before it met again he succeeded in securing a majority in the commons to back the executive. He did this by exploiting the greed and ambitions of discontented politicians, mostly from the ranks of the lesser gentry, who had failed to benefit from the patronage controlled by the undertakers and who were jealous of the wealth which a few, mainly from the leading families, had gained as a result. Townshend skilfully worked on this to gain their support by promises of his own, strengthened by the new political stability in London which guaranteed his continuing presence in Dublin and thus his continuing control over patronage. When parliament reassembled in February 1771, not only had the lord lieutenant succeeded in building up what was in effect a 'castle party' in the commons, but the opposition facing him was disunited and to some extent in disarray.

As a result of Townshend's success, the parliamentary session which lasted until May witnessed an unprecedented series of large government majorities in favour of bills. Of the 25 divisions in the commons between 26 February and 18 May, the average number of members supporting the government was 100 as against an average of 63 in opposition. A new speaker, a nominee of the government, was elected and the power of the old undertakers was broken. During the years following, until he left Ireland in 1772, Townshend was able to consolidate the castle party in the commons, though this required the disciplining of some of his supporters who, as he wrote, 'would be the manager in their turn'. Given the fact that the lord lieutenant himself was absent from parliament and that the Dublin executive was quite separate from it, managers, under the control of the castle, were still necessary to secure continuing support in the commons. The success of Townshend can be seen in the continuance of his system to the end of the century, despite the constitutional change of 1782, and indeed it was largely responsible for effecting the act of union with Britain in 1800. Control of patronage was the key. There were many, even among the patriots, who could be bought, provided the price was high enough. One astonishing statistic illustrates the extent of the patronage dispensed: between 1767 and 1785 no less than 50 new Irish peerages were created and shared out.

Among those members of parliament who, for one reason or another, found themselves in opposition to the government and the castle party was a motley collection of individuals who were called patriots. They had no agreed programme, apart from limiting the life of parliament and winning legislative independence for Ireland, were not organized as a party and the composition of the group changed regularly. Some were radical, like the famous Dublin apothecary Charles Lucas, who had caused so much trouble in 1749 that he was declared to be an enemy of Ireland by the House of Commons and had to flee to avoid imprisonment. Back home in Dublin after his exile he was elected to parliament where he continued to denounce the British claim to legislate for Ireland and promoted the ideas of Molyneux and Swift. In 1763 he founded the *Freeman's Journal* which became the mouthpiece of the opposition in parliament and he used it to mould public opinion. In this way what he called 'wise and virtuous, honest and free electors would choose members worthy of themselves'. None of the other members were as radical as Lucas, who promoted the notion of parliament lasting for only three years and vigorously attacked the pension list which he claimed consisted of 'drones who consume the fruits of the labours of the industrious'. But they all had one aim in common and that was to strengthen the role of the House of Commons, which for many meant challenging the English view of Ireland as a dependent colony and its parliament as subject to the superior legislative authority of the British parliament.

The argument propounded by Molyneux was still effective and among the critics most vocal on the issue in the House of Commons and elsewhere, and in particular on the manner in which Poynings' law was abused, was Henry Flood. A graduate of Trinity College, where Edmund Burke had been a contemporary, Flood was a trained lawyer, though he never practised, and had a sound grasp of constitutional law. From county Kilkenny, where he inherited from his father, the chief justice Warden Flood, an estate reputedly worth £5,000 a year, he first entered parliament in 1759. A brilliant orator, he quickly gained a reputation for his grasp of difficult constitutional matters, his ability to expound clearly issues which were problematic, and the moral tone he customarily adopted when denouncing abuse. He was, as a friend of Grattan's said, 'a gentleman of gigantic abilities'. When in 1769 Molyneux's *The Case* was reprinted in Dublin it contained a new introduction which impressed by the vigour and power of the anti-English argument, an essay which it was generally believed had been written by Flood. He, with Lucas, was at the forefront of the group which campaigned vigorously for the introduction of a septennial act limiting the life of parliament to seven years.

If there had been a certain charisma attached to him in the 1760s, climaxed with the passing of the Octennial Act in 1768, his reputation became tarnished when he accepted the vice-treasurership in 1775. This office was almost a sinecure, since the vice-treasurer had no real function in the executive. The fact that it added considerably to Flood's income, with the common view being that the holder of such an office would almost necessarily be corrupted, destroyed Flood's leadership of the patriots. Lord Charlemont, later general of the Volunteers, condemned the holding of office in Ireland: 'It was not a situation held for Ireland, but held for the English government, often in collision with, and frequently hostile to Ireland'.

But Flood never lost his skills in parliament and his ability to organize public opinion in favour of reform. In 1779, for example, he made what was called 'free trade' an issue, arguing that Ireland should be equal to Britain in foreign (including colonial) trade – a concession which was conceded in December 1779. Three years later the Dublin Chamber of Commerce was founded. He remained a radical in his view of the constitutional relationship between Britain and Ireland. For him the Westminster parliament must totally renounce its right to legislate for Ireland. When the British parliament in June 1782 repealed the declaratory act of 1720 (6 George I) and amended Poynings' law to the extent that bills approved in Dublin by both houses of parliament must be sent to England without any further alteration, Flood was one of the few who protested that this was far from what was required.

England must be prepared to renounce altogether its superior position and the logic of this would mean a repeal of Poynings' law.

Thanks largely to Flood's continuing public campaign, on 17 April 1783 the British parliament did promulgate the renunciation act, which formally acknowledged the exclusive right of the Irish parliament to legislate for Ireland:

> '. . . be it declared and enacted, that the said right claimed by the people of Ireland to be bound only by laws enacted by his majesty and the parliament of that kingdom in all cases whatever, and to have all actions and suits at law or in equity, which may be instituted in that kingdom, decided in his majesty's courts therein finally and without appeal from thence, shall be and is hereby declared to be established and ascertained for ever, and shall at no time hereafter be questioned or questionable'.

It was by way of a bonus that the exclusive jurisdiction of the Irish courts was accepted. But Poynings' law remained on the statute book.

Flood also involved himself in the Volunteers (the military organization formed some years previously when invasion was threatened) and in 1783 even appeared in the commons in uniform to present the moderate proposals for parliamentary reform (mostly devised by himself) which had been accepted by the Volunteer convention held in Dublin's Rotunda in November. This and other motions which he sponsored were thrown out by the commons and that probably helped to convince Flood that his future in politics lay at Westminster. That he was ambitious is undoubted. But it is likely, too, that he was unwilling to be party to the more radical view of many patriots on the future of Catholics in Ireland. He was willing to overturn many of the popery laws, but not to allow Catholics any political power. He said himself in parliament the Catholics should be allowed to purchase lands, 'but we should carefully guard against their possessing any power in the state'.

Like many of his contemporaries, especially among the patriots, Flood encouraged an interest in Ireland's history and was a founder member of the Royal Irish Academy. He even left his Kilkenny estate to Trinity College to create a professorship of Irish and to help the library acquire important Irish manuscripts. Two other founder members of the Academy in 1785 were Henry Grattan and Lord Charlemont (the first president, in whose house the first meeting was held), the latter publishing an essay in the first volume of *Transactions* on 'The antiquity of the woollen manufacture in Ireland, proved from a passage of an ancient Florentine poet'. Grattan and Charlemont, his patron, took over as leaders of the patriots in parliament and it was Grattan in particular who was responsible for organizing the forces, both within and outside parliament, which brought about the 1782 constitutional change.

Grattan entered parliament in December 1775 and joined the patriot opposition. He proved to be a master of debate and thrived in the many confrontations with the castle party and administration, rapidly establishing himself as one of the most important patriots in the commons. In January 1780 he showed his skill in mustering public opinion when he proclaimed that he would 'strain every nerve' to have Poynings' law modified and, more important, 'secure this country against the illegal claims of the British parliament'. This open declaration of war on the English claim to legislate for Ireland, with major implications for the Irish economy because of the mercantilist nature of parliamentary restrictions on Irish trade, was calculated to whip up support in Dublin for the patriots. Grattan made good his promise when parliament reassembled. In an important speech in the commons on 19 April he argued that 'the king's most excellent majesty, lords and commons of Ireland' were 'the only powers competent to make laws to bind this kingdom'. Even though his motion was finally defeated by 136 votes to 97, his great speech was effective in making the question of Irish legislative independence the number one priority for the patriots in parliament.

It was Grattan, with Charlemont (the commander-in-chief) and Flood, who carefully manipulated the Volunteer convention which met at Dungannon on 15 February 1782 and composed the motions which would establish the constitutional independence of Ireland in the forefront of Volunteer political aspirations. This would restore the medieval constitutional position, as Grattan subsequently made plain in the House of Commons on 16 April: 'The crown of Ireland is an imperial crown inseparably annexed to the crown of Great Britain'. He was no republican and the new constitution of 1782, while it repealed the declaratory act of 1720 (6 George I), modified Poynings' law, made the House of Lords the final court of appeal for Ireland and established the independence of the Irish judges, it left the link with the crown intact. In his famous speech to the commons on 16 April 1782, in which he described how the nation had progressed 'from injuries to arms, and from arms to liberty', Grattan said that 'Ireland is now a nation. In that character I hail her, and being in her august presence I say *Esto perpetua* (be it so for ever)'. Later, when revising his speeches for publication, he added to the text of what he had actually said in Dublin on that day: 'Spirit of Swift, spirit of Molyneux, your genius has now prevailed. Ireland is now a nation'. But in 1782 he had added that if the crown of Ireland was inseparably united to that of England, the kingdom of Ireland was separate and distinct.

Grattan was now the darling of the public and the hero of parliament. Adulation was expressed in the most practical way when the House of Commons voted him the enormous sum of £50,000, which not only bought him an estate suitable to his rank, but would make him financially secure for life. It is no wonder that to nationalist historians and politicians in the next century the parliament which sat under the new 1782 constitution was known simply as 'Grattan's parliament'.

But this unique tribute to Grattan in Irish historiography was misplaced, for the 1782 constitution was fatally flawed, as Flood had realized. England still controlled legislation because the Dublin administration was composed of Englishmen at the highest levels and a majority of MPs could still be bought when their votes were needed. When Grattan failed to convince the Volunteers that Ireland now had legislative independence, he moved aside and it was Flood, as we have seen, who used public opinion to force the British parliament in 1783, in the renunciation act, to recognize the exclusive right of the Irish parliament to legislate for Ireland. Grattan tried to maintain an independent stance in parliament, sometimes supporting the government in legislation which he believed to be necessary, even if this meant incurring public odium for seemingly betraying his liberal principles. Worse, he could suffer physical assault, as happened when on one occasion his home was attacked by a Dublin mob. But he never entirely abandoned the opposition in the commons and in 1785 he joined with Flood and Charlemont in defeating Pitt's proposed bill for regulating Irish trade – a bill which Grattan described as 'subversive of . . . the free constitution of Ireland'. He unsuccessfully attempted to push tithe reform through the commons. In 1789 he supported the cause of the Prince of Wales in the Irish parliament during the regency crisis in England and gained much political influence as a result.

When the Catholic demand for relief asserted itself in 1792 Grattan was faced with a difficult choice. In the past he had actively supported Catholic emancipation. In 1782 it was he, unknown to Flood, who had submitted a proposal to the Volunteers at Dungannon urging the 'relaxation of the penal laws against our Roman Catholic fellow subjects'. It is significant that Grattan referred to 'penal' laws and not 'popery' laws. Even more important, by insisting that Catholics were 'fellow subjects' and not simply 'papists', he was applying a doctrine of equality which, if given effect, would substitute a new Irish nation for the hitherto exclusively Protestant one. It was a proposal far more radical than the one for constitutional reform. Now, in 1792, he was being asked to support a Catholic demand for equality which would challenge what Grattan himself called a 'Protestant ascendancy' in Ireland. Even if it meant alienating many of those who in the past had valued his leadership and driving into a frenzy the extreme element which was determined to maintain Protestant ascendancy, Grattan remained true to his earlier liberal principles. In the commons he supported 'the removal of all disabilities' affecting Catholics. In the event, the resulting legislation was very limited indeed and Grattan's ineffective opposition was cruelly exposed.

He now mistrusted the extreme radicalism of the United Irishmen (the movement established in Belfast and Dublin in 1791) and the growing influence of what he regarded as insidious notions coming from revolutionary France. Not surprisingly he backed the war against France. But despite this support of the government, he was unable to prevent the severe repressive legislation which was successfully pushed through parliament. He continued to press for Catholic emancipation and supported the foundation of the new seminary at Maynooth in 1795. Even though this earned him the respect of Catholics and radicals alike, he again failed to secure the necessary legislation which would give Catholics equal rights as subjects. This not only alarmed the defenders of the Protestant ascendancy, so that he became an object of suspicion as a subversive, it also alienated the more extreme radical elements in Ireland who not only adopted republicanism and the revolutionary notions imported from France, but saw in violence the only hope of reform.

When the administration in 1796 embarked on a policy of extreme repression in an insurrection act, Grattan despaired. 'There are now two constitutions in Ireland', he wrote, 'one for the rich and another for the poor'. He denounced the majority who backed the government in the commons: they had, he said, 'the spirit of planters, not of country gentlemen'. In disgust he withdrew from parliament and in 1797 did not seek re-election. But after the rebellion of 1798, for which the most extreme Protestant element held him partly responsible – a letter from a county Meath landowner to a former chief secretary for Ireland in December 1798 called him 'that arch-traitor' and blamed him for bringing

> 'that rebellion into the field, and then like a scoundrel and a coward he shamefully fled, leaving the loyalists to fight the battles which he had occasioned and his own partisans to be most plentifully cut up'

– he bought his way back into parliament via a safe borough seat. He was determined to prevent Pitt, the prime minister, from procuring an act of union. But Grattan was now a spent force and could do nothing to prevent the union. He retired from politics a defeated man. He lost his place on the privy council, his portrait was removed from its honoured place in Trinity College, he was expelled from the merchants' guild, and in Cork Grattan street was given a new name.

There is another legacy of Grattan's time in parliament which is usually forgotten: it achieved a unique measure of social reform. For example, between 1784 and 1787 legislation on prison reform was enacted which was so radical that not for another generation was it to be matched in Britain. In making such legislation not only 'radicals' were prominent, but 'reactionaries' like John Foster and John Fitzgibbon. Ascendancy members such as they could cooperate with patriots like Grattan in trying to improve the lot of the people, while maintaining a steady hostility where constitutional matters were concerned.

When Grattan appeared in his Volunteer uniform on the last occasion he graced the House of Commons, he was publicly proclaiming the significant role which that organization had played in bringing about the constitution of 1782. The Volunteers were a unique phenomenon. An armed body, highly organized throughout the kingdom, independent and outside the control of the government, tolerated by Dublin castle, they became a dominant force in Irish politics, not least because of the potential threat they posed to the rule of law. They were not a rabble but were firmly controlled by upper class officers, mostly gentry who had the means to finance the corps, with the ranks composed of businessmen and farmers who could afford the high cost of equipment and, indeed, the entertainment that became part of the business of the Volunteers. Membership became a status symbol, not only of one's Protestantism (though some Catholics in more remote parts did join), but of a useful member of the community, prepared to do one's duty in the defence of the kingdom and when that was not necessary in helping to maintain law and order.

Established in 1778, the Volunteers were a response to the need to protect Ireland from a possible French invasion. But much earlier, with the great rise in rural disturbance and agrarian unrest from the 1760s and onwards, especially in Munster, local companies of rangers were established to protect property. A letter from a Youghal resident in 1762 described the formation of a local Protestant militia, supplied with arms, with 70 men on guard each night and patrols through the town every two hours. When a large band of Whiteboys (rural agitators) attacked the town, they were driven back by 'the mayor and several other gentlemen, in number forty-one, well mounted and accoutered'. In 1776 a Limerick Union was formed of leading citizens, consisting of troops of cavalry and a company of foot, to protect the town and put down disturbers. Similar bodies of armed men sprang up in many parts of the country, all at no cost to the government. The outbreak of war in America and the departure in 1775 of 4,000 regular troops from Ireland to serve there dangerously weakened the army. When war with France broke out in March 1778 and with England soon at war with much of Europe, the problem of defence against a potential invasion became acute. Because of the serious financial situation – the lord lieutenant reported to the prime minister, Lord North, in England that there was 'no balance in the treasury' – it was decided to solve the problem by encouraging the formation of more independent companies in the localities, financed by local gentry and others with the necessary resources. It was out of these companies that the Volunteer movement was born and to be a Volunteer quickly became the fashion.

It was in Belfast, on 17 March 1778, that the first Volunteer company was established. Others quickly followed and by August 1779 the numbers had climbed to 40,000, with a centralized structure of command being fashioned as the companies were formed into regiments and battalions. In 1779 parliament voted a message of thanks to them for helping to protect the country against the threat of invasion. But when that threat was removed the Volunteers did not disband. Instead, they turned to internal matters and became political agents, outside the control of the government. On 4 November, the birthday of William III, the duke of Leinster led thousands of Dublin Volunteers to the king's statue on College Green. There they demonstrated in favour of free trade for Ireland, then being debated in the parliament building opposite to where they assembled. With banners proclaiming 'Free Trade' and 'Glorious Revolution', some cannon carrying the sign 'Free trade or this', and the men brandishing guns and other weapons, they made it quite plain to Lord North and the British government, not to mention Dublin castle, that physical force might achieve what disputed authority would not concede. Lord North made concessions and, flushed with success, some Volunteer companies went further in their demands. In December, for example, the Newry Volunteers asserted that Ireland should be independent of the British parliament. The captain of the Armagh company was even more explicit when he published *A letter to Lord North*, urging him to accept the legislative independence of Ireland before it was taken by force, namely the Volunteers.

This assumption of a political role by the Volunteers, coupled with their independence of governmental control, frightened and alienated many members of the Irish parliament. In August 1780 when a controversial mutiny bill came back from England with a new clause added which would make the act perpetual, Grattan and other patriots protested and opposed the bill. But, despite that, the commons accepted the bill by 114 votes to 62. On the next day the Dublin merchants' company of Volunteers denounced the act at a public meeting, declaring that by accepting it the commons had subverted the constitution.

Further afield the spirit of the Volunteers won admiration in the most unlikely quarter. The *Belfast Newsletter* reported on 27 March 1781 that at St James' palace the king had ceremoniously celebrated St Patrick's day in a Volunteer uniform, wearing sprigs of shamrock in his hat. This was in keeping with the fashionable view of the Volunteers almost as gentlemen's clubs, dressing up, parading, and generally enjoying themselves in public. Numbers had escalated over the years, from 40 to 60,000 by 1780, 80,000 the year following, and to as many as 100,000 by the time the duke of Portland came as lord lieutenant in 1792. With only 5,000 regular troops under his control, it is no wonder that Portland would write, not long after his arrival: 'It is no longer the parliament of Ireland that is to be managed or attended to – it is the whole of the country'. Given such high numbers, it seems that despite the popery laws which forbade them to carry weapons, some Catholics who could afford the expense of providing a uniform joined the organization, as was reported by government spies in 1784.

It was significant that Tom Paine, the great author of *The Rights of Man* (1791), who was to have such an influence on the circulation of revolutionary ideas in Ireland, regarded the Volunteers as the only genuine revolutionary group in Ireland. They showed something of revolutionary fervour late in 1781 when the Armagh battalion of which Lord Charlemont (the commander-in-chief of the Volunteers) was colonel, issued an invitation to all the companies in Ulster to elect delegates to a convention in Dungannon on 15 February 1782. The election of representatives gave the meeting a quasi-parliamentary character. The purpose, as reported in the *Belfast Newsletter*, could not have been more avowedly political: they were to assemble 'then and there to deliberate on the present alarming situation of public affairs'. Delegates from 143 companies turned up, 'conspirators for the common good', as the *Newsletter* put it. Lord Charlemont presided and other prominent patriots, such as Flood and Grattan, were present. It was no coincidence that Molyneux's *The Case of Ireland* was reprinted in Belfast and, because it was considered relevant to the issues of the day, was sold for only 6d a copy.

The convention soon showed its revolutionary spirit in the resolutions passed. The claim of the British parliament 'to make laws to bind this kingdom' was condemned as 'unconstitutional, illegal and a grievance'. So, too, were 'the powers exercised by the privy councils of both kingdoms under Poynings' law'. It was also resoundingly proclaimed, almost as a fact which no British parliament could change, that 'the ports of Ireland are open to all ships of countries not at war with his majesty'. Then came the famous motion drafted by Grattan and accepted by the convention, rejoicing at the relaxation of penal laws against Catholics. There was a far more radical proposal from the Bishop of Derry, Frederick Augustus Hervey, who was also Earl of Bristol. He suggested that Catholics and dissenters, both discriminated against in law, should unite together to achieve complete freedom under the law.

Hervey was a larger-than-life figure who had travelled widely in Catholic Europe, studying the relationship between church and state in Catholic countries. He was convinced that a *modus vivendi* could be worked out with Catholics, among whom he had many friends, which would secure their loyalty to the state, protect the Protestant position, and thus enable the popery laws to be completely abolished. Dismissed by many as unbalanced and not to be taken seriously, he does illustrate the important fact that radicals included members of the nobility and gentry as well as middle class professionals, businessmen and artisans. Neither was his suggestion that dissenters should join with Catholics as outrageous as it might seem on first sight. Pitt had told the duke of Buckingham in Ireland in 1760 that

> 'the Presbyterian dissenters in general must ever deserve to be considered, in opposition to the church of Rome, as a very valuable branch of the reformation, and that with regard to their civil principles, that respectable body have in all times shown themselves . . . firm and zealous supporters of the glorious revolution under King William, and of the present happy establishment'.

But in Ireland they saw that the 'glorious revolution' had not been honoured as far as they were concerned and since Pitt wrote many of them, particularly in Ulster, had assumed a more radical stance, seeking reform of laws which penalized them almost as much as Catholics. In the process many of them were willing to cooperate with Catholics in seeking redress and in the end were to join in a revolution designed to establish a French-style republic in Ireland.

Many Ulster Presbyterians had strong connections with America and when the War of Independence broke out there in April 1775 there was a huge surge of support for the rebels. Benjamin Franklin, when he visited Ireland in 1771, had sessions with the leading patriots in Dublin where parliament was sitting. He later wrote:

'I found them disposed to be friends of America, in which I endeavoured to confirm them with the expectation that our growing weight might in time be thrown into their scale, and by our joining our interests with theirs, a more equitable treatment from this nation [England] might be obtained for themselves as well as for us'.

Four years later there was enormous interest in and support for the colonists in their fight against the British. Newspapers regularly published all the manifestos of the colonists. In Dublin Napper Tandy, the famous radical, later told his son that 'when America revolted against the tyranny of Great Britain my heart rejoiced within me and I should at that time have joined her standard if not prevented'. In Ennis a schoolmaster wrote a poem in Irish celebrating Washington's victories in 1776 and in Dublin in December a public fast was proclaimed in support of the colonists.

The dissemination from America of notions of liberty and freedom had a profound effect on many Volunteers. The Ulster Presbyterian William Drennan, the man who later coined the phrase 'the emerald isle' and who was one of the founders of the United Irishmen, saw in the armed Volunteers what he called in 1783 'the buried majesty of the people'. This kind of attitude alienated the moderates, fearful of what such a large armed force might demand if controlled by extremists. In the euphoria created by the new 1782 constitution, moderate patriots in parliament found Volunteer support increasingly embarrassing. When a national convention of Volunteers in Dublin's Rotunda pressed for parliamentary reforms in 1783, it was seen as a threat by many in the commons. On 17 November the convention accepted a plan which would give some Catholic representation in parliament. Henry Flood rushed to the House of Commons which was still in session. Still in his Volunteer uniform, he tried to introduce a bill 'for the more equal representation of the people in parliament'. But many of the MPs, even if they supported the notion of some form of Catholic emancipation, were alarmed at the prospect of being intimidated by armed Volunteers. John Fitzgibbon, the future Earl of Clare and later a dominant figure in government, put it clearly and succinctly: 'I do not think life worth holding at the will of an armed demagogue'. After a heated debate, which continued until 3 a.m. on Sunday morning, the commons rejected Flood's bill by 157 votes to 77. This really marked the end of the Volunteer–parliament alliance. In effect, by rejecting by a large majority a reform bill which was supported by the Volunteers, parliament was reclaiming power for itself and turning its back on the threat posed by armed Volunteers to the sovereignty of parliament.

But the Volunteer movement was far from dead. In August 1785, for example, the viceroy, Lord Camden, told Pitt that what he called 'popular clamour' and more especially the Volunteers 'with the certainty . . . [that] assistance from France gives Ireland such an accession of strength as to make her own conceit more than a match for England under our present circumstances' might bring about a rebellion to secure independence from England. The outbreak of the French revolution in 1789 gave a huge impetus to the Volunteers, especially in Ulster, in the early 1790s. On 14 July 1791 the fall of the Bastille was commemorated in Belfast and a large banner depicted Hibernia in chains being introduced by a Volunteer to Liberty. An address delivered to the Volunteers assembled before the Linen Hall included a declaration that the meeting not only wished for 'a real representation of the national will', but also desired to see 'all evil and religious intolerance annihilated in this land'. In Dublin on the same day the Volunteers, led by Colonel James Napper Tandy, paraded through the streets to St Stephen's Green under a banner which read: 'We do not rejoice because we are slaves; but we rejoice because of the French being free'. The wish expressed by the Belfast Volunteers for the removal of the penal laws was later matched in Dublin when the Volunteers there proclaimed the hope 'that we and our Roman Catholic brethren would unite like citizens and claim the rights of man'.

All through the summer of 1791 radicals were busy forming new companies of Volunteers or revitalizing old ones. In Ulster the revival spread rapidly. A 'military fund' was established which would help to buy arms and ammunition for Volunteers, to enable 'our poorer brethren to act'. A convention assembled at Dungannon in February 1793 and although it rejected republicanism, it sought parliamentary reform and fair representation 'by extending the franchise equally to persons of every religious persuasion'. In Dublin, too, Volunteer activity was increasingly evident and parades of armed men through the streets began to cause alarm. This was increased when the Dublin Society of United Irishmen in December 1792 published a declaration addressed to the Volunteers: 'Citizen-soldiers, to arms!'.

The government reacted by running an arms bill through parliament, which not only banned the unlicensed import of arms, ammunition and powder, but also prohibited their distribution throughout the country. A convention act also made illegal the holding of assemblies like the Dungannon one and finally a militia act, while not designed to undermine the Volunteer, effectively did so by making recruiting almost impossible. Already in many places Volunteers had been encouraged as a local police force, companies being formed to help deal with rural disturbances, not least those occasioned by dangerous organizations like the Catholic Defenders. Indeed this had the effect of bringing some conservatives with strong anti-Catholic feelings into the ranks of the Volunteers for the first time. When asked why he had joined the force, one Volunteer recruit replied that he 'would never suffer Ireland to become a popish country'. Even in Belfast there was evidence that some Volunteers were at best ambivalent in their attitude towards Catholics. Intelligence reported to Dublin castle that although they were 'disposed much to republicanism', the Belfast Volunteers 'do not in general relish the admission of Roman Catholics to a participation of their power'.

This was a far cry from the heyday of the Volunteers, when the emancipation of Catholics had been a central part of their political aims, not least among the radical Presbyterians of Ulster. When the new Catholic cathedral of St Mary's was opened in Belfast on 30 May 1784, the Volunteers there provided a guard of honour. The movement was supported and praised generally by Catholics, even though the majority were excluded from active participation. In 1782 a Clare poet praised the Volunteers in Irish verses for 'freeing Ireland from the Saxon yoke'.

There was one important medium through which Catholics and Protestants could meet and share together the new attitudes which the European enlightenment had generated so forcibly. Freemasonry entered Ireland early in the eighteenth century and despite condemnation by the papacy, many Catholics were members of lodges. The official history of the Irish Grand Lodge actually has a Catholic majority among the members in the late eighteenth century, including Daniel O'Connell at the very end. Sharing a common Masonic ideology, Protestants (and especially dissenters) and Catholics were able to come together on equal terms. It was inevitable that the notion of emancipation from penal legislation should gain ground.

This was possible because the Catholics came to be seen as not necessarily a threat to the achievements of the 'glorious revolution' in Ireland. Unlike their co-religionists in England and Scotland, Irish Catholics in general did not respond actively to Jacobite intrigues. There had been no Irish involvement in the rising of 1715, neither was there any response to the Jacobite rising in Scotland, led by Prince Charles himself, in 1745. In 1759 during the Seven Years' War they presented the lord lieutenant with an address of loyalty to the king and when war broke out with Spain the bishops ordered all Catholics to pray for a British victory. When a small French force under Thurot landed in Ulster in February 1760 and captured Carrickfergus, not only was he resisted by locals, but there was no Catholic supportive action anywhere in Ireland. Perhaps most significant of all, the papal recognition of George III as the rightful king after the death of the Old Pretender in 1766 enabled moderate Protestants to accept Catholic protests of loyalty as genuine.

Anxious to free themselves from the stigma of 'popery' (in a political rather than a religious sense), Catholic historians began to lay stress on the independence of the early Irish church from Rome, as did Charles O'Connor in his influential *Dissertations on the ancient history of Ireland* (1753). Some even argued that it was the Normans who had introduced the notion of papal authority into Ireland when Henry II sought the sanction of the pope for his invasion of Ireland. When the English translation of Geoffrey Keating's *History of Ireland* was published in Dublin in 1717 (and later in London in 1723 and 1732), it emphasized Ireland's freedom from Roman interference, which Keating's insistence on the dominant position of Armagh in the early Irish church facilitated. The term 'catholic' was hardly used and, more startling, the term 'parliament' was introduced to stress the long history of that institution in an independent Ireland. This view of Ireland's past fitted in well with the new sense of Irish identity which was to be fostered by the patriots in parliament. In *An essay on the ancient and modern state of Ireland* (1760), the Protestant Henry Brooke not only interpreted Ireland's past in a fashion in tune with patriot politics, using such terms as 'constitution' and even 'patriot' freely in writing of the distant past, he even argued that a thousand years before Julius Caesar brought 'civility' to England, Ireland was civilized and even had what he termed a 'truly parliamentary system of government'. He also had an interest in and helped to make available early Irish mythology and although he never seems to have followed up his resolution to learn Irish, his daughter Charlotte did and left in her *Reliques of Irish poetry* (1789) what was perhaps the most influential of all the literary works produced in Ireland in the late eighteenth century.

Even earlier in the century the discovery of early Irish civilization had aroused enormous enthusiasm not only in Ireland but in England as well. It meant that prejudiced views which for many generations had emphasized Irish barbarism were given a severe jolt. William Nicolson, who became Bishop of Derry in 1718, accepted Keating's argument that even pre-Christian Ireland had been literate and had preserved historical records. His *Irish historical library* presented a view of early Irish Christianity which fore-shadowed the later 'island of saints and scholars' and argued that not only was Irish civilization the equal of that of the Greeks, but that the Olympic games were but 'mirrors of the triennial festivals of our Taragh (Tara)'.

This pride in the past and sense of Irish identity was to help the patriots in their struggle for parliamentary independence and to encourage a more tolerant concept of the Irish nation that would include Catholics in an active role. In tune with the Romantic movement sweeping Europe, and more particularly the Ossianic mania first generated by Macpherson's forgeries, many Protestants, including patriots, became increasingly interested in their Irish heritage. A Gaelic revival resulted, which enabled Protestants to overcome the tradition which simply identified them as foreigners who had conquered Ireland and continued to dominate hostile natives. But by fitting themselves into a scheme of history which saw waves of settlers shaping the Irish nation as it existed in the late eighteenth century, they saw the incongruity of excluding Catholics, the majority of the people, from that nation and preserving the penal code which maintained that exclusion. When Volunteers sang, in translation, an Irish poem 'The tears of Hibernia for the battle of Aughrim', which began:

> Mourn lost Hibernia ever mourn
> thy freedom lost, thy laurels torn,
> thy warriors sunk on Aughrim's plains,
> and Britain loading thee with chains

they were aware that it was the Catholics who had lost the battle. Interestingly, too, John Ashton's verse tragedy, *The Battle of Aughrim* of 1756, written on the model of Dryden, was popularly performed by amateur players to Catholic as well as Protestant audiences, even though a Catholic defeat was its subject. It is evident that at a popular level, if sectarian religious works are excluded, Catholics and Protestants enjoyed much the same common store of literature.

The influence of the enlightenment is also undoubted, not least among the educated middle class. Lord Charlemont, so prominent among the Volunteers and in the patriot opposition in parliament, wrote in his memoirs that 'the spirit of toleration was lately gone abroad . . . it is now grown fashionable to be tolerant'. French influence was particularly strong in eighteenth century Ireland and it was inevitable that the works of the leading *philosophes*, as well as Voltaire and Rousseau, were in demand. Dublin bought 13 sets of the famous *Encyclopédie*, just as many as did London. When radicals, too, came to believe in the contract theory of government, in notions of liberty and freedom imported from America and France, in the importance of Irish identity, and in the rich native civilization which they had inherited, it necessarily meant that the majority of the 'natives', the Catholics, must be made part of the political nation. This the radical Protestants accepted, so they made emancipation from penal legislation a part of their political programme.

Gradually laws were changed. In 1774 an oath of allegiance in tune with the Catholic conscience was devised and in 1778, the year the first Volunteer company was formed in Belfast, parliament passed a Catholic relief act which enabled them to take leases for 999 years and to inherit, without division of estates, in the same way as Protestants. After the Volunteer convention in Dungannon in 1782 and the publication of Edmund Burke's famous statement on Catholic emancipation (*A letter to a peer of Ireland on the penal laws against Irish Catholics*) in the same year, parliament granted further relief: Catholics were now allowed to hold land, 'advowsons, and manors and boroughs returning members to parliament excepted', on the same terms as Protestants; the laws against bishops, priests and religious orders were removed; and Catholics were allowed to open schools.

In 1791 a young Dublin barrister, Theobald Wolfe Tone, published an influential pamphlet, *An Argument on behalf of the Catholics of Ireland*. Intended mainly for Presbyterians, though it enjoyed wide circulation, he therein argued for a reformed parliament in which Catholics would play an essential role. But this could only be achieved by Catholic and Protestant opponents of 'the present despotism' working in harmony together. 'Irishmen of all denominations' must oppose the 'boobies and blockheads' in government and demand reform of parliament. William Drennan had earlier asked if Catholics were fit for freedom: 'Are Roman Catholics generally or partially *capaces libertatis* [fit for freedom] and if not, what are the speediest means of making them so?'. Tone replied that Catholics were not 'incapable of liberty' and until they united with Protestants there would be no true liberty for any in Ireland. If Protestants continued to resist emancipating Catholics, then they must 'cease to murmur at the oppression of the government which grinds us'.

Such a Protestant–Catholic alliance would be a powerful force in Irish politics and the very prospect alarmed the lord lieutenant, the Earl of

Westmoreland. He recommended Tone's pamphlet as 'a pretty specimen of the sentiments of Irish reformers' and tried to prevent the question of the franchise for Catholics from coming before parliament. But in 1792 a petition from the Catholic Committee (founded as far back as 1760 by Catholic gentlemen in Dublin to press their claims) calling 'the attention of parliament to the grievances of Roman Catholics' and asking that 'their capital grievance', exclusion from parliament and denial of the franchise, should be 'alleviated or finally done away' was presented to the commons and was defeated by 208 votes to 25. Later in the same parliament minor concessions were made to Catholics: they were allowed to marry Protestants, to practise law, and education was freed from all restriction. In 1793 the British cabinet promoted a new Catholic relief bill which admitted Catholics to vote on the same terms as Protestants in parliamentary and municipal elections. Subject to certain qualifications, they were given the right to bear arms and, with some few exceptions (the office of lord lieutenant and other high offices in the civil and legal administration), all military (below the rank of general) and civil posts were now available to them, but they remained excluded from membership of parliament. Using all its resources the government got this legislation through a reluctant parliament and in the end got a surprisingly high majority in its favour.

After the bill became law it was reported that Catholics were celebrating a great victory and Westmoreland wrote that in many areas they had 'assumed an insolence and shown a dislike to Protestants which occasioned great alarm'. When the Catholic Committee voted a sum of £1,500 to Wolfe Tone, as well as publishing a declaration demanding further parliamentary reform, Westmoreland saw this as support for extreme radicals like the United Irishmen and confirmation of his view that, as he put it, 'there can be no end to their demands'. He determined to 'take away from them the power of doing mischief' by making it impossible for them in future to hold 'such assemblies and parliaments' as had swung the Catholic population behind them in the past and given them a mandate for action. So in August 1793 the 'convention act' made it impossible for assemblies like the 'Back Lane parliament' of December 1792 to meet in future.

This famous assembly had been responsible for the petition for Catholic emancipation sent directly to the king in England and thus initiating the events which led to the relief legislation of 1793. It was the climax to the work of the Catholic Committee and it marked a major step forward in the process by which the Catholic population at large was politicized. The Catholic Committee had been formed by a group of gentry in 1760, including Charles O'Connor. He had attributed part of the blame for Ireland's economic problems to the penal laws and in a letter of 1756 he expounded on 'the evil consequences of the penal laws on the prosperity of the kingdom'. Later, in 1777, he was supported in his view by no less a person than Adam Smith, the famous author of the influential *Wealth of Nations*, who was quite blunt about the potential of the Irish economy. Ireland was divided, he wrote, 'between two hostile nations, the oppressors and the oppressed, the Protestants and the papists', so there was no hope of real development without reconciliation between the two.

This perceptive view of an intelligent and informed outsider strengthened the more radical elements against the conservative aristocratic control of the Catholic Committee. As middle class radicals took over, influenced by French revolutionary ideals, they began to demand the end of penal laws as a right and not just a favour granted to loyal subjects. When Lord Kenmare and the other conservatives decided to present an address of loyalty to the lord lieutenant at the end of 1791, the Catholic Committee, now dominated by radicals, condemned it as an 'invidious and servile address'. When the members of the Committee were denounced as unrepresentative of Catholic Ireland and were condemned in parliament as 'shop keepers and shop lifters' or as 'men of low and mean parentage', they replied on 17 March 1792 by publishing a declaration which stated, among other matters, that excommunication by the pope did not automatically allow subjects to depose their rulers. Most important of all, it renounced 'all interest in, and title to, all forfeited lands resulting from any rights of our ancestors, or any claim, title, or interest therein'. It also stated that if the franchise were restored to Catholics, they would not use that right 'to disturb and weaken the establishment of the Protestant religion or Protestant government in the kingdom'.

This attempt to allay Protestant fears was widely circulated around the country and signatures were collected in support. The help of the clergy was important and it seems that strong measures were taken to make sure that those who were reluctant agreed to be cooperative. John Keogh, one of the leaders of the Catholic Committee, reported that 'the people seem well inclined to give' the clergy who were not cooperative 'the French cure'. Enormous numbers of signatures in support of the declaration were secured. In county Waterford alone above 20,000 signed and many thousands more all over Ireland. It was a great success and, most significantly, it gave the Catholic Committee what could be interpreted as a mandate from the Catholic population and showed how popular support could be enrolled for Catholic rights.

The printed word was also widely used for propaganda purposes. Thousands of copies of Edmund Burke's influential *A letter to Sir Hercules Langrishe MP* of January 1792, in which he asserted Catholic rights, and of Tone's *Argument* and other literature supportive of the Catholic claim to equality were circulated by the radicals. Not only does the success of this nation-wide propaganda exercise among Catholics show a high degree of literacy among the people, it also demonstrates that the Catholic Committee now controlled a highly efficient organization throughout the country, which was soon put to good use when it was decided to hold a national convention of Catholics in Dublin.

During the summer and autumn of 1792 elections were held throughout the country. Meetings were held in chapels, where representatives were chosen to attend county conventions. There delegates were elected to represent the county in Dublin and the bigger towns, too, elected representatives in the same way. By early November the elections had been completed in 25 counties and all the larger towns. When the convention finally assembled in Dublin on 3 December, 229 elected representative were present: 128 from the 32 counties and 101 from 40 cities and towns. The clergy were represented by Archbishop Troy of Dublin and Bishop Moylan of Cork. It was in a very real sense an assembly representative of the whole of Catholic Ireland and it declared itself 'the only power competent to speak the sense of the Catholics of Ireland'.

Luke Teeling, a linen draper from Lisburn, demanded that the convention should petition the king for 'nothing short of total emancipation' and that they should make clear that they accepted not even 'one fragment of that unjust and abominable system, the penal code'. Others insisted that they should not send their petition in the normal way via Dublin castle – 'we will not, like African slaves, petition our task-masters' – but send it straight to the king and that was what happened. A delegation travelled to England, via Belfast (where their coach was drawn by Protestant sympathizers) because of contrary winds, and was favourably received and presented to George III on 2 January. The result of this delegation, and of the lobbying on their behalf by Edmund Burke, Henry Grattan and others in London, was the Catholic relief legislation introduced at the cabinet's behest in the Irish parliament of 1793.

During the debates in parliament which preceded the legislation, it was notable that many members emphasized the importance of what they termed the 'Protestant ascendancy' in Ireland. In a letter of 2 February 1792 the Bishop of Cloyne condemned the proposed Catholic relief as endangering 'the Protestant interest in Ireland' and denounced 'this wretched compromise of the Protestant ascendancy'. Indeed it was the same bishop, Richard Woodward, who seems to have first coined the phrase in his *The present state of the Church of Ireland* (1787). His diocese had been hard hit by rural disturbances associated with Catholic activists and he was worried, too, that following the example of America moves might be made to disestablish the anglican church in Ireland. There was, he wrote, a choice for Ireland in 'the ascendancy of either the Church of Ireland, or the Church of Rome'. It was possible that 'Protestant ascendancy' would be replaced by a Catholic ascendancy. Woodward's pamphlet was popular, nine editions being rapidly published. It gave the notion of Protestant ascendancy wide currency and by 1792 it had become a rallying-cry for militant Protestants opposed to granting further relief to Catholics who were now seen as a threat to that ascendancy.

It was Dublin corporation which gave the most famous definition of what the term implied. Repudiating what parliament had done, it proclaimed that 'the Protestants of Ireland should not be compelled by any authority whatever to abandon that political situation which their forefathers won with their swords and which is therefore their right'. In a resounding passage the declaration pronounced the rights of every Protestant in the state as derived 'from that constitution which his ancestors acquired, when they overthrew the popish tyrant . . . it is secured by the law, he is possessed of it, and we know of no power under heaven authorised to eliminate our most valuable inheritance'. They swore to defend

> 'a Protestant King of Ireland, a Protestant parliament, a Protestant hierarchy, Protestant electors and government, the benches of justice, the army and the revenue through all their branches and detail Protestant; and this system supported by a connection with the Protestant realm of England'.

Other corporations and grand juries followed the Dublin initiative and the term 'Protestant ascendancy' quickly became the symbol of a more aggressive anti-Catholic attitude among members of the established church.

Reporting on reaction to the introduction of a Catholic relief bill, allowing them to practise as lawyers, in parliament in 1792 the *Morning Post* recounted how some Protestants even proposed the use of 'gunpowder and bayonet' as 'the only specific remedies' against Catholics agitating for reform. On 14 January *Faulkeners Dublin Journal* contained an account of what it called 'Protestants of spirit' who were preparing by 'cleaning their firelocks'. When a Volunteer MP, George Ogle from Wexford, saw further relief for Catholics as a threat to the Protestant interest, then a serious polarization had clearly taken place. 'Nor can I think it within the power of human wisdom to do anything for Roman Catholics without endangering ascendancy in church and state', he declared in parliament.

Even some members of the government feared that further concessions to Catholics might result in civil war. Outraged by the sectarian speeches in defence of the Protestant ascendancy in parliament, some Volunteers refused to participate in the annual parade to the statue of William III, celebrated as the founding father of that ascendancy, demanding that the French revolution should be celebrated instead. Then, in late 1795, the Orange Order was founded, which not only excluded Catholics but had as its avowed purpose the maintenance of the Protestant ascendancy, by whatever means. Sectarian polarization was a fact of life in Ireland henceforth and memories of old persecutions were rekindled. When in December 1796 the Defender James Weldon was executed for high treason, it was reported that he and his fellow-conspirators had planned 'to repeat another Protestant massacre of the last century in this country'. Even earlier, in the aftermath of the relief act, Westmoreland wrote to a friend: 'You cannot have an idea of the alarm in every part of the country, man woman and child dream of 1641'.

To understand how Protestants could have once again come to see the Catholics as a real threat to their dominance in Ireland, it is necessary to discern the conjunction of events which not only seemed to strengthen the

Catholic position, but to endanger the very lives of conservative Protestants themselves. In November 1791 Westmoreland warned the cabinet in London:

> 'In a country where every man holds his estate and political consequence by dispossession of Catholics, allowance must be made for even unreasonable apprehension; it is a common conversation that if the Protestant interest must have a struggle for their property, it is wiser to resist in the first interest'.

No matter what the radicals might say, or the Catholic Committee proclaim, the fear of ancient claims by Catholics to landed property remained a reality to the Protestant landed interest. But there were also more immediate dangers which the emergence of Catholic Ireland into the political arena posed. An alliance with radical dissenters, manifested most obviously on the growth of the United Irishmen movement, was one obvious cause of alarm. So, too, was the possibility of French intervention, once war with revolutionary France became a reality in 1793.

But no less serious was the politicization of Catholics throughout Ireland and the emergence of activists at a popular level. When the Bishop of Cloyne wrote his pamphlet in 1787 his diocese, and indeed much of Munster, was suffering from a Catholic campaign against the excessive tithes levied on their crops. Known as Whiteboys, the agitators were following a tradition of violence which had a long history in rural Ireland. Much of this had its origin in the terrible poverty of most of the Catholics outside the towns. Despite the growth in prosperity which resulted from an expanding trade and increased manufacture of certain goods in the larger towns, only the few had benefited. The bulk of the population never enjoyed any increase in their standard of living and the gradual change in diet from dairy products, which began to be valuable commercially and increasingly exported, to the potato which was surplus to the requirements of trade, placed the rural poor at risk from famine if that crop failed.

This is what happened in 1740–1. Famine was by no means rare in Ireland. Generally harvests were poor and adverse weather conditions could lead to a serious shortage of food. All too easily famine could result. In 1674, for example, many died of hunger. In Armagh Oliver Plunket remarked in June on the 'hundreds and hundreds of starved skeletons, rather than men, walking the roads' and by September over 500 were dead in his diocese. But in 1740–1 famine was on an unprecedented scale. For seven weeks, until the middle of February 1740, there was a continuous frost which maintained the lowest temperatures ever recorded. If the frozen lakes and rivers provided some with the opportunity to indulge in novel sports – a hurling match was played on the Shannon, for example – the weather inflicted a cruel hardship on the inhabitants of town and country alike. It also destroyed the potato crop, so that prices rocketed; around Lough Ennel potatoes which normally sold for 8–10s: a barrel fetched 32s.; in county Roscommon the increase was even sharper, from 3s. in 1738 to 18s. in 1741. In Dublin there were bread riots on three consecutive days from 31 May to 2 June. But worse was to come. Spring came six weeks later than usual, the summer continued cold and by early autumn the frosty weather had returned. A poor harvest was the result and the famine got worse. An epidemic of 'fever' (probably typhus) and 'bloody flux' (dysentery) spread throughout Ireland, affecting mainly the poor, though even the rich did not escape, and reaching its peak later in 1741 when the weather was unusually dry, with a rare hot summer. This was the *bliadhain an áir* (year of slaughter). If a contemporary estimate that 'one third part, by a moderate computation, of the common people' died seems much too high, there is no doubt that in some areas the death rate was very much higher than in other parts. It is generally accepted that between 200,000 and 400,000 is a likely figure over all. What is undoubted is that it was a catastrophe burned into folk consciousness, not to be erased until the 1840s produced another great famine.

After 1741 the population began to grow again. When 'improving' land-lords began to enclose what had traditionally been common land, it produced a furious reaction from people who had for generations exploited those lands to help feed themselves. An expanding population had also increased competition for land, so that rents became prohibitive and eviction a threat. The payment of tithes to the established church was also resented, at a time when many lived barely above starvation level. When the Speaker of the House of Commons in Dublin complained in 1747 that 'the bulk of the people in Ireland live so miserably that no two million of people besides of any country in Europe consume so little of the commodities which they raise themselves', he spoke no more than the truth.

The enclosure of commons, but more especially the heavy tithes exacted on potato crops in Munster, led to a great outburst of agrarian protest which began with the Whiteboy movement in county Tipperary in 1761. The movement spread rapidly to counties Kilkenny, Cork and Waterford before being finally suppressed in 1765. While few murders were committed by the subversives, many were assaulted, some even tortured, and much property was destroyed. On 1 November the Catholic Bishop of Ossory issued instructions condemning Whiteboy activity, to be read aloud at mass on three successive Sundays and explained in Irish. If any had grievances, the bishop said, then recourse to the law was the answer: 'They ought to be amenable to the laws of the nation, and not provoke the government, which is mild beyond expression'. If the government in fact was 'mild' it was because it was faced with a conspiracy of silence, with the people in support of the activists, which made it virtually impossible to bring offenders to justice.

There were many other secret organizations engaged in rural protests, grouped on a regional basis and using distinctive descriptive names, such as Hearts of Oak, Oakboys, Hearts of Steel and Steelboys in Ulster. But the Whiteboys made such an impression that down to the end of the next century the term 'Whiteboyism' was commonly used to describe all kinds of agrarian protest in Ireland. There were new outbursts of disturbance in the 1780s, starting with the Rightboys in county Cork in 1785, quickly spreading through Munster and into counties Leix, Offaly and Kilkenny. Once again the exaction of tithes was the primary target. But they were no radicals, seeking a total abolition. What they sought was reform, particularly of the level of exaction. Neither were they sectarian, they objected just as vehemently to the level of dues which they had to pay to the Catholic clergy. In 1786 they established what they considered to be equitable rates:

> 'potatoes, 4s. per acre; wheat and barley, 1s.6d. per acre; oats and meadows, 1s. per acre – Roman Catholic clergy to receive for marriages 5s., for baptism 1s.6d., for anointing and visitation of the sick 1s., for mass 1s., for confession 6d. . . . .'.

It should be noted that in the diocese of Ossory, where disturbance was widespread, Bishop Troy in September of the same year regulated 'the collection of dues' which more than matched the rates proposed by the Rightboys. For marriages, for example, the dues varied from 11s. 4½d. 'from the richest person' to 'nothing . . . from the real poor'. For 'unctions for the wealthy' the rates were 1s. 1d.; 'from the poor, nothing'. Again, for baptism, 'from the real poor what they can afford or nothing'. Through violence and intimidation the Rightboys tried to enforce their scale of fees. Inevitably the more extreme among the Protestants used this as evidence of an attack on 'the Protestant establishment in church and consequently in state', as one of them put it in 1786. He was George Ogle and in the same speech he warned that 'the landed property of the kingdom' as well as 'the Protestant ascendancy' were endangered by such agrarian disturbances and he demanded protection from the government.

In response 2,000 troops were sent to Munster, but with little effect. This caused alarm, so that some feared another 1641 and others the possibility of what one official in Dublin castle called 'real rebellion'. A spate of pamphlets urged strong action, denouncing the disturbances as attempts to destroy the rights to which Protestants were entitled. Patrick Duigenan, a convert from Catholicism, was vitriolic. Writing as 'Theophilus', he went so far as to say that if what he conceived as this Catholic attack on Protestants was not stemmed, then not only would all the penal laws be repealed and the Williamite settlement undone, but a Catholic monarch would succeed and initiate a 'civil war' with Britain, which might result in 'the destruction of Great Britain, the monarchy, Protestantism and the liberties of Europe'.

If this hysterical outburst was not really typical of the reaction to the agrarian outrages, the paper war and the public debate which ensued helped to establish more firmly the notion of a Protestant ascendancy under threat. Associated with that went the conviction that the penal laws were a necessary support of that ascendancy. Arthur Browne summed it up in a pamphlet in which he wrote that the penal laws were necessary for the Protestants in order 'to preserve their estates . . . their religion and . . . the Protestant ascendancy'. Later, in 1793, Westmoreland wrote to the home secretary in England to explain the problem of getting parliament to agree to further Catholic relief legislation and said that it was all the more difficult because 'at this moment a most daring insurrection prevails among the lower Catholics in neighbouring counties for the purpose of disarming the Protestants which is generally believed to be part of the intimidating system of their committee'.

Westmoreland was in fact referring to Defender raids for arms. The Defenders had originated in troubles which broke out in Armagh in the 1780s. County Armagh was roughly divided between anglicans in the north, Presbyterians in the middle, and Catholics in the south. If sectarian violence ever took root, this was an explosive mix and was liable to lead to widespread trouble. With a virtual population explosion in the second half of the century, competition for land became acute, worsened by the new freedoms which relief acts gave Catholics in the scramble for leases. The growth of the linen industry was another source of antagonism which bred animosities. When Catholics, despite the prohibitions of penal laws, began openly to carry arms, sometimes with the connivance of Volunteers or of local landlords like Lord Gosford, who used armed Catholics to guard his orchards, local Protestants were outraged. They regarded the bearing of arms as a prized prerogative of Protestants, so they retaliated against this challenge to their ascendancy. Trouble erupted and Catholics had to defend themselves. Lord Gosford in February 1788 told how

'acts of violence are perpetrated by a low sort of fellows, who call themselves Protestant dissenters and who with guns and bayonets and other weapons break open the houses of Roman Catholics and as I am informed treat many of them with cruelty, and take from them such eatables and drink as they find and this under the pretence of searching for arms'.

The Defenders not only protected Catholics, but met violence with violence. Reports were received in Dublin of widespread disturbance and acts of terrorism, but there was much exaggeration. A Presbyterian clergyman of Armagh, William Campbell, wrote to the Earl of Charlemont that 'peace and tranquillity' in fact reigned in places where it had been reported that 'violent outrages were continuing'. He said that in some 'remote parts of the county, or among the mountains' there may have been trouble, though he had heard of none. 'But this I know, that every drunken quarrel, or rescue of cattle, or unfortunate accident that happened, is immediately ascribed to these parties, though in no sort connected with them'. On the other hand another letter to Charlemont a year later, from local magistrate, John Moore, describes a state of 'absolute rebellion and confusion', with the Defenders out every night, lying in wait 'behind ditches, to murder and destroy every Protestant that appears' and recounting his own experience of this. He described how 'thousands of the popish party' had assembled from as far away as Drogheda 'and by what I can find their whole intent is not to leave a Protestant alive'. He claimed that there was no ammunition left in the county because the Catholics had bought it up and made an appeal for arms and ammunition 'for heaven's sake'.

The reported fear of a Protestant massacre, reminiscent of 1641, was a genuine reflection of an increasingly widespread belief. It was used to justify sectarian violence against Catholics. In Armagh the Protestant Peep-o'-Day-Boys, as they called themselves, continued to attack Catholic homes and the Defenders became involved in this sectarian violence. An incident in Forkhill in south Armagh became a byword for their cruelty. Some years previously a landowner had left 3,000 acres in the area to be 'colonized by Protestants', which aroused fierce resentment among Catholics. The Reverend Edward Hudson, one of the trustees appointed to administer the will, told the Earl of Charlemont in December 1789 of the local Catholic reaction to the proposed redistribution of land: 'The idea of its being let therefore set them mad'. Earlier in the same letter he had described how he had tried to introduce 'some decent manufacturing and I hope to make our savages happy against their wills by establishing trade and industry amongst them'. The use of the term 'savage' is significant, as is the notion that industrialization and civilization went hand-in-hand. Hudson explained further: even though they were 'so little removed from the least part of the kingdom', he told Charlemont,

> 'your lordship will hardly believe how little appearances of civilisation there are here . . . many traces of savage life still remain among us: the same laziness and improvidence, the same unrelenting ferocity in their combats, the same love of intoxication, the same hereditary enmities handed down from generation to generation'.

Loss of land, then, was bound to produce a savage reaction.

But it was the appointment in 1791 of a Protestant schoolmaster, Andrew Barclay, which was the catalyst, because the catechism would no longer be taught to the local Catholic children in their own language, Irish. A group of 60 Defenders attacked his house one night, tore out his tongue and cut off his fingers. They also mutilated his wife and her 14-year-old brother and then openly paraded through the district with lighted torches. The incident aroused Protestant anger and even pro-Catholic reformers protested. William Drennan denounced the Catholics as 'savages' and said that what had happened at Forkhill would 'put off the day of general freedom'.

But it was after 1791 that the violence escalated and the Defender organization began to spread. In another violent incident near Drumsna in county Leitrim in April 1795, revenue officers were pursued by local Defenders, took refuge in a building which was then set on fire and 11 officers were hacked to death as they fled the flames. Defenderism and violence became almost synonymous. But it was often a response to violence used against them, not least the horror tactics which the government pursued in an attempt to frighten would-be agitators. The public execution of a noted Defender, the schoolmaster Laurence O'Connor, at Naas in 1795 is a good example. Found guilty of administering 'an oath of love, liberty and loyalty', his execution was designed to frighten off would-be subversives. He was not only hanged, but then disembowelled, quartered, and his head was displayed on a pike over Naas jail. The terror worked for, as an observer recounted, 'the Roman Catholic clergy refused to attend him at the time of his execution, or to administer the sacraments to him'.

By the time O'Connor was executed Defenderism had spread to at least 13 of the other counties. The 1793 militia act had produced a furious reaction in many counties with widespread rioting: at least 230 were killed, more than five times the number killed during the disturbances of the previous 30 years. There was a bloody repression and the level of violence escalated. Then came a famous incident in county Armagh which was to have a profound effect on subsequent history. In September 1795 a 'battle' took place at the Diamond in county Armagh, between Peep-o'-Day-Boys and other Protestant groups and Catholic Defenders. The Defenders were completely routed. At the end of celebrations, the victorious Protestants met and formed themselves into the Orange Society, later the Orange Order, to maintain Protestant ascendancy over Catholics. In the original oath this was made clear: 'I . . . do solemnly swear that I will, to the utmost of my power, support and defend the king and his heirs as long as he or they support the Protestant ascendancy'.

The new Orange Order spread rapidly and by the end of the century there were over 170,000 members. More immediately a pogrom against Catholics in Ulster saw many driven from their homes in counties Armagh, Down, Fermanagh and Tyrone, estimated by some to have reached as many as 10,000. About 4,000 of those fled to Connacht and some even to as far away as Kerry. Wherever they went the refugees spread the story of Orange terror, backed by the government, and thus helped to generate sectarian as well as anti-government feelings. As Camden, the lord lieutenant, put it in a letter of 6 August 1796, 'they related their sufferings and I fear excited a spirit of revenge among their Catholic brethren'. Worse, it led to Defenders forming alliances with United Irishmen. In another letter Camden explained how Defenders swore not only to be true to each other 'but to unite and correspond with the society of United Irishmen'.

By 1795, then, the Defenders had become not only a well-organized subversive movement, anti-English and anti-settler, but anti-Protestant as well. In the long term they provided a link between the conservative underground movements of earlier decades and the revolutionary, subversive movements of the nineteenth century. More immediately, they were an important agent in helping to introduce the people to politics, supporting Thomas Russell's denial of 'the infamous intolerable proposition . . . that the mass of the people have no right to meddle in politics' and his assertion that it was 'not only the right, but the essential duty of every man to interest himself in the conduct of government'. They were crucial in helping to provide the organization which was exploited by the United Irishmen in reaching the people. They were also republican, looked to France for military aid, and in this way they helped to change the United Irishmen from a reform club, limited to parts of Ulster and Dublin, into a nation-wide revolutionary movement, with international connections. The emergence of Catholic Ireland as a political, even a revolutionary force, at a popular level was to have a decisive impact on the future. A polarization had taken place which was to last for generations.

12 Revolution and emancipation

In 1795 it was reported that the Defenders swore to 'quell all nations, dethrone all kings, and plant the true religion that was lost since the reformation'. Because their aim was a Catholic restoration, a direct, open Defender alliance with the avowedly non-sectarian United Irishmen was not possible. It was out of the liberal Presbyterian ethos that the first society of United Irishmen was founded in October 1791 in Belfast, established as 'a union of Irishmen of every religious persuasion in order to obtain a complete reform of the legislature, founded on the principles of civil, political, and religious liberty'. At a time when the Volunteers in Armagh had become sectarian, in response to Catholic militancy, middle-class Protestants, mostly Presbyterians, agreed at a meeting in Belfast in January 1792 to send a petition to parliament:

> 'We therefore pray, that the legislature may be pleased to repeal all penal and restrictive statutes at present in existence against the Roman Catholics of Ireland; and that they thus may be restored to the rank and consequence of citizens'.

From the beginning, then, the Belfast United Irishmen highlighted Catholic emancipation as one of their aims. But they also wished for radical political reform. William Drennan, the Belfast born Presbyterian who was one of the founders of the Dublin Society of United Irishmen and later its secretary and president, had written in 1785 that he saw three choices for Ireland: the 'commercial treaty' proposed by Pitt; a union; or 'disunion':

> 'And I hope to God that a short time will show the expediency, necessity and sublimity of the last choice, without which Ireland will never become a great or a happy people. And why should we not be as America, I have never seen any substantial reason'.

So, for some at least among the United Irishmen political separatism – 'disunion' – was an aspiration.

They did not advocate the use of military force to achieve that end. William

Orr, a Protestant farmer from county Antrim, the first United Irishman to be executed for treason under the insurrection act in October 1797, issued what he called a 'dying declaration' from Carrickfergus gaol in which he protested his innocence:

> 'My comfortable lot and industrious course of life, best refute the charge of being an adventurer for plunder: but if to have loved my country, to have known its wrongs, to have felt the injuries of the persecuted Catholic, and to have united with them and all other religious persons in the most orderly and least sanguinary means of procuring redress – if these be felonies, I am a felon, but not otherwise'.

Yet a year later, in 1798, the United Irishmen were in open rebellion and attempting to establish a republic in Ireland. 'Remember Orr' was used as a battle-cry by many of them and his name had inspired others far away from Ulster into joining the rebels. Gold rings with the motto 'Remember Orr' inscribed on them were in wide circulation and popular songs, above all Drennan's *The Wake of William Orr*, popularized his name:

> Hapless nation, rent and torn,
> Thou were early taught to mourn;
> Warfare of six hundred years!
> Epochs marked with blood and tears!

On 20 January 1798 a traveller on the road from Roscrea to Limerick reported that there was 'not a village on the road in which the name William Orr and the cause for which he died is not as well known as in the town of Carrickfergus'.

How did the United Irishmen become a republican and revolutionary organization which plotted a rebellion to secure independence for Ireland? To some extent they were revolutionary from the beginning. Wolfe Tone, who was the real inspiration behind the Belfast society, wrote in his 1791 *Argument* that 'a new age had dawned. These were the days of illumination at the close of the eighteenth century'. The impact of the European enlightenment would bring necessary change in Ireland. The revolution in France had shown to all that the most Catholic country in Europe could overthrow the burden of the past. It was therefore not only possible, but essential, that Ireland's Catholics too should be fully admitted to the body politic and as members of a new, representative Irish parliament help to change Ireland and end despotism. As was reported to Dublin castle, the United Irishmen believed that 'with a parliament thus reformed, everything is possible'. The Catholic relief acts of the early 1790s seemed to show that reform at long last was under way, even if the Protestant ascendancy as represented in parliament was unwilling to make too many concessions. Prominent members of the Catholic Committee, such as John Keogh, were also active in the Dublin society of United Irishmen. When Tone was appointed as assistant secretary of the Catholic Committee in July

1792, the close relationship between the two organizations began to worry the Government. The success of the Catholic convention in December 1792 caused further worry. When war with France broke out in February 1793 it alienated many in the society still further from the Government.

Meanwhile the United Irishmen had deliberately been attempting to educate the people into 'citizenship' and to propagate the idea of accountable government. Through satires like *Billy Bluff and Squire Firebrand*, written by the radical Presbyterian minister the Reverend James Porter and first published in the United Irishman newspaper the *Northern Star*, the corrupt gentry ascendancy and the tradition of rights of property were savagely attacked. This work enjoyed such popularity that it remained in print to the end of the next century and when Porter was later hanged as a United Irishman it was commonly believed that it was really because he was the author of the famous satire. Squire Firebrand is aggrieved because of the great change that has taken place in Ireland: 'O what a happy country we had before men turned their thoughts to thinking', he laments. But now

'your Catholic college – your Catholic schools – your Catholic emancipation – your Sunday schools – your charter schools – your book societies – your pamphlets, and your books, and your one h-ll or another are all turning people's heads, and setting them a thinking about this, that and t'other'.

The United Irishmen in Dublin and Belfast were able to avail of a good network of printing and publishing houses. In Dublin more than 50 printers were available, many others were at work in the provinces, especially in Ulster, and an astonishing forty newspapers were published. In particular, the Belfast society of United Irishmen had at its disposal the *Northern Star*, one of the great newspapers until it was suppressed in 1797. Its circulation of 5,000 was larger than that enjoyed by the *Times* of London. Its avowed aim, it said, was 'to cultivate a knowledge of the rights of man, to diffuse political information, and to promote uncertainty and concord amongst Irishmen'. •

The United Irishmen circulated a veritable flood of literature, simply written so that 'the common man' could readily understand, promising that reform, Catholic emancipation, and not least the achievements of the revolutionaries in France would soon bring profit and gain to all. The government was informed in 1796 that these pieces of propaganda were 'disseminated so industriously so as to find their way to every village, fair and market' and through them the United Irishmen 'had been incessantly inculcating on the multitude that they were the most wretchedly abused, oppressed people under the canopy of heaven, that their misery arose solely from a political cause, the radically bad government under which they lived'. Propaganda was thus easily produced and widely distributed through a well-established network, even to the most isolated areas. Ideas disseminated in this way helped the societies in 'making every man a politician' as Thomas Addis Emmet expressed it. The people became educated as to their rights.

But this had its dangers for the more conservative elements and helped to give the more radical the initiative. Men like Thomas Russell, the great friend of Tone, Samuel Neilson or Henry Joy McCracken began to move towards a closer relationship with the Defenders and others. Issues such as tithes, rents, taxes, living conditions, even class structure, and above all poverty, were increasingly politicized in the propaganda and by 1795 something like a merger with the Defenders was on the cards. By then, too, United Irishmen had begun to organize themselves along military lines, using not only existing Defender lodges, but infiltrating Masonic lodges as well. Henry Joy McCracken, for example, became a Mason in 1795. Republican ideals were increasingly dominant and it was natural for leaders to look to France not only for inspiration but also for military help. Early in 1794 the French Government, now at war with England, sent an agent to make contact with subversives in Ireland, he was an anglican clergyman, William Jackson. Although born in Ireland. He was English educated, a radical who had moved to Paris and became part of a group of English-speaking Francophiles, which included Thomas Paine and, for a time, Lord Edward Fitzgerald. Although Pitt in England was made aware of this mission, he allowed it to go ahead because it included a friend of Jackson's, John Cokayne, who unknown to him was in English pay and kept Pitt informed of all that was going on in Ireland. A rather confused plan, in which Tone was implicated, was devised to present the French with evidence of support in Ireland if ever they invaded. With the plot revealed, arrests were made. But as Westmoreland admitted, not 'a tittle of evidence' could be brought against Tone on a charge of treason and he was still at large when Jackson was brought to trial in April 1795. Found guilty of treason, Jackson spectacularly committed suicide with poison while in the dock awaiting sentence. Tone, who was an embarrassment to the government, was allowed to leave Ireland and he sailed for America in June.

By now the apparent threat to the Protestant ascendancy was the dominant concern of most MPs and fears of a massacre of Protestants were deliberately and widely propagated, particularly in the south. Already, in May 1794, the Dublin Society of United Irishmen had been suppressed and driven underground. From then on the United Irishmen moved ever closer to an alliance with France, aimed at getting military help to establish an Irish republic. Tone went from America to France in 1796 and became active in persuading the government to invade Ireland, the traditional 'backdoor to England'. A popular ballad celebrated that 'the French are on the sea' and that after they landed:

Yes, Ireland shall be free,
From the centre to the sea,
Then hurra! for Liberty,
Says the Shan Van Vocht.

The failure of the Fitzwilliam initiative in the early months of 1795 to win Catholic emancipation had a major impact in Ireland. Not only did it confirm the supporters of Protestant ascendancy in power, it convinced many reformers, even among conservatives, that there was no hope in looking for redress of grievances through constitutional channels. It galvanized many Catholics into action and the ranks not only of the Defenders but also the United Irishmen were swollen by new members. The endowment of the Royal College of St Patrick at Maynooth in 1795, far from allaying the Catholic fear that reform would never come, confirmed the sectarian polarization that was taking place at the top. The college was established to allow seminarians to be trained at home and not in France, as had been the norm, where the government rightly feared that they would be influenced by revolutionary ideas. It was never intended as an anticipation of full Catholic emancipation. Maynooth was to have a profound influence on the way the Catholic church developed in Ireland, and indeed throughout the English-speaking world. But in 1795 it was seen as yet another sign that emancipation of Catholics was some way off in the future.

In February 1796 the parliament passed an insurrection act, making the administration of an unlawful oath a capital offence. Worse, the government was given the power to 'proclaim' a district in which a curfew could be imposed and gave the magistrates extensive powers to conduct a search for arms and to send suspected persons, without benefit of trial, to serve in the fleet. The *habeas corpus* act was suspended and a largely Protestant force of yeomen established. The impact of these changes was soon felt in the localities, when the rule of law was virtually suspended at times.

That the government had cause for alarm was made abundantly clear in December when a French fleet set sail for Ireland from Brest. Aboard were 15,000 men, commanded by Hoche, one of the best of the French generals. Fortunately for the British government the fleet was scattered by bad weather. One part, with Hoche, was driven out into the Atlantic and never even saw Ireland. Only about 6,000 men were aboard the ships that finally managed to reach Bantry Bay. Even so, if they had been able to get ashore they would have posed a real problem for the Dublin government. Tone was aboard and he recorded his frustration that continuous bad weather prevented the troops from landing: 'We have now been six days in Bantry Bay within 500 yards of the shore without being able to effect a landing; we have been dispersed four times in four days'. The best they could hope for was to get safely back to France, eventually managing to do so, and although most of the ships had been damaged, none had been lost. For the Westminster government the worst aspect of the expedition was not just the threat posed, but the failure of the vaunted British navy to prevent the troops from reaching Ireland and getting back safely to France. It was time to make sure that if ever another French army managed to reach Ireland it would find little or no support once it got ashore.

In the first place this meant disarming the United Irishmen, now organized as a widespread, oath-bound, secret society. In Ulster General Lake set to work in March 1797 to disarm the province. He gave his army complete freedom in the search for weapons and the result was flogging, torture, shootings and burned houses. Thousands were deported to the navy and although Lake succeeded in collecting 5,400 guns and many bayonets and other arms, the terror was widely condemned, even at Westminster. Since many of the Defender lodges were now integrated into the movement, numbers grew alarmingly. The informer Boyle reported to Dublin in May 1797 that there were now 117,917 United Irishmen in Ulster, well over 99,000 of these in Antrim, Down and Derry. The search for guns continued and with it the brutality and terror that were now part of a deliberate government programme. At the end of March 1797 General Knox had written: 'I look upon Ulster to be a La Vendée and that it will not be brought into subjection but by the same means adopted by the republicans in power – namely spreading devastation through the most disaffected parts'. What he said of Ulster could equally well apply to other parts of Ireland and the comparison with peasant risings in rural France was telling. General Lake was even more blunt: 'Nothing but terror will keep them in order' and on 24 May 1798, after rebellion had broken out, he ordered General Loftus that if he had occasion to attack 'the villains, take no prisoners'.

Attempts by moderates like Grattan in the Irish parliament or Fox in England to halt the terror and repeal the coercive legislation came to nothing. When Grattan's proposal was finally defeated on 15 May 1797 by 143 votes to 19 he and others left in despair, as did some MPs in England, and the terror continued. News from Europe in the summer increased the tension. A Dutch fleet carrying 15,000 Dutch and 6,000 French troops was being prepared for an invasion of Ireland. It was to be joined by a French fleet from Brest, carrying a further 6–8,000 under General Hoche. Mutinies in the British fleets made the situation even more dangerous. But these subsided in time and the unexpected death of Hoche in September threw the invasion plans into disarray. The defeat of the Dutch fleet at the battle of Camperdown on 11 October made a successful invasion of Ireland impossible. By the time action was taken the following year, it was too little and much too late. On 6 August Humbert set sail with only 1,019 man and the fleet which sailed from Brest on 6 September had less than 3,000, not all troops. Humbert succeeded in landing at Killala Bay and enjoyed a remarkable but brief success. After what passed into folklore as 'the races of Castlebar', when the English army fled in disarray, a local Catholic, John Moore, was appointed first president of the 'provisional government of Connacht'. But lacking further armed support, Humbert was finally forced into surrender in September. The second expedition was defeated in Lough Swilly before a single man could get ashore. It hardly mattered since by then the rebellion was crushed and the leaders dead or in prison.

Among those taken prisoner in Lough Swilly was Wolfe Tone. His captors refused to recognize his rank in the French army and treat him as a prisoner-of-war. He was separated from the other officers and taken away as a common criminal in chains. That he had now lost his right to life Tone accepted; but he believed and asserted his right to be treated as a captured army officer at war. Instead, he was regarded as a traitor and a rebel. Brought in chains to Dublin, he was tried by a military court in the Royal Barracks on 10 November. Dressed in his French military uniform, he admitted the charge against him. 'The great object of my life has been the independence of my country' he said when he addressed the court, and ended: 'I have failed in the attempt; my life is in consequence forfeited and I submit; the Court will do their duty and I shall endeavour to do mine'. He asked to be executed by firing squad, the death due to a soldier of France. But on the evening of 11 November he learned that he was to be publicly hanged the following day. During the night he cut his throat and died over a week later on the morning of 19 November. His family received the body for burial, but only 'on the express condition', as Castlereagh the chief secretary put it, 'that no assemblage of people shall be permitted and that he be interred in the most private manner'. On 21 November Tone was buried in Bodenstown in the family plot.

To this day that grave is still the symbol of physical force republicanism in Ireland. But Tone's famous declaration of 1796 that his object was 'to break the connection with England' and that his means were 'to unite the whole people of Ireland, to abolish the memory of all past dissensions, and to substitute the common name of Irishman, in the place of the denominations of Protestant, Catholic and Dissenter' remained unrealized and, as events were to prove, unattainable.

The United Irishmen had been strengthened by the severe repressive measures imposed by the government and from a largely middle class society had become a more popularly based movement, with large numbers in both towns and country joining. The leaders of the Dublin society had always been aware of what political reform would necessarily mean. In 1793 they had warned that if they gave what they called 'political value and station to the majority of the people', it meant extending to them the franchise, and that would mean 'a more equal distribution of the benefits and blessings of life through the lowest classes of the community, the stamina of society'. Ireland seemed ready for radical politicization. Sales of Tom Paine's *The Rights of Man* reached 40,000 in Ireland at a time when sales in Scotland and England combined barely came to 17,000. In 1791 alone 13 editions were published, and four newspapers printed most of the book in long extracts in April and May. Not only did the United Irishmen distribute large numbers of the book free, they even managed to produce an Irish translation. Small wonder that Paine was enormously popular in Ireland or that he was elected an honorary member of the Dublin society of United Irishmen.

Dublin city was now second only to London and by 1798 its population had reached about 180,000. It was natural that it should assume direction of events that would ultimately lead to separation from England. The spread of the Defenders in Dublin was such that by 1795 they were 4,000 strong. When absorbed, like the Masons, by the United Irishmen they helped to build up a strong armed force within the city. By May 1798 the official return for the city listed 9,889 armed men. Some of the members lived in Church Street where they worked in the foundry which, during 1797, was largely operating primarily as a secret munitions factory. They manufactured pike-heads, heavy shot, and what were called 'cats', metal spikes to be used as traps against cavalry in street-fighting. A military committee was appointed in early 1798 to plan the rebellion and Lord Edward Fitzgerald, a trained soldier – he had joined the army during the American war – was appointed commander-in-chief. He drew up a plan of action, stressing the importance of guerrilla warfare and, more interestingly, of street fighting in the cities. It was agreed that the seizure of Dublin castle would begin the rebellion in Dublin and that if military camps were similarly attacked in the country many of the Catholic militia would join the rebels. It never happened.

The government was kept well informed of what was happening, where meetings were held (mostly in public houses in Dublin), and what was planned. From March onwards arrests were regularly made. One United Irishman, William Sampson, wrote: 'I remained in Dublin until the 16th of April, when the terror became so atrocious that humanity could no longer bear it . . . men were taken at random without process or accusation'. The leadership was removed. On 12 March as a result of an informer's report, a detachment of soldiers surrounded the house of Oliver Bond and his warehouse in Bridge Street where a meeting of delegates of the 'Leinster Directory' of the United Irishmen was in progress. Delegates from Meath, Dublin, Kildare, Carlow and Queen's county were taken, including Bond himself. On the same day another raid captured most of the other leaders, Lord Edward Fitzgerald escaped and went into hiding, but was later captured with the remaining leaders. In the struggle he was fatally wounded. According to papers found on him a total of 279,896 had taken the oath as United Irishmen before 1798, an extraordinary achievement for the late eighteenth century. Dublin was placed under martial law on 20 May and when the rebellion was due to begin on the night of 23 May, the city was saturated with troops. A reign of terror ensued, the streets were cleared, a house-by-house search for weapons produced 20,000 pikes. There was no insurrection in Dublin.

Without Dublin and the central direction the captured leaders would have provided, the rebellion was spasmodic and uncoordinated. It was not without some successes, particularly in the south-east where the military organization had been thorough. In county Wexford, for example, the people had long since been politicized. In 1792 no less that 20,000 signed a petition on Catholic loyalty and three years later 22,252 signed an address, circulated by William Hay, to Fitzwilliam. So it was easy enough to organize regiments and battalions of United Irishmen.

By 1798 at least six colonels presided over nearly 8,000 men, with perhaps as many as 60 captains, ready to answer a call-to-arms. Even some of the Catholic clergy were active militarily. Of 85 priests in the county, as many as 10 joined the rebellion. Good organization meant a speedy mobilization of men so that, by the end of May, most of the county was in rebel hands with a committee, under the presidency of Bagenal Harvey, 'to manage the affairs of the people of the county of Wexford'. They failed to extend the area under their control, however, despite some victories in the field and their main force was smashed at Vinegar Hill by General Lake on 21 June. Although some took refuge in the Wicklow mountains and in some other areas where they managed to hold out for a time, the rebellion was effectively over before the end of July.

Closer to Dublin the rebels enjoyed some success in counties Dublin, Kildare and Carlow, but in the end the superior government forces regained control. The same thing happened in some other areas, most notably in Antrim and north Down. More than anything else it was the use of artillery, the 'whiff of grapeshot', which checked the insurgents at a number of decisive points. Early in 1797 the government imported artillery in anticipation of a rebellion and 'battalion guns' were given to a number of regiments. In addition a body of troops from the recently formed horse artillery was shipped to Ireland. Losses on both sides were heavy. A total of 512 from 37 militia regiments were killed, in addition to an unknown number in regular units.

On the other side the losses were much more horrendous. The best contemporary estimate put the figure at 30,000, the overwhelming proportion of whom were non-combatants. General Lake's comment on the determination of his troops 'to destroy everyone they think is a rebel' as being 'beyond description' seems, if anything, an understatement. Most were killed in one month. In Quaker Ballitore in county Kildare, Mary Leadbeater described the horror: cannon were brought into the village, 'the trumpet was sounded, and the inhabitants were delivered up for two hours to the unbridled license of the furious soldiery'. She pictured two smiths, Owen Finn and his brother, 'hand-cuffed and weeping', walking behind the car which carried all their equipment. Several families were whipped publicly 'and the torture was excessive. The village once so peaceful exhibited a scene of tumult and dismay, the air rang with the shrieks of the sufferers and the lamentations of those who beheld them suffer'. At least 69 Catholic churches, mainly in south Leinster, were damaged or destroyed. Before the end of 1799 at least a further 1,500 men were condemned by the courts, including the military tribunals. By comparison with the Vendée in France, where the Catholics rose in revolt against the republic, the numbers killed and tortured in Ireland may seem small. In 1794 the republicans, so much admired by Irish radicals, killed some 300,000 in that rebellion. At the village of Les Lucs, for example, 564 villagers who had taken refuge in the church were slaughtered. But such a comparison is not sustainable, given the huge difference in populations, and in Ireland the impact of the slaughter was just as traumatic.

But it was not all onesided, as Tone later admitted in his speech from the dock when he said that 'very great atrocities have been committed on both sides'. Later claims for damage to property came to well over one million pounds. The rebels, too, committed atrocities which further enraged the soldiers opposing them. In Ballitore, for example, after 300 United Irishmen, armed with pikes, knives and pitchforks took over the village, Mary Leadbeater describes how the son of a local squire 'was brought in a prisoner, and despite the efforts of Priest Cullen was piked and shot'. Houses were set on fire by the rebels and locals were rounded up as prisoners, to be used in front of the rebels as protection against the shot of the army. An American Quaker who visited Enniscorthy in June 1798 was told by the Quakers there that during the four-week siege they suffered much, not least from 'the frequent solicitation to change their religion and embrace the tenets of the Romish Church' and 'being told "there must be but one religion in Ireland"'. Two men who refused to become Catholics had been murdered by the rebels. But the most famous atrocity of all occurred at Scullabogue when the rebels burned perhaps as many as 200 Protestants (and a few Catholics) held prisoner in a barn. In Wexford town 70 prisoners were stripped naked, tied to the bridge, piked, and then thrown into the river. No wonder memories of 1641 were revived and fierce anti-Catholic hatreds were expressed. The rebellion was easily construed as what the Speaker of the commons called 'a popish conspiracy' designed to end the Protestant ascendancy.

While there is undoubtedly some truth in the assertions that many of the atrocities were sectarian, the government refused to accept that the rebellion itself was purely sectarian in nature or purpose. With the rebellion finally crushed, it tried to withdraw from the use of terror and began to woo the Catholics. But it was too late to convince Catholics that they were not the victims of Protestant, and in particular Orange Order, savagery and this was the memory of 1798 which survived among the Catholic population.

In England Pitt was now convinced that only a union of the two kingdoms would guarantee the security of Britain. Those Protestants who opposed the notion in Ireland must be persuaded or, if necessary, bought off and commercial interests must be convinced that a union would be beneficial. In a sense what might be called a commercial union already existed for, by 1800, over 85 per cent of all exports from Ireland went to Britain and nearly 80 per cent of all imports came from Britain. Economic theory favoured a union. In 1785 Adam Smith, in his *An enquiry into the nature and causes of the wealth of nations*, presented powerful arguments in favour of union and that the only rational alternative was what he called 'total separation'.

But it was the 1798 rebellion which clearly demonstrated that the dominant Protestant ascendancy in Ireland, partly contaminated by the growth of radicalism, was unable to control the island and make secure the backdoor to England. When Cornwallis, a soldier of repute as well as a politician, was appointed to the new combined office of lord lieutenant and commander-in-chief at the outbreak of rebellion, Pitt was quite explicit in ordering that he 'must ultimately and as soon as possible have in view some permanent settlement which may provide for the internal peace of the country and secure its connection with Great Britain . . . by an Union'.

The only secure way to make Ireland safe in the face of potential French aggression was to unite the two kingdoms and this the English government proceeded to do. Protestant opposition in Ireland to such a union, largely from elements which in the past had gained political influence and material gain from an independent parliament, encouraged Catholics to accept union as their best hope of gaining full emancipation, a hope which the government positively encouraged. Even Presbyterians, if not actively welcoming union, at least remained neutral.

The attitude of the Catholics, and particularly of the bishops, was crucial. During the recent rebellion the rebels had been unambiguously condemned by the bishops. Even before the outbreak both the United Irishmen and the Defenders had been denounced by the hierarchy. Archbishop Troy of Dublin excommunicated all Catholics who joined the rebels and while some priests had defied the ban, less than 60 of approximately 1,800, or just over three per cent, gave open support. Some paid a heavy price. On Christmas Day 1797 a priest was murdered in Kildare because, the government was informed, he had 'exhorted his congregation to abstain from disloyalty'.

Over the years the laws against Catholics had been largely ignored and between 1778 and 1783 there had been substantial legislation in the Irish parliament which abolished most of the penal laws. Tolerance had been growing, perhaps never better exemplified than on a public occasion on 5 May 1789. In thanksgiving for the recovery of George III from the illness which had precipitated the regency crisis, a solemn high mass, followed by a *Te Deum*, was celebrated in the Catholic church in Francis Street in Dublin. Apart from Catholic notables who attended, also present were the duke of Leinster and nine other peers; six MPs, including Thomas Conolly and Henry Grattan; the lord mayor and sheriffs of Dublin; and many more.

But at the end of the century, when the perceived threat to the Protestant ascendancy by Catholics was openly denounced in the Dublin parliament, it became clear that an Irish parliament would never tolerate full emancipation for Catholics. The suppression of the rebellion further alienated Catholics from a kingdom in which they thought a Protestant ascendancy had been confirmed as permanent. When Protestants who opposed union began to call themselves 'loyalists' it alienated Catholics still further. What Francis Moylan, the Catholic Bishop of Cork, wrote about the union to the home secretary, Thomas Pelham, on 9 March 1799 represented the views of most Catholics: 'God grant that it may soon take place! The tranquillity and future welfare of this poor distracted country rest in a great degree thereon. The earlier it is accomplished the better. May God give a blessing to it!'

The promise of full emancipation and of state salaries for Catholic clergy was, of course, an important inducement. More than anything else, the prospect of emancipation procured Catholic support for the government. The new parliament of the united kingdom would do what no Protestant

Irish parliament was prepared to do and enact legislation granting full emancipation. This is what Pitt preferred to do and most Catholics agreed with him. As early as December 1798, the lord lieutenant, Cornwallis, reported that the Catholic Lord Fingall preferred that there should be no debates in the Dublin parliament over the Catholic question – it 'should rest till it can be submitted in quieter times to the unprejudiced decision of the united parliament'.

By now Catholics outnumbered Protestants in Ireland by five to one. For supporters of the Protestant ascendancy this made defence of that ascendancy increasingly difficult. In a new united kingdom, however, the ratio would change drastically: Protestants would now outnumber Catholics by 14 to three and the kingdom would remain permanently under the legislation of a Protestant parliament. It was difficult to argue against that. Those with vested interests could be bought off and in the end the proprietors of boroughs which lost the franchise were compensated by the enormous sum of £1,260,000. During the parliamentary recess of 1799, when the Dublin government was busy procuring a parliamentary majority in favour of union, the chief secretary, Viscount Castlereagh, wrote from the Phoenix Park in July about the 'complicated negotiations' involved. 'Every individual is now playing his game as if it were his last stake, and it is most difficult to meet their expectations in any degree, keeping within the possibility of accomplishment'. He warned London that it 'must be prepared for having the favours and patronage of the crown most deeply engaged to the actors in this contest'. This realistic view of the position in Dublin, that bribery in one form or another was at the heart of the matter, was borne out by events. When challenged, one of the 'actors' was reported to have said that he could only thank God that he had a country to sell!

Not all members of parliament acted out of greed or self-interest. For many, on both sides, it remained a matter of principle and even divided families. Viscount Gosford of Armagh was strongly in favour of union; but his son, Major Acheson, who held a seat in the commons on the strength of his father's estate, remained firmly against the union to the end, despite all efforts to persuade or bribe him to the contrary. Outside parliament, many genuinely believed that, like the 'middle nation' of the medieval lordship, they were of the land of Ireland, separate from England, though under the crown, and with their own parliament which represented them fully. When the Irish Bar debated the union on 9 December 1799, those against the union won by 166 votes to 32. One leading counsel was loudly cheered when he protested that though 'there are 40,000 British troops in Ireland, with 40,000 bayonets at my breast', no British government would:

'plant another Sicily in the bosom of the Atlantic. Our patent to be a state, not a shire, came direct from heaven. The almighty has, in majestic characters, signed the great charter of our independence. The great creator of the world has given our beloved country the gigantic outlines of a kingdom. The God of nature never intended that Ireland should be province, and by God she never shall'.

The historical references to Sicily and *magna carta* were telling. But such arguments meant nothing to those MPs who were more interested in material gain. Castlereagh had expressed it succinctly in 1799 when he said that the government's task was 'to buy out, and secure to the crown for ever, the fee simple of Irish corruption'. This was done and by the time parliament met again in 1800 the government had secured the necessary majority. On 15 January there was high drama and the debate continued through the night. Near dawn it reached a climax when the sick Grattan appeared in his old Volunteer uniform, almost carried into the chamber. He spoke for two hours, but to no avail. When a vote was taken at 10 a.m. the opposition amendment, that an independent Irish parliament be maintained, was defeated by 138 votes to 96, a government majority of 42.

This majority was never lost. When Castlereagh submitted a motion on 6 February that a union should be seriously considered, it was passed in the commons by 160 votes to 117, a majority of 43; and 11 days later, when the largest division ever taken in the Irish parliament resulted in another win for the government, the majority was 46. From then on it was a matter of hammering out the details. It is significant that there was little or no public reaction on the streets of Dublin, even though a record number of books and pamphlets debated the matter in print. In December 1759, when it was only rumoured that a union was imminent, there had been a quick reaction by the Dublin mob. On 9 December they actually invaded the parliament, terrified those present and forced some of the more important, including the lord chancellor and the chief justice of the king's bench, to swear 'to be true to their country'. There were no such high feelings expressed on the streets of Dublin in 1800. The English writer de Quincy happened to be visiting a friend in Dublin in 1800 and was present in the visitors' gallery at the last session of the Irish parliament. He was angry at what he witnessed, as he wrote, when the union was ratified 'without a muttering, or a whispering, or the protesting echo of a sigh'. More than 500 years of parliamentary institutions was swept aside. From now on Ireland was to be represented in the Westminster parliament by 32 peers (including four Church of Ireland bishops) in the upper house and 100 MPs in the commons. There were provisions for free trade, for retaining a distinct Irish exchequer and its own national debt and for uniting the Church of Ireland and the Church of England. 'The United Kingdom of Great Britain and Ireland' was by law established and came into being on 1 January 1801. But nowhere was there mention of Catholics or emancipation.

In England there was some opposition to union which was the result of age-old prejudice against all things Irish. As Lord Sheffield in his attack on the union exclaimed: 'I do not think any of our country gentlemen would venture into parliament if they were to meet a hundred Paddies'. Such hatred was largely sectarian and reflected a latent fear of a Catholic ethos being introduced into the very bastion of the established church. In Ireland Protestant fears that relaxation of the penal laws had led to the rebellion of 1798 and would destroy the Protestant ascendancy if not halted were very real. In November 1799 a former chief secretary wrote to Pitt that 'as you cannot extirpate' the Catholics, who would always be unsatisfied, they could only be controlled if 'the state, the parliament, and the church should be exclusively Protestant'.

In England in November 1799 two cabinet meetings had favoured emancipation for Catholics, with the only doubts expressed concerning their admission to the very highest offices. Indeed Castlereagh was authorized to offer emancipation if he felt such an offer was necessary to secure full Catholic support for the union. But when he returned to England in December 1800 the situation had changed and while the cabinet in January 1801 agreed that the Catholic question should be supported by the Government, the king refused to entertain the proposal.

George III had long been fiercely anti-emancipation. In June 1798 he had declared publicly that:

> 'there could be only one national church, whose members must therefore have a monopoly of government, and that no country can be governed where there is more than one established religion; the others may be tolerated, but that cannot extend further than leave to perform their religious duties according to the tenets of their church, for which indulgence they cannot have any share in the government of the state'.

Now, in 1801, he showed that his views had not changed one whit: 'What is this Catholic emancipation which this young lord, this Irish secretary has brought over that you are going to throw at my head?', he exclaimed in public. 'I will tell you that I shall look on every man as my personal enemy who proposes that question to me'. The king asked that a new government be formed in England, Pitt resigned, as did Cornwallis and Castlereagh in Ireland, and the question of Catholic emancipation was postponed indefinitely with long-term disastrous political results.

In Ireland the coming into effect of the union on 1 January 1801 made very little impact. Dublin castle government was still preserved virtually intact and the new lord lieutenant, the Earl of Hardwicke, prevented the Catholic question from emerging as even a matter for discussion. The peace of Amiens not only ended the war with France but was 'a dismay to traitors', as the new chief secretary expressed it. No potential rebel could hope for help from that quarter. All seemed tranquil, even drab. But suddenly government complacency was rudely shattered on the night of Saturday 23 July 1803 by disturbances on the streets of Dublin during which men were killed. Much more serious was the murder of the chief justice, Lord Kilwarden, and a Custom House official called Leech, who were dragged from their coaches and piked to death. Kilwarden's daughter was with him in the coach and was not molested. But not so lucky was his nephew, Reverend Richard Wolfe, who was also killed. These deaths were the result of a rebellion which had been long planned by Robert Emmet, younger brother of the United Irishman leader Thomas Addis Emmet, but which had gone disastrously astray.

Robert Emmet has passed into Irish romantic folklore and his rebellion, while admired for its daring and bravery, has commonly been dismissed as foolhardy and little more than a farce in its execution. Indeed Emmet himself, before he died, was of the opinion that it was not entitled to 'the respectability of an insurrection'. But General Fox, the army supreme commander, insisted that it could have had the most serious consequences. Later he was proud of 'the easy and almost instant suppression of an insurrection which at the time appeared as formidable in its preparation and means of doing mischief as any in history'. If that is an exaggeration, it does confirm the military view of the danger posed. Myles Byrne, one of the leaders, had no doubt of what would have happened had Emmet's plan been carried through. Had Dublin castle been taken, he insisted, 'the citizens would have flocked to the standard of independence hoisted on this movement' and then Dublin would have fallen into rebel hands. 'Not for centuries had Ireland so favourable an opportunity of getting rid of the cruel English yoke'.

Even as a lad of 17 Robert Emmet had enjoyed such a reputation as a nationalist and a brilliant orator that the Trinity College authorities actively tried to counteract his influence in the college Historical Society. Later, in 1798, Lord Clare, on an official visitation to the college, discovered no fewer than four branches of the United Irishmen in Trinity, with Emmet as the secretary of one branch. He was summarily expelled and later went to France where he established contact with many United Irishmen and tried to organize yet another French expeditionary force to invade Ireland. Back in Dublin in October 1802, he immediately began secret preparations for a new rebellion. There were still large numbers of United Irishmen in Ireland, anxious to break the connection with England. Even former leaders, such as Russell, Byrne and Hamilton, were available.

Across the water in England there was a strong underground republican movement, including United Irishmen, Corresponding Societies (such as that of London), the Secret Committee of England, and even United Britons. Plans were made for a simultaneous rebellion in England and Ireland, encouraged by the French who promised help and then an invasion. Associated, wrongly, with Edward Despard, a member of an Anglo-Irish landed family, who was later executed for his 'conspiracy', the English republican plans came to nothing in the end.

Back in Ireland the young Emmet made a huge impression. Myles Byrne recounted how in his first meeting Emmet's 'powerful, persuasive language, and sound reason, all coming from the heart, left it impossible for any Irishman, impressed with a desire for his country's independence, to make any objection to his plans'. He was also much loved by many of his elders. Denis

Lambert Redmond, a coal factor of Coal Quay in Dublin, was one of those later brought to trial and executed. When he left directions for his burial, he asked that he be put 'as near my dear friend Emmet as possible; I never can be put too close to him'.

However much a shambles the rebellion turned out to be in the end, its planning was meticulous and potentially dangerous to the government and Emmet was the brain behind it. As the attorney general, Standish O'Grady said at the trial, he was 'a gentleman to whom the rebellion may be traced, as the origin, the life, the soul of it'. Not only was a large supply of arms manufactured and successfully stored away, special pikes were devised for use in street-fighting and dangerous explosive devises which would be deadly against cavalry on the narrow streets. He even successfully experimented with a new type of rocket which had devastating effects. Hurling clubs were set up in many parts of Dublin so that, under cover of sport, drill practice could take place without interference by the authorities.

But in the end it was all to no avail and a series of mishaps and misunderstandings blew apart all the careful plans. When Emmet finally led his tiny force against the castle on the night of 23 July, dressed in his elaborate general's uniform and brandishing his sword, the end was inevitable. He escaped from Dublin and remained at large until he was arrested on 25 August. He was brought to trial on 19 September and after a long day in the dock was sentenced to be hanged, drawn and quartered the following day. In the course of a long statement from the dock, interspersed with heated exchanges with Lord Norbury, who presided, Emmet made a final speech which moved all who heard it (even Norbury, who is reported to have shed tears when passing sentence) and which has ever since been a standard for generations of Irish patriots:

> 'I have parted with everything that was dear to me in this life for my country's cause, and abandoned another idol I adored in my heart – the object of my affections. My race is run – the grave opens to receive me, and I sink into its bosom. I am ready to die – I have not been allowed to vindicate my character. I have but one request to ask at my departure from this world – it is the charity of its silence. Let no man write my epitaph; for as no man who knows my motives dares now to vindicate them, let not prejudice or ignorance asperse them. Let them rest in obscurity and peace; my memory be left in oblivion and my tomb remain uninscribed, until other times and other men can do justice to my character. When my country takes her place among the nations of the earth, then, and not till then, let my epitaph be written. I have done.'

That night the Newgate chaplain, Reverend Gamble, visited Emmet in his cell. He reported that Emmet had denounced deism and protested his Christianity. More surprisingly, he said that Emmet had denounced Bonaparte 'as the most savage unprincipled tyrant by whom earth was ever disgraced'. They prayed together. Emmet received 'the sacrament of the lord's supper' and having 'protested his ignorance and abhorrence of Lord Kilwarden's murder . . . besought the forgiveness of heaven for having been the instrument of plunging so many of his deluded fellow creatures in guilt and misery'.

If in retrospect Emmet's rising assumes a tragi-comic guise, the foolish escapade of a misguided 25 year old, in reality it produced a fierce reaction. It was condemned in particular by those who opposed the union with England and by the Catholic hierarchy. Daniel O'Connell joined a special corps of yeomanry, made up of lawyers, formed to combat the rising and to help maintain law and order. During a house raid he seized a blunderbuss and in later years proudly displayed it among his most cherished possessions. He denounced the rising 'as wild as anything in romance' and said that 'no madder scheme was ever devised'.

In the immediate aftermath Emmet's rebellion was seen by many, not least some of those in high office in Dublin, as yet another example of Catholic determination to overthrow Protestant ascendancy and even to massacre as many innocent Protestants as possible. In the heated atmosphere generated by the publication of Sir Richard Musgrave's fiercely anti-Catholic *Memoirs of the Different Rebellions in Ireland* in 1801, fears of another Protestant massacre were easily aroused. Even the lord lieutenant, the Earl of Hardwicke, believed that the Catholic hierarchy possessed prior knowledge of the rebellion and only denounced it after it had failed. So, in the years following the union, despite all attempts by those who favoured granting emancipation to Catholics, it became clear that the English parliament, and in particular the House of Lords, was adamantly against any such legislation. By 1807, when a new government was installed in England as a result of an election during which 'no popery' had become a winning slogan, the position remained hopeless, especially with the king as averse as ever. The chief secretary in Ireland told a leading Catholic peer that this was now the case, though he sweetened the pill by adding that the surviving penal laws 'would be administered with mildness and good temper'.

The growth of sectarian strife did not help matters. The yeomanry, now almost wholly Protestant and nearly exclusively Orange, was involved in open sectarian atrocities. The militia was in many places largely Catholic and sectarian clashes between them and the yeomanry were recorded. The growth of new underground societies in the countryside, and indeed increasingly in the towns, mostly militantly Catholic in membership, made the situation worse. Although they were not overtly sectarian, and were, for example, as vehemently opposed to the fees charged by Catholic priests as they were to the traditional tithes levied by the anglican church, they were perceived as sectarian.

During the early nineteenth century Protestant evangelicalism led to a sustained attempt to convert the poor of Ireland from the errors of popery and Bible societies supplied the missionaries with the literature they needed to carry out their work. Not only Bibles, but religious tracts of all kinds were supplied in astonishing numbers. In 10 years four and a half million tracts were given away throughout Ireland. Such missionary activity, and the conversions which followed, forced the Catholic church to give a greater priority to education and to teaching the faithful more about the truths of the religion they professed. More attention was paid to the organization of the church in the localities and to a public display of the predominance of Catholicism in Ireland. This in turn made Catholics more conscious than ever of the discrimination practised against them, even where the law made them equal with Protestants. While most offices in the administration, apart from the most senior, were by law open to Catholics after the act of 1793, in practice discrimination against them was still the norm. Evidence produced by the Catholic Association in 1828 was incontrovertible. It listed 1,314 posts in the administration of justice, of which only 39 were held by Catholics. Another area of administration showed even greater discrimination: of 3,033 offices listed only 134 were held by Catholics.

Such continued discrimination and the sustained refusal of the government to even consider Catholic emancipation, quickly alienated the vast majority of Catholics, even those who had been most eager to support the union. The controversy over the proposal that the government should have the power of veto over the appointment of bishops brought the breach with the government into sharp focus. While the Catholic hierarchy in the aftermath of rebellion in 1799 might have been willing to accept the notion of a veto, especially with the prospect of Catholic emancipation dangled before them, there was no way that most of them, or indeed of the Catholic people under their direction, were willing to accept what in 1801 was regarded as an outrage. The passionate opposition to the notion of a veto was, proclaimed Daniel O'Connell, the result of 'the hereditary hatred which seven centuries of oppression have inspired in the Irish mind'. The emphasis on long centuries of oppression, however nonsensical in fact, was to become typical of the new Catholic nationalism which this controversy and the new anti-union feelings were to engender.

By the early nineteenth century the Catholic vote in the counties, where most of the MPs were elected, was something which no politician could ignore. In line with the extraordinary increase which had taken place in the size of the Catholic population, the number of Catholic 40-shilling freeholders eligible to vote had risen to 100,000 and then doubled by the second decade of the century. Once these Catholic voters were made aware of their power, and persuaded to break free of the control exercised by their landlords, they formed a formidable and even decisive power-bloc in most constituencies. The process of politicization, which brought these voters into the mainstream of Irish politics, was the result of the organization which petitions against the remaining penal laws, and opposition to the veto, required.

In early 1807, with the help of the bishops, an appeal for signatures to a petition to parliament was organized nationally for the first time since 1792.

In the years following more petitions were circulated, with bishops supplying parochial clergy to help. The organizational power of the Catholic church was quickly exploited by politicians who supported what was loosely called 'the Catholic cause'. In 1811 elections for a national convention of Catholics were organized on a county basis, usually in churches, and even though the government invoked the Convention Act of 1793 to prohibit the meeting, the process of election had clearly shown not only the strength of Catholic opinion once it was organized, but also how efficiently the church could be exploited in that situation.

Despite the extent of grievance among the people, however, the Catholic leaders were unable to make anything of the situation. This was, in part, because Robert Peel, the new chief secretary who arrived in 1812, was vehemently anti-emancipation and was more than a match for those leaders. But the failure was, in the main, the result of dissensions among those same leaders. What Charles Butler, a leading spokesman for the English Catholics, wrote in 1818 was the bald truth: 'our greatest misfortunes are our dissensions among ourselves'. It was only when Daniel O'Connell was able to assume a dominance in the movement for emancipation that an organized and coherent plan of campaign emerged which was to open the way to not only Catholic involvement in politics at the highest level, but to the more fundamental aspiration of repeal of the union.

Daniel O'Connell was typical of the new Catholic leaders emerging in nineteenth century Ireland in that he was middle class, professional and with a landed background. His Kerry ancestors had managed to hold onto their lands, with the connivance of Protestant friends, and his uncle, to whose lands and fortune Daniel was heir, had also, like so many other Catholics, moved into commerce with great success, greatly helped by his involvement in the smuggling trade with Europe. Partly educated in France, where he witnessed the horrors of the early revolutionary terror, and which gave him a life-long aversion to the use of any kind of violence in the pursuit of political ends, he studied law in London and Dublin, was called to the bar, and became one of the most successful junior counsels in Ireland: by 1805 he was earning over £1,000 per annum, which soon climbed to £3,500. It was partly for professional reasons that, like most lawyers, he became a Volunteer early in 1797, though he was well aware of the dangers of a French invasion which would, as he saw it, destroy all true liberty in Ireland: 'The altar of liberty totters when it is cemented only with blood, when it is supported only with carcasses'.

He was naturally opposed to the 1798 rebellion and later publicly repudiated the proposed union with Britain. He helped to organize a meeting of Catholics in Dublin in January 1800, the purpose of which was to denounce what he called 'so horrible a calumny'. In an impassioned speech against the use of force he proclaimed 'that if the alternative were offered' to any man who felt as he did 'of union, or the re-enactment of the penal code in all its pristine horrors, that he would prefer without hesitation the latter, as the lesser and more sufferable evil'. He concluded by insisting that 'he would rather confide in the justice of his brethren, the Protestants of Ireland, who had already liberated him, than lay his country at the feet of foreigners'.

A deist for a time, he returned to his inherited religion with a zeal and conviction which lasted to his death. But his extensive reading of works such as William Godwin's *Political Justice*, or indeed novels like Henry Mackenzie's *The Man of Feeling*, left an indelible impression of humanitarianism and helped to form the radicalism that was to remain with him all his life. He supported the emancipation of Jews, was at the forefront of the anti-slavery movement, denounced colonialism and its victims wherever it existed, preached 'the brotherhood of man' with conviction and denounced sectarianism (though his own public speeches, even in court, might often suggest the opposite). He became a model for liberal Catholics in Europe, as Montalambert told him in Paris in 1847, not long before his death:

> 'We are all your children, or rather, your pupils. You are not just a man for one nation, you are a man for all Christendom . . . Wherever Catholics return to the practice of civil virtues and dedicate themselves to the conquest of their legitimate rights, after God, this is your work. Wherever religion strives to emancipate itself from the yoke that many generations of sophists and legists have forged for it, it is to you, after God, that it owes it'.

His reputation in contemporary Europe was immense. When he died in Italy, the solemn obsequies in Rome, at the church of Sant' Andrea della Valle, lasted for two days.

But it was in Ireland that O'Connell was to give full rein to his radical and egalitarian beliefs. By 1808 he was playing a leading role in the affairs of the Catholic Committee, using the public debate over the veto question to enhance his public reputation. The previous year at a public meeting he had argued the justice of Catholic claims – 'the new score of justice', he had called it, significantly adding that it was that same justice 'which would emancipate the Protestant in Spain and Portugal, the Christian in Constantinople'.

But during the veto debate he was much more aggressive and when in September 1808 the Catholic hierarchy rejected the concession of a veto, it marked the extent of O'Connell's public influence. By the time the veto question became an issue again, during the negotiations concerning the restoration of the papal states at the Congress of Vienna, it was O'Connell again who led the opposition. Despite the concession of a veto by the pope, and its acceptance by the English bishops, the Irish church showed its independence by refusing to yield. On 24 January 1815 O'Connell organized a public meeting at the Clarendon Street church in Dublin to oppose the granting of the veto by Rome or the Irish bishops. 'Let our determination [to resist] reach Rome', he said from the altar steps, and protested that he would continue resisting to the end. 'I am sincerely a Catholic but I am not a papist'.

He warned the Irish bishops that if 'the present clergy should descend from the high station they hold to become the vile slaves of the castle', then they must 'look to their masters for support, for the people will despise them too much to contribute'. This produced great applause from the audience. 'The people would imitate their forefathers', he continued, and what he called 'the castle clergy' would then 'preach to still thinner numbers than attend in Munster or Connaught the reverend gentlemen of the present established church'.

This invocation of the power of the people was to become a cornerstone of O'Connell's future politics and was to be demonstrated with devastating effect. On 25 April 1823 he proposed the creation of a new Catholic Association, with an annual subscription of one guinea. Significantly, priests were given *ex officio* membership, a sure indication of the important role they were to play. While emancipation was a primary aim, it was intended that all Catholic grievances would be addressed. O'Connell put this clearly. The new association, he said, 'would apply a new secret of healing – that wonderful power of sympathy with the sufferer, of fellow interest in the grievance, which would do more than statutes or armies to restore the quality'. He added that 'it was dangerous to leave the people without some body of recognised friends, to whom they could at least vent their complaints'.

At a time when agrarian grievances were widespread and aggressive secret societies abounded, O'Connell spoke the truth. But it was the step taken early in 1824 which revolutionized the movement. For payment of one penny a month, a 'catholic rent' as it became known, associate members were admitted in large numbers. With episcopal backing the movement quickly spread. First Bishop James Doyle of Kildare and Leighlin gave the scheme his backing, supplying O'Connell with a list of priests who would help with the collection of the rent. Other bishops quickly followed suit. The collections were mostly taken up at chapel gates on a Sunday and by October 1824 there were already hundreds of thousands paying the rent, many of them holding regular meetings in hired rooms. Political views were discussed at those meetings and soon local problems were arbitrated, grievances publicized, and examples of discrimination against Catholics attacked.

These thousands, and those well organized local bodies, were now at the disposal of O'Connell and his planned agitations. Now he became a national leader – the 'incorporation of his people' as Balzac later called him – unchallenged in his popularity throughout Ireland. Eventually perhaps as many as half a million individuals were associate members and provided O'Connell with the nucleus of the first genuinely popular democratic movement in Europe. The income from the rent also provided him with a fund which he was able to use for political purposes, as well as to help to protect voters against their landlords when this new popular strength was exploited in parliamentary elections.

Priests were of vital importance in helping to organize this popular movement. But so, too, were the thousands who had returned from active military service and provided the expertise which their experience had given them. The militarization of Ireland in years past was of enormous importance. Between 1793 and 1815 as many as 159,000 joined the British army from Ireland, as well as a further 40,000 and more who went into the navy. Indeed, they constituted such a large proportion of the armed forces that in 1798, when the lord lieutenant requested regiments of soldiers to be sent from England to crush the rebellion, the home secretary informed him that there were no specifically 'English' regiments available since 'so large a part of our regular infantry is composed of recruits or men raised in Ireland'. When most returned to Ireland, they provided well-disciplined Catholics all over the island, to be used as needed by O'Connell. A letter from the Earl of Rosse to Lord Redesdale in 1822, describing why 'the lower orders are much more formidable now than they ever were in this island', listed 'the habit of organisation and the taste they have got for it, also from the numbers of disbanded soldiers and militia'.

These militias also provided another important ingredient. When they were organized on a county basis in 1790 and later, they were moved around the island so that they would not serve in their home or adjoining counties. The result was not only to provide many such Catholics with a knowledge of areas which most of them would otherwise never have visited, but also to awaken in them a deeper 'national' sense than was ever possible in the past when so few people were aware of the full extent of Ireland.

The Waterford election of 1826 marked a decisive turning point in Irish politics. The county was largely under the control of the Beresford family, fiercely anti-Catholic and representative of the Protestant ascendancy at its worst. Thomas Wyse, of a local prominent Catholic mercantile family, furious at what he called 'the discordancy between the electors and the elected', was determined to try to unseat the Beresford interest. Together with Father Sheehan, a local priest, he devised a strategy to win the seat at the next election. He persuaded a liberal Protestant, Henry Villiers Stuart, to stand and organized a campaign in the general election of 1826. They hired paid agents, employed lawyers to examine voters' qualifications, made good use of the press for propaganda, and procured the active support of the Catholic clergy. Because of the fear that landlords would punish any freeholder who voted for Stuart, a fund was created to help possible victims and, even more of an innovation, alternative holdings of land were made available. O'Connell came south towards the end of the campaign, electioneering vigorously through the county. The results were spectacular. By the time Beresford withdrew Stuart was leading by 1357 votes to 527, which probably represented a majority of three to one if the uncounted votes were taken into the reckoning.

Inspired by what was happening in Waterford, Catholics in other counties attempted at the last minute to mobilize support for liberal candidates in the general election. In Louth, it was not until 10 days before the ballot that a candidate was found who was willing to challenge the powerful Foster family. Despite the lack of time and the inadequacy of the resources available, the

Catholics procured the help of the Archbishop of Armagh and very nearly carried the day. Foster had only five votes to spare after the count and explained his humiliation to Peel by blaming the priests. They had told the Catholic voters, he said, that what was at stake was their 'eternal salvation'. On the day when the poll commenced, he said, 'all the priests of the county were collected and distributed through the different booths where they stood with glaring eyes opposite to the voters of their respective flocks as they were severally brought up'. The Association was also successful in counties Armagh, Monaghan, Westmeath, Cavan and Mayo. From now on the Catholic vote was the key element in any parliamentary election. As Lord Donoughmore put it in a letter to Hely Hutchinson in July, where he tried to explain what these successes meant for Catholics:

'Hereafter no man will ever have a quiet election in an Irish county who does not support them. This is to be the most formidable and the most unexpected symptom of strength which our Catholic leaders have ever yet displayed . . . the county elections are placed entirely in their hands'.

This revolt of the Catholic freeholders represented the emergence of a 'catholic nation', whose existence and strength could no longer be denied. In the next general election that 'nation' would have to be placated and this meant, above all else, emancipation. In the end even Peel, the most committed opponent of emancipation among senior politicians, had to face this reality. On 17 January 1828 nearly three-quarters of the Catholic parishes in Ireland held rallies demanding emancipation, a show of strength and organizational capacity which impressed all. Then a vacancy occurred in Clare when the promotion of William Vesey Fitzgerald to cabinet rank meant that by law he had to stand for re-election. On 24 June O'Connell dropped a bombshell. He announced that he would stand in the Clare by-election, the first time since the penal laws were inaugurated at the end of the seventeenth century that a Catholic would contest a parliamentary election.

Straight away in his electoral address O'Connell made clear what the issue was, so as to win the Catholic vote in Clare. He would never take the oath required by law: 'That the sacrifice of the mass and the invocation of the Blessed Mary and other saints, as now practised in the Church of Rome, are impious and idolatrous'. But Fitzgerald 'has often taken that horrible oath; he is ready to take it again, and asks your votes to enable him so to swear. I would rather be torn limb from limb than take it'. The electors would have a clear choice 'between that sworn libeller of the Catholic faith and one who has devoted his early life to your cause, who has consumed his manhood in a struggle for your liberties'.

Given the issue, it is not surprising that almost all the priests campaigned vigorously for O'Connell. Typical was the parish priest of Corofin, Father John Murphy. An onlooker has described how as soon as mass was over, he threw off his vestments and addressed the congregation in Irish, telling them that they must sacrifice themselves for O'Connell as well as for faith and fatherland. At the close of his speech:

> 'he became inflamed by the power of his emotions, and while he raised himself into the loftiest attitude to which he could ascend, he laid one hand on the altar, and shook the other in the spirit of almost prophetic admonition, and as his eyes blazed and seemed to start from his forehead, thick drops fell down his face, and his voice rolled through his lips, livid with passion and covered with foam'.

The listening crowd burst into loud applause and shouts of acclamation and, reported the onlooker, 'would have been ready to mount a battery roaring with cannon at his command'. Two days later Father Murphy led the tenants into Ennis and there each man voted for O'Connell.

In the end, O'Connell gained 67 per cent of the votes, a famous victory which threw down the gauntlet to the government. As he told the Association at a meeting on 10 July: 'They must either crush us or conciliate us. There is no going on as we are'. There could be no question now of 'crushing' the Catholics of Ireland, so emancipation must come, sooner rather than later. The triumphal return of O'Connell from Clare, with multitudes of supporters thronging the whole way to Dublin, and band, banners and all the trappings of victory widely in evidence, symbolized what was expected. Even more threatening was the inscription on the side of the car which carried O'Connell:

> Hereditary bondsmen! know ye not,
> Who would be free themselves must strike the blow?

In England Wellington, the prime minister, decided that he must move quickly. He prevailed upon the king that he must face reality and in the king's speech at the opening of parliament on 5 February 1829 there was a clear signal that an emancipation bill would be introduced. To prepare the way a bill suppressing the Catholic Association was published eight days later and then another which abolished the right of the 40-shilling freeholders to vote. Instead, the vote was confined to £10 freeholders which significantly changed the Catholic electorate from 230,000 to 14,000, out of a population (very largely Catholic) of seven million. Finally, on 13 March the king, even if reluctantly, signed the emancipation bill and the 'act for the relief of His Majesty's Roman Catholic subjects' became law.

A new oath, which obliged Catholics to 'adjure any intention to subvert the present church establishment as settled by law . . . or weaken the Protestant religion or Protestant government in the United Kingdom', though offensive, did not contravene the religious beliefs of practising Catholics and opened the way to parliament and to all offices (except those of regent, chancellor and lord lieutenant). A host of relatively minor restrictions were retained – for example, Catholics could worship only in their own churches or in private, no habit or vestments might be worn in public, no registered Catholic church could have a bell or steeple. But there was no veto on the appointment of bishops and the only ones to suffer serious deprivation were the 40-shilling freeholders, when the county freehold franchise was raised to £10.

It was regarded as a great victory, won by priests and laity acting together as a massive and highly organized pressure group, led by O'Connell, the liberator of Catholics. Popular feeling was summed up by the reported reaction of one peasant:

> 'We may have a light if we please now; and we walk about without being stopped by soldiers; and it'll not be long before we get law and justice, and Catholic magistrates that will believe the truth from a Catholic. Oh! the devil fly away with Protestant magistrates that find all Catholics guilty'.

13 The genesis of home rule

Catholic emancipation was a titanic achievement and the celebrations which resulted were a public acknowledgement of that fact. Liberal Protestants also celebrated. Down in county Limerick Aubrey De Vere joined in the demonstrations and helped to light bonfires on the hills around Adare where he lived. But later, when the popular euphoria had passed, there was a growing disillusion with the results. As one priest reported a parishioner saying: 'We die of starvation just the same'. The harsh reality was that for the vast majority of Catholics emancipation made no difference to their daily lives and for some, the 40-shilling freeholders, it may even have hastened their downfall, now that they no longer had a vote which was at the disposal of their landlords.

The struggle for emancipation also had the effect of helping to make Irish nationalism more markedly Catholic and therefore sectarian in nature. When Alexis de Toqueville came to Ireland in 1835, he remarked that the Catholic bishops 'were as much the leaders of a party as the representatives of a church'. He detected 'a note of triumph', as if they had already emerged as leaders of political opinion on the island. Clergy and laymen, he saw, were closely bound together by political as well as religious ties.

O'Connell had often been intemperate in his speeches and had alienated Protestants by references to the persecution of Catholics by Cromwell and the slaughter of innocents. But times had changed and this treatment of Catholics was no longer possible. 'We were a paltry remnant in Cromwell's time. We are nine millions now'. He even went so far as to say that if ever the support of Britain was withdrawn, the Protestant minority would 'sink' into the Irish nation.

The Catholic potential in politics was well understood. In an article in the *Edinburgh Review* in 1844, Nassau Senior put it bluntly, when he wrote that since Irish Catholics had now become a nation, 'Ireland can never be controlled while to be a Catholic is a badge of exclusion'. Later in the 1840s, Macauley was to point the potential impact of this emergence of Catholic political strength by arguing that if a House of Commons which was Protestant had proved that it could not be trusted to legislate equitably for a Catholic Ireland, 'how can an Irish House of Commons, chiefly elected by

Catholics, be trusted to legislate for Protestant Ulster?'. Many Protestants who had supported emancipation now became alienated, fearing the impact of a politicized and well-organized Catholic people. The situation was made worse because Catholics now saw that there was no real hope of long-standing grievances being redressed in an English parliament and so they turned to agitate for a repeal of the union and a parliament of their own. What had been regarded as the 'Catholic question' in England now became simply the 'Irish question'. Because emancipation had been so grudgingly conceded, and only at the last minute owing to English fears of civil war in Ireland, it had the effect of convincing many Irish that the only way to win redress of grievances from England was by what Macauley called 'turbulence'. Peel had warned, even before the emancipation bill was introduced in parliament, that 'the settlement of the Catholic question would not be the settlement of Ireland'. Time was to prove how right he was.

Protestant ascendancy in Ireland had rested in large measure not only on possession of land, but also on control of parliament and the instruments of government. Union with Britain had not changed that. But the admission of Catholics to the Westminster parliament after 1829 and the increase in their voting power in the boroughs after the reform act of 1832 posed a threat which was very real. That same act also marginally increased the number of Irish seats from 100 to 105. In the general election of 1835 65 of those who won seats could be classed as 'anti-Tory' and O'Connell was able to command the votes of at least 60 of those.

In the famous 'Lichfield House compact' of that year, though nothing was committed to paper, an agreement was made promising the Whig leader Russell these votes, in return for some influence over measures affecting Ireland and over appointments there, Ireland would benefit and in particular the Catholic majority. Repeal of the union was to be put on the back burner, but it was always there, to be invoked if the Whigs reneged on what Russell later called 'an alliance on honourable terms of mutual cooperation'. It was an extraordinary achievement for O'Connell, so soon after entering parliament, and it marked a crucial stage in the emergence of Catholic political power. Lord Beresford's baleful forecast that the effect of 1829 would be to 'transfer from Protestants to Roman Catholics the ascendancy of Ireland' was given substance.

One result of the struggle to achieve Catholic emancipation and the consequent admission of Irish Catholics to parliament was the creation of a new, radical political party which was well in advance of its time. The 'repeal party' (it adopted different names through the years because of legislation-banning meetings and the like) set a new standard, even a model, of organization. It was not just centrally controlled under a party leader, who was provided with an income by a fund raised nationally by party activists. During elections, pledges were procured from candidates by the electorate and the local elections were skilfully organized by election agents, most often the local Catholic priests. In the *Freeman's Journal*, the *Register* and the *Pilot* the party was provided with a popular and highly effective press to propagate its views and elicit support. In the 1832 election the party won 39 seats, as against 36 Whigs and 29 Tories. Not all of these were Catholic: 13 were Protestants who had supported emancipation in the past.

On 6 April 1830 O'Connell had founded a Society of the Friends of Ireland of all Religious Persuasions to fight for a number of causes of which one was repeal of the union. For him repeal, to be achieved with liberal Protestant as well as Catholic support, meant what he defined himself in 1833 as 'an Irish parliament, British connection, one king, two legislatures'. Basic to his anti-union politics was the avoidance of all physical-force methods and a total reliance on parliamentary democracy. In February 1830 his political philosophy was unambiguously stated when he outlined the 'principal means of attaining our constitutional objects' and gave first place to:

> 'the perpetual determination to avoid anything like physical force or violence and by keeping in all respects within the letter as well as the spirit of the law, to continue peaceable, rational, but energetic measures so as to combine the wise and the good of all classes, stations and persuasions in one determination to abolish abuse and renovate the tone and strength of the representative system'.

He also emphasized the importance of popular participation – 'The people should incessantly call for reform until their cry is heard and *felt* within the walls of Westminster' – and of an 'efficacious treasury' supplied by the regular collection of sums of money, however tiny, from the people at large. Such employment and control of popular support on a massive scale was unprecedented.

For the full realization of his plans to galvanize popular support in this manner, to involve the Catholic masses in constitutional politics, O'Connell could hardly do without the assistance of the Catholic parochial clergy, a fact already demonstrated during the agitation for Catholic emancipation. Despite the strictures of the hierarchy, and later of Rome, the Catholic clergy almost to a man supported O'Connell in organizing the people on a national scale. He had already proclaimed in 1830: 'I go to parliament to form the party of the people'. He would fight for a constitution 'which would secure for every man his right to select his representative, and to protect him by the secrecy of his ballot in the exercise of that selection'. During the debate on reform in parliament in 1832 he publicly demanded universal male suffrage and a secret ballot. If the resultant legislation fell far short of O'Connell's ideal, it did help to loosen the control exercised by the landlords and others in the different constituencies. In the election which followed, O'Connell's Repeal Party won 39 of the seats, larger than the number of Liberals (36) or Conservatives (29) returned.

But the Repealers were quickly brought back to reality in 1834 when an attempt by O'Connell to have the union and its effects on Ireland debated in the commons was defeated by 523 votes to 38. Not only did this overwhelming defeat reveal the futility of hoping for repeal in parliament in the near future, it also exposed the reality that the great majority of Irish MPs still favoured union with Britain.

O'Connell had thus no alternative but to use his party in parliament to try to win other reforms for Ireland. He even went so far as to declare after this that he was 'opposed to repeal if justice is done to Ireland'. In 1826 he argued that the union could benefit Ireland: 'a union of prosperity, and the rights of justice and of benefits'. The people of Ireland 'are ready to become portion of the Empire, provided they be made so in reality, and not in name alone; they are ready to become a kind of West Britons, if made so in benefits and justice'. So, while still retaining leadership over his own repeal party, he formed a coalition of anti-Tory, Whig and liberal Irish politicians to fight elections and win redress of outstanding grievances in parliament.

Ireland at that time, the early 1830s, was a land of violent crime and disorder. Violence, murder, injury and destruction of property were endemic. Crime was widespread, law and order in disarray in many places and secret societies proliferated. The first item on any agenda of reform must be to deal with this. But it was also recognized that these social disorders were symptoms of other problems which had to be tackled. This was explicitly admitted by Thomas Drummond, a Scottish Presbyterian who became under secretary in 1835. Probably the greatest public servant to serve in Ireland in the nineteenth century, Drummond had worked for the Ordnance Survey and was familiar as few men were with the state of affairs in the Irish countryside. In a letter of 1838 he wrote: 'Property has its duties as well as its rights; to the neglect of these duties in times past is mainly to be ascribed that disordered state of society in which such crimes take their rise'. The answer, he believed, lay not in 'statutes of extraordinary severity, but chiefly in the better and more faithful performance of those duties, and the more enlightened and human exercise of those rights'. A new and more accepted police system (the RIC) was put in place by him. He attacked the Orange Order and specifically prohibited all public display calculated to provoke a Catholic reaction. Magistrates were no longer to be appointed on the recommendation of local interests, but as the central administration judged to be most suitable. Catholics were made judges, new jury lists were compiled which would not simply reflect local sectarian interests, and even the problem of excessive drinking was tackled.

The major source of the problem of disorder was the system of tithes and the methods of enforcement and collection. Bishop James Doyle of Kildare and Leighlin (the famous JKL) in his pastoral of 1831 had denounced them as 'this devouring impost' and said that they should be opposed 'with all the means which the law allows'. But Bishop Doyle had always been relentless in his condemnation of secret societies and the violence they engendered. Like O'Connell, he always urged his people to follow legal and peaceful ways in removing injustice. Now in 1838 legislation was introduced at

Westminster to tackle the problem of tithes and though falling far short of what he and his party would have liked, it was accepted by O'Connell. Tithes were now to be converted into a money charge or rent, payable by the landlord who recovered the cost from his tenants. The lowest and poorest classes of tenant were exempted and all arrears of tithe were annulled. Limited as it was, the 1838 act effectively ended the tithe problem. But the political associations which the campaign against tithes had generated remained in place and continued to support repeal and liberal candidates in parliamentary elections.

The problem of poverty was also tackled. The Poor Law Act of 1838 set up workhouses and within three years the island was divided into 130 poor law unions or districts, each with a workhouse, supported by poor law valuations. Three out of four of the 'guardians' who sat on the board which managed each union were elected, thus extending the notion of popular franchise still further through local communities. The Catholic influence in local politics was further strengthened in 1840 when the Municipal Corporation Act was passed through Westminster. Although this came nowhere near reaching the changes which O'Connell and his supporters had demanded, and was way behind the radical measures which reformed municipal government in England and Scotland, it nevertheless ended absolute Protestant control of municipalities in Ireland. The franchise was confined to £10 householders and not given to all who paid rates. But even that was enough to guarantee that liberal and Catholic control would emerge. Protestant ascendancy was ended in yet another quarter. In Dublin, for example, the first election after the 1840 act saw only 13 Tories elected, as against 47 repealers and liberals. The election of O'Connell in 1841 as the first Catholic Lord Mayor since the end of the seventeenth century was a fitting and appropriate symbol of the change that had occurred.

Both at Westminster and in Dublin castle, then, the new alignment of O'Connell and the Whigs seemed to work and reflected the growth of Catholic nationalism in Ireland. Even educational reform, which the London government had tried to establish on a purely non-sectarian basis, had been compromised so that in effect it was organized on sectarian lines. This was to suit the established church as well as Catholic and Presbyterian interests. O'Connell seemed well on the way to achieving his avowed aim of restoring Ireland to the Irish, which in reality meant to the Catholics.

In 1841, however, the Whig Government was defeated and Sir Robert Peel, who had been a bitter opponent of Catholic emancipation, became prime minister. During the election campaign in Ireland O'Connell tried to keep repeal on the agenda, without alienating Whigs and radicals who favoured the union, and so he urged voters in the *Freeman's Journal*: 'Oppose the Tories everywhere, and in everything'. The result was that the Tories won only 38 seats, the repealers twenty and other anti-Tories the remaining 47. In England, however, the Tories won an overall majority of more than 80. Not only did Peel become head of a government with a comfortable majority,

Russell, the Whig leader, decided that nothing more could be gained from the Lichfield House compact and he broke with O'Connell.

There was now no alternative for the Irishman but to make repeal once again the open objective. 'Repeal is the sole basis the people will accept', he wrote. 'We attempted half measures . . . and failed, although we had the patronage of government'. He now concentrated his energies on Ireland. After his election as Lord Mayor of Dublin late in 1841, he used the corporation as an opportunity to prove that Irishmen, and especially Catholics, were well capable of governing themselves. His term in office ended on 31 October 1842, on 28 February 1843 he introduced a motion in favour of repeal and after three days' debate, widely reported, it was carried by 41 votes to 15.

After leaving the mayoralty O'Connell turned his attention to overhauling the organization of the repeal movement. Parish-by-parish membership of the Repeal Association was expanded with such success that O'Connell was able to announce a goal of three million members. Most of the Catholic bishops not only became members, but active supporters as well. Before the end of 1842 O'Connell had been able to declare that '1843 is and shall be the great Repeal year'. 'Monster meetings' (the term invented by the *Times*), about 40 in all, were held in almost every county, with an estimated 300,000 or more at many of them. On 13 August 1843 the *Times* (no friend of repeal) reported that about one million people had assembled at Tara.

These crowds were always well controlled and throughout the campaign O'Connell was careful to remain within the law, making it impossible for the Dublin administration, or Peel in London, to do anything to call a halt to these mass public demonstrations of demand for repeal. In May O'Connell announced that within three months elections would be held and a 'Council of Three Hundred' would meet in Dublin and would, as he put it, draw up 'Bill no. 1' to repeal the union and 'Bill no. 2' to establish a new Irish House of Commons. This the government could not ignore and by September O'Connell could see that such a council, in effect an Irish parliament, would be prevented by force if necessary. A final monster meeting was planned for Clontarf on 8 October. But in the printed notices advertising the meeting military language was rashly used which Dublin castle was able to construe as seditious. Even though O'Connell repudiated the notice on 2 October, it was too late. On the afternoon of 7 October, the day before the Clontarf meeting was to take place, it was banned and the military were deployed to prevent it. O'Connell submitted and late as it was, printed notices were quickly in circulation asking all to accept the ban. On each of the main roads leading to Dublin prominent members of the association turned back the crowds converging on the capital. Two days later O'Connell and eight others were arrested and charged with sedition – of attempting 'by means of intimidation and the demonstration of great physical force to procure and effect changes to be made in the government, laws, and constitution of this realm'. Early in 1844 O'Connell was sentenced to a year in prison and sent to the Bridewell.

But a successful appeal to the House of Lords, supported by a national novena which all the Catholic bishops recommended, saw him released after six months. In the pro-cathedral in Dublin the archbishop presided at a solemn *Te Deum* 'in thanksgiving to Almighty God for the deliverance of the beloved Liberator to his country, and his fellow-martyrs from unjust captivity'. He was now an old man of 70 and leadership was soon to pass to younger hands.

O'Connell's belief that, as he himself put it, 'we are arrived at a stage of society, in which the peaceable combination of a people can easily render its wishes omnipotent' had clearly been proved to be wrong. Faced with the implacable determination of Peel to maintain the union, no matter what the cost ('Deprecating as I do all war, but above all, civil war, yet there is no alternative which I do not think preferable to the dismemberment of this empire'), there was no way that peaceful demonstrations by 'monster meetings' was ever going to achieve repeal. A more militant approach was soon demanded by younger members of the Repeal Association. Dissensions tore the movement asunder and by the time of O'Connell's death in 1847 it was obvious that his methods of winning repeal had failed utterly. New ideas became dominant, not least those propagated by the group known as Young Ireland, led by Thomas Davis.

A Trinity educated Protestant of mixed English and Irish parentage, Davis articulated a concept of Irish nationality which was to have a lasting influence right down to the present day. Both Tone and O'Connell had stressed that Catholic and Protestant alike made up the Irish nation. Davis went further in advocating 'a nationality which may embrace Protestant, Catholic and Dissenter – Milesian and Cromwellian – the Irishman of a hundred generations and the stranger who is within our gates'. The notion of bringing Orange and Green together was to be symbolized in a new national flag. He not only rejected outright the Swiftean concept that the Irish nation was exclusively Protestant, he (unlike O'Connell) defended the place of the Irish language as an essential ingredient, because without a distinctive language nationality could not survive. 'A nation should guard its language more than its territories', he wrote. To impose another language, English, on the Irish was 'to cut off the entail of feeling, and separate the people from their forefathers by a deep gulf'. The past had produced the nation and knowledge of that history was vital.

Together with another Trinity graduate, the Catholic John Blake Dillon, and the northern Catholic Charles Gavan Duffy (who had attended a Presbyterian school) a new newspaper, the *Nation*, was founded to disseminate the new Young Ireland concepts of nationality. The first issue on 15 October 1842 clearly set out what the aims of Davis, Dillon and Duffy were:

'Nationality is their first great object, a nationality which will not only raise our people from their poverty, by securing to them the blessings of a domestic legislature, but inflame and purify them with a lofty and heroic love of country . . . a nationality which may embrave Protestant, Catholic and Dissenter, Milesian and Cromwellian'.

Duffy, with experience of journalism in Belfast, became editor and it was his influence which led to poetry being given prominent space in the paper. The first number came out on 15 October 1842 and, despite the very high cover price of sixpence, the 12,000 copies printed sold out immediately. It retained this huge circulation of over 10,000, the largest of any Irish newspaper to that time, reaching an audience of at least 250,000 people throughout the country. Given this influence, and the ideas propagated, the launch of the *Nation* was certainly one of the most significant events in the history of Irish journalism.

Davis poured his heart out in a flood of poetry and essays, giving voice to his views on nationality. When an edition of his poems was published after his death in 1848 the editor wrote that 'here, youth of Ireland, in this little book is a Psalter of Nationality'. Ballads like 'A nation once again', 'The west's asleep', or 'Lament for the death of Owen Roe O'Neill' were calculated to arouse strong feelings against the English. In the O'Neill ballad, for example, he wrote in the very first stanza that him 'they feared to meet with steel' (O'Neill) they 'slew with poison' and the poet cried:

> May God wither up their hearts! May their blood cease to flow!
> May they walk in living death, who poisoned Eoghan Ruadh.

Had O'Neill not been poisoned 'our dear country had been free'; but because he is dead it is 'slaves we'll ever be'.

Many others wrote patriotic ballads in the *Nation*, calculated to revive memories of past glories, even if such memories were bordering on the seditious and thus an embarrassment to O'Connell and most of his followers. On 1 April 1843 'The memory of the dead' was printed. This revolutionary ballad commemorating the 1798 rising was written by John Kells Ingram, a young Trinity scholar, and it set out to remind people that not too long ago 'the brave' had risen 'in dark and evil days to right their native land'. But because 'Might can conquer Right' they had failed. Their memory lives on:

> may it be
> For us a guiding light,
> To chart our strife for liberty,
> And teach us to unite.

The ballad suddenly brought the 1798 rebellion into focus as a political model to be copied. Indeed it was later included as evidence when Duffy of the *Nation* was charged, with others, of 'unlawful seditious opposition . . . to government and constitution'. It was immensely popular, was included in *The Spirit of the Nation*, a collection of ballads published in June 1843, and led O'Connell in July to denounce 1798 as unrepresentative of the nation. The rebels, he said, were the 'unfortunate dupes of British policy'. Davis, in reply, defended what he called 'just war' and urged that if a man takes arms to defend 'truth, country and freedom, may glory sit upon his tomb'. Those Irish who had made the name of the United Irishmen 'a name of reproach' he denounced as slaves who simply reflected their 'master's calumny'.

At the other end of the social scale from Ingram was John Keegan, a Catholic peasant and a product of a 'hedge school' education, who gives us a unique access to the kind of thinking which the ordinary lower class Catholic of rural Ireland voiced in his locality. In 'The Irish Reaper's Harvest Hymn', addressed to Holy Mary, he shows a depth of hatred which borders on the blasphemous. He wanders far from home

> To toil for the dark-haired, cold hearted foe,
> Who mocks me, and hates me, and calls me a slave,
> An alien, a savage – all names but a knave.
>> But, blessed be Mary!
>> My sweet, holy Mary!
> The bodagh he never dare call me a knave.

It is only Mary who keeps his 'rough hand from red murder' and from revenge on tyrants:

> But sure in the end our dear freedom we'll gain
> And wipe from the green flag each Sassanach stain.

He prays that Mary will 'give hearts to the timid'

>> And then, Mother Mary!
>> Our own blessed Mary!
> Light Liberty's flame in the heart of the slave!

Another Davis, the Presbyterian Francis (the Belfastman, as he called himself) also wrote for the *Nation*, again trying to keep alive the unity of all Irishmen, no matter what their religion, and in poems like 'My Southern Brother' commented on the loneliness of division, urging all to 'sing our wild anthems of freedom together'. In another poem he proclaimed:

> Our island has wakened to freedom again;
> 'Twas only in slumber she thought of a chain!

Bad as most of the poetry in the *Nation* was, it had enormous political importance. Not only did it popularize Irish songs and Irish history, it inspired the Catholic people whom O'Connell was trying to galvanize into action in support of repeal. Davis and the other leading Young Irelanders had joined the Repeal Association in 1841 and played a leading part in the organization of the movement. It was the perception of increasing Catholic, and particularly clerical, dominance which began to alienate them. O'Connell had consistently remained true to his firm belief in non-sectarian politics, notwithstanding his own deep Catholic religious beliefs. In July 1840 he had declared that the question to be asked by all repealers was 'not to what religion a man belongs, but whether he is a true-born Irishman'. Even earlier, in 1833, he had gone so far as to proclaim that he wished 'to obviate the possibility of a Catholic ascendancy' in Ireland. He was one of the most vociferous in parliament speaking on behalf of the Presbyterians who were attempting to establish the legality of marriages between them and Anglicans and he kept up the pressure until a new law was enacted in 1844. But as the repeal movement gathered momentum in the 1840s he found it increasingly difficult to maintain a real independence of the Catholic hierarchy in all political matters. Dependence on the bishops, and more especially the lower clergy in the day-to-day activities of the repeal movement, limited his options.

Education, always a sensitive subject for the Catholic hierarchy, revealed the problem. The creation of the 'Irish national system of education' in 1831, far ahead of anything available in England for nearly 40 years, had seen upwards of 4,500 schools provide a largely state-funded education for over 511,000 pupils by 1850. Intended to be non-denominational and therefore a potential source of conflict with the Catholic church, these national schools had rapidly become sectarian at the wish of the different denominations, with the manager in each case the local Catholic priest, the appropriate rector or minister or, occasionally, landlord. But the proposal in 1845 to establish new non-denominational university colleges in Ireland brought a confrontation in which O'Connell and the Repeal Association became involved. Led by Archbishop MacHale of Tuam, a faction of the Catholic bishops opposed the proposals vigorously and demanded denominational colleges. In his Lenten pastoral in 1846, MacHale even blamed the famine on these 'godless colleges'. In December 1844 O'Connell had already publicly argued that 'education in literature and religion should not be separated' and in May 1845 he described the new colleges as 'godless' and 'infidel'. Worse, in recounting the events of the session of parliament in which the proposal was debated, he used the term 'old Irish' to describe those who were opposed to the legislation, revealing a latent belief that those who were not Catholic and Gaelic were at best 'new Irish' and thus somehow lacking in true Irishness.

Increasingly 'Irish' and 'Catholic' were being identified, the very opposite to the kind of secular nation which Davis and Young Ireland advocated. When the Repeal Association publicly debated the new colleges on 26 May 1845, the bigotry of one speaker (Michael Conway, an old Trinity friend of Davis), denouncing the 'theories of Young Ireland' who were 'masked infidels', was tumultuously applauded, even by O'Connell, not least when he said that any attempt (such as, by implication, the new colleges) to restore a Protestant ascendancy must be resisted. Davis and the other Young Irelanders present were shocked and though O'Connell later tried to make peace, it was too late. He insisted that those who still favoured the 'godless colleges' should resign from the Association, but as Davis wrote in a letter in June he and the other Young Irelanders refused to do so 'to avert disaster for our cause and country'.

When Thomas Davis died suddenly on 16 September 1845, still only 30 years old, O'Connell was genuinely heart-broken. But the breach became unbridgeable. In July 1846 the Association accepted O'Connell's declaration that 'the principles of the Association to be the utter and total disclaimer of the contemplation of physical force' and he told the general meeting that his resolution was intended 'to draw a marked line between the Young Ireland and the Old Ireland'. The Young Irelanders began to withdraw, a conference in December 1846 failed to bring about a reunion and in January 1847 they set up a new association of their own, the Irish Confederation. They still had the *Nation* to propagate their ideas and when those proved too moderate for the radical Ulster Presbyterian, John Mitchel, he founded his own newspaper, *United Irishman*, in February 1848.

Mitchell had already outraged O'Connell when he published in the *Nation* guidelines on how best to ambush military on the move along railway lines. In his own paper he now resurrected the notion of an Irish republic and even suggested revolution. In April 1848 he called on the people 'to strike for a republic . . . to raise the Irish tricolour, orange, white and green, over a forest of Irish pikes'. And a month later he wrote that what Ireland needed was '*not* a return to our "ancient constitution" . . . but an Irish republic one and indivisible'.

The outbreak of revolution in France and the attempt of a delegation of Irish nationalists to win the support of the new revolutionary government in Paris galvanized the London government into action. Mitchel, Smith O'Brien (a Protestant landlord who had led that delegation) and Thomas Francis Meagher were charged with sedition. Mitchel was convicted and was sentenced to be transported for 14 years. The public outcry brought about a new alignment of dissident repealers into the Irish League (formed by uniting the Irish Confederation with the Loyal National Repeal Association), with the use of force no longer absolutely forbidden and members of the clubs arming themselves. When *habeas corpus* was suspended on 22 July and membership of Confederate clubs made illegal, the leaders decided that armed rebellion was the only possible answer.

Preparations were minimal, though not entirely hopeless. Help had been promised, for example, from the Clyde area of Scotland and Thomas D'Arcy Magee, who had become secretary of the Confederation in 1847, went to arrange shipping for armed volunteers who were to land at Killala, scene of the French invasion in 1798. But before he had got very far he was recognized and fled to Donegal where he tried to continue with the preparations. But everywhere the people failed to respond in any numbers and the planned rebellion came to an abrupt halt when the leaders, lacking the ruthless streak necessary for successful revolutions, surrendered to the police at Balingarry in county Tipperary, rather than burn them out of the Widow McCormak's house and destroy her in the process. Thus ended the 'cabbage patch' revolution.

But it was not without effect. The leaders, including O'Brien and Meagher, were convicted and transported to join Mitchel in exile. Many other Young Irelanders made their escape to North America, where they contributed to the fierce hostility to English misrule in Ireland. James Stephens and others reached Paris and later helped to found the Fenian movement which was to keep alive the tradition of rebellion against British injustice. The legacy of 1848 was to live on. John Mitchel, in his *Jail Journal*, insisted that as a result of the rebellion:

> 'the breach [with England] is every way widened and deepened; arms are multiplied, notwithstanding proclamations and searches; a fund of treason and disaffection is laid up for future use; and it will burn into the heart of the country till it find vent'.

One reason for the failure of the rebels to excite a rural society long accustomed to peasant revolution of one sort or another was that the countryside was suffering from the most horrific natural disaster to hit Ireland since the Black Death of the fourteenth century, the great famine. In what Oscar Wilde later described as a 'famine-murdered land', the struggle to stay alive took precedence over all else. Early in September 1845 a fungal disease, now simply called the potato blight, hit the potato crop during a particularly wet harvest season. Less than one third of the crop was lost, enough to put many lives in danger. But in 1846 the blight appeared in July and the disaster was nearly total. As early as 7 August, in a letter to Trevelyan, the assistant secretary to the English treasury, the famous Father Mathew ('apostle of temperance') said that 'the food of a whole nation has perished'. Even though the blight did not return in 1847, it was too late. So few potatoes had been planted that the crop was small. The blight was back in 1848 and hardly any potatoes were harvested. Less severe in 1849, it had virtually disappeared in 1850. Other crops, too, had suffered from the bad weather. Even the number of sheep and pigs fell dramatically. The impact was widespread and disastrous.

Most Irish people were dependent on the potato for food and survival, a highly dangerous situation which was potentially life-threatening. An eminent Dublin physician, Dominic Corrigan, had witnessed the disastrous effect of food shortage in 1826. Huge numbers died of related diseases and he warned the government that 'a pestilence and disease of unprecedented magnitude will befall us' if the people were not provided with an alternative to the potato as a source of food, because sooner or later there would be a blight. The Devon commission, established in 1843 to inquire into land occupation, had estimated that there were at least 326,000 occupying land plots insufficient to support a family of five. Ireland was on the brink of disaster and the crop failure of 1845 initiated a trauma that was to change the island forever. The devastating impact can most easily be measured by the decline in population revealed by census figures. In 1821 there were nearly seven million people in Ireland. In 1831 this had increased by over 14 per cent to nearly 7,800,000. Ten years later it was over 8,100,000, an increase of over 5 per cent. But in

1851, this had fallen to just over six and a half million, a loss of nearly 20 per cent. This decline continued, with each census showing a fall, so that by 1901 there was just under four and a half million people in Ireland, approaching half the number before the famine. It is clear that while deaths were responsible for some of this decline, emigration played its part. In 1841, for example, there were nearly 290,000 Irish-born people living in England and Wales, with another 126,000 in Scotland. Even before the famine, then, emigration from Ireland was already substantial. But flight from hunger inflated the figures. In 1850 nearly 962,000 Irish-born people were living in the USA; and in 1852 the number in Britain had jumped to nearly 730,000. By 1860 the numbers had increased to 1,600,000 in the USA and well over 800,000 in Britain.

There had been disasters before. In August 1816 crop failure had resulted in famine. An outbreak of typhus in September became endemic, lasted for three years, and led to 50,000 deaths. But the great famine resulted in a million deaths, partly from starvation but more from different diseases which were associated with the hunger. This was a catastrophe on a scale which numbed the imagination. Peel's government made an immediate response to the first outbreak, when it appeared that the scale of the disaster was much less than it turned out to be. He not only established a scientific commission to investigate the causes of the blight, he secretly purchased about £100,000 worth of Indian meal in the USA to be used in emergency in Ireland. Between September 1846, when the full scale of the tragedy became obvious, and the end of 1847, the main form of assistance was through public works. At its peak, this provided wages for 715,000 men, which supported some three and a half million people. In 1847, too, the government established soup kitchens all over Ireland and each day gave rations of food to about three million people. Logistically this was an almost unbelievable achievement and helped greatly to reduce mortality. But it did not last. Late in 1847 the kitchens closed and people starved again.

Altogether the British government spent over nine million pounds on various projects to counteract the effects of the famine, a tiny fraction of what was needed. It was believed that had they stopped food leaving the country, people might not have starved in such numbers. In 1782–4 during an earlier shortage, a Dublin government had closed down the ports. But widespread notions of free trade and other economic arguments made it nearly impossible for the government to do this in 1846. In any case it might not have achieved much, or so the argument goes. In 1847 only 10 per cent of the total production of oats was exported. But much of this came from the areas worst affected. Between January and September 1847 for example, 75 ships left Tralee, mostly loaded with grain which they landed in Liverpool. Some of this was sold on to Europe, where prices were particularly high. In all, nearly 4,000 vessels carrying different kinds of life-saving food left Ireland. Small wonder that the unofficial estimate of the constabulary was that 400,000 people died during the winter.

In England the common view, especially among liberals, was that not only the peasants, but the landlords as well, were useless and state intervention would only encourage them to do nothing to help themselves. They would not even show gratitude for any social welfare provided by the state, a view which the 1848 rebellion seemed to confirm. Much more serious was the belief in some quarters that the loss of people would be of economic benefit in the long run and the misguided conviction of others that what had happened was the will of God, not to be challenged. In August 1847 Lord Clarendon, the lord lieutenant, wrote to the prime minister in England: 'We shall be equally blamed for keeping [the Irish] alive or letting them die and we have only to select between the censures of the Economists or the Philanthropists – which do you prefer?'

In Ireland the horrors which were daily revealed were in themselves a condemnation. The famous war correspondent William Russell, a graduate of Trinity, was sent to Ireland by the *Times* to report and wrote an account of what he witnessed during his journey through the west 'in an agony of suffering and death'. Later he wrote that 'in all my subsequent career . . . breakfasting, dining and supping full of horrors in the tide of war I never beheld sights so shocking as those which met my eyes in that famine tour of mine in the West'. The stories which were published horrified readers everywhere and charitable donations poured in, not just from England but from all over the world. Private soup kitchens were organized, especially by groups such as the Society of Friends, and these saved many lives. But for some it became almost a sideshow. From London came the famous French chef of the Reform Club, Alexis Soyer, who set up a soup kitchen in the Phoenix Park in Dublin in 1847. There he dispensed a soup to his own recipe at a charge of only £1 per 100 gallons. Dublin's elite came to watch, paying well for the privilege. On 6 April the *Freeman's Journal* reported:

> 'Dublin society pays 5 shillings each to see paupers feed on Soyer's soup. Five shillings each to watch the burning blush of shame chasing pallidness from poverty's cheek! When the animals in the Zoological Gardens can be inspected at feeding time for sixpence!'

Whole families were wiped out and many more broken up for ever. On the Blasket islands a woman, known afterwards as Grey Bridie, lost her husband and eight children. She had to bury them herself in the graveyard at Ballynahown. When she finally buried the last, she blessed them all:

> 'Rest in peace, dear children and gentle husband. You need have no fear of wakening till the sea flows from the north and the raven turns white . . . I leave you at rest in God's grace till the Angel sounds the trumpet on the last day'.

In January 1850 the workhouses were caring for no less than 119,628 children who knew neither their surnames or if any of their parents were alive. Even many of those who managed to escape and find their way towards England or America were unlucky. In December 1846, for example, a steamer (*Londonderry*) which left Sligo port with a mixed cargo of emigrants and cattle ran into a storm at sea. The 178 emigrants on board were forced below to where the cattle were housed and before the ship reached Liverpool it was discovered that 89 of them had suffocated. No wonder that 'coffin ships' became the common name applied to many of the vessels plying this trade in emigrants.

For this, too, the authorities were blamed. Wherever the truth lies, the English were widely condemned for what had happened in Ireland. John Mitchel forcefully expressed the common belief that England had deliberately encouraged the conditions which brought about starvation and death in Ireland, for her own economic benefit: 'Without famine in Ireland, England could not live as she had a right to expect; and the exact complement of a comfortable family dinner in England, is a coroner's inquest in Ireland: verdict, *Starvation*'. In her poem *The Famine Year*, Speranza (later Lady Wilde) finished with lines that for years afterwards were quoted in hatred of those believed to have been responsible:

> But our whitening bones against ye shall rise as witnesses,
> From the cabins and the ditches, in their charred uncoffin'd masses,
> For the Angel of the Trumpet will know them as he passes.
> A ghastly spectral army, before great God we'll stand,
> And arraign ye as our murderers, the spoilers of our land.

To this day the landscape in many parts of the island, particularly in the west, still shows the scars of this disaster – deserted cottages, even villages; abandoned lazybeds on hillsides; a network of tiny roads built as public works. In a very short time Irish society was changed for ever. Most of the small-holders vanished, as did the landless labourers. By 1851 more than 26 per cent of the tenants had holdings of over 30 acres (as against only 7 per cent in 1841). Larger holdings of land meant that pasture replaced tillage on much land, with stock providing an increasing family income. Tenants either married later, or remained bachelors, so that family size fell and family holdings of land increased; all of this was in some degree the result of another terrible legacy of the great famine. For various reasons, not least because landlords were unwilling to pay the rates for which they were liable on all holdings under £4 in valuation, huge numbers of small-holders were evicted, often in the most shocking of circumstances. In 1849 no less than 13,384 families were evicted and over 14,500 a year later. While the numbers declined thereafter, eviction became commonplace in the Irish countryside.

Evictions brought to the fore the vexed question of security of tenure for tenants and reform of the land system in general. It became an ingredient in the mix which was to dominate Irish politics in the future. As early as 1848 James Fintan Lalor had urged that repeal should be linked 'like a railway carriage to a train' to the more popular cause of land reform. In 1859 John Mitchel, for long a protagonist of revolutionary republicanism, wrote that he was 'no republican doctrinaire . . . I am convinced, and long have been, that the mass of the Irish people cannot be roused in an quarrel less than social revolution, destruction of landlordism, and denial of all title and tenure derived from English sovereigns'. In the years after the famine the land question did replace repeal as the primary political target and attracted politicians who believed in constitutional methods, as well as others who were convinced that only the use of physical force, or revolutionary methods, would compel England to reform the land system in Ireland.

Many landlords, for various reasons, had faced bankruptcy for years and the added cost of famine relief, with which they were charged by the English government, ruined them. Their estates were unproductive and opinion in England was that what were called 'nominal and embarrassed proprietors' by an English economist in 1849 should make way for new landlords with the capital and initiative to make the land pay. The encumbered estates acts of 1848 and 1849 made it possible for lands to be sold and it was even hoped by some that tenants might be able to purchase their holdings. But it was mainly speculators who moved in, determined to make a quick profit on their investments, at the expense of the smaller tenants where necessary. 'Tenant right' quickly became a matter of public concern. In 1850 the Tenant League was formed by Duffy, with the intent of legalizing what became known as the '3 Fs' (fair rent, fixity of tenure, freedom of sale) and extending it throughout Ireland.

In the 1852 general election supporters of the League did well and a conference in Dublin, attended by 41 MP's, agreed that they should remain 'independent of, and in opposition to' any government which did not give legal effect to the demands of the Tenant League. In parliament about 48 Irish MP's eventually joined what amounted to an independent Irish party, intending to exploit the situation at Westminster. Known as 'The Irish Brigade', and later, more significantly, as 'The Pope's Brass Band', they failed to stay united. Some, most notably two of the leaders, Sadleir and Keogh, were bribed by office into conformity, and others were swayed by the growing opposition in some ecclesiastical quarters, especially from Cullen, the Catholic Archbishop of Dublin. The number of MP's who remained loyal to the League continued to decline until in 1859 only five voted according to the pledge of tenant right which they had accepted seven years previously. The Tenant League disappeared and with it the independent Irish party at Westminster.

By then the seeds sown in 1848 had come to fruition with the founding of what became known as the Irish Republican Brotherhood (IRB), or more popularly the Fenian movement, in 1858. Looking back from 1896, the famous Fenian leader John O'Leary had no doubt that 'Fenianism was the natural, or at least a natural, outcome of Young Irelandism'. Despite his admiration for Lalor and Mitchel, both of whom had inspired him as a young revolutionary in 1848, he could not believe that the 'land question' had any part in 'an Irish insurrectionary movement'. Sympathy for the wretched condition of the peasantry, and contempt for the cruelty of landlords, was natural. But he firmly believed that 'the full remedy for that wretchedness and those wrongs could only come from freedom . . . English rule remaining, I saw little chance of the satisfactory settlement of the land question, or, indeed, of any question'. He, and some of the other founders of Fenianism (James Stephens, John O'Mahony, Thomas Luby, Charles Kickham and Martin Doheny), had been implicated in the 1848 rising and were firm believers in the use of physical force to achieve independence.

A secret military society was organized on a national basis, the members swearing 'allegiance to the Irish Republic, now virtually established'. Though concentrated on the workers in town and country, the Young Ireland tradition of appeal to middle class intellectuals was not neglected. Edmund O'Donovan, a younger son of the famous Irish scholar John O'Donovan, became a Fenian while still at Trinity, like his brother before him who had founded a 'circle' (as the basic unit of organization was called) in the college. Edmund was appointed the 'centre', or head, of that circle by James Stevens himself, when it contained between 80 and 100 members.

When Terence Bellew Mac Manus, one of the revolutionary leaders of 1848, died in California in 1861, his body was brought home for burial. Cardinal Cullen banned it from the Pro-Cathedral and it was believed that no Catholic church in Dublin would receive the corpse. From the Mechanics' Institute, where the body had lain in state for over a week, the funeral procession to Glasnevin took place on 10 November. Up to 8,000 marched behind the hearse and as many as ten times that number crowded the streets. At the graveside Luby delivered a passionate oration and gave voice to the Fenian hope that the example of the dead hero would give 'us faith and stern resolve to do the work for which Mac Manus died'. This great funeral not only demonstrated the apparent level of popular support for the Fenian aspiration of independence, but also inaugurated what became thereafter a republican tradition of exploiting the funerals of all dead heroes.

Fenianism had been established in New York on the very same day as in Dublin, with the expectation of exploiting not only the anti-English sentiments of the huge Irish population in the USA, but also of drawing on the military experience of many of those Irish. At its strongest, as many as 45 thousand had joined the brotherhood there and these included many in the famous New York Irish regiment, the 'Fighting 69th', as well as in other regiments. It was also essential that the same Irish would make available the funds and arms which were necessary before any revolution could be contemplated in Ireland when the opportunity arose. In the event very little money ever came from America.

But the American IRB engaged in a spectacular attack on British North America when they invaded Canada in June 1866. No less than 24,000 veterans of the civil war were involved, with some artillery and supported by three former US warships. The aim was to occupy territory which then could be used when future negotiations took place with the British for Irish independence. The IRB troops actually defeated the British in two military engagements and caused such anxiety that the Westminster government entered into negotiations with President Johnson for help in curtailing the invasion, promising $15 million in compensation for supporting the south in the civil war and ceding claims to some territories in dispute. More important, when the Dominion of Canada was recognized in May 1867, the premier of New Brunswick acknowledged that had the IRB invasion not taken place, the British would never have agreed to the union of the Canadian provinces. Far from being the farce so often depicted, this IRB invasion might easily have strengthened the hand of the Irish Fenians in their pursuit of Irish freedom.

By 1864 it was estimated that up to 54,000 had taken the oath in Ireland, of whom no less than 8,000 were said to be serving in the British army regiments stationed there. Such was their public impact that in that same year 'Fenianism' was added to the index of registered papers in the chief secretary's office in Dublin castle. Preparations were well in hand for rebellion, with rifles being purchased in Britain. When Stephens announced that 1865 would witness the founding of the republic, the government reacted. In September he and other Fenian leaders were arrested and though he escaped, making his way to New York, the opportunity to take advantage of the ending of the Civil War in America was lost. It was an American Fenian, Thomas Kelly, a former captain in the Federal army, who took charge of preparations. With other Irish-American officers he came to England and planned a rebellion in February 1867. They also established a provisional Republican government. But plans went hopelessly astray. An attempt to seize arms from Chester castle on 11 February and a premature rising in Kerry on 12 February alerted the government and many Fenians were arrested, including Kelly and other leaders. But on the night of 4–5 March the rebellion went ahead as planned. In Dublin it was estimated by the police that as many as 8,000 Fenians had mustered on Tallaght hill, despite the bitter cold and adverse weather conditions. But without leadership most of those took no part in any action and made their way back into the city in the morning. One group captured two small police barracks, some others exchanged fire with the police, and that was the end. There was some action in counties Cork, Clare, Limerick, Tipperary, Louth and Queen's County. The police estimate that the total number of deaths on both sides was 12 gives the best indication of how limited the military action really was. After the rebellion Fenianism seemed dead.

But it was given new life by events in England. During a raid on a police van in Manchester in September 1867, in an attempt to rescue the head of the IRB and another Fenian, one of the guards, Sergeant Brett, was accidentally killed by the shot which broke the lock. Three men were brought to trial, convicted, and executed on 23 November. The three, Allen, Larkin and O'Brien, became known as the 'Manchester martyrs' and provided Fenianism with popular heroes who helped to keep Republican sentiments alive. A ballad written by T.D. Sullivan, 'God save Ireland', the cry of the three martyrs in the dock, became a national anthem. In December 1867 another attempt to rescue a Fenian prisoner, Richard O'Sullivan Burke, from Clerkenwell, using gunpowder to demolish a wall, killed 12 people and further outraged public opinion in England. Michael Barret was tried for his part in the killing, convicted, and executed at Newgate on 26 May 1868, the last public execution in England. When the supreme council of the IRB met in Dublin on 24 April 1868, however, it had unreservedly condemned the Clerkenwell explosion as:

> 'this dreadful and deplorable event . . . No language we could employ would express our horror and indignation respecting this event; and were the perpetrators within our control, and amenable to our laws, their punishment would be commensurate with our sense of justice'.

When a viceregal proclamation of 12 December 1867 declared 'Manchester martyr' funeral processions illegal, it was a sure indication of the popular level of Fenian sentiment sweeping Ireland. Down in Kerry, in his sermon on Sunday 17 February, after the Fenian rising near Caherciveen, Bishop Moriarty castigated what he called 'the heads of the Fenian conspiracy' in words which have remained famous ever since: '. . . we must acknowledge that eternity is not long enough nor hell hot enough to punish such miscreants'. In January 1868 he issued a letter to his clergy forbidding masses to be celebrated for the 'Manchester martyrs'. But all over Ireland masses were said, even in public, and in Dublin Cullen told his priests that it was right to pray for the dead Fenians and even to say masses for them in private.

The priests now once again became increasingly involved in nationalist politics supporting the movement for the release of Fenian convicts. Even Cullen interceded, successfully, for the reprieve of Thomas Burke, who had been sentenced to death for his role in the Fenian risings. Popular support for Fenian convicts was manifested by collections taken up at mass in many churches during 1869, especially on St Patrick's day. An Irish MP, J.F. Maguire, told Gladstone that popular demand for the release of the Fenians was the reason for the lack of Irish support for him: 'The most loyal Catholics – Bishops, Priests, Magistrates, men of wealth and station – earnestly desire their freedom'. Gladstone himself was aware that change was desperately needed, not least in the land system, and admitted in parliament that 'the Fenian conspiracy had an important influence with respect to Irish policy', precipitating a new programme of reform. For that reason, if for no other, Fenianism had a positive effect in determining the future course of events.

Even before the famine, in 1845, the young Gladstone had stated his belief that Ireland's unhappy condition was the result of 'cruel, inveterate, and half-atoned injustice'. Now that he was prime minister he set himself to redress this injustice, and in the process to gain the support of Catholic Ireland. One sign that a new era had arrived was the appointment of Thomas O'Hagan in 1868 as the first Catholic lord chancellor since the reign of James II. In March 1868 in the commons Gladstone proposed the disestablishment of the Church of Ireland. One year later, after the general election which made him prime minister, he introduced his Irish church bill and on 22 July 1869 the Irish Church Act was passed in the commons. Even though about half of the temporalities and church property, worth about eight million pounds, was retained by the Church of Ireland, the legislation was seen by many Irish Protestants as a betrayal, even an attack on the union itself of which, it was argued, a united Church of Great Britain and Ireland was an integral part. But the Catholic reaction was positive, seeing disestablishment as a confirmation of hopes raised by Gladstonian liberalism and justifying their support for Liberals in the 1868 election, when they won 66 of the 105 seats in Ireland. It indicated that it was within the union, and not in any republic, even if one could be achieved, that Ireland's political future lay.

Gladstone himself said that there was what he called a 'group of questions' relating to Ireland which together made up 'the many branches from one trunk, and that trunk is the tree of what is called the Protestant ascendancy'. One of these 'questions' had already been answered by the disestablishment and disendowment of the Church of Ireland, which in one way ended its privileged position. Other 'questions' were 'the land of Ireland' and 'the education of Ireland', supporting a privileged ascendancy, and both of these had to be addressed. In 1870 he introduced his first land act, which attempted for the first time to give some protection in law to tenants. It fell far short of what was demanded, even though it gave Irish tenants rights which were not enjoyed elsewhere in the United Kingdom or even in Europe. But it did indicate that landlordism as it existed could only be reformed through parliamentary legislation and strengthened the growing belief that constitutional politics was the only way through which justice for Ireland might be procured.

University education provided Gladstone with another opportunity to meet Catholic claims. But his university bill of 1873 satisfied neither Catholic or Protestant interests and provoked such antagonism that it was defeated in parliament. The general election which followed in 1874 saw the Conservatives, under Disraeli, returned to power and in Ireland the total defeat of the Liberals, who won only 10 of the 105 seats. This was the first general election to be fought under the ballot act of 1872, which introduced secret voting for the first time. Thirty-three Conservatives were returned. But most significantly of all, what were called 'home rulers' won no less than 60 seats. Of these, 46 were Catholics; but only six were landowners and one the younger son of a landowner, an enormous change in the social mix of elected MP's. Most of them had already declared their support for denominational education, in opposition to the non-sectarian character of Gladstone's legislation; and they also supported fixity of tenure for all tenants. They thus gained the backing of the local Catholic clergy, as well as the support of the tenant farmers, powerful assets when elections had to be fought.

It was Isaac Butt who had set this home rule movement in motion. From being an arch Conservative while at Trinity, the founder of the *Dublin University Magazine* and the defender of Protestant ascendancy against the Catholic threat represented by O'Connell and his repeal politics, he had become a believer in the notion that a new federal United Kingdom was the only way to secure Protestant rights in Ireland. By 1848, when he was briefed to defend Meagher and O'Brien against the charge of sedition, he argued that they were not guilty of the charge of contempt of the crown, but of contempt of the union. In his defence the basis of his argument was a justification of repeal and because of this he became something of a national hero, praised in the *Nation*: 'No man since Grattan has a greater career open to him if he be true to the principles he himself has taught'. His experience in defending Fenians had made him think deeply on what he described as 'the depth, the breadth, the sincerity of that love of fatherland that misgovernment had tortured into disaffection and misgovernment', and which 'driving men to despair, had exaggerated into revolt'.

Elected to parliament in 1852, his experiences in the House of Commons convinced him that Irish affairs were neglected and by the time he lost his seat in 1865 he was converted to the view that only in an Irish parliament could this be rectified. He again achieved prominence as the leading barrister for the Fenians during their trials. Even though he did not agree with their republican and separatist notions, their sincerity impressed him and helped him to clarify further his notions of federalism. In 1868 he founded the Amnesty Association to procure the release of Fenian prisoners. In March 1870 he published under his own name a pamphlet which had enormous influence: *Ireland's appeal for amnesty: a letter to W.E. Gladstone*. The Government established a commission, chaired by the Earl of Devon, and as a result many Fenians (including such notables as O'Leary, Luby, Devoy, Mulcahy and O'Donovan Rossa) were released in January 1871.

In 1870, too, Butt published his *Home government for Ireland: Irish federalism, its meaning, its objects, and its hopes*. He was able to declare: 'I have long since had the conviction forced upon me that it is equally essential to the safety of England and the happiness and tranquillity of Ireland, that the right of self-government should be restored to this country'. He now outlined how the United Kingdom might be federalized. In the Irish parliament, the House of Lords would have the power of veto, thus preventing legislation like the 1869 and 1870 acts relating to church and land which had caused such distress to Protestant interests.

He organized a meeting in Dublin in May 1870, to consider his proposals for Irish self-government. Out of it came the Home Government Association, with the aim of setting up a new federal system, including an Irish parliament dealing with the affairs of Ireland. 'All questions affecting the imperial crown and government' would still be settled by the Westminster parliament, in which Ireland would continue to be represented. Soon this was identified as a policy of 'home rule' and that was the title which eventually became common. Although some home rule candidates contested by-elections between 1870 and 1874, they met with success only where tenant right and denominational education were added to the policy advocated. In this way home rule quickly became identified with Catholic rather than Protestant concerns. When Mitchell Henry was returned unopposed in the Galway by-election of 1871, it was because in addition to making home rule his political goal, he had added 'denominational education' and, most markedly, the maintenance in Italy of 'the dignity and independence of the pope'.

Liberals, too, were increasingly attracted to the home rule organization, especially when the widespread opposition to the non-denominational nature of Gladstone's educational programme became apparent. On 20 September 1873 A.M. Sullivan wrote in the *Nation* of 'the necessity of enlisting in the home rule cause the whole strength of the country'. A reorganization was called for. The Catholic Bishop of Cloyne in the same issue of the *Nation* proposed 'the holding of an aggregate meeting in Dublin of the representatives of all interested in this great question – and they are the entire people, without distinction of class or creed'. And Sullivan wrote that the new organization would be one 'which will embrace the whole manhood and intellect of the home rule within its fold, and which will strike its roots deep in the population of every barony and every parish'. It was to be a return to the days of O'Connell and the political mobilization of the rural population in a manner unique in Europe.

On 18 November 1873 a meeting was held in the Rotunda in Dublin, with 800 attending, but it represented many more than that. At Butt's suggestion, the proposal to summon the meeting had been widely circulated and was returned with 25,000 signatures. The night before, a meeting of Fenian leaders was held and it was agreed to support Butt. Four years before this the supreme council of the IRB had adopted what it called 'the constitution of the Irish Republic'; but then on 12 January 1870 the Fenians had been condemned by the Holy Office in Rome. In the same month, in an 'Address of the IRB supreme council to the people of Ireland', the leadership advised members that 'common sense would also point out to us the advisability of giving preference to our friends in all our dealings', a Masonic principle which was to govern members in commercial as well as political activities. In the 17 March 1873 amended constitution of the IRB it was explicitly laid down that it 'shall confine itself in time of peace to the exercise of moral force'; that 'the IRB shall await the decision of the Irish nation, as expressed by a majority of the Irish people, as to the fit hour of inaugurating a war against England', in the meanwhile lending 'its support to every movement calculated to advance the cause of Irish independence'. This constitution implicitly condemned the 1867 rising and the Clerkenwell explosion, and would have made the future 1916 rising unlawful. More important at the time, it cleared the way to support Butt and home rule and some leading Fenians attended the Rotunda meeting, speaking to endorse Butt's proposals.

Now the Home Rule League was established and set out its policy, as reported in a journal, 'in the significant order of denominational education, land without rent, and home rule'. Political realism had at last impinged on Butt. The result was the extraordinary success, with the minimum of preparation, but with the local support of Fenian and clerical organizations alike, in the general election of 1874. The new MP's met in Dublin and constituted themselves a 'separate and distinct party in the House of Commons'. A great new era in Irish politics was inaugurated.

Butt was determined, as he said himself in 1875, 'to press upon the British parliament the legislation which we believe the pressing wants of our country need'. In pursuit of this, he adopted a policy of putting a superfluity of Irish business on the order book. In 1876 home rulers gave notice of 16 bills and of 15 in 1877. Where other legislation was seen to be against Irish interests, opposition was prolonged. On 25 July 1874 a bill was introduced which contained, among other matters, the retention of special powers for preserving the peace in Ireland; the Irish members fought it for seven hours, causing the house to divide three times. A week later they again opposed the committee stage, arguing until 3.45 a.m. and causing the house to divide eight times. Not until late the following night was the bill finally carried, after substantial amendments. Such activity, however, produced little that was positive, largely because the Irish party was badly organized, lacking discipline, and with too few members willing to pursue it energetically. One MP, Joseph Biggar of Belfast, decided to adopt a 'filibustering' policy which would further delay bills. On 22 April 1875, for example, he spoke for nearly four hours. In this policy of using the rules of the house to obstruct the passage of bills, Biggar was quickly joined by other home rulers. On 6 March 1876 they caused the house to divide 17 times. By 1877 they were intervening in debates on bills which had no Irish connection.

Butt refused to accept the validity of this new approach, believing as he did in the dignity of the commons and that it would only 'bring discredit and disgrace upon the proceedings'. Obstruction of this kind, he said, was 'the abandonment of constitutional action, and the adoption of unconstitutional action in its stead'. His attempts to prevent the use of obstructionist tactics not only failed, but led in the end to serious divisions within the party and among supporters. His death on 5 May 1879 was sincerely mourned, but his passing did not heal the divisions which plagued the party of which his leadership had become increasingly nominal. In the *Nation* on 10 May the young Timothy Healy wrote:

> 'He gave practical direction to national aspirations, kindled patriotic fire, and then, aided by the spirit he evoked, then? – Then he failed. Before his death so long had he accustomed Irish patriots to look elsewhere for a leader, that now these men will miss him least'.

The new leader was to be Charles Stewart Parnell, who had earlier emerged as Butt's leading opponent in defence of the obstructionist tactics being employed in parliament, which he himself had pursued almost from the first day he took his seat in the House of Commons. In the general election of 1880, 61 home rulers were returned and at a meeting in the City Hall in Dublin in May Parnell was elected party leader.

Parnell was one of the most charismatic figures to emerge in the public life of Ireland in the nineteenth century. On the main street of the capital city the monument to his memory stands at one end, with that to O'Connell at the other. Inscribed are the words which still resonate through nationalist Ireland and which keep his memory alive: 'No man has the right to set a boundary to the march of a nation'. He was a Protestant who became the leader – 'the chief', as he was popularly known – of Catholic Ireland; a landlord who could command rural Ireland; a conservative who secured Fenian support; an enthusiastic cricketer who came to represent Irish Ireland in a way few had achieved before him. But his family had been politically active in Ireland since the eighteenth century. Sir John Parnell, his great-grandfather, had been a minister in Grattan's parliament, favoured Catholic emancipation, and vigorously opposed the union. His son Henry also served in the Irish parliament in 1797 and subsequently at Westminster, supporting Catholic emancipation (in 1808 he published the influential *History of the penal laws against Catholics*) and serving as a minister in a number of Whig Governments. Parnell's grandfather, William, was also an MP at Westminster, published influential writings on the causes of popular discontent in Ireland and in the family tradition also argued strongly in favour of Catholic emancipation. Parnell's mother, the American Delia Tudor Stewart, also came from a family which had played a prominent role in American politics since the War of Independence.

One can say, then, that politics was in his blood and that some sense of Irish nationality was equally deep-rooted. He was rusticated from Cambridge in disgrace in 1869 and had no interest in books, especially those on Irish history in the well-stocked library at his home in Avondale in county Wicklow, where the poet Thomas Moore wrote 'The meeting of the waters' while staying there as a guest. No deep thinker, a notably poor public speaker, he seemed to be incapable of formulating original political ideas. Yet it was he who became the 'Uncrowned King of Ireland', with over a hundred thousand people attending his funeral in Dublin, even though he had died in public disgrace. Because Parnell had the necessary ruthlessness which Butt lacked and the determination to brook no opposition, he brought to the remnants of the home rule party what it had been lacking under Butt and that was a discipline and purpose which made it a cohesive and powerful force in politics. He also had a clear and consistent vision of what he meant by home rule as he clearly expressed it in 1885, in a famous speech in Cork in January. After asking for 'the restitution of that which was stolen from us towards the close of the last century' he continued:

'We cannot ask for less than the restitution of Grattan's Parliament, with its important privileges and wide and far-reaching constitution. We cannot under the British constitution ask for more than the restitution of Grattan's Parliament but no man has a right to say to his country "Thus far shalt thou go and no further" and we have never attempted to fix the *ne plus ultra* to the progress of Ireland's nationhood and we never shall'.

After failing in the Dublin by-election in 1874, he was successful the following year in Meath. In his maiden speech in the commons on 27 March he nailed his nationalist colours firmly to the mast: 'Why should Ireland be treated as a geographical fragment of England . . .? Ireland was not a geographical fragment, but a nation'. But it was his emotional outburst a year later in parliament, when a government spokesman attacked the notion that home rule would liberate those whom he called 'the Manchester murderers', that won Parnell prominence. After shouting 'No! No!' he went on to interject deliberately and coldly: 'I wish to say as publicly and directly as I can that I do not believe, and never shall believe, that any murder was committed at Manchester'. Even Fenians began to look on him as an asset and although both Michael Davit and John Dillon failed to recruit him into the IRB in 1878, his attitude was ambiguous to say the least. He knew that without Fenian support he would never succeed in leadership.

In 1879 he sailed to America to persuade the Fenian organization there, Clan na Gael, to offer financial support. In a public statement he displayed what at best could be construed as an ambiguous attitude to the use of physical force:

'A true revolutionary movement in Ireland should, in my opinion, partake both of constitutional and an illegal character. It should be both and open and a secret organisation, using the Constitution for its own purposes, but also taking advantage of its secret combination'.

Later still, in 1882, there is evidence that Parnell at his own request took the IRB oath in the library of Trinity College. This cannot be absolutely proved. But there is no doubt that what became known as 'the new departure' – a term first used in the New York *Herald* in October 1878 to describe the informal support of the Fenians for Parnell – was of vital importance in Irish politics.

Strong support across rural Ireland was also an essential element in making Parnell's leadership of the home rule movement a potent force in politics. A series of bad harvests produced an agricultural crisis which not only threatened famine, but saw thousands of tenants in default over payment of rents and facing eviction on a scale not seen since the 1840s. In October 1879 a new rural organization, the Irish National Land League, was established. The prime mover in this was Michael Davitt, who had moved from Mayo to Lancashire as a young boy after his family had been evicted from their holding. While working in the local cotton mill he lost his right arm in an accident. So, at the age of 11, unable to work, he turned to schooling. Later converted to Fenianism, he was sentenced to 15 years penal servitude for taking part in the attack on Chester castle in 1870. Released in 1877, he was filled with hatred of the British domination of Ireland, and even more of the dominance of English landlordism. Back in his native Mayo he began to organize the tenants and persuaded Parnell to address a mass-meeting at Westport on 8 June 1879. Parnell told them: 'You must show the landlords that you intend to keep a firm grip of your homesteads and lands. You must not allow yourselves to be dispossessed as you were dispossessed in 1847'. Parnell had addressed mass-meetings of tenants before and had already begun to win their support. At Ballinasloe in November 1878 a letter was read to the meeting from the redoubtable Archbishop MacHale of Tuam, praising Parnell as 'the sterling hereditary advocate of Irish interests'. When Davitt formed the Irish National Land League in October it was no surprise that he asked Parnell to become the first president.

The League engaged in what became known as 'The Land War' of 1879–92. A mass-movement which surpassed even that of O'Connell's greatest days, it supported tenants and fought landlords at every level. Violence was still endemic in many parts of rural Ireland and outrages were frequent. Land was what mattered to most people. The novelist George Bermingham was told by a local nationalist: 'Damn Home Rule! What we're out for is the land. The land matters. All the rest is talk'. It was this passion that Parnell and Davitt tried to tap. The terrible weapon of the boycott was developed to ostracize not only errant landlords and their agents (such as the unfortunate Captain Charles Boycott, of Lough Mask House in county Mayo, after whom the term was first coined), but any person who violated the code of behaviour laid down by the League. Addressing a meeting of farmers in Ennis, Parnell told them that:

'when a man takes a farm from which another has been evicted you must shun him on the roadside when you meet him, you must shun him in the streets of the town, you must shun him at the shop-counter, you must shun him in the fair and in the market-place, and even in the house of worship'.

The success of The Land War can be measured simply by Gladstone's land act of 1881, which initiated a process which successive governments developed over the years through further legislation, by which the old landlord ascendancy was ended and Ireland became a land of peasant proprietors. The tenants became owners of their lands, a social revolution which transformed Ireland. Its achievement was the result of the political and popular agitation led by Parnell and the League. The general election of 1880 which returned Gladstone to power was critical. Tenant rights and land reform had been the election issue in Ireland and Gladstone was made well aware that its solution must be his primary objective. Still determined to do justice to Ireland – as late as 1892 he wrote to a friend: 'I am as fast bound to Ireland as Ulysses was to his mast' – he proceeded to tackle the problem.

In doing so he refused to tolerate the illegalities perpetrated by the Land League (such as the League courts which virtually paralysed the ordinary administration of justice in the countryside) and using special coercive powers he arrested the leaders, including Parnell, and the League was proclaimed illegal. Not even the extraordinary assumption of power by Parnell's sister Anna, who established the Ladies' Land League, diverted him. Eventually in 1882 the so-called Kilmainham treaty saw Parnell released and a new agreement between the two leaders. The murder of the new chief secretary, Lord Frederick Cavendish, and the under-secretary. T.H. Burke, in the Phoenix Park by the Invincibles on 6 May exposed the continuing danger of the proponents of physical force. But it did not divert Gladstone, or Parnell, from the course they were pledged to follow.

The Land War had hardened Parnell's determination to win home rule and had provided him with the popular basis he needed. It had been a great movement of the nation asserting its rights, a great and powerful movement of mass democracy, and it must now be translated into a demand for home rule. The Land League was replaced by a new National League in October 1882, effectively controlled by Parnell and linked to his parliamentary party. Using it to impose party discipline throughout the constituencies, the choice of candidates to contest elections was carefully controlled. Each was made to take a pledge that if elected he would 'sit, act and vote with the Irish parliamentary party' and that if ever he broke this pledge he would resign his seat. In the 1885 general election the party won 85 seats (17 of them in Ulster) and the result persuaded Gladstone that the time had come to introduce a home rule bill in parliament, which he did in 1886. The Conservatives opposed it as not only denying Protestant interests in Ireland, particularly in Ulster, but as a threat to the unity of the empire itself. Some Liberals, too, defected and the bill was defeated. Gladstone had to fight an election specifically on the home rule issue and was soundly beaten. The Conservatives remained in power, except for a brief return of Gladstone in 1892–3, for the next 20 years and assiduously opposed Home Rule.

The great achievement of Parnell was to place home rule firmly on the agenda of English politics. One measure of his success and consequent stature was the attempt of the London *Times* in 1889 to ruin him, and other home rulers, by producing a series of articles purporting to prove their complicity in murder and violence during The Land War. Most spectacular of all was the publication on 18 April of a letter in facsimile, under his own signature, which linked Parnell to the notorious Phoenix Park murders of 1882. A commission of inquiry was established by the government and subsequently the letter was proved to be a forgery, concocted for money by Richard Pigott, a down-at-heel journalist.

Parnell's vindication made him more popular than ever. When next he took his seat in the House of Commons he received a standing ovation from the other members, including the opposition and in July he received the freedom of Edinburgh. His star was clearly in the ascendant. But all was shattered in November 1890, when he was cited as co-respondent in a divorce case. His long-standing relationship with Mrs Katharine O'Shea, wife of a member of his own party, was made public and quickly destroyed him. Victorian England would not tolerate the publicity and Gladstone demanded, for political reasons, that he resign the leadership of his party, even if only temporarily. Parnell refused. In Ireland the party split and Parnell was eventually left with only about one-third of the MPs willing to accept him as leader. On a popular level, too, opinion in Ireland was divided. The Catholic clergy were now ranged against him and 'the chief' travelled the country in a relentless and exhausting campaign to rally support. He suddenly collapsed on 2 October 1891 and died four days later, still only 45 years old.

On the face of it, his behaviour during that last year of his life seems to show that he was an unprincipled opportunist who put himself before the welfare of his party and the cause of home rule. Joseph Chamberlain had said of him that he was 'unscrupulous like all great men'. He was ruthless, as was necessary, and firmly (and rightly) believed that his own leadership was necessary. He knew that none of his possible successors could hold the party together. One, John Dillon, wrote in his diary in the summer of 1880 that he was 'lacking in intensity and continuity of purpose', which indicated his lack of leadership qualities. Parnell's political intelligence convinced him that retirement or any compromise would be a disaster in the long run regardless of the short term. Gladstone's verdict – 'Parnell was the most remarkable man ever met' – was a vindication. Not for nothing was he popularly known as 'the chief'.

He was brought back to Ireland on 11 October and after a massive funeral through the streets of Dublin, he was buried in Glasnevin. A huge boulder of Wicklow granite was later placed over the grave, engraved with the single word *Parnell*. He remained an icon in Irish history subsequently, not just to believers in the constitutional way to win independence, or even to many republicans of the physical force tradition, but to all Irish nationalists. 'Mourn the ivy leaf' (the symbol of the lost leader) became an appropriate epitaph.

14 The struggle for independence

The death of Parnell left the Irish parliamentary party shattered and fragmented during a period which William O'Brien described as 'years of hellish strife'. The *United Irishman*, in the first issue to appear after his death, expressed the belief of those who still remained loyal to him that he had been 'sacrificed by Irishmen on the altar of English liberalism . . . Murdered he has been as surely as if the gang of conspirators had surrounded him and hacked him to death'. There was to be no quick peace between the rival Parnellite factions. John Redmond, who succeeded to the leadership of the minority still loyal to 'the chief', was roundly defeated in Cork when he stood in the by-election to fill Parnell's vacant seat. At the end of December he scraped home in Waterford against Michael Davitt. In July of 1892 the full extent of the catastrophe was revealed in the general election, when the nationalists (as the home rulers were now commonly called) won 80 seats, but of these no less than 71 were anti-Parnellite.

While the anti-Parnellite majority urged continued support for Gladstone and the Liberals, now returned to power in Westminster, Redmond and his faction argued that because Gladstone had tried to remove Parnell from the leadership he could no longer be trusted and support was therefore out of the question. This widened the breach. and it was worsened by the almost total backing of the Catholic hierarchy and clergy for the anti-Parnellites, seen in their vociferous support at all levels during the 1892 election campaigns. The *United Irishman* of 16 July said in a leader that 'gross clerical intimidation, servile obedience to the priests on the part of the illiterate voters, clergymen canvassing in support of whiggery in the parishes or acting as personating agents in the polling booths' were what brought about defeat for the Parnellites. Putting it more bluntly, one wit suggested that 'were a broomstick nominated by the clergy it would sweep away any division in Ireland'. When Archbishop Walsh of Dublin asked John Dillon in June 1893, during the debates on home rule in the commons, 'how anyone can regard them (the 'Irish parliamentary party') as a body in whose hands any public interest would be safe', he was voicing the views of many. 'So far as I am concerned, the party has committed suicide'.

The squabbles and bickerings continued, especially between the supporters of John Dillon and Tim Healy, damaging the home rule movement further and making it impossible to apply on Westminster the kind of political pressure which Parnell so successfully had exercised. Gladstone did introduce a home rule bill in February 1893 and on 2 September it passed its third reading in the commons. But a week later it was heavily defeated (419 to 41) in the lords. Home rule was now a hopeless cause, especially after Gladstone resigned in 1894. His successor, the Earl of Rosebery, made this plain in his first speech in the commons, when he said that 'before Irish home rule is conceded by the imperial parliament, England, as the predominant partner in the Three Kingdoms, will have to be convinced of its justice and equity'.

When a new parliament assembled after the 1895 elections, now dominated by Conservatives and Unionists, a new policy of 'killing home rule with kindness' was initiated. The phrase was used by Gerald Balfour (brother of the more illustrious Arthur) in a policy speech made in October 1895, after his appointment as chief secretary for Ireland. In a letter in 1899 he explained how he had been misunderstood:

> 'This phrase has been repeatedly quoted since, as if it had been a formal declaration on the part of the incoming Irish government that "to kill home rule" was the alpha and omega of their policy. What I really said was that we intended to promote measures having for their object an increase in the material prosperity of the country; that if we could thereby kill home rule with kindness, so much the better; but that the policy stood on its merits irrespective of any ulterior consequences'.

Social and economic reforms to the benefit of Ireland were backed by all Irish members. But 1897 exposed just how feeble that all-party cooperation really was. The Childers Committee on the Financial Relations of England and Ireland revealed in 1896 that ever since the union Ireland had been overtaxed by nearly three million pounds annually. An all-Ireland committee was established in 1897 to seek redress, but it broke up in disorder when the Unionists broke ranks and let the government off the hook. The centenary commemorations of 1798 further exposed the bitter divisions among the nationalists and their inability to unite even for such an important historical event.

In 1897 a failure of the potato crop in Connacht caused widespread agitation, which, in January, led to the founding of the United Irish League by William O'Brien, one of the anti-Parnellite leaders. With land reform as its primary objective, it also pursued wider economic objectives and within three years there were nearly 1,000 branches country-wide, with about 100,000 members. Its success naturally attracted the politicians and under its auspices the nationalist factions came together in January 1900. In February John Redmond was chosen as leader of the new grouping. A convention in Dublin in June elected Redmond as chairman of the League (in December he assumed the presidency), endorsed his leadership in parliament and accepted the

League as a party electoral organization. The general election in October saw 76 nationalists (as well as five independent nationalists) returned, a resounding success for the new arrangement and the discipline it imposed. Home rule dominance was assured among Ireland's representatives at Westminster.

The land question, which for so long had been a dominant factor in Irish politics, was now well on the way to solution. Increasing numbers of independent small farmers emerged, to provide the hard nucleus of political movements in the future. The Local Government Act of 1898 created new county, urban, and rural district councils which were elected on a popular suffrage, in which women for the first time voted, and which were largely under Catholic and nationalist control, the impact was enormous. As Redmond said of the effect of the new legislation: 'It worked a social revolution: it completely disestablished the old ascendancy class from its position of power and made the mass of the Irish people masters of all the finance and the local affairs of Ireland'.

Part of this 'social revolution' was the work of Sir Horace Plunkett, the third son of Lord Dunsaney of Meath. Ten years as a rancher in Wyoming had opened his eyes to the economic problems which beset those working the land in Ireland. Cooperation would enable the farmers to help themselves economically. His slogan became 'Better farming, Better business, Better living'. In 1889 he founded his first cooperative society at Doneraile and five years later, when there were more than 30 cooperatives working in Ireland, he founded the Irish Agricultural Organization Society and under its auspices there were 876 societies in existence by 1904 and over 1,000 10 years later. Plunkett was a unionist (though by 1911 he was openly describing himself as a home ruler) and a Protestant. But he insisted that agricultural improvement had nothing to do with politics or religion, a view that won him widespread support.

Among those who helped was the poet George Russell ('AE'), who edited the *Irish Homestead* for Plunkett. Here Russell not only promoted the economic aspects of Plunkett's crusade, but also what he saw as its Celtic character, a kind of return to Ireland's Celtic past. New cultural forces, laying a new emphasis on the importance of Ireland's Gaelic heritage, had been sweeping Ireland and were to have a profound effect on politics.

In 1884, while Parnell was still in the ascendant, the Gaelic Athletic Association had been founded. The aim was 'the preservation and cultivation of national pastime'. Archbishop Croke of Cashel who, together with Parnell and Davitt, had been invited to become a patron of the new association, wrote that

> 'we are daily importing from England, not only her manufactured goods . . . but, together with her fashions, her accents, her vicious litera-ture, her music, her dances and her manifold mannerisms, her games also and her pastimes, to the utter discredit of our own grand national sports . . . as though we were ashamed of them'.

The new association quickly spread. Soon it banned from membership not only those who played or watched what it called 'foreign games', but members of the RIC and the army as well. It became intensely anti-English. Cusack called rugby football 'a denationalising plague'.

The Gaelic Athletic Association (GAA) had a political dimension from the start, with the IRB exercising a strong influence. Of the 10 members elected to the national executive in 1885, five were Fenians. The following year John O'Leary was invited to become patron and the IRB were in virtual control. After the decisive convention at Thurles in November 1887 it was reported to Dublin castle that an IRB member had said that 'they were proud the priests had been put out, that the clubs were composed of Fenians, and not of rotten nationalists, and if the priests had left long ago they would have less trouble in organising their men'. Many members took the Fenian oath and GAA clubs became not only political agents, but active in promoting a distinctive 'Gaelic' culture as a basis for a new kind of nationalism.

Even more important in this development was the founding of the Gaelic League in 1893. Eugene O'Growney, the professor of Irish at Maynooth, together with Douglas Hyde (a Trinity educated Protestant) and Eoin MacNeill (an Ulster Catholic who later became an eminent professor in the new University College, Dublin) were the prime movers. Shortly before the League was founded, Hyde gave an important public lecture with the arresting title: 'The necessity of de-anglicising the Irish people'. The aim, therefore, was not just to stop the seemingly inexorable spread of English as the language of the people, preserve the remaining few Irish-speaking areas, and restore spoken Irish to as many parts of Ireland as possible. The League was also, like the GAA, separatist in the cultural sense. But from the beginning it proclaimed that it was non-political, which was one reason why it took no part in any of the celebrations of the centenary of 1798.

Like Davis and the Young Irelanders, Hyde believed that without its own language Ireland could never be recognized as a separate nation. A new literature, history, and even games must give expression to that nationality through the medium of the Irish language. A major step in this attempt to restore Irish was to have the language taught in the schools. By 1909, out of about 9,000 primary schools in Ireland, Irish was being taught in 3,000, an extraordinary achievement in so short a time.

Many of the most gifted young people, Protestant as well Catholic, joined the Gaelic League. Branches sprang up throughout the island, so that by 1908 there were no fewer than 599, with at least one in every county. Even though the number of activists was never huge, they had a local influence way beyond their number. Not surprisingly, political separatists found attractive the notion of Ireland a distinct nation because of its culture and argued that Ireland should therefore be a separate nation-state. This went completely against all that Hyde, president since the foundation of the League, believed in. In 1915 at the Árd Fheis (annual convention) at Dundalk he protested: 'My ambitions had always been to use the language as a neutral field upon which all Irishmen could meet . . . So long as we remained non-political there was no end to what we could do'.

In this spirit the Gaelic League had been non-sectarian and non-political. Even the infamous banning of the Church of Ireland Canon Hannay (the novelist George Bermingham) from the feis committee of Tuam in September 1906, on the grounds that he had insulted Catholics in two of his novels – in denouncing him, the parish priest in Tuam said that in his novels he had attacked 'catholics and Irishmen as such' – failed to make the League sectarian. Hannay himself earlier in that year had written that 'there is no religious strife or religious bitterness' inside the League and remarked that it was 'an amazing thing' that there was in Ireland 'an organization where men and women of different creeds meet in friendliness; where priest and parson love one another'. He was elected to the national executive in August and was fully supported at the executive meeting in November. The weekly journal of the League, *An Claidheamh Soluis*, in its edition of 10 October, clearly expressed the official view in condemning the action in Connacht. The editor, Patrick Pearse, insisted that 'a man is entitled to his opinions; and a Gaelic Leaguer, as such, ought not to be penalized for any acts or views of his ... which are not inconsistent with his faith as a Gaelic Leaguer'. Hyde consistently continued to insist that the League was not sectarian. In June 1913 he wrote that he 'never knew . . . the opinion of any member to be shaken or biased one iota by sectarian considerations'.

But by 1915 all had changed and the image that the League now projected was of an institution that was not only Gaelic and Catholic, but politically nationalist as well. Even as early as 1913 Patrick Pearse wrote in *An Claidheamh Soluis*, in an article called 'The coming revolution', that the League was 'a spent force'; but he added that 'the vital work to be done in the new Ireland will be done . . . by men and movements that have sprung from the Gaelic League'. He made it plain what he meant when he wrote that 'nationhood is not achieved otherwise than in arms'. Hyde had to face the reality that the League had become what General Richard Mulcahy later called 'a spawning bed' for independence and he resigned his presidency. A year later, 1916, six of the seven signatories of the proclamation of a republic 'on behalf of the Provisional Government' were members of the Gaelic League.

This attempt to revive the language and give Ireland a distinct Gaelic culture of its own was matched by an extraordinary explosion of literary creation in English. There had for long been a strong sense of identification with Ireland among Anglo-Irish writers. Lady Wilde (Speranza) had been stridently nationalistic and she passed on to her son, the more famous Oscar Wilde, not only her patriotism, but a willingness to give it public expression. While touring the USA in 1882 he had voiced some extreme opinions. Ireland, he said, had once been the university of Europe. 'But with the coming of the English, art in Ireland came to an end and it had no existence for over seven hundred years. I am glad it has not, for art could not live and flourish under a tyrant'. Not only did he look forward to Ireland, 'the Niobe of nations', regaining her independence, he did so as a Republican: 'Yes, I am a thorough republican. No other form of government is so favourable to the growth of art'.

But the literary renaissance which began in late nineteenth-century Ireland will always be associated with the names of W.B. Yeats, Lady Gregory and others who founded the Irish Literary Theatre in 1898, out of which the famous Abbey Theatre was to come. This was just as important a part of the cultural revolution which changed the face of Ireland as was the GAA or the Gaelic League. Here, too, Hyde had an important part to play in helping to make the tradition and poetry of the Irish countryside more accessible. Yeats, Lady Gregory and others like George Moore not only built on this and made popular the mythical heroes of Irish history like Cuchulainn, but they gave a European dimension to this great Irish renaissance.

In so doing they frequently came into conflict with conservative elements at home. Inspired by the centenary celebration of 1798, Yeats wrote a patriotic play, *Cathleen ni Houlihan*, where the title was in the Gaelic literary tradition of representing Ireland (and national sovereignty) as a woman. Played by the beautiful Maud Gonne, the old woman asked young men to rise up, throw the strangers out of her house, and give her back her four green fields, Leinster, Munster, Ulster and Connacht. The poet later worried that his play may have inspired some young men to die for Ireland:

> Did that play of mine send out
> Certain men the English shot?

But when it was given its first performance in 1899, it outraged conservative Catholics and there was a near-riot in the theatre, with police keeping order in the auditorium.

The plays of J.M. Synge, drawn from his own experiences of the Irish countryside, were especially condemned as insulting to the Irish nation. On the first night (28 January 1907) of his *The Playboy of the Western World*, Lady Gregory informed Yeats in a famous telegram, 'Audience broke up in disorder at the word shift'. The second night witnessed the beginning of a week of organized riots in the theatre, despite the heavy police presence, which have never been equalled since. On 2 February in a review of the play in his paper *Sinn Féin*, Arthus Griffith condemned it as 'a vile and inhuman story told in the foulest language we have ever listened to from a public platform'. When the play was performed in America during the first Abbey tour in 1911–12 it encountered the same kind of organized protests in many cities. In Philadelphia the actors were actually arrested and charged with participating in what was classed as an immoral performance.

There can be no doubt that most people objected on political grounds, because they saw the play as perpetuating the notion that the Irish peasant was brutal and savage, and thus not fit for self-government. But the Abbey Theatre had also been instrumental in providing a platform for nationalist plays. In 1908 *When the Dawn is Come*, written by Thomas MacDonagh, one of the signatories of the 1916 proclamation, with a future Irish revolution as its theme, was performed. When Yeats and Lady Gregory won a court decision against censorship imposed by Dublin castle, and most especially when they kept the Abbey open in 1910 on the night King Edward died, they won the support of the most separatist political organization of the time. This was Sinn Féin, a movement initiated in 1907 when a number of clubs, under the influence of Arthur Griffith, came together at a convention in Dundalk.

In 1897, at the age of 26, Arthur Griffith left Dublin for South Africa, partly for health reasons (a fear of tuberculosis) and partly because a depression in the printing trade forced him to look for work abroad. His sojourn there had a profound effect on him. He helped to establish the Irish Transvaal Society to celebrate 1798, met John MacBride who remained a friend, became intensely pro-Boer and made Paul Kruger his hero, and under that influence became more determined than ever to liberate Ireland from Britain. At home in Ireland again when the Boer war broke out in October 1899, he helped to organize public opinion against the British. All Irish nationalists condemned the 'persecution' of the Boers, none more vociferously than John Dillon at Westminster. Early in 1900 he told the House of Commons that 'we know from long and bitter experience' what was meant by a member of the government who had said that the British race would be predominant in South Africa:

> 'It is an infamous object; the conscience of humanity will be against you in this struggle, and although for a time you may beat down these people by overwhelming numbers, you are but creating for yourselves, as a result of this war, far away in the southern seas, 7,000 miles away from your shores, another Ireland.'

Michael Davitt walked out of the commons and resigned his seat in protest. A 'Transvaal Committee', which Maude Gonne helped to found and in which Griffith took a leading part, as did James Connolly, organized practical support for the Boers and for the military unit, led by John MacBride, which the Irish Society provided to fight against the British in South Africa, and which incidentally learnt the strategy of using small, mobile groups against the British army which was to prove so successful later in Ireland.

Earlier in 1899, Griffith had started a newspaper, to which he gave the significant title of *United Irishman*. In the first issue he made even plainer where his political sympathies lay, when he proclaimed that 'we accept the nationalism of '98, '48 and '67 as the true nationalism' – militant republicanism, in effect – though his admiration for Swift and Emmet, expressed in the same issue, showed that his attitude was by no means clearcut. Thomas Davis, too, had always been an inspiration. Griffith for a short time was a member of the IRB, but his involvement with a wider political spectrum soon modified his views. Friendship with Maude Gonne not only brought him into the literary and political circle dominated by Yeats (of whom Griffith wrote: 'Mr Yeats sings of what he knows and sings more beautifully than ever Irish sang before'), but also the acquaintance of people as diverse as Douglas Hyde, James Connolly the socialist and, not least, the veteran Fenian John O'Leary.

Gradually his ideas of separatism matured and in October 1902 he demanded that Irish members of parliament should follow what he called the 'Hungarian policy', absenting themselves from London, and that they must 'remain at home to help in promoting Irish interests and to aid in guarding its national rights'. Then, in 1904, he ennunciated his policy more clearly in a pamphlet, *The resurrection of Hungary, a parallel for Ireland*, which sold 30 thousand copies and enormously influenced young people in particular, like Richard Mulcahy who later said that reading it was like 'a quiet blood-transfusion'. The pamphlet was published in translation in India, where it was also widely influential. Even newspapers there disseminated Griffith's ideas and Gandhi was only one of many who fell under their influence.

Griffith wrote that in Hungary Kossuth had 'realized that language alone cannot make a nation – that no nation can endure deprived of political institutions' and so in Ireland 'the language itself is not an end but a means to an end'. Though he had sympathy with Kossuth's republicanism and the physical force he resorted to in the unsuccessful rebellion of 1848, it was the more moderate monarchist nationalism of other Hungarians which he adopted. Griffith, in effect, sought a return to O'Connell's 'repeal of the union' and accepted the concept of a dual monarchy. But he argued that the Renunciation Act of 1783 was still valid, in which England renounced any right to legislate for Ireland, a matter which had been debated since the fourteenth century, and it must therefore be the starting point for all political relations between Britain and Ireland.

He abandoned his membership of the IRB in 1906 and then in 1907 came the formation of the Sinn Féin league, followed in September by a wider amalgamation under the simple Sinn Féin name. Griffith had already, in 1905, described his separatist policy as 'Sinn Féin' ('Ourselves'), which may have been borrowed from an earlier poem written by Douglas Hyde ending with *Sinn Féin amháin* ('ourselves alone').

In fact this Sinn Féin policy of abstentionism was not altogether new. It had been anticipated in some detail as early as February 1848 by Charles Gavan Duffy, by George Sigerson in 1868, and (rather more ironically) by John Dillon in 1877–8, when in his diary he set out a plan 'for bringing about the final crisis between England and Ireland, by withdrawing our representation, setting up a parliament in Dublin and obstructing the carrying out of English acts'. But it had never been adopted by Irish parliamentarians. Now it was put to the test when the young C.J. Nolan, MP for North Leitrim, read Griffith's pamphlet, was converted to Sinn Féin policy, resigned his seat in parliament, and in February 1908 contested the by-election as a Sinn Féiner. Even though heavily defeated by 3,103 votes to 1,157, Griffith insisted that this showed a great public swing in favour of his abstentionist policy. But the

Irish party at Westminster was not convinced. The return of the Liberals to government at Westminster in the general election of 1906 strengthened the position of the home rulers. Redmond was now in an unassailable position, heading a group of 83 nationalists at Westminster. As the result of the North Leitrim by-election in 1908 seemed to show, he now enjoyed the support of the great majority of the Irish electorate.

A large Liberal majority at Westminster naturally convinced most nationalists in Ireland that what to Gladstone had been an almost sacred commitment, to grant home rule, would become a reality. But not all Liberals were now committed to home rule and some, like Lord Rosebery, who in 1894 had shown apathy, now went further and condemned it outright. In October 1905 he issued a warning that:

> 'the policy of placing home rule in the position of a reliquary, and only exhibiting it at great moments of public stress, as Roman Catholics are accustomed to exhibit the relics of a saint, is not one which will earn sympathy or success in this country'.

The subsequent introduction of the Irish Council bill in parliament on 7 May 1907 showed the home rulers what they might expect – no parliament of their own, control over education, agriculture and local government only, with the lord lieutenant enjoying power of veto, and ultimate authority still reposing at Westminster. No wonder it was outrightly rejected by a nationalist convention a fortnight later or that the bill itself was withdrawn on 3 June. Later legislation enabling land to be purchased for evicted tenants, in particular the 1909 Land Act, or the 1908 Universities Act which created the National University of Ireland and the new Queen's University in Belfast, did little to assuage nationalist feelings of betrayal.

When the election held early in 1910 left the nationalists holding a balance of power at Westminster it seemed that nothing could now prevent home rule finally reaching the statute book. But the House of Lords, still dominated by unionists, continued to hold the right of veto. Before anything could be done about the Irish problem that right of veto had to be addressed. Through months of argument and discussion the government tried to get some kind of agreement on this and some other controversial issues, but without any success. The Liberals decided that before addressing such a potentially dangerous problem they should go to the country again. The result, in the general election of December 1910, was even more favourable to the Irish nationalists who increased their seats to 84, putting them in an even stronger position to exercise pressure on the Liberals who were now reduced to 271 seats. Finally, on 18 August 1911 the Parliament Act enacted that the power of veto was restricted to two years and, on 11 April the following year, the prime minister, Asquith, introduced his home rule bill in the House of Commons. After long debates, public protests and demonstrations, and attempts through amendment to exclude Ulster counties from the legislation, the bill passed the commons by 352 votes to 243 on 7 July 1913, only to be rejected a week later by the lords by 305 votes to 64. But that rejection could last only for two years after which home rule would become law. On 18 September 1914 the royal assent was finally given.

Earlier, Asquith had informed Redmond that in proceeding with his government of Ireland bill the position of Ulster would have to be considered before it became operative. If necessary, parliament must be given the opportunity to introduce amending legislation. An amendment to the home rule bill was, in fact, moved by a Liberal MP in June 1912, that four counties (Armagh, Down, Derry and Antrim) should be excluded. It was defeated by 320 votes to 251. 'I have never heard that orange bitters will mix with Irish whiskey' was how the proposer put it in his speech to the house.

Much more seriously, the cabinet had already decided in February of that year that the government must make whatever concessions were necessary to Ulster if circumstances seemed to warrant them and had told Redmond of its decision. At the end of July a mass demonstration in London protested against home rule and Andrew Bonar Law, the Canadian-born leader, with Ulster ancestry, of the Conservative party, told the crowd that what he called 'a corrupt parliamentary bargain' must not be allowed to deprive the Protestants of Ulster of what he insisted was their 'birthright'. There were, he said, 'things stronger than parliamentary majorities' and if parliament forced through home rule 'I can imagine no length of resistance to which Ulster will go in which I should not be prepared to support them' and which would not be 'supported by the overwhelming majority of the British people'. He had, in fact, already publicly given a pledge to a mass meeting at Balmoral in early April that Ulster resistance to home rule would be supported by British unionists. More than 100,000 attended that meeting, the surest sign that the Protestants of Ulster, supported by unionists outside the province, would never accept home rule.

The man who emerged as leader of the Ulster unionists, Sir Edward Carson, was a Dublin-born barrister who had no Ulster connections. Famous as the man who demolished Oscar Wilde in court, he was reluctant to get so involved in politics that his career as an eminent barrister would suffer, even though he was an active MP representing Dublin University at Westminster. But he was a convinced unionist, certain in his mind that separation from Great Britain would destroy not only Ulster, but Ireland itself. It was he who now became the chief architect of unionist resistance to home rule, with the assistance of James Craig who had a proven record as an organizer of great skill. That was demonstrated for all to see when on 23 September 1911 he organized a massive anti-home rule march of 50,000 Ulster unionists from Belfast to Craigavon, to join thousands more already assembled there. The huge meeting was addressed by Carson, who accepted leadership – 'the responsibility' – that they put on him that day and said that 'I now enter into a compact with you, and with the help of God you and I joined together . . . will yet defeat the most nefarious conspiracy that has ever been hatched against a free people.' He ended by saying that they must be prepared 'the morning home rule passes', themselves to 'become responsible for the Government of the Protestant province of Ulster'.

What 'being prepared' meant was quickly made evident. Traditional, long-standing Presbyterian and episcopalian differences were put aside and on 28 September 1912 the Solemn League and Covenant was signed. In all 470,000 (2,000 of them in Dublin) pledged that they would use 'all means which may be found necessary to defeat the present conspiracy to set up a Home Rule parliament in Ireland'. In Belfast Carson was given a silk banner which was supposedly carried before William III at the battle of the Boyne and the emotion was palpable as he held it up and proclaimed: 'May this flag ever float over a people that can boast of civil and religious liberty'. When Carson and other public figures signed the Covenant, it was filmed and subsequently the film was circulated widely to audiences in the country, but also in England to convince the authorities of the extent of support for unionists.

A further step was taken in 1913 when 500 delegates of the Ulster union-ist Council, which had been formed in 1905 to bring together all the unionist associations, nominated a provincial government which would take office, as Carson had said, 'the morning home rule passes'. This went far beyond what was promised in the home rule bill, for under it the Unionists in Ulster would take full control over all revenues, the post office, customs, law, education and, most importantly, the army with which they would resist home rule. The Ulster Volunteer Force (UVF) was established and by March 1914 it num-bered over 84 thousand men. Because a legal anomaly allowed two justices of the peace to licence drilling and military displays in their area, to defend the constitution of the United Kingdom, there was no problem in authorizing military activities all over the province. Arms were imported and legally held under licence. By the end of 1913 it was estimated that about 10,000 rifles had been distributed. In April 1914 a spectacular achievement was the landing of 24,000 German rifles and three million rounds of ammunition, most of it at Larne, without any interference from the civil or military authorities. These, too, were widely distributed all over Ulster, often with military and police help.

The secret password used by the Larne gun-runners was 'Gough', a refer-ence to General Sir Hubert Gough, commander of the Third Cavalry Brigade, who shortly before had been involved in a famous incident which quickly became known as 'the Curragh mutiny'. Alarmed at what had been happening in Ulster, the government, in December 1913, had issued royal proclamations forbidding the importation of arms or ammunition. In March 1914 it decided that a military force must be constantly on the alert in the Curragh, ready to intervene if Ulster exploded into violence. The comman-der-in-chief of the army in Ireland demanded that any officer who expressed an unwillingness to invade Ulster must be dismissed from the forces. Gough told him that he could not see his way to use arms against his friends in Ulster and no less than 58 of the officers stationed at the Curragh made it known that if ordered to move against the northern province they would refuse. This 'Curragh mutiny', as it came to be called, made headlines in London and Dublin, raising suspicions that the Ulster unionists enjoyed considerable support in the British army. About 130 of the officers stationed in Ireland submitted their resignations rather than march against Ulster. Colonel Arthur Parker, who commanded the Fifth Lancers, a regiment stationed at the Curragh, later told the Adjutant General of the army in London: 'I would not take part in anything that would lead to the coercion of Ulster'. It quickly became apparent that not only were many officers in the army in England supportive of the unionists, but many in the navy, too, said that they would not act against Ulster.

Gough made his way to Westminster and secured a written promise from the secretary-of-state for war that the government would never use the army in Ireland 'to crush political opposition to the policy or principle of the home rule bill'. He told the editor of the *Morning Post*: 'I dictated the terms, and wrote them with my own hand'. Even though Asquith, the prime minister, quickly repudiated this promise, the government had been made vividly aware of how dangerous was the situation in Ireland.

Ulster unionists used history and symbols to present their defence of a Protestant nation under siege since the seventeenth century. The Orange Order came into its own, providing not only the symbolic trappings to represent Protestant defiance, but through their organization and the network of halls scattered throughout the province and beyond they made it easier to organize all aspects of the anti-home rule movement. Even earlier, when the Land League began to expand in Ulster, it was not only Catholic tenants who supported the demand for land reform. Landlords became alarmed when Protestant tenants joined the clamour for 'the three Fs' (fair rent, fixity of tenure, free sale), as in January 1881 when 22,000 Protestant tenants, most of them Orangemen and none connected with the Land League, petitioned Gladstone. But the very success of the Land League quickly frightened many Protestants. It was construed by many in the Orange order as a Catholic movement to gain dominance. In October 1880 the lodge in Fermanagh ordered its members to acquire arms and drill, so as to be prepared to prevent the expansion of this southern nationalist movement. A meeting of the Grand Orange Lodge of Ireland in Dublin on 3 November 1880 denounced what it called 'a sinister conspiracy' and warned that it had 'the ulterior purpose of uprooting and extinguishing Protestantism and, with it, civil and religious liberty in Ireland'. This was how home rule came to be perceived in Ulster. It was an assertion of Catholic power, which would destroy Protestant Ireland. The belief that home rule was Rome rule became dominant.

When Rome issued the *Ne temere* decree in November 1907, it ended what up to then had been an old relaxed tradition towards mixed marriage in Ireland. Now the local Catholic bishop had to give a dispensation. Then the two had to sign a solemn agreement that all children would be baptised as

Catholics, that the Catholic partner must try 'in every reasonable way to bring the non-Catholic partner to the faith', and that 'the parties shall not present themselves, either before or after the Catholic marriage, before a non-Catholic minister of religion for any religious ceremony'. This confirmed the worst fears of most Protestants and a famous case in 1911 revealed all. A Belfast Catholic, Alexander McCann, had married a Presbyterian in her church. Now the local priest told him that for his marriage to be valid he would have to be remarried in the Catholic church. His wife refused, so he abandoned her and took the children with him, acclaimed by the Catholic clergy.

More than ever before, politics became sectarian and Catholic-Protestant polarization was copper fastened in Ulster. When the battle of the Boyne was commemorated with Orange marches on 12 July, or the raising of the siege of Derry by Apprentice Boys marching in August, it pointed up the sectarian differences and frequently led to riots and bloodshed.

There had always been dangerous confrontations in Belfast in particular, such as in 1864 when the unveiling of the O'Connell memorial in Dublin produced such a reaction that there was rioting for 18 days in which 12 people were killed and a hundred injured. Worse were the riots of 1886 when 32 were killed and 371 seriously injured. Randolph Churchill (who later coined the famous motto 'Ulster will fight and Ulster will be right') had addressed a meeting in February, rousing the crowd with his insistence that the issue 'means honour, religion, liberty, and, I should say, when I think of the days of 1641, it means possibly to you all that is worth living for'. Hearing the speech, the French consul reported: 'Une invitation à la guerre civile'. No wonder there were riots. Catholics were driven out of their homes and places of work (especially the shipyards, where the same thing was to happen again in 1893, 1912 and 1920), so as to ensure that a Protestant population would survive. The migration of large numbers of Catholics into the city to meet the demand for labour only made the situation worse. By the beginning of the twentieth century they made up about a quarter to one third of the total population of Belfast. The old cry of 'no surrender' was now taken up with such unanimity and resolve that few liberals were willing to put it to the test.

In asserting the Protestant cultural character of Ulster, the unionists ignored the Catholics, mainly home rulers, as if they did not have any rights. But Protestants, although in a majority, amounted to only 56.33 per cent of the population in 1911, enjoying an outright majority in only four counties. Reality did not matter. The extent of their military organization and the sheer number of arms, with appropriate ammunition, widely distributed throughout the province – this was what mattered and forced the British government to tread warily. In January 1915 the RIC reported that the number of rifles held was 53,341, with more arms in Belfast alone than the total held by the Irish Volunteers in the other three provinces.

The success of the UVF convinced the nationalists that just as the Ulster unionists had successfully armed themselves in defence of the union, they, too, should organise themselves militarily to achieve separation from Great Britain. In Dublin Eoin MacNeill published an article, 'The North Began', on 1 November 1913 in *An Claidheamh Soluis*. The title was taken from a poem by Thomas Davis in which he said 'our freedom's won' because of 'the Volunteers the North began'. MacNeill claimed that 'the Ulster Volunteer movement is essentially and obviously a home rule movement' and that Carson 'had knocked the bottom out of Unionism'. He accepted Carson's boast that not even the British army could suppress the UVF, but pointed out that those Volunteers were confined mainly to four counties. There was 'nothing to prevent the other twenty-eight counties from calling into existence citizen forces'. These, like the Volunteers of 1782, would then become 'the instrument of establishing self-government and Irish prosperity'.

MacNeill was persuaded to chair a committee which would organize the setting up of this force 'to ensure and maintain the rights and liberties common to all the people of Ireland without distinction of creed, class or politics'. A mass meeting was held in the Rotunda in Dublin and 4,000 men were enrolled in the new army. Six months later the number had reached 75,000 and very shortly after it was 180,000. The commander-in-chief was Colonel Maurice Moore, who had led the Connacht Rangers.

Another former army officer, Captain J.R. White, had helped to organize workers who were locked out during the great strike in Dublin in 1913. An army of a few hundred was drilled and trained by him, to ward off the police if they adopted the tactics earlier employed in attacking striking workers. After the strike, in March 1914, it was reconstituted as the Irish Citizen Army (ICA), with a socialist programme written by Sean O'Casey, the great playwright of the future. While what he called 'the first and last principle' was that 'the ownership of Ireland, moral and material, is vested of right in the people of Ireland', the leaders, who included the Countess Markievicz as well as James Connolly, agreed that an independent Ireland was necessary before a workers' republic could be established.

There was yet another army in existence, the IRB, which though only numbering about 2,000, was able to infiltrate and in some cases even to dominate other nationalistic organizations. They constituted 12 members of the committee which launched the Volunteers and by the autumn of 1914 exactly half of the committee were members of the IRB. When the committee was replaced by a general council in October, the IRB strengthened its position. While MacNeill was appointed Chief-of-Staff, despite his total ignorance of military matters, Bulmer Hobson and the O'Rahilly (both IRB) were made quartermaster and director of arms respectively. Even more important was the more immediate control over recruits given to three other IRB members: Patrick Pearse as director of military organization; Joseph Plunkett as director of military operations; and Thomas MacDonagh as director of training.

Women, too, had organized themselves militarily, spurred on by their experience in the suffragette movement. In 1912 Hanna Sheehy Skeffington, sentenced with some other suffragettes to two months imprisonment in

Mountjoy prison for throwing stones through the windows of government buildings, went on hunger strike, the first time this weapon was used in Ireland. On 5 April 1914 Cumann na mBan ('Association of women') was founded by republican women, led by Agnes O'Farrelly, 'to assist in arming and equipping a body of Irishmen for the defence of Ireland'. This meant not only raising money through a 'Defence of Ireland' fund, but acquiring skills in first aid, in military tactics, and in the dissemination of information, so that they might be real auxiliaries to the men in arms.

In what later became known as the Howth gun-running, women, too, played a central role. On 26 July *Asgard*, a yacht owned and captained by Erskine Childers (veteran of the Boer War, former clerk in the House of Commons, author of the best selling *Riddle of the Sands* and recent convert to home rule) landed 900 German rifles and 26,000 rounds of ammunition under the eyes of the government in Howth harbour. Two extraordinary women helped him to crew his yacht, his wife Molly Childers and Mary Spring Rice. Another 600 rifles and 20,000 rounds of ammunition were also safely landed further south at Kilcoole. Planned, financed and executed in the main by Anglo-Irish Protestants, led by Childers, Sir Roger Casement and Mrs Alice Stopford Green, this successful gun-running gave an enormous boost to the Volunteer and the home rule movement. A thousand Volunteers openly paraded back into Dublin carrying the guns, defying police and army forces which failed to stop them. As British soldiers marched in disgrace back to barracks crowds everywhere jeered and insulted them. On the quays at Bachelor's Walk the Scottish Borderers turned on the crowd without warning, opened fire, killed three civilians (one a woman) and wounded 35 (including four boys). A man and a woman were bayoneted.

This incident further inflamed public opinion against the English. A new ballad was now sung in the streets of Dublin:

> God rest the souls of those who sleep apart from earthly sin,
> Including Mrs Duffy, James Brennan and Patrick Quinn;
> But we will yet avenge them and the time will surely come
> That we'll make the Scottish Borderers pay for the cowardly deeds they
>   done.

In the House of Commons John Redmond did not mince his words:

> 'Let the House clearly understand that four-fifths of the Irish people will not submit any longer to be bullied, or punished, or shot, for conduct which is permitted to go scot-free in the open light of day in every county in Ulster by other sections of their fellow countrymen'.

In the autumn of 1914, then, before the royal assent was given to the home rule legislation, the militarization of Ireland by groups who were politically opposed created a situation in which civil war was nearly inevitable. Home rule would be forcibly resisted by the UVF who would defend a new Ulster as part of the United Kingdom. Conservative support for the unionists was so strong in Britain that English involvement in an armed struggle could not be ruled out. Addressing Conservatives at Bristol in January 1914 Bonar Law had said 'we are drifting inevitably to civil war' and emphasized the determination of Ulster 'to resist by force if necessary' the imposition of Home Rule.

> 'The ground on which our American Colonies took up arms seems to me utterly trivial in comparison with the wrong with which Ulster is threatened. We have given a pledge that if Ulster resists we will support her in her resistance. We intend, with the help of the Almighty, to keep the pledge, and the keeping of it involves more than the making of speeches'.

The Irish Volunteers, nominally under the control of Redmond and the Irish nationalists, would insist on a separate parliament for the whole of Ireland, based in Dublin and enjoying control over important functions of government, while acknowledging the monarchy. The IRB, already exerting extensive, if secret, control in all the leading separatist political and cultural organizations, would go further and with the support of the ICA and dissident Volunteers would aim to create the republic championed by Tone and his Fenian heirs.

When the king addressed an all party conference which he had summoned to Buckingham Palace on 21 July he expressed his fears:

> 'For months we have watched with deep misgivings the course of events in Ireland. The trend had been surely and steadily toward an appeal to force and today the cry of civil war is on the lips of the most responsible and sober-minded of my people'.

But then, on 4 August, Britain declared war on Germany and even though home rule received the royal assent in September it was immediately suspended, with Redmond's agreement, until the war was brought to a conclusion. Redmond in anticipation had already in the House of Commons promised the services of the Volunteers. 'If it is allowed to us', he said, 'in comradeship with our brothers in the North, we will ourselves defend the shores of Ireland'. His offer won high praise – in America John Devoy remarked in dismay on 'the almost universal approval of John's pledge'. Then after home rule was put on the Statute Book on 18 September he decided to go further. Addressing a parade of Volunteers at Woodenbridge on 20 September he said that it:

> 'would be a disgrace forever to our country, a reproach to her manhood, and a denial of the issues of history, if young Irishmen confined their efforts to remaining at home to defend the shores of Ireland from unlikely invasion'.

They must be prepared, he insisted, to go 'wherever the firing line extends'.

Even though MacNeill, O'Rahilly and others immediately repudiated Redmond's call to arm and Sinn Féin and the republicans broke ranks, most Volunteers remained with Redmond. The 2,000 who broke away (inflated to 11,000 by 1915) retained the old name 'Irish Volunteers', though they also became known as the 'Sinn Féin Volunteers', or more popularly simply as the 'Shinners'. The 170,000 who remained with Redmond now became the 'National Volunteers' and many were recruited for the war in Europe.

There was a long tradition in Ireland of serving in the army. The first two Victoria crosses had been awarded to Irishmen. Now both Redmond and Carson tried to persuade Lord Kitchener, a product of the Anglo-Irish unionist tradition who had recently been appointed secretary of state for war, to have both sets of Volunteers officially accepted as integral parts of the British army. He instantly refused to allow them to be organized as separate units under their own commands, although shortly afterwards he authorized the 36th (Ulster) Division which was based on the UVF and retained a distinct Protestant and unionist identity. But he held firm against Redmond.

Because of this, recruitment from nationalist ranks was slow to gain momentum. Even so, between August 1914 and the end of February 1915, 50,107 had volunteered in Ireland. During the following year 45,036 joined up. By the time the war ended 140,460 Irish had been recruited, not counting those who joined in Britain and elsewhere. There is no doubt that many of them volunteered because they believed that their brand of nationalism demanded, as Redmond had expressed it at Woodenbridge, that they should fight 'in defence of right and freedom and religion in this war'. The Meath poet, Francis Ledwidge, who died in the war, wrote that he had joined the Enniskilling Fusiliers 'because she [England] stood between Ireland and an enemy to our civilization, and I would not have her say that she defended us while we did nothing at home but pass resolutions'. Many, like the two MPs Willie Redmond (brother of John) and Tom Kettle, sincerely believed that by serving together with Ulster unionists – holding hands, as Redmond put it – they would discover a common Irish identity which would help to sort out political problems in Ireland once the war was over. Kettle wrote that 'this tragedy of Europe', as he called it, 'must be the prologue to the two reconciliations of what all statesmen have dreamed, the reconciliation of Protestant Ulster with Ireland, and the reconciliation of Ireland with Great Britain'. In the slaughter of the Somme, in particular, many of them did find common cause.

It is not possible now to be absolutely certain of how many were killed. Altogether about 35,000 died in the war, including the elderly MP Willie Redmond – the man who won the resultant by-election in Clare was Eamonn de Valera, who was to become the dominant figure in Irish politics for the next 40 years. Shortly before he was killed at Guinchy in September 1916, Tom Kettle wrote a sonnet for his baby daughter ('my darling rosebud') explaining why he had abandoned her 'to dice with death'. With the guns thundering around him, he told her:

> Know that we fools, now with the foolish dead,
> Died not for flag, nor King, nor Emperor,
> But for a dream, born in a herdsman's shed,
> And for the secret Scripture of the poor.

Even though many were serving right to the end of the war, playing a prominent role in the Fifth Army (which Lord Birkenhead later said was instrumental in winning the war) and suffering huge losses at the crucial battle of St Quentin in March 1918, the slaughter at the Somme and Gallipoli had dampened whatever enthusiasm for the war existed in Ireland. Worse, in the official reports of Gallipoli no specific mention was made of the Irish contribution and this caused an outcry back home where many felt betrayed. Writing about Irish losses and this failure to mention their gallantry the poet Katharine Tynan wrote: 'We felt that their lives had been thrown away and their heroism had gone unrecognized'. Redmond went further and said that there had been what he called a 'systematic suppression' of any mention of the gallantry of Irish troops.

There seems no doubt that this disillusion helped to augment the growing support for the strong Sinn Féin opposition to Redmond's insistence on Volunteer participation in the war. Later, when this reached its height with the 1916 rising, Asquith, the prime minister, told Kitchener that there was still a 'good deal of bitterness in Ireland about Suvla'. Many were anxious that advantage should be taken of the war to strike at Britain at home – to give effect to the old adage that 'England's difficulty is Ireland's opportunity'.

As early as 1912 Sir Roger Casement had published an article, 'Ireland, Germany, and the Next War' in *The Irish Review*, in which he suggested that Ireland should take full advantage of the war that was certain to come, proclaim neutrality, and argue that because of the island's position of strategic importance in the Atlantic it might gain international support which would guarantee its independence. After helping to organize the Howth gun-running, he went to America to raise money for more arms and after war broke out he went to the German ambassador in Washington in an attempt to secure a promise that if Germany won the war it would recognize Irish independence. Then he made his way to Germany to recruit Irish prisoners of war to form an 'Irish Brigade' which would fight for Ireland against Britain. He failed miserably in this, meeting with positive hostility from many soldiers and generally finding support for Redmond. But he was more successful in his second objective of procuring a public promise of German support for Irish independence. On 20 November 1914 the German government, through the chancellor, issued an official statement that it would never invade Ireland 'with a view to its conquest or the overthrow of any native institutions'. If, in the future, German troops did land in Ireland, it would be 'as the forces of a government that is inspired by goodwill towards a country and a people for whom Germany desires only prosperity and national freedom'.

Back in Ireland, those who had broken with Redmond and the home rulers over his policy of supporting Britain in the war effort, were divided as to the possibility of a rebellion during the war. MacNeill quoted Thomas Davis to support his view that in the past Ireland had lost 'through inadequate preparation' and that what he called 'distinct revolutionary action' would be justified only when there is 'deep and widespread popular discontent'. But following John Devoy in America, who informed the German ambassador that his Clan na Gael organization intended to support a rebellion in Ireland, the supreme council of the IRB decided to plan a rising before the end of the war, even if Germany failed to respond. They already dominated the Irish Volunteers, even though MacNeill was nominally Chief-of-Staff; and with Connolly now in charge of the ICA and militant separatists prominent in Cumann na mBan, support for a rising was assured.

As early as 8 August, only four days after Britain had declared war on Germany, Connolly openly proposed armed rebellion in the *Irish Worker*. Urging an uprising for national independence, he wrote that this would 'set the torch to a European conflagration that will not burn out until the last throne and the last capitalist bond and debenture will be shrivelled in the funeral pyre of the last war lord'. But the less radical leaders of the IRB agreed that if conscription was imposed on Ireland, or if the Germans landed, a rebellion would be immediately organized. In any event, they would plan a rebellion to take place before the end of the war.

The impact of the coalition government formed by Lloyd George in May 1915, in which the most vehement unionists and anti-home rulers (Bonar Law, Carson and F.E. Smith) were given cabinet places, helped the republicans in Ireland to persuade more people that home rule was, as Carson put it, nothing more than 'a scrap of paper'. In July the IRB procured the election of members (including republicans who were then in prison) to the executive committee (Coiste Gnótha) of the Gaelic League during the Ard Fheis at Dundalk, causing the moderate Douglas Hyde to resign his presidency. Diarmuid Lynch, an IRB member of that committee, later explained that at a time 'when the stage was being secretly set for insurrection against Britain', it was essential that what he called the 'Left Wing' should become dominant.

Present at that Dundalk meeting were the wife and daughter of the veteran Fenian O'Donovan Rossa. Two weeks later at his funeral on 1 August Patrick Pearse delivered a graveside oration which was designed to inflame the feelings of the thousands of men in uniform and the many thousands of others who had gathered at Glasnevin. He told his listeners that 'the seeds sown by the young men of '65 and '67 are coming to their miraculous ripening today'. The British 'think they have pacified Ireland'; but, he told them in words which have reverberated ever since, 'the fools, the fools, the fools! – they have left us our Fenian dead, and while Ireland holds these graves, Ireland will never be at peace'.

The audience was deeply moved, but very few were willing to answer a call to armed rebellion. Pearse realized this and knew that only a small army could be assembled for any rising. To die for Ireland was a sacrifice which not many, even in the IRB, were willing to make. As early as May 1915 the IRB leaders agreed on what Seán MacDermott, later a member of the secret military council, called 'a blood sacrifice for a principle'. Those who were supposedly in control of the Irish Volunteers, under MacNeill, saw the force in a different way. It was defensive, until home rule was finally achieved. It was to be used in action against the British government only if that were denied, of if threatened with conscription during the war, or if any attempt were made to seize their arms. They must train, be on their guard, and have a strategy prepared to meet an emergency, but a hopeless rebellion was never given serious consideration.

In May 1915 a secret military council was established, first with Pearse, the poet Plunkett, and the young Eamonn Ceannt (whose brother, ironically, was to be killed fighting in France in April 1916), who had come into the IRB through membership of the Keating branch of the Gaelic League which attracted young men with revolutionary nationalist beliefs. A few months later Thomas Clarke (the former Fenian who had served 15 years in prison in England and had galvanized the IRB after his return to Dublin) and Seán MacDermott were included. Connolly became a member in January 1916 and in April Thomas MacDonagh, the poet and academic, was co-opted. It was these same seven who were signatories of the proclamation of an Irish republic as members of the provisional government established later that year.

Away in Germany Casement had continued his futile attempts to recruit an Irish Brigade which, despite all his efforts, numbered a mere 50 men. He was joined in April 1915 by Plunkett, who was to negotiate a shipment of arms to Ireland the following spring, to arrive in time to service an armed rebellion. After his return to Ireland Plunkett and the other members of the military council decided early in 1916 that the rising would take place at Easter and the German War Office was asked to land the arms at Fenit in county Kerry at the end of Holy Week. By March the Germans had made the necessary arrangements so that the arms (20,000 rifles and ammunition) would be landed between 20 and 23 April as requested. They would be carried in the *Aud*. Later, on 7 April, it was agreed that Casement and others would travel separately to Ireland by submarine.

With this guarantee of German help the IRB secret military council went ahead with its plans. As early as the autumn of 1915 Pearse and the others had planned that Volunteers in counties Cork, Kerry, Limerick, Clare and Galway would link up with each other and hold the line of the Shannon, joined by volunteers from Ulster. By January 1916 they had persuaded Connolly to give up any plan of independent military action and to cooperate, with his ICA, in their plans for a rising. That rising was then fixed for Easter Sunday and a strategy for Dublin and the provinces was worked out.

MacNeill, the Chief-of-Staff, and other Volunteer officers were kept in the dark about all this. However, suspicions had been aroused and at a meeting of the 'headquarters staff' of the Volunteers on 5 April it was agreed that no orders would be issued without MacNeill's countersignature. But the plans still went ahead. It was not until Holy Thursday night (20 April) that MacNeill discovered that manoeuvres already sanctioned for Easter were in fact to be the mustering for an insurrection. With the plans now in the open, MacNeill became convinced that it was too late to do anything, especially when he was told that German arms were about to be landed in Kerry. Earlier in the week it had been revealed to him that the British government had plans ready to put Dublin under military occupation, disarm the Volunteers and arrest all persons to whom any shadow of suspicion was attached and this helped his capitulation to agree to a rising.

But by the end of the week he became convinced that this 'revelation' was bogus, designed simply to convince him and other moderates that insurrection was necessary. The news of the seizure of the *Aud* by the British on Good Friday, resulting in the total loss of the German arms, and the capture of Casement on the same day, after he had been put ashore in Ballyheigue Bay, finally made up MacNeill's mind that the insurrection must be called off. Late on Saturday night he sent orders by special messengers and in the *Irish Independent* of Sunday 23 April, as Chief-of-Staff, he inserted an order (dated 22 April) which was printed in bold type:

'Owing to the very critical position, all orders given to the Irish Volunteers for tomorrow, Easter Sunday, are hereby rescinded, and no parades, marches, or other movements of Irish Volunteers will take place. Each individual Volunteer will obey this order strictly in every particular'.

Pearse and the other leaders met at Liberty Hall on Sunday, decided to go ahead with the rising as planned for Dublin but to postpone it for a day, and then informed MacNeill that his orders had been obeyed. But on Easter Monday, while Dubliners and many army officers were enjoying themselves at the Fairyhouse races, the Volunteers and Citizen Army took up their strategic positions as planned in different parts of the city. By the time the government realized what was happening, four battalions of the Volunteers and the Citizen Army had occupied areas in a ring around the city based on Jacob's factory, Boland's mills, St Stephen's Green (which shortly after was vacated for the College of Surgeons), the Mendicity Institution, the General Post Office, and the Four Courts.

At the GPO two flags were raised in place of the British ones – a green one, with a golden harp in the centre and carrying the inscription 'Irish Republic'; the other was the green, white and orange tricolour which the Irish Free State later adopted as the national flag. Patrick Pearse, as the newly chosen president of the Irish Republic, then moved outside and read aloud to the people who happened to be passing by in Sackville Street the proclamation of that republic: 'In the name of God and of the dead generations from which she derives her old tradition of nationhood, Ireland, through us, summons her children to her flag and strikes for her freedom'. Having set out the role of the IRB, the Volunteers, the ICA, and the support given by 'her exiled children in America and by gallant allies in Europe', he went on to declare 'the right of the people of Ireland to the ownership of Ireland and to the unfettered control of Irish destinies, to be sovereign and indefeasible'. Despite 'long usurpation of that right by a foreign people' it had not been lost and had been asserted by every generation of the people of Ireland. Now asserting that right again 'in arms in the face of the world, we hereby proclaim the Irish Republic as a Sovereign Independent State' and he demanded the 'allegiance of every Irishman and Irishwoman'. Religious and civil liberty were guaranteed and the Republic would be 'cherishing all the children of the nation equally'. A 'permanent National Government' of Ireland would be 'elected by the suffrages of all her men and women'. And 'the cause' was placed under God's protection. The proclamation was signed on behalf of the provisional government by Clarke, MacDermot, MacDonagh, Pearse, Ceannt, Connolly and Plunkett.

Stephen MacKenna, the Greek scholar and friend of Pearse, was listening in the street and he later described the reaction of the audience: 'the response was chilling; a few thin, perfunctory cheers, no direct hostility just then; but no enthusiasm whatever'. The hostility, especially from middle-class Dublin, was not slow in coming. As the week wore on, lives were lost, buildings destroyed, and generally much of the centre of Dublin became a war zone. Reaction against the insurgents became increasingly bitter, not least among the women who queued up at the GPO to collect their army allowances, only to be told that the new Irish Republic had abolished these British payments. Looting, too, became widespread in Sackville Street and a mob quickly went out of control. In some areas there does seem to have been a degree of support. A Canadian journalist who happened to be in Dublin during that week and who condemned the rising, reported that while 'the open and strong sympathy of the mass of the population was with the British troops . . . in the better parts of the city', what he himself saw 'in the poorer districts' was the opposite. There he witnessed 'a vast amount of sympathy with the rebels, particularly after the rebels were defeated'.

By the time Pearse decided to surrender unconditionally on Saturday morning – 'in order to prevent the further slaughter of Dublin citizens, and in the hope of saving the lives of our followers, now surrounded and hopelessly outnumbered', as he put it in the order sent to the different Volunteer stations – terrible damage had been done and many lives had been lost. Altogether about 500 were killed and over 2,500 injured, of which more than 300 and 2,000 respectively were civilian casualties, many of them ruthlessly cut down by British soldiers and Volunteers. James Stephens witnessed a carter shot dead by Volunteers when he tried to recover his cart, which he needed for his work, from a barricade they had erected in Stephens Green.

But of the civilians killed, it was the murder of Sheehy-Skeffington after his arrest by the Cork-born Captain Bowen-Colthurst, whom he witnessed killing a boy for breaking curfew, which caused the biggest outcry. A well known pacifist who had strongly opposed the rising – 'Once bloodshed is started in Ireland, who can say where it will end', he exclaimed – he had tried to control the looters and help the civilian wounded. After keeping him in jail overnight the deranged officer had him executed, together with two innocent journalists, for which he was later found guilty (but insane) of murder. He was committed to a lunatic asylum for 20 months, before being allowed to emigrate to Canada.

Far from being a military shambles and the misconceived plot of poets and idealists intent on a blood-sacrifice, the organization of the rising in Dublin was praised subsequently by the British. The Chief Commissioner of the Dublin Metropolitan Police said that the military articles published in *The Irish Volunteer* before the rising were worthy of praise and that the conduct of the rising itself was 'all done very well'. No less a person than General Maxwell reported to the war office in London that 'the fighting qualities so far displayed by the rebels gives evidence of better training and discipline than they have been credited with'. A member of the royal commission set up to investigate the rising, Sir Mackenzie Chalmers, was convinced by the evidence that it was 'exceedingly well arranged'; and Sir Mathew Nathan, a former soldier who became Under Secretary for Ireland, told the commission that 'the conduct of the insurrection showed greater organizing power and more military skill than had been attributed to the Volunteers'.

The original plans had been carefully worked out, but had to be modified when the German arms failed to be delivered and when MacNeill's influence caused most of the intending participants to withdraw, so that only about 1,800 in all came out in Dublin. By the time that Pearse, Connolly and the other leaders occupied their carefully chosen garrisons in Dublin, the most they could hope for was to hold out for a week or so and forcibly bring the notion of a sovereign Irish republic before the eyes of the world. Their strategy was original, unlike that normally practised by revolutionaries. Wimborne, the lord lieutenant, commented afterwards: 'There was no conflict in the streets. The ordinary tactics of revolutionaries, which I imagine to be barricades and so on, were not resorted to . . . at the very start they took to the houses and house-tops'.

Even had larger numbers of Volunteers joined in, the lack of arms would have been a disaster. On St Patrick's Day, when a grand Volunteer parade was held, the police carefully counted all those on parade, which came to 4,555; but only 1,817 of these were armed, half with old rifles and the rest with shotguns. Outside Dublin the rising took place only in a few scattered places in counties Galway, Wexford and Dublin, and there, too, the lack of arms was a disaster. In Galway, for example, where Liam Mellows had been promised 3,000 German rifles from the *Aud*, the 1,400 Volunteers who joined the rising (more than fought in Dublin) had, according to a police report, only seven rifles, 86 shotguns and seven revolvers. No wonder Liam Mellows said later: 'I had to send many of them home. I never knew the blackness of despair until then'.

Under those circumstances, then, what was achieved was beyond what poets and academics might be expected to achieve. There is no doubt that Patrick Pearse was consumed with the notion of being a new Cú Chulainn, prepared to sacrifice himself for Ireland. But he was also the author of *The Murder Machine*, an important work on education, and the founder of St Enda's, a school under lay management, where his theories were put into practice. He was not just a visionary, but a capable editor, teacher and organizer who gave the British government a fright and nearly caused a crisis in the middle of the war.

After the surrender, when the destruction and loss of life were there for all to see, the *Irish Times* demanded that 'the rapine and bloodshed of the past week must be punished with a severity which will make any repetition of them impossible for many generations to come'. At Westminster Redmond told the House of Commons that 'the overwhelming mass of the Irish people' condemned the rising 'with a feeling of detestation and horror'. Martial law had already been proclaimed and on Friday, before the surrender, General Sir John Maxwell took charge. He immediately ordered the arrest of all who were suspected of complicity in the rising and nearly 3,500 men and 80 women were thrown into jail. Many were sent to internment in Britain, many more were released after interrogation, and 170 (including the Countess Markievicz and Eamonn de Valera, as well as all the leaders) were court-martialled.

The military courts, held in private, began immediately on the Monday. The accused were given copies of the charges against them, of 'rebellion with the intent of assisting the enemy', were given no legal aid and were not allowed to call witnesses. On Tuesday Pearse, Clarke and MacDonagh were brought to trial, found guilty, brought to Kilmainham gaol, and at 3:30 on Wednesday morning were shot. For 12 days the trials went on, followed by executions in which 14 in all were shot dead in Dublin, with another one in Cork. Plunkett was allowed to marry and, guarded by soldiers, was given 10 minutes with his wife before his execution. Connolly was so wounded that he could not stand and so faced the firing squad tied to a chair. Finally, on 3 August, Casement was hanged in London, after a trial during which his reputation was destroyed by the release of evidence of homosexual experiences preserved in his diary and despite the many protests and pleas for mercy from famous men and women.

The impact of all this on public opinion was immense. Condemnation of the rising gave way to sympathy and outright anti-British sentiments. Not since Robert Emmet in 1803 had a rebel been executed in Ireland and very quickly those of 1916 were given heroic status. A letter from George Bernard Shaw to the *Daily Mail* on 10 May left no doubt of what would happen: 'The shot Irishmen will now take their places beside Emmet and the Manchester Martyrs in Ireland, and beside the heroes of Poland and Serbia and Belgium in Europe; and nothing in Heaven or earth can prevent it'. Even the British government was very quickly made aware that more executions would further inflame Ireland. As early as 6 May the cabinet, with Maxwell in attendance, agreed that while it should be left 'to his discretion the dealing with particular cases', only 'ringleaders and proved murderers' should be shot and 'that it is desirable to bring the executions to a close as soon as possible'. But once back in Dublin, Maxwell ruthlessly continued to execute non-leaders, such as Edward Daly and Sean Heuston.

On 11 May John Dillon, who had been in Dublin, almost under siege in his house, during the rising and then witnessed the growing condemnation of the executions, made an impassioned speech in the House of Commons, expressing his pride in 'these men', even if they had been foolish and misled:

> 'I say I am proud of their courage, and if you were not so dense and stupid, as some of you English people are, you would have had these men fighting for you . . . It is not murderers who are being executed, it is insurgents who have fought a clean fight, a brave fight, however misguided'.

His outburst caused a sensation, Asquith left immediately for Ireland to prevent further executions. His experience there convinced him that immediate action was necessary and he gave Lloyd George the task of finding some way of bringing home rule into effect. He organized a conference and a manner of implementing home rule was agreed. The unionists demanded the exclusion of Ulster but Redmond and the Irish party at Westminster would have none of this. 'Irish nationalists can never be assenting parties to the mutilation of the Irish nation', said Redmond. 'The two-nation theory is to us an abomination and a blasphemy'. But Lloyd George knew that a concession to the unionists was necessary. A private meeting with Redmond secured his agreement, however reluctant, that this necessarily meant an exclusion, for a very limited period, of the six north-eastern counties: Antrim, Armagh, Down, Fermanagh, Londonderry and Tyrone. But meeting separately with Carson, Lloyd George gave him a written guarantee that this exclusion would be 'permanent and enduring'. He made it clear that 'at the end of the provisional period Ulster does not, whether she likes it or not, merge with the rest of Ireland'. A cabinet meeting on 19 July decided that 'Sir E. Carson's claim for the definitive exclusion of Ulster could not be resisted'.

When Redmond discovered this, he withdrew his agreement to temporary partition and ended all hope of any rapid implementation of home rule. But it was too late for him and the Irish party at Westminster. The way quickly became open for Griffith and Sinn Féin to assume leadership of the nationalists in Ireland. As early as July Maxwell reported the profound change which was taking place in Ireland, where Sinn Féin was in the ascendant as the organization the people should support 'because it has . . . done more for Ireland than Mr Redmond and the constitutional party; in other words, rebellion pays'. By September John Dillon could say bluntly:

'Enthusiasm and trust in Redmond and the party is dead, so far as the mass of the people is concerned'.

Back in Ireland, within weeks of the executions, masses were being celebrated for the dead of 1916 in many churches, filled with worshippers who were raising the dead patriots almost to the level of martyrs. When Father John Blowick was moving through Ireland in his efforts to generate support for the proposed Maynooth mission to China, he found that many young people 'had been aroused into a state of heroism and zeal by the Rising of 1916 and by the manner in which the leaders had met their death'. Many lower clergy praised the efforts of the insurgents and in June a nun told the Bishop of Limerick, Edward O'Dwyer, how 'the hearts of the people are turning towards the poor fellows who fell in Dublin. Their deaths have touched a cord of religion and nationality that were hardly ever more beautifully united'. The bishop himself publicly condemned the executions and England's 'misgovernment of this country'. He said that the rising had 'galvanized the dead bones in Ireland and breathed into them the spirit with which England has had to reckon'.

Meanwhile the release of those interned without trial in Britain had begun. Arthur Griffith, who had been a prisoner at Reading, was back in Dublin for Christmas 1916. He quickly discovered that the confusion which had linked the name of Sinn Féin to the rising was generating an enthusiasm for the organization which led to many new branches being formed around the country. Thousands joined, disillusioned with what they perceived as the failure of Redmond and the Irish parliamentary party at Westminster. By July 1917 the police had listed 166 clubs with a membership of 11,000 and by the end of August there were 22,000 members of nearly 400 clubs. Two months later there were 1,300 clubs with 250,000 members.

The extent of the disillusionment with the home rulers was made vividly clear in the North Roscommon by-election on 3 February 1917. Count Plunkett, father of the executed 1916 leader, stood in what had always been a safe home rule seat. Even before the 1916 Rising he had been sworn into the IRB and carried a letter to Casement in Germany with necessary information. He also visited Pope Benedict XV in Rome and brought back what he claimed to be a papal blessing for the Volunteers. By the time of his candidature in North Roscommon he was already a committed separatist. He was easily elected and he immediately declared that he would not take his seat at Westminster. This support for the Sinn Féin abstentionist policy won wide approval. The position of the Irish parliamentary party worsened in May when they lost another safe seat to Sinn Féin in the Longford by-election. In July the Irish Convention, designed to hammer together a scheme of government acceptable to all, was brought together by Lloyd George, now prime minister, under the chairmanship of Count Plunkett. But with the unionists still insisting on partition, and the absence of Sinn Féin and the other organizations which were now gaining political control, it had no hope of success.

By then all Irish political prisoners still in jail in England had been released. Chief among those to arrive back in Ireland was Eamon de Valera, who was the winner in the Clare by-election of July. As the only surviving commander of a military post to survive 1916, de Valera enjoyed enormous prestige and influence. In October, with the cooperation of Griffith, he was elected president of Sinn Féin, where radicals were now in the ascendant, at the annual Ard Fheis (convention) and the following day he was also elected president of the Volunteers. At the Ard Fheis, too, Sinn Féin adopted as official policy the compromise solution proposed by de Valera: 'Sinn Féin aims at receiving international recognition of Ireland as an independent Irish Republic. Having achieved that status the Irish people may by referendum freely choose their own form of government'.

The death of Redmond in March 1918 was quickly followed by the withdrawal of the Irish parliamentary party (now led by Dillon) from Westminster because of the proposal on 9 April to introduce conscription into Ireland. On 27 March Henry Duke, chief secretary for Ireland, had not minced his words when he told the cabinet that conscription was out of the question: 'We might almost as well conscript Germans', he said, and prophesied that Ireland would be lost as a result. But to no avail. Back in Dublin, Dillon and the Irish parliamentary party took part in an anti-conscription conference, attended by representatives of all the nationalist groups, and supported by the clergy. At that meeting in the Mansion House on 18 April, backed by Dillon and his party, a resolution was unanimously agreed to: 'Taking our stand on Ireland's separate and distinct nationhood . . . we deny the right of the British Government or any external authority to impose compulsory military service in Ireland against the clearly expressed will of the Irish people'. The passing of the Conscription Act in the commons 'must be regarded as a declaration of war on the Irish nation'. Significantly, Dublin Protestants organized their own protest against conscription, which they called 'a violation of the law of God'.

But Lloyd George went ahead with his proposals. A new lord lieutenant, Lord French, was sent to Dublin with wide powers. On 17 May nearly all the Sinn Féin leaders were arrested, accused of treasonable conspiracy with the Germans. All public meetings were banned and Sinn Féin, the Volunteers, Cumann na mBan and the Gaelic League were proclaimed to be illegal organizations.

But it was too late. After the war ended in November, a general election was held on 14 December. The electorate had been dramatically enlarged by the act of 6 February which enfranchised all men over 21 and most women over 30. As a result, nearly two million voters (mostly Catholic and nationalists) came onto the register in place of the more than 700,000 who had voted in the last election. The new voters were mainly young and Sinn Féin supporters. When the results were declared on 28 December, Sinn Féin, in the words of the *Irish Times*, 'swept the board' and 'the defeat of the Nationalist party is crushing and final'. Sinn Féin won a total of 73 seats 'and none of them for the present, at any rate, will attend the Imperial Parliament. In other words, the country outside North-East Ulster . . . is virtually disenfranchised. It is an impossible situation as Sinn Féin will soon discover . . .'. Among those elected was Countess Markievicz, who became the first woman elected to the House of Commons. In addition to Sinn Féin, six other nationalists won seats, and only 26 unionists.

Early in January 1919 Count Plunkett, as 'Chairman of meeting of Republican Representatives', sent an invitation to all elected members to attend the opening of An Dáil Éireann. He informed them that at a meeting on 7 January in the Mansion House 'of the Republican representatives of Ireland', a motion was adopted that 'we, the Republican members of the Irish constituencies, in accordance with the National Will, are empowered to call together Dáil Éireann'. On 21 January the Dáil met in the Mansion House, though only 27 Sinn Féin MPs were present. Most of the others, including Griffith and de Valera, were in prison, and the six nationalists, as well as the unionists of course, took their seats at Westminster. In a 'Declaration of Independence', recorded in the official minutes in Irish and French, the republic established in 1916 was ratified and Ireland, the Dáil said, called 'upon every free nation to uphold her national claim to complete independence as an Irish Republic, against the arrogant pretentions of England'. Three delegates (de Valera, Griffith and Count Plunkett) were chosen to argue that case at the Paris peace congress. But even though the senate in Washington supported Irish sovereignty and tried to secure a hearing for 'the case of Ireland' in Paris, it was to no avail. British opposition prevailed.

Cathal Brugha was elected acting President of the new Dáil. But on 1 April, after his spectacular escape from Lincoln jail, de Valera became the new President. The Dáil was not satisfied with the symbols of authority but proceeded to form an alternative government. The President (or *priomh aire* as he was called officially) chose a number of ministers: Arthur Griffith – Home Affairs; Cathal Brugha – Defence; Michael Collins – Finance; Count Plunkett – Foreign Affairs; Eoin MacNeill – Industry; Countess Markievicz – Labour; Liam Cosgrave – Local Government. Two 'heads of department' were also appointed – Ginnell in Propaganda and Barton in Agriculture. The President was to be paid £1,000 a year and each minister a maximum of £500.

Cosgrove and his deputy, Kevin O'Higgins, had an extraordinary success in reorganizing local government so that within a short time nearly all the boroughs in the 26 counties recognized the new Dáil's Department of Local Government. Home assistance was provided for many poor; others were sent to new county homes (formerly workhouses); rates were paid to Dáil collectors. But perhaps an even more extraordinary success were the newly established Dáil courts. The cabinet in London was told that the whole country was 'going over to Sinn Féin, horse, foot and baggage'. Even substantial landowners were using the new courts, so much so that in Donegal an IRA (Irish Republican Army) brigade led by Peadar O'Donnell decided to suppress the courts 'because', he said, 'they are taking the landlords' side'.

These Sinn Féin courts, as they were popularly known, were in every corner of Ireland, available to all and administering the justice of the new government in Dublin. They rejected English law and imposed their own form of punishments. In Clare, for example, two men had been brought to a local Sinn Féin court and ordered to re-build a wall which they had previously demolished. When the court subsequently discovered that they had failed to carry out its sentence, the local IRA rounded them up and marooned them on an island for three weeks as a punishment. The RIC intervened and launched a boat on the sea to rescue them. But to their astonishment they were stoned by the castaways, insulted, and told to clear off because they were 'prisoners of the Republic'.

In a letter to the *Times* Lord Dunraven explained that popular dissatisfaction was not with law and order, but rather with the origins of that law. Eventually there was a court in every parish, district courts, and a supreme court in Dublin. Even when martial law was proclaimed and the courts were driven underground, they still carried on. Many were arrested by the RIC, such as Judge Crowley in Ballina, who was thrown into prison for 13 months and stripped of his pension as a former customs officer. The most famous arrest was that of Terence MacSwiney in Cork, who had arranged for foreign press reporters to witness the courts in action. He was arrested when he was caught presiding at the district court in Cork and eventually deported to Brixton prison in England, where he died on hunger-strike after 74 days without food.

MacSwiney had also been involved in the Dáil loan, launched by Collins as a way of raising money, at home and abroad, to help finance the new government. It officially closed at the end of July 1920. Even though much of the money promised had still to be collected, Collins told MacSwiney that the total in hand then was over £355,000. De Valera had gone to America to raise more money, as well as to court diplomatic and political help, and while it is not now known exactly how much came in, it is believed to be about five million dollars. Coincidentally, Russian revolutionaries were on the same mission and the Irish had sympathy for a new government which, like themselves, was trying to win world recognition. When the two delegations accidentally met, the Irish contributed $20,000 to the Russians, receiving as collateral Romanov jewels which had been seized by the communists. The Catholic Irish, then, made the first foreign loan to the new communist state and it was not until 1948 that the jewels were returned and the loan repaid.

The new Dáil needed a regular income if the administration it had established was to work with any efficiency. Local rates were of particular importance. But all too frequently the local IRA sympathized with local opposition to rates and helped to organize resistance, even to the extent of tacit support of official RIC attempts to prevent the rates reaching Dublin.

The successful operation of the Dáil courts also depended on local IRA cooperation. In theory all IRA units were under the central control of Dublin. But in practise most of them operated quite independently, often in direct contradiction of government policy.

Coincidentally, on the same day that the new Dáil assembled in Dublin, Volunteers in Tipperary ambushed a train at Soloheadbeg, shooting dead two members of the RIC who were guarding gelignite on its way to a quarry. Dan Breen, one of the leaders of the ambush, later said that it was a deliberate action 'to light the fuse', the first shot in what later became known as the War of Independence, or more popularly simply as 'The Troubles'. 'Our only regret was that the escort consisted of only two peelers instead of six. If there had to be dead Peelers at all, six would have created a better impression than a mere two'. Many soldiers, including officers, returning from the war joined the Volunteers, now officially called Óglaigh na hÉireann, and unofficially as the Irish Republican Army, or the IRA. They supplied an expertise which had previously been lacking, and under the direction of Michael Collins, who had given new life to the IRB, a ruthless war against British forces and their supporters in Ireland was initiated.

Collins had come back from back from England, where he had joined the IRB, in time to take part in the 1916 rising and had gained prestige as *aide-de-camp* to Plunkett in the GPO. He was one of the more than 1,800 interned in the former prisoner of war camp for Germans at Frongoch in Wales. There, in what the MP Tim Healy called 'a Sinn Féin university', he organized most of the internees into avid revolutionaries, through lectures, debates, and even training sessions. Many of the key figures later in the IRA, like Collins himself who became Director of Intelligence as well as chief organizer, or Richard Mulcahy who became Chief-of-Staff, were Frongoch 'graduates' who provided the hard core of disciplined men ready to organize armed resistance as soon as they were back in Ireland. While still at Frongoch they were also organized into units under IRB control.

When Collins returned to Ireland his genius at organization was given full scope not only in the military sphere, but in establishing an intelligence network which reached into Dublin castle itself and kept Sinn Féin fully aware of British plans. For example, de Valera, Griffith and others who were arrested in 1918 were told in advance by Collins the very hour when they would be seized and they allowed themselves to be taken, because it would greatly influence public opinion in their favour and be politically advantageous to conduct policy from jail. But Collins himself, and others who were essential for the military organization of the Volunteers, successfully evaded capture.

Collins had already made clear, in a manner deliberately reminiscent of Patrick Pearse, his insistence that only through the gun would Ireland win her freedom. On 25 September 1917 Thomas Ashe had died on hunger-strike in Mountjoy. Emotions were high and the IRB were determined to exploit fully the occasion. At the funeral on 1 October, Volunteers, including Collins, openly paraded with arms in full uniform, firing three volleys over the grave. Then Collins stepped forward to deliver the funeral oration at the graveside. It could not have been shorter or more explicit: 'Nothing additional remains to be said. That volley which we have just heard is the only speech which it is proper to make above the grave of a dead Fenian'. The gun was to be the means of forcing the British to recognize the new Irish Republic.

Ten days after the two RIC men were killed in Tipperary, Cathal Brugha issued an order in *An tÓglach*, the official publication of the Volunteers, authorizing the killing of 'soldiers and policemen of the English usurper' if necessary. No policeman was safe thereafter. De Valera did not help matters when he denounced the RIC – 'Their history is a continuity of brutal treason against their own people' – and proposed a motion in the Dáil on 19 April that they be 'ostracized socially and publicly by the people of Ireland'. When 17-year-old Sean Hogan was taken prisoner on 12 May he was dramatically rescued from a train at Knocklong and two more RIC men were killed. At the inquest later the jury refused to return a verdict of murder and blamed the government for 'exposing the police to danger'. It was the RIC who suffered most as their barracks became primary targets in the desperate search for arms and very many police were killed. The pattern was quickly established with local IRA units operating independently.

The number of active IRA men remained low, never more than 3,000 at their strongest. But using guerrilla tactics, often out of uniform so as to take the enemy by surprise, operating 'flying columns', they caused terrible problems to the government. Irish ex-servicemen, often incapacitated because of war injuries, provided easy targets. Before the end of July 1921 at least 82 were brutally murdered, the majority of them Catholics, mostly on the charge that they were informers. On only five occasions were the murders denounced by the local clergy and generally there was no public condemnation in Ireland.

The numbers of police began to fall drastically, partly because of death or injury in service, but also because local boycotting of families caused many to resign. The cabinet decided to reinforce the RIC and recruited about 8,000, mainly ex-servicemen, in England to serve in Ireland. Because RIC uniforms were scarce, the recruits dressed in army khaki, with the distinctive police black belt and green cap and they quickly became known as 'Black and Tans', after a famous pack of hounds in Limerick. Additional recruits were found among army ex-officers and organized separately as 'Auxiliary Cadets'. They, too, came to augment the RIC and were popularly known as 'Auxiliaries'.

These two military groups introduced a new militant spirit into the police in 1920 and 1921, operating in a more ruthless, and at times even barbarous, fashion. Tomás MacCurtain, the Commandant of the Cork IRA brigade who had been elected Lord Mayor, was murdered in his home, in front of his wife and family, in the early hours of 20 March 1920. At the coroner's inquest the jury returned that he had been 'wilfully murdered under circumstances of most callous brutality' and that 'the murder was organized and carried out by the Royal Irish Constabulary, officially directed by the British Government'. On the night of 14 November 1920, the young Father Michael Griffin was lured from his residence in Galway city on a bogus sick call and was then murdered by the Black and Tans.

The number of atrocities on both sides escalated, with the civilian population caught in the middle. Michael Collins, as president of the IRB, was particularly concerned with the British intelligence force which supplied information to the police and he formed a special group of hand-picked men to eliminate as many intelligence officers as necessary. Known as 'The Gang', the chosen men carried out their work efficiently and ruthlessly. On the morning of Sunday 21 November 1920 they conducted their most famous operation, when 10 were killed, mostly in their beds, some in front of their wives or children. Four more were wounded, of whom one died later; and another three innocents, mistakenly identified, were murdered.

The reaction was horrendous. Three prisoners in Dublin castle were shot dead. That afternoon lorries filled with Auxiliaries burst into Croke Park, where a GAA match was in progress, and opened fire on the crowd of onlookers and the players. A Tipperary player was killed, 14 others, including women, were shot dead, and many more seriously injured in the panic. Known ever since as 'Bloody Sunday', this particular atrocity inflamed the situation even more. A climax was reached on the night of 10–11 December when a large part of Cork was deliberately burnt by the Auxiliaries by way of retaliation for the killing of 18 of their number at Kilmichael.

Most of the commanders of local IRA units were only in their 20s in 1920. For example, Tom Barry was 24, Dan Breen 26, Ernie O'Malley only 22. Those who followed them were even younger, many of them teenagers. As a result they were difficult to control from Dublin, operating frequently as independent units, and all too often were motivated by local considerations. The official policy of martial law and coercion, which too often prevented whole localities from going about their normal business, produced retaliation in which many innocent people suffered. Assassinations followed by retaliations continued on both sides. Many 'big houses' were also deliberately destroyed and in some areas Protestants were killed.

But the idea that there was some kind of pogrom against Protestants has no foundation. Outside of Ulster, Protestants generally did not view the local IRA units as avowedly sectarian. In June 1920 the moderator of the Presbyterian church publicly protested that 'it is a notable fact that nowhere has a hand been raised against one of our isolated Church buildings, nor against a single Presbyterian in the South and West'. A month later, another Protestant, a wealthy unionist in Munster, wrote to the *Irish Times* about the reports of Catholic sectarian actions: 'I feel it my duty to protest most strongly against this slander of our Catholic neighbours'.

The British government consistently insisted that there was no popular widespread popular support for IRA activity, which in essence was the work of only a handful of fanatics and terrorists. There is no doubt that it never was in any real sense a popular movement in which the mass of the people were seriously involved. But one indication of the popularity of political separatism was the result of the 1920 local elections, when (as was freely admitted at the time) proportional representation (PR) was introduced to reduce Sinn Féin success. But in 28 of the 32 counties they won an overwhelming majority; and even in those four Ulster counties the introduction of PR enabled nationalists to win more seats than expected. In Derry, for the first time since 1691, the unionists lost control of the corporation; and in Belfast the nationalist minority was very substantially increased.

Another indication of widespread support for the new Dáil was industrial action, purely for political ends, in which the public resisted the government passively. Between May and December 1920 a railway strike created severe difficulty for the government when the movement of troops and munitions was interfered with. More important, it demonstrated extensive moral support for Sinn Féin and the repudiation of British rule. So did the two day general strike of April 1920, which helped to procure the release of Sinn Féin prisoners on hunger strike in Mountjoy.

Outside of Ireland, too, support for the new Sinn Féin was growing. News of the atrocities committed by government forces in Ireland were spread abroad. In India young men serving in the first battalion of the Connaught Rangers were so appalled by what they heard that they mutinied, replaced Union Jacks with Tricolours in the areas controlled by them, protested against what the government was doing at home, and demanded freedom for Ireland. Quickly put down, the mutineers faced court-martials, severe penal servitude sentences, and in one case (Jim Daly) the death sentence. Before his execution, in a letter to his mother telling her he was going to die, Daly wrote: 'What harm, it is all for Ireland'.

Meanwhile public opinion in Britain, and not just among the Irish, was being organized by Sinn Féin against what they condemned as a brutal war of oppression in Ireland. Many important people, including MPs, churchmen and other public figures, were independently converted to the view that England would be shamed by what was happening in Ireland and that peace must be restored there. In America, too, de Valera's propaganda campaign – he addressed a total of at least half a million people at 17 meetings during his first coast-to-coast campaign – had focused much public attention on Ireland. He not only raised the huge sum of five million dollars, without which the IRA campaign in Ireland could not have been sustained, but by the time he returned to Ireland in December 1920 he had galvanized public sympathy for the cause of Irish independence.

By that time the British government had already begun to face reality. In the spring of 1920 the administration in Dublin castle had been reformed, so that the nucleus of a peace party emerged there. Lloyd George proposed two parliaments for Ireland, one for the six counties in Ulster, the other for the rest of the Ireland, each with limited powers. A council of Ireland, made up of representatives of both parliaments, would provide a bridge which eventually, it was hoped, would end partition. On 23 December 1920 the government of Ireland act passed into law, to come into effect by mid-June 1921.

But this new legislation had no effect on the war and produced a massive reaction in Ulster where many Catholics had been killed, or driven from their homes and the Belfast shipyards, and sectarian divisions were made worse than ever. By the time elections to the new parliaments were held in May, in which the unionists won 40 of the 52 seats in the north and Sinn Féin were returned unopposed in every constituency in the south (apart from the four Dublin University seats), war weariness had set in on all sides.

But before the peace-makers could make much progress, on 25 May the IRA had a spectacular success when they attacked the Custom House in the heart of Dublin, exposing the inability of the government to cope. New initiatives were called for. When King George V opened the Northern Ireland parliament on 22 June 1921, he finished his address by emphasizing that 'the future lies in the hands of my Irish people themselves' and ended:

> 'May this historic gathering be the prelude of a day in which the Irish people, North and South, under one Parliament or two, as those Parliaments may themselves decide, shall work together in common love for Ireland upon the sure foundation of mutual justice and respect'.

Then Lloyd George followed by offering a peace conference, significantly dropping his earlier demand of an IRA surrender of arms as a necessary precondition. General Smuts, the great South African leader who was greatly admired in Ireland, was engaged as an arbitrator, went to Dublin on 5 July, and under his persuasion a truce was signed, to take effect on 11 July.

When de Valera, accompanied by Griffith, Barton, Plunkett, Stack and Childers, arrived in London on 12 July to begin negotiations for a permanent settlement, he began a series of four meetings with Lloyd George and others which tried to solve insoluble problems. How could apparently irreconcilable positions be reconciled? The British were willing to go further than the old home rule solution and offer dominion status; the Irish nationalists wanted nothing less than complete 32 counties independence; the Ulster unionists would hold on to the six county partition already achieved. For when Lloyd George managed to get the government of Ireland act on the statute book in December 1920, the new administration which was established in Belfast from Dublin (in which, incidentally, Catholics were excluded from all key positions), coupled with the creation of the special Ulster constabulary, effectively made partition a permanent reality. This had been recognized at the time, when the *Irish Times* observed that the government 'in passing this Bill will pass a measure for the permanent division of Ireland'. Even the *Times* of London protested that 'the Bill as presented to Parliament, bears . . . evidence of painstaking adjustment to the susceptibilities of Sir Edward Carson and his followers', and went on to condemn the government because it had 'even been prepared to jeopardize every chance of conciliating nationalist opinion by the prodigality of their provisions for Ulster unionism'.

Apart from the Ulster problem, the British feared that if they gave way to Irish demands and recognized an Irish republic, they would establish a precedent which, as the cabinet was told on 20 July, 'might then prove impossible to resist in the case of India'. The future of the British Empire was now an issue. Dominion status (or 'dominion home rule' as it was more generally termed) was the most that could be offered, involving an oath of allegiance to the king. Lloyd George insisted, too, that the new state must fully recognize 'the existing powers and privileges of the parliament of Northern Ireland, which cannot be abrogated except by their own consent'. When the Dáil met on 16 August it unanimously rejected the British proposals. Then, in a significant gesture, on 26 August it elected de Valera, until then the Prime Minister (*príomh aire*), President of the Republic of Ireland and all the deputies swore an oath of allegiance to that republic.

After a long exchange of letters between Lloyd George and de Valera, who had been promoting his notion of a relationship of what he called 'external association' between the republic and the British Commonwealth, the English prime minister wrote to him on 29 September with what he called a 'fresh invitation to a conference in London on October 11th, where we can meet your delegates or spokesmen of the people whom you represent with a view to ascertaining how the association of Ireland with the community of nations known as the British Empire may be reconciled with Irish national aspirations'. The following day de Valera replied, agreeing that 'conference, not correspondence, is the more practical and hopeful way to an understanding' and accepted the invitation.

Acting 'in virtue of the authority vested in me by Dáil Éireann', he appointed Griffith, Collins, Barton, Duggan and Gavan Duffy as:

> 'envoys plenipotentiaries for the elected Government of the Republic of Ireland to negotiate and conclude on behalf of Ireland, with representatives of his Britannic Majesty George V a treaty or treaties of settlement, association and accommodation between Ireland and the community of nations, known as the British Commonwealth'.

Although officially classed as 'plenipotentiaries', the delegates were also obliged to consult the cabinet in Dublin before decisions were made on what was called, rather obscurely, 'the main question', and to submit a 'complete text of the draft treaty' to Dublin and await a reply. Since de Valera, for reasons best known to himself, did not head the delegation to London (probably because he believed that he would be more in control if he remained in Dublin, especially since die-hard republicans in the cabinet needed constant persuasion to a more moderate stance), it was obviously essential that no final decision about a settlement be taken without prior reference back to Dublin.

In the event, this was to prove a fatal flaw in the arrangements and the ambiguity in the statement of the delegates' powers was to be a disaster for the future history of Ireland. During the protracted and almost continuous negotiations between 11 October and 6 December in London, three main issues were debated: the relationship of the new Irish state to King and Commonwealth (the dominant issue on the British side, as Lloyd George made clear in his invitation on 19 September); partition (on which the Irish delegates had instructions to break off the negotiations if necessary); and the provision of naval and military facilities in Ireland to secure Britain's defensive and security needs (which surprisingly caused no problems then or during the later debates in the Dáil).

Lloyd George soon realized that ceding the principle of Irish unity was necessary if acceptance of the crown was to be achieved. But how could the intransigent Ulster unionists or others in the House of Commons, whose support his minority government needed, ever be persuaded to yield on this? When Craig arrived in London from Ulster on 5 November, he refused to budge and insisted that the 1920 legislation, which virtually guaranteed partition, remain in place. In desperation Lloyd George came up with the idea of a boundary commission which would transfer to the jurisdiction of the Dáil areas with a nationalist majority. This would make the remainder of unionist Ulster economically unviable and ensure the ultimate failure of partition.

By late November both sides seemed as far apart as ever. In desperation Lloyd George offered a further concession: the form of the oath of allegiance would become even more innocuous and the dominion status of Canada would serve as a model. But time was running out. Lloyd George had promised Craig a definite answer by 6 December. On 29 November Craig told parliament in Belfast that 'in the meantime, the rights of Ulster will be in no way sacrificed or compromised'. Griffith and the other delegates returned to Dublin to discuss what Lloyd George had offered and found the cabinet split on the oath. By the time they returned to London the delegates themselves were split. While their new instructions were, as happened so often, confused, there seems no doubt that the cabinet had agreed that the form of the oath, as offered, must be amended; if there was a stalemate, then the Ulster issue was to be made the occasion of a breakdown; and no agreement must be signed until it had first been accepted in Dublin.

On 5 December a new form of oath was offered:

'I . . . do solemnly swear true faith and allegiance to the Constitution of the Irish Free State as by law established and that I will be faithful to H.M. King George V, his heirs and successors by law, in virtue of the common citizenship of Ireland with Great Britain and her adherence to and membership of the group of nations forming the British Commonwealth of Nations'.

This was the first time that the new term 'British Commonwealth' was used, an indication of how far Lloyd George was willing to go in softening the impact of the controversial oath. Some minor concessions on defence and trade were also made. Then Lloyd George told the delegates that he had to inform Craig of the decision on the very next day at the latest. He showed them two letters, the first explaining that articles of agreement had been signed; the second that negotiations had broken down, which would mean war within three days. Contingency plans for a war in Ireland and the protection of loyalists had long since been laid down. On 31 October instructions were verbally conveyed to the troops in Dublin that 'certain suitable buildings should be selected' to house loyalists' families. The prime minister now demanded to know immediately which letter he would post to Belfast that same day. The Dáil delegates argued and discussed among themselves. They could not contact de Valera who was in Limerick inspecting troops and the urgency created by Lloyd George made delay impossible. No further concessions could be won and the threat of immediate war was very real. Collins had already told the IRB supreme council in November that the IRA had not 'an average of one round of ammunition for each weapon we had' and that they could not carry on fighting for much longer. So, at 2:10 a.m. on the morning of 6 December, the articles of agreement for a treaty were signed at 10 Downing Street.

The treaty had still to be ratified by the Dáil and if it proved unacceptable it would be scrapped. De Valera, as president, issued a statement after a cabinet meeting on 7 December referring to 'the proposed treaty with Great Britain'. On the same day the Cabinet in London advised the king that 4,000 internees should be released immediately: 'it would be more difficult for the Irish Parliament to reject the Articles of Agreement if the internees had been released, as an act of clemency immediately after the signature of those articles'. It seems clear, then, that both sides accepted that until the articles had been accepted by the Dáil they had no validity in law.

A long and acrimonious debate followed in the Dáil. The central issue was not partition, which was hardly mentioned, but the loss of republican status, epitomized in the controversial oath which every member of the Dáil in the new state would have to swear. That controversial oath (which was subsequently incorporated, word-for-word, in the constitution of the new Irish Free State) differed in fact from that in every other dominion, where allegiance was sworn to the crown. In Ireland 'true faith and allegiance' was first sworn to 'the Constitution of the Irish Free State as by law established' and only then did the elected deputy swear to 'be faithful' to the crown. The crown was the common link between the two separate states – exactly the position which had been set out so long ago in the proclamation of the Irish parliament in 1460.

It was of crucial importance that, on 10 December, Collins persuaded the supreme council of the IRB to back the treaty and support its ratification by the Dáil. His argument, as he expressed it later in the Dáil on 19 December, was that it offered the freedom to achieve freedom. When the Dáil adjourned for Christmas on 22 December it was still not clear what way the vote would go. Public opinion seemed to be favouring the treaty, but when the Dáil debate resumed on 3 January the outcome was still uncertain. The vote, when it was finally taken on 7 January, was close, 64 to 57 in favour of ratifying the treaty. De Valera resigned his presidency, led his anti-treaty supporters from the Dáil, and Griffith was elected as new president.

Under the terms of the treaty a provisional government was established, with a new cabinet, pending a general election when the people would be given their chance to vote for or against the treaty. The new Dáil would then enact a new constitution, it would be confirmed by the British parliament, and the Irish Free State would be by law established. At long last independence would be achieved.

15 Towards a Republic

The terms of the treaty had stipulated that the 'members of Parliament elected to constituencies in Southern Ireland' under the 1920 act were to be summoned and were to establish a provisional government. The British government would then 'take the steps necessary to transfer to such provisional Government the powers and machinery requisite for the discharge of its duties'. On 14 January the elected members of that parliament, without de Valera and his republican followers, established the provisional government under Michael Collins as chairman. Two days later the last of the viceroys, Viscount Fitzalan, formally surrendered powers of government, symbolized by the handing over of Dublin castle which for centuries, since its institution in 1204, had been the centre of English rule – 'that dread Bastille of Ireland', as Collins called it.

The administration based in the castle now came under the new government. While 300 officials volunteered to transfer to Belfast, 21,000 civil servants remained, with their files of records, to serve the new state. All military barracks were slowly evacuated and, with arms and ammunition, were handed over to the IRA, still nominally under the leadership of Richard Mulcahy as Chief-of-Staff. Bound by their oath to the Dáil, most units remained loyal to the new government. But others, led by anti-treaty republicans such as Liam Mellows, Rory O'Connor and Ernie O'Malley, posed a dangerous threat to the peace.

A split which had occurred in the IRA following the defeat of the republicans in the Dáil now became institutionalized. On 5 February Cumann na mBan rejected both the treaty and the new provisional government. On 26 March members of the IRA met in convention, despite a ban by Mulcahy, who was now Minister of Defence. There were 233 delegates present, representing over 112,000 members, and on a vote they rejected the new government, took a new oath to the Republic, as distinct from the Dáil, and established an army executive as their new authority. Commonly called 'irregulars' by supporters of the treaty, the dissidents soon caused trouble in many areas. Some newspapers which supported the treaty were attacked, even wrecked, and in one case in Clonmel had its press smashed and the type melted down. Barracks were raided to procure arms, government forces were attacked, and by 6 May eight soldiers had already been killed and as many as 49 wounded. Many post offices around the country were attacked and money stolen. In Dublin a raid on the Bank of Ireland yielded £50,000 and some buildings in the city centre were occupied by irregulars. Then on 14 April a unit lead by Rory O'Connor seized the Four Courts in the heart of Dublin and openly challenged the government. The country now seemed to be heading towards civil war.

In a desperate attempt to provide for some sort of coalition government, Collins and de Valera made a pact on 20 May whereby agreed Sinn Féin candidates, chosen for each constituency in proportion to their strength in the current Dáil, would contest the forthcoming election. This blatant anti-democratic arrangement was condemned by many. Colonel Maurice Moore (brother of George Moore the novelist), later elected to the new senate of the Free State, wrote to Mulcahy on 9 May and told him bluntly that 'political parties have no right to impose such a rule on the people, it is really an anti-democratic manoeuvre, and even more degrading than the imposition of a military despotism and the prevention of elections'. But despite this agreement, which admittedly broke down in some areas, in the election on 16 June the anti-treaty party won only 36 seats, as against 58 pro-treaty Sinn Féin, a surprising 17 for labour, seven for the farmers, and 10 independents – altogether 92 for the treaty. There could be no question now of what was the democratically expressed wish of the Irish people.

But for the die-hard Republicans this did not matter. During the treaty debates in the Dáil it had become clear that it was the republic, and not partition, that was the issue. Anything less was regarded as a betrayal. When Ernie O'Malley warned Cathal Brugha that the people had not been consulted, implying that their wish should settle the matter, the ominous reply had been that 'if so, we never would have fired a shot'. The gun must now decide the outcome. Already the irregulars had made this clear. In mid-February they had killed 27 in Belfast and wounded 68; another attack in May left 14 dead. By the end of May a total of 87 Protestants had been killed, as well as 150 Catholics, in what the occupiers of the Four Courts regarded as 'the war in the North'.

Then on 22 June, less than a week after the election, Field Marshal Sir Henry Wilson was assassinated in London by two members of the IRA. A former Chief of the Imperial Staff who had been elected a unionist MP for North Down only five months previously, his murder came as a terrible blow to the peace movement in Ireland. Even though rumours at the time, and ever since, linked the name of Collins to the killing, there seems no doubt that it was carried out by what the British government at the time called 'irregular elements of the IRA'. As chairman of the provisional government in Dublin Collins received a strongly worded protest from London, in which the prime minister told him that 'documents have been found upon the murderers of Sir Henry Wilson which clearly connect the assassins with the Irish Republican army, and which further reveal the existence of a definite conspiracy against the peace and order of this country'. Then in a bitter speech in parliament on 26 June Churchill warned the Irish that 'if through weakness, want of courage or some other less charitable reason' the Four Courts in Dublin were not immediately brought back under government control, then this failure would be regarded by the British government as a formal violation of the treaty. Lloyd George, too, demanded that Rory O'Connor should no longer 'be permitted to remain with his followers and his arsenal in open rebellion in the heart of Dublin in possession of the Courts of justice, organising and sending out from this centre enterprises of murder'. The implication was clear – the London assassination had been organized from the Four Courts. He insisted that 'the necessary action will be taken by your government without delay' and offered 'the necessary pieces of artillery' and any other assistance which might be required.

Even before this the British government had been making contingency plans for coping with the possible defeat of the provisional government in Ireland by the irregulars. On 8 April General Boyd, the Commander-in-Chief of British troops still in the Dublin area, was given secret instructions for the occupation of Dublin in the event of a *coup d'etat*. Early in May further plans were made for action in the event of what the director of military intelligence called 'the declaration of a republic of Ireland and the overthrow or absorption of the provisional government'. These involved not only the landing of troops from England, but plans were made for air raids, the bombing of specific coastal towns, as well as the rescue of 'loyal persons and their families living in the interior' and an embargo on exports from Ireland.

Collins had been reluctant to move against the irregulars, knowing that the use of force against them would inevitably lead to civil war. Even the implied threat of war by Lloyd George failed to rouse him to immediate action. He appeared to be ambiguous in his attitude: chairman of the provisional government, with the responsibility for upholding the rule of law; yet at the same time retaining his connection as president with the secret IRB, which he was later to reorganize while helping to arm the IRA in the north. On 3 August he wrote to Cosgrave: 'I am forced to the conclusion that we may yet have to fight the British in the northeast'. After his death the IRB, which he had reorganized, amended its constitution, with a clause which pledged it to be not only the custodian of the republican ideal, but also to organize the nation militarily to achieve the republic in conjunction with the national Free State army which now existed.

But when the irregulars in the Four Courts took prisoner General J.J. 'Ginger' O'Connell, assistant Chief-of-Staff, on 27 June and held him hostage, Collins was left with no choice. The irregulars ignored his ultimatum to surrender and at 4 a.m. on 28 June the shelling of the Four Courts began. On 30 June, those in occupation surrendered, but not before they had caused the loss of nearly all the records stored in the Public Record office there, one of the finest archives in Europe. Twenty years later Ernie O'Malley related how a burning volume fell before him, which contained the record of payments by the government to informers in 1798. More than seven hundred years of irreplaceable records were lost in the explosion. Thus did the terrible civil war begin.

Many republicans were driven by ideological fantasies and unrealistic dreams. During the treaty debates in the Dáil Mary MacSwiney had exclaimed that 'the fight' (which she said the pro-treaty republicans had betrayed) had been:

> 'essentially a spiritual fight . . . a fight of right against wrong, a fight of small people struggling for a spiritual ideal against a mighty, rapacious and material empire; and as the things of the spirit have always prevailed, they prevail now'.

Cardinal Logue, in June 1923, put it bluntly: 'the people of Ireland are running wild after dreams and chimera and turning the country upside down in the process'. But in fact the revolutionary republicanism and socialism which had inspired 1916 and which animated the leaders of the subsequent struggle for freedom was in the main urban and bourgeois, even in its literary manifestations. Rural Ireland, and indeed much of Ireland outside Dublin, was not deeply touched by these sentiments. The great mass of the people were never involved as they had been in the drive for Catholic emancipation behind O'Connell. Religion mattered far more than abstractions like nationalism. The land mattered even more and had made Davitt and Parnell the charismatics of a new Ireland. Maurice Moore wrote to Mulcahy from Mayo in May 1922 to tell him that Protestants were being driven from their homes and their lands occupied. He said that this was because they were landlords, and not because they were Protestants. He claimed that republicans were 'making a bid for support through an agrarian movement'. He added: 'The people of the west have no anti-Protestant feeling, but they have a very strong desire to take the land, and that is being utilized to raise an agrarian agitation, to popularize the anti-Treaty party'. Most of those who did choose the gun were young, often driven by material considerations rather than any ideology, and thus not averse to using the disturbances for personal gain or private vendetta. The vast majority of the people chose the ballot box.

John Dillon, the former MP, was in Dublin when the government finally began forcibly to repossess buildings, including the Four Courts, occupied by the anti-treaty forces. He described the scale of destruction vividly in a letter of 28 June, where he said that the night before 'was quite as bad as, if not worse than, the hottest night of 1916'. A week later he said that the destruction was in fact worse than what had happened in 1916:

> 'Yesterday the sniping around this house was the worst we had during the fight. And at 12 o'clock last night O'Connell Street was a perfect sea of

fire – an appalling spectacle. Looking from our top windows, and listening to the explosions as the ammunition dumps were reached by the flames, it seemed as if the whole city must be destroyed'.

A war of destruction had truly begun.

By the time Dublin, Cork, Limerick and other main centres were firmly under government control, there was no hope that anti-treaty forces could win the war. There was no real coherence between the different units. One unit, for various reasons, was often unable to cooperate with or help another. Republicans in Cork and Tipperary, where many of the most active units operated, found it difficult to reinforce each other. Local particularism was very strong: the further away from Dublin, the more independent the local unit. Lacking central control, they all too often engaged in actions which served no other purpose beyond the locality. The civil war quickly degenerated into localized and largely disconnected incidents of violence.

Meanwhile two deaths occurred which had an enormous bearing on the political outcome. On 12 August Arthur Griffith, worn out by the stress of government, died from a cerebral haemorrhage. For so long the protagonist of home rule and the man who, as President of the Dáil, was responsible for maintaining the democratic process in politics, Griffith was a key figure in the winning of independence. But the loss of Collins was a major disaster. Killed in an ambush at Bealnablath in county Cork on 22 August, his death removed the man who was best placed to negotiate some kind of settlement with de Valera and the less radical wing of the anti-treaty republicans. At the same time it must be said that his role in recent months had been causing some unrest. Despite pressure after the general election on 16 June, he had failed to summon the new Dáil, even after the Labour party in July threatened to withdraw unless it was convened, and suspended it on a fortnightly basis. He was replaced as Chairman of the provisional government by William Cosgrave on 25 August and it is significant that one of the first decisions of the new government was to put aside Collins's suspension and to summon the third Dáil to meet on 9 September.

The other side, too, lost leaders. On 5 July Cathal Brugha, who had refused to surrender in the Hamman Hotel until he was forced out, was shot and died two days later. Erskine Childers was captured in Wicklow, found to be in possession of a revolver (it was in fact a small, ornamental weapon, a gift of Michael Collins), and on that technicality was condemned to death and executed on 24 November, even though he had lodged a *habeas corpus* appeal. As he told his wife in a letter from prison: 'I am full of intense love for Ireland'; and he had proved that love many times over since the day he landed the priceless shipment of guns at Howth harbour. Now his heroism was forgotten and a terrible revenge exacted for his refusal to deny his republican commitments.

To help suppress what it construed as an armed rebellion, the Dáil had agreed on 28 September to establish military courts with power to inflict the death penalty for a wide range of offences, including unauthorized possession of arms. From then to the end of the war 77 irregulars were executed by firing squads. The most infamous executions happened on 8 December, as a reprisal for the shooting dead of a member of the Dáil, Sean Hales. Four prisoners, representing the fours provinces, were chosen: Rory O'Connor, Liam Mellows, Joseph McKelvey and Dick Barrett, all of whom had been in prison since the surrender of the Four Courts and none of whom had been found guilty of any crime. The year before, O'Connor had been best man at the wedding of Kevin O'Higgins who, now in cabinet as Minister for Justice, was nominally responsible and agreed to his execution, which he always defended in the interest of the state. It saddened him, but he added: 'It was done deliberately, and in the belief that only by that method could representative government and democratic institutions be preserved here. It was at once curative and deterrent'. In a letter to his sister, written at 7 a.m. just before his execution, O'Connor told her: 'I forgive all my enemies. I have never felt any feelings of revenge'.

But others thought differently and exacted terrible revenge. The executions were widely condemned, even by government supporters. John Dillon told a friend in a letter: 'Even amongst supporters of the government I think the predominant feeling is hostile. And really so far as I can recollect there is no exact precedent for such a proceeding in the annals of any modern civilized government'. A week after the executions a letter from the Hales family was published in the *Cork Examiner*, expressing their horror at the reprisals, condemning the executions which could only lead to further murders. But on 11 February 1923 O'Higgins's father was murdered in front of his wife and daughter in his own home.

A terrible blow to the anti-treaty forces was a joint pastoral letter issued by the Catholic bishops on 10 October: 'the guerilla warfare now being carried out by the irregulars is without moral sanction, and therefore the killing of national soldiers in the course of it is murder before God'. Anyone involved was guilty of grave sin and therefore forbidden confession or holy communion and excommunicated if they persevered in such evil. Some left the church as a result, never to return.

But it did not halt the killings or the widespread destruction. Government forces, too, retaliated and were responsible for some terrible atrocities. At Knocknagoshal in Kerry three officers and two soldiers were killed in a trap laid by irregulars. On 7 March by way of retaliation, nine republican prisoners were tied to a mine which was then exploded. Miraculously one of them escaped death. And so it went on, reaching levels of depraved behaviour which even the Black and Tans had never attempted.

One sad aspect of the conflict was that close friends were often on opposing sides. Michael Collins cried when he heard that Harry Boland, who had been shot when trapped in a hotel in Skerries, had died. In an ambush in county Sligo, Sean Adair of the Free State army was killed in an ambush which was led by Frank Carty. But in May 1921, when Carty, after his arrest in Scotland, was being transferred from court to prison in Glasgow, a rescue attempt by the IRA resulted in the killing of a policeman. It was Sean Adair who was arrested, tried for murder, acquitted on a technicality, only to be killed later by the very man he had tried to rescue.

Meanwhile as the struggle continued with increasing ferocity, the elements of a new state had to be stitched together. A constitution was drafted, approved in principle by the British, accepted by the Dáil on 25 October, and ratified by act of the English parliament, together with the treaty, on 5 December 1922. Saorstát Éireann (the Irish Free State) was now legally in being and on 6 December T.M. Healy was sworn in as first Governor General, the Dáil approved an executive council, and the first official postage stamp (2d.) was issued. The Oireachtas (legislature) consisted of the Dáil and the Senate. A new police force, the Gárda Síochána (Civic Guards), already in being, was greatly expanded. As an unarmed police force it was unusual in the circumstances and so it has remained, one of the great achievements of the Free State. The army, too, expanded rapidly, reaching 55,000 before the end of the war.

Even though the balance had tilted decisively in favour of the government, the demands of the war were straining resources to the limit. By the spring of 1923 about 12,000 republicans had to be maintained in prison. The deliberate policy of destruction pursued by the republicans, in addition to the more familiar guerrilla tactics, not only meant the burning of enemy houses, but the sabotage of railways and public services generally. Costs continued to mount.

But the die-hard republicans refused to be moved. When de Valera tried to suggest that the Irish people should be 'the ultimate court of appeal' and vote on the issue, he was told by Mary MacSwiney that he was wrong:

> 'If that is granted, our civil war had no sanction; the bishops are quite justified; and so is everything the Free Staters have said to us. And if it is right now to submit to majority rule on this point, it was equally right last July. What have all the lives been lost for?'.

Still the position of the republicans continued to deteriorate. While the hard-liners dominated the army council there was no hope that any peace moves initiated by de Valera could succeed. But the death of Liam Lynch, Chief-of-Staff, in April, removed the most adamant of the no-surrender brigade and hard bargaining with Cosgrave's government began.

The army council met again and decided on what they called a 'simple quit' – not a surrender, but a simple ending of the armed struggle. So Frank Aiken, the new Chief-of-Staff, issued orders that all arms must be dumped and a cease-fire come into operation immediately. On 28 April the *Irish Times* published a proclamation from 'Dáil Éireann' and 'Government of the Republic of Ireland' ordering a cease-fire, signed by de Valera as President. He had already sent a message to the 'troops', which the newspapers published on 23 April:

'Soldiers of the Republic! Legion of the Rearguard! The Republic can no longer be defended successfully by your arms. Further sacrifice of life would be vain, and continuance of the struggle in arms unwise in the National interest. Military victory must be allowed to rest for the moment with those who have destroyed the Republic'.

He thanked them for having 'saved the Nation's honour' and asked them to accept the sufferings which were bound to come 'in a manner worthy of men who were ready to give their lives for their cause'. The civil war ended, but it was not forgotten. It left a legacy of hatred and distrust which was to colour Irish politics down to the present time. Over 800 soldiers had been killed on the pro-treaty side and perhaps as many as 5,000 republicans, not counting civilian deaths. The army of the republic had not been dissolved and formed the nucleus of the new Sinn Féin party which was to contest the general election in August 1923, the first under the new constitution of the Irish Free State. Before then republicans who had not surrendered, but chose to go on the run, faced the risk of execution without trial for possession of arms, if they were captured. As late as October 1923 the body of Noel Lemass was found in the Dublin mountains, even though he had been arrested three months previously. When de Valera stood for Clare in the election, he was arrested on 15 August (the date deliberately chosen because it was the feast of the Assumption) on the platform in Ennis where he addressed the thousands gathered to cheer him. He was then held as a prisoner, without trial, until he was finally released on 16 July 1924. By then he had been elected to the new Dáil on 23 August 1923, when the Clare electors had given him 17,762 votes as against 8,196 for his nearest pro-treaty challenger.

In that election the republicans, standing as Sinn Féin, had enjoyed a remarkable success, in spite of lack of money and the campaigning difficulties of the candidates. They won 44 seats, an improvement on the 36 gained in the last election, though this time from a larger total of 153 (as against 128) seats. The government candidates, now standing as members of Cumann na nGaedheal, the new political party founded by Cosgrave in April 1923, won 63 seats. The farmers won 15, Labour 14 and Independents a surprising 16. There could be no doubt in anyone's mind now what the wish of the Irish people was.

Because Sinn Féin continued to pursue an abstentionist policy, refusing to take the oath required by law, Cosgrave and his party formed the new government. The challenge was immense. The war had cost the new state as much as 20 million pounds, at a time when the huge damage to railways, roads, bridges, and buildings everywhere had to be repaired. Public order had to be restored, justice had to be administered, a new framework of courts and judges provided, and a civil service organized to meet the needs of the new state. The police force continued to develop, with new training provided. But it was difficult to cope with the problems, particularly in rural Ireland, where suspicion of all police officers died hard. The army, too, had to be reduced in numbers and changed into a professional force to replace the thousands of untrained amateurs who had largely made up the army of the state during the civil war. But the reduction in numbers, from nearly 50,000 to about 20,000, inevitably caused problems with those who were to be demobilized. There was also some resentment at the employment of former British army recruits. Most serious of all, an IRB element in the army, loyal to the memory of Collins, argued that the government was betraying the republican ideal. A crisis developed when an ultimatum was delivered to the government in March 1924. This, the 'army mutiny', was successfully confronted by the government and the upshot was not only a radical pruning of republican sympathizers, but the permanent restoration of the principle of army subordination to the Irish government. Given what happened so often in other states which won their independence, and often were plunged into civil war which resulted in military dictatorships, this, together with the establishing of an unarmed police force, was a crucial outcome of Ireland's civil war.

The government soon faced a new crisis in that same year. The long-awaited boundary commission, promised in the treaty and supposedly guaranteeing the cession of northern areas to Ireland which might make the northern state unviable, was finally established. A judge of the South African supreme court, Richard Feetham, was appointed Chairman and Arbitrator of Claims. But when the final decision on transfers of land and population was made in October 1925 it was way below what the Irish had expected. Only something over 180,000 acres (with a population of 27,834 Catholics and 3,476 others) was to be transferred to the south, which in turn would have to yield nearly 50,000 acres (with a population of 2,764 Catholics and 4,830 others) to Northern Ireland. For the most part this was confined to parts of south Armagh (going south) and east Donegal (going north). It ignored the clams of nationalists in parts of Derry (including the city) and south Down, as well as in other areas along the border, to be included in the Free State. Eoin MacNeill, the southern representative, resigned in disgust from the commission and on 2 December 1925 the governments of the Free State, Northern Ireland, and Britain formally agreed to suppress the commission's report, let the boundary as it was stand unchanged, and (as a sop to the Irish) modify some of financial provisions of the treaty in favour of the Free State.

In Northern Ireland there was, naturally, jubilation, not least because the possibility of 'Rome rule' seemed to be removed for good. Special church services in thanksgiving were announced in the *Belfast Telegraph* of 5 December. They had good reason to give thanks, for the new southern state had begun to assume the character of a Catholic dominion. Eoin MacNeill had long since expressed the conviction that Catholicism was an essential element in the new Irish nation, just as the Irish language was. The new Irish state, which represented that nation, would therefore be Catholic as well and this was a view shared by many of those who were to shape the new Ireland. A Catholic ethos must predominate.

As early as 24 February 1921 Cosgrave proposed that 'there should be a sort of Upper House in the Dáil consisting of a theological board which would decide whether any enactments of the Dáil were contrary to faith and morals or not'. The pope should also be given a guarantee that the Dáil would not make laws contrary to the teaching of the Catholic church. Although these proposals got short shrift, and even though the provisional government in 1922 had refused to insert in the new constitution a statement that 'the Irish State shall recognise, as heretofore, the inviolable sanctity of the marital bond', it did include a qualification in the guarantee of 'freedom of conscience and the free profession and practice of religion' that this was 'subject to public order and morality'.

Subsequently, when petitions for divorce were lodged with the Oireachtas, the Catholic Archbishop of Dublin was consulted and he told the government's representative that the Catholic church claimed 'sole jurisdiction' with regard to marriage. In October 1923 a meeting of the Catholic bishops declared that 'it would be altogether unworthy of an Irish legislative body to sanction the concession of such divorce, no matter who the petitioners might be'. In an interview on 7 February 1924 with Archbishop Byrne of Dublin, Cosgrave discussed the matter and a few days later was sent a definitive statement of the reasons why divorce must be refused not only to Catholics, but to 'heretics, schismatics, and apostates, in a word all Christians'. On 11 February Cosgrave told the Dáil that 'the whole fabric of our special organization is based upon the sanctity of the marriage bond' and the meeting agreed to rule out of order the introduction of any bill allowing divorce in the state. The only protest recorded in the Dáil came from the Trinity College deputies.

The fact was that the foundation of the Irish Free State coincided with the advent of a more authoritarian papacy in Rome, with the election of Pius XI in 1922 and his successor Pius XII in 1939. The statement in the Catholic catechism that 'outside the church there is no salvation' was to be taken seriously. The 1926 census revealed that out of a population of 2,971,992 in the Free State there were 2,751,269 who were Catholics. Many Protestants left the state rather than live under a regime which denied what Professor Thrift had called, during the Dáil debate on divorce, 'fair play to all sections of the community'. He also warned that such discrimination 'will raise up one more barrier against a possible union between the north of Ireland and the south of Ireland'. In the Senate the great poet W.B. Yeats echoed this:

'It is perhaps the deepest political passion with this nation that north and south should be united into one nation. If it ever comes that north and south unite, the north will not give up any liberty which she already possesses under her constitution. You will then have to grant to another people what you refuse to grant those within your borders'.

He called the measure 'grossly oppressive' to 'a minority of this nation' – the people of Burke, Grattan, Swift, Emmet and Parnell. But the process of imposing a Catholic ethos continued, with the censorship of films, the disaster of book censorship, culminating in the 1937 constitution, when 'the special position' of the Catholic church passed into law.

That constitution was the work of de Valera, who in 1925 had unambiguously proclaimed that 'Ireland remains a Catholic nation, and as such, sets the eternal destiny of man above the issues and idols of the day'. He had been released from prison in July 1924. Tired, and somewhat disillusioned with politics, he made his way to Rome, disguised as a priest, the following summer. There his friend Monsignor Hagan, rector of the Irish college, advised him of the theological niceties involved in taking the disputed oath of allegiance which barred him and the other elected Sinn Féin members from taking their seats in the Dáil. He now felt certain that sooner rather than later Sinn Féin must get around the oath and enter the Dáil.

After his return to Dublin the Sinn Féin executive called an extraordinary Árd-fheis on 9 March to consider proposals along this line from the president. But an amendment by Father O'Flanagan – 'That it is incompatible with the fundamental principle of Sinn Féin to send representatives into any usurping legislature set up by English law in Ireland' – was only narrowly defeated by 179 votes to 177 (with 85 abstentions), while another O'Flanagan resolution effectively barring Sinn Féin from the Dáil was carried by 233 votes to 218. Clearly the die-hards were still in control. De Valera immediately resigned as president and the following May established a new political party, Fianna Fáil (Soldiers of Destiny) in Dublin. Significantly, its official title was Fianna Fáil – the Republican Party, a title it still holds today. Even though he attracted most of the leading members of Sinn Féin, many still remained loyal (as they saw it) to the republic. The IRA, too, was split, not for the last time – as Brendan Behan, drawing on his own experiences of the IRA as a young man, later cynically put it: 'The first item on the agenda (of any IRA meeting) is the split'.

When a general election was held on 9 June 1927 the government won 47 seats, the new Fianna Fáil won 44, labour 22, the farmers 11, and others 29 (including five Sinn Féin). But when the new Dáil assembled on 23 June and Fianna Fáil tried to take their seats without taking the controversial oath, they were locked out. Then, on 10 July, Kevin O'Higgins, Minister for Justice, was shot dead while on his way to mass. It seems certain that the murder was committed by three IRA members without the sanction or knowledge of the army council; and despite intense efforts by the government no person was ever brought to trial. O'Higgins survived for five hours after the shooting and, like Erskine Childers before him, he forgave his murderers before he died. But, as in the case of Childers, this did nothing to mollify those bent on revenge.

The crime was denounced by Cosgrave as 'the fruit of the steady, persistent attack against the state and its fundamental institutions'. Within days the government introduced a public safety bill which would give it power to establish new military courts with draconian powers, suppress periodicals, and proclaim as unlawful any 'association' seen as a threat to the rule of law. Even more important for the future was a bill which would require all candidates before nomination in an election to the Dáil to declare that if they were elected they would take the oath prescribed by law. This posed an immediate problem for de Valera and the Fianna Fáil deputies. But if, as he continued to insist, the oath was 'a mere formality', there was no reason why they should not accept the formality. The party issued a public statement saying that they regarded 'the declaration', as they called it, 'as an empty formality ' and they repeated that their 'only allegiance is to the Irish nation, and that it will be given to no other power or authority'. On 11 April they entered Leinster House, pushed the Bible aside, and having covered the copy of the oath on the page in front of them, each of them signed the page.

Having taken this momentous step, de Valera was in a position to join with other Dáil members in voting on a motion of no confidence in the government. It ended in a tie (70–70) and only the casting vote of the Speaker saved the government. Cosgrave had little option but to call a general election, held on 15 September. His party won 62 seats, but Fianna Fáil had a spectacular success in winning 57, and the others 34. Cosgrave was able to form a new minority government, but de Valera was now the leader of the kind of vigorous opposition which the Dáil had so far not witnessed. The emergence of a two-party system as the dominant feature of the Dáil was a hugely important step in strengthening the parliamentary democracy which had become dominant in independent Ireland at a time when it was under threat in so many places elsewhere.

The IRA may have gone into decline and lost direction after Fianna Fáil chose constitutional politics, but it did not disintegrate. Cumann na mBan remained particularly active, not least in conducting a propaganda campaign to win support for republicanism. The gun was still used. Spies were occasionally executed – as Patrick J. Carroll of the Dublin brigade on 30 January 1931 – and the Gárda Síochána received a shock when Superintendent Curtin, who was trying to bring to court IRA members found drilling in Tipperary, was shot outside his home some weeks later. There was also some movement towards radical socialism, with the launching of Saor Éire (Free Ireland) in 1931, which was immediately denounced as communist by church and state alike and gave rise to what became known as the 'red scare'. But the most serious worry to the government was the violence, and particularly the shootings and intimidation of juries, which persisted. When the IRA organized a parade to Wolfe Tone's grave at Bodenstown in county Kildare for Sunday 31 June, the government banned it. All bus and train services to the area were cancelled, the roads to the cemetery were sealed off by the army, and every effort was made to prevent republicans from reaching the graveside. But thousands assembled at Sallins and marched to the grave in such numbers that the army lost control. Thousands more had already assembled there, among them de Valera and a Fianna Fáil contingent. The result of this failure to control the republicans, the continuance of widespread illegal drilling, the intimidation of juries and the increase in violence generally, convinced the government that new and more drastic measures were demanded. In October a new Public Safety Act became law, establishing a military tribunal with the power to impose the death penalty, and from whose decisions there could be no appeal. On 20 October the IRA, Saor Éire, Cumann na mBan and nine other organizations were banned and many were arrested and thrown into jail.

Meanwhile Ireland, like other states, was experiencing the effects of the great depression following the 1929 crash. In September 1931 Patrick McGilligan, the Minister for Industry and Commerce, summed up the resulting problems which the Free State now faced: 'falling revenue, increasing demands for services, falling prices, increasing unemployment, absence of emigrants' remittances and almost entire failure of dividends from foreign investments'. He argued that 'it would be sheer madness to think of trying to operate repressively throughout a miserable and poverty-stricken twelve months'. Cosgrave agreed and went to the country in February 1932.

As a party Cumann na nGael was poorly organized, with an electorate largely confined to the better-off farmers, businessmen and the middle class generally. Fianna Fáil with a superb system of local organization, based on the cumann in almost every parish and incorporating many of the old Sinn Féin contacts, was in a much better way to fight an election. The result showed this clearly: Fianna Fáil won 72 seats, the government party 56, and all the others only 24 between them. But small as it was, the Labour success in winning seven seats was enough to secure the election of Eamonn de Valera as president on 9 March. A Fianna Fáil government was formed and the party was to remain in power for the next 16 years.

Despite the terrible social, economic and political problems confronting them when they came into office, Cosgrave and his Cumann na nGael governments had achieved much during the 10 years since they attempted to establish an independent Ireland. Before the 1929 recession the economy prospered, in particular farming: the export of agricultural products in 1926 was not again equalled until 1960. The 1923 Land Act which made provision for the compulsory purchase of land still held on lease, meant that by 1929 the percentage of owner-occupied land rose from the 62 per cent of 1916 to more than 97 per cent. The creation of the ESB (Electricity Supply Board) in 1927, and the successful completion of the Shannon hydro-electric scheme, made electricity more widely available than ever before. When a national radio station (2RN) began broadcasting from Dublin on 1 January 1926 it ushered in a new age in mass communication.

But from a political perspective, perhaps the most important achievement of the government was the winning of international recognition of Ireland as an independent state, separate from Britain. When it was given membership of the League of Nations in September 1923 the new state was given a status which set it apart from the other members of the Commonwealth. This status was confirmed when it sent an ambassador to the USA in 1924. When Cosgrave addressed the opening meeting of the Imperial Conference in London in October 1923, he set a pattern for the future, where Ireland was to play an increasingly important role. By joining with Canada and South Africa in demanding that dominion status should be placed on an equal footing with Britain, they procured the Balfour declaration in 1926 that they were 'autonomous communities within the British Empire, equal in status, in no way subordinate one to another'. Four years later Patrick McGilligan played a leading role in the Imperial Conference in drafting what became the statute of Westminster. This crucial piece of legislation enacted that 'no law hereafter made by the Parliament of the United Kingdom shall extend to any of the said Dominions . . . otherwise than at the request and with the consent of that Dominion'; and that 'the Parliament of a Dominion has full power to make laws having extra territorial operation'. Here at last was a vindication of the pro-treaty argument of Collins and others that the treaty gave 'freedom to win freedom'.

But de Valera was far from satisfied and on 16 March, when he outlined to the press some of the reforms he planned to introduce in government, the abolition of the controversial oath of allegiance was still top of his list. He introduced a bill to remove the oath from the constitution on 20 April; but although passed by the Dáil, it was returned by the Senate and held up until May 1933 before it finally became law. The delay made de Valera determined to abolish the Senate as soon as possible.

Before then the Government had begun the release of republican prisoners, which gave rise to fears that the IRA might now be allowed to reassert itself in the Irish countryside. When the Public Safety Act was suspended, the military tribunal abolished, and the ban on the IRA and other organizations lifted, fears were increased. Anglo-Irish relations came under strain. The Governor General, James McNeill, was deliberately snubbed by members of the government who saw his office as a symbol of the monarchy in Ireland. He was particularly humiliated when during the 1932 Eucharistic Congress in Ireland, an event which got world-wide attention, he was kept in the background and was not even invited to attend the reception which the government hosted for important overseas delegates who were in attendance. Finally, de Valera secured the appointment of an old supporter, Domhmall Ó Buachalla, a 1916 veteran who ran a small shop in Maynooth, as Governor General. Ó Buachalla refused to take up his official residence in the magnificent Viceregal Lodge in the Phoenix Park. Instead, he moved into a small house in the suburbs, refused to discharge duties in public, and never entertained officially. Not only did this insult the office, it finally brought it to an end.

In September 1932 de Valera travelled to Geneva where he presided over a meeting of the council of the League of Nations. He was required to address the assembly, normally a harmless welcome to international delegates. But he astonished the assembly by putting aside the speech prepared by the secretariat and launching into a vigorous defence of the Convention, which had been openly flouted by Japan when she invaded Manchuria:

> 'No state should be permitted to jeopardize the common interest by self-ish action contrary to the Covenant, and no state is powerful enough to stand long against the League if the governments in the League and their peoples are determined that the Covenant shall be upheld'.

His speech was applauded in the international press. The London *Daily Herald* reporter said that it was 'the best speech I ever heard from a President of the League' and wrote that this was 'not only my own judgement', but was the opinion held by every journalist to which he spoke. No-one referred to the fact that years before de Valera had exploited that same Convention while in America, to try to win support for the Republic and, by implication, to denounce the partition of Ireland. That implication was still there and his Geneva speech could be interpreted, and in some quarters was, as an attack on Britain supposedly flouting the same Convention by imposing partition on Ireland. He was still determined to restore a 32 counties Republic.

But it was not partition which he now rigorously pursued as head of government in Ireland, but the abolition of the controversial oath of allegiance and the payment of land annuities to Britain. Under the treaty it had been agreed that the Free State government would repay these loans, made to Irish tenants years before to help them to purchase their lands. Now de Valera refused to continue the repayments of about two million pounds annually. After protracted negotiations, to no avail, the London government decided, in compensation, to impose a duty of 20 per cent *ad valorem* on all produce from Ireland entering Britain. What became known as the 'Economic War' began and had an important effect on Irish agriculture. It helped to achieve what de Valera favoured, to change many farmers from grazing to tillage, to produce what could be sold on the home market. But for the people in general it was a disaster, leading to much unemployment and consequent hardship. By the time agreement was finally reached with Britain in 1938 The economic war had cost the Irish state about £48,000,000. Under the agreement the Irish paid a lump sum of £10,000,000 to Britain. But in return, de Valera gained the right of duty-free entry to the British markets, while at the same time retaining the right to protect Irish industry. Hardly less significant, and of crucial importance in enabling Dublin to pursue a policy of neutrality in World War II, was the return to Ireland of the ports ceded to Britain under the 1922 agreement.

The release of political prisoners in 1932 had convinced many who had been pro-treaty in previous years that the de Valera government now enjoyed the active support of the IRA. When the Dublin brigade in June 1932, now swollen to 2,000 members, organized a march to Bodenstown for the Wolfe Tone commemoration, there was a strong Fianna Fáil delegation in official attendance. Free speech was threatened by the physical force tradition and indeed opponents of the new government were frequently heckled and even physically assaulted at political meetings in town and country. A new group, the Army Comrades' Association, was formed in 1931 to protect free speech and when General O'Duffy was dismissed as Gárda Commissioner by de Valera early in 1933, he took over as leader of the new movement. The members soon became known as 'Blueshirts' because of the uniform they wore and for a time they became a central force in Irish politics. Numbers grew rapidly, from about 8,000 in late 1932, to 38,000 in March 1934 and as high as 48,000 by the following August, the result of the charismatic leadership of O'Duffy. A year later they fell to 4,000 and then the movement rapidly disappeared.

Bitterly opposed to Fianna Fáil, most of the members were young, largely of middle-farmer (30 to 60 acre farms) background, mostly supporters of Cumann na nGael (later Fine Gael), and generally of the better educated. They were largely of the stock which had felt the impact of the economic war with Britain and this undoubtedly helped to recruit some. But they were not typical of the fascist movements which were threatening democracy elsewhere, whatever ideological aspirations some of the leaders may have had. Quite the opposite, in fact, because it was their perception of the IRA threat to free speech and their perceived influence over Fianna Fáil, which urged the majority to join. Their youthful ideology responded to the propaganda of O'Duffy and to the kind of sentiments which he expressed in speeches like that delivered on 30 July 1933:

> 'I believe there is a feeling in the country generally, and amongst the youth in particular, that economic measures of a really lasting and constructive character will prove unduly difficult, if not impossible, without political changes which will tend to substitute unity for sectionalism, and without a national spiritual awakening'.

The impact of the papal encyclical *Quadragessimo Anno* promulgated in 1931 undoubtedly had an influence. But the need to find protection against what a speaker in the Dáil in 1934 called the 'man-handling of a number of persons who did not agree with Fianna Fáil', which he said made 'numbers of nervous persons . . . afraid to go to meetings', was much more important.

When the government decided to ban Blueshirt parades and to prohibit the wearing of the uniform there was a bitter debate in the Dáil. One member accused the government of supporting 'those persons who wish to set up their views by physical force' and at the same time 'putting a ban on moral force' represented by 'an organized body of the best amongst the young men and women of our country, a body which is putting moral force against physical violence'. In a bitter attack he quoted a statute of 1539 in which the government of Henry VIII forbade the wearing of certain forms of dress or hairstyle and said that 'it is pretty obvious where President de Valera went for his precedent. King Henry VIII objected to the colour saffron, and President de Valera objects to the colour blue'. He also quoted a statute of Henry VII which forbade the use of cries like *Cromabo* or *Butlerabo* and said that he supposed 'we will shortly have some legislation making "Up Cosgrave" or "Up O'Duffy" a criminal offence'.

The bill was passed by the Dáil in 1934 after a bitter debate. But it was rejected by the senate, still dominated by Cumann na nGael (soon to become the new party of Fine Gael). By the time it would become law, it was superfluous. The Blueshirt movement fell apart. O'Duffy led an Irish brigade of 700 volunteers to Spain late in 1936, in support of Franco in the Civil War against the Government there, where they achieved little before returning home a year later. But they had fought in the battle of Jarama in February, where an IRA unit was supporting the communist government on the opposite side. Under the leadership of Frank Ryan, 300 of them left to support the communist government in Spain, where they joined the International Brigade.

But back in Ireland the IRA had finally been outlawed by the Fianna Fáil government. The horrendous murder on 24 March of 72-year-old Vice-Admiral Somerville at his home in Skibereen – a small card pinned to the body read: 'This English Agent sent fifty-two Irishmen to the British Army in the last seven weeks' – followed a month later by the callous execution of a young man on the street in Dungarvan, finally made the government react to the public condemnations. IRA leaders were arrested, the movement was proclaimed an unlawful association, all parades (including the annual one to Bodenstown) were banned. Toleration was at an end.

At that time de Valera had other serious matters on his mind, for he was now deep into preparations for a new constitution for Ireland. In December 1936, taking advantage of the crisis produced by the abdication of Edward VIII, he introduced a bill in the Dáil, removing all references to the crown and the Governor General from the Free State constitution and on 1 May following he published the draft of his new constitution, which was approved by the Dáil on 14 June. The Dáil was then dissolved and in the subsequent general election on 1 July Fianna Fáil won 69 seats, as against 48 for Fine Gael, 13 for Labour, and eight others. But, much more importantly, a referendum held on the same day accepted the new constitution by 685,105 votes to 526,945.

The 1937 constitution has remained as probably the most contentious piece of legislation to emerge from the de Valera era. It reflects his view of Ireland and its ethos, Catholic and Gaelic. De Valera once said that 'if I were told tomorrow, "You can have a united Ireland if you give up the idea of restoring the national language to be the spoken language of the majority of the people", I would, for myself, say no'. He wanted his people to realize that Irish was 'the language of Ireland, the language of their forefathers, and the bards and heroes who went before them, the language of Padraig Pearse, Thomas McDonagh and others whose policy was to Gaelicize Ireland so that it would be a true nation'. Romantic as the notion may have been, he never lost his dream of a Catholic, Irish-speaking Ireland, which would preserve what he considered to be the best part of the island's heritage from the past. As he expressed it in his famous broadcast of 17 March 1943:

> 'That Ireland which we dreamed of would be the home of a people who valued material wealth only as the basis of right living, of a people who were satisfied with frugal comfort and devoted their leisure to the things of the spirit; a land whose countryside would be bright with cosy homesteads, whose fields and villages would be joyous with the sounds of industry, with the romping of sturdy children, the contests of athletic youths, the laughter of comely maidens, whose firesides would be forums for the wisdom of serene old age. It would, in a word, be the home of a people living the life that God desires that men should live'.

In preparing the early drafts of the new constitution, de Valera was under fierce pressure to give due recognition to the place of the Catholic church in the state. He was pressurized to include the statement that 'the State acknowledges . . . that the Church of Christ is the Catholic Church' and to give no recognition to any other church or religion. He consulted a wide spectrum of Christian opinion, Church of Ireland, Presbyterian, Methodist, as well as Catholic. As a result, while the final version did include the famous article 44: 1.2.: 'The State recognizes the special position of the Holy Catholic Apostolic and Roman Church as the guardian of the Faith professed by the great majority of its citizens'; it also recognized not only the other christian churches and 'the Jewish congregations', but also 'the other religious denominations existing in Ireland'. The article which forbade the passing of any law 'providing for the grant of a dissolution of marriage' was also approved by those he consulted.

Irish was made the first language of the state, whose name henceforth was to be Éire. But much more contentious, then and ever since, was Article 2: 'The national territory consists of the whole island of Ireland, its islands and the territorial seas'; and Article 3: 'Pending the re-integration of the national territory, and without prejudice to the right of the Parliament and Government established by this Constitution to exercise jurisdiction over the whole of this territory, the laws enacted by that parliament shall have the like area and extent of application as the laws of Saorstát Éireann and the like extra-territorial effect'. This attempt to ignore the fact of partition has led to constant bitter denunciation by unionists which soured relations between the two governments.

Hardly less contentious at the time was the fact that only three women among the 152 members of the Dáil – known as the 'Silent Sisters' – were able to comment on the drafts. A number of women's organizations protested against some articles, which they argued were offensive to the dignity of womanhood. De Valera was adamant, however, in retaining his belief that the role of a woman was to be wife and mother, full-time, in an indissoluble marriage. But however anti-feminist his views might have been, the fact is that through the years since 1937 the courts have shown that his constitution had the capacity to advance women's rights and has resulted in giving the women of Ireland rights which are in some respects superior to those in England and even the USA.

For all its faults, de Valera's constitution did provide a stability which was lacking in many other parts of the world. The will of the people, as expressed in the constitution, did predominate in the future and no government could arbitrarily alter the rules to suit itself. The constitution, interpreted by independent judges in public courts, was there to prevent that.

To replace the Governor General of the old constitution, Ireland was now to have an Uachtaráin (President) who would reside in the old Viceregal lodge, henceforth to be known as Áras an Uachtaráin. It is significant that the man chosen to fill that office was Douglas Hyde, a Protestant, who was elected unopposed. This created problems, well illustrated when the parish priest of Aughrim Street, in which the Áras lay, demanded that the President should pay annual 'dues' as his predecessor inhabiting the house had done. When it was pointed out to him that Hyde was not a Catholic, he said it did not matter. He argued that 'the President's house was the home of the Head of a Catholic nation, the occupant of which had been appointed under a Constitution which was wholly Catholic in its outlook' and so the payment of dues was 'therefore a matter of duty and not of generosity'. He also insisted that, as with the Governor General, a Catholic chaplain should be attached to the house, even if the present occupant was a Protestant, 'inasmuch as he is the head of a Catholic country'.

The full irony of a Protestant presiding over a Catholic state was only fully revealed when Hyde died in 1949. On the day of his funeral, all the Catholic members of the government, including the taoiseach, remained outside St Patrick's cathedral until the service was over, before joining the funeral as it moved off to Roscommon. Canon law took precedence over their political duty and would not allow them to attend a Protestant religious service.

Having banished the king from the constitution, made Irish the first language of the state, and given formal, legal recognition to the special place of the Catholic church in Éire, de Valera gave northern unionists the ammunition they needed to brand what was in effect a new republic as sectarian and anti-Protestant. It strengthened their determination to preserve forever their place in the United Kingdom. There had been incidents which seemed to confirm the unionist view. In 1931 a Protestant woman, a graduate of Trinity College, had been refused appointment as Mayo County Librarian solely on religious grounds. Such sectarianism was not untypical of the Cumann na nGael government then in power. But de Valera, too, despite his anxiety to attack the government on every possible occasion, had defended this decision because, he argued, a Catholic community was entitled to demand the appointment of a Catholic in sensitive areas like education or health. Catholics were forbidden by their church from entering Trinity College. The censorship of films, but especially books, was another indication of the Catholic ethos which prevailed.

Just how trivial the reason for censorship could be was illustrated in the Senate when it was revealed that Kate O'Brien's *Land of Spices* was banned because she used the word 'pederast' and in one sentence ('she saw Etienne and her father, in the embrace of love') alluded to a homosexual act. A tragic example of censorship was the case of a window commissioned by the Cosgrave government from the artist Harry Clarke. It was intended to be a gift from the government to the office of the International Labour Conference of the League of Nations in Geneva. Despite having to go to Switzerland to try to cure the TB which eventually killed him, Clarke finished the elaborate window in 1930, only to have it turned down by Cosgrave. The series of panels celebrated the achievements of twentieth century Irish writers, who had brought fame to the new state. One panel depicted a scene from a story by Liam O'Flaherty, showing a nude girl dancing before Mr Gilhooley. Cosgrave told Clarke that it would 'not be desirable to include the panel which contains a representation from the books of Liam O'Flaherty', a banned author. After Clarke's death his widow had to refund the fee of £400 which he had been paid. When she approached the de Valera government in 1932 and asked Seán Lemass, the new Minister for Industry and Commerce, for help in the matter, she fared no better. Indeed she was told by an official that she was lucky she was not charged interest.

Later, the same kind of prejudice was evident when attempts were made to persuade the Irish government to offer asylum to Jewish refugees. When the Irish Coordinating Committee for Refugees was established in November 1938, at a time when many Jewish refugees were desperately trying to escape from Nazi persecution, it decided that only Christian refugees were to be accepted into Ireland.

But in Northern Ireland Catholics fared even worse under the unionist, Protestant regime there. Right from the very beginning of the Northern State, the unionists were determined that Catholics would be prevented from exercising the kind of influence their numbers in the community would support. Not only were constituencies organized to give unionist majorities by the process which became known as 'gerrymandering', but the new government there quickly set about getting rid of the system of proportional representation which had been introduced by Westminster in 1919. The secretary of the Tyrone Unionist Association said it all when he wrote to his opposite number in April 1922: 'I suppose you are engaged in preparing a scheme to make Fermanagh boundaries safe . . . [I am] gerrymandering at night . . . it is the hardest job I ever undertook . . . We have a big Nationalist majority against us'. But despite that majority, the constituency became a safe unionist seat.

The 1922 Special Powers act gave the Minister for Home Affairs the ability to prohibit all 'meetings, assemblies . . . or processions in public places' without cause. It was used ruthlessly against Catholics. While 12 July was soon designated a national holiday, Easter processions by Catholics were quickly attacked. In 1928 eight men were arrested at Milltown cemetery in Belfast because they refused to take flowers out of their lapels which the police decided were emblems of nationalism. Under the 1922 act they were then held in prison for three weeks without charge. From 1929 to 1935 Easter processions were banned and again from 1936 to 1948. Sir Basil Brooke, the future prime minister, in an infamous speech to an Orange parade on 12 July 1933 gave public expression to what most unionists believed. It was reported in the *Fermanagh Times*:

> 'There was a great number of Protestants and Orangemen who employed Roman Catholics. He felt that he could speak freely on this subject as he had not a Roman Catholic about his own place . . . Roman Catholics were endeavouring to get in everywhere and were out with all their force and might to destroy the power and constitution of Ulster. There was a definite plot to overpower the vote of Unionists in the North. He would appeal to Loyalists therefore, wherever possible, to employ good Protestant lads and lassies'.

Attitudes such as that, which continued to dominate successive northern governments, caused a polarization of politics on religious grounds which proved impossible to eradicate.

Meanwhile the IRA was determined to end unionist domination of the north by the use of force. When the Army Convention met in 1936, Tom Barry made a fiery speech and urged immediate war to drive the British out of Northern Ireland. The Convention was convinced and swept with emotion decided to begin the war with a raid on the military barracks in Armagh. Barry's own Cork brigade was to provide the nucleus of the unit and preparations went ahead. But just before the unit, dressed as civilians, was preparing to board the train for Dundalk, a representative from Cumann na mBan arrived at army headquarters. She said that her organization had resolved that they, too, should take part in this military operation against Armagh. It then emerged that this highly secret military operation had not only been openly discussed by the women at their meeting in Dublin, but was common gossip in Belfast and elsewhere. There was no option but to cancel the raid and Barry's grandiose plan for a great northern campaign was over without a shot being fired.

This comic opera incident caused no great surprise. The fact was that the IRA by then was in a state of complete disarray, split into rival factions, unable to plan adequately, much less execute, an operation which demanded united action and absolute secrecy. The arrest of Maurice ('Moss') Twomey in May 1936 and his subsequent imprisonment had deprived the group of its main organizing strength. On 18 June the IRA was banned by the government as an illegal organization and most of the leaders had to go on the run. Two years later the government was sufficiently confident that the

IRA no longer posed a serious threat to the rule of law and the release of political prisoners began, the last of them gaining freedom in May 1938.

But slowly the militants began to regroup under new leadership. In December 1938 a document was published, signed by seven men claiming to be the 'Executive Council of Dáil Éireann', transferring their authority to the Army Council of the IRA. Henceforward that council claimed to be acting on behalf of the second Dáil, which had never (they said) dissolved itself and which therefore was now the only authority still representing the people of Ireland. The result was quickly seen when the IRA, as 'the Government of the Irish Republic', on 4 January 1939 issued an ultimatum to the British government demanding the 'withdrawal of all British armed forces stationed in Ireland'. They announced that 'the Irish people' would 'in no event take part in a war of aggression against any people' who came into conflict with Britain.

By then it was clear to all that war in Europe was inevitable. On 19 February de Valera announced that it was government policy 'to preserve our neutrality in the event of war'. The British government was preparing for war, and a bill to introduce conscription was prepared. But under pressure from de Valera, Chamberlain announced on 4 May that Northern Ireland would be excluded from the legislation. On 2 September, the day before Britain and France formally declared war on Germany, de Valera once more announced that it was the intention of his government to remain neutral in any European war. Next day Ireland entered a period which was graphically described as 'the emergency'. The Dáil resolved 'that a national emergency exists'. An Emergency Powers Act was passed on 3 September 'for securing the public safety and the preservation of the state in time of war', giving the government power to regulate supplies, control prices, exercise censorship to protect neutrality, intern suspects, and generally deal with the problems caused by the new wartime situation. A new Ministry for Supplies was created, with Sean Lemass as Minister, and Aiken was made Minister for Coordination of Defensive Measures. Petrol rationing was introduced on 13 September.

Unlike other countries which remained neutral, Ireland was in no fit state to protect herself. With the army fully mobilized it could barely reach 19,000 (7,000 regulars and a reserve of 12,000), poorly equipped and with inadequate resources. There was virtually no navy – two small vessels and three torpedo boats – and her skies could not be protected with her tiny air force. She was at the mercy of the warring states, if they chose to attack or protect her neutrality. But after Poland had been divided between the Germans and Russians, a lull occurred. The period known as 'the phoney war' began and all immediate danger seemed to be removed. By March 1940 5,000 had been demobilized.

But then came the occupation of Norway, Denmark, Belgium, Holland and finally the fall of France in June 1940. The situation had changed dramatically and Ireland suddenly became strategically significant because of her position as an island in the Atlantic flanking Britain. If Hitler now pushed on and invaded Britain then clearly not only would the defence of Ireland become imperative, but fear of a British intervention became a reality. Churchill's speech in the commons on 6 November 1940 showed how real the danger was, when he complained of the lack of support from Ireland: 'The fact that we cannot use the South and West coasts of Ireland to refuel our flotillas and aircraft, and thus protect the trade by which Ireland as well as Britain lives, that fact is a most grievous burden and one which should never have been placed on our shoulders, broad though they be'. The reply of de Valera in the Dáil on the same day showed determination not to give way to any threat:

'I want to say to our people that we may be – I hope not – facing a grave crisis. If we are to face it, then we shall do it, anyhow, knowing that our cause is right and just and that, if we have to die for it, we shall be dying in a good cause'.

When questioned by Mulcahy about what he would do if British ships entered Irish ports uninvited, de Valera replied that they would be fired on. If the Germans invaded, he said, British help would be sought only as a last resort.

But the reality was that Ireland could do nothing except enlarge her armed forces and hope for the best. By Easter 1941 the Air Corps had been augmented, the marine service expanded, a Local Security Force (which soon became the Local Defence Force) created, all of which brought the services to about 250,000. Everywhere people got involved, if not in the armed forces then in the Red Cross and other ancillary organizations. A Department of External Affairs record shows that in 1941 there was a real fear of a German invasion and it commented: 'If and when our forces have reached a point at which they are no longer able to resist an actual invasion', then British aid is to be invited.

But before the end of 1941 the main centre of the war changed from Western to Eastern Europe, removing most of the pressure from Ireland. From the British perspective, too, that fact that she was able to use Northern Ireland meant that there was not the same need to find other bases to use in Ireland. From Derry, for example, entry to the Mersey or the Clyde could be adequately protected. And when the USA finally entered the war at the end of 1941 she was able to base many troops in the north and use Derry as her naval base. Ironically, then, the fact of partition probably saved Irish neutrality at a crucial stage in the war.

Safe as she was, Ireland had to endure considerable hardship as a result of the war. Grain could no longer be imported and the system of compulsory tillage which was introduced not only failed to make up what was lacking, but produced a very inadequate and poor quality substitute. Sugar, tea and fuel were severely rationed, as were bread (no white bread was available until the war was well over) and clothing. Coal became nearly unobtainable, so that supplies of gas and electricity were seriously curtailed. With severe rationing of petrol private motors more or less disappeared for the duration. Public transport, too, was seriously affected. Trains ran to Cork only twice a week, with the journey taking anything between eight and 12 hours and in the summer of 1944 the tram service in Dublin was suspended. It was estimated that in 1943 only small proportions of what had been available for popular consumption before the war were now to be had: 25 per cent of normal tea consumption; 20 per cent of petrol; 14 per cent of paraffin; 16 per cent of coal (for gas only – none for the home); 22 per cent of textiles. Shortages continued even after the war – rationing did not end until 1947 and some commodities remained in short supply until 1949.

Ireland suffered in other ways too. On 26 August 1940, for example, German bombs destroyed the creamery at Campile in county Wexford, killing three people. During January 1941 bombs were dropped in seven other counties. But the worst tragedy of all was to happen on 31 May, when the North Strand in Dublin was bombed. Thirty-four people were killed, 90 others seriously injured, 25 houses completely destroyed and 300 damaged to such a degree that many hundreds were made homeless.

The hardships of the war years brought Irish people together in a way not really seen since the struggle for independence and the first Dáil. But the IRA still had some supporters and some of those who believed (as many did in the early stages of the war) that Germany and the Axis would win were ready to accept the argument that the opportunity should be taken to attack England and end partition. Safe houses were provided, safe locations for drilling and war manoeuvres were found, and even a means of communicating with Germany by wireless was made available. After the 4 January 1939 ultimatum produced no reaction, the IRA had initiated a bombing campaign in England. On 16 January seven explosions damaged power stations and electrical distribution lines. More bombs followed on the London underground in February, resulting in serious injury, and the bombing campaign continued until 25 August when a bomb in Coventry killed five people and injured 70. Two men were convicted of the crime and were hanged in February 1940, despite a plea from de Valera to commute the sentences to imprisonment. Before the end of August 1939 there had been 130 explosions, resulting in seven deaths and many injured. By then all Irish living in England were suspect, many were arrested, homes searched, and the intensity of police activity made it nearly impossible for the IRA to continue with the bombing campaign in England.

Back in Ireland the government had decided on tough measures against the militants. In June 1939 an Offences Against the State Act provided for the internment of prisoners without trial. The need for harsh methods of repression was made embarrassingly clear when on 23 December a raid on the Magazine Fort in the Phoenix Park in Dublin saw the IRA get away with 13 lorry loads of ammunition, 1,084,000 rounds in all, which was the great bulk of the army's reserve supply. Even though all of this, and indeed even more, was recovered as a result of extensive raids and searches in January, it gave the government the excuse to rush through more repressive legislation in January 1940 which resulted in more IRA members being interned. Nine of these went on hunger strike in late February, two of whom died before the strike was ended on 19 April.

Contacts had been established before this with Germany and on 5 May Herman Goertz parachuted into county Meath and was given safe refuge deep in Wicklow by the wife of Francis Stuart, who was used by the Nazis (like the more famous William Joyce, Lord Haw-Haw) to broadcast propaganda in English from Germany. Goertz remained at large until 27 November 1942, without achieving anything. The Germans were really not anxious to get involved in Ireland and found the IRA contacts more of an embarrassment than anything else. All interest failed after Sean Russell, the Chief-of-Staff who had been trying to involve the Nazis, died in a submarine near Galway when returning from Germany.

Even though nothing came of those contacts with Germany, de Valera could take no chances with the IRA and a policy of ruthless suppression was followed during the war years. As a result of the work of the Special Branch, key figures were isolated and arrested, some were shot in gun battles, others were executed – such as the two (one a 1916 veteran) who were sentenced to death by a military tribunal after a shoot-out in Rathgar on 17 August and executed by firing squad in Mountjoy on 16 September 1940. None of those arrested were released after serving their prison sentences in Mountjoy or Arbour Hill, but were interned in the Curragh Camp until the government decided that the emergency was over. There most of them sat out the war, often in great hardship, creating a legacy of bitterness towards de Valera and his government which was to have serious repercussions in later times.

While the Irish government was punctilious in maintaining the strict law of neutrality, there was no doubt that whatever about de Valera's public utterances to the contrary, or actions like the visit to the German Legation to offer sympathy on the death of Hitler in 1945, that neutrality was heavily biased in favour of the Allies. On 24 May 1941 the Department of External Affairs prepared a document entitled: 'Help given by Irish Government to the British in Relation to the Actual Waging of the War', which set out in some detail for the government precisely how regular, in some cases daily, information was supplied from intelligence sources; from the elaborate coast-watching services monitoring the activities of German planes and submarines; and detailed meteorological reports. There was no protest over the regular overflying of national territory, and indeed an air corridor was provided to allow planes to get over the Atlantic more speedily and safely. Altogether 163 planes, English, American and German, crashed in Ireland during the war and 607 of the crew members died. But 223 survived and while the Germans remained interned for the duration, many of the others were allowed to return home. While the British Legation was allowed to maintain 'two secret wireless sets and a private line to London and Belfast', the

Germans were eventually compelled to hand over their transmitter. There was also no attempt to prevent migration from Ireland to a warring state. Huge numbers went to England, as many as 250,000, where they provided a crucial element in the labour force required to keep some industries going which were essential to the war effort. As many as 50,000 from Ireland joined the British armed services.

Perhaps the single most important gesture came in April and May 1941, when Belfast suffered two massive air raids in which almost 1,000 people died, many more were seriously injured, and 15,000 lost their homes. The Dublin Government replied in the most positive way. Not only were fire brigades rushed north to help, but relief centres were established to cater for refugees and money was collected to help the homeless in Belfast. De Valera made no bones about this: 'We are one and the same people . . . any help we can give them in the present time we will give them wholeheartedly, believing that were the circumstances reversed, they would also give us their help wholeheartedly'.

It may be that knowledge of the atrocities being committed by the Nazis helped to bias the government in favour of the Allies. While censorship kept this knowledge away from the public at large until the war was over, the government knew from early on what was happening in the concentration camps. The Minister responsible, Frank Aiken, later said: 'What was going on in the camps was pretty well known to us early on, but the Russian were as bad – you had only to look at what happened in Katyn forest [referring to the murder of an estimate 12,000 Polish officers by the Russians]. There are photographs to prove that'. Anti-English feelings still persisted. After the war Gerald Boland, Minister for Justice in the war cabinet, also made reference to Katyn, Dresden, Hiroshima and Nagasaki and marvelled at those responsible 'having the cheek to try anyone for war crimes'.

Churchill was only one of many British and American statesmen who were never satisfied with what they considered to be the adverse effects of Irish neutrality, despite the positive way it had been biased in favour of the Allies. On 13 May he broadcast a famous victory speech in which he made it clear that 'had it not been for the loyalty and friendship of Northern Ireland, we should have been forced to come to close quarters with Mr de Valera, or perish for ever from the earth'. De Valera replied on 17 May. It was not, as he said himself, 'the answer that springs to the lips of every man of Irish blood who heard or read that speech, no matter in what circumstances or in what part of the world he found himself'. Nor was it 'the reply I would have given a quarter of a century ago'. He staunchly, but in moderate terms, defended Irish neutrality. Having accepted that 'Mr Churchill is proud of Britain's stand alone, after France had fallen and before America entered the war', he went on with emotion:

'Could he not find in his heart the generosity to acknowledge that there is a small nation that stood alone not for one year or two, but for several hundred years against aggression; that endured spoilations, famines, massacres in endless succession; that was clubbed many times into insensibility, but that each time on returning consciousness, took up the fight anew; a small nation that could never be got to accept defeat and has never surrendered her soul?'

If this speech struck a chord with the emotions of the nationalist people of Ireland, it did nothing to counter the antagonisms which had been generated by de Valera's insistence in offering condolence to Hempel, the German Minister in Dublin, on the death of Hitler. Even though he insisted that as a neutral he was only doing what he had done two weeks previously, when he had gone to the embassy of the United States to offer similar condolences on the death of Roosevelt, relations with the British and American governments were cooled as a result. It did not help Ireland's application in August 1946 to join the United Nations, which was vetoed by the Soviet Union. Gromyko, the Foreign Minister, defended the veto because while the war lasted Ireland had continued to maintain friendly relations with fascist states. 'Her behaviour is hardly calculated to help her to admission to the United Nations'. He did not mention de Valera's support of the entry of the Soviet Union into the pre-war League of Nations, nor the early recognition and financial support given to his country by republican Ireland, money which was not repaid until January 1948. But the veto was not removed until 1955 as part of a package deal and Ireland was at last admitted to the UN. She did, however, participate in some UN operations, those organized by the Food and Agriculture Organisation, for example.

In Europe, despite the hostility initially generated by her neutrality, Ireland came to play a useful role. Hardly was the war over, and despite the poverty and hardship which Ireland endured, when the government sent food and clothing, worth over three million pounds, to help Germany and other suffering peoples and agreed to take refugees. Later, after the Marshal Plan was inaugurated, Ireland played a part in the Organisation for European Economic Co-operation. Even more important, she was a founder member of the Council of Europe in 1950. But she refused to participate in the negotiations which led to the North Atlantic Treaty in 1949. Even though the government opposed communism and was entirely supportive of the west in the Cold War in Europe, the continuing fact of partition made involvement impossible. On 10 July 1948 the position was made clear in the Dáil, by Seán MacBride: 'Our sympathies lie clearly with Western Europe . . . but the continuance of partition precludes us from taking our rightful place in the affairs of Europe'.

Partition was, and remained, the justification for neutrality. So long as part of the national territory was occupied by a foreign power, Ireland could not reasonably become a party to any military policy which involved that power. So the argument went. But as neutrality became an essential part of Ireland's foreign policy, so the notion grew that a small and more or less defenceless state like Ireland could do more good in international affairs as a neutral. The end of the war had not brought the hardship endured by the people of Ireland to an end. The wet summer of 1946, followed by the coldest winter on record, created such a shortage of essential food supplies that further rationing was necessary. Emigration continued at around 30,000 a year, unemployment increased, and unrest was growing, epitomized by a strike of national teachers in Dublin in 1946 which lasted for seven months. Members of the IRA who were still held without trial now became a source of further embarrassment to the government. Many of the leaders had refused to wear prison uniforms and continued to insist that they should not be treated like criminals. Denied even the freedom of criminals, they remained in solitary confinement. While the war lasted, censorship prevented news of their condition from reaching the public. But once that censorship was lifted, public sympathy for them grew. One of the leaders, Seán McCaughey, went on hunger strike in Portaloise prison in April 1946, by which time he had spent over four years in solitary confinement. On 11 May, after 31 days without food, and 12 without water, he died. That same month the Northern government released David Fleming, who had also been on hunger strike, to save his life.

The contrast with the Irish government's harsh policy caused a public outrage among those with republican sympathies and led to a growing antagonism towards de Valera and his Fianna Fáil party, even among many of his old supporters. In July a new political party was founded, Clann na Poblachta ('Children of the Republic'), with Seán MacBride as leader. Son of John MacBride, executed in 1916, and Maude Gonne, a veteran of the civil war, a former Chief-of-Staff in the IRA, an experienced lawyer who had fought in the courts for many of the interned IRA, MacBride made an appeal not only to convinced republicans, but to many young intellectuals who were disillusioned with the character of Irish politics. The new party had arisen out of what had been known as 'the republican university', when people like Máirtín O Cadhain and others had provided education for prisoners in the Curragh and elsewhere to pass away the interminable hours. After the war, committees had been formed to help the internees and it was these which provided the nucleus of the Clann. Not only radical republicanism, but a new blend of economic and social reforms featured in the manifesto. Accused of being communist, the members were for the most part, protagonists of Catholic social doctrines and indeed (like MacBride himself) antagonistic towards the spread of communism in Europe, not least in Italy. During an election campaign the party promised that a social insurance plan put together by Bishop Duignan of Clonfert would be implemented by them in government.

De Valera was still confident that despite the catalyst provided by the new party, and the growing disaffection in the country at large, that his government would survive any opposition. In August 1947 a radical Health Act was introduced. In particular it sought to control the problem of infectious diseases and provided a free medical service (with some compulsory elements) for mothers and children to the age of 16, which was not to be means-tested. But many doctors condemned what they saw as state intrusion into what should be essentially private matters. The Catholic hierarchy agreed, construing this part of the legislation as 'anti-family' and a confrontation between church and state seemed to be in the offing.

A public scandal, involving the sale of Locke's distillery in county Westmeath, resulted in the setting up of a tribunal of inquiry in November 1947. The public debate and the political ramifications did not help the Government. Defeated by the new Clann na Poblachta party in two by-elections, de Valera was shaken by what he perceived as the potential alienation of many Fianna Fáil supporters by the new Republican revival, as well as by the hostility generated by the controversial health legislation and the scandal of the Locke's distillery affair. He decided to hold an election, even though his government still had over a year to run in office, fearful of a disaster if he gave the new party time to organize itself among the grass-root voters throughout the country.

In the event, in the general election of February 1948 the Fianna Fáil party retained 68 seats (having lost eight) and remained by far the largest party in the new Dáil. Clann na Poblachta's ambitions were shown to be hollow. Fielding 93 candidates, it won only 10 seats. Fine Gael won 31; Labour 14; the new Farmers' party (Clann na Talamhn – 'Children of the land') seven; National Labour (which later was reunited with the Labour party) five; and Independents twelve. For the first time in 16 years de Valera was unable to form a government. A new leader of Fine Gael, John A. Costello, was elected Taoiseach after policy agreements were made with the other parties and some of the Independents. A new era in Irish politics was seen to begin.

The new Coalition government, the first in Irish history, faced a formidable task, the maintenance of agreement between so many different, and potentially conflicting, interests was bound to create tensions. The presence of Seán MacBride, now Minister of External Affairs, guaranteed that partition would be at the top of any political agenda. A massive propaganda campaign was planned, especially in America but also throughout the world through a new Irish News Agency financed and controlled by the government. In office, MacBride complained: 'I have no staff whose function it is to deal with partition'. Of 32,171 civil servants employed by the government, not one dealt with the problem; and while the government spent over 70,000,000 pounds on state services, he said, 'not one penny is devoted to dealing with this vital problem'. But even though the government allocated £25,000 to the new agency, it failed.

The annual commemoration by the British Legion of Armistice Day in Dublin was another source of controversy. For years the Legion had been subject to problems created by restrictions placed on the use of banners and decorations, and on numbers allowed to participate. There was much public opposition and were frequent incidents. No representative of the government ever took part, even though as early as 1924 Colonel Maurice Moore had laid a wreath on behalf of the government. Between 1928 and 1931, too, the government had been officially represented. The advent of de Valera ended all that. But with the new Coalition the matter was raised again in 1948 and Costello showed some willingness to change. Civil servants in his office officially recorded: 'In view of the constitutional changes which have been announced, he feels that any objection to such representation no longer exists'. However, when a civil servant in 1949 reminded Costello of his undertaking to consider representation at the forthcoming commemoration at Islandbridge, he backed down. 'He decided', his office recorded, 'that no action should be taken in the matter in the absence of any request for such representation'. Commemorating the Irish who fell in the war was still contentious and no government wished to risk the condemnations that would certainly result from official participation.

The precise nature of Ireland's constitutional position in relation to Great Britain and the Commonwealth was another question which was bound to arise with the new government. While still nominally a member of the Commonwealth, Ireland in fact had not participated in any Imperial Conference for years. De Valera left no doubt as to how he regarded the question of Ireland's membership: 'If being in the Commonwealth implied in any way allegiance or acceptance of the British King as King here, we are not in the Commonwealth'. The British government, and indeed the Dominion governments as well, continued to regard Ireland as a member. For them the 1937 constitution, and the External Relations Act of 1936, had not fundamentally changed that fact. The conflict of opinion was to be resolved in a very radical way by the new Coalition government.

On 5 September 1948 the *Sunday Independent* published a headline, 'External Relations Act to Go', which caused a sensation. The article referred to a speech by MacBride in the Dáil in July in which he said that the substance of Anglo-Irish relations required more precise definition: 'Outward forms which are only reminders of a historically unhappy past can only act as irritants'. In August William Norton, the tánaiste (deputy prime minister), went even further: 'It would do our national self-respect good at home and abroad if we were to proceed without delay to abolish the External Relations Act'. It seems clear that the cabinet had decided, before Costello left on an official visit to Canada, to repeal the act. He was to deliver a lecture, 'Ireland in International Affairs', and it seems that the text of this was approved before he left Dublin because it, too, would hint at the repeal. But after the revelation in the *Sunday Independent* Costello had little option but to give a positive answer to the inevitable questions which he would face at a press conference on 7 September. On the day he did admit that it was the intention of his government to repeal the act and as a result faced a barrage of criticism for making such an important declaration in Canada and not at home in Ireland.

Speaking in the Dáil on 24 November during the debate on the bill,

Costello made the government's position clear: 'This Bill will end, and end forever in a simple, clear and unequivocal way, this country's long and tragic association with the institution of the British Crown and will make it manifest beyond equivocation or subtlety that the national and international status of this country is that of an independent Republic'. He refused to accept the criticism that the proposed legislation would in fact make partition permanent and insisted that 'this Bill, by creating conditions on which that goodwill [towards Britain] can increase, will help towards the solution of the problem of partition. We hold out, as I said earlier today, the hand of friendship to the decent people of Northern Ireland'.

But in 1949 the Ireland Act, which the British parliament enacted on 2 June, while declaring that citizens of Éire were not to be regarded as aliens, would be given citizens' rights while in Britain, and that Ireland was not to be regarded as a foreign country, also enacted that Northern Ireland 'remains part of His Majesty's dominions and of the United Kingdom and it is hereby affirmed that in no event will Northern Ireland or any part thereof cease to be part of His Majesty's dominions and of the United Kingdom without the consent of the Parliament of Northern Ireland'. In a sense, then, the proclamation of a republic did lead to making partition more permanent.

With that problem out of the way the Coalition government was free to proceed with the programme of reform adopted after the general election. The terrible devastation of the scourge of tuberculosis was successfully attacked by the new Minister for Health, Noel Browne of Clann na Poblachta, appointed to office at the age of 32 and on his first day in the new Dáil. Using money provided by the Hospitals Sweeps, founded in 1929, a network of sanatoria provided the beds needed for treatment. By July 1950 an extra 2,000 beds had been made available. The death rate had been cut from 123 per 100,000 in 1947 to seventy-three in 1951. A blood transfusion service was created and other medical innovations suggested that a National Health Service would soon be able to tackle the worst of the medical problems, especially among the poor of Ireland.

But when the government attempted to introduce what became known as 'the mother and child scheme' it soon ran into trouble. In 1950 Noel Browne proposed free medical care for all expectant mothers and for children up to the age of 16, but the Catholic hierarchy resisted the proposed legislation. The bishops were uneasy at what they saw as state interference, part of a wider problem in the growth of state power which had been perceived during the Fianna Fáil era. As with the Fianna Fáil Health Act of 1947, this new legislation was viewed as anti-family. After a meeting in Maynooth on 10 October the bishops told Costello in no uncertain terms of their opposition:

> 'The powers taken by the state in the proposed Mother and Child Health Service are in direct opposition to the rights of the family and of the individual and are liable to very great abuse . . . If adopted in law they would constitute a ready-made instrument for future totalitarian aggression'.

There were other grounds for objection, not least the fact that 'doctors trained in institutions in which we have no confidence may be appointed as medical officers under the proposed services, and may give gynaecological care not in accordance with Catholic principles'.

Discussion dragged on and in March 1951 Costello told Browne that he and other colleagues 'would not be party to any proposals affecting moral questions which would or might come into conflict with the definite teaching of the Catholic Church'. Eventually at a cabinet meeting on 6 April it was decided to abandon the scheme and to go ahead with an alternative which would 'be in conformity with Catholic social teaching'. Four days later MacBride, as Leader of Clann na Poblachta, demanded the resignation of Browne and the Minister then sent his resignation to Costello. The *Irish Times* commented wryly: 'The Roman Catholic Church would seem to be the effective government of this country'.

The Coalition government, like others before them, was unwilling to challenge the Catholic hierarchy when legislation was construed as being offensive to faith and morals. From the very beginning this was clear. At its very first cabinet meeting it was agreed to send a telegram to the pope in Rome, informing him of the wish 'to repose at the feet of your Holiness the assurance of our filial loyalty and of our devotion to your August Person, as well as our firm resolve to be guided in all our work by the teaching of Christ, and to strive for the attainment of a social order in Ireland based on Christian principles'. When the bishops heard that a bill was to be introduced in the Dáil abolishing the Sunday closure of pubs in rural Ireland, they condemned the notion on 22 June 1948 and on 14 July the bill was defeated by 106 votes to 23. Even on a more mundane level the bishops were respected and even cultivated. Early in 1949 Costello actually went on a trial run himself around Merrion Square in a Panhard car which had been specially imported from America for presentation to Archbishop McQuaid.

So when someone like Archbishop Kinnane of Cashel spoke on public matters, as he did on 2 June 1951, they listened:

> 'Bishops are the authoritative teachers of faith and morals. It follows that their teaching is binding and that their Catholic subjects must obey it . . . subjects should not oppose their Bishop's teaching by word, by act, or in any other way . . . political and social activities, quite as much as those which are purely personal and private, are subject to God's moral law, of which the Church is the divinely constituted interpreter and guardian'.

At the crucial cabinet meeting of 6 April it was Seán MacBride who told his colleagues that the

> 'science of government involves the task of ensuring a harmonious relationship between the churches and the civil government . . . Even if, as Catholics, we were prepared to take the responsibility of disregarding

their views, which I do not think we can do, it would be politically impossible to do so. We must therefore accept the views of the hierarchy in this matter'.

Coming from what was supposed to be the most radical member of the cabinet, representing the most radical party, it was no surprise that in the new republic, whose foundation was symbolically celebrated in front of the Dublin GPO at Easter 1949, the Catholic church was given a role in politics which seemed to deny the very essence of what that republic should have stood for. When the government decided to issue a special stamp to commemorate the Holy Year in 1950, a correspondent protested in a memorandum which was brought to the cabinet. Outlining the history of Rome's interference in Ireland in the twelfth century and papal support for English oppression of the Irish – he told them that if 'politicians in speaking of our past must refer to "our ancient enemy" they might at least, in the interests of truth and accuracy, use the plural' – he protested against the manner in which the government had 'gone out of its way to emphasize the relations existing between Rome and Ireland. It is the more nauseating that it should have been done by the government that declared Ireland a Republic'.

Browne and other idealistic young men left Clann na Poblachta and created the situation where the first Coalition Government was unable to continue in office. A general election in May 1951 saw de Valera and Fianna Fáil return to power and witnessed the virtual destruction of Clann na Poblachta who gained only two seats. The government of which they had been a part had lost support not only because of the mother and child affair, but also because of public scandals like what became known as 'the battle of Baltinglass'. This revealed one of the Labour Ministers, Everett, using his office to secure a sinecure (a sub-post office) for an influential party supporter in his constituency at the expense of the family who had been successfully discharging the function of postmaster for 80 years. The opposition, national as well as local, forced the government to back down and did immense harm to their reputation.

The Republic of Ireland had at last been achieved. But for many the ideals (however romantic they may seem in retrospect) which had inspired earlier generations in the struggle to achieve it seemed tarnished by the actions of that first republican Government. The notion of Wolfe Tone that

'the emancipated and liberated Irishman, like the emancipated and liberated Frenchman, may go to mass, may tell his beads, or sprinkle his mistress with holy water; but neither the one or the other will attend to the rusty and extinguished thunderbolts of the Vatican, or the idle anathemas'

seemed further away than ever. Pearse had adopted Tone's determination 'to substitute the common name of Irishman in place of the denominations of

Protestant, Catholic, and dissenter'. But in placing Tone beside the legendary figure of Cú Chulainn in his pantheon of Irish heroes, he demonstrated that dying for Ireland, the use of physical force to achieve the dream of an independent Ireland, was what counted in the end. This part of the legacy of Pearse lived on in some parts of Ireland. The failure to end partition, despite the achievement of a Republic and separation from Britain, continued to provide justification in some minds for maintaining what they chose to call 'the armed struggle'. But for the majority of Irish people the proclamation of the Republic and the dissociation with Britain and the Commonwealth which followed, was the culmination of what their ancestors had fought for. Although with partition in place on a seemingly permanent basis, it may have fallen short of the ideals which had motivated so many, in this limited way Ireland was seen as free at last and the Irish nation master of its own destiny.

Epilogue
The new Ireland

In the 1950s the Republic seemed to continue along the path which had been marked out by the older politicians who had been dominant since the 1930s. De Valera's vision of an Ireland that was not only Gaelic, but Catholic as well had been given reality. Even if the Gaelic element had been compromised with the passage of time – the number of native Irish speakers declined to about 70,000 by 1961, or about a fifth of what it had been in 1922; by 1980 it had fallen to about 32,000 – the Catholic ingredient was, if anything, strengthened. The new leader of the Labour party, Brendan Corish addressing the Dáil in 1953, could hardly have been more precise:

> 'I am an Irishman second; I am a Catholic first . . . If the Hierarchy gives me any direction with regard to Catholic social teaching, or Catholic moral teaching, I accept without qualification in all respects the teaching of the Hierarchy and the Church to which I belong'.

The confessional nature of the new state seemed to be taken for granted. But this slowly changed. When Brian Lenihan as Minister of Justice in 1966 proposed to change the censorship laws, he told the Cabinet that 'standards of propriety do change'. Despite the public opposition of the Bishop of Cork, who argued that the existing laws were in fact too lax and demanded that it should be made a criminal offence to publish 'corrupting works', the government went ahead with its reforms. This was only one sign of a major change which was taking place, from a confessional to a more pluralist society. It was all the more remarkable because the people of Ireland were still 90 per cent staunchly Catholic. When Pope John Paul II came to Ireland in 1979, the huge crowds who turned out to salute him were a witness to that fact. About one and a quarter million assembled in Dublin's Phoenix Park, and altogether an estimated two-thirds of the population attended the different ceremonies. Yet despite the staunchly Catholic ethos which prevailed, a referendum in 1972 deleted the article in the constitution which recognized 'the special position' of the Catholic church; censorship of books was effectively ended in 1966; contraceptives were allowed to be imported and legally sold from 1979; and a Supreme Court judgement in 1992 allowed abortion in limited cases, where there was a real danger that refusal might lead to suicide. Three years later the constitutional ban on divorce, the subject of passionate debate in the Dáil of 1925, was finally removed by referendum.

The modernization of Ireland can probably be best epitomized in the politics of Seán Lemass, who became taoiseach in 1959. He was one of the old conservative school of politicians, a convinced republican, old IRA, veteran of the civil war, founder member of Fianna Fáil, heir to de Valera. He was also a Catholic of the old school. Like four members of the coalition cabinet which in 1951 had confronted Browne over the mother and child bill, he was a member of the Knights of St Columbanus. Deferential to the Catholic hierarchy, his attitude is well illustrated by his response to the objections raised by McQuaid, the Archbishop of Dublin, to the National Library of Ireland being extended into the grounds of Trinity College. At the final stages of the project, he told his cabinet that it must be held up until 'the proper authorities' were consulted. His secretary was then ordered to arrange a meeting with McQuaid, who was being difficult. The archbishop was told that the taoiseach would meet him at his convenience, at any time, day or night. As a result of that meeting the cabinet was next informed that the whole project was being called off.

But it was the same Lemass who backed the revolutionary economic proposals of T.K. Whittaker, Secretary of the Department of Finance, which led to the expansion of the Irish economy. Ireland in the 1950s still suffered from heavy emigration, high unemployment, and slow growth in every aspect of the economy. Before Lemass became taoiseach the annual rate of emigration had climbed to over 40,000, mostly across the water to Britain. By 1961 nearly 400,000 people of Irish birth (with a population of under three million in Ireland) were living abroad. Such a catastrophe could not easily be halted until employment was provided for those seeking work at home. The publication of Whitaker's *Economic Development* in December 1958 contained his ideas which had an important impact on government policy – first in the 1958 First Programme for Economic Expansion, and later in the Second Programme of 1964. These helped to revolutionize the Irish economy, by focusing attention on economic planning, and gave substance to what Lemass had told the Dáil in 1959, that 'the historic task of this generation is to secure the economic foundation of independence'.

Even though Ireland failed to gain admission to the EEC in 1962 – she was not admitted until 1972 – the country began to prosper. The growing economic achievement was well summed up by President Kennedy during his memorable visit in 1963, when he addressed the two houses of the Oireachtas on 28 June: 'You have modernised your economy, harnessed your rivers, diversified your industry, liberalised your trade, electrified your farms, accelerated your rate of growth, and improved the living standards of your people'. When Lemass retired from politics in 1969, the level of foreign borrowings had fallen to a mere 50 million pounds; and of this the post-war Marshall Plan loan, still being repaid, accounted for 31 million pounds.

An average growth rate of 4 per cent in the economy was maintained right through the 1960s and 1970s. Agriculture was given a huge boost after admission to the EEC was achieved and the flow of money from Europe created a new prosperity in rural Ireland. Industry, too, developed as foreign companies were attracted to Ireland and provided more employment. The population began to increase again, from about 2,800,000 in 1961 to 3,440,000 in 1981. More importantly, this was a younger population, with nearly half under the age of 25. Important developments in education became possible, when it was provided free at second level and, even more important, with free transport in rural areas hitherto cut off, leading to an expansion from 143 thousand pupils in 1965 to over 300,000 in 1980.

In other ways, too, a new Ireland was beginning to emerge and began to make some impact on the world stage. The election of Frederick Boland to the presidency of the UN general assembly in September 1960 was an indication of the growing respect which Ireland now enjoyed as an independent state in the Cold War. Even though condemning the policy of aggression which China was pursuing in Tibet, Ireland still supported the proposal that her admission to the UN should be discussed in the assembly. Then, in 1961, she voted against that admission. Long before that, in 1950, Ireland had signed the European Convention on Human Rights and fully accepted the European Court of Human Rights as well as the European Commission of Human Rights.

But it was in peace-keeping operations of the UN that Ireland made the biggest impact. In 1958 officers of the Irish army served for the first time as UN observers in the Lebanon, and after that in Cyprus, the Middle East, New Guinea, on the India–Pakistan border, and in other sensitive areas. This involved sacrifice. In 1960 two battalions of Irish troops were sent to the Congo in support of UN peace-keeping operations there. In addition, General Seán Mac Eoin acted as Commander-in-Chief. In an ambush on 8 November 10 Irish soldiers were killed. Notwithstanding that, Irish troops continued to serve in Africa, with more loss of life in service. They earned the special thanks of U Thant, the Secretary General, in 1965: 'The United nations and the world are in debt to them for the services they have rendered . . .'

One result of Ireland's greater involvement in the world outside was that a new rapprochement with Westminster became possible. The signing of an Anglo-Irish trade agreement in December 1965 by Wilson and Lemass was one important sign. But the most potent symbols of this new relationship were the return of the remains of Roger Casement on 23 February 1965, when he was buried in an emotional ceremony at Glasnevin; and of the flag which flew over the GPO in 1916, which had since reposed in the Imperial War Museum in London, but which was returned by Wilson's government in time to be flown again over the GPO during the special anniversary commemoration in 1966. The attitude of goodwill prevailed, despite the many incidents of violence which were to come. After the British embassy in Dublin was burned by a protesting crowd on 2 February 1972, the Scottish and Welsh rugby teams refused to come to Lansdowne Road to play Ireland. But a year later the English team came and were greeted with a five minutes' standing ovation by an emotional crowd. An even more significant sign of the change which had taken place was the removal by the GAA of its infamous ban on 'foreign games', which in fact were the English games of cricket, hockey, rugby and soccer. This was achieved at a historic meeting in Belfast on 11 April 1971. Then, on Sunday 15 October 1979, the Reverend Canon John Austin Baker preached a sermon at Westminster Abbey in which he told the congregation that Britain should admit her 'sins towards Ireland . . . The real miracle of modern Ireland is that the vast majority of the Irish people are so ready to forgive and forget, and to treat individual British as friends'.

But not all were ready to 'forgive and forget'. Five weeks prior to the 1916 commemoration in 1966, Nelson Pillar in the heart of Dublin was wrecked by an explosion, the work of the IRA. In Belfast a Catholic barman was killed by UVF gunmen on 26 June and two others seriously wounded. The bitter antagonisms which had been bred through the generations were still active and finding expressions in violence. The 'armed struggle' of the IRA for what they perceived as the freedom of Ireland, still to be achieved, continued. It was opposed by the terrorist organizations on the unionist side, determined to preserve the union with the United Kingdom, no matter what the cost. The people, the politicians and the churchmen were caught in between the terrorists, unable to preserve the rule of law, much less to find a way to end the violence.

If the Republic manifested some of the characteristics of a confessional state, Northern Ireland showed many signs of sectarianism. The classic statement of Protestant bigotry was made in 1933 by a future prime minister, Brookeborough, addressing an annual Orange Order parade. Despite the fact that about one third of the population was Catholic, the unionist government made no attempt to hide its avowedly sectarian attitude. Craig told the parliament at Stormont in 1934: 'I have always said that I am an Orangeman first and a politician and a member of this Parliament afterwards ... All I boast is that we have a Protestant Parliament and a Protestant State'. Catholics might vote for unionists, but they were barred from the Unionist Party or the Orange Order. The 'Special Forces' established in 1920 (A-Specials; B-Specials, the most infamous; and C-Specials) were also exclusively Protestant. Even in the RUC Catholics rarely rose above 10 per cent. If many decent people ignored this kind of prejudice, there was a definite bias against Catholics in state employment, where no attempt was made to pretend otherwise. Patrick Shea, a Catholic who was attached to the Ministry of Education, wrote of the day in 1958 when the Permanent Secretary sent for him. He was told of the many occasions on which he had figured in discussions about promotion and why he was always passed over: 'Because you are a Roman Catholic you may never get any further promotion. I'm sorry'.

By the time legislation was introduced against this kind of discrimination, it was too late. Politics had become, irrevocably it seemed, sectarian. When the Northern Ireland Civil Rights Association was established in January 1969 to fight discrimination against Catholics, it tried to break with this tradition. While its membership was largely Catholic, it also had communists, socialists, liberals, trade unionists, independents, and even the leader of the Young Unionist group among its members. It fought for civil rights for everyone in the north, not for any political motives and it was linked with the National Council for Civil Liberties in England. Above all, the members were inspired by civil rights movements elsewhere, especially in America. They regularly used as an anthem the great chant of 'We shall overcome', associated in particular with the charismatic Martin Luther King. But on 5 October 1968 in Derry a peaceful civil rights demonstration was viciously attacked by the police. Shown to the world on television, it exposed the continuing brutality of the anti-Catholic bias still prevailing in the north, associated with the permanent unionist domination in government at all levels.

The abolition of proportional representation – for parliamentary elections in 1922 and local elections in 1929 – meant that unionists dominated Stormont thereafter. They never held fewer that 33 of the 52 seats; indeed at least 40 per cent of all seats, and sometimes more, were never contested. The situation was even worse in the local elections, especially after successful gerrymandering. In 1967 nationalists controlled only eight out of 68 local authorities. This continuing lack of balance in the political situation strengthened the stance of activists who argued that nothing would be achieved by nationalists through the ballot box alone. The IRA had not disappeared. In December 1956 a new campaign was initiated against military targets in the north, in which six RUC and eight IRA, as well as five civilians, were killed before it was called off in 1962. The funeral of Seán South, killed in an attack on a barracks in Fermanagh, showed in the thousands who lined the streets as the procession passed through Dublin on its way to Limerick, that the cult of 'martyrs for the cause' was still far from dead in the Republic. Even though the campaign was called off in 1962, the IRA still pledged itself to 'the cause'. The notice in the *United Irishman* in March carried the declaration: 'The Irish Resistance Movement renews its pledge of eternal hostility to the British Forces of Occupation in Ireland'.

Efforts to promote understanding between the two communities were given a boost in 1965 when on the initiative of the northern prime minister, Terence O'Neill, Lemass visited Stormont to discuss reforms face-to-face. O'Neill in turn visited Dublin. But he paid the price in 1969 when he was forced from office and hard-line unionists ruled again. By then the UVF had become active again – they killed a Catholic barman, and wounded two others, in Belfast in 1969 – and the IRA initiated a series of bomb attacks. An Orange hall was burned in July 1969 and a UVF bomb exploded in Dublin in August. A 'peace line' was erected by the government in Belfast between Catholic and Protestant housing estates. Many Catholics felt under siege and in May 1970 two ministers in the Fianna Fáil government were put on trial on charges of being implicated in the illegal importation of arms into the Republic, supposedly to be used by republicans in the north. No charges were proved, but the reaction among many Fianna Fáil supporters showed that not all were willing to see nationalists in the north continue under oppression, as they put it, without practical help.

Meanwhile the IRA had split again, into 'Officials' and 'Provisionals' (or Provos, as they became known), fighting each other in Belfast in May 1971, when some were killed. From now on it was the Provos who spearheaded the campaign in the north and the increased military activity led to the introduction of internment without trial by Stormont on 9 August. As a result 342 were arrested and imprisoned. There was a violent reaction, which led to the destruction of many homes and, worst of all, 17 deaths. Refugees poured out of the north and were given shelter in the Republic. Violence escalated again, climaxing on 30 January 1972 in Derry. Known ever since as 'Bloody Sunday', it saw English paratroopers open fire on civil rights demonstrators, killing 13 in all. When the Irish government in response proclaimed 2 February a day of national mourning a mob attacked and burned the British embassy in Dublin. 'Bloody Sunday' was burned into the national consciousness and became a rallying cry for republicans. Seven years later, when Earl Mountbatten and others were murdered while boating at Mullaghmore in Sligo, among the graffiti which celebrated the slaughter was one with these verses:

> Thirteen dead but not forgotten
> We got eighteen and Mountbatten.

Still the violence and massacre of innocents continued. In 1972 Belfast had its 'Bloody Friday', when IRA bombs killed 11 and injured 130, Loyalist bombs in Dublin killed two and injured 127. England did not escape from this bombing campaign and many were killed there too. But it was in Dublin, on 17 May 1974, that the worst single incident occurred, when three explosions in the centre of the city, at rush hour, killed 24 civilians and seriously injured over 100 people.

It seemed that nothing could be done to bring the violence to a halt and prevent the further useless killing of innocent people. When a Belfast magistrate, with his wife and daughter, were leaving church after attending mass on 8 April 1984, they were ambushed by two gunmen. He was shot six times in the chest, back and lower body; his 22-year-old daughter, a teacher, was shot in the heart and died instantly; his wife escaped injury because she threw herself weeping on the two bleeding bodies. The magistrate survived the attack. Later the provisional IRA admitted responsibility for the execution and justified it because the magistrate was an enemy in the employ of the British.

Far from helping to secure 'freedom' for Ireland, the violence in fact strengthened partition. The border was guarded and watched over by police and military forces on both sides. Some roads and bridges were permanently blocked, causing unnecessary hardship to many local communities. When the UK refused to join a European Monetary System in 1979 and the Republic did, a further line was drawn because the Irish púnt was for the first time separated from the English pound sterling, helping to strengthen partition still further.

But there were other ways in which barriers between the two communities were breached. Election of members to the European parliament helped to bring the representatives of north and south together in Europe when common interests were at stake. Some important sports continued to ignore partition when representing the whole of Ireland in international games. Trade unions spanned the border, economic cooperation, especially where agriculture was concerned, often worked to the interests of both communities. Politicians, too, continued to play their part in attempting to bring some kind of peace to Northern Ireland. The unionist government reluctantly agreed to a 'power-sharing' assembly in place of the traditional parliament in July 1973. A conference at Sunningdale in England later that year resulted in an Anglo-Irish agreement that no change could take place in the constitutional status of Northern Ireland within the United Kingdom without the consent of a majority of the people there; and that a new Council of Ireland would be formed from representatives elected by the new Assembly in Belfast and the Dáil in Dublin. But the scheme quickly fell apart, as did other attempts to solve the problem along constitutional lines. The violence continued. By 1983 over 2,300 had lost their lives in Northern Ireland and the numbers mounted through the years that followed. In recent times, however, an IRA ceasefire has raised hopes. The advent of a new Labour government in England, with a huge majority and a more positive approach to the problem of Northern Ireland, has led to a major turnabout. Now the political parties are meeting to find a peaceful solution and for the first time since 1922 republicans, nationalists and unionists are meeting together for talks and negotiations.

At the same time the Republic continued to flourish. Not only were economic advances achieved which produced increased wealth and attracted many who had emigrated back to a more confident Ireland – what later became known in popular parlance later as 'the Celtic tiger' – but there was a corresponding growth in many other aspects of Irish life. Literature flourished. Since 1923, when Yeats was awarded the Nobel prize, Shaw (1926), Beckett (1969) and Heaney (1995) have been similarly honoured. Irish drama has won worldwide recognition and the arts generally have manifested the growth in national confidence as prosperity increased. Even popular music, and not least the native music of the countryside, has won a huge international audience. Political stability has been maintained, enabling Ireland to play a role in international affairs way beyond what might be expected of such a small society. What Cromwell long ago described as 'that bleeding nation' may still retain an element to give some justification to his description. But modern Ireland has been transformed and today the words of Donatus, the ninth century Irish Bishop of Fiesole in Italy, seem more appropriate. In exile he looked to what he called 'the best of lands' in the far west – 'called Scotia in the ancient books' – which is 'rich in goods, in silver and gems, in cloth and gold'. We can still hear the envy in his voice as he wrote of the Irish who are worthy to live in that fair land. Five hundred years later another Irish poet, this time in English, expressed the exhilaration of living in Ireland:

> Icham of Irlaund
> Ant of the holy londe of irlonde.
> Gode sir pray ich ye
> for of saynte charite
> come ant daunce wyt me
> in Irlaund.

Further reading

A New History of Ireland, 9 volumes (Oxford, 1976–96), is a large multi-authored history, with extensive bibliographies which will be brought up to date periodically. Two volumes, I and VII, await publication. Volume VIII is a useful detailed chronology of Irish history to 1976. Volume IX contains useful maps in addition to comprehensive genealogical tables, succession lists, parliaments from 1264, and parliamentary elections from 1801.

Other general multi-volume histories are: J.F. Lydon and Margaret MacCurtain (eds), *The Gill History of Ireland*, 11 volumes (Dublin 1972–5); and Art Cosgrove and Elma Collins (eds), *The Helicon History of Ireland*, 10 volumes (Dublin, 1981–7).

Good general histories are: Edmund Curtis, *A History of Ireland* (London, 1950); J.C. Beckett, *A Short History of Ireland* (London, 1981); and R.F. Foster (ed.) *The Oxford Illustrated History of Ireland* (Oxford, 1989). T.W. Moody and F.X. Martin (eds), *The Course of Irish History* (Cork, 1984) has an excellent topical bibliography.

Of great interest is the ongoing series of county histories, under the general editorship of Wiallam Nolan, of which 10 have been published (Dublin, 1981–97).

Jonathan Bardon, *A History of Ulster* (Belfast, 1992) is by far the best history of the northern province.

L.M. Cullen, *Life in Ireland* (London, 1968) is a good general social history.

P.J. Corish (ed.), *A History of Irish Catholicism* (Dublin, 1967) was first initiated by the Irish Catholic Historical Committee during the Patrician Year of 1961, but it was never completed and a series of separate fascicles has been issued. They are invaluable.

Patrick J. Corish, *The Irish Catholic Experience: A historical survey* (Dublin, 1985) is the best general study.

The most useful short collection of sources is Edmund Curtis and R.B. McDowell (eds), *Irish Historical Documents, 1172–1922* (London, 1968).

Early Ireland

Ludwig Bieler, *Ireland, Harbinger of the Middle Ages* (London, 1963).
F.J. Byrne, *Irish Kings and High-Kings* (London, 1973).
N.K. Chadwick, *The Age of the Saints in the Early Celtic Church* (London, 1961).
Myles Dillon (ed.), *Early Irish Society* (Dublin, 1954).
Myles Dillon and Nora K. Chadwick, *The Celtic Realms* (London, 1972).
Máire and Liam de Paor, *Early Christian Ireland* (London, 1958).
Robin Flower, *The Irish Tradition* (Oxford, 1947).
R.P.C. Hanson, *Saint Patrick, his Origins and Career* (Oxford, 1968).
Françoise Henry, *Early Christian Irish Art* (Dublin, 1954).
—— *Irish Art in the Early Christian Period to AD 800* (London, 1965).
—— *Irish Art During the Viking Invasions, 800–1020 AD* (London, 1967).
—— *Irish Art in the Romanesque Period, 1021–1170 AD* (London, 1070).
Kathleen Hughes, *The Church in Early Irish Society* (London, 1966).
—— *Early Christian Ireland: Introduction to the Sources* (London, 1972).
J.F. Kenney, *Sources for the Early History of Ireland: Ecclesiastical* (Ithaca, NY, 1966).
Eoin MacNeill, *Phases of Irish History* (Dublin, 1919).
Dáibhí Ó Cróinín, *Early Medieval Ireland, 400–1200* (London, 1995).
T.F. O'Rahilly, *Early Irish History and Mythology* (Dublin, 1947).
John Ryan, *Irish Monasticism: Origins and early development* (Dublin, 1934).
A.B. Scott, *Malachy* (Dublin, 1976).

Medieval

Olive Armstrong, *Edward Bruce's Invasion of Ireland* (London, 1923).
P.W.A. Asplin, *Medieval Ireland, c.1170–1495: A bibliography of secondary works* (Dublin, 1971).
Terry Barry, *The Archaeology of Medieval Ireland* (London, 1987).
Terry Barry, Robin Frame and Katharine Simms (eds), *Colony and Frontier in Medieval Ireland* (London, 1995).
Donough Bryan, *The Great Earl of Kildare, 1456–1513* (Dublin, 1933).
Agnes Conway, *Henry VIII's Relations with Scotland and Ireland, 1485–98* (Cambridge, 1932).
Colmcille Conway, *The Story of Mellifont* (Dublin, 1958).
Edmund Curtis, *A History of Medieval Ireland* (Dublin, 1923, and London, 1938).
—— *Richard II in Ireland, 1394–5* (Oxford, 1937).
Seán Duffy, *Ireland in the Middle Ages* (London, 1997).
Steven Ellis, *Reform and Revival: English Government in Ireland, 1470–1534* (London, 1986).
Marie Therese Flannagan, *Irish Society, Anglo-Norman Settlers, Angevin Kingship: Interactions in Ireland in the late twelfth century* (Oxford, 1989).

Robin Frame, *English Lordship in Ireland, 1318–61* (Oxford, 1981).

J.T. Gilbert, *History of the Viceroys of Ireland* (Dublin, 1865).

Alice Stopford Green, *The Making of Ireland and its Undoing* (London, 1908).

Aubrey Gwynn, *The Irish Church in the Eleventh and Twelfth Centuries* (Dublin, 1993).

G.J. Hand, *English Law in Ireland, 1290–1234* (Cambridge, 1967).

H.G. Leask, *Irish Castles and Castellated Houses* (Dundalk, 1941).

J.F. Lydon, *The Lordship of Ireland in the Middle Ages* (Dublin, 1972).

James Lydon (ed.), *England and Ireland in the Later Middle Ages* (Dublin, 1981).

—— *The English in Medieval Ireland* (Dublin, 1984).

Barry W. O'Dwyer, *The Conspiracy of Mellifont, 1216–31* (Dublin, 1970).

Timothy O'Neill, *Merchants and Mariners in Medieval Ireland* (Dublin, 1987).

G.H. Orpen, *Ireland under the Normans 1169–1333*, 4 volumes (Oxford, 1911–20).

M.D. O'Sullivan, *Italian Merchant Bankers in Ireland in the Thirteenth Century* (Dublin, 1962).

A.J. Otway-Ruthven, *A History of Medieval Ireland* (London, 1968).

H.G. Richardson and G.O. Sayles, *The Irish Parliament in the Middle Ages* (Philadelphia, 1952).

—— *Parliament in Medieval Ireland* (Dundalk, 1964).

St. John J. Seymour, *Anglo-Irish Literature, 1200–1582* (Cambridge, 1929).

Katharine Simms, *From Kings to Warlords: The changing political structures of Gaelic Ireland in the later middle ages* (Woodbridge, 1987).

Alfred P. Smith, *Celtic Leinster: Towards a historical geography of early Irish civilisation, AD 500–1600* (Dublin, 1982).

R.A. Stalley, *The Cistercian Monasteries of Ireland* (London, 1987).

—— *Architecture and Sculpture in Ireland, 1150–1350* (Dublin, 1971).

John A. Watt, *The Church and the Two Nations in Medieval Ireland* (Cambridge, 1970).

Ireland to 1800

Richard Bagwell, *Ireland under the Tudors*, 4 volumes (London, 1885–90).

—— *Ireland under the Stuarts*, 3 volumes (London, 1909–16).

Thomas Bartlett, *The Rise and Fall of the Irish Nation: The catholic question, 1690–1830* (Dublin, 1992).

J.C. Beckett, *Protestant Dissent in Ireland, 1681–1780*, (London, 1948).

—— *The Making of Modern Ireland, 1625–42* (London, 1966).

T.C. Bernard, *Cromwellian Ireland: English government in Ireland, 1649–60* (Oxford, 1975).

Henry Boylan, *Wolfe Tone* (Dublin, 1981).

Brendan Bradshaw, *The Dissolution of the Religious Houses in Ireland under Henry VIII* (Cambridge, 1974).

Brendan Bradshaw, *The Irish Constitutional Revolution of the Sixteenth Century* (Cambridge, 1979).

Ciaran Brady, *The Chief Governors: The rise and fall of reform government in Tudor Ireland* (Cambridge, 1994).

—— *Shane O'Neill* (Dublin, 1996).

Ciaran Brady and Raymond Gillespie (eds), *Natives and Newcomers, the Making of Irish Colonial Society, 1534–1641* (Dublin, 1986).

N.P. Canny, *The Formation of an Old English Elite in Ireland* (Dublin, 1975).

—— *The Elizabethan Conquest of Ireland: A pattern established, 1565–1576* (Hassocks, 1976).

—— *The Upstart Earl: A study of the social and mental life of Richard Boyle, first Earl of Cork, 1566–1643* (Cambridge, 1982).

Aidan Clarke, *The Old English in Ireland, 1625–42* (London, 1966).

—— *Thr Graces, 1625–41* (Dundalk, 1968).

L.M. Cullen, *An Economic History of Ireland Since 1600* (London, 1978).

—— *The Emergence of Modern Ireland, 1600–1900* (London, 1981).

Louis Cullen, *The Hidden Ireland: Reassessment of a concept* (Dublin, 1988).

Nancy Curtin, *The United Irishmen: Popular politics in Ulster and Dublin, 1791–1798* (Oxford, 1993).

David Dickson (ed.), *The Gorgeous Mask: Dublin 1700–1850* (Dublin, 1987).

David Dickson, Dáire Keogh and Kevin Whelan (eds), *The United Irishmen: Republicanism, radicalism and rebellion* (Dublin, 1993).

R. Dudley Edwards, *Church and State in Tudor Ireland* (Dublin, 1935).

Marianne Elliott, *Partners in Revolution: The United Irishmen and France* (London, 1992).

—— *Wolfe Tone: Prophet of Irish independence* (London, 1989).

Steven Ellis, *Tudor Ireland: Crown, community and the conflict of cultures* (London, 1985).

R.F. Foster, *Modern Ireland, 1600–1972* (London, 1988).

Richard Hayes, *The Last Invasion of Ireland* (Dublin, 1979).

Denis Johnston, *In Search of Swift* (Dublin, 1959).

Edith M. Johnston, *Great Britain and Ireland, 1760–1800: A study in political administration* (Edinburgh, 1989).

Frederick M. Jones, *Mountjoy, 1563–1606: The last Elizabethan Deputy* (Dublin, 1958).

James Kelly, *Prelude to Union: Anglo-Irish politics in the 1780s* (Cork, 1992).

—— *Henry Grattan* (Dublin, 1993).

Dáire Keogh, *The French Disease: The catholic church and radicalism in Ireland, 1790–1800* (Dublin, 1993).

W.E.H. Lecky, *Ireland in the Eighteenth Century*, 5 volumes (London, 1892).

Colm Lennon, *Richard Stanihurst the Dubliner, 1547–1618* (Dublin, 1979).

—— *Sixteenth-Century Ireland: The incomplete conquest* (Dublin, 1989).

Laurence McCorristine, *The Revolt of Silken Thomas* (Dublin, 1978).

Margaret MacCurtain and Mary O'Dowd (eds), *Women in Early Modern Ireland* (Dublin, 1991).

G.A. Hayes-McCoy, *Scots Mercenary Forces in Ireland* (Edinburgh, 1937).

R.B. McDowell, *Ireland in the Age of Imperialism and Revolution, 1760–1800* (Oxford, 1979).

—— *Irish Public Opinion, 1750–1800* (London, 1944).

J.L. Macracken, *The Irish Parliament in the Eighteenth Century* (Dundalk, 1971).

W.A. Macguire (ed.), *Kings in Conflict: The revolutionary war in Ireland and its aftermath, 1689–1750* (Belfast, 1990).

A.P.W. Malcomson, *John Foster: The politics of the Anglo-Irish ascendancy* (Oxford, 1978).

Hiram Morgan, *Tyrone's rebellion: The outbreak of the nine years war in Tudor Ireland* (Dublin, 1993).

Michael MacCarthy-Murrough, *The Munster Plantation: English migration to Southern Ireland, 1583–1611* (Oxford, 1986).

Gerard O'Brien (ed.), *Parliament, Politics and People: Essays in eighteenth-century Irish history* (Dublin, 1989).

Leon Ó Broin, *The Unfortunate Mr. Robert Emmet (Dublin, 1958)*.

Mary O'Dowd, *Power, Politics and Land: Sligo, 1568–1688* (Belfast, 1981).

Thomas Pakenham, *The Year of Liberty: The great Irish rebellion of 1798* (Dublin, 1969).

Sir Charles Petrie, *The Great Tyrconnel: A chapter in Anglo–Irish relations* (Cork, 1972).

J.P.P. Prendergast, *The Cromwellian Settlement of Ireland* (London, 1870).

D.P. Quinn, *The Elizabethans and the Irish* (Ithaca, NY, 1966).

Myles Ronan, *The Reformation in Dublin, 1536–48* (London, 1926).

J.J. Silke, *Kinsale: The Spanish intervention in Ireland at the end of the Elizabethan wars* (Liverpool, 1970).

J.G. Simms, *The Williamite Confiscation in Ireland, 1690–1703* (London, 1958).

—— *The Treaty of Limerick* (Dundalk, 1965).

—— *The Jacobite Parliament of 1689* (Dundalk, 1966).

—— *Jacobite Ireland, 1685–91* (London, 1969).

—— *Colonial Nationalism, 1698–1776* (Dublin, 1976).

—— *William Molyneux of Dublin* (Dublin, 1982).

Jim Smith, *The Men of No Property: Irish radicals and popular politics in the late eighteenth century* (Dublin, 1992).

Bernard Tucker, *Jonathan Swift* (Dublin, 1983).

Maureen Wall, *The Penal Laws* (Dundalk, 1961).

Philip Wilson, *The Beginnings of Modern Ireland* (London, 1920).

Ireland from 1800

James Bower Bell, *The Secret Army: History of the Irish Republican Army, 1916–79* (Dublin, 1979).

Paul Bew, *Land and the National Question in Ireland, 1858–82* (Dublin, 1978).

R.D. Collinson Black, *Economic Thought and the Irish question, 1817–70* (Cambridge, 1960).

John Bowman, *De Valera and the Ulster Question, 1917–79* (Oxford, 1972).

D. George Boyce, *Nineteenth-Century Ireland: The search for stability* (Dublin, 1990).

—— *Ireland 1828–1923: From ascendancy to democracy* (Oxford, 1992).

Patricia Boyne, *John O'Donovan (1806–61): A biography* (Kilkenny, 1987).

Terence Brown, *Ireland: A social and cultural history, 1922–79* (London, 1981).

Basil Chubb, *The Government and Politics of Ireland* (London, 1992).

Samuel Clarke, *Social Origins of the Irish Land War* (Princeton, 1979).

Samuel Clarke and J.S. Donnelly Jnr. (eds), *Irish Peasants: Violence and political unrest, 1780–1914* (Madison, 1983).

R.V. Comerford, *The Fenians in Context: Irish politics and society, 1848–82* (Dublin, 1985).

K.H. Connell, *Irish Peasant Society* (Oxford, 1968).

S.J. Connolly, *Priests and People in Pre-Famine Ireland, 1780–1845* (Dublin, 1982).

—— *Religion and Society in Nineteenth-Century Ireland* (Dundalk, 1985).

John Cooney, *The Crozier and the Dáil: Church and state, 1922–86* (Dublin, 1986).

L.M. Cullen (ed.), *The Formation of the Irish Economy* (Cork, 1968).

Mary E. Daly, *The Famine in Ireland* (Dundalk, 1986).

R. Davis, *The Young Ireland Movement* (Dublin, 1987).

R.P. Davis, *Arthur Griffith* (Dublin, 1976).

R. Dudley Edwards and T.D. Williams (eds), *The Great Famine: Studies in Irish history, 1845–52* (Dublin, 1956).

Ruth Dudley Edwards, *Patrick Pearse: The Triumph of failure* (London, 1977).

T. Ryle Dwyer, *De Valera: The Mind and the myths* (Dublin, 1991).

Brian Farrell, *Seán Lemass* (Dublin, 1983).

David Fitpatrick, *Politics and Irish Life, 1913–21: Provincial experience of war and revolution* (Dublin, 1977).

David Fitzpatrick (ed.), *Ireland and the First World War* (Dublin, 1986).

—— *Revolution? Ireland 1917–23* (Dublin, 1990).

C.D. Greaves, *The Life and Times of James Connolly* (London, 1961).

Robert Mitchell Henry, *The Evolution of Sinn Féin* (Dublin n.d.).

Edgar Holt, *Protest in Arms: The Irish Troubles, 1916–23* (London, 1960).

Michael Hopkinson, *Green against Green: The Irish civil war* (Dublin, 1988).

K.T. Hoppen, *Ireland Since 1800: Conflict and conformity* (Essex, 1989).

Dermot Keogh, *Ireland and the Vatican: The politics of church–state relations, 1922–60* (Cork, 1995).

—— *Twentieth-century Ireland: Nation and state* (Dublin, 1994).

D.A. Kerr, *Peel, Priests and Politics: Sir Robert Peel's administration and the Roman Catholic Church in Ireland* (Oxford, 1982).

Michael Laffan, *The Partition of Ireland, 1911–25* (Dundalk, 1983).
Emmet Larkin, *James Larkin Irish Labour Leader, 1876–1947* (London, 1963).
J.J. Lee, *Ireland 1912–75* (Cambridge, 1980).
J.J. Lee (ed.), *Ireland, 1945–70* Dublin, 1979).
F.S.L. Lyons, *The Fall of Parnell, 1890–91* (London, 1960).
—— *John Dillon: A biography* (London, 1968).
—— *Ireland Since the Famine* (London, 1973).
—— *Charles Stewart Parnell* (London, 1977).
F.S.L. Lyons and R.A.J. Hawkins (eds), *Ireland Under the Union: Varieties of tension* (Oxford, 1980).
J.B. Lyons, *The Enigma of Tom Kettle* (Dublin, 1983).
Dorothy Macardle, *The Irish Republic* (Dublin, 1937).
Donal McCartney (ed.), *The World of Daniel O'Connell* (Dublin, 1980).
—— *Parnell: The politics of power* (Dublin, 1991).
R.B. McDowell, *Public Opinion and Government Policy in Ireland, 1801–46* (London, 1952).
Oliver Macdonagh, *The Union and its Aftermath* (London, 1977).
—— *States of Mind: A study of Anglo-Irish conflict, 1780–1980* (London, 1983).
—— *The Hereditary Bondsman: Daniel O'Connell, 1775–1829* London, 1988).
—— *The Emancipist: Daniel O'Connell, 1830–49* (London, 1989).
Roger McHugh (ed.), *Dublin 1916* (London, 1976).
Francis MacManus (ed.), *Thomas Davis and Young Ireland* (Dublin, 1945).
—— *The Years of the Great Test, 1926–39* (Cork, 1967).
Laurence McCaffrey, *The Irish Question, 1800–1922* (Lexington, 1968).
W.F. Mandle, *The Gaelic Athletic Association and Irish Nationalist Politics* (Dublin, 1987).
Nicholas Mansergh, *Ireland in the Age of Reform and Revolution* (London, 1940).
—— *The Irish Question, 1840–1921* (London, 1965).
—— *The Unresolved Question: The Anglo-Irish settlement and its undoing, 1912–72* (London, 1991).
F.X. Martin (ed.), *The Irish Volunteers, 1913–15* (Dublin, 1963).
—— *The Howth Gun-Running and the Kilcoole gun-running, 1914: Recollections and documents* (Dublin, 1964).
—— *Leaders and Men of the Easter Rising: Dublin, 1916* (London, 1967).
Arthur Mitchell and Pádraig Ó Snodaigh (eds), *Irish Political Documents, 1919–49* (Dublin, 1985).
Joel Mokyr *Why Ireland Starved?* (1983).
John N. Molony, *A Soul Came to Ireland: Thomas Davis, 1814–45* (Dublin, 1995).
T.W. Moody, *Davitt and Irish Revolution, 1846–82* (Oxford, 1981).
T.W. Moody (ed.), *The Fenian Movement* (Cork, 1968).
T.W. Moody and J.C. Beckett (eds), *Ulster Since 1800: A political and economic survey* (London, 1957).

Christopher Morash (ed.), *The Hungry Voice: The poetry of the Irish famine* (Dublin, 1989).

Brian P. Murphy, *Patrick Pearse and the Lost Republican Ideal* (Dublin, 1991).

E.R. Norman, *The Catholic Church and Ireland in the Age of Rebellion, 1859–73* (London, 1965).

K.B. Nowlan, *Charles Gavan Duffy and the Repeal Movement* (Dublin, 1963).

—— *The Politics of Repeal: A study in the relations between Great Britain and Ireland, 1841–50* (London, 1965).

K.B. Nowlan (ed.), *The Making of 1916: Studies in the history of the rising* (Dublin, 1969).

K.B. Nowlan and T.D. Williams (eds), *Ireland in the War Years and After, 1939–51* (Dublin, 1969).

C. Cruise O'Brien, *Parnell and his Party* (Oxford, 1944).

C. Cruise O'Brien (ed.) *The Shaping of Modern Ireland* (London, 1960).

Leon Ó Broin, *Dublin castle and the 1916 Rising* (Dublin, 1966).

—— *Revolutionary Underground: The story of the Irish Republic Brotherhood* (Dublin, 1976).

—— *The Chief Secretary: Augustine Birrell in Ireland* (Hamden, Connecticut, 1970).

—— *Protestant Nationalists in Revolutionary Ireland: the Stopford connection* (Dublin, 1985).

Emmet O'Connor, *A labour history of Ireland, 1841–1960* (Dublin, 1992).

Frank O'Connor, *The Big Fellow* (Dublin, 1965).

Sean O'Faolain, *King of the Beggars* (London, 1938).

Fergus O'Ferrall, *Daniel O'Connell* (Dublin, 1981).

Cormac Ó Gráda, *A New Economic History, 1780–1939* (Oxford, 1994).

Clare O'Halloran, *Partition and the Limits of Irish Nationalism* (Dublin, 1987).

James O'Shea, *Priest, Politics and Society in Post-Famine Ireland: a study of county Tipperary 1850–91* (Dublin, 1983).

Edd W. Parks and Aileen W. Parks, *Thomas MacDonagh* (Athens, Georgia, 1967).

Sam Pollock, *Mutiny for the Cause* (London, 1969).

B.L. Reid, *The Lives of Roger Casement* (Yale, 1976).

Hereward Senior, *Orangeism in Ireland and Britain, 1795–1836* (London, 1966).

Jeanne Sheehy, *The Rediscovery of Ireland's past: The Celtic revival, 1830–1930* (London, 1980).

James Stephens, *The Insurrection in Dublin* (Dublin, 1966).

A.T.Q. Stewart, *The Narrow Ground: Aspects of Ulster, 1609–1969* (London, 1977).

Rex Taylor, *Michael Collins* (London, 1958).

William Irwin Thompson *The Imagination of an Insurrection: Dublin, Easter 1916* (New York, 1967).

Michael Tierney (ed.) *Daniel O'Connell: nine centenary essays* (Dublin, 1949).

W.E. Vaughan, *Landlords and Tenants in Ireland, 1848–1904* (Dublin, 1984).
—— *Landlords and Tenants in mid-Victorian Ireland* (Oxford, 1994).
Margaret Ward, *Maud Gonne: A life* (San Francisco, 1993).
Trevor West, *Horace Plunkett: Co-operation and politics: an Irish biography* (Gerrards Cross, 1986).
J.H. Whyte, *Church and State in Modern Ireland, 1923–79* (Dublin, 1984).
T.D. Williams (ed.), *The Irish Struggle, 1916–26* (London, 1966).
Carlton Younger, *Ireland's Civil War* (London, 1968).
—— *Arthur Griffith* (Dublin, 1981).

Index

Please note that sub-lists to entries are ordered chronologically.